THE ILIAD *of* HOMER

THE

ILIAD *of* HOMER

TRANSLATED WITH AN INTRODUCTION BY

Richmond Lattimore

THE UNIVERSITY OF CHICAGO PRESS

CHICAGO & LONDON

THE UNIVERSITY OF CHICAGO PRESS, CHICAGO 60637

The University of Chicago Press, Ltd., London

ISBN: 0-226-46940-9 (paperback)
LCN: 62-19604

10 09 08 07 06   46 47 48 49 50 51 52 53

⊗ The paper used in this publication meets the minimum requirements
of the American National Standard for Information Sciences—
Permanence of Paper for Printed Library Materials, ANSI Z39.48–1992.

TO
MY MOTHER AND FATHER

These dull notes we sing
Discords neede for helps to grace them

IN MAKING this translation I have used the Oxford text of D. B. Monro and T. W. Allen (3rd edition, 1919), and have not knowingly failed to follow its readings except in a very few cases, viz.: In 8. 328 I would either read νεῦρον instead of νευρήν, or, better perhaps, take νευρή here to mean nerve, sinew, or tendon, *not* bowstring. Where the Oxford editors have numbered, but excluded from their text, 8. 548 and 8. 550–552, I have included these lines. I have translated, but bracketed, 16. 614–615.

Further, I have, in the interests of clarity and English usage, occasionally given personal names instead of personal pronouns. As regards formula and repeat, I have, with the help of Schmidt's *Parallel-Homer* and Cunliffe's admirable *Lexicon of the Homeric Dialect*, tried to preserve something of the formulaic character, but have not systematically attempted to render all identical passages in Greek by identical passages in English.

I wish to thank the editors and the staff of the University of Chicago Press for their sympathy and their belief in this project from its very beginnings; David Grene and Mabel Lang for reading the translation and offering valuable advice and criticism; Rhys Carpenter for very helpful criticism of the introduction; Alice Lattimore for her help in preparing the manuscript; and finally, all those friends who have sustained me in the belief that this work was worth doing, and refrained from asking: 'Why do another translation of Homer?'; a question which has no answer for those who do not know the answer already.

NOTE

Three passages from the Iliad in my translation appeared in *War and the Poet*, edited by Richard Eberhart and Selden Rodman, New York, Devin-Adair, 1945. The passages in question are: 6. 441–465; 12. 310–328; and 21. 97–119; they appear in *War and the Poet* on pages 7–8, 10, and 11. Thanks are due to the Devin-Adair Company for permission to reproduce (with some revisions) these passages.

CONTENTS

CONTENTS

I HAVE tried in this introduction to put before the reader the information that will help him to a more complete understanding of the translation. 'Information', though, if it concerns Homer, means controversy; so I have had to cut a rather sweeping path through a mass of difficult or insoluble problems, working from the text and not from the literature on the subject. The exposition will of course not have the authority of a properly documented monograph. Some of my interpretations I should like, in some more appropriate place, to elaborate and defend. Still, all this aside, the introduction represents the translator's ideas about the Iliad.

Even a select bibliography is, accordingly, not called for here, but I may mention a few works, some of which I have referred to briefly in the following pages, which will be particularly helpful to the general student:

T. W. ALLEN: *Homer: Origins and Transmissions*, Oxford, Clarendon Press, 1924.

S. E. BASSETT: *The Poetry of Homer*, Berkeley, University of California Press, 1938.

C. M. BOWRA: *Tradition and Design in the Iliad*, Oxford, The Clarendon Press, 1930.

From Virgil to Milton, London, Macmillan, 1945.

RHYS CARPENTER: *Folk Tale, Fiction, and Saga in the Homeric Epics*, Berkeley and Los Angeles, University of California Press, 1946.

E. DRERUP: *Homerische Poetik: Das Homerproblem in der Gegenwart*, Wurzburg, 1921. (This is the authoritative account of Homeric theory and controversy up to the time of its publication.)

H. G. Evelyn-White: *Hesiod, the Homeric Hymns, and Homerica*, London and Cambridge, Mass., Heinemann and Harvard University Press, revised edition 1936. (The Loeb edition of Hesiod and the fragments of the Epic Cycle, Greek text with English translation.)

Gilbert Murray: *The Rise of the Greek Epic*, Oxford University Press and London, Humphrey Milford, fourth edition 1934.

J. A. Scott: *The Unity of Homer*, Berkeley, University of California Press, 1921.

A. Shewan: *Homeric Essays*, Oxford, Blackwell, 1935.

THE STORY OF THE FALL OF TROY

The Greeks of the post-Homeric period, the 'classical' Greeks and their successors, that is, those Greeks who were literate and have left articulate records of their beliefs, considered that one of the episodes in the early history of their own race was the Trojan War. As to the details of this war, as to the interpretation of its causes and its meaning, there might be disagreement; but for most persons at least, it was a piece of history, not a piece of legend or myth; and the main characters and the essential course of events were matters of general agreement.

This essential story may be summarized as follows: Paris, also called Alexandros, was the son of Priam, who was King of Troy, a city in the north-west corner of Asia Minor. Paris on an overseas voyage was entertained by Menelaos in Sparta, and from there carried away, with her full consent, Helen, the wife of Menelaos. He took her back with him to Troy, where she lived with him as his wife. The princes of Greece thereupon raised a force of a thousand or more ships, manned by fighters, with a view to forcing the return of Helen. The armada was led by Agamemnon, elder brother of Menelaos, the King of Mykenai; it included many lords or kings from the Peloponnese, Central Greece, Thessaly, and certain islands, and each prince personally led his own following. The fleet assembled at Aulis in Boiotia and made for Troy. There the Greeks landed after a fight, but were unable to take the city. For nine years they remained before Troy, keeping the Trojans on the defensive, and storming and plundering various places in the vicinity. In the tenth year, Agamemnon, the most powerful chief, quarrelled with Achilleus, his most powerful fighting man. Achilleus withdrew from the fighting, and kept his followers idle as well. In his absence, the Trojans, led by Hektor (a son of Priam and brother of Paris), temporarily got the better of their enemies and threatened to destroy the ships. Achilleus returned to the fighting, killed Hektor and routed the Trojans. Achilleus himself fell soon afterwards, but his death did not save Troy, which was presently taken. Most of the defenders were killed, the non-combatant population was carried into slavery, and the kingdom of Troy was obliterated. The lords of Greece made their way back, beset by weather, quarrels, and the hostility of those they had left at home years before. The destruction of Troy was brought about by the design and will of the gods.

Such is the basic story of Troy: and I call it 'basic' because, while further details or episodes *may* have found universal acceptance *later*, all Greek writers so far as we know accepted *at least* so much.

THE HOMERIC POEMS

The story outlined above derives its authority from the fact that everything in it is contained in the Iliad or the Odyssey of Homer. The Greeks regarded Homer as their first, and greatest, poet. They might speak of other names which pretended to greater antiquity, but they had no text to quote. For Homer they did. The Iliad and the Odyssey were unequivocally ascribed to him; other epics more doubtfully, as, for instance, 'the *Sack of Troy*, by Homer or Arktinos'.[1] For the Iliad and Odyssey, full and reasonably sound texts were available from at least the end of the sixth century B.C.; possibly, and I would say probably, from long before that.[2] Side by side with the transcription and dissemination of written texts went dissemination through recital, the business of professional reciters and interpreters of Homer, called rhapsodes.

At any rate, Homer, for the Greeks, stood at the head of their literary tradition. All knew him, few challenged his greatness. Hesiod, alone of the

---

[1] To be discussed a little later.

[2] There is considerable late evidence for some sort of editorial work performed at Athens in the time of Peisistratos, who was tyrant from 560 to 528 B.C. The tradition is, however, confused, and the pieces of evidence frequently contradict each other. For a statement of the evidence see Allen, pp. 225-248. It is quite possible that the text was edited at Athens in the time of Peisistratos; that this text was the original transcription seems to me very unlikely.

poets who have survived in more than name, was sometimes thought of as his contemporary and his equal; but Hesiod was far less widely quoted.

Of the two great Homeric epics, the Iliad deals with the story of Troy, the Odyssey with the homecoming of the Greek heroes after the capture of the city: in particular, the homecoming of Odysseus, the adventures, temptations, and dangers he went through before he made his way back to Ithaka and restored order in his own house. It thus concerns itself with heroic material chronologically later than that of the Iliad; and it has usually, in antiquity as in modern times, been thought of as the later of the two compositions.

THE STORY IN THE ILIAD

The Iliad is a poem of 15,693 lines, written in dactylic hexameter. It has been divided, as has the Odyssey, into twenty-four books, which range in length from 424 to 909 lines. This division was made long after, not only the first written version of the Iliad, but long after the time of Plato, perhaps early in the third century B.C. But the division was made well, the terminations mark clear and crucial points in the narrative, and the book numbers are regularly used in modern editions of the text.

The contents of the Iliad are as follows. Chryses, priest of Apollo in Chryse, a small place near Troy, comes to the camp of the Greeks to ask for the return of his daughter, Chryseis, who has been captured and allotted to Agamemnon as his concubine. Agamemnon refuses, and Chryses prays to Apollo to avenge him. Apollo inflicts a plague upon the Greeks. When there is no end in sight and the people are dying, Achilleus calls an assembly of the chiefs to consider what can be done. With the support and encouragement of Achilleus, Kalchas the soothsayer explains the wrath of Apollo. Agamemnon, though angry, agrees to give the girl back and propitiate the god, but demands that some other leader give up his mistress to him, in place of Chryseis. When Achilleus opposes this demand, Agamemnon takes away Briseis, the concubine of Achilleus. Achilleus does two things. He withdraws himself and all his men from the fighting; and he prays to his mother, Thetis, a divinity of the sea, that she will use her influence with Zeus and the Olympians to see that the Achaians are defeated in his absence, so that they may learn how necessary he has been to their fortunes, and so that Agamemnon in particular must realize what a man he has dishonoured. Thetis communicates her son's prayer to Zeus, who reluctantly promises to carry out the wish of Achilleus.

Such is the situation at the end of the first book, and from the quarrel here set forth the rest of the action is generated. In the second book, Agamemnon's army, with Achilleus missing, is after some delays and confusion marshalled and set in motion against the Trojans. A day of fighting on which fortunes vary opens with an indecisive duel between Menelaos and Paris in Book 3 and closes with an indecisive duel between Aias and Hektor in Book 7. But the Greeks are sufficiently shaken to take advantage, during a truce, of the opportunity to build a wall, which will defend their camp and their ships.

On the next day of fighting, the Trojans with the assistance of Zeus gain the upper hand, and by the end of the day (end of Book 8) they are encamped on the plain, confident that next day they can storm the defences of their enemies and sweep them into the sea. Agamemnon and his chief men are correspondingly discouraged and fearful. Before his assembled council, Agamemnon acknowledges his own fault in the quarrel with Achilleus. He proposes to give back Briseis, whom he swears he has never touched, and to offer many other gifts and honours as well, if Achilleus will come back. Odysseus, Aias, and Phoinix convey this message to Achilleus, who greets them and entertains them as friends, but is still too angry to accept. The account of these dealings takes up the ninth book. The tenth is devoted to a scouting expedition undertaken by Odysseus and Diomedes, which is represented as taking place on the same night as the embassy to Achilleus.

Book 11 opens a great and eventful day of fighting, which does not end until Book 18. The Achaians begin well, but one after another the great champions are disabled (Agamemnon, Diomedes, Odysseus, as well as Eurypylos and Machaon) until Aias is the only Greek of the first rank left in the field. The Trojans drive the Achaians back and Hektor smashes in the gate of the wall, and leads the attack until the Achaians are fighting to save their ships from destruction. Hektor calls for fire, and sets one ship ablaze, but now a new turn occurs and the Greeks are unexpectedly rescued. Achilleus, while still keeping out of the fight, has been watching it, and his dearest friend, Patroklos, has become increasingly distressed and alarmed for the sake of the whole army. He persuades Achilleus to lend him his armour and his men and let him go into battle to save the ships (beginning of Book 16).

Patroklos is fresh and eager, and wears the superior armour of Achilleus. His Myrmidons are rested and spoiling for a fight. But the Trojans have fought all day and are battle-weary, nor are they sure that the newcomer is not Achilleus himself (16. 280–282). They break, and are swept back on their city wall. Patroklos performs enormous exploits until at last, taken at a disadvantage, he is killed by Hektor. The fighting turns in favour of the Trojans once more. Hektor captures the armour of Achilleus from the corpse of Patroklos, but the Achaians rescue the body itself. That is all they can do; by the end of Book 17 they are in full retreat.

But by now Achilleus has heard the news. Shocked and furious as he is, he cannot go at once into battle, for he has no armour. But the gods transfigure him, and by merely showing himself and shouting his war cry he turns back the Trojans, and the Achaians escape. The day's fighting is over. Hephaistos, at the asking of Thetis, forges new, immortal armour for Achilleus. Next day Achilleus calls an assembly of the Achaians and declares the end of his quarrel with Agamemnon and his return to battle. The armies encounter. Achilleus leads the attack, slaughters many, and at last drives the main body of the Trojans inside their walls. Hektor refuses to take refuge and awaits Achilleus. At the last moment, his nerve fails and he runs, with Achilleus in pursuit. The gods agree that Hektor must not escape, and Athene tricks him into standing his ground. Hektor goes down fighting, is stripped and dragged by the heels from Achilleus' chariot to the ships.

Such is the position at the end of Book 22. The fighting of the Iliad is over, but the two great dead men, Patroklos and Hektor, still lie unburied. Patroklos is burned and buried with much ceremony and sacrifice, and elaborate games are held in his honour. These events occupy Book 23. Meanwhile, Hektor's corpse has been shamefully treated, but the gods defend it from harm. Priam, guided by Hermes, goes to the shelter of Achilleus at night to ask for the return of his son's body. Achilleus pities the old man, and gives it back; and the Iliad ends with the burial of Hektor by the Trojans.

THE ILIAD AND THE STORY OF TROY

If we now measure the story of the Iliad against the entire story of the Fall of Troy, as it was outlined above, we can at once see important differences. The Iliad is not the story of Troy. Neither the beginning nor the end of the war is narrated in the Iliad. We begin in the tenth year of the siege (2. 134) and we end, some weeks later, still in the tenth year, with the city still untaken. Moreover, the main plot of the Iliad is something narrower than would be the chronicle of a piece out of the siege-time. It is the story of Achilleus; or more precisely, it is, as has been frequently seen, the tragedy of Achilleus, which develops through his quarrel with Agamemnon and withdrawal from battle, the sufferings of the Greeks in his absence, the death of Patroklos who tried to rescue the Greeks from the plight into which Achilleus had put them, and the vengeance taken by Achilleus on Hektor, who killed Patroklos. This is not chronicle but tragedy, with beginning, middle, and end. It is the story of a great man who through a fault in an otherwise noble character (and even the fault is noble) brings disaster upon himself, since the death of Patroklos is the work of free choice on the part of Achilleus, and the anger of Achilleus, turned first against Agamemnon, then against Hektor, is at last resolved in a grudging forgiveness when the body of Hektor is given back to the Trojans. This, not the fall of Troy, closes the story. In fact, Achilleus did not, in the Iliad or anywhere else, take Troy; he died first, but his death is not told in the Iliad, though it is foreseen.[1] The fighting during the absence of Achilleus is not ordinary fighting such as we are to understand took place continually during the ten years' siege, but an extraordinary counter-attack by the Trojans which could be made only in the absence of Achilleus.[2]

So the Iliad is the story of Achilleus. But it cannot be completely torn loose from the story of Troy, or of Achaians and Trojans. There is much in the Iliad that has nothing to do with Achilleus. Furthermore, his personal actions have effects which go beyond his own story or his own aims. In avenging Patroklos, he saves the Greeks. In killing Hektor, he dooms Troy.

Further: granted that the Iliad does not tell the story of Troy, there must have been some previous account, or more than one such account, that did. The Iliad is a work of art evolved within the scope of a chronicle; it is not the chronicle itself.

---

[1] 18. 95–100; 22. 356–366, and elsewhere.

[2] This is made plain by Homer, Iliad, 9. 352–359. See also the speech of Pouly-damas, 18. 254–265.

THE RELATIVE DATE OF HOMER

This can be seen most clearly if we consider the chronological relation between Homer and his material, i.e. the Trojan War. Greek historians were at their weakest when it came to chronology, yet the tradition seems good enough for our purposes. A group of dates is given by Greek authors for the fall of Troy, and the dates range from 1334 B.C. to 1150 B.C. The most noteworthy are Eratosthenes' 1184 B.C., which has prevailed as the 'traditional date'; and Herodotus' (2. 145) approximate date of 1250 B.C. All these dates are approximations based on genealogical material. We do not know which date is right, if any one is. We do not, for that matter, know whether there was a Trojan War.[1] But we can see where tradition put it. When we consider the evidence for Homer's date, we find a more drastic set of variations. Some thought him a contemporary of the events he chronicled, others made him active sixty, or a hundred, or more, years later. Herodotus (2. 53) put him '400 years before my own time, at the most', that is, about 850 B.C.[2]

This Herodotean date may thus appear to be 'minimal', that is, the latest we can accept. Actually, it is more likely to be maximal. Homer could not have lived at, or very near, the time of the events he tells about. For one thing, he himself makes it quite plain that what he speaks of happened long ago, when men were different from the men of his own age, and could lift easily weights no two men now could lift (12. 445–449 and elsewhere). Such, too, is the drift of his appeal to the remembering Muses, who must bring to life what must otherwise be a rumour confused in time (2. 484–493). But further: between the time of Homer's story and the time of Homer, Greek legend, which must, however confusedly, perpetuate historical fact, has placed two great events: the Dorian invasion and the Ionian colonization. The Trojan War came before these; Homer came after.

According to the tradition, upheavals and mass rival migrations followed the Trojan War. New tribes pushed into Greece, driving out or overwhelming old ones. A race of invaders called Thessalians occupied Thessaly, and dislodged the Boiotians; these in turn occupied the territory of the Kadmeians, thereafter called Boiotia. Dorians, in conjunction with

---

[1] But something happened which gave rise to the legend, however remote the legend may be from historical fact.

[2] See Allen, 11–41, with data on the life of Homer tabulated, p. 32.

the Herakleidai (the 'sons of Herakles'), came from the north to win Sparta, Messenia, Argos, and other places in the Peloponnese. Whether these movements were sudden or gradual we do not always know. There is much evidence that the newcomers sometimes established themselves by way of peaceful compromise rather than outright conquest. But establish themselves they did. The result was a further series of dislocations and migrations, of which the most significant for our purposes was the occupation of the coast of Asia Minor and the adjacent islands by Hellenes. The most important of these Hellenic groups were called Ionians and Aiolians. They came from Thessaly, Boiotia, and the Peloponnese; those areas where the invasions had taken place.

We do not know where Homer was born any more than we know when he was born. We do not know whether he was an Ionian or an Aiolian; Chios and Smyrna, where the two strains are hardest to separate, have the strongest claims on him. But of one thing we can, I think, be sure. He was born on or near the coast of Asia Minor. Homer, therefore, comes after the Ionian migration; the Ionian migration comes after the Dorian invasion; and the Dorian invasion comes after the Trojan War. Regardless of dates, the relative sequence is secure.

But the Iliad is pre-Dorian. Homer, himself an Asiatic Greek, deals with an age when there were no Greeks in Asia. The people of what in his day were Ionia and Aiolia fight in the Iliad on the side of Troy. Miletos is in the hands of 'the Karians of the outland speech' (2. 867). Homer does not call the men of Greece Greeks (Graikoi) as we do, nor again Hellenes, as they called themselves.[1] He calls them Achaians, Argives, and Danaans. His Argives are not necessarily from what was later Argos, nor are his Achaians necessarily from what was later Achaia; they, like the Danaans, are just 'Greeks'. He avoids the term 'Dorians', which appears once in the Odyssey (19. 177); and he avoids 'Thessalians'. The term Hellene is closely associated with the term Dorian. Its opposites, Pelasgian, Karian, and barbarian, he knows also, but regularly avoids them.

The conclusion is, I think, quite clear. Homer knew—how could he help it?—that the Dorians and the others had come and driven his people

---

[1] He does use, sparingly, the terms Hellas, Hellenes, Panhellenes. These terms seem, with the exception of one phrase found in the Odyssey, to be used of a particular locality, Achilleus' country, Phthia in Thessaly, rather than of all Greece. Anachronisms and mistakes are possible, though, here as elsewhere.

across the water to Asia. But he ignored this, because he went back to an age generations before, when the ancestors of his audience, doubtless his own ancestors as well, were lords of Greece and went to Asia not as fugitives to colonize but as raiders to harry and destroy. He betrays himself now and again through anachronisms, but he is trying to reconstruct the remote past.

We have not, it is true, emerged from these considerations with a positive date for Homer. All we have is relative, attached to the date of the Trojan War, a date which itself cannot be fixed. We have, though, established that a considerable stretch of time elapsed between the date of Homer and the period he chose to describe. And I hope that we thus dispose of any proposal to put him back in the immediate neighbourhood of the Trojan War. Herodotus' 850 B.C. is certainly in better case than it first appeared to be, and it may be that we can find some help at the other end, counting not forward to Homer but back to Homer. But first, we should go back to the problem that led us into this chronological consideration, that is, the problem of Homer's relation to his material.

THE RELATION OF HOMER TO HIS MATERIAL

At the near end, we have the finished product, our Iliad. What do we have at the far end? Plainly, the historical counterpart of the fictitious Trojan War. This war may not have been much like what we hear about; it may not have been a ten years' war, it may not have been pan-Achaian in scale, it may not have been waged against Troy, and it may have been a defeat, not a victory. Personally, I think it was a viking-raid, or several such combined into one. But it *was something* which, justifiably or not, *generated* the story of Troy we know. From the event, the legend, and from the legend, Homer; but between the event and Homer, we see now, the legend had time to grow.

In what way? It is a question seriously debated whether Homer, comparatively late in the tradition, could write. Certainly, his most remote predecessors could not. If we look at the text of the Iliad, we find illustrations of the way a legend could begin. Phoinix, in order to point his moral, relates to Achilleus a piece of recent history, the story of Meleagros (9. 529–605). Nestor, with a blandness that becomes almost unendurable, recites again and again the heroic exploits of himself when young.

Glaukos has the history of his ancestor, Bellerophontes, all in his mind, and is ready to pass it on to Diomedes as they pause and converse in the middle of a great battle (6. 144–211). Or again: when the peacemakers come to the shelter of Achilleus, they find him singing of the famous exploits of men, and accompanying himself on a lyre (9. 186-189).[1]

The last case is noteworthy, because Achilleus is singing. Nestor and the others tell their tales, of course, in Homer's hexameters, but are not making poetry. Simultaneously after the event, the tradition begins in prose saga and in verse. Neither kind of record is written down; both kinds are communicated and perpetuated by word of mouth.

Imagine this process repeating itself through the generations that string out between the event and Homer, and you have some idea of what his material was. Note that tales change in the telling, so that what reached Homer may have been very different from what really happened, through the fault of no particular individual. Note again that among the mixed lot of story-tellers and poets there would probably be some more talented and more influential than the general ruck. This would mean that certain aspects of the story would be emphasized, and prejudices might count. There is opportunity for selection within limits.

And selection within limits was the privilege of Homer, too, when he set out to compose, within the story of Troy, the story of Achilleus. Within limits; the tradition must by now have fixed certain events in the story in all the authority of fact. So Homer could not make Achilleus take Troy any more than he could make Troy win the battle and survive. He could not save Achilleus, and he could not kill Odysseus. We have, therefore, the presumption of what we may call a basic story, which Homer knew, and which at the same time stimulated and limited his invention. He could emphasize or develop some parts, episodes, characters in the story, barely acknowledge others, omit others entirely. But he could not contradict the legends.

For although Homer has selected a series of events occupying a few weeks in the tenth year of the war, and does not deal with either beginning

[1] There is something comparable in the picture of Helen working into the design she weaves 'numerous struggles of Trojans, breakers of horses, and bronze-armoured Achaians' (3. 126-127): the history that is being made at the moment outside the city walls. And this in turn reminds us of the up-to-date Tyrian settlers who have got the story of Troy on their temple wall by the time Aeneas arrives to look at it (*Aeneid*, 1. 453-493). See Drerup, 75.

or end, he knows the beginning and the end. The **Achaians** came for the sake of Menelaos, to win back Helen whom Paris had carried off. That is understood, and alluded to quite often. And he knows, and all the characters in his story pretty well know, that Troy will fall. At the same time, these parts of the story are not brought into the poem in any forthright way, as something that must be explained to an audience. The flight of Helen is alluded to in various contexts, and rather casually. She is first mentioned in Hera's speech to Athene, when the Achaians seem to be demoralized and on the point of going home (2. 158–162):

> as things are, the Argives will take flight homeward over
> the wide ridges of the sea to the land of their fathers,
> and thus they would leave to Priam and to the Trojans Helen
> of Argos, to glory over, for whose sake many Achaians
> lost their lives in Troy far from their own native country.

No further explanation. So the audience *knew* who Helen was, what she did. We have struck material in what I have called the basic story. And here is the first introduction of Hektor. It occurs in Achilleus' threat to Agamemnon (1. 241–243):

> Then stricken at heart though you be, you will be able
> to do nothing when in their numbers before manslaughtering Hektor
> they drop and die.

One could, I suppose, gather from this that Hektor was a formidable Trojan; but scarcely more. And Patroklos? He first appears simply as Menoitiades, that is, *the son of Menoitios!* [1] Hektor and Patroklos, so introduced, can hardly have been inventions of Homer. They came down to him in the tradition, and his audience knew who they were. And so, once more, we strike the basic story which tradition handed on to Homer.

Of such major fixed characters, Helen, who is far more important in the story of Troy than Patroklos, and even Achilleus, is far less important in the Iliad. This emphasizes the selection within limits, and leads us to consider the use or discard of usable material.

---

[1] 1. 307. In my translation I have here called him 'Patroklos, the son of Menoitios' so as not to be puzzling. But 'Patroklos' is not in the Greek until thirty lines later. Such introductions (or non-introductions) seem to me to be decisive against the views that either Hektor or Patroklos was a fictitious character invented by Homer.

The stories told by Glaukos, Phoinix, Nestor, which we referred to above, are pieces out of the whole complex of legend in which the story of Troy itself is only one big episode. They are unassimilated lumps of saga, from near the story but not of it. They relate to the heroes of the Iliad and can be brought in, at discretion: marginal material. But while these tales of Meleagros and Bellerophontes are not part of the story of Troy, there is more material, marginal to the Iliad, which *is* part of the story of Troy, and this material concerns our problem very nearly.

MARGINAL MATERIAL

We must consider certain episodes which form part of the ultimate story of Troy, concerning which we get little or no information in the Iliad. One such episode, the flight of Helen, we have already noticed, and we have seen that Homer knew it and accepted it, but made relatively little of Helen because she is not important in that part of Troy's story which is the Iliad. If, however, we start from the story as it has come down to *us*, we may state the following propositions and try to verify them in Homer:

(*a*) The ultimate cause of the Trojan War was the judgment of Paris.

(*b*) The Achaian heroes were suitors for the hand of Helen. Her father, Tyndareus, made them swear to stand by her husband, whichever of them it might be, in case someone should carry her off.

(*c*) The Achaian fleet was weatherbound at Aulis because of the anger of Artemis. Agamemnon sacrificed his daughter, Iphigeneia, to Artemis in order to appease her.

(*d*) Thetis dipped the infant Achilleus in the Styx, in order to make him invulnerable. But the heel where she held him did not touch the water and remained a mortal spot. Achilleus died of an arrow wound in the heel.

(*e*) Troy was taken by means of a wooden horse.

These five propositions form part of a tradition which has certainly grown very familiar indeed. But how much is there in the Iliad to support them?

(*a*) There is one statement (24. 25–30) that Hera, Poseidon, and Athene hated Ilion and its people 'because of the sin of Paris, who insulted the goddesses when they came to his courtyard, and praised that one who gave him disastrous lust'. This can hardly be anything except an allusion to the judgment of Paris.[1] The episode is, however, mentioned only here, in the last book of the Iliad, when most of the action is over; and it is mentioned in a queer, allusive fashion, with the names of Helen and Aphrodite suppressed. The judgment of Paris seems to be a part of Homer's tradition which he did not care to emphasize. The place where it would properly be brought into the Iliad is after 4. 31–33, where Zeus asks Hera why she hates the Trojans, and gets no answer.

(b) The oath of the suitors to Tyndareus is not mentioned in the Iliad. There are allusions to oaths. The name of Tyndareus does not appear.

(c) Iphigeneia is not named in the Iliad.

(d) Achilleus in the Iliad is neither more vulnerable nor invulnerable than anybody else. Hektor, dying, predicts that Paris and Apollo will kill him (22. 359) and we are presumably meant to understand that he is right. There is no reference to a wound in the heel.

(e) There is no reference to a wooden horse in the Iliad. It is mentioned several times in the Odyssey (4. 272; 8. 493–494; 11. 523) and is said to have been built by Epeios (8. 493; 11. 523). Epeios comes into the Iliad once (23. 665) as an undistinguished warrior but a champion boxer.

These last four episodes appear to be post-Iliad, if not post-Homeric. If they were parts of Homer's tradition, he rejected them. Yet they appear in the later tradition, which is richer in episodes than the Iliad. The appearance of the Homeric poems, or at least of the Iliad, seems to have been followed by a group of continuations in a process designed to tell the complete story of Troy in a series of epic poems. Most familiar additions to Homer are found in this series, commonly known as the Epic Cycle; a few others come from random sources, sometimes much later.

THE EPIC CYCLE AND OTHER CONTINUATIONS

The group of poems is called a cycle possibly because together they round out, bring to completion, the story of the heroic age. The poems themselves have not come down to us, but we have, in addition to fragments (random lines or passages quoted by other authors), a summary

---

[1] The way out is to follow an ancient grammarian and declare these lines an interpolation. That way madness lies.

prose account of the contents[1] the general accuracy of which there is no reason to doubt. The important points concerning those parts of the Cycle which concern us[2] may be conveniently set down as follows, with the Homeric poems in their position among them (see next page).

In addition to the above, there are various works which seem to have dealt with the material of Troy, in particular a group of catalogues which have been attached by tradition to the name of Hesiod. From these, as from the Cycle, material was drawn by the great lyric poets, Stesichoros, Simonides, Pindar, and by the tragic poets of Athens. But the Cycle, as given above, represents the systematic completion of the Trojan story in verse form.

The Cycle is post-Homeric, and this can be said positively. In the first place, ancient tradition on this point is firm and unanimous. But the conclusion can be defended from analysis. If there is any character of the Cycle as a whole which is indisputable, it is the businesslike manner in which the story is told from beginning to end, without gaps. But if Homer had come later than the Cycle, there would have been such a gap, for there would have been no account either of the anger of Achilleus or the death of Hektor, nor of the homecoming of Odysseus, since this was apparently not part of the *Returns*. But if the Iliad was already there before the Cycle began, all is clear. The author of the *Cypria* took the story up to the beginning of the Iliad, then stopped short; and the *Aithiopis* obediently picks the story up again immediately after the point where the Iliad closes.

Let us return to our episodes, considered above. The judgment of Paris, which gets into the Iliad by the back door, is apparently put in its right place in the *Cypria*. The wooden horse comes up in his proper chronological position in the *Sack of Ilion* (and the *Little Iliad*, which seems to overlap the two works of Arktinos). So, too, other episodes alluded to by Homer, the death of Achilleus, the flight of Helen, the retirement and return of Philoktetes (2. 716–725), the death of Protesilaos (2. 695–710), find their appropriate places in the chronicle of the Cycle.

But did the later poets add new material, which was not part of the

[1] Actually, the summary of a summary; the outline of Proclus, summarized by Photius. The material is found, Greek with good English translation, in *Hesiod, the Homeric Hymns, and Homerica*, ed. Evelyn-White, London and Cambridge, Mass. (Loeb series), new and revised edition 1936.

[2] There is evidence for a good deal of material, sometimes included in the Cycle, which has nothing directly to do with the story of Troy; but this may have been considered as a kind of prologue to the story.

Part of Story Covered	Name of Work	Name of Author	Date [1]	No. of Books
From the decision of the gods to cause the Trojan War to the quarrel between Achilleus and Agamemnon	Cypria	Stasinos of Cyprus (or Hegesias or Homer)	Not given	11
From the anger of Achilleus to the burial of Hektor	Iliad	Homer	In question	24
From the coming of the Amazons to the suicide of Aias	Aithiopis	Arktinos of Miletos	776 B.C. 744 B.C.	5
From the death of Achilleus to the fall of Troy and the departure of the Achaians	Little Iliad	Lesches of Lesbos (or Thestorides or Kinaithon or Diodoros or Homer)	Evidence obscure, conflicting	4
From the building of the wooden horse to the fall of Ilion and the departure of the Achaians	Sack of Ilion	Arktinos of Miletos	776 B.C. 774 B.C.	2
The returns of the various heroes	The Returns	Agias of Troizen (or an unnamed Kolophonian or Homer)		5
The return of Odysseus	Odyssey	Homer	In question	24
From the return of Odysseus to his death	Telegony	Eugammon of Kyrene (or Kinaithos of Lakedaimon)	568 B.C.	2

[1] Dates (traditional) are, as usual, absolutely unreliable, but may be relatively sound.

basic story known to Homer? It seems unlike the workmen of the Cycle, and yet Homer betrays no knowledge of the sacrifice of Iphigeneia, told in the *Cypria* and familiar ever since. His story, however, permits him to ignore this episode, which may conceivably have been invented in order to motivate more fully Agamemnon's murder by Klytaimestra (this last is mentioned in the Odyssey). Outside of the Cycle, however, additions seem to have been made. The oath of the suitors to Tyndareus comes from the *Catalogue of Women* attributed to Hesiod; but it is a minor motive and could have been in the *Cypria* and left out by its epitomizer. The vulnerable heel of Achilleus seems to be a late invention, and first appears in the form familiar to us in Servius' commentary on the *Aeneid*, though less familiar variants can be found earlier.[1]

Further speculations would be inappropriate to an introduction of this sort, but enough has perhaps been given to show how the tradition might have formed itself. The conjectural stages may be summed up as follows:

1. The event.

2. Immediate record and elaboration in hearsay and oral poetry.

3. Formation of a fixed legend and formation, perhaps over the same period, of hexameter verse.

4. The Iliad of Homer.

The Odyssey of Homer. Both recognized as authoritative, whether because of their excellence and elaboration, or because they were the first poems to be written down, or both.

5. The completion of the Trojan Story in the Epic Cycle, exhausting pre-Homeric material not exhausted by Homer, but avoiding the areas in the legend dealt with by Homer.

---

[1] In its earliest traceable form, the story is that Thetis tried to make all her children immortal. Thus Apollonius of Rhodes (early third century B.C.), 4. 869. On the other hand, the legend that Aias was invulnerable except in one part of his body is at least as early as Aeschylus, and the Achilleus story may have been borrowed from this. It is to be noted that all these episodes *explain* something which Homer left unexplained or problematical. The judgment of Paris explains the rape of Helen and the hostility of Hera and Athene to the Trojans. The oath of the suitors explains the participation of chiefs from all over Greece in what might have appeared to be a private quarrel between Menelaos and Paris. The sacrifice of Iphigeneia explains more fully the murder of Agamemnon. The mortal heel of Achilleus explains how Paris could kill him when Hektor could not (and may have been suggested by Paris' disabling of Diomedes with an arrow shot in the foot). The wooden horse explains how the Achaians took Troy without Achilleus, although they could not do it with his help.

6. Elaboration and interpretation of material not used by Homer in choral poetry, tragedy, late epic.

DATES

The author of the most authoritative history of Greek literature[1] has stated flatly that, in view of the confusion among the ancients themselves, we shall never know when Homer lived. With this one must agree. But the student can hardly avoid having an opinion, and an introduction in which the Iliad is analysed does seem to call for some statement, however guarded and personal, of belief. What follows is an opinion, and nothing more.

Consider first, that the appearance of the Homeric poems is followed by (1) the Epic Cycle, (2) Hesiod and the Hesiodic continuations, (3) short personal poems, elegy or lyric. All three developments are generally post-Homeric according to Greek tradition, and all three use or modify the hexameter, in whose history the Homeric poems seem to have marked an epoch. Now, are these three developments contemporary? Possibly; but tradition, at least, would put Archilochos, Kallinos, and Terpander after Hesiod and after Arktinos and Stasinos; and the forms, which employ and modify hexameter and break with the epic tradition of narrative, speak for innovation and relative lateness. If we put Homer before Hesiod and Stasinos, and these before the lyricists and elegists, we can compute back to a misty species of date. Because Archilochos, Kallinos, and Terpander were dated, after a fashion. The first two are made roughly contemporary, so that Archilochos carries Kallinos with him; and Archilochos is put by the majority in the earlier half of the seventh century. Terpander of Lesbos is dated as having been active at dates ranging from 676 to 645 B.C.

If we work back from these, we get an eighth-century Homer, and there are a few bits of evidence that tend to make this more likely. A late authority gives for Terpander the surprisingly brief genealogy: Homer-Euryphon-Boios of Phokis-Terpander, which would mean a Homer born early in the eighth century. Let us also reconsider Herodotus, who dated Homer '400 years before my time, no more'. Why did Herodotus think he knew this? There is a probability that he calculated from the number of generations he believed to have elapsed between Homer and himself.

---

[1] W. Schmid, *Geschichte der griechischen Literatur*, I. I (Munich, 1929), 83.

We know from a statement he made elsewhere (2. 142) that Herodotus reckoned three generations as one hundred years: $33\frac{1}{3}$ years as an average from father to son seems rather long, to involve too late an age at marriage. But twelve generations *might* be correct. If so, by subtracting 60 to 100 years for over-reckoning of generations we come out once more with an eighth-century Homer. A possible synchronization between Hesiod and a man prominent in the Lelantine War, generally dated about 700 (Hesiod, *Works and Days*, 654–662), suggests that the order Homer-Hesiod-Archilochos is the right one.

One more consideration. The works of Archilochos and Kallinos certainly, of Arktinos, Stasinos, Hesiod probably, were written down. In spite of the certainty that Iliad and Odyssey were preserved through rhapsodes, or reciters, their authority also almost demands that these two poems also were written down, whether by Homer himself or by a contemporary or immediate successor. If so, we can go back so far.[1]

No one knows better than I that such evidence as I have just referred to is none too stout. I have given merely the reasons why I believe that Homer composed in the eighth (conceivably into the seventh) century.

THE UNITY OF HOMER

And did he write both Iliad and Odyssey? This is not a soluble problem and it is not, to me, a very interesting one; it is the work, not the man or men who composed the work, which is interesting. But Greek tradition down to the time of the Alexandrians is unanimously in favour of single authorship. If someone not Homer wrote the Odyssey, nobody had a name to give him. Later authors quote Iliad and Odyssey constantly; other poems of the Cycle are less well known. *They* may be attributed to Homer; but not vice versa. The special position of Iliad and Odyssey, under the name of Homer, in Greek tradition, puts the burden of proof on those who would establish separate authorship, and I have not encountered any arguments strong enough to alter that situation.

[1] See Carpenter, 11–16. Mr. Carpenter would put Homer before Hesiod, but considers that Hesiod wrote, while Homer composed orally. Therefore, Hesiod-in-writing is earlier than Homer-in-writing. He would date the composition of the Iliad 'close to 700 B.C.' (p. 179), and would put the Odyssey almost fifty years later. My own preference is for a date a little earlier, but not much.

THE PATTERN OF THE ILIAD

The Iliad is the elaboration of a stretch in the story of Troy, a stretch running from the quarrel of Agamemnon and Achilleus to the death and burial of Hektor. In the whole story it is not a long stretch. If the essential narrative contents of the Iliad were summarized, as the narrative contents of the poems in the Cycle were summed up, we should appear to have a very short story. In fact, we do not; we have a very long one. To put it rather differently: it would be easy to think of an epic that set forth the essential plot of our Iliad in three books, thus:

1. Quarrel of Achilleus and Agamemnon. Withdrawal of Achilleus.
2. Defeat of the Achaians by the Trojans and Hektor.
3. Intervention and death of Patroklos. Return of Achilleus. Defeat of the Trojans. Death of Hektor.

This is the irreducible plot. But the Iliad contains not three books, but twenty-four.[1]

Book 1 of our real Iliad is identical with Book 1 of the hypothetical work outlined above. At its close Achilleus is out of the action, and Zeus has promised Thetis to see that the Achaians are defeated. In order to do this, he sends a dream to Agamemnon informing him that if he attacks he may take Troy.

This is at the opening of the second book, and so far all is in order. Homer has thoroughly motivated a headlong attack led by Agamemnon which will be disastrously repulsed, thus showing how Agamemnon cannot get along without Achilleus. This is what the audience must have expected.

And this is precisely what does not happen. Instead, Agamemnon calls a meeting of the chiefs and proposes to test out the spirit of his army by inviting them to go home. They take him literally, and are barely rallied by Odysseus and Nestor, with the inspiration of Athene. Still, rallied they are, and advance, while the poet pauses to enumerate the chiefs and contingents on both sides. By the opening of the third book, the armies are on the point of collision.

But they do not encounter. Instead, a duel is arranged between Menelaos

[1] By way of comparison, consider the enormous amount of 'history' that has got crammed into the eleven books of the *Cypria*: from the beginning of the beginning through all the preparations and the first nine years of the war down to the quarrel.

and Paris, the winner to have Helen, while the others swear peace and friendship. As Paris is in danger of death or capture, Aphrodite miraculously snatches him away and sets him down in Ilion. But Paris is clearly beaten, and by the terms of the treaty Helen must go to Menelaos. The war will be over and Troy will survive. Hera and Athene will not let this pass, and by the gods' consent Athene induces Pandaros, a Trojan ally, to break the treaty by trying to kill Menelaos. Again the armies prepare to attack and the battle, long anticipated and twice deferred, at last begins (4. 446).

It does not, however, result in any defeat for the Achaians. Instead, the fighting sways back and forth; the Achaians, led by the unheralded Diomedes, get rather the better of it. The battle closes with a duel between Aias and Hektor (7. 54–312). The only reminder that this day's battle should have been a defeat is seen in the fact that the Achaians now fortify their camp.

A subsequent battle results in an Achaian defeat (Book 8). The unsuccessful embassy to Achilleus (Book 9), the night spying expedition of Odysseus and Diomedes (Book 10), carry us to the great battle which at last brings on the assault of Hektor on the ships (Book 15), the intervention and death of Patroklos (Book 16); so that the position forecast in Book 1 has at last been reached. The intervention of Achilleus and death of Hektor are attended by further delays, but we have seen enough to perceive how the pattern works.

Plainly, the Iliad sees through the anger of Achilleus much of the whole story of Troy. The catalogues, of the ships and of the Trojan allies, widen the scope of the poem. The episodes of the third book take us to actors' even more nearly concerned in the basic story than Agamemnon and Achilleus; namely, to Helen, Menelaos, and Paris. And thus material like the duel between Menelaos and Paris, which ought by right to come at the beginning of the war, gets incorporated into the story of Achilleus without interfering with it, and though beginning and ending in the tenth year we have a sense of the beginning and end of the war.

Moreover, the Iliad was composed for a Hellenic audience, of the upper class, among which many claimed to trace their ancestry back to the heroes of the Trojan War. The pro-Hellenic bias is plain, though not crude, though tempered by a considerate sympathy for the Trojans; and the pro-Hellenic bias involves the reputation of the Achaian heroes.

The *logical* structure of the Achilleus story is the brief one outlined above. But immediate and utter rout of the Achaians on the withdrawal of Achilleus leaves no very glorious part open to the other heroes. Homer's dilemma ran thus: he must maintain the truth of Achilleus' dictum: 'Without me you cannot cope with Hektor and the Trojans.' And at the same time he must maintain the claims to greatness of Diomedes, Aias, Agamemnon, Odysseus, and the Achaians in general. He cannot do both in short compass; he must be more devious.

It is not only that with Achilleus out of action the other Achaians have a better chance to show their valour (a special show of valour by an individual is called *aristeia*), since sooner or later they must retreat. The ancients called the first great battle the *aristeia* of Diomedes; the battle is drawn. But through the second and third battles, where the Achaians must be losing, the 'Achilleus situation' (rout of the Achaians stemmed by one man) is repeated again and again. In the first battle, a Trojan charge led by Hektor is stemmed by Diomedes. In the eighth book, Zeus announces that the other gods (and he means the 'pro-Achaians') must stay out of action. He lightens and thunders from Ida, and the lords of the Achaians turn and run (8. 75–79). The expected rout is on. But Diomedes turns to rescue Nestor from danger, brings down Hektor's charioteer, and *would have routed the Trojans* (8. 130–131) had not Zeus once more thundered and lightened. Back go the Achaians again in headlong flight, beaten into their defences by Hektor; and he would have burnt their ships, had not Hera inspired Agamemnon to rally them. By the day's end the Achaians are beaten, but not irrevocably, and the close of the eighth book motivates the embassy to Achilleus. But it is not soon enough for Achilleus to give in; the danger has not come close enough, Hektor has not stormed the defences or fired the ships; so we get one more day of fighting.

During this day, the pattern of rout and rally continues, until, like Diomedes and Agamemnon in the eighth book, Diomedes (11. 312–321), Eurypylos (11. 575), Polypoites and Leonteus (12. 145) have had their chances to play Achilleus, but all in vain, because Zeus favours the Trojans. So the amusing episode of Zeus beguiled by the charms of Hera is not merely an episode, because in Zeus' absence the Achaians rally and defeat their enemies once more. It takes Zeus to make good Achilleus' statement.

We might feel that such men as the Achaians could take care of themselves under any circumstances. *Do* they need Achilleus after all? They must, and way is made for him as his rivals are cleared away, one by one. Agamemnon opened this day by leading an irresistible charge, but is at length wounded and has to withdraw. Diomedes repulses Hektor, but is put out by an arrow wound in the foot. Odysseus is stabbed by one of his victims. Paris, who had wounded Diomedes, disables Eurypylos with another arrow, then Machaon. These men are not considered defeated. Agamemnon and Odysseus kill the men who wound them; the others are victims of archery, not overcome in fair fight. Still, in spite of Diomedes' finely expressed contempt for the bow (11. 385–395), he and his fellow victims fight no more in the Iliad.

By the end of the eleventh book, the only Achaian of the first magnitude left in the fighting is Aias. He does not break, but he can only sustain, cannot beat off, the Trojan attack. At the end of Book 15 he is fighting, tired, overmatched, bravely but hopelessly, from the ships. The desired moment for the entry of Patroklos, representative and forerunner of Achilleus, has been reached.

Without, however, permitting us to escape feeling that the Achaians are better men. Consider the close of the long eleventh book. Wounded Eurypylos gives a gloomy report to Patroklos (11. 823–827); the Trojans are winning, the Achaians are doomed. Yet, if we look back over the course of the battle through which this position was reached, we find that, in addition to five big heroes wounded, nine Achaians were killed, and twenty-eight Trojans.

Whether such legerdemain indicates the hand of a single author, I leave it to my readers to decide. But note that the dilemma—vindicate Achilleus but do not dishonour the Achaians—has been solved.

HEKTOR AND *ARISTEIA*

There is one figure in the Achilleus story to whom we have not yet given full attention. This is the enemy hero. The Achaians are not being defeated by, Achilleus does not rescue them from, any horde of nameless Trojans. The hero must have a worthy opponent: a gigantic warrior, a Goliath of Gath.

In the Iliad, this is Hektor. What his part should be in the Achilleus story, we may see from parallels which lie near at hand and which express the basic pattern of the *Achilleis*. After the death of Hektor, according to Arktinos, 'the Amazon Penthesilea, the daughter of Areas and of Thracian birth, comes to aid the Trojans'. She fights bravely (*aristeia*) but is killed by Achilleus. It is perhaps only inference that Penthesileia routed the Achaians before Achilleus disposed of her, though the language suggests it. But the case is clearer for Memnon. 'Next Memnon, the son of Eos (Dawn), wearing armour made by Hephaistos, comes to help the Trojans. . . .' In the battle which follows Antilochos is killed by Memnon and Memnon by Achilleus. That Memnon routed the Achaians before Achilleus intervened seems clear from Pindar's *Sixth Pythian*. Still another leader of the Trojans slain by Achilleus was Kyknos, the son of Poseidon. Kyknos, Memnon, and Hektor are grouped as the three greatest victims of Achilleus by Pindar (*Olympia* 2; *Isthmia* 5).

The best parallel, though, is the Telephos story. Stasinos, according to the summary, told in the *Cypria* how the Achaians on their first expedition put in at Teuthrania, in Mysia, down the coast from Troy. They thought the city was Ilion and tried to sack it, but the Mysians came out against them. Telephos, their leader, killed Thersandros, an Achaian chief, but Achilleus then wounded Telephos. Pindar is more explicit, for he tells us how Patroklos

> brought with the sons of Atreus
> in the plain of Teuthras stood his ground alone with Achilleus
> when Telephos, bending back the rest of the valiant Danaans,
> hurled them against their own beached ships.[1]

Clearly, it is no great exaggeration to say that Hektor *is* Telephos. He performs the same function in the same script. Only Homer, as we already saw, has complicated the script.

For Hektor, as the giant who leads the defence, should be the greatest warrior on either side, with the exception of Achilleus. Achilleus should defeat him only after a struggle, and perhaps only with help.[2]

---

[1] *The Odes of Pindar*, R. Lattimore, Chicago, University of Chicago Press, 1947, p. 29 (*Ninth Olympian*).

[2] This last is interesting. Note that in the story of Memnon, the hero kills Antilochos (Achilleus' second-best friend) before he falls. Telephos, in the *Cypria*, killed Thersandros before he was defeated. According to the *Little Iliad*, Neoptolemos, the son of Achilleus, called to Troy to help the Achaians, fought Eurypylos, the son of Telephos, who had come to help the Trojans. Eurypylos was killed; but he killed Machaon first. When the Asian hero claimed his victim before going down, was that victim

In the Iliad, Hektor both does and does not appear as such a hero, and in such stature. Achilleus insists, as we have seen, that the other Achaians cannot stand against him. He is a bogey with which to frighten Agamemnon and the rest. But Achilleus has no doubts that he, himself, can handle him (9. 351–354).

Not so the other Achaians. Agamemnon claims that Achilleus has been reluctant to fight Hektor (7. 112–114). Odysseus appeals to Achilleus to save them from Hektor, and their bravest constantly show fear of him, doubt if they can stop him (15. 636–637; 10. 47–52; 18. 149–150). When he challenges any Achaian to single combat, not one man is willing to fight him. Menelaos at last volunteers, for shame, and is roundly told that he would have no chance. Only after a characteristic scolding by Nestor do the bravest Achaians rise up and say that they are ready. And yet Aias, chosen by lot from the volunteers, clearly defeats Hektor, and he does so once more for their other combat (14. 402–437). Similarly, Diomedes is frankly afraid of him, but smashes him back in their brief encounter (11. 345–356). So Hektor himself is inclined to brag, and anticipate more than he can do (e.g. 8. 535–541; 13. 824–832; 18. 293–309), but he himself is constantly being heckled by some other prince, as Sarpedon (5. 472–481) or Glaukos (16. 538–547; there are numerous similar passages). Plainly, the reputation of Hektor continually surpasses his achievements. These are great. He is the heart and soul of the Trojan defence, and when he falls the Trojans feel their chances are gone. He kills many. But his only really great victim is Patroklos; and from Patroklos he runs, and must be rallied to fight him; and Apollo stuns and disarms Patroklos, and Euphorbos spears him in the back, before Hektor runs up to dispatch a helpless man, and boast that he has beaten him. Much of what he does is by divine favour. Apollo picks him up when he is down, and Zeus is behind his charges. He runs in panic from Achilleus, until Athene, disguised as Deïphobos, brings him to stand and fight. He is beaten by Aias and repulsed by Diomedes. Agamemnon and Odysseus he does not meet, so that his only advantage against a major Achaian warrior

helping the Achaian hero, and so enabling him to win? In Pindar's story, Patroklos and Achilleus fought Telephos together. In a pre-Homeric version, was Patroklos helping Achilleus when Hektor killed him, and Achilleus killed Hektor? And did Homer alter it, for the greater glory of Achilleus, and consequent diminution of Hektor, and in order to motivate the return of Achilleus through desire for honourable revenge?

[35]

is the tainted triumph over Patroklos. His moment of highest grandeur comes when he smashes in the *gate*: 'no man could have stopped him then', but no Aias stands in his path to be shamed.

Whatever his failures, he remains a figure of terror to the Achaians:

> *so Hektor*
> *followed close on the heels of the flowing-haired Achaians,*
> *killing ever the last of the men; and they fled in terror.*
> *But after they had crossed back over the ditch and the sharp stakes*
> *in flight, and many had gone down under the hands of the Trojans,*
> *they reined in and stood fast again beside their ships, calling*
> *aloud upon each other, and to all of the gods uplifting*
> *their hands each man of them cried out his prayers in a great voice,*
> *while Hektor, wearing the stark eyes of a Gorgon, or murderous*
> *Ares, wheeled about at the edge his bright-maned horses*
>
> (8. 340–349).

> *With this in mind he (Zeus) drove on against the hollow ships Hektor*
> *Priam's son, though Hektor without the gods was in fury*
> *and raged, as when destructive fire or spear-shaking Ares*
> *rages among the mountains and dense places of the deep forest.*
> *A slaver came out around his mouth, and under the lowering*
> *brows his eyes were glittering, the helm on his temples*
> *was shaken and thundered horribly to the fighting of Hektor*
>
> (15. 603–609).

And he does what he must do. Knocked out, beaten off, he comes back, and with gods' help or no help he does, almost single-handed, pile the Achaians back on their ships and begin to fire the fleet. Here, from another view, is that same sleight of hand by which the great Achaians, never surpassed in *aristeia*, are yet shattered and beaten in on their ships, and army and fleet are lost without Achilleus.

Two ways, again. Homer's success is somewhat left-handed. He has so industriously diminished his Goliath for the sake of others that we sense deception, and feel that Hektor 'really was' greater than Patroklos or any other Achaian except Achilleus. For this Hektor, Homer's Hektor, who brags outrageously, who sometimes hangs back when the going is worst, who bolts from Achilleus, is still the hero who forever captures the affection and admiration of the modern reader, far more strongly than his conqueror has ever done.[1] Such are the accidental triumphs of Homer.

STYLE: FORMAL ELEMENTS AND FORMULA

The narrative character of the Iliad, which is free invention working on and within advanced but still fluid tradition, is reflected also in the style of the Iliad. And as Homer took over details of person and act from his predecessors, he also took over from them exact phrases by which to characterize the person, or narrate the act.

We can perhaps best understand Homeric style if we state two mutually dependent propositions. First: the Iliad is essentially oral composition, since, *whether or not* Homer himself wrote it down, it was intended to be recited aloud, not read silently, and since it builds on a deep-piled tradition of oral recitations. Second: all statement is dominated by the metre, which is dactylic hexameter, so that ready-made phrases which fit the metre tend to be retained, while possible innovations are subject to rejection if they do not fit.

With this in mind, consider the following passage, taken almost at random (3. 67–75):

67 *Now though, if you wish me to fight it out and do battle,*
make the rest of the Trojans sit down, and all the Achaians,
and set me in the middle with Menelaos the warlike
70 *to fight together for the sake of Helen and all her possessions.*
That one of us who wins and is proved stronger, let him
take the possessions fairly and the woman, and lead her homeward.
But the rest of you, having cut your oaths of faith and friendship
dwell, you in Troy where the soil is rich, while those others return home
75 *to horse-pasturing Argos, and Achaia the land of fair women.*

The passage may be called padded, in that the underscored words and phrases are not necessary to the minimum meaning which is to be communicated. Homer had not been told to be concise or terse, or that having once said 'fight it out' he need not, therefore should not, add 'and do

---

[1]   *If this be so, then bragless let it be.*
                 Great Hector was a man as good as he.

Shakespeare has deliberately made Achilleus' triumph over Hektor even hollower than Homer made Hektor's triumph over Patroklos.

battle'. A passage like this (and it is typical enough) shows no preoccupation with brevity, and no ambition to be original. The superfluous words and phrases are, on the other hand, *metrically* necessary and since they fall into position in the cadences of the line, they are employed not only here, but anywhere else in the poem where they suit both text and metre.

A leisurely style, and one that does not avoid saying a thing in a practically desirable way merely because the thing has been said that way before. On the contrary. Lines 71 and 72 are repeated, 73 virtually repeated, when Hektor passes on this proposal to the Achaians.

Such repeats are frequent in Homer. Even the casual reader will notice them, but only the careful student will find a pattern of repetition so all-pervasive that it creates an essential texture of language without which Homer would not be Homer.

But repeats are of various orders. In the first place, an entire passage, often of considerable length, may be repeated. When Agamemnon after the first Achaian defeat proposes to abandon the siege and go home (9. 17–28), he borrows his entire speech from the text of the previous speech in which he was 'testing' the Achaians (2. 110–141),[1] except for the first line, which had opened a still earlier speech (2. 79), and which is used six times in the Iliad. His appearance, in tears, is described in terms used later to present the weeping Patroklos (9. 14–15 = 16. 3–4, beginning of first line adjusted). All repeats are founded on the principle that a thing once said in the right way should be said again in the *same* way when occasion demands. Agamemnon proceeds to enumerate the gifts through which he offers to propitiate Achilleus (9. 122–157). When Odysseus transmits the offer to Achilleus (9. 264–299), he does it in the exact words of Agamemnon, except that he must shift from first to third person, and that one line, involving Agamemnon's long name, must be more drastic-ally altered. Aias' spear-throw against Hektor is described in the terms of Menelaos' spear-throw against Paris (3. 356–360 = 7. 250–254).

Such repeats of a few lines are exceedingly numerous, but far more numerous are repeats of single lines. Highly characteristic are hexameters for the introduction of a speech, as

Then in turn the Gerenian horseman Nestor answered him,

or for the address to an individual:

[1] Note that the original speech is longer. What Agamemnon has borrowed is the beginning and the end.

Son of Laertes and seed of Zeus, resourceful Odysseus,
or a death in battle:

He fell, thunderously, and his armour clattered upon him.

Finally, there is the word group of less than a line which forms a metrical unit adaptable to any place where sense demands, and the metre will accommodate.[1] This can be most easily illustrated through the noun-adjective or name-adjective combinations, involving the fixed epithet, although such combinations by no means exhaust the varieties of formula. Names, or nouns, carry with them descriptive terms, of varying appropriateness, which adhere so closely that they are scarcely more than extensions of the noun. Examples are: innocent children, strong-greaved Achaians, grey-eyed Athene, generous Troad.

The metrical significance of such formulae may be illustrated as follows. Suppose a name closes a line, and that the line is filled except for the last two feet, so that what is desired is $- \cup \cup - -$.

Formulae involving the names of Odysseus, Hektor, and Zeus are as follows:

> dios Odysseus (brilliant Odysseus),
> phaidimos Hektor (glorious Hektor),
> metieta Zeus (Zeus of the counsels),
> euryopa Zeus (Zeus of the wide brows).

But now suppose the syllables desired are $\cup \cup \,|\, - \cup \cup \,|\, - -$, we get

> polymetis Odysseus (resourceful Odysseus),
> korythaiolos Hektor (Hektor of the shining helm),
> nephelegerata Zeus (Zeus the cloud-gatherer),

and for three and a half feet, $\cup \,|\, - - \,|\, - \cup \cup \,|\, - -$, we get

> polytlas dios Odysseus (long-suffering brilliant Odysseus),
> megas korythaiolos Hektor (tall Hektor of the shining helm),
> pater andron te theon te (the father of gods and men).

Note how Zeus changes from counsellor to storm-mountain-god to

[1] In the discussion which follows, I make no claim to originality. The analysis and application of formula in Homer is the work of Milman Parry; his methods and conclusions have revolutionized Homeric studies. All I have tried to do is illustrate some of his findings for the benefit of those who do not know Greek. My entire interpretation of the formal elements in style is based on Parry. His chief publications on this material are: *L'Épithète traditionelle dans Homère*, Paris, 1928; and 'Studies in the Epic Technique of Oral Verse-Making', *Harvard Studies in Classical Philology*, 41 (1930), 73–147; 43 (1932), 1–50.

paternal god, *not* in connection with what he is doing, but at the dictates of metre. He is not *nephelegereta Zeus* when he is gathering clouds, but when he is filling the metrical unit ∪ ∪ − ∪ ∪ − −. Just so, Achilleus, whose name is the exact metrical equivalent of Odysseus (∪ − −), shares with him the rather general epithet *dios*. And Menelaos and Diomedes get the odd epithet 'of the great war cry' not because they are noisier than anybody else, but because their metrically identical names can usefully terminate a line beginning − − − ∪ ∪ − ∪ with

boen agathos (Menelaos)
(Diomedes).

Now such an epithet is (metre aside) neither specially appropriate nor yet inappropriate. Elsewhere, though, the formula trails its adjective into surprising contexts. So Aigisthos, of all people, is 'blameless'. Aphrodite is 'laughing' when she voices a complaint (5. 375) in tears. If Helen will be the 'beloved wife' of the rival who wins her (3. 138) this implies no archness or slyness on the part of the speaker. 'Beloved' goes with 'wife'.

It is the manipulation of such counters that makes up, in part, the Homeric style. Parry's contention that the formulae are too numerous to be the work of a single man, while probably right, is not demonstrably so. But it does not seem possible that the same man could have invented all these formulae *and* the metre which they involve, as it involves them. Formulae are words, and they come down in the tradition, though many may be the work of a single man, and in the incredible skill of their manipulation in the Iliad we may be justified in seeing a single, original poet. But not original in the sense that he would throw away a ready-made phrase for the sake of making a new one, his own. In this respect later Greek poets, such as Pindar and Aeschylus, are as remote from Homer as are Donne, Crashaw, and Browning.

STYLE: THE SIMILE

The formulaic aspect of Homer represents the traditional as the fixed story represents the traditional. He did not make this style, he used it. It needs no defence. Padded, adjectival, leisurely, routine, it works.

But formula does not exhaust the style, since there are passages which, unique, non-standardized, non-formulaic, show the operations of original technique as clearly as do the characterizations of Hektor and others.

The escape of the individual from the impersonal may be shown in the intensely characteristic similes.

In Homer, as in Greek literature generally, direct and detailed description is rare. In the Iliad, only one person receives full physical characterization, and this is the grotesque Thersites (2. 216–219) who receives it precisely because he varies from the august standards of the characteristic hero. Elsewhere, single adjectives as 'huge', 'fair-haired', 'glancing-eyed', 'deep-girdled', or adherent epithets as 'ox-eyed', etc., suffice, nor does Homer describe the details of a situation directly as such. Indirectly, though, description can be communicated through effect (the beauty of Helen, the strength of Achilleus). Or through comparison.

I would, briefly, distinguish metaphor and simile thus: In simile, you say that A is like B. In metaphor, you say that A is B, or you introduce A as B without making any specific equation. This is an insufficient account, but will serve here because Homer does not use metaphor extensively, and when he does the use is confined to simple phrases as 'dikes of battle' or 'this pestilence, Hektor' or, of a mountain, 'mother of sheepflocks', of which the last two are deliberate personifications, the first probably a primeval and fossilized phrase whose meaning might have been as lost to Homer as it is to us. Intensification of such metaphors would lead to the difficult austere figures of a Pindar or Sophocles, in which the reader or listener must make the transition from A to B himself; where an act of sorcery and transmutation has taken place and A is no longer A but has turned into B. Homer carries metaphor no farther than the simple figures shown above. He develops the more explicit simile.

Simple similes appear. Aias carries his shield which is like a wall, men attack like wolves or lions, fight like fire, the island of the Phaeacians lies like a shield in the sea. But a simile may develop itself, and development takes place not of A, the thing described, but B, that to which it is referred. Consider the wound of Menelaos (4. 141–147):

141 *As when some Maionian woman or Karian with purple*
   colours ivory, to make it a cheek piece for horses;
   it lies away in an inner room, and many a rider
   longs to have it, but it is laid up to be a king's treasure,
145 *two things, to be the beauty of the horse, the pride of the horseman:*
   so, Menelaos, your shapely thighs were stained with the colour
147 *of blood, and your legs also and the ankles beneath them.*

White skin, blood-stained; like a stained cheek piece. The cheek piece has a history of its own, and this is told before we return to our subject. This shows the construction. A is like B (141); B has such and such a history, progresses in such and such a manner (141–145); and (we repeat) it is like A (146–147).

The development of the form begins where we enter the history of B, which is, from the point of view of narrative, superfluous. Development need not take place. In a place which comes a little before the simile of the cheek piece, Athene brushes the arrow away from its mark (4. 130–131).

> She brushed it away from his skin as lightly as when a mother
> brushes a fly away from her child who is lying in sweet sleep.

This simile, which stops at A is like B, is not developed. It is complete in itself.

In simile, we are referred from the scene in the Iliad to a scene which is not part of the Iliad; sometimes to the supernatural, more often to the everyday world. Such passages represent in part an escape from the heroic narrative of remote events which is the poet's assignment and the only medium we know of through which he could communicate his craft. It is perhaps such a liberation that wittingly or not vitalizes the development within the simile (4. 452–456):

> As when rivers in winter spate running down from the mountains
> throw together at the meeting of streams the weight of their water
> out of the great springs behind in the hollow stream-bed,
> and far away in the mountains the shepherd hears their thunder;
> such, from the coming together of men, was the shock and the shouting.

Such similes are landscapes, direct from the experience of life, and this one is humanized by the tiny figure of the shepherd set against enormous nature.

So the development may sweep on for its own sake until it ends even by contradicting the effect which it was introduced in order to achieve. Consider the following: a volley of missiles from men defending a wall (12. 278–289):

> And they, as storms of snow descend to the ground incessant
> on a winter day, when Zeus of the counsels, showing
> before men what shafts he possesses, brings on a snowstorm
> and stills the winds asleep in the solid drift, enshrouding

the peaks that tower among the mountains and the shoulders out-jutting,
and the low lands with their grasses, and the prospering work of men's
*   hands,*
and the drift falls along the grey sea, the harbours and beaches,
and the surf that breaks against it is stilled, and all things elsewhere
it shrouds from above, with the burden of Zeus' rain heavy upon it;
so numerous and incessant were the stones volleyed from both sides,
some thrown on Trojans, others flung against the Achaians
by Trojans, so the whole length of the wall thundered beneath them.

What the missiles have in common with the snow is, of course, descent in infinite quantity, but the snowfall, described first, builds a hushed world from which we wake with a shock to the crashing battle. The ultimate effect is not of likeness, but contrast.

Simile offers the most natural and frequently used, but not the only, escape from the heroic. Consider (11. 86–90):

But at that time when the woodcutter makes ready his supper
in the wooded glens of the mountains, when his arms and hands have
*   grown weary*
from cutting down the tall trees, and his heart has had enough of it,
and the longing for food and for sweet wine takes hold of his senses;
at that time the Danaans by their manhood broke the battalions.

This is to indicate the time of day, but the time of day has been indicated as we end line 86. What follows is gratuitous. It has the *form* of the simile, as well as the content: unheroic but interesting woodcutter, a moment out of his life and feeling. And in this spirit Homer takes advantage of Achilleus' new shield to illustrate, under form of a rehearsal of its decorations, scenes representing the life of his day. In this series the sense of description is so strong that the inert images on the shield come to life and move in time and space before our eyes.

I take such passages to be non-traditional and original. For as an essential characteristic of the formula is repeat, an essential of simile is uniqueness.[1] Therefore, it happens that when a very minor figure is set into the narrative, appearing once (often in order to be one of the victims of a major

---

[1] Very few similes are repeated. The most notable case is 6. 506–511 = 15. 263–268; 16. 482–486 repeats 13. 389–393. There are a few cases where a later simile borrows a line or two from an earlier, 16. 299–300 = 8. 557–558; 16. 4 with previous half-line repeats 9. 15 with previous half-line. See Shewan, 219–220.

hero), he may trail after him a few lines of personal history constructed
after the manner of the simile, since then he enters in a capacity similar
to that of the stained cheek piece that describes Menelaos' wound. Con-
sider this battle-sequence (5. 49–68):

> *While Menelaos son of Atreus killed with the sharp spear*
> 50 *Strophios' son, a man of wisdom in the chase, Skamandrios,*
> *the fine huntsman of beasts. Artemis herself had taught him*
> *to strike down every wild thing that grows in the mountain forest.*
> *Yet Artemis of the showering arrows could not now help him,*
> *no, nor the long spearcasts in which he had been pre-eminent,*
> 55 *but Menelaos the spear-famed, son of Atreus, stabbed him*
> *as he fled away before him, in the back with a spear thrust*
> *between the shoulders and driven through to the chest beyond it.*
> *He dropped forward on his face and his armour clattered upon him.*
> *Meriones in turn killed Phereklos, son of Harmonides,*
> 60 *the smith, who understood how to make with his hand all intricate*
> *things, since above all others Pallas Athene had loved him.*
> *He it was who had built for Alexandros the balanced*
> *ships, the beginning of the evil, fatal to the other*
> *Trojans, and to him, since he knew nothing of the god's plans.*
> 65 *This man Meriones pursued and overtaking him*
> *struck in the right buttock, and the spearhead drove straight*
> *on and passing under the bone went into the bladder.*
> *He dropped, screaming, to his knees, and death was a mist about him.*

Skamandrios and Phereklos are people of no importance. In narrative,
they are just cannon-fodder for Menelaos and Meriones. There are in-
numerable battle-victims like them in the Iliad. Did all these people and
their names make their way down the tradition to Homer? We cannot
tell, but invention seems probable. In any case, note that Menelaos'
success could well end at line 50, Meriones' at 59. The huntsman par-
ticularly, a prototype of Hippolytos, offers a brief escape into individual
lines and matter, before his death is described in the ghastly formulae for
death in battle (55–58). Such passages with their incidental pathos are in
the manner of similes, with which they can unobtrusively stand in com-
bination (a good example is Simoesios, 4. 473–489).

Simile, with its relatives, is as essential to Homer as formula. It has been
more frequently noticed, but even more seriously misunderstood. Simile

in Homer is not decoration; it is dynamic invention, and because of this no successor has been able to swing it in the same grand manner.[1]

THE PEOPLE OF THE ILIAD

The Iliad is a story, and the strength of a story, as such, depends to a great extent on its characters. The actions and achievements of the great Homeric characters might have been fixed in tradition, or twisted by *tendenz*, but within the frame-work of fact the personality of the hero might remain plastic. Not the 'what', but the 'how' and 'why', gave the poet some option.

THE DEFENDER: HEKTOR

Against the tragedy of Achilleus is set the tragedy of Troy, and the two strands are closely involved. The hero of the Trojan tragedy is Hektor. We looked at him once before, from the Achaian point of view; to them he was a figure of terror even for their bravest, over-rated perhaps, but deadly enough in his actions as well as his menaces. But Goliath of Gath might have looked to the wives and mothers of the Philistines very different from the monster seen by Saul and Abner. It shows a significant difference between epic and chronicle when Homer takes us over to the other side and lets us see Hektor as the Trojans saw him.

In Troy, Hektor was beloved. Homer interrupts his narrative to take him back to Troy and show him with mother, brother and sister-in-law, wife and child, all affectionate and concerned. Priam and Hekabe consider him far the best and dearest of their sons. Helen testifies that where others were hateful (an exaggeration characteristic of Helen) Hektor was always kind (24. 762–775).

Hektor's tragedy is that of Troy. He, like it, is destroyed fighting a quarrel unworthy of him. He does not believe in Paris' quarrel, and he does not like to fight. When Andromache beseeches him not to go back into open battle, the beginning of his answer is revealing (6. 441–445):

[1] This is not to detract from Virgil, Dante, Milton, and others who have made magnificent original use of the tradition. Dante is particularly fortunate, but quite different from Homer in that he combines simile with metaphor of quite un-Homeric sophistication and depth. I should have liked to go further into such distinctions. See Bowra's valuable chapter on oral and literary epic, *From Virgil to Milton*, 1–32.

yet I would feel deep shame
before the Trojans, and the Trojan women with trailing garments
if like a coward I were to shrink aside from the fighting;
and the spirit will not let me, since I have learned to be valiant
and to fight always among the foremost ranks of the Trojans.

Perhaps one should not stress too much the implications of 'I have learned', but the close of Hektor's speech to Paris a little later shows the same tendency (6. 526–529):

Let us go now; some day hereafter we will make all right
with the immortal gods in the sky, if Zeus ever grant it,
setting up to them in our houses the wine-bowl of liberty
after we have driven out of Troy the strong-greaved Achaians.

Not bloodthirsty enough to be a natural warrior, he fights finely from a sense of duty and a respect for the opinions of others, a respect which Paris notoriously lacks (3. 43–45; 56–57).

Surely now the flowing-haired Achaians laugh at us,
thinking you are our bravest champion, only because your
looks are handsome, but there is no strength in your heart, no courage.

No, but the Trojans are cowards in truth, else long before this
you had worn a mantle of flying stones for the wrong you did us.

The sneer sticks to Hektor himself. Some hidden weakness, not cowardice but perhaps the fear of being called a coward, prevents him from liquidating a war which he knows perfectly well is unjust.[1] This weakness, which is not remote from his boasting, nor from his valour (6. 407), is what kills him.

ACHILLEUS: THE TRAGIC HERO

The function of Achilleus in the Iliad of itself necessitates certain qualities. The necessary man must be a supreme warrior, but in station and as a king he ranks below Agamemnon. As a hero of tragedy, he is great, but human and imperfect. His tragedy is an effect of free choice by a will that falls short of omniscience and is disturbed by anger.

[1] Shakespeare sees the difficult question: 'Why do not the Trojans return Helen, in spite of Paris?', and has his own answer. His Hektor, as intelligent as brave, demolishes the arguments of Paris and Troilus, then gives way in a spirit of chivalry.

In the Iliad his supremacy as a warrior is scarcely challenged, and is insisted upon at all times. After Patroklos' death he terrifies the battle-weary Trojans by appearing, unarmed (18. 202–231). But his supremacy is powered by gods who favour, strengthen, and protect him. In the scene just mentioned, he is supernaturally attended. When he shouts, Athene shouts with him, and when he appears he is surrounded in a flaming nimbus lit by Athene. Thetis carries his case to Zeus, and it is put through against the will of powerful goddesses. Hephaistos makes him immortal armour. When Hektor at last fights him, he fights at a gross disadvantage, swindled by Athene and deserted by Apollo, with inferior body armour and with no spear. Achilleus goes so well guarded by gods that Aineias, himself a divine favourite, can justly complain; none can meet Achilleus on fair terms (20. 97–102).

Nevertheless, Achilleus is not in any sense immortal. The legend of almost complete invulnerability is either unknown to Homer or discarded by him. He is closer to the gods than other heroes, but defers to them generally; one failure to do so, in his fight with the river, almost brings him to an abrupt and undignified ending, from which he is saved only by the intervention of stronger divinities. Achilleus is prescient beyond others, but his knowledge has limitations, and his character can be invaded by the human emotions of grief (18. 22–27), fear (20. 259–266), a passage which makes plain that he is neither semi-divinity nor superman (16. 126–129), and, above all, anger.

It is the anger of pride, the necessary accompaniment of the warrior's greatness, that springs the tragedy of the Iliad. We see it in the treatment of Hektor's body and the slaughter of captives; we see it motivate the quarrel of the first book, where the fourth word of the first line is 'anger'. He dares Agamemnon, makes it almost impossible for the latter to act except as he does. Yet as he leaves to pray for the defeat of his friends, though this prayer amounts to outright treason, we feel, as we are meant to feel, that he is in the right. In the ninth book, the burden shifts. Agamemnon has never touched the girl Briseis, and now he will give her back and offers abundant gifts in addition. The offer is conveyed by three of Achilleus' best friends. Odysseus warns him against pride and anger, and appeals to him in the name of friendship, but Achilleus rejects all appeals. Then Aias reproaches him, not with treachery or lack of patriotism, but with bad friendship, and Achilleus answers (9. 645–647):

all that you have said seems spoken after my own mind.
Yet still the heart in me swells up in anger, when I remember
the disgrace that he wrought upon me before the Argives.

He has now put himself in the wrong. Anger has clouded a high intelligence, and Achilleus acts uncertainly. Before, he had announced his intention of sailing home, but instead stayed by his ships and watched the fighting, torturing himself and the others by his inaction. Now, again, he threatens to go home; but shifts again, and refuses to fight until Hektor reaches the ships of the Myrmidons. Such a moment is near, when Achilleus at last gives way to Patroklos and lets him go in his place. He is again uncertain (16. 60–65):

still we will let all this be a thing of the past; and it was not
in my heart to be angry forever; and yet I did say
I would not give over my anger until that time came
when the fighting with all its clamour came up to my own ships.
So do you draw my glorious armour about your shoulders;
lead the Myrmidons whose delight is battle into the fighting.

There is no reason now why Achilleus should not fight himself. His action makes no sense, and is fatal to Patroklos. So Achilleus admits to his mother (18. 74–82). The tragedy is his, the result of his own choice.

Apollo, outraged at the treatment of his friend Hektor, practically describes Achilleus as a brute and a barbarian (24. 33–54). He is not. He is a man of culture and intelligence; he knows how to respect heralds, how to entertain estranged friends. He presides over the games with extraordinary courtesy and tact. He is not only a great fighter but a great gentleman, and if he lacks the chivalry of Roland, Lancelot, or Beowulf, that is because theirs is a chivalry coloured with Christian humility which has no certain place in the gallery of Homeric virtues. Above all, Achilleus is a real man, mortal and fallible, but noble enough to make his own tragedy a great one.

AGAMEMNON: THE KING

Most of the greater Achaian heroes are kings in their own right, but the greatest king among them is Agamemnon. Whether he is emperor of the Achaians, or general of the army, or the king with most subjects, whose friends stand by him in his brother's quarrel (unless he insults them), is a question apparently as obscure to the heroes of the Iliad as it is to us. But essentially a king is what he is; not the biggest Achaian, says Priam to Helen, but the kingliest; a bull in a herd of cattle; a lord who must be busy while others rest, marshalling his men for ordered assault. In the quarrel with Achilleus, he demands recognition of his kingly stature, as if afraid of losing his position if he lacks what others have, in this case a captive mistress. So he comes off badly, yet even here, while he reviles Kalchas and beats down Achilleus, his first thought is for the army.

Here, in his position, is the key to Agamemnon's character. As brave and effective a personal fighter as one could ask (Achilleus' strictures are manifestly untrue), Agamemnon is a worried, uncertain man. Beyond others, he drifts in his thinking. He invites the Achaians to go home in order to 'make trial' of them, but ends up as if he had outwitted himself and believed his own falsehoods. Certainly, he stands helpless in front of the confusion he has caused, and it is Odysseus, backed by Hera and Athene, who pulls the situation around. His panic, when Menelaos is treacherously wounded, causes a similar drift of thought: he begins with the assurance that the Trojans must die for their treachery (4. 158–168) and ends by visualizing a triumphant Trojan jumping on the grave of Menelaos (4. 176–182). He veers between the two poles of thought: that he can take Troy at once, without Achilleus; that he will be lucky if he gets any of his men home alive. Twice after his test of the second book he proposes mass flight, at once (9. 9–28, compare 10. 1–20; 14. 74–81). In all moods of despair, he must be rallied and propped up by Odysseus, Nestor, and Diomedes, who are tougher than he. But the uncertainty is that of a king, with whom Homer's aristocratic audience may well have sympathized, and it is his 'kingliness', his concern for those he leads, which grounds his uncertainty.[1] Nevertheless, irresolution and consequent anger combine with the anger of Achilleus to motivate tragedy.

[1] That tyranny corrupts character, so breeds tragedy, becomes a commonplace for Herodotus and the tragic poets. Sophocles' Kreon is the clearest case: a good man, inadequate to monarchy, whose disqualification ruins him and others. Kreon and Agamemnon alike make one rash statement, after which their rebellious opponents give them no chance to escape.

ODYSSEUS: THE PRUDENT COUNSELLOR AND COMPLETE MAN

Odysseus of the Iliad foreshadows Odysseus of the Odyssey not only in his epithets (resourceful, long-suffering, etc.) but in his whole character. I do not know whether this means that the same man composed both Iliad and Odyssey; but it does mean that the author of the Odyssey thoroughly understood the Odysseus of the Iliad. We can, I think, argue from one work to the other.

Odysseus is crafty, resourceful, daring, and merciless. These characteristics have usually been taken as essentials of his personality, from which stem the stop-at-nothing politician of Sophocles, or Dante's treacherous captain (*Inferno*, Canto 26). But guile and unscrupulousness are only secondary characteristics of the Homeric Odysseus.

Essentially, he can be described by the Greek word *sophron* (though the word is not Homeric). This is untranslatable. It means, not necessarily that you have superior brains, but that you make maximum use of whatever brains you have got. Odysseus is the antithesis of Achilleus. Achilleus has a fine intelligence, but passion clouds it; Odysseus has strong passions, but his intelligence keeps them under control. Achilleus, Hektor, and Agamemnon, magnificent as they are, are flawed with uncertainty and can act on confused motives; Odysseus never. So those three are tragic heroes, but Odysseus, less magnificent but a complete man, is the hero of his own romantic comedy, the *Return of Odysseus*, or *Odyssey*.

A single purpose guides Odysseus in the Iliad. The expedition against Troy must succeed. Whether this motive grows out of personal affection for Agamemnon is not clear. But this is the end toward which the demoralized army must be rallied, Thersites chastised, Achilleus propitiated, Agamemnon braced. A single purpose guides Odysseus through the Odyssey as well. He must get home and put his house and kingdom in order. To do this, he must drive his men and himself, outwit and outlast trial by danger and trial by pleasure, leave the blandishing goddesses, fight down his joy at seeing home and wife for fear joy might give him away prematurely, fight down, for the same reason, rage at seeing the disorder in his household.

A man who could win through all this is a man supremely adequate, in mind and body; therefore, by corollary, resourceful, much enduring.

Odysseus can be most eloquent, but he wastes no eloquence on Thersites —who has an unanswerable argument—but beats him up and makes him cry, which is far more effective. He can build a raft and sail it, or build a bed, or plough a field. He has no recklessness, but does have stark courage when that is needed; the Odysseus who makes the plans for others to fight by is post-Homeric. Always equal to the occasion, he startles the Trojans who think he looks like a fool and can be no orator, as he startles the suitors who take him for a broken-down tramp. Not the noblest or stateliest of Homer's heroes, he is the one who survives.

AIAS: THE SOLDIER

Greatest of the warriors after Achilleus is Aias. Homer is very firm about this (2. 768–769), although Diomedes at times seems to surpass anything that Aias can do. Diomedes in his *aristeia* fights under the protection of Athene, and Achilleus is constantly attended and favoured by divinities; but Aias carries on, from beginning to end, without benefit of supernatural aid.

A huge man, he is compared to a wall, and carries a great shield of seven-fold ox-hide. He is not the man to sweep the enemy back in a single burst, as Diomedes, Agamemnon, Achilleus, or Hektor can do; rather, his fighting qualities appear in a comparison drawn by Idomeneus (13. 321–325):

> *Nor would huge Telamonian Aias give way to any man*
> *who was mortal and ate bread, the yield of Demeter,*
> *one who could be broken by the bronze and great stones flung at him.*
> *He would not make way for Achilleus who breaks men in battle,*
> *in close combat. For speed of feet none can strive with Achilleus.*

Lack of inspired brilliance may go with the failure, in Aias' case, of that divine aid lavished on other heroes. He fights as a big man, with no aura of the supernatural about him; best on defence and when the going is worst. With the other great Achaians out of action, he keeps the Achaian retreat from becoming a rout, defends the wall, and then the ships. At the last moment before Patroklos and the Myrmidons come to the rescue, we find him leading the defence of the ships, baffled by Hektor, beaten, sweating, and arm-weary, without hope, but still fighting. Lacking the glamour of others, never the greatest leader, Aias remains throughout the best soldier of them all.

PEOPLE OF THE ILIAD IN LATER TRADITION

Space will not allow further analysis of Homeric persons, and such a study has in any case frequently been made. My purpose has been to illustrate, briefly, the coherence of these persons as they appear *in the text of the Homeric poems*, particularly the Iliad. It was necessary to do this, because we too often observe the Homeric hero through a disfiguring mist, and with preconceptions which lead us into error.

The political situation in the Achaian army, as implied in the Iliad, becomes explicitly developed and exploited in later tradition, until we find something like the following. An unscrupulous king, backed by a little group of politicians, not only leads Hellas into a disastrous, un-necessary war, but consistently slights and outrages his noblest warriors. Homer's story of Achilleus, the analogous, unused story of Philoktetes, the post-Homeric tale of Palamedes—Odysseus' rival, a truly wise man, done to death by chicanery[1]—show the trend. The people of the epic become, in the fifth century, counters for political propaganda and the exploitations of intra-Hellenic hatreds. To Pindar, Aias is an Aiginetan; to Sophocles, an Athenian. Menelaos, the courtly and considerate *grand seigneur* (and millionaire!) of Iliad and Odyssey, becomes the vulgar villain of Sophocles' *Aias*, the personification of Spartan *machtpolitik* in Euripides' *Andromache*.[2] Euripides can use Kalchas to vent his spleen against soothsayers, Talthybios to convey an almost equally potent aversion for heralds.[3]

Such manipulations passed, of course, as 'historical interpretations', and are merely developments, sometimes outrageous, of a situation inherent in the story-pattern of the necessary man. A clear case is the rivalry of Odysseus and Aias. In the Iliad, it does not exist, or at least goes unrecog-nized. But in the Odyssey, we find allusion[4] to the story of how the armour of dead Achilleus was awarded to Odysseus, rather than Aias,

---

[1] See Evelyn-White, *Hesiod*, pp. 493, 495, 505. The story, with variants, was told in the Cycle, and was the subject of a tragedy by Euripides.

[2] See also Euripides, *Orestes, Iphigeneia in Aulis*, and *Trojan Women*.

[3] *Helen*, 744–757; *Trojan Women*, 424–426.   [4] II. 543–551.

and how Aias died as a result. How and why Aias died Homer does not tell us, even in the Odyssey; but according to the Cycle, he went mad and killed himself.

By the time Pindar and the tragic poets get to work, the opposed heroes have come to represent the man of counsel and the man-at-arms. Odysseus, his valour and devotion forgotten, has stood ever since for the crafty, treacherous politician.[1] Aias does not come off much better. The story of the armour, *in itself*, demands a character different from that of the hero in the Iliad,[2] for the Iliad's Aias is as soberly sane as anyone in the epic. The reasoning must be something like this: Aias died as a result of not being awarded the armour. Nobody is known to have killed him, he must have killed himself. If so, he must have been mad; and if capable of insanity over such a point of honour, therefore naturally proud, vain, and choleric.[3] The bare negative fact of the Iliad, that Aias fought so well without divine protection, becomes twisted into a positive story that he arrogantly despised the proffered help of the gods, particularly Athene, the protectress of Diomedes and Odysseus.[4] Therefore, she wrecked him with delusions which drove him to slaughter cattle in the belief they were his enemies. Here we may have a contamination with Aias' namesake, the Lokrian, who 'defied the lightning' and came to so violent an end. At all events, we have the materials for Shakespeare's unbelievably believable caricature in *Troilus and Cressida*. This is an example of tradition, character, interpretation, and new tradition in the life of Homeric figures.

THE GODS IN THE ILIAD

I have said little in this introduction about the part played by the gods in the story of Troy; partly because the modern reader will generally be

[1] Sophocles' interpretation in his *Aias* is ultimately favourable to Odysseus, but even here he is no warrior. To Euripides (*Iphigeneia in Aulis, Trojan Women* particularly) Odysseus is responsible for all the deceptions and most of the brutalities perpetrated by the Achaians.

[2] If Homer composed the Odyssey, did he know, when he composed the Iliad, of the fate of Aias? The probability is that, in any case, he did, for there is no variant story which we can trace. If so, he suppressed the episode, with a view to making Aias the sort of person he did make him. The episode could be suppressed, or rather need not be introduced, because it lay outside the proper scope of the Iliad.

[3] With exactly those faults for which Aias, in the Iliad, so effectively reproaches Achilleus.   [4] Sophocles, *Ajax*, 758–777.

more interested in human than divine character; partly because the question is too complicated to be discussed in brief compass. But I will state briefly a few conclusions.

(1) The gods of Homer are mainly immortal men and women, incomparably more powerful than mortals, but like mortals susceptible to all human emotions and appetites, therefore capable of being teased, flattered, enraged, seduced, chastised. As immortal people, they may *also* represent projections of feelings or activities in the observed world. Thus, Ares is an immortal person, son of Zeus, protector of Troy, a brutal and blustering character. Ares is also war (Ares in lower-case, so to speak) and as such he is a force, a fact, and has no character at all. The two concepts may be combined. When Helen protests to Aphrodite, who has dragged her off to Troy for the sake of an unworthy man, I think she is doing two things at once. First, she is appealing to a supernatural person who is making her do what that person wants. Second, she is talking to herself, to that susceptibility (her Aphrodite) which has made her behave in a manner which the excellent mind of Helen considers idiotic.

(2) These gods have, in relation to men, absolute power. God may be overborne by god. The strongest is Zeus, who can do as he pleases, but often refrains from so doing for fear of unpleasantness. Zeus is *not* subject to fate. When Hera protests against his notion of saving Ilion or rescuing Sarpedon, against fate, she implies that he can do these things if he insists. The weighing of destinies on scales, apparently impersonal (8. 69; 22. 209), is a ceremony representing compromise with a different view.

(3) We simply do not know how seriously Homer took his Olympian gods, to what extent they are his divinities, or those of his tradition, or those of his audience. For narrative, they are enormously useful. They can turn events, reconcile otherwise impossible motives, rescue people who have got to be rescued. But one thing the gods-as-persons of Homer do not do: they do not change human nature. They manipulate Achilleus, Aineias, Paris, but they do not make them what they are. The choices are human; and in the end, despite all divine interferences, the Iliad is a story of people.

A NOTE ON THE TRANSLATION

My aim has been to give a rendering of the Iliad which will convey the meaning of the Greek in a speed and rhythm analogous to the speed and rhythm I find in the original. The best metre for my purpose is a free six-beat line. My line can hardly be called English hexameter. It is less regular than that of Longfellow, or the recent Smith-Miller translation of the Iliad. It is not based on a quantitative theory (or any other theory) as is Robert Bridges' rendering of part of the *Aeneid*. I have allowed anapaests for dactyls, trochees and even iambs for spondees. The line is to be read with its natural stress, not forced into any system.

Matthew Arnold has stated[1] that the translator of Homer must bear in mind four qualities of his author: that he is rapid, plain and direct in thought and expression, plain and direct in substance, and noble. Even one who does not agree in all details with Arnold's very interesting essay must concede that Homer has these qualities. I have tried as hard as I could to reproduce the first three. I do not think *nobility* is a quality to be directly striven for; you must write as well as you can, and then see, or let others see, whether or not the result is noble. I have used the plainest language I could find which might be adequate, and mostly this is the language of contemporary prose. This usage is not 'Homeric'. Arnold points out that Homer used a poetic dialect, but I do not draw from this the conclusion, which Arnold draws, that we should translate him into a poetical dialect of English. In 1951, we do not have a poetic dialect, and if I used the language of Spenser or the King James Version, I should feel as if I were working in Apollonius of Rhodes, or at best Arktinos, rather than Homer. I must try to avoid mistranslation, which would be caused by rating the word of my own choice ahead of the word which translates the Greek. Subject to such qualification, I must render Homer into the best English verse I can write; and this will be in my own 'poetical language', which is mostly the plain English of today.

[1] *On the Study of Celtic Literature* and *On Translating Homer*; p. 149 in Macmillan edition of 1910.

THE ILIAD *of* HOMER

SING, goddess, the anger of Peleus' son Achilleus
and its devastation, which put pains thousandfold upon the
    Achaians,
hurled in their multitudes to the house of Hades strong souls
of heroes, but gave their bodies to be the delicate feasting
of dogs, of all birds, and the will of Zeus was accomplished   5
since that time when first there stood in division of conflict
Atreus' son the lord of men and brilliant Achilleus.

What god was it then set them together in bitter collision?
Zeus' son and Leto's, Apollo, who in anger at the king drove
the foul pestilence along the host, and the people perished,   10
since Atreus' son had dishonoured Chryses, priest of Apollo,
when he came beside the fast ships of the Achaians to ransom
back his daughter, carrying gifts beyond count and holding
in his hands wound on a staff of gold the ribbons of Apollo
who strikes from afar, and supplicated all the Achaians,   15
but above all Atreus' two sons, the marshals of the people:
'Sons of Atreus and you other strong-greaved Achaians,
to you may the gods grant who have their homes on Olympos
Priam's city to be plundered and a fair homecoming thereafter,
but may you give me back my own daughter and take the ransom,   20
giving honour to Zeus' son who strikes from afar, Apollo.'

Then all the rest of the Achaians cried out in favour
that the priest be respected and the shining ransom be taken;
yet this pleased not the heart of Atreus' son Agamemnon,

25 but harshly he drove him away with a strong order upon him:
'Never let me find you again, old sir, near our hollow
ships, neither lingering now nor coming again hereafter,
for fear your staff and the god's ribbons help you no longer.
The girl I will not give back; sooner will old age come upon her
30 in my own house, in Argos, far from her own land, going
up and down by the loom and being in my bed as my companion.
So go now, do not make me angry; so you will be safer.'

So he spoke, and the old man in terror obeyed him
and went silently away beside the murmuring sea beach.
35 Over and over the old man prayed as he walked in solitude
to King Apollo, whom Leto of the lovely hair bore: 'Hear me,
lord of the silver bow who set your power about Chryse
and Killa the sacrosanct, who are lord in strength over Tenedos,
Smintheus, if ever it pleased your heart that I built your temple,
40 if ever it pleased you that I burned all the rich thigh pieces
of bulls, of goats, then bring to pass this wish I pray for:
let your arrows make the Danaans pay for my tears shed.'

So he spoke in prayer, and Phoibos Apollo heard him,
and strode down along the pinnacles of Olympos, angered
45 in his heart, carrying across his shoulders the bow and the hooded
quiver; and the shafts clashed on the shoulders of the god walking
angrily. He came as night comes down and knelt then
apart and opposite the ships and let go an arrow.
Terrible was the clash that rose from the bow of silver.
50 First he went after the mules and the circling hounds, then let go
a tearing arrow against the men themselves and struck them.
The corpse fires burned everywhere and did not stop burning.

Nine days up and down the host ranged the god's arrows,
but on the tenth Achilleus called the people to assembly;
55 a thing put into his mind by the goddess of the white arms, Hera,
who had pity upon the Danaans when she saw them dying.
Now when they were all assembled in one place together,
Achilleus of the swift feet stood up among them and spoke forth:
'Son of Atreus, I believe now that straggling backwards
60 we must make our way home if we can even escape death,
if fighting now must crush the Achaians and the plague likewise.
No, come, let us ask some holy man, some prophet,

even an interpreter of dreams, since a dream also
comes from Zeus, who can tell why Phoibos Apollo is so angry,
if for the sake of some vow, some hecatomb he blames us,   65
if given the fragrant smoke of lambs, of he goats, somehow
he can be made willing to beat the bane aside from us.'

He spoke thus and sat down again, and among them stood up
Kalchas, Thestor's son, far the best of the bird interpreters,
who knew all things that were, the things to come and the things past,   70
who guided into the land of Ilion the ships of the Achaians
through that seercraft of his own that Phoibos Apollo gave him.
He in kind intention toward all stood forth and addressed them:
'You have bidden me, Achilleus beloved of Zeus, to explain to
you this anger of Apollo the lord who strikes from afar. Then   75
I will speak; yet make me a promise and swear before me
readily by word and work of your hands to defend me,
since I believe I shall make a man angry who holds great kingship
over the men of Argos, and all the Achaians obey him.
For a king when he is angry with a man beneath him is too strong,   80
and suppose even for the day itself he swallow down his anger,
he still keeps bitterness that remains until its fulfilment
deep in his chest. Speak forth then, tell me if you will protect me.'

Then in answer again spoke Achilleus of the swift feet:
'Speak, interpreting whatever you know, and fear nothing.   85
In the name of Apollo beloved of Zeus to whom you, Kalchas,
make your prayers when you interpret the gods' will to the Danaans,
no man so long as I am alive above earth and see daylight
shall lay the weight of his hands on you beside the hollow ships,
not one of all the Danaans, even if you mean Agamemnon,   90
who now claims to be far the greatest of all the Achaians.'

At this the blameless seer took courage again and spoke forth:
'No, it is not for the sake of some vow or hecatomb he blames us,
but for the sake of his priest whom Agamemnon dishonoured
and would not give him back his daughter nor accept the ransom.   95
Therefore the archer sent griefs against us and will send them
still, nor sooner thrust back the shameful plague from the Danaans
until we give the glancing-eyed girl back to her father
without price, without ransom, and lead also a blessed hecatomb
to Chryse; thus we might propitiate and persuade him.'   100

He spoke thus and sat down again, and among them stood **up**
Atreus' son the hero wide-ruling Agamemnon
raging, the heart within filled black to the brim with anger
from beneath, but his two eyes showed like fire in their blazing.
105 First of all he eyed Kalchas bitterly and spoke to him:
'Seer of evil: never yet have you told me a good thing.
Always the evil things are dear to your heart to prophesy,
but nothing excellent have you said nor ever accomplished.
Now once more you make divination to the Danaans, argue
110 forth your reason why he who strikes from afar afflicts them,
because I for the sake of the girl Chryseis would not take
the shining ransom; and indeed I wish greatly to have her
in my own house; since I like her better than Klytaimestra
my own wife, for in truth she is no way inferior,
115 neither in build nor stature nor wit, not in accomplishment.
Still I am willing to give her back, if such is the best way.
I myself desire that my people be safe, not perish.
Find me then some prize that shall be my own, lest I only
among the Argives go without, since that were unfitting;
120 you are all witnesses to this thing, that my prize goes elsewhere.'
   Then in answer again spoke brilliant swift-footed Achilleus:
'Son of Atreus, most lordly, greediest for gain of all men,
how shall the great-hearted Achaians give you a prize now?
There is no great store of things lying about I know of.
125 But what we took from the cities by storm has been distributed;
it is unbecoming for the people to call back things once given.
No, for the present give the girl back to the god; we Achaians
thrice and four times over will repay you, if ever Zeus gives
into our hands the strong-walled citadel of Troy to be plundered.'
130   Then in answer again spoke powerful Agamemnon:
'Not that way, good fighter though you be, godlike Achilleus,
strive to cheat, for you will not deceive, you will not persuade me.
What do you want? To keep your own prize and have me sit here
lacking one? Are you ordering me to give this girl back?
135 Either the great-hearted Achaians shall give me a new prize
chosen according to my desire to atone for the girl lost,
or else if they will not give me one I myself shall take her,
your own prize, or that of Aias, or that of Odysseus,

going myself in person; and he whom I visit will be bitter.
Still, these are things we shall deliberate again hereafter.   140
Come, now, we must haul a black ship down to the bright sea,
and assemble rowers enough for it, and put on board it
the hecatomb, and the girl herself, Chryseis of the fair cheeks,
and let there be one responsible man in charge of her,
either Aias or Idomeneus or brilliant Odysseus,   145
or you yourself, son of Peleus, most terrifying of all men,
to reconcile by accomplishing sacrifice the archer.'
    Then looking darkly at him Achilleus of the swift feet spoke:
'O wrapped in shamelessness, with your mind forever on profit,
how shall any one of the Achaians readily obey you   150
either to go on a journey or to fight men strongly in battle?
I for my part did not come here for the sake of the Trojan
spearmen to fight against them, since to me they have done nothing.
Never yet have they driven away my cattle or my horses,
never in Phthia where the soil is rich and men grow great did they   155
spoil my harvest, since indeed there is much that lies between us,
the shadowy mountains and the echoing sea; but for your sake,
o great shamelessness, we followed, to do you favour,
you with the dog's eyes, to win your honour and Menelaos'
from the Trojans. You forget all this or else you care nothing.   160
And now my prize you threaten in person to strip from me,
for whom I laboured much, the gift of the sons of the Achaians.
Never, when the Achaians sack some well-founded citadel
of the Trojans, do I have a prize that is equal to your prize.
Always the greater part of the painful fighting is the work of   165
my hands; but when the time comes to distribute the booty
yours is far the greater reward, and I with some small thing
yet dear to me go back to my ships when I am weary with fighting.
Now I am returning to Phthia, since it is much better
to go home again with my curved ships, and I am minded no longer   170
to stay here dishonoured and pile up your wealth and your luxury.'
    Then answered him in turn the lord of men Agamemnon:
'Run away by all means if your heart drives you. I will not
entreat you to stay here for my sake. There are others with me
who will do me honour, and above all Zeus of the counsels.   175
To me you are the most hateful of all the kings whom the gods love.

[63]

Forever quarrelling is dear to your heart, and wars and battles;
and if you are very strong indeed, that is a god's gift.
Go home then with your own ships and your own companions,
180 be king over the Myrmidons. I care nothing about you.
I take no account of your anger. But here is my threat to you.
Even as Phoibos Apollo is taking away my Chryseis.
I shall convey her back in my own ship, with my own
followers; but I shall take the fair-cheeked Briseis,
185 your prize, I myself going to your shelter, that you may learn well
how much greater I am than you, and another man may shrink back
from likening himself to me and contending against me.'
    So he spoke. And the anger came on Peleus' son, and within
his shaggy breast the heart was divided two ways, pondering
190 whether to draw from beside his thigh the sharp sword, driving
away all those who stood between and kill the son of Atreus,
or else to check the spleen within and keep down his anger.
Now as he weighed in mind and spirit these two courses
and was drawing from its scabbard the great sword, Athene descended
195 from the sky. For Hera the goddess of the white arms sent her,
who loved both men equally in her heart and cared for them.
The goddess standing behind Peleus' son caught him by the fair hair,
appearing to him only, for no man of the others saw her.
Achilleus in amazement turned about, and straightway
200 knew Pallas Athene and the terrible eyes shining.
He uttered winged words and addressed her: 'Why have you come now,
o child of Zeus of the aegis, once more? Is it that you may see
the outrageousness of the son of Atreus Agamemnon?
Yet will I tell you this thing, and I think it shall be accomplished.
205 By such acts of arrogance he may even lose his own life.'
    Then in answer the goddess grey-eyed Athene spoke to him:
'I have come down to stay your anger—but will you obey me?—
from the sky; and the goddess of the white arms Hera sent me,
who loves both of you equally in her heart and cares for you.
210 Come then, do not take your sword in your hand, keep clear of fighting,
though indeed with words you may abuse him, and it will be that way.
And this also will I tell you and it will be a thing accomplished.
Some day three times over such shining gifts shall be given you
by reason of this outrage. Hold your hand then, and obey us.'

Then in answer again spoke Achilleus of the swift feet: 215
'Goddess, it is necessary that I obey the word of you two,
angry though I am in my heart. So it will be better.
If any man obeys the gods, they listen to him also.'

He spoke, and laid his heavy hand on the silver sword hilt
and thrust the great blade back into the scabbard nor disobeyed   220
the word of Athene. And she went back again to Olympos
to the house of Zeus of the aegis with the other divinities.

But Peleus' son once again in words of derision
spoke to Atreides, and did not yet let go of his anger:
'You wine sack, with a dog's eyes, with a deer's heart. Never   225
once have you taken courage in your heart to arm with your people
for battle, or go into ambuscade with the best of the Achaians.
No, for in such things you see death. Far better to your mind
is it, all along the widespread host of the Achaians
to take away the gifts of any man who speaks up against you.   230
King who feed on your people, since you rule nonentities;
otherwise, son of Atreus, this were your last outrage.
But I will tell you this and swear a great oath upon it:
in the name of this sceptre, which never again will bear leaf nor
branch, now that it has left behind the cut stump in the mountains,   235
nor shall it ever blossom again, since the bronze blade stripped
bark and leafage, and now at last the sons of the Achaians
carry it in their hands in state when they administer
the justice of Zeus. And this shall be a great oath before you:
some day longing for Achilleus will come to the sons of the Achaians,   240
all of them. Then stricken at heart though you be, you will be able
to do nothing, when in their numbers before man-slaughtering Hektor
they drop and die. And then you will eat out the heart within you
in sorrow, that you did no honour to the best of the Achaians.'

Thus spoke Peleus' son and dashed to the ground the sceptre   245
studded with golden nails, and sat down again. But Atreides
raged still on the other side, and between them Nestor
the fair-spoken rose up, the lucid speaker of Pylos,
from whose lips the streams of words ran sweeter than honey.
In his time two generations of mortal men had perished,   250
those who had grown up with him and they who had been born to
these in sacred Pylos, and he was king in the third age.

He in kind intention toward both stood forth and addressed them:
'Oh, for shame. Great sorrow comes on the land of Achaia.
255 Now might Priam and the sons of Priam in truth be happy,
and all the rest of the Trojans be visited in their hearts with gladness,
were they to hear all this wherein you two are quarrelling,
you, who surpass all Danaans in council, in fighting.
Yet be persuaded. Both of you are younger than I am.
260 Yes, and in my time I have dealt with better men than
you are, and never once did they disregard me. Never
yet have I seen nor shall see again such men as these were,
men like Peirithoös, and Dryas, shepherd of the people,
Kaineus and Exadios, godlike Polyphemos,
265 or Theseus, Aigeus' son, in the likeness of the immortals.
These were the strongest generation of earth-born mortals,
the strongest, and they fought against the strongest, the beast men
living within the mountains, and terribly they destroyed them.
I was of the company of these men, coming from Pylos,
270 a long way from a distant land, since they had summoned me.
And I fought single-handed, yet against such men no one
of the mortals now alive upon earth could do battle. And also
these listened to the counsels I gave and heeded my bidding.
Do you also obey, since to be persuaded is better.
275 You, great man that you are, yet do not take the girl away
but let her be, a prize as the sons of the Achaians gave her
first. Nor, son of Peleus, think to match your strength with
the king, since never equal with the rest is the portion of honour
of the sceptred king to whom Zeus gives magnificence. Even
280 though you are the stronger man, and the mother who bore you was
      immortal,
yet is this man greater who is lord over more than you rule.
Son of Atreus, give up your anger; even I entreat you
to give over your bitterness against Achilleus, he who
stands as a great bulwark of battle over all the Achaians.'
285   Then in answer again spoke powerful Agamemnon:
'Yes, old sir, all this you have said is fair and orderly.
Yet here is a man who wishes to be above all others,
who wishes to hold power over all, and to be lord of
all, and give them their orders, yet I think one will not obey him.

[66]

And if the everlasting gods have made him a spearman, 290
yet they have not given him the right to speak abusively.'
    Then looking at him darkly brilliant Achilleus answered him:
'So must I be called of no account and a coward
if I must carry out every order you may happen to give me.
Tell other men to do these things, but give me no more 295
commands, since I for my part have no intention to obey you.
And put away in your thoughts this other thing I tell you.
With my hands I will not fight for the girl's sake, neither
with you nor any other man, since you take her away who gave her.
But of all the other things that are mine beside my fast black 300
ship, you shall take nothing away against my pleasure.
Come, then, only try it, that these others may see also;
instantly your own black blood will stain my spearpoint.'
    So these two after battling in words of contention
stood up, and broke the assembly beside the ships of the Achaians. 305
Peleus' son went back to his balanced ships and his shelter
with Patroklos, Menoitios' son, and his own companions.
But the son of Atreus drew a fast ship down to the water
and allotted into it twenty rowers and put on board it
the hecatomb for the god and Chryseis of the fair cheeks 310
leading her by the hand. And in charge went crafty Odysseus.
    These then putting out went over the ways of the water
while Atreus' son told his people to wash off their defilement.
And they washed it away and threw the washings into the salt sea.
Then they accomplished perfect hecatombs to Apollo, 315
of bulls and goats along the beach of the barren salt sea.
The savour of the burning swept in circles up to the bright sky.
    Thus these were busy about the army. But Agamemnon
did not give up his anger and the first threat he made to Achilleus,
but to Talthybios he gave his orders and Eurybates 320
who were heralds and hard-working henchmen to him: 'Go now
to the shelter of Peleus' son Achilleus, to bring back
Briseis of the fair cheeks leading her by the hand. And if he
will not give her, I must come in person to take her
with many men behind me, and it will be the worse for him.' 325
    He spoke and sent them forth with this strong order upon them.
They went against their will beside the beach of the barren

salt sea, and came to the shelters and the ships of the Myrmidons.
The man himself they found beside his shelter and his black ship
330 sitting. And Achilleus took no joy at all when he saw them.
These two terrified and in awe of the king stood waiting
quietly, and did not speak a word at all nor question him.
But he knew the whole matter in his own heart, and spoke first:
'Welcome, heralds, messengers of Zeus and of mortals.
335 Draw near. You are not to blame in my sight, but Agamemnon
who sent the two of you here for the sake of the girl Briseis.
Go then, illustrious Patroklos, and bring the girl forth
and give her to these to be taken away. Yet let them be witnesses
in the sight of the blessed gods, in the sight of mortal
340 men, and of this cruel king, if ever hereafter
there shall be need of me to beat back the shameful destruction
from the rest. For surely in ruinous heart he makes sacrifice
and has not wit enough to look behind and before him
that the Achaians fighting beside their ships shall not perish.'
345   So he spoke, and Patroklos obeyed his beloved companion.
He led forth from the hut Briseis of the fair cheeks and gave her
to be taken away; and they walked back beside the ships of the Achaians,
and the woman all unwilling went with them still. But Achilleus
weeping went and sat in sorrow apart from his companions
350 beside the beach of the grey sea looking out on the infinite water.
Many times stretching forth his hands he called on his mother:
'Since, my mother, you bore me to be a man with a short life,
therefore Zeus of the loud thunder on Olympos should grant me
honour at least. But now he has given me not even a little.
355 Now the son of Atreus, powerful Agamemnon,
has dishonoured me, since he has taken away my prize and keeps it.'
    So he spoke in tears and the lady his mother heard him
as she sat in the depths of the sea at the side of her aged father,
and lightly she emerged like a mist from the grey water.
360 She came and sat beside him as he wept, and stroked him
with her hand and called him by name and spoke to him: 'Why then,
child, do you lament? What sorrow has come to your heart now?
Tell me, do not hide it in your mind, and thus we shall both know.'
    Sighing heavily Achilleus of the swift feet answered her:
365 'You know; since you know why must I tell you all this?

We went against Thebe, the sacred city of Eëtion,
and the city we sacked, and carried everything back to this place,
and the sons of the Achaians made a fair distribution
and for Atreus' son they chose out Chryseis of the fair cheeks.
Then Chryses, priest of him who strikes from afar, Apollo,   370
came beside the fast ships of the bronze-armoured Achaians to ransom
back his daughter, carrying gifts beyond count and holding
in his hands wound on a staff of gold the ribbons of Apollo
who strikes from afar, and supplicated all the Achaians,
but above all Atreus' two sons, the marshals of the people.   375
Then all the rest of the Achaians cried out in favour
that the priest be respected and the shining ransom be taken;
yet this pleased not the heart of Atreus' son Agamemnon,
but harshly he sent him away with a strong order upon him.
The old man went back again in anger, but Apollo   380
listened to his prayer, since he was very dear to him, and let go
the wicked arrow against the Argives. And now the people
were dying one after another while the god's shafts ranged
everywhere along the wide host of the Achaians, till the seer
knowing well the truth interpreted the designs of the archer.   385
It was I first of all urged then the god's appeasement;
and the anger took hold of Atreus' son, and in speed standing
he uttered his threat against me, and now it is a thing accomplished.
For the girl the glancing-eyed Achaians are taking to Chryse
in a fast ship, also carrying to the king presents. But even   390
now the heralds went away from my shelter leading
Briseus' daughter, whom the sons of the Achaians gave me.
You then, if you have power to, protect your own son, going
to Olympos and supplicating Zeus, if ever before now
either by word you comforted Zeus' heart or by action.   395
Since it is many times in my father's halls I have heard you
making claims, when you said you only among the immortals
beat aside shameful destruction from Kronos' son the dark-misted,
that time when all the other Olympians sought to bind him,
Hera and Poseidon and Pallas Athene. Then you,   400
goddess, went and set him free from his shackles, summoning
in speed the creature of the hundred hands to tall Olympos,
that creature the gods name Briareus, but all men

Aigaios' son, but he is far greater in strength than his father.
405 He rejoicing in the glory of it sat down by Kronion,
and the rest of the blessed gods were frightened and gave up binding him.
Sit beside him and take his knees and remind him of these things
now, if perhaps he might be willing to help the Trojans,
and pin the Achaians back against the ships and the water,
410 dying, so that thus they may all have profit of their own king,
that Atreus' son wide-ruling Agamemnon may recognize
his madness, that he did no honour to the best of the Achaians.'
      Thetis answered him then letting the tears fall: 'Ah me,
my child. Your birth was bitterness. Why did I raise you?
415 If only you could sit by your ships untroubled, not weeping,
since indeed your lifetime is to be short, of no length.
Now it has befallen that your life must be brief and bitter
beyond all men's. To a bad destiny I bore you in my chambers.
But I will go to cloud-dark Olympos and ask this
420 thing of Zeus who delights in the thunder. Perhaps he will do it.
Do you therefore continuing to sit by your swift ships
be angry at the Achaians and stay away from all fighting.
For Zeus went to the blameless Aithiopians at the Ocean
yesterday to feast, and the rest of the gods went with him.
425 On the twelfth day he will be coming back to Olympos,
and then I will go for your sake to the house of Zeus, bronze-founded,
and take him by the knees and I think I can persuade him.'
      So speaking she went away from that place and left him
sorrowing in his heart for the sake of the fair-girdled woman
430 whom they were taking by force against his will. But Odysseus
meanwhile drew near to Chryse conveying the sacred hecatomb.
These when they were inside the many-hollowed harbour
took down and gathered together the sails and stowed them in the black
      ship,
let down mast by the forestays, and settled it into the mast crutch
435 easily, and rowed her in with oars to the mooring.
They threw over the anchor stones and made fast the stern cables
and themselves stepped out on to the break of the sea beach,
and led forth the hecatomb to the archer Apollo,
and Chryseis herself stepped forth from the sea-going vessel.
440 Odysseus of the many designs guided her to the altar

and left her in her father's arms and spoke a word to him:
'Chryses, I was sent here by the lord of men Agamemnon
to lead back your daughter and accomplish a sacred hecatomb
to Apollo on behalf of the Danaans, that we may propitiate
the lord who has heaped unhappiness and tears on the Argives.'   445
    He spoke, and left her in his arms. And he received gladly
his beloved child. And the men arranged the sacred hecatomb
for the god in orderly fashion around the strong-founded altar.
Next they washed their hands and took up the scattering barley.
Standing among them with lifted arms Chryses prayed in a great voice: 450
'Hear me, lord of the silver bow, who set your power about
Chryse and Killa the sacrosanct, who are lord in strength over
Tenedos; if once before you listened to my prayers
and did me honour and smote strongly the host of the Achaians,
so one more time bring to pass the wish that I pray for.   455
Beat aside at last the shameful plague from the Danaans.'
    So he spoke in prayer, and Phoibos Apollo heard him.
And when all had made prayer and flung down the scattering barley
first they drew back the victims' heads and slaughtered them and skinned
        them,
and cut away the meat from the thighs and wrapped them in fat,   460
making a double fold, and laid shreds of flesh upon them.
The old man burned these on a cleft stick and poured the gleaming
wine over, while the young men with forks in their hands stood about
        him.
But when they had burned the thigh pieces and tasted the vitals,
they cut all the remainder into pieces and spitted them   465
and roasted all carefully and took off the pieces.
Then after they had finished the work and got the feast ready
they feasted, nor was any man's hunger denied a fair portion.
But when they had put away their desire for eating and drinking,
the young men filled the mixing bowls with pure wine, passing   470
a portion to all, when they had offered drink in the goblets.
All day long they propitiated the god with singing,
chanting a splendid hymn to Apollo, these young Achaians,
singing to the one who works from afar, who listened in gladness.
    Afterwards when the sun went down and darkness came onward   475
they lay down and slept beside the ship's stern cables.

But when the young Dawn showed again with her rosy fingers,
they put forth to sea toward the wide camp of the Achaians.
And Apollo who works from afar sent them a favouring stern wind.
480 They set up the mast again and spread on it the white sails,
and the wind blew into the middle of the sail, and at the cutwater
a blue wave rose and sang strongly as the ship went onward.
She ran swiftly cutting across the swell her pathway.
But when they had come back to the wide camp of the Achaians
485 they hauled the black ship up on the mainland, high up
on the sand, and underneath her they fixed the long props.
Afterwards they scattered to their own ships and their shelters.

But that other still sat in anger beside his swift ships,
Peleus' son divinely born, Achilleus of the swift feet.
490 Never now would he go to assemblies where men win glory,
never more into battle, but continued to waste his heart out
sitting there, though he longed always for the clamour and fighting.

But when the twelfth dawn after this day appeared, the gods who
live forever came back to Olympos all in a body
495 and Zeus led them; nor did Thetis forget the entreaties
of her son, but she emerged from the sea's waves early
in the morning and went up to the tall sky and Olympos.
She found Kronos' broad-browed son apart from the others
sitting upon the highest peak of rugged Olympos.
500 She came and sat beside him with her left hand embracing
his knees, but took him underneath the chin with her right hand
and spoke in supplication to lord Zeus son of Kronos:
'Father Zeus, if ever before in word or action
I did you favour among the immortals, now grant what I ask for.
505 Now give honour to my son short-lived beyond all other
mortals. Since even now the lord of men Agamemnon
dishonours him, who has taken away his prize and keeps it.
Zeus of the counsels, lord of Olympos, now do him honour.
So long put strength into the Trojans, until the Achaians
510 give my son his rights, and his honour is increased among them.'
She spoke thus. But Zeus who gathers the clouds made no answer
but sat in silence a long time. And Thetis, as she had taken
his knees, clung fast to them and urged once more her question:
'Bend your head and promise me to accomplish this thing,

or else refuse it, you have nothing to fear, that I may know   515
by how much I am the most dishonoured of all gods.'
    Deeply disturbed Zeus who gathers the clouds answered her:
'This is a disastrous matter when you set me in conflict
with Hera, and she troubles me with recriminations.
Since even as things are, forever among the immortals   520
she is at me and speaks of how I help the Trojans in battle.
Even so, go back again now, go away, for fear she
see us. I will look to these things that they be accomplished.
See then, I will bend my head that you may believe me.
For this among the immortal gods is the mightiest witness   525
I can give, and nothing I do shall be vain nor revocable
nor a thing unfulfilled when I bend my head in assent to it.'
    He spoke, the son of Kronos, and nodded his head with the dark brows,
and the immortally anointed hair of the great god
swept from his divine head, and all Olympos was shaken.   530
    So these two who had made their plans separated, and Thetis
leapt down again from shining Olympos into the sea's depth,
but Zeus went back to his own house, and all the gods rose up
from their chairs to greet the coming of their father, not one had courage
to keep his place as the father advanced, but stood up to greet him.   535
Thus he took his place on the throne; yet Hera was not
ignorant, having seen how he had been plotting counsels
with Thetis the silver-footed, the daughter of the sea's ancient,
and at once she spoke revilingly to Zeus son of Kronos:
'Treacherous one, what god has been plotting counsels with you?   540
Always it is dear to your heart in my absence to think of
secret things and decide upon them. Never have you patience
frankly to speak forth to me the thing that you purpose.'
    Then to her the father of gods and men made answer:
'Hera, do not go on hoping that you will hear all my   545
thoughts, since these will be too hard for you, though you are my wife.
Any thought that it is right for you to listen to, no one
neither man nor any immortal shall hear it before you.
But anything that apart from the rest of the gods I wish to
plan, do not always question each detail nor probe me.'   550
    Then the goddess the ox-eyed lady Hera answered:
'Majesty, son of Kronos, what sort of thing have you spoken?

Truly too much in time past I have not questioned nor probed you,
but you are entirely free to think out whatever pleases you.
555 Now, though, I am terribly afraid you were won over
by Thetis the silver-footed, the daughter of the sea's ancient.
For early in the morning she sat beside you and took your
knees, and I think you bowed your head in assent to do honour
to Achilleus, and to destroy many beside the ships of the Achaians.'
560   Then in return Zeus who gathers the clouds made answer:
'Dear lady, I never escape you, you are always full of suspicion.
Yet thus you can accomplish nothing surely, but be more
distant from my heart than ever, and it will be the worse for you.
If what you say is true, then that is the way I wish it.
565 But go then, sit down in silence, and do as I tell you,
for fear all the gods, as many as are on Olympos, can do nothing
if I come close and lay my unconquerable hands upon you.'
     He spoke, and the goddess the ox-eyed lady Hera was frightened
and went and sat down in silence wrenching her heart to obedience,
570 and all the Uranian gods in the house of Zeus were troubled.
Hephaistos the renowned smith rose up to speak among them,
to bring comfort to his beloved mother, Hera of the white arms:
'This will be a disastrous matter and not endurable
if you two are to quarrel thus for the sake of mortals
575 and bring brawling among the gods. There will be no pleasure
in the stately feast at all, since vile things will be uppermost.
And I entreat my mother, though she herself understands it,
to be ingratiating toward our father Zeus, that no longer
our father may scold her and break up the quiet of our feasting.
580 For if the Olympian who handles the lightning should be minded
to hurl us out of our places, he is far too strong for any.
Do you therefore approach him again with words made gentle,
and at once the Olympian will be gracious again to us.'
     He spoke, and springing to his feet put a two-handled goblet
585 into his mother's hands and spoke again to her once more:
'Have patience, my mother, and endure it, though you be saddened,
for fear that, dear as you are, I see you before my own eyes
struck down, and then sorry though I be I shall not be able
to do anything. It is too hard to fight against the Olympian.
590 There was a time once before now I was minded to help you,

and he caught me by the foot and threw me from the magic threshold,
and all day long I dropped helpless, and about sunset
I landed in Lemnos, and there was not much life left in me.
After that fall it was the Sintian men who took care of me.'
    He spoke, and the goddess of the white arms Hera smiled at him,   595
and smiling she accepted the goblet out of her son's hand.
Thereafter beginning from the left he poured drinks for the other
gods, dipping up from the mixing bowl the sweet nectar.
But among the blessed immortals uncontrollable laughter
went up as they saw Hephaistos bustling about the palace.   600
    Thus thereafter the whole day long until the sun went under
they feasted, nor was anyone's hunger denied a fair portion,
nor denied the beautifully wrought lyre in the hands of Apollo
nor the antiphonal sweet sound of the Muses singing.
    Afterwards when the light of the flaming sun went under   605
they went away each one to sleep in his home where
for each one the far-renowned strong-handed Hephaistos
had built a house by means of his craftsmanship and cunning.
Zeus the Olympian and lord of the lightning went to
his own bed, where always he lay when sweet sleep came on him.   610
Going up to the bed he slept and Hera of the gold throne beside him.

```
┌─────────────────────────────────┐
│ ┌─────────────────────────────┐ │
│ │        BOOK  TWO            │ │
│ └─────────────────────────────┘ │
└─────────────────────────────────┘
```

Now the rest of the gods, and men who were lords of chariots,
slept night long, but the ease of sleep came not upon Zeus
who was pondering in his heart how he might bring honour
to Achilleus, and destroy many beside the ships of the Achaians.
5 Now to his mind this thing appeared to be the best counsel,
to send evil Dream to Atreus' son Agamemnon.
He cried out to the dream and addressed him in winged words:
'Go forth, evil Dream, beside the swift ships of the Achaians.
Make your way to the shelter of Atreus' son Agamemnon;
10 speak to him in words exactly as I command you.
Bid him arm the flowing-haired Achaians for battle
in all haste; since now he might take the wide-wayed city
of the Trojans. For no longer are the gods who live on Olympos
arguing the matter, since Hera forced them all over
15 by her supplication, and evils are in store for the Trojans.'
    So he spoke, and Dream listened to his word and descended.
Lightly he came down beside the swift ships of the Achaians
and came to Agamemnon the son of Atreus. He found him
sleeping within his shelter in a cloud of immortal slumber.
20 Dream stood then beside his head in the likeness of Nestor,
Neleus' son, whom Agamemnon honoured beyond all
elders beside. In Nestor's likeness the divine Dream spoke to him:
'Son of wise Atreus breaker of horses, are you sleeping?
He should not sleep night long who is a man burdened with counsels
25 and responsibility for a people and cares so numerous.

Listen quickly to what I say, since I am a messenger
of Zeus, who far away cares much for you and is pitiful.
Zeus bids you arm the flowing-haired Achaians for battle
in all haste; since now you might take the wide-wayed city
of the Trojans. For no longer are the gods who live on Olympos   30
arguing the matter, since Hera forced them all over
by her supplication, and evils are in store for the Trojans
from Zeus. Keep this thought in your heart then, let not forgetfulness
take you, after you are released from the kindly sweet slumber.'

    So he spoke and went away, and left Agamemnon   35
there, believing things in his heart that were not to be accomplished.
For he thought that on that very day he would take Priam's city;
fool, who knew nothing of all the things Zeus planned to accomplish,
Zeus, who yet was minded to visit tears and sufferings
on Trojans and Danaans alike in the strong encounters.   40
Agamemnon awoke from sleep, the divine voice drifting
around him. He sat upright and put on his tunic,
beautiful, fresh woven, and threw the great mantle over it.
Underneath his shining feet he bound the fair sandals
and across his shoulders slung the sword with the nails of silver,   45
and took up the sceptre of his fathers, immortal forever.
Thus he went beside the ships of the bronze-armoured Achaians.

    Now the goddess Dawn drew close to tall Olympos
with her message of light to Zeus and the other immortals.
But Agamemnon commanded his clear-voiced heralds to summon   50
by proclamation to assembly the flowing-haired Achaians,
and the heralds made their cry and the men were assembled swiftly.

    First he held a council session of the high-hearted princes
beside the ship of Nestor, the king of the race of Pylos.
Summoning these he compacted before them his close counsel: 55
'Hear me, friends: in my sleep a Dream divine came to me
through the immortal night, and in appearance and stature
and figure it most closely resembled splendid Nestor.
It came and stood above my head and spoke a word to me:
"Son of wise Atreus breaker of horses, are you sleeping?   60
He should not sleep night long who is a man burdened with counsels
and responsibility for a people and cares so numerous.
Now listen quickly to what I say, since I am a messenger

[77]

from Zeus, who far away cares much for you and is pitiful.
65 Zeus bids you arm the flowing-haired Achaians for battle
in all haste; since now you might take the wide-wayed city
of the Trojans. For no longer are the gods who live on Olympos
arguing the matter, since Hera has forced them all over
by her supplication, and evils are in store for the Trojans
70 by Zeus' will. Keep this within your heart." So speaking
the Dream went away on wings, and sweet sleep released me.
Come then, let us see if we can arm the sons of the Achaians.
Yet first, since it is the right way, I will make trial of them
by words, and tell them even to flee in their benched vessels.
75 Do you take stations here and there, to check them with orders.'
  He spoke thus, and sat down again, and among them rose up
Nestor, he who ruled as a king in sandy Pylos.
He in kind intention toward all stood forth and addressed them:
'Friends, who are leaders of the Argives and keep their counsel,
80 had it been any other Achaian who told of this dream
we should have called it a lie and we might rather have turned from it.
Now he who claims to be the best of the Achaians has seen it.
Come then, let us see if we can arm the sons of the Achaians.'
  So he spoke and led the way departing from the council,
85 and the rest rose to their feet, the sceptred kings, obeying
the shepherd of the people, and the army thronged behind them.
Like the swarms of clustering bees that issue forever
in fresh bursts from the hollow in the stone, and hang like
bunched grapes as they hover beneath the flowers in springtime
90 fluttering in swarms together this way and that way,
so the many nations of men from the ships and the shelters
along the front of the deep sea beach marched in order
by companies to the assembly, and Rumour walked blazing among them,
Zeus' messenger, to hasten them along. Thus they were assembled
95 and the place of their assembly was shaken, and the earth groaned
as the people took their positions and there was tumult. Nine heralds
shouting set about putting them in order, to make them cease their
clamour and listen to the kings beloved of Zeus. The people
took their seats in sober fashion and were marshalled in their places
100 and gave over their clamouring. Powerful Agamemnon
stood up holding the sceptre Hephaistos had wrought him carefully.

Hephaistos gave it to Zeus the king, the son of Kronos,
and Zeus in turn gave it to the courier Argeïphontes,
and lord Hermes gave it to Pelops, driver of horses,
and Pelops again gave it to Atreus, the shepherd of the people.   105
Atreus dying left it to Thyestes of the rich flocks,
and Thyestes left it in turn to Agamemnon to carry
and to be lord of many islands and over all Argos.
Leaning upon this sceptre he spoke and addressed the Argives:
'Fighting men and friends, o Danaans, henchmen of Ares: 110
Zeus son of Kronos has caught me fast in bitter futility.
He is hard; who before this time promised me and consented
that I might sack strong-walled Ilion and sail homeward.
Now he has devised a vile deception, and bids me go back
to Argos in dishonour having lost many of my people.   115
Such is the way it will be pleasing to Zeus, who is too strong,
who before now has broken the crests of many cities
and will break them again, since his power is beyond all others.
And this shall be a thing of shame for the men hereafter
to be told, that so strong, so great a host of Achaians   120
carried on and fought in vain a war that was useless
against men fewer than they, with no accomplishment shown for it;
since if both sides were to be willing, Achaians and Trojans,
to cut faithful oaths of truce, and both to be numbered,
and the Trojans were to be counted by those with homes in the city,   125
while we were to be allotted in tens, we Achaians,
and each one of our tens chose a man of Troy to pour wine for it,
still there would be many tens left without a wine steward.
By so much I claim we sons of the Achaians outnumber
the Trojans—those who live in the city; but there are companions   130
from other cities in their numbers, wielders of the spear, to help them,
who drive me hard back again and will not allow me,
despite my will, to sack the well-founded stronghold of Ilion.
And now nine years of mighty Zeus have gone by, and the timbers
of our ships have rotted away and the cables are broken   135
and far away our own wives and our young children
are sitting within our halls and wait for us, while still our work here
stays forever unfinished as it is, for whose sake we came hither.
Come then, do as I say, let us all be won over; let us

140 run away with our ships to the beloved land of our fathers
since no longer now shall we capture Troy of the wide ways.'
     So he spoke, and stirred up the passion in the breast of all those
who were within that multitude and listened to his counsel.
And the assembly was shaken as on the sea the big waves

145 in the main by Ikaria, when the south and south-east winds
driving down from the clouds of Zeus the father whip them.
As when the west wind moves across the grain deep standing,
boisterously, and shakes and sweeps it till the tassels lean, so
all of that assembly was shaken, and the men in tumult

150 swept to the ships, and underneath their feet the dust lifted
and rose high, and the men were all shouting to one another
to lay hold on the ships and drag them down to the bright sea.
They cleaned out the keel channels and their cries hit skyward
as they made for home and snatched the props from under the vessels.

155   Then for the Argives a homecoming beyond fate might have
been accomplished, had not Hera spoken a word to Athene:
'For shame, now, Atrytone, daughter of Zeus of the aegis.
As things are, the Argives will take flight homeward over
the wide ridges of the sea to the land of their fathers,

160 and thus they would leave to Priam and to the Trojans Helen
of Argos, to glory over, for whose sake many Achaians
lost their lives in Troy far from their own native country.
But go now along the host of the bronze-armoured Achaians.
Speak to each man in words of gentleness and draw him backward

165 nor let them drag down to the salt sea their oarswept vessels.'
     So she spoke, nor did the goddess grey-eyed Athene
disobey her, but went in speed down the peaks of Olympos,
and lightly she arrived beside the fast ships of the Achaians.
There she came on Odysseus, the equal of Zeus in counsel,

170 standing still; he had laid no hand upon his black, strong-benched
vessel, since disappointment touched his heart and his spirit.
Athene of the grey eyes stood beside him and spoke to him:
'Son of Laertes and seed of Zeus, resourceful Odysseus:
will it be this way? Will you all hurl yourselves into your benched ships

175 and take flight homeward to the beloved land of your fathers,
and would you thus leave to Priam and to the Trojans Helen
of Argos, to glory over, for whose sake many Achaians

lost their lives in Troy far from their own native country?
Go now along the host of the Achaians, give way no longer,
speak to each man in words of gentleness and draw them backward,   180
nor let them drag down to the salt sea their oarswept vessels.'
    So she spoke, and he knew the voice of the goddess speaking
and went on the run, throwing aside his cloak, which was caught up
by Eurybates the herald of Ithaka who followed him.
He came face to face with Agamemnon, son of Atreus,   185
and took from him the sceptre of his fathers, immortal forever.
With this he went beside the ships of the bronze-armoured Achaians.
    Whenever he encountered some king, or man of influence,
he would stand beside him and with soft words try to restrain him:
'Excellency! It does not become you to be frightened like any   190
coward. Rather hold fast and check the rest of the people.
You do not yet clearly understand the purpose of Atreides.
Now he makes trial, but soon will bear hard on the sons of the Achaians.
Did we not all hear what he was saying in council?
May he not in anger do some harm to the sons of the Achaians!   195
For the anger of god-supported kings is a big matter,
to whom honour and love are given from Zeus of the counsels.'
    When he saw some man of the people who was shouting,
he would strike at him with his staff, and reprove him also:
'Excellency! Sit still and listen to what others tell you,   200
to those who are better men than you, you skulker and coward
and thing of no account whatever in battle or council.
Surely not all of us Achaians can be as kings here.
Lordship for many is no good thing. Let there be one ruler,
one king, to whom the son of devious-devising Kronos   205
gives the sceptre and right of judgment, to watch over his people.'
    So he went through the army marshalling it, until once more
they swept back into the assembly place from the ships and the shelters
clamorously, as when from the thunderous sea the surf-beat
crashes upon the great beach, and the whole sea is in tumult.   210
    Now the rest had sat down, and were orderly in their places,
but one man, Thersites of the endless speech, still scolded,
who knew within his head many words, but disorderly;
vain, and without decency, to quarrel with the princes
with any word he thought might be amusing to the Argives.   215

[81]

This was the ugliest man who came beneath Ilion. He was
bandy-legged and went lame of one foot, with shoulders
stooped and drawn together over his chest, and above this
his skull went up to a point with the wool grown sparsely upon it.
220 Beyond all others Achilleus hated him, and Odysseus.
These two he was forever abusing, but now at brilliant
Agamemnon he clashed the shrill noise of his abuse. The Achaians
were furiously angry with him, their minds resentful.
But he, crying the words aloud, scolded Agamemnon:
225 'Son of Atreus, what thing further do you want, or find fault with
now? Your shelters are filled with bronze, there are plenty of the choicest
women for you within your shelter, whom we Achaians
give to you first of all whenever we capture some stronghold.
Or is it still more gold you will be wanting, that some son
230 of the Trojans, breakers of horses, brings as ransom out of Ilion,
one that I, or some other Achaian, capture and bring in?
Is it some young woman to lie with in love and keep her
all to yourself apart from the others? It is not right for
you, their leader, to lead in sorrow the sons of the Achaians.
235 My good fools, poor abuses, you women, not men, of Achaia,
let us go back home in our ships, and leave this man here
by himself in Troy to mull his prizes of honour
that he may find out whether or not we others are helping him.
And now he has dishonoured Achilleus, a man much better
240 than he is. He has taken his prize by force and keeps her.
But there is no gall in Achilleus' heart, and he is forgiving.
Otherwise, son of Atreus, this were your last outrage.'
    So he spoke, Thersites, abusing Agamemnon
the shepherd of the people. But brilliant Odysseus swiftly
245 came beside him scowling and laid a harsh word upon him:
'Fluent orator though you be, Thersites, your words are
ill-considered. Stop, nor stand up alone against princes.
Out of all those who came beneath Ilion with Atreides
I assert there is no worse man than you are. Therefore
250 you shall not lift up your mouth to argue with princes,
cast reproaches into their teeth, nor sustain the homegoing.
We do not even know clearly how these things will be accomplished,
whether we sons of the Achaians shall win home well or badly;

yet you sit here throwing abuse at Agamemnon,
Atreus' son, the shepherd of the people, because the Danaan   255
fighters give him much. You argue nothing but scandal.
And this also will I tell you, and it will be a thing accomplished.
If once more I find you playing the fool, as you are now,
nevermore let the head of Odysseus sit on his shoulders,
let me nevermore be called Telemachos' father,   260
if I do not take you and strip away your personal clothing,
your mantle and your tunic that cover over your nakedness,
and send you thus bare and howling back to the fast ships,
whipping you out of the assembly place with the strokes of indignity.'

So he spoke and dashed the sceptre against his back and   265
shoulders, and he doubled over, and a round tear dropped from him,
and a bloody welt stood up between his shoulders under
the golden sceptre's stroke, and he sat down again, frightened,
in pain, and looking helplessly about wiped off the tear-drops.
Sorry though the men were they laughed over him happily,   270
and thus they would speak to each other, each looking at the man next
        him:
'Come now: Odysseus has done excellent things by thousands,
bringing forward good counsels and ordering armed encounters;
but now this is far the best thing he ever has accomplished
among the Argives, to keep this thrower of words, this braggart   275
out of assembly. Never again will his proud heart stir him
up, to wrangle with the princes in words of revilement.'

So the multitude spoke, but Odysseus, sacker of cities,
stood up holding the staff, and beside him grey-eyed Athene
in the likeness of a herald enjoined the people to silence,   280
that at once the foremost and the utmost sons of the Achaians
might listen to him speaking and deliberate his counsel.
He in kind intention toward all stood forth and addressed them:
'Son of Atreus: now, my lord, the Achaians are trying
to make you into a thing of reproach in the sight of all mortal   285
men, and not fulfilling the promise they undertook once
as they set forth to come here from horse-pasturing Argos,
to go home only after you had sacked strong-walled Ilion.
For as if they were young children or widowed women
they cry out and complain to each other about going homeward.   290

In truth, it is a hard thing, to be grieved with desire for going.
Any man who stays away one month from his own wife
with his intricate ship is impatient, one whom the storm winds
of winter and the sea rising keep back. And for us now
295 this is the ninth of the circling years that we wait here. Therefore
I cannot find fault with the Achaians for their impatience
beside the curved ships; yet always it is disgraceful
to wait long and at the end go home empty-handed.
No, but be patient, friends, and stay yet a little longer
300 until we know whether Kalchas' prophecy is true or is not true.
For I remember this thing well in my heart, and you all are
witnesses, whom the spirits of death have not carried away from us;
yesterday and before, at Aulis, when the ships of the Achaians
were gathered bringing disaster to the Trojans and Priam,
305 and we beside a spring and upon the sacred altars
were accomplishing complete hecatombs to the immortals
under a fair plane tree whence ran the shining of water.
There appeared a great sign; a snake, his back blood-mottled,
a thing of horror, cast into the light by the very Olympian,
310 wound its way from under the altar and made toward the plane tree.
Thereupon were innocent children, the young of the sparrow,
cowering underneath the leaves at the uttermost branch tip,
eight of them, and the mother was the ninth, who bore these children.
The snake ate them all after their pitiful screaming,
315 and the mother, crying aloud for her young ones, fluttered about him,
and as she shrilled he caught her by the wing and coiled around her.
After he had eaten the sparrow herself with her children
the god who had shown the snake forth made him a monument,
striking him stone, the son of devious-devising Kronos,
320 and we standing about marvelled at the thing that had been done.
So as the terror and the god's monsters came into the hecatomb
Kalchas straightway spoke before us interpreting the gods' will:
"Why are you turned voiceless, you flowing-haired Achaians?
Zeus of the counsels has shown us this great portent: a thing late,
325 late to be accomplished, whose glory shall perish never.
As this snake has eaten the sparrow herself with her children,
eight of them, and the mother was the ninth, who bore them,
so for years as many as this shall we fight in this place

and in the tenth year we shall take the city of the wide ways."
So he spoke to us then; now all this is being accomplished. 330
Come then, you strong-greaved Achaians, let every man stay
here, until we have taken the great citadel of Priam.'
    So he spoke, and the Argives shouted aloud, and about them
the ships echoed terribly to the roaring Achaians
as they cried out applause to the word of godlike Odysseus. 335
Now among them spoke the Gerenian horseman, Nestor:
'Oh, for shame! You are like children when you hold assembly,
infant children, to whom the works of war mean nothing.
Where then shall our covenants go, and the oaths we have taken?
Let counsels and the meditations of men be given to the flames then, 340
with the unmixed wine poured and the right hands we trusted.
We do our fighting with words only, and can discover
no remedy, though we have stayed here a long time. Son of Atreus,
do you still as before hold fast to your counsel unshaken
and be the leader of the Argives through the strong encounters; 345
let them go perish, these one or two, who think apart from
the rest of the Achaians, since there will be no use in them
until they get back again to Argos without ever learning
whether Zeus of the aegis promises false or truly.
For I say to you, the son of all-powerful Kronos 350
promised, on that day when we went in our fast-running vessels,
we of Argos, carrying blood and death to the Trojans.
He flashed lightning on our right, showing signs of favour.
Therefore let no man be urgent to take the way homeward
until after he has lain in bed with the wife of a Trojan 355
to avenge Helen's longing to escape and her lamentations.
But if any man is terribly desirous to go home,
let him only lay his hands on his well-benched black ship,
that before all others he may win death and destruction.
Come, my lord: yourself be careful, and listen to another. 360
This shall not be a word to be cast away that I tell you.
Set your men in order by tribes, by clans, Agamemnon,
and let clan go in support of clan, let tribe support tribe.
If you do it this way, and the Achaians obey you,
you will see which of your leaders is bad, and which of your people, 365
and which also is brave, since they will fight in divisions,

and might learn also whether by magic you fail to take this
city, or by men's cowardice and ignorance of warfare.'
    Then in answer again spoke powerful Agamemnon:
370 'Once again, old sir, you surpass the sons of the Achaians
in debate. O father Zeus, Athene, Apollo:
would that among the Achaians I had ten such counsellors.
Then perhaps the city of lord Priam would be bent
underneath our hands, captured and sacked. But instead
375 Zeus of the aegis, son of Kronos, has given me bitterness,
who drives me into unprofitable abuse and quarrels.
For I and Achilleus fought together for a girl's sake
in words' violent encounter, and I was the first to be angry.
If ever we can take one single counsel, then no longer
380 shall the Trojans' evil be put aside, not even for a small time.
Now go back, take your dinner, and let us gather our warcraft.
Let a man put a good edge to his spear, and his shield in order,
let each put good fodder before his swift-footed horses,
and each man look well over his chariot, careful of his fighting,
385 that all day long we may be in the division of hateful Ares.
There will not even for a small time be any respite
unless darkness come down to separate the strength of the fighters.
There will be a man's sweat on the shield-strap binding the breast to
the shield hiding the man's shape, and the hand on the spear grow weary.
390 There will be sweat on a man's horse straining at the smoothed chariot.
But any man whom I find trying, apart from the battle,
to hang back by the curved ships, for him no longer
will there be any means to escape the dogs and the vultures.'
    So he spoke, and the Argives shouted aloud, as surf crashing
395 against a sheer ness, driven by the south wind descending,
some cliff out-jutting, left never alone by the waves from
all the winds that blow, as they rise one place and another.
They stood up scattering and made for the ships; they kindled
the fires' smoke along the shelters, and took their dinner,
400 each man making a sacrifice to some one of the immortal
gods, in prayer to escape death and the grind of Ares.
But Agamemnon the lord of men dedicated a fat ox
five years old to Zeus, all-powerful son of Kronos,
and summoned the nobles and the great men of all the Achaians,

Nestor before all others, and next the lord Idomeneus,   405
next the two Aiantes and Tydeus' son Diomedes,
and sixth Odysseus, a man like Zeus himself for counsel.
Of his own accord came Menelaos of the great war cry
who knew well in his own mind the cares of his brother.
They stood in a circle about the ox and took up the scattering   410
barley; and among them powerful Agamemnon spoke in prayer:
'Zeus, exalted and mightiest, sky-dwelling in the dark mist:
let not the sun go down and disappear into darkness
until I have hurled headlong the castle of Priam
blazing, and lit the castle gates with the flames' destruction;   415
not till I have broken at the chest the tunic of Hektor
torn with the bronze blade, and let many companions about him
go down headlong into the dust, teeth gripping the ground soil.'
    He spoke, but none of this would the son of Kronos accomplish,
who accepted the victims, but piled up the unwished-for hardship.   420
    Now when all had made prayer and flung down the scattering barley,
first they drew back the victim's head, cut his throat and skinned him,
and cut away the meat from the thighs and wrapped them in fat,
making a double fold, and laid shreds of flesh above them.
Placing these on sticks cleft and peeled they burned them,   425
and spitted the vitals and held them over the flame of Hephaistos.
But when they had burned the thigh pieces and tasted the vitals
they cut all the remainder into pieces and spitted them
and roasted all carefully and took off the pieces.
Then after they had finished the work and got the feast ready   430
they feasted, nor was any man's hunger denied a fair portion.
But when they had put away their desire for eating and drinking
the Gerenian horseman Nestor began speaking among them:
'Son of Atreus, most lordly and king of men, Agamemnon,
let us talk no more of these things, nor for a long time   435
set aside the action which the god puts into our hands now.
Come then, let the heralds of the bronze-armoured Achaians
make proclamation to the people and assemble them by the vessels,
and let us together as we are go down the wide host
of the Achaians, to stir more quickly the fierce war god.'   440
    He spoke, nor did the lord of men Agamemnon neglect him,
but straightway commanded the clear-voiced heralds to summon

by proclamation to battle the flowing-haired Achaians;
and the heralds made their cry and the men were assembled swiftly.

445 And they, the god-supported kings, about Agamemnon
ran marshalling the men, and among them grey-eyed Athene
holding the dear treasured aegis, ageless, immortal,
from whose edges float a hundred all-golden tassels,
each one carefully woven, and each worth a hundred oxen.

450 With this fluttering she swept through the host of the Achaians
urging them to go forward. She kindled the strength in each man's
heart to take the battle without respite and keep on fighting.
And now battle became sweeter to them than to go back
in their hollow ships to the beloved land of their fathers.

455   As obliterating fire lights up a vast forest
along the crests of a mountain, and the flare shows far off,
so as they marched, from the magnificent bronze the gleam went
dazzling all about through the upper air to the heaven.
These, as the multitudinous nations of birds winged,

460 of geese, and of cranes, and of swans long-throated
in the Asian meadow beside the Kaÿstrian waters
this way and that way make their flights in the pride of their wings, then
settle in clashing swarms and the whole meadow echoes with them,
so of these the multitudinous tribes from the ships and

465 shelters poured to the plain of Skamandros, and the earth beneath their
feet and under the feet of their horses thundered horribly.
They took position in the blossoming meadow of Skamandros,
thousands of them, as leaves and flowers appear in their season.
Like the multitudinous nations of swarming insects

470 who drive hither and thither about the stalls of the sheepfold
in the season of spring when the milk splashes in the milk pails:
in such numbers the flowing-haired Achaians stood up
through the plain against the Trojans, hearts burning to break them.
These, as men who are goatherds among the wide goatflocks

475 easily separate them in order as they take to the pasture,
thus the leaders separated them this way and that way
toward the encounter, and among them powerful Agamemnon,
with eyes and head like Zeus who delights in thunder,
like Ares for girth, and with the chest of Poseidon;

480 like some ox of the herd pre-eminent among the others,

a bull, who stands conspicuous in the huddling cattle;
such was the son of Atreus as Zeus made him that day,
conspicuous among men, and foremost among the fighters.

    Tell me now, you Muses who have your homes on Olympos.
For you, who are goddesses, are there, and you know all things,   485
and we have heard only the rumour of it and know nothing.
Who then of those were the chief men and the lords of the Danaans?
I could not tell over the multitude of them nor name them,
not if I had ten tongues and ten mouths, not if I had
a voice never to be broken and a heart of bronze within me,   490
not unless the Muses of Olympia, daughters
of Zeus of the aegis, remembered all those who came beneath Ilion.
I will tell the lords of the ships, and the ships numbers.

    Leïtos and Peneleos were leaders of the Boiotians,
with Arkesilaos and Prothoenor and Klonios;   495
they who lived in Hyria and in rocky Aulis,
in the hill-bends of Eteonos, and Schoinos, and Skolos,
Thespeia and Graia, and in spacious Mykalessos;
they who dwelt about Harma and Eilesion and Erythrai,
they who held Eleon and Hyle and Peteon,   500
with Okalea and Medeon, the strong-founded citadel,
Kopai, and Eutresis, and Thisbe of the dove-cotes;
they who held Koroneia, and the meadows of Haliartos,
they who held Plataia, and they who dwelt about Glisa,
they who held the lower Thebes, the strong-founded citadel,   505
and Onchestos the sacred, the shining grove of Poseidon;
they who held Arne of the great vineyards, and Mideia,
with Nisa the sacrosanct and uttermost Anthedon.
Of these there were fifty ships in all, and on board
each of these a hundred and twenty sons of the Boiotians.   510

    But they who lived in Aspledon and Orchomenos of the Minyai,
Askalaphos led these, and Ialmenos, children of Ares,
whom Astyoche bore to him in the house of Aktor
Azeus' son, a modest maiden; she went into the chamber
with strong Ares, who was laid in bed with her secretly.   515
With these two there were marshalled thirty hollow vessels.

    Schedios and Epistrophos led the men of Phokis,
children of Iphitos, who was son of great-hearted Naubolos.

These held Kyparissos, and rocky Pytho, and Krisa
520 the sacrosanct together with Daulis and Panopeus;
they who lived about Hyampolis and Anamoreia,
they who dwelt about Kephisos, the river immortal,
they who held Lilaia beside the well springs of Kephisos.
Following along with these were forty black ships,
525 and the leaders marshalling the ranks of the Phokians set them
in arms on the left wing of the host beside the Boiotians.
    Swift Aias son of Oïleus led the men of Lokris,
the lesser Aias, not great in size like the son of Telamon,
but far slighter. He was a small man armoured in linen,
530 yet with the throwing spear surpassed all Achaians and Hellenes.
These were the dwellers in Kynos and Opoeis and Kalliaros,
and in Bessa, and Skarphe, and lovely Augeiai,
in Thronion and Tarphe and beside the waters of Boagrios.
Following along with him were forty black ships
535 of the Lokrians, who dwell across from sacred Euboia.
    They who held Euboia, the Abantes, whose wind was fury,
Chalkis, and Eretria, the great vineyards of Histiaia,
and seaborne Kerinthos and the steep stronghold of Dion,
they who held Karystos and they who dwelt about Styra,
540 of these the leader was Elephenor, scion of Ares,
son of Chalkodon and lord of the great-hearted Abantes.
And the running Abantes followed with him, their hair grown
long at the back, spearmen furious with the out-reached ash spear
to rip the corselets girt about the chests of their enemies.
545 Following along with him were forty black ships.
    But the men who held Athens, the strong-founded citadel,
the deme of great-hearted Erechtheus, whom once Athene
Zeus' daughter tended after the grain-giving fields had born him,
and established him to be in Athens in her own rich temple;
550 there as the circling years go by the sons of the Athenians
make propitiation with rams and bulls sacrificed;
of these men the leader was Peteos' son Menestheus.
Never on earth before had there been a man born like him
for the arrangement in order of horses and shielded fighters.
555 Nestor alone could challenge him, since he was far older.
Following along with him were fifty black ships.

Out of Salamis Aias brought twelve ships and placed them
next to where the Athenian battalions were drawn up.

They who held Argos and Tiryns of the huge walls,
Hermione and Asine lying down the deep gulf,   560
Troizen and Eïonai, and Epidauros of the vineyards,
they who held Aigina and Mases, sons of the Achaians,
of these the leader was Diomedes of the great war cry
with Sthenelos, own son to the high-renowned Kapaneus,
and with them as a third went Euryalos, a man godlike,   565
son of Mekisteus the king, and scion of Talaos;
but the leader of all was Diomedes of the great war cry.
Following along with these were eighty black ships.

But the men who held Mykenai, the strong-founded citadel,
Korinth the luxurious, and strong-founded Kleonai;   570
they who dwelt in Orneai and lovely Araithyrea,
and Sikyon, where of old Adrestos had held the kingship;
they who held Hyperesia and steep Gonoëssa,
they who held Pellene and they who dwelt about Aigion,
all about the sea-shore and about the wide headland of Helike,   575
of their hundred ships the leader was powerful Agamemnon,
Atreus' son, with whom followed far the best and bravest
people; and among them he himself stood armoured in shining
bronze, glorying, conspicuous among the great fighters,
since he was greatest among them all, and led the most people.   580

They who held the swarming hollow of Lakedaimon,
Pharis, and Sparta, and Messe of the dove-cotes,
they who dwelt in Bryseiai and lovely Augeiai,
they who held Amyklai and the seaward city of Helos,
they who held Laas, and they who dwelt about Oitylos,   585
of these his brother Menelaos of the great war cry
was leader, with sixty ships marshalled apart from the others.
He himself went among them in the confidence of his valour,
driving them battleward, since above all his heart was eager
to avenge Helen's longing to escape and her lamentations.   590

They who dwelt about Pylos and lovely Arene,
and Thryon, the Alpheios crossing, and strong-built Aipy;
they who lived in Kyparisseeis and Amphigeneia,
Pteleos and Helos and Dorion, where the Muses

595 encountering Thamyris the Thracian stopped him from singing
as he came from Oichalia and Oichalian Eurytos;
for he boasted that he would surpass, if the very Muses,
daughters of Zeus who holds the aegis, were singing against him,
and these in their anger struck him maimed, and the voice of wonder
600 they took away, and made him a singer without memory;
of these the leader was the Gerenian horseman, Nestor,
in whose command were marshalled ninety hollow vessels.

They who held Arkadia under the sheer peak, Kyllene,
beside the tomb of Aipytos, where men fight at close quarters,
605 they who dwelt in Orchomenos of the flocks, and Pheneos,
about Rhipe and Stratia and windy Enispe;
they who held Tegea and Mantineia the lovely,
they who held Stymphalos, and dwelt about Parrhasia,
their leader was Angkaios' son, powerful Agapenor.
610 Sixty was the number of their ships, and in each ship
went many men of Arkadia, well skilled in battle.
Agamemnon the lord of men himself had given
these for the crossing of the wine-blue sea their strong-benched vessels,
Atreus' son, since the work of the sea was nothing to these men.

615 They who lived in Bouprasion and brilliant Elis,
all as much as Hyrmine and Myrsinos the uttermost
and the Olenian rock and Alesion close between them,
of these there were four chieftains, and with each man ten swift
vessels followed, with many Epeian men on board them.
620 Of two tens Thalpios and Amphimachos were leaders,
of Aktor's seed, sons one of Kteatos, one of Eurytos.
Ten more were led by Amaryngkeus' son, strong Diores,
and of the fourth ten godlike Polyxeinos was leader,
son of lord Agasthenes, of the race of Augeias.
625 They who came from Doulichion and the sacred Echinai,
islands, where men live across the water from Elis,
Meges was the leader of these, a man like Ares,
Phyleus' son, whom the rider dear to Zeus had begotten,
Phyleus, who angered with his father had settled Doulichion.
630 Following along with him were forty black ships.

But Odysseus led the high-hearted men of Kephallenia,
those who held Ithaka and leaf-trembling Neriton,

those who dwelt about Krokyleia and rigged Aigilips,
those who held Zakynthos and those who dwelt about Samos,
those who held the mainland and the places next to the crossing.   635
All these men were led by Odysseus, like Zeus in counsel.
Following with him were twelve ships with bows red painted.

   Thoas son of Andraimon was leader of the Aitolians,
those who dwelt in Pleuron and Olenos and Pylene,
Kalydon of the rocks and Chalkis beside the sea-shore,   640
since no longer were the sons of high-hearted Oineus living,
nor Oineus himself, and fair-haired Meleagros had perished.
So all the lordship of the Aitolians was given to Thoas.
Following along with him were forty black ships.

   Idomeneus the spear-famed was leader of the Kretans,   645
those who held Knosos and Gortyna of the great walls,
Lyktos and Miletos and silver-shining Lykastos,
and Phaistos and Rhytion, all towns well established,
and others who dwelt beside them in Krete of the hundred cities.
Of all these Idomeneus the spear-famed was leader,   650
with Meriones, a match for the murderous Lord of Battles.
Following along with these were eighty black ships.

   Herakles' son Tlepolemos the huge and mighty
led from Rhodes nine ships with the proud men of Rhodes aboard them,
those who dwelt about Rhodes and were ordered in triple division,   655
Ialysos and Lindos and silver-shining Kameiros.
Of all these Tlepolemos the spear-famed was leader,
he whom Astyocheia bore to the strength of Herakles.
Herakles brought her from Ephyra and the river Selleëis
after he sacked many cities of strong, god-supported fighters.   660
Now when Tlepolemos was grown in the strong-built mansion,
he struck to death his own father's beloved uncle,
Likymnios, scion of Ares, a man already ageing.
At once he put ships together and assembled a host of people
and went fugitive over the sea, since the others threatened,   665
the rest of the sons and the grandsons of the strength of Herakles.
And he came to Rhodes a wanderer, a man of misfortune,
and they settled there in triple division by tribes, beloved
of Zeus himself, who is lord over all gods and all men,
Kronos' son, who showered the wonder of wealth upon them.   670

Nireus from Syme led three balanced vessels,
Nireus son of Aglaia and the king Charopos,
Nireus, the most beautiful man who came beneath Ilion
beyond the rest of the Danaans next after perfect Achilleus.
675 But he was a man of poor strength and few people with him.
They who held Nisyros and Krapathos and Kasos,
and Kos, Eurypylos' city, and the islands called Kalydnai,
of these again Pheidippos and Antiphos were the leaders,
sons both of Thessalos who was born to the lord Herakles.
680 In their command were marshalled thirty hollow vessels.
Now all those who dwelt about Pelasgian Argos,
those who lived by Alos and Alope and at Trachis,
those who held Phthia and Hellas the land of fair women,
who were called Myrmidons and Hellenes and Achaians,
685 of all these and their fifty ships the lord was Achilleus.
But these took no thought now for the grim clamour of battle
since there was no one who could guide them into close order,
since he, swift-footed brilliant Achilleus, lay where the ships were,
angered over the girl of the lovely hair, Briseis,
690 whom after much hard work he had taken away from Lyrnessos
after he had sacked Lyrnessos and the walls of Thebe
and struck down Epistrophos and Mynes the furious spearmen,
children of Euenos, king, and son of Selepios.
For her sake he lay grieving now, but was soon to rise up.
695 They who held Phylake and Pyrasos of the flowers,
the precinct of Demeter, and Iton, mother of sheepflocks,
Antron by the sea-shore, and Pteleos deep in the meadows,
of these in turn fighting Protesilaos was leader
while he lived; but now the black earth had closed him under,
700 whose wife, cheeks torn for grief, was left behind in Phylake
and a marriage half completed; a Dardanian man had killed him
as he leapt from his ship, far the first of all the Achaians.
Yet these, longing as they did for their leader, did not go leaderless,
but Podarkes, scion of Ares, set them in order,
705 child of Iphikles, who in turn was son to Phylakos
rich in flocks, full brother of high-hearted Protesilaos,
younger born; but the elder man was braver also,
Protesilaos, a man of battle; yet still the people

lacked not a leader, though they longed for him and his valour.
Following along with Podarkes were forty black ships. 710
   They who lived by Pherai beside the lake Boibeis,
by Boibe and Glaphyrai and strong-founded Iolkos,
of their eleven ships the dear son of Admetos was leader,
Eumelos, born to Admetos by the beauty among women
Alkestis, loveliest of all the daughters of Pelias. 715
   They who lived about Thaumakia and Methone,
they who held Meliboia and rugged Olizon,
of their seven ships the leader was Philoktetes
skilled in the bow's work, and aboard each vessel were fifty
oarsmen, each well skilled in the strength of the bow in battle. 720
Yet he himself lay apart in the island, suffering strong pains,
in Lemnos the sacrosanct, where the sons of the Achaians had left him
in agony from the sore bite of the wicked water snake.
There he lay apart in his pain; yet soon the Argives
beside their ships were to remember lord Philoktetes. 725
Yet these, longing as they did for their leader, did not go leaderless,
but Medon, the bastard son of Oileus, set them in order,
whom Rhene bore to Oïleus the sacker of cities.
   They who held Trikke and the terraced place of Ithome,
and Oichalia, the city of Oichalian Eurytos, 730
of these in turn the leaders were two sons of Asklepios,
good healers both themselves, Podaleirios and Machaon.
In their command were marshalled thirty hollow vessels.
   They who held Ormenios and the spring Hypereia,
they who held Asterion and the pale peaks of Titanos, 735
Eurypylos led these, the shining son of Euaimon.
Following along with him were forty black ships.
   They who held Argissa and dwelt about Gyrtone,
Orthe and Elone and the white city Oloösson,
of these the leader was Polypoites, stubborn in battle, 740
son of Peirithoös whose father was Zeus immortal,
he whom glorious Hippodameia bore to Peirithoös
on that day when he wreaked vengeance on the hairy beast men
and drove them from Pelion and hurled them against the Aithikes;
not by himself, for Leonteus was with him, scion of Ares, 745
Leonteus, son of high-hearted Koronos the son of Kaineus.

Following in the guidance of these were forty black ships.
    Gouneus from Kyphos led two and twenty vessels,
and the Enienes and the Perrhaibians stubborn in battle
750 followed him, they who made their homes by wintry Dodona,
and they who by lovely Titaressos held the tilled acres,
Titaressos, who into Peneios casts his bright current:
yet he is not mixed with the silver whirls of Peneios,
but like oil is floated along the surface above him:
755 since he is broken from the water of Styx, the fearful oath-river.
    Prothoös son of Tenthredon was leader of the Magnesians,
those who dwelt about Peneios and leaf-trembling
Pelion. Of these Prothoös the swift-footed was leader.
Following along with him were forty black ships.
760   These then were the leaders and the princes among the Danaans.
Tell me then, Muse, who of them all was the best and bravest,
of the men, and the men's horses, who went with the sons of Atreus.
    Best by far among the horses were the mares of Eumelos
Pheres' son, that he drove, swift-moving like birds, alike in
765 texture of coat, in age, both backs drawn level like a plumb-line.
These Apollo of the silver bow had bred in Pereia,
mares alike, who went with the terror of the god of battle.
Among the men far the best was Telamonian Aias
while Achilleus stayed angry, since he was far best of all of them,
770 and the horses also, who carried the blameless son of Peleus.
But Achilleus lay apart among his curved sea-wandering
vessels, raging at Agamemnon, the shepherd of the people,
Atreus' son; and his men beside the break of the sea-beach
amused themselves with discs and with light spears for throwing
775 and bows; and the horses, standing each beside his chariot,
champed their clover and the parsley that grows in wet places,
resting, while the chariots of their lords stood covered
in the shelters, and the men forlorn of their warlike leader
wandered here and there in the camp, and did no fighting.
780   But the rest went forward, as if all the earth with flame were eaten,
and the ground echoed under them, as if Zeus who delights in thunder
were angry, as when he batters the earth about Typhoeus,
in the land of the Arimoi, where they say Typhoeus lies prostrate.
Thus beneath their feet the ground re-echoed loudly

to men marching, who made their way through the plain in great speed. 785
    Now to the Trojans came as messenger wind-footed Iris,
in her speed, with the dark message from Zeus of the aegis.
These were holding assembly in front of the doors of Priam
gathered together in one place, the elders and the young men.
Standing close at hand swift-running Iris spoke to them, 790
and likened her voice to that of the son of Priam, Polites,
who confident in the speed of his feet kept watch for the Trojans
aloft the ancient burial mound of ancient Aisyetes,
waiting for the time when the Achaians should move from their vessels.
In this man's likeness Iris the swift-running spoke to them: 795
'Old sir, dear to you forever are words beyond number
as once, when there was peace; but stintless war has arisen.
In my time I have gone into many battles among men,
yet never have I seen a host like this, not one so numerous.
These look terribly like leaves, or the sands of the sea-shore, 800
as they advance across the plain to fight by the city.
Hektor, on you beyond all I urge this, to do as I tell you:
all about the great city of Priam are many companions,
but multitudinous is the speech of the scattered nations:
let each man who is their leader give orders to these men, 805
and let each set his citizens in order, and lead them.'
    She spoke, nor did Hektor fail to mark the word of the goddess.
Instantly he broke up the assembly; they ran to their weapons.
All the gates were opened and the people swept through them
on foot, and with horses, and a clamour of shouting rose up. 810
    Near the city but apart from it there is a steep hill
in the plain by itself, so you pass one side or the other.
This men call the Hill of the Thicket, but the immortal
gods have named it the burial mound of dancing Myrina.
There the Trojans and their companions were marshalled in order. 815
    Tall Hektor of the shining helm was leader of the Trojans,
Priam's son; and with him far the best and the bravest
fighting men were armed and eager to fight with the spear's edge.
    The strong son of Anchises was leader of the Dardanians,
Aineias, whom divine Aphrodite bore to Anchises 820
in the folds of Ida, a goddess lying in love with a mortal:
not Aineias alone, but with him were two sons of Antenor,

Archelochos and Akamas, both skilled in all fighting.
They who lived in Zeleia below the foot of Mount Ida,
825 men of wealth, who drank the dark water of Aisepos,
Trojans: of these the leader was the shining son of Lykaon,
Pandaros, with the bow that was actual gift of Apollo.

They who held Adresteia and the countryside of Apaisos,
they who held Pityeia and the sheer hill of Tereia,
830 these were led by Adrestos and Amphios armoured in linen,
sons both of Merops of Perkote, who beyond all men
knew the art of prophecy, and tried to prevent his two sons
from going into the battle where men die. Yet these would not
listen, for the spirits of dark death were driving them onward.

835 They who dwelt in the places about Perkote and Praktion,
who held Sestos and Abydos and brilliant Arisbe,
their leader was Asios, Hyrtakos' son, a prince of the people,
Asios, son of Hyrtakos, whom huge and shining
horses carried from Arisbe and the river Selleëis.

840 Hippothoös led the tribes of spear-fighting Pelasgians,
they who dwelt where the soil is rich about Larissa;
Hippothoös and Pylaios, scion of Ares, led these,
sons alike of Pelasgian Lethos, son of Teutamos.

Akamas led the men of Thrace with the fighter Peiroös,
845 all the Thracians held within the hard stream of the Hellespont.

Euphemos was leader of the Kikonian spearmen,
son of Troizenos, Keas' son, the king whom the gods loved.

Pyraichmes in turn led the Paionians with their curved bows,
from Amydon far away and the broad stream of Axios,
850 Axios, whose stream on all earth is the loveliest water.

Pylaimones the wild heart was leader of the Paphlagones,
from the land of the Enetoi where the wild mules are engendered,
those who held Kytoros and those who dwelt about Sesamos,
those whose renowned homes were about Parthenios river,
855 and Kromna and Aigialos and high Erythinoi.

Odios and Epistrophos led the Halizones
from Alybe far away, where silver was first begotten.

Chromis, with Ennomos the augur, was lord of the Mysians;
yet his reading of birds could not keep off dark destruction
860 but he went down under the hands of swift-running Aiakides

in the river, as he slew other Trojans beside him.
    Phorkys and godlike Askanios were lords of the Phrygians
from Askania far away, eager to fight in the onfall.
    Mesthles and Antiphos were leaders of the Maionians,
sons of Talaimenes, who was born of the lake Gygaian: 865
these led the Maionian men whose home was beneath Mount Tmolos.
    The Karians of the outland speech were led by Nastes,
they who held Miletos and the leaf-deep mountain of Phthiron,
the waters of Maiandros and the headlong peaks of Mykale;
of these the two leaders were Amphimachos and Nastes,   870
Nastes and Amphimachos, the shining sons of Nomion.
Nastes came like a girl to the fighting in golden raiment,
poor fool, nor did this avail to keep dismal death back;
but he went down under the hands of swift-running Aiakides
in the river, and fiery Achilleus stripped the gold from him.   875
    Sarpedon with unfaulted Glaukos was lord of the Lykians
from Lykia far away, and the whirling waters of Xanthos.

BOOK THREE

Now when the men of both sides were set in order by their
leaders,
the Trojans came on with clamour and shouting, like wildfowl,
as when the clamour of cranes goes high to the heavens,
when the cranes escape the winter time and the rains unceasing
5   and clamorously wing their way to the streaming Ocean,
bringing to the Pygmaian men bloodshed and destruction:
at daybreak they bring on the baleful battle against them.
But the Achaian men went silently, breathing valour,
stubbornly minded each in his heart to stand by the others.
10   As on the peaks of a mountain the south wind scatters the thick mist,
no friend to the shepherd, but better than night for the robber,
and a man can see before him only so far as a stone cast,
so beneath their feet the dust drove up in a stormcloud
of men marching, who made their way through the plain in great speed.
15   Now as these in their advance had come close together,
Alexandros the godlike leapt from the ranks of the Trojans,
as challenger wearing across his shoulders the hide of a leopard,
curved bow and sword; while in his hands shaking two javelins
pointed with bronze, he challenged all the best of the Argives
20   to fight man to man against him in bitter combat.
Now as soon as Menelaos the warlike caught sight of him
making his way with long strides out in front of the army,
he was glad, like a lion who comes on a mighty carcass,
in his hunger chancing upon the body of a horned stag

or wild goat; who eats it eagerly, although against him   25
are hastening the hounds in their speed and the stalwart young men:
thus Menelaos was happy finding godlike Alexandros
there in front of his eyes, and thinking to punish the robber,
straightway in all his armour he sprang to the ground from his chariot.

   But Alexandros the godlike when he saw Menelaos   30
showing among the champions, the heart was shaken within him;
to avoid death he shrank into the host of his own companions.
As a man who has come on a snake in the mountain valley
suddenly steps back, and the shivers come over his body,
and he draws back and away, cheeks seized with a green pallor;   35
so in terror of Atreus' son godlike Alexandros
lost himself again in the host of the haughty Trojans.

   But Hektor saw him and in words of shame rebuked him:
'Evil Paris, beautiful, woman-crazy, cajoling,
better had you never been born, or killed unwedded.   40
Truly I could have wished it so; it would be far better
than to have you with us to our shame, for others to sneer at.
Surely now the flowing-haired Achaians laugh at us,
thinking you are our bravest champion, only because your
looks are handsome, but there is no strength in your heart, no courage.   45
Were you like this that time when in sea-wandering vessels
assembling oarsmen to help you you sailed over the water,
and mixed with the outlanders, and carried away a fair woman
from a remote land, whose lord's kin were spearmen and fighters,
to your father a big sorrow, and your city, and all your people,   50
to yourself a thing shameful but bringing joy to the enemy?
And now you would not stand up against warlike Menelaos?
Thus you would learn of the man whose blossoming wife you have taken.
The lyre would not help you then, nor the favours of Aphrodite,
nor your locks, when you rolled in the dust, nor all your beauty.   55
No, but the Trojans are cowards in truth, else long before this
you had worn a mantle of flying stones for the wrong you did us.'

   Then in answer Alexandros the godlike spoke to him:
'Hektor, seeing you have scolded me rightly, not beyond measure—
still, your heart forever is weariless, like an axe-blade   60
driven by a man's strength through the timber, one who, well skilled,
hews a piece for a ship, driven on by the force of a man's strength:

such is the heart in your breast, unshakable: yet do not
bring up against me the sweet favours of golden Aphrodite.
65 Never to be cast away are the gifts of the gods, magnificent,
  which they give of their own will, no man could have them for wanting
    them.
  Now though, if you wish me to fight it out and do battle,
  make the rest of the Trojans sit down, and all the Achaians,
  and set me in the middle with Menelaos the warlike
70 to fight together for the sake of Helen and all her possessions.
  That one of us who wins and is proved stronger, let him
  take the possessions fairly and the woman, and lead her homeward.
  But the rest of you, having cut your oaths of faith and friendship,
  dwell, you in Troy where the soil is rich, while those others return home
75 to horse-pasturing Argos, and Achaia the land of fair women.'
    So he spoke, and Hektor hearing his word was happy
  and went into the space between and forced back the Trojan battalions
  holding his spear by the middle until they were all seated.
  But the flowing-haired Achaians kept pointing their bows at him
80 with arrows and with flung stones striving ever to strike him
  until Agamemnon lord of men cried out in a great voice:
  'Argives, hold: cast at him no longer, o sons of the Achaians.
  Hektor of the shining helm is trying to tell us something.'
    So he spoke, and they stopped fighting and suddenly all fell
85 silent; but Hektor between them spoke now to both sides:
  'Hear from me, Trojans and strong-greaved Achaians, the word
  of Alexandros, for whose sake this strife has arisen.
  He would have all the rest of the Trojans and all the Achaians
  lay aside on the bountiful earth their splendid armour
90 while he himself in the middle and warlike Menelaos
  fight alone for the sake of Helen and all her possessions.
  That one of them who wins and is proved stronger, let him
  take the possessions fairly and the woman, and lead her homeward
  while the rest of us cut our oaths of faith and friendship.'
95   So he spoke, and all of them stayed stricken to silence;
  but among them spoke out Menelaos of the great war cry:
  'Listen now to me also; since beyond all others this sorrow
  comes closest to my heart, and I think the Argives and Trojans
  can go free of each other at last. You have suffered much evil

for the sake of this my quarrel since Alexandros began it.   100
As for that one of us two to whom death and doom are given,
let him die: the rest of you be made friends with each other.
Bring two lambs: let one be white and the other black for
Earth and the Sun God, and for Zeus we will bring yet another.
Bring, that he may seal the pledges, the strength of Priam: 105
Priam himself, for his sons are outrageous, not to be trusted;
lest some man overstep Zeus' oaths, and make them be nothing.
Always it is, that the hearts in the younger men are frivolous,
but when an elder man is among them, he looks behind him
and in front, so that all comes out far better for both sides.'   110
     So he spoke, and the Trojans and Achaians were joyful,
hoping now to be rid of all the sorrow of warfare.
They pulled their chariots into line, and themselves dismounted
and stripped off their armour which was laid on the ground beside them,
close together, so there was little ground left between them.   115
Hektor sent away to the citadel two heralds
lightly to bring down the lambs, and to summon Priam;
and powerful Agamemnon in turn sent Talthybios
to go down to the hollow ships, with orders to bring two
lambs: he did not disobey the order of great Agamemnon.   120
     Now to Helen of the white arms came a messenger, Iris,
in the likeness of her sister-in-law, the wife of Antenor's
son, whom strong Helikaon wed, the son of Antenor,
Laodike, loveliest looking of all the daughters of Priam.
She came on Helen in the chamber; she was weaving a great web,   125
a red folding robe, and working into it the numerous struggles
of Trojans, breakers of horses, and bronze-armoured Achaians,
struggles that they endured for her sake at the hands of the war god.
Iris of the swift feet stood beside her and spoke to her:
'Come with me, dear girl, to behold the marvellous things done   130
by Trojans, breakers of horses, and bronze-armoured Achaians,
who just now carried sorrowful war against each other,
in the plain, and all their desire was for deadly fighting;
now they are all seated in silence, the fighting has ended;
they lean on their shields, the tall spears stuck in the ground beside them. 135
But Menelaos the warlike and Alexandros will fight
with long spears against each other for your possession.

You shall be called beloved wife of the man who wins you.'
Speaking so the goddess left in her heart sweet longing
140 after her husband of time before, and her city and parents.
And at once, wrapping herself about in shimmering garments,
she went forth from the chamber, letting fall a light tear;
not by herself, since two handmaidens went to attend her,
Aithre, Pittheus' daughter, and Klymene of the ox eyes.
145 Rapidly they came to the place where the Skaian gates stood.
Now those who sat with Priam: Panthoös and Thymoites,
Lampos and Klytios, Hiketaon, scion of Ares,
with Antenor and Oukalegon, both men of good counsel:
these were seated by the Skaian gates, elders of the people.
150 Now through old age these fought no longer, yet were they excellent
speakers still, and clear, as cicadas who through the forest
settle on trees, to issue their delicate voice of singing.
Such were they who sat on the tower, chief men of the Trojans.
And these, as they saw Helen along the tower approaching,
155 murmuring softly to each other uttered their winged words:
'Surely there is no blame on Trojans and strong-greaved Achaians
if for long time they suffer hardship for a woman like this one.
Terrible is the likeness of her face to immortal goddesses.
Still, though she be such, let her go away in the ships, lest
160 she be left behind, a grief to us and our children.'
So they spoke: but Priam aloud called out to Helen:
'Come over where I am, dear child, and sit down beside me,
to look at your husband of time past, your friends and your people.
I am not blaming you: to me the gods are blameworthy
165 who drove upon me this sorrowful war against the Achaians.
So you could tell me the name of this man who is so tremendous;
who is this Achaian man of power and stature?
Though in truth there are others taller by a head than he is,
yet these eyes have never yet looked on a man so splendid
170 nor so lordly as this: such a man might well be royal.'
Helen, the shining among women, answered and spoke to him:
'Always to me, beloved father, you are feared and respected;
and I wish bitter death had been what I wanted, when I came hither
following your son, forsaking my chamber, my kinsmen,
175 my grown child, and the loveliness of girls my own age.

It did not happen that way: and now I am worn with weeping.
This now I will tell you in answer to the question you asked me.
That man is Atreus' son Agamemnon, widely powerful,
at the same time a good king and a strong spearfighter,
once my kinsman, slut that I am. Did this ever happen?'   180
    This she said, and the old man spoke again, wondering at him:
'O son of Atreus, blessed, child of fortune and favour,
many are these beneath your sway, these sons of the Achaians.
Once before this time I visited Phrygia of the vineyards.
There I looked on the Phrygian men with their swarming horses,   185
so many of them, the people of Otreus and godlike Mygdon,
whose camp was spread at that time along the banks of Sangarios:
and I myself, a helper in war, was marshalled among them
on that day when the Amazon women came, men's equals.
Yet even they were not so many as these glancing-eyed Achaians.'   190
    Next again the old man asked her, seeing Odysseus:
'Tell me of this one also, dear child; what man can he be,
shorter in truth by a head than Atreus' son Agamemnon,
but broader, it would seem, in the chest and across the shoulders.
Now as his armour lies piled on the prospering earth, still he   195
ranges, like some ram, through the marshalled ranks of the fighters.
Truly, to some deep-fleeced ram would I liken him
who makes his way through the great mass of the shining sheep-flocks.'
    Helen, the daughter descended of Zeus, spoke then in answer:
'This one is Laertes' son, resourceful Odysseus,   200
who grew up in the country, rough though it be, of Ithaka,
to know every manner of shiftiness and crafty counsels.'
    In his turn Antenor of the good counsel answered her:
'Surely this word you have spoken, my lady, can be no falsehood.
Once in the days before now brilliant Odysseus came here   205
with warlike Menelaos, and their embassy was for your sake.
To both of these I gave in my halls kind entertainment
and I learned the natural way of both, and their close counsels.
Now when these were set before the Trojans assembled
and stood up, Menelaos was bigger by his broad shoulders   210
but Odysseus was the more lordly when both were seated.
Now before all when both of them spun their speech and their counsels,
Menelaos indeed spoke rapidly, in few words

but exceedingly lucid, since he was no long speaker
215 nor one who wasted his words though he was only a young man.
But when that other drove to his feet, resourceful Odysseus,
he would just stand and stare down, eyes fixed on the ground beneath him,
nor would he gesture with the staff backward and forward, but hold it
clutched hard in front of him, like any man who knows nothing.
220 Yes, you would call him a sullen man, and a fool likewise.
But when he let the great voice go from his chest, and the words came
drifting down like the winter snows, then no other mortal
man beside could stand up against Odysseus. Then we
wondered less beholding Odysseus' outward appearance.'
225   Third in order, looking at Aias, the old man asked her:
'Who then is this other Achaian of power and stature
towering above the Argives by head and broad shoulders?'
    Helen with the light robes and shining among women answered him:
'That one is gigantic Aias, wall of the Achaians,
230 and beyond him there is Idomeneus like a god standing
among the Kretans, and the lords of Krete are gathered about him.
Many a time warlike Menelaos would entertain him
in our own house when he came over from Krete. And I see them
all now, all the rest of the glancing-eyed Achaians,
235 all whom I would know well by sight, whose names I could tell you,
yet nowhere can I see those two, the marshals of the people,
Kastor, breaker of horses, and the strong boxer, Polydeukes,
my own brothers, born with me of a single mother.
Perhaps these came not with the rest from Lakedaimon the lovely,
240 or else they did come here in their sea-wandering ships, yet
now they are reluctant to go with the men into battle
dreading the words of shame and all the reproach that is on me.'
    So she spoke, but the teeming earth lay already upon them
away in Lakedaimon, the beloved land of their fathers.
245   Now through the town the heralds brought the symbols of oaths
        pledged,
two young rams, and cheerful wine, the yield of the tilled land
in a goatskin wine sack, while another carried the shining
mixing bowl (the herald Idaios) and the golden wine-cups.
Standing beside the aged man he spoke words to arouse him:
250 'Son of Laomedon, rise up: you are called by the chief men

of Trojans, breakers of horses, and bronze-armoured Achaians
to come down into the plain that you may seal the oaths pledged.
For warlike Menelaos and Alexandros are to fight
with long spears against each other for the sake of the woman.
Let the woman go to the winner, and all the possessions.   255
Let the rest of them, cutting their oaths of faith and friendship,
dwell, we in Troy where the soil is rich, while those others return home
to horse-pasturing Argos and Achaia the land of fair women.'
    So he spoke, and the old man shuddered, but called his companions
to yoke the horses to the car, and they promptly obeyed him.   260
And Priam mounted into the car and gathered the reins back
as Antenor beside him stepped into the fair-wrought chariot.
Through the Skaian gates to the plain they steered the swift horses.
    Now when these had come among the Trojans and Achaians,
they stepped down on the prospering earth from their car with horses   265
and made their way striding among the Achaians and Trojans.
On the other side rose up the lord of men, Agamemnon,
and the resourceful Odysseus rose up. Meanwhile the proud heralds
led up the victims for the gods' oaths, and in a great wine-bowl
mixed the wine, and poured water over the hands of the princes.   270
Atreus' son laid hands upon his work-knife, and drew it
from where it hung ever beside the mighty sheath of his war sword
and cut off hairs from the heads of the lambs; and the heralds thereafter
passed these about to all the princes of the Trojans and Achaians.
Atreus' son uplifting his hands then prayed in a great voice: 275
'Father Zeus, watching over us from Ida, most high, most honoured,
and Helios, you who see all things, who listen to all things,
earth, and rivers, and you who under the earth take vengeance
on dead men, whoever among them has sworn to falsehood,
you shall be witnesses, to guard the oaths of fidelity.   280
If it should be that Alexandros slays Menelaos,
let him keep Helen for himself, and all her possessions,
and we in our seafaring ships shall take our way homeward.
But if the fair-haired Menelaos kills Alexandros,
then let the Trojans give back Helen and all her possessions,   285
and pay also a price to the Argives which will be fitting,
which among people yet to come shall be as a standard.
Then if Priam and the sons of Priam are yet unwilling

after Alexandros has fallen to pay me the penalty,
290 I myself shall fight hereafter for the sake of the ransom,
here remaining, until I have won to the end of my quarrel.'
    So he spoke, and with pitiless bronze he cut the lambs' throats,
letting them fall gasping again to the ground, the life breath
going away, since the strength of the bronze had taken it from them.
295 Drawing the wine from the mixing bowls in the cups, they poured it
forth, and made their prayer to the gods who live everlasting.
And thus would murmur any man, Achaian or Trojan:
'Zeus, exalted and mightiest, and you other immortals,
let those, whichever side they may be, who do wrong to the oaths sworn
300 first, let their brains be spilled on the ground as this wine is spilled now,
theirs and their sons', and let their wives be the spoil of others.'
    They spoke, but none of this would the son of Kronos accomplish.
Now among them spoke Priam descended of Dardanos also:
'Listen to me, you Trojans and you strong-greaved Achaians.
305 Now I am going away to windy Ilion, homeward,
since I cannot look with these eyes on the sight of my dear son
fighting against warlike Menelaos in single combat.
Zeus knows—maybe he knows—and the rest of the gods immortal
for which of the two death is appointed to end this matter.'
310   He spoke, a godlike man, and laid the lambs in the chariot,
and mounted into it himself, and pulled the reins backward.
Antenor beside him stepped up into the fair-wrought chariot.
These two took their way backward and made for Ilion.
Hektor now, the son of Priam, and brilliant Odysseus
315 measured out the distance first, and thereafter picked up
two lots, and put them in a brazen helmet, and shook them,
to see which one of the two should be first to cast with his bronze spear,
and the people on each side held up their hands to the gods, and prayed
to them. Thus would murmur any man, Achaian or Trojan:
320 'Father Zeus, watching over us from Ida, most high, most honoured,
whichever man has made what has happened happen to both sides,
grant that he be killed and go down to the house of Hades.
Let the friendship and the sworn faith be true for the rest of us.'
    So they spoke, and tall Hektor of the shining helm shook
325 the lots, looking backward, and at once Paris' lot was outshaken.
All the rest sat down in their ranks on the ground, at the place where

the glittering armour of each was piled by his light-footed horses,
while one of them put about his shoulders his splendid armour,
brilliant Alexandros, the lord of lovely-haired Helen.
First he placed along his legs the fair greaves linked with   330
silver fastenings to hold the greaves at the ankles.
Afterwards he girt on about his chest the corselet
of Lykaon his brother since this fitted him also.
Across his shoulders he slung the sword with the nails of silver,
a bronze sword, and above it the great shield, huge and heavy.   335
Over his powerful head he set the well-fashioned helmet
with the horse-hair crest, and the plumes nodded terribly above it.
He took up a strong-shafted spear that fitted his hand's grip.
In the same way warlike Menelaos put on his armour.

   Now when these two were armed on either side of the battle,   340
they strode into the space between the Achaians and Trojans,
looking terror at each other; and amazement seized the beholders,
Trojans, breakers of horses, and strong-greaved Achaians.
They took their stand in the measured space not far from each other
raging each at the other man and shaking their spearshafts.   345
First of the two Alexandros let go his spear far-shadowing
and struck the shield of Atreus' son on its perfect circle
nor did the bronze point break its way through, but the spearhead bent
     back
in the strong shield. And after him Atreus' son, Menelaos,
was ready to let go the bronze spear, with a prayer to Zeus father: 350
'Zeus, lord, grant me to punish the man who first did me injury,
brilliant Alexandros, and beat him down under my hands' strength
that any one of the men to come may shudder to think of
doing evil to a kindly host, who has given him friendship.'

   So he spoke, and balanced the spear far-shadowed, and threw it   355
and struck the shield of Priam's son on its perfect circle.
All the way through the glittering shield went the heavy spearhead
and smashed its way through the intricately worked corselet;
straight ahead by the flank the spearhead shore through his tunic,
yet he bent away to one side and avoided the dark death.   360
Drawing his sword with the silver nails, the son of Atreus
heaving backward struck at the horn of his helmet; the sword-blade
three times broken and four times broken fell from his hand's grip.

Groaning, the son of Atreus lifted his eyes to the wide sky:
365 'Father Zeus, no God beside is more baleful than you are.
Here I thought to punish Alexandros for his wickedness;
and now my sword is broken in my hands, and the spear flew vainly
out of my hands on the throw before, and I have not hit him.'
He spoke, and flashing forward laid hold of the horse-haired helmet
370 and spun him about, and dragged him away toward the strong-greaved
        Achaians,
for the broidered strap under the softness of his throat strangled Paris,
fastened under his chin to hold on the horned helmet.
Now he would have dragged him away and won glory forever
had not Aphrodite daughter of Zeus watched sharply.
375 She broke the chinstrap, made from the hide of a slaughtered bullock,
and the helmet came away empty in the heavy hand of Atreides.
The hero whirled the helmet about and sent it flying
among the strong-greaved Achaians, and his staunch companions
        retrieved it.
He turned and made again for his man, determined to kill him
380 with the bronze spear. But Aphrodite caught up Paris
easily, since she was divine, and wrapped him in a thick mist
and set him down again in his own perfumed bedchamber.
She then went away to summon Helen, and found her
on the high tower, with a cluster of Trojan women about her.
385 She laid her hand upon the robe immortal, and shook it,
and spoke to her, likening herself to an aged woman,
a wool-dresser who when she was living in Lakedaimon
made beautiful things out of wool, and loved her beyond all others.
Likening herself to this woman Aphrodite spoke to her:
390   'Come with me: Alexandros sends for you to come home to him.
He is in his chamber now, in the bed with its circled pattern,
shining in his raiment and his own beauty; you would not think
that he came from fighting against a man; you would think he was going
rather to a dance, or rested and had been dancing lately.'
395   So she spoke, and troubled the spirit in Helen's bosom.
She, as she recognized the round, sweet throat of the goddess
and her desirable breasts and her eyes that were full of shining,
she wondered, and spoke a word and called her by name, thus:
'Strange divinity! Why are you still so stubborn to beguile me?

Will you carry me further yet somewhere among cities   400
fairly settled? In Phrygia or in lovely Maionia?
Is there some mortal man there also who is dear to you?
Is it because Menelaos has beaten great Alexandros
and wishes, hateful even as I am, to carry me homeward,
is it for this that you stand in your treachery now beside me?   405
Go yourself and sit beside him, abandon the gods' way,
turn your feet back never again to the path of Olympos
but stay with him forever, and suffer for him, and look after him
until he makes you his wedded wife, or makes you his slave girl.
Not I. I am not going to him. It would be too shameful.   410
I will not serve his bed, since the Trojan women hereafter
would laugh at me, all, and my heart even now is confused with sorrows.'
    Then in anger Aphrodite the shining spoke to her:
'Wretched girl, do not tease me lest in anger I forsake you
and grow to hate you as much as now I terribly love you,   415
lest I encompass you in hard hate, caught between both sides,
Danaans and Trojans alike, and you wretchedly perish.'
    So she spoke, and Helen daughter of Zeus was frightened
and went, shrouding herself about in the luminous spun robe,
silent, unseen by the Trojan women, and led by the goddess.   420
    When they had come to Alexandros' splendidly wrought house,
the rest of them, the handmaidens went speedily to their own work,
but she, shining among women, went to the high-vaulted bedchamber.
Aphrodite the sweetly laughing drew up an armchair,
carrying it, she, a goddess, and set it before Alexandros,   425
and Helen, daughter of Zeus of the aegis, took her place there
turning her eyes away, and spoke to her lord in derision:
'So you came back from fighting. Oh, how I wish you had died there
beaten down by the stronger man, who was once my husband.
There was a time before now you boasted that you were better   430
than warlike Menelaos, in spear and hand and your own strength.
Go forth now and challenge warlike Menelaos
once again to fight you in combat. But no: I advise you
rather to let it be, and fight no longer with fair-haired
Menelaos, strength against strength in single combat   435
recklessly. You might very well go down before his spear.'
    Paris then in turn spoke to her thus and answered her:

'Lady, censure my heart no more in bitter reprovals.
This time Menelaos with Athene's help has beaten me;
440 another time I shall beat him. We have gods on our side also.
Come, then, rather let us go to bed and turn to love-making.
Never before as now has passion enmeshed my senses,
not when I took you the first time from Lakedaimon the lovely
and caught you up and carried you away in seafaring vessels,
445 and lay with you in the bed of love on the island Kranae,
not even then, as now, did I love you and sweet desire seize me.'
    Speaking, he led the way to the bed; and his wife went with him.
So these two were laid in the carven bed. But Atreides
ranged like a wild beast up and down the host, to discover
450 whether he could find anywhere godlike Alexandros.
Yet could none of the Trojans nor any renowned companion
show Alexandros then to warlike Menelaos.
These would not have hidden him for love, if any had seen him,
since he was hated among them all as dark death is hated.
455   Now among them spoke forth the lord of men Agamemnon:
'Listen to me, o Trojans, Dardanians and companions:
clearly the victory is with warlike Menelaos.
Do you therefore give back, with all her possessions, Helen
of Argos, and pay a price that shall be befitting,
460 which among people yet to come shall be as a standard.'
    So spoke Atreus' son, and the other Achaians applauded him.

Now the gods at the side of Zeus were sitting in council
over the golden floor, and among them the goddess Hebe
poured them nectar as wine, while they in the golden drinking-cups
drank to each other, gazing down on the city of the Trojans.
Presently the son of Kronos was minded to anger   5
Hera, if he could, with words offensive, speaking to cross her:
'Two among the goddesses stand by Menelaos,
Hera of Argos, and Athene who stands by her people.
Yet see, here they are sitting apart, looking on at the fighting,
and take their pleasure. Meanwhile laughing Aphrodite forever   10
stands by her man and drives the spirits of death away from him.
Even now she has rescued him when he thought he would perish.
So, the victory now is with warlike Menelaos.
Let us consider then how these things shall be accomplished,
whether again to stir up grim warfare and the terrible   15
fighting, or cast down love and make them friends with each other.
If somehow this way could be sweet and pleasing to all of us,
the city of lord Priam might still be a place men dwell in,
and Menelaos could take away with him Helen of Argos.'
    So he spoke; and Athene and Hera muttered, since they were   20
sitting close to each other, devising evil for the Trojans.
Still Athene stayed silent and said nothing, but only
sulked at Zeus her father, and savage anger took hold of her.
But the heart of Hera could not contain her anger, and she spoke forth:
'Majesty, son of Kronos, what sort of thing have you spoken?   25

How can you wish to make wasted and fruitless all this endeavour,
the sweat that I have sweated in toil, and my horses worn out
gathering my people, and bringing evil to Priam and his children.
Do it then; but not all the rest of us gods will approve you.'
30   Deeply troubled, Zeus who gathers the clouds answered her:
'Dear lady, what can be all the great evils done to you
by Priam and the sons of Priam, that you are thus furious
forever to bring down the strong-founded city of Ilion?
If you could walk through the gates and through the towering ramparts
35 and eat Priam and the children of Priam raw, and the other
Trojans, then, then only might you glut at last your anger.
Do as you please then. Never let this quarrel hereafter
be between you and me a bitterness for both of us.
And put away in your thoughts this other thing that I tell you:
40 whenever I in turn am eager to lay waste some city,
as I please, one in which are dwelling men who are dear to you,
you shall not stand in the way of my anger, but let me do it,
since I was willing to grant you this with my heart unwilling.
For of all the cities beneath the sun and the starry heaven
45 dwelt in by men who live upon earth, there has never been one
honoured nearer to my heart than sacred Ilion
and Priam, and the people of Priam of the strong ash spear.
Never yet has my altar gone without fair sacrifice,
the libation and the savour, since this is our portion of honour.'
50   Then the goddess the ox-eyed lady Hera answered:
'Of all cities there are three that are dearest to my own heart:
Argos and Sparta and Mykenai of the wide ways. All these,
whenever they become hateful to your heart, sack utterly.
I will not stand up for these against you, nor yet begrudge you.
55 Yet if even so I bear malice and would not have you destroy them,
in malice I will accomplish nothing, since you are far stronger.
Yet my labour also should not be let go unaccomplished;
I am likewise a god, and my race is even what yours is,
and I am first of the daughters of devious-devising Kronos,
60 both ways, since I am eldest born and am called your consort,
yours, and you in turn are lord over all the immortals.
Come then, in this thing let us both give way to each other,
I to you, you to me, and so the rest of the immortal

gods will follow. Now in speed give orders to Athene
to visit horrible war again on Achaians and Trojans,   65
and try to make it so that the Trojans are first offenders
to do injury against the oaths to the far-famed Achaians.'

    She spoke, nor did the father of gods and men disobey her,
but immediately he spoke in winged words to Athene:
'Go now swiftly to the host of the Achaians and Trojans   70
and try to make it so that the Trojans are first offenders
to do injury against the oaths to the far-famed Achaians.'

    Speaking so he stirred up Athene, who was eager before this,
and she went in a flash of speed down the pinnacles of Olympos.
As when the son of devious-devising Kronos casts down   75
a star, portent to sailors or to widespread armies of peoples
glittering, and thickly the sparks of fire break from it,
in such likeness Pallas Athene swept flashing earthward
and plunged between the two hosts; and amazement seized the beholders,
Trojans, breakers of horses, and strong-greaved Achaians.   80
And thus they would speak to each other, each looking at the man next
    him:
'Surely again there will be evil war and terrible
fighting, or else now friendship is being set between both sides
by Zeus, who is appointed lord of the wars of mortals.'

    Thus would murmur any man, Achaian or Trojan.   85
She in the likeness of a man merged among the Trojans assembled,
Laodokos, Antenor's son, a powerful spearman,
searching for godlike Pandaros, if she might somewhere come on him.
She found the son of Lykaon, a man blameless and powerful,
standing still, and about him were the ranks of strong, shield-armoured   90
people, who had followed him from the streams of Aisepos.
Speaking in winged words she stood beside him and spoke to him:
'Wise son of Lykaon, would you now let me persuade you?
So you might dare send a flying arrow against Menelaos
and win you glory and gratitude in the sight of all Trojans,   95
particularly beyond all else with prince Alexandros.
Beyond all beside you would carry away glorious gifts from him,
were he to see warlike Menelaos, the son of Atreus,
struck down by your arrow, and laid on the sorrowful corpse-fire.
Come then, let go an arrow against haughty Menelaos,   100

but make your prayer to Apollo the light-born, the glorious archer,
that you will accomplish a grand sacrifice of lambs first born
when you come home again to the city of sacred Zeleia.'
   So spoke Athene, and persuaded the fool's heart in him.
105 Straightway he unwrapped his bow, of the polished horn from
a running wild goat he himself had shot in the chest once,
lying in wait for the goat in a covert as it stepped down
from the rock, and hit it in the chest so it sprawled on the boulders.
The horns that grew from the goat's head were sixteen palms' length.
110 A bowyer working on the horn then bound them together,
smoothing them to a fair surface, and put on a golden string hook.
Pandaros strung his bow and put it in position, bracing it
against the ground, and his brave friends held their shields in front of him
for fear the warlike sons of the Achaians might rise up and rush him
115 before he had struck warlike Menelaos, the son of Atreus.
He stripped away the lid of the quiver, and took out an arrow
feathered, and never shot before, transmitter of dark pain.
Swiftly he arranged the bitter arrow along the bowstring,
and made his prayer to Apollo the light-born, the glorious archer,
120 that he would accomplish a grand sacrifice of lambs first born
when he came home again to the city of sacred Zeleia.
He drew, holding at once the grooves and the ox-hide bowstring
and brought the string against his nipple, iron to the bowstave.
But when he had pulled the great weapon till it made a circle,
125 the bow groaned, and the string sang high, and the arrow, sharp-pointed,
leapt away, furious, to fly through the throng before it.
Still the blessed gods immortal did not forget you,
Menelaos, and first among them Zeus' daughter, the spoiler,
who standing in front of you fended aside the tearing arrow.
130 She brushed it away from his skin as lightly as when a mother
brushes a fly away from her child who is lying in sweet sleep,
steering herself the arrow's course straight to where the golden
belt buckles joined and the halves of his corselet were fitted together.
The bitter arrow was driven against the joining of the war belt
135 and passed clean through the war belt elaborately woven;
into the elaborately wrought corselet the shaft was driven
and the guard which he wore to protect his skin and keep the spears off,
which guarded him best, yet the arrow plunged even through this also

and with the very tip of its point it grazed the man's skin
and straightway from the cut there gushed a cloud of dark blood.   140
   As when some Maionian woman or Karian with purple
colours ivory, to make it a cheek piece for horses;
it lies away in an inner room, and many a rider
longs to have it, but it is laid up to be a king's treasure,
two things, to be the beauty of the horse, the pride of the horseman: 145
so, Menelaos, your shapely thighs were stained with the colour
of blood, and your legs also and the ankles beneath them.
   Agamemnon the lord of men was taken with shuddering
fear as he saw how from the cut the dark blood trickled downward,
and Menelaos the warlike himself shuddered in terror;   150
but when he saw the binding strings and the hooked barbs outside
the wound, his spirit was gathered again back into him. Agamemnon
the powerful spoke to them, groaning heavily, and by the hand held
Menelaos, while their companions were mourning beside them:
'Dear brother, it was your death I sealed in the oaths of friendship,   155
setting you alone before the Achaians to fight with the Trojans.
So, the Trojans have struck you down and trampled on the oaths sworn.
Still the oaths and the blood of the lambs shall not be called vain,
the unmixed wine poured and the right hands we trusted.
If the Olympian at once has not finished this matter,   160
late will he bring it to pass, and they must pay a great penalty,
with their own heads, and with their women, and with their children.
For I know this thing well in my heart, and my mind knows it.
There will come a day when sacred Ilion shall perish,
and Priam, and the people of Priam of the strong ash spear,   165
and Zeus son of Kronos who sits on high, the sky-dwelling,
himself shall shake the gloom of his aegis over all of them
in anger for this deception. All this shall not go unaccomplished.
But I shall suffer a terrible grief for you, Menelaos,
if you die and fill out the destiny of your lifetime.   170
And I must return a thing of reproach to Argos the thirsty,
for now at once the Achaians will remember the land of their fathers;
and thus we would leave to Priam and to the Trojans Helen
of Argos, to glory over, while the bones of you rot in the ploughland
as you lie dead in Troy, on a venture that went unaccomplished.   175
And thus shall some Trojan speak in the proud show of his manhood,

leaping lightly as he speaks on the tomb of great Menelaos:
"Might Agamemnon accomplish his anger thus against all his
enemies, as now he led here in vain a host of Achaians

180 and has gone home again to the beloved land of his fathers
with ships empty, and leaving behind him brave Menelaos."
Thus shall a man speak: then let the wide earth open to take me.'
    Then in encouragement fair-haired Menelaos spoke to him:
'Do not fear, nor yet make afraid the Achaian people.

185 The sharp arrow is not stuck in a mortal place, but the shining
war belt turned it aside from its course, and the flap beneath it
with my guard of armour that bronze-smiths wrought carefully for me.'
    Then in answer again spoke powerful Agamemnon:
'May it only be as you say, o Menelaos, dear brother!

190 But the physician will handle the wound and apply over it
healing salves, by which he can put an end to the black pains.'
    He spoke, and addressed Talthybios, his sacred herald:
'Talthybios, with all speed go call hither Machaon,
a man who is son of Asklepios and a blameless physician,

195 so that he may look at Menelaos, the warlike son of
Atreus, whom someone skilled in the bow's use shot with an arrow,
Trojan or Lykian: glory to him, but to us a sorrow.'
    He spoke, and the herald heard and did not disobey him,
but went on his way among the host of bronze-armoured Achaians

200 looking about for the warrior Machaon; and saw him
standing still, and about him the strong ranks of shield-bearing
people, who had come with him from horse-pasturing Trikka.
He came and stood close beside him and addressed him in winged words:
'Rise up, son of Asklepios; powerful Agamemnon calls you,

205 so that you may look at warlike Menelaos, the Achaians'
leader, whom someone skilled in the bow's use shot with an arrow,
Trojan or Lykian: glory to him, but to us a sorrow.'
    So he spoke, and stirred up the spirit within Machaon.
They went through the crowd along the widespread host of the Achaians.

210 But when they had come to the place where fair-haired Menelaos
had been hit, where all the great men were gathered about him
in a circle, and he stood in the midst of them, a man godlike,
straightway he pulled the arrow forth from the joining of the war belt,
and as it was pulled out the sharp barbs were broken backwards.

He slipped open the war belt then and the flap beneath it   215
with the guard of armour that bronze-smiths wrought carefully for him.
But when he saw the wound where the bitter arrow was driven,
he sucked the blood and in skill laid healing medicines on it
that Cheiron in friendship long ago had given his father.

    While they were working over Menelaos of the great war cry   220
all this time came on the ranks of the armoured Trojans.
The Achaians again put on their armour, and remembered their warcraft.

    Then you would not have seen brilliant Agamemnon asleep nor
skulking aside, nor in any way a reluctant fighter,
but driving eagerly toward the fighting where men win glory.   225
He left aside his chariot gleaming with bronze, and his horses,
and these, breathing hard, were held aside by a henchman,
Eurymedon, born to Ptolemaios, the son of Peiraios.
Agamemnon told him to keep them well in hand, till the time came
when weariness might take hold of his limbs, through marshalling so   230
    many.
Then he, on foot as he was, ranged through the ranks of his fighters.
Those of the fast-mounted Danaans he found eager, he would
stand beside these and urge them harder on with words spoken:
'Argives, do not let go now of this furious valour.
Zeus the father shall not be one to give aid to liars,   235
but these, who were the first to do violence over the oaths sworn,
vultures shall feed upon the delicate skin of their bodies,
while we lead away their beloved wives and innocent
children, in our ships, after we have stormed their citadel.'

    Any he might see hanging back from the hateful conflict   240
these in words of anger he would reproach very bitterly:
'Argives, you arrow-fighters, have you no shame, you abuses?
Why are you simply standing there bewildered, like young deer
who after they are tired from running through a great meadow
stand there still, and there is no heart of courage within them?   245
Thus are you standing still bewildered and are not fighting.
Or are you waiting for the Trojans to come close, where the strong-
    sterned
ships have been hauled up along the strand of the grey sea,
so you may know if Kronos' son will hold his hand over you?'

    Thus he ranged through the ranks of his men and set them in order.   250

[119]

On his way through the thronging men he came to the Kretans
who about valiant Idomeneus were arming for battle.
Idomeneus, like a boar in his strength, stood among the champions
while Meriones still urged along the last battalions.
255 Agamemnon the lord of men was glad as he looked at them
and in words of graciousness at once spoke to Idomeneus:
'I honour you, Idomeneus, beyond the fast-mounted
Danaans whether in battle, or in any action whatever,
whether it be at the feast, when the great men of the Argives
260 blend in the mixing bowl the gleaming wine of the princes.
Even though all the rest of the flowing-haired Achaians
drink out their portion, still your cup stands filled forever
even as mine, for you to drink when the pleasure takes you.
Rise up then to battle, be such as you claimed in time past.'
265   Then in turn Idomeneus lord of the Kretans answered him:
'Son of Atreus, I will in truth be a staunch companion
in arms, as first I promised you and bent my head to it.
Rouse up rather the rest of the flowing-haired Achaians
so that we may fight in all speed, since the Trojans have broken
270 their oaths: a thing that shall be death and sorrow hereafter
to them, since they were the first to do violence over the oaths sworn.'
    So he spoke, and Atreides, cheerful at heart, went onward.
On his way through the thronging men he came to the Aiantes.
These were armed, and about them went a cloud of foot-soldiers.
275 As from his watching place a goatherd watches a cloud move
on its way over the sea before the drive of the west wind;
far away though he be he watches it, blacker than pitch is,
moving across the sea and piling the storm before it,
and as he sees it he shivers and drives his flocks to a cavern;
280 so about the two Aiantes moved the battalions,
close-compacted of strong and god-supported young fighters,
black, and jagged with spear and shield, to the terror of battle.
Agamemnon the lord of men was glad when he looked at them,
and he spoke aloud to them and addressed them in winged words:
285 'Aiantes, o leaders of the bronze-armoured Argives,
to you two I give no orders; it would not become me
to speed you, now that yourselves drive your people on to fight strongly.
Father Zeus, and Athene, and Apollo, if only

[120]

such a spirit were in the hearts of all of my people.
Then perhaps the city of lord Priam would be bent   290
underneath our hands, captured and utterly taken.'
    So he spoke, and left them there, and went among others.
There he came upon Nestor, the lucid speaker of Pylos,
setting in order his own companions and urging them to battle,
tall Pelagon with those about him, Alastor and Chromios,   295
Haimon the powerful, and Bias, shepherd of the people.
First he ranged the mounted men with their horses and chariots
and stationed the brave and numerous foot-soldiers behind them
to be the bastion of battle, and drove the cowards to the centre
so that a man might be forced to fight even though unwilling.   300
First he gave orders to the drivers of horses, and warned them
to hold their horses in check and not be fouled in the multitude:
'Let no man in the pride of his horsemanship and his manhood
dare to fight alone with the Trojans in front of the rest of us,
neither let him give ground, since that way you will be weaker.   305
When a man from his own car encounters the enemy chariots
let him stab with his spear, since this is the stronger fighting.
So the men before your time sacked tower and city,
keeping a spirit like this in their hearts, and like this their purpose.'
    Thus the old man wise in fighting from of old encouraged them.   310
Agamemnon the lord of men was glad when he looked at him
and he spoke aloud to him and addressed him in winged words:
'Aged sir, if only, as the spirit is in your bosom,
so might your knees be also and the strength stay steady within you;
but age weakens you which comes to all; if only some other   315
of the fighters had your age and you were one of the young men!'
    Nestor the Gerenian horseman spoke and answered him:
'Son of Atreus, so would I also wish to be that
man I was, when I cut down brilliant Ereuthalion.
But the gods give to mortals not everything at the same time;   320
if I was a young man then, now in turn old age is upon me.
Yet even so I shall be among the riders, and command them
with word and counsel; such is the privilege of the old men.
The young spearmen shall do the spear-fighting, those who are born
of a generation later than mine, who trust in their own strength.'   325
    So he spoke, and Atreides, cheerful at heart, went onward.

He came on the son of Peteos, Menestheus, driver of horses,
standing still, and about him the Athenians, urgent for battle.
Next to these resourceful Odysseus had taken position,
330 and beside him the Kephallenian ranks, no weak ones,
were standing, since the men had not heard the clamour of battle
but even now fresh set in motion moved the battalions
of Achaians and Trojans, breakers of horses; so these standing
waited, until some other mass of Achaians advancing
335 might crash against the Trojans, and the battle be opened.
Seeing these the lord of men Agamemnon scolded them
and spoke aloud to them and addressed them in winged words, saying:
'Son of Peteos, the king supported of God: and you, too,
you with your mind forever on profit and your ways of treachery,
340 why do you stand here skulking aside, and wait for the others?
For you two it is becoming to stand among the foremost
fighters, and endure your share of the blaze of battle;
since indeed you two are first to hear of the feasting
whenever we Achaians make ready a feast of the princes.
345 There it is your pleasure to eat the roast flesh, to drink
as much as you please the cups of the wine that is sweet as honey.
Now, though, you would be pleased to look on though ten battalions
of Achaians were to fight with the pitiless bronze before you.'
    Then looking at him darkly resourceful Odysseus spoke to him:
350 'What is this word that broke through the fence of your teeth, Atreides?
How can you say that, when we Achaians waken the bitter
war god on Trojans, breakers of horses, I hang back from
fighting? Only watch, if you care to and if it concerns you,
the very father of Telemachos locked with the champion
355 Trojans, breakers of horses. Your talk is wind, and no meaning.'
    Powerful Agamemnon in turn answered him, laughing,
seeing that he was angered and taking back the word spoken:
'Son of Laertes and seed of Zeus, resourceful Odysseus:
I must not be niggling with you, nor yet give you orders,
360 since I know how the spirit in your secret heart knows
ideas of kindness only; for what you think is what I think.
Come now, I will make it good hereafter, if anything evil
has been said; let the gods make all this come to nothing.'
    So he spoke, and left him there, and went among others.

He came on the son of Tydeus, high-spirited Diomedes,   365
standing among the compacted chariots and by the horses,
and Kapaneus' son, Sthenelos, was standing beside him. At sight
of Diomedes the lord of men Agamemnon scolded him
and spoke aloud to him and addressed him in winged words, saying:
'Ah me, son of Tydeus, that daring breaker of horses,   370
why are you skulking and spying out the outworks of battle?
Such was never Tydeus' way, to lurk in the background,
but to fight the enemy far ahead of his own companions.
So they say who had seen him at work, since I never saw nor
encountered him ever; but they say he surpassed all others.   375
Once on a time he came, but not in war, to Mykenai
with godlike Polyneikes, a guest and a friend, assembling
people, since these were attacking the sacred bastions of Thebe,
and much they entreated us to grant him renowned companions.
And our men wished to give them and were assenting to what they asked 380
    for
but Zeus turned them back, showing forth portents that crossed them.
Now as these went forward and were well on their way, and came
to the river Asopos, and the meadows of grass and the deep rushes,
from there the Achaians sent Tydeus ahead with a message.
He went then and came on the Kadmeians in their numbers   385
feasting all about the house of mighty Eteokles.
There, stranger though he was, the driver of horses, Tydeus,
was not frightened, alone among so many Kadmeians,
but dared them to try their strength with him, and bested all of them
easily, such might did Pallas Athene give him.   390
The Kadmeians who lash their horses, in anger compacted
an ambuscade of guile on his way home, assembling together
fifty fighting men, and for these there were two leaders,
Maion, Haimon's son, in the likeness of the immortals,
with the son of Autophonos, Polyphontes stubborn in battle.   395
On these men Tydeus let loose a fate that was shameful.
He killed them all, except that he let one man get home again,
letting Maion go in obedience to the god's signs.
This was Tydeus, the Aitolian; yet he was father
to a son worse than himself at fighting, better in conclave.'   400
    So he spoke, and strong Diomedes gave no answer

in awe before the majesty of the king's rebuking;
but the son of Kapaneus the glorious answered him, saying:
'Son of Atreus, do not lie when you know the plain truth.
405 We two claim we are better men by far than our fathers.
We did storm the seven-gated foundation of Thebe
though we led fewer people beneath a wall that was stronger.
We obeyed the signs of the gods and the help Zeus gave us,
while those others died of their own headlong stupidity.
410 Therefore, never liken our fathers to us in honour.'
    Then looking at him darkly strong Diomedes spoke to him:
'Friend, stay quiet rather and do as I tell you; I will
find no fault with Agamemnon, shepherd of the people,
for stirring thus into battle the strong-greaved Achaians;
415 this will be his glory to come, if ever the Achaians
cut down the men of Troy and capture sacred Ilion.
If the Achaians are slain, then his will be the great sorrow.
Come, let you and me remember our fighting courage.'
    He spoke and leapt in all his gear to the ground from the chariot,
420 and the bronze armour girt to the chest of the king clashed terribly
as he sprang. Fear would have gripped even a man stout-hearted.
    As when along the thundering beach the surf of the sea strikes
beat upon beat as the west wind drives it onward; far out
cresting first on the open water, it drives thereafter
425 to smash roaring along the dry land, and against the rock jut
bending breaks itself into crests spewing back the salt wash;
so thronged beat upon beat the Danaans' close battalions
steadily into battle, with each of the lords commanding
his own men; and these went silently, you would not think
430 all these people with voices kept in their chests were marching;
silently, in fear of their commanders; and upon all
glittered as they marched the shining armour they carried.
But the Trojans, as sheep in a man of possessions' steading
stand in their myriads waiting to be drained of their white milk
435 and bleat interminably as they hear the voice of their lambs, so
the crying of the Trojans went up through the wide army.
Since there was no speech nor language common to all of them
but their talk was mixed, who were called there from many far places.
Ares drove these on, and the Achaians grey-eyed Athene,

and Terror drove them, and Fear, and Hate whose wrath is relentless,   440
she the sister and companion of murderous Ares,
she who is only a little thing at the first, but thereafter
grows until she strides on the earth with her head striking heaven.
She then hurled down bitterness equally between both sides
as she walked through the onslaught making men's pain heavier.   445

    Now as these advancing came to one place and encountered,
they dashed their shields together and their spears, and the strength
of armoured men in bronze, and the shields massive in the middle
clashed against each other, and the sound grew huge of the fighting.
There the screaming and the shouts of triumph rose up together   450
of men killing and men killed, and the ground ran blood.
As when rivers in winter spate running down from the mountains
throw together at the meeting of streams the weight of their water
out of the great springs behind in the hollow stream-bed,
and far away in the mountains the shepherd hears their thunder;   455
such, from the coming together of men, was the shock and the shouting.

    Antilochos was first to kill a chief man of the Trojans,
valiant among the champions, Thalysias' son, Echepolos.
Throwing first, he struck the horn of the horse-haired helmet,
and the bronze spearpoint fixed in his forehead and drove inward   460
through the bone; and a mist of darkness clouded both eyes
and he fell as a tower falls in the strong encounter.
As he dropped, Elephenor the powerful caught him by the feet,
Chalkodon's son, and lord of the great-hearted Abantes,
and dragged him away from under the missiles, striving in all speed   465
to strip the armour from him, yet his outrush went short-lived.
For as he hauled the corpse high-hearted Agenor, marking
the ribs that showed bare under the shield as he bent over,
stabbed with the bronze-pointed spear and unstrung his sinews.
So the spirit left him and over his body was fought out   470
weary work by Trojans and Achaians, who like wolves
sprang upon one another, with man against man in the onfall.

    There Telamonian Aias struck down the son of Anthemion
Simoeisios in his stripling's beauty, whom once his mother
descending from Ida bore beside the banks of Simoeis   475
when she had followed her father and mother to tend the sheepflocks.
Therefore they called him Simoeisios; but he could not

render again the care of his dear parents; he was short-lived,
beaten down beneath the spear of high-hearted Aias,
480 who struck him as he first came forward beside the nipple
of the right breast, and the bronze spearhead drove clean through the
    shoulder.
He dropped then to the ground in the dust, like some black poplar,
which in the land low-lying about a great marsh grows
smooth trimmed yet with branches growing at the uttermost tree-top:
485 one whom a man, a maker of chariots, fells with the shining
iron, to bend it into a wheel for a fine-wrought chariot,
and the tree lies hardening by the banks of a river.
Such was Anthemion's son Simoeisios, whom illustrious
Aias killed. Now Antiphos of the shining corselet,
490 Priam's son, made a cast at him in the crowd with the sharp spear
but missed Aias and struck Leukos, a brave companion
of Odysseus, in the groin, as he dragged a corpse off,
so that the body dropped from his hand as he fell above it.
For his killing Odysseus was stirred to terrible anger
495 and he strode out among the champions, helmed in bright bronze,
and stood close to the enemy hefting the shining javelin,
glaring round about him; and the Trojans gave way in the face
of the man throwing with the spear. And he made no vain cast,
but struck down Demokoön, a son of Priam, a bastard,
500 who came over from Abydos, and left his fast-running horses.
Odysseus struck him with the spear, in anger for his companion,
in the temple, and the bronze spearhead drove through the other
temple also, so that a mist of darkness clouded both eyes.
He fell, thunderously, and his armour clattered upon him.
505 The champions of Troy gave back then, and glorious Hektor,
and the Argives gave a great cry, and dragged back the bodies,
and drove their way far forward, but now Apollo watching
from high Pergamos was angered, and called aloud to the Trojans:
'Rise up, Trojans, breakers of horses, bend not from battle
510 with these Argives. Surely their skin is not stone, not iron
to stand up under the tearing edge of the bronze as it strikes them.
No, nor is Achilleus the child of lovely-haired Thetis
fighting, but beside the ship mulls his heartsore anger.'
    So called the fearful god from the citadel, while Zeus' daughter

Tritogeneia, goddess most high, drove on the Achaians,   515
any of them she saw hanging back as she strode through the battle.
    Now his doom caught fast Amaryngkeus' son Diores,
who with a jagged boulder was smitten beside the ankle
in the right shin, and a lord of the Thracian warriors threw it,
Peiros, son of Imbrasos, who had journeyed from Ainos.   520
The pitiless stone smashed utterly the tendons on both sides
with the bones, and he was hurled into the dust backwards
reaching out both hands to his own beloved companions,
gasping life out; the stone's thrower ran up beside him,
Peiros, and stabbed with his spear next the navel, and all his guts poured 525
out on the ground, and a mist of darkness closed over both eyes.
    Thoas the Aitolian hit Peiros as he ran backward
with the spear in the chest above the nipple, and the bronze point fixed
in the lung, and Thoas standing close dragged out the heavy
spear from his chest, and drawing his sharp sword struck him   530
in the middle of the belly, and so took the life from him,
yet did not strip his armour, for his companions about him
stood, Thracians with hair grown at the top, gripping their long spears,
and though he was a mighty man and a strong and proud one
thrust him from them so that he gave ground backward, staggering.   535
So in the dust these two lay sprawled beside one another,
lords, the one of the Thracians, the other of the bronze-armoured
Epeians; and many others beside were killed all about them.
    There no more could a man who was in that work make light of it,
one who still unhit and still unstabbed by the sharp bronze   540
spun in the midst of that fighting, with Pallas Athene's hold on
his hand guiding him, driving back the volleying spears thrown.
For on that day many men of the Achaians and Trojans
lay sprawled in the dust face downward beside one another.

HERE to Tydeus' son Diomedes Pallas Athene
granted strength and daring, that he might be conspicuous
among all the Argives and win the glory of valour.
She made weariless fire blaze from his shield and helmet
5   like that star of the waning summer who beyond all stars
rises bathed in the ocean stream to glitter in brilliance.
Such was the fire she made blaze from his head and his shoulders
and urged him into the middle fighting, where most were struggling.
    There was a man of the Trojans, Dares, blameless and bountiful,
10   priest consecrated to Hephaistos, and he had two sons,
Phegeus and Idaios, well skilled both in all fighting.
These two breaking from the ranks of the others charged against him
riding their chariot as Diomedes came on, dismounted.
Now as in their advance these had come close to each other
15   first of the two Phegeus let go his spear far-shadowing.
Over the left shoulder of Tydeus' son passed the pointed
spear, nor struck his body, and Diomedes thereafter
threw with the bronze, and the weapon cast from his hand flew not vain
but struck the chest between the nipples and hurled him from behind
20   his horses. And Idaios leaping left the fair-wrought chariot
nor had he the courage to stand over his stricken brother.
Even so he could not have escaped the black death-spirit
but Hephaistos caught him away and rescued him, shrouded in darkness,
that the aged man might not be left altogether desolate.
25   But the son of high-hearted Tydeus drove off the horses

and gave them to his company to lead back to the hollow vessels.
Now as the high-hearted Trojans watched the two sons of Dares,
one running away, and one cut down by the side of his chariot,
the anger in all of them was stirred. But grey-eyed Athene
took violent Ares by the hand, and in words she spoke to him: 30
'Ares, Ares, manslaughtering, blood-stained, stormer of strong walls,
shall we not leave the Trojans and Achaians to struggle
after whatever way Zeus father grants glory to either,
while we two give ground together and avoid Zeus' anger?'

    So she spoke, and led violent Ares out of the fighting   35
and afterwards caused him to sit down by the sands of Skamandros
while the Danaans bent the Trojans back, and each of the princes
killed his man. And first the lord of men Agamemnon
hurled tall Odios, lord of the Halizones, from his chariot.
For in his back even as he was turning the spear fixed   40
between the shoulders and was driven on through the chest beyond it.
He fell, thunderously, and his armour clattered upon him.

    Idomeneus killed Phaistos the son of Maionian Boros,
who had come out of Tarne with the deep soil. Idomeneus
the spear-renowned stabbed this man just as he was mounting   45
behind his horses, with the long spear driven in the right shoulder.
He dropped from the chariot, and the hateful darkness took hold of him.

    The henchmen of Idomeneus stripped the armour from Phaistos,
while Menelaos son of Atreus killed with the sharp spear
Strophios' son, a man of wisdom in the chase, Skamandrios,   50
the fine huntsman of beasts. Artemis herself had taught him
to strike down every wild thing that grows in the mountain forest.
Yet Artemis of the showering arrows could not now help him,
no, nor the long spearcasts in which he had been pre-eminent,
but Menelaos the spear-famed, son of Atreus, stabbed him,   55
as he fled away before him, in the back with a spear thrust
between the shoulders and driven through to the chest beyond it.
He dropped forward on his face and his armour clattered upon him.

    Meriones in turn killed Phereklos, son of Harmonides,
the smith, who understood how to make with his hand all intricate   60
things, since above all others Pallas Athene had loved him.
He it was who had built for Alexandros the balanced
ships, the beginning of the evil, fatal to the other

Trojans, and to him, since he knew nothing of the gods' plans.
65 This man Meriones pursued and overtaking him
struck in the right buttock, and the spearhead drove straight
on and passing under the bone went into the bladder.
He dropped, screaming, to his knees, and death was a mist about him.
    Meges in turn killed Pedaios, the son of Antenor,
70 who, bastard though he was, was nursed by lovely Theano
with close care, as for her own children, to pleasure her husband.
Now the son of Phyleus, the spear-famed, closing upon him
struck him with the sharp spear behind the head at the tendon,
and straight on through the teeth and under the tongue cut the bronze
    blade,
75 and he dropped in the dust gripping in his teeth the cold bronze.
    Eurypylos, Euaimon's son, killed brilliant Hypsenor,
son of high-hearted Dolopion, he who was made Skamandros'
priest, and was honoured about the countryside as a god is.
This man Eurypylos, the shining son of Euaimon,
80 running in chase as he fled before him struck in the shoulder
with a blow swept from the sword and cut the arm's weight from him,
so that the arm dropped bleeding to the ground, and the red death
and destiny the powerful took hold of both eyes.
    So they went at their work all about the strong encounter;
85 but you could not have told on which side Tydeus' son was fighting,
whether he were one with the Trojans or with the Achaians,
since he went storming up the plain like a winter-swollen
river in spate that scatters the dikes in its running current,
one that the strong-compacted dikes can contain no longer,
90 neither the mounded banks of the blossoming vineyards hold it
rising suddenly as Zeus' rain makes heavy the water
and many lovely works of the young men crumble beneath it.
Like these the massed battalions of the Trojans were scattered
by Tydeus' son, and many as they were could not stand against him.
95   Now as the shining son of Lykaon, Pandaros, watched him
storming up the plain scattering the battalions before him,
at once he strained the bent bow against the son of Tydeus,
and shot, and hit him as he charged forward, in the right shoulder
at the hollow of the corselet; and the bitter arrow went straight through
100 holding clean to its way, and the corselet was all blood-spattered.

And the shining son of Lykaon cried aloud in a great voice:
'Rise up, Trojans, o high-hearted, lashers of horses.
Now the best of the Achaians is hit, and I think that he will not
long hold up under the strong arrow, if truly Apollo
lord and son of Zeus stirred me to come forth from Lykia.'   105

So he spoke, vaunting, but the swift arrow had not broken him,
only he drew back again to his chariot and horses,
and stood there, speaking to Sthenelos, son of Kapaneus:
'Come, dear friend, son of Kapaneus, step down from the chariot,
so that you may pull out from my shoulder this bitter arrow.'   110

So he spoke, and Sthenelos sprang to the ground from his chariot
and standing beside him pulled the sharp arrow clean through his
     shoulder
and the blood shot up spurting through the delicate tunic.
Now Diomedes of the great war cry spoke aloud, praying:
'Hear me now, Atrytone, daughter of Zeus of the aegis: 115
if ever before in kindliness you stood by my father
through the terror of fighting, be my friend now also, Athene;
grant me that I may kill this man and come within spearcast,
who shot me before I could see him, and now boasts over me, saying
I cannot live to look much longer on the shining sunlight.'   120

So he spoke in prayer, and Pallas Athene heard him.
She made his limbs light again, and his feet, and his hands above them,
and standing close beside him she spoke and addressed him in winged
     words:
'Be of good courage now, Diomedes, to fight with the Trojans,
since I have put inside your chest the strength of your father   125
untremulous, such as the horseman Tydeus of the great shield
had; I have taken away the mist from your eyes, that before now
was there, so that you may well recognize the god and the mortal.
Therefore now, if a god making trial of you comes hither
do you not do battle head on with the gods immortal,   130
not with the rest; but only if Aphrodite, Zeus' daughter,
comes to the fighting, her at least you may stab with the sharp bronze.'

She spoke thus, grey-eyed Athene, and went, while Tydeus'
son closed once again with the champions, taking his place there;
raging as he had been before to fight with the Trojans,   135
now the strong rage tripled took hold of him, as of a lion

whom the shepherd among his fleecy flocks in the wild lands
grazed as he leapt the fence of the fold, but has not killed him,
but only stirred up the lion's strength, and can no more fight him
140 off, but hides in the steading, and the frightened sheep are forsaken,
and these are piled pell-mell on each other in heaps, while the lion
raging still leaps out again over the fence of the deep yard;
such was the rage of strong Diomedes as he closed with the Trojans.
  Next he killed Astynoös and Hypeiron, shepherd of the people,
145 striking one with the bronze-heeled spear above the nipple,
and cutting the other beside the shoulder through the collar-bone
with the great sword, so that neck and back were hewn free of the
    shoulder.
He left these men, and went on after Polyidos and Abas,
sons of the aged dream-interpreter, Eurydamas;
150 yet for these two as they went forth the old man did not answer
their dreams, but Diomedes the powerful slew them. Now he
went after the two sons of Phainops, Xanthos and Thoön,
full grown both, but Phainops was stricken in sorrowful old age
nor could breed another son to leave among his possessions.
155 There he killed these two and took away the dear life from them
both, leaving to their father lamentation and sorrowful
affliction, since he was not to welcome them home from the fighting
alive still; and remoter kinsmen shared his possessions.
  Next he killed two children of Dardanian Priam
160 who were in a single chariot, Echemmon and Chromios.
As among cattle a lion leaps on the neck of an ox or
heifer, that grazes among the wooded places, and breaks it,
so the son of Tydeus hurled both from their horses
hatefully, in spite of their struggles, then stripped their armour
165 and gave the horses to his company to drive to their vessels.
  Now as Aineias saw him wrecking the ranks of warriors
he went on his way through the fighting and the spears' confusion
looking to see if he could find Pandaros the godlike;
and he came upon the strong and blameless son of Lykaon.
170 He stood before him face to face and spoke a word to him:
'Pandaros, where now are your bow and your feathered arrows;
where your fame, in which no man here dare contend with you
nor can any man in Lykia claim he is better?

Come then, hold up your hands to Zeus, and let go an arrow
at this strong man, whoever he be, who does so much evil   175
to the Trojans, since many and great are those whose knees he has broken.
Unless this be some god who in wrath with the Trojans for offerings
failed afflicts them. The wrath of a god is hard to deal with.'
    Then in answer the shining son of Lykaon spoke to him:
'Aineias, charged with the counsels of the bronze-armoured Trojans,   180
I liken him in all ways to the valiant son of Tydeus,
going by his shield and the hollow eyes of his helmet
and by the look of his horses; but it may be a god, I am not sure;
and if this is a man, as I think, and the valiant son
of Tydeus, yet not without god does he rage so, but some one   185
of the immortals, mantling in mist his shoulders, stands close beside him
who turned my flying arrow as it struck, elsewhere, away from him.
For I have shot my shaft already, and hit him in the shoulder,
the right one, hard driven through the hollow of his corselet,
and I said to myself I had hurled him down to meet Aidoneus,   190
yet still I have not beaten him; now this is some god who is angered.
But I have no horses nor chariot I could mount in, and yet
somewhere in the great house of Lykaon are eleven chariots,
beauties, all new made, just finished, and over them blankets
lie spread, and beside each chariot one brace of horses   195
stand there, champing their white barley and oats. But Lykaon
the aged spearman spoke to me over and over, as I was
on my way from the house well compacted, advising me;
he told me to take my horses and chariots, and riding
there to be lord among the Trojans in the strong encounters.   200
I did not let him persuade me, and that would have been far better,
sparing my horses, who had grown accustomed to eating all
they wished, from going hungry where the men were penned in a small
        place.
So I left them and made my way on foot to Ilion
trusting my bow, a thing that was to profit me nothing.   205
For now I have drawn it against two of their best men, Tydeus'
son, and the son of Atreus, and both of these I hit
and drew visible blood, yet only wakened their anger.
So it was in bad luck that I took from its peg the curved bow
on that day when I carried it to lovely Ilion   210

at the head of my Trojans, bringing delight to brilliant Hektor.
Now if ever I win home again and lay eyes once more
on my country, and my wife, and the great house with the high roof,
let some stranger straightway cut my head from my shoulders
215 if I do not break this bow in my hands and throw it in the shining
fire, since as a wind and nothing I have taken it with me.'
      Then in turn Aineias, lord of the Trojans, answered him:
'Speak no more this way; there will be no time for changing
before you and I must face this man with horses and chariot
220 and strength against strength fight it out with our weapons. Therefore
mount rather into my chariot, so that you may see
what the Trojan horses are like, how they understand their
plain, and how to traverse it in rapid pursuit and withdrawal.
These two will bring us safe to the city again, if once more
225 Zeus grants glory to Diomedes the son of Tydeus.
Come then, taking into your hands the goad and the glittering
reins, while I dismount from my chariot and carry the fighting;
or else yourself encounter this man, while I handle the horses.'
      Then in answer the shining son of Lykaon spoke to him:
230 'Keep yourself, Aineias, the reins and your horses. These will
carry better the curved chariot under the driver
they know best, if we must give way before the son of Tydeus;
for fear they might go wild with terror and not be willing
to carry us out of the fighting, as they listen and long for your voice,
235 for fear the son of high-hearted Tydeus charging upon us
might kill us both and drive away the single-foot horses.
Rather drive yourself your own horses and your own chariot
while with my sharp spear I encounter this man as he comes on.'
      They spoke so, and mounting the wrought chariot held
240 their fast-running horses against the son of Tydeus, in fury.
And Sthenelos the shining son of Kapaneus seeing them
swiftly uttered his winged words to the son of Tydeus:
'Son of Tydeus, you who delight my heart, Diomedes,
look, I see two mighty men furious to fight with you.
245 Their strength is enormous, one of them well skilled in the bow's work,
Pandaros, who claims his right as son of Lykaon,
and the other Aineias, who claims he was born as son to
Anchises the blameless, but his mother was Aphrodite.

Come then, let us give way with our horses; no longer storm on
so far among the champions, for fear you destroy your heart's life.'   250
    Then looking at him darkly strong Diomedes spoke to him:
'Argue me not toward flight, since I have no thought of obeying you.
No, for it would be ignoble for me to shrink back in the fighting
or to lurk aside, since my fighting strength stays steady forever.
I shrink indeed from mounting behind the horses, but as I am   255
now, I will face these. Pallas Athene will not let me run from them.
These two men, their fast-running horses shall never carry them
both back away from us, even though one man may escape us.
And put away in your thoughts this other thing I tell you.
If Athene of the many counsels should grant me the glory   260
to kill both, then do you check here these fast-running horses,
ours, tethering them with the reins tied to the chariot's rail and thereafter
remember to make a dash against the horses of Aineias,
and drive them away from the Trojans among the strong-greaved
        Achaians.
These are of that strain which Zeus of the wide brows granted   265
once to Tros, recompense for his son Ganymedes, and therefore
are the finest of all horses beneath the sun and the daybreak;
and the lord of men Anchises stole horses from this breed,
without the knowledge of Laomedon putting mares under them.
From these there was bred for him a string of six in his great house.   270
Four of these, keeping them himself, he raised at his mangers,
but these two he gave to Aineias, two horses urgent of terror.
If we might only take these we should win ourselves excellent glory.'
    Now as these were speaking things like this to each other,
the two came fast upon them driving their swift-running horses.   275
First to Diomedes called out the shining son of Lykaon:
'Valiant and strong-spirited, o son of proud Tydeus,
you were not beaten then by the bitter arrow, my swift shot.
Now I will try with the throwing-spear to see if I can hit you.'
    So he spoke, and balanced the spear far-shadowed, and threw it,   280
and struck the son of Tydeus in the shield, and the flying
bronze spearhead was driven clean through and into the corselet,
and the shining son of Lykaon cried aloud in a great voice:
'Now are you struck clean through the middle, and I think that you will
        not

[135]

285 hold up for much longer; you have given me great claim to glory.'
  Then strong Diomedes answered, not frightened before him:
  'You did not hit me, you missed, but I do not think that you two
  will go free until one or the other of you has fallen
  to glut with his blood Ares the god who fights under the shield's guard.'
290 He spoke, and threw; and Pallas Athene guided the weapon
  to the nose next to the eye, and it cut on through the white teeth
  and the bronze weariless shore all the way through the tongue's base
  so that the spearhead came out underneath the jawbone.
  He dropped then from the chariot and his armour clattered upon him,
295 dazzling armour and shining, while those fast-running horses
  shied away, and there his life and his strength were scattered.
  But Aineias sprang to the ground with shield and with long spear,
  for fear that somehow the Achaians might haul off the body,
  and like a lion in the pride of his strength stood over him
300 holding before him the perfect circle of his shield and the spear
  and raging to cut down any man who might come to face him,
  crying a terrible cry. But Tydeus' son in his hand caught
  up a stone, a huge thing which no two men could carry
  such as men are now, but by himself he lightly hefted it.
305 He threw, and caught Aineias in the hip, in the place where the hip-bone
  turns inside the thigh, the place men call the cup-socket.
  It smashed the cup-socket and broke the tendons both sides of it,
  and the rugged stone tore the skin backward, so that the fighter
  dropping to one knee stayed leaning on the ground with his heavy
310 hand, and a covering of black night came over both eyes.
  Now in this place Aineias lord of men might have perished
  had not Aphrodite, Zeus' daughter, been quick to perceive him,
  his mother, who had borne him to Anchises the ox-herd;
  and about her beloved son came streaming her white arms,
315 and with her white robe thrown in a fold in front she shielded him,
  this keeping off the thrown weapons lest some fast-mounted Danaan
  strike the bronze spear through his chest and strip the life from him.
  She then carried her beloved son out of the fighting.
  Nor did Sthenelos son of Kapaneus forget the commandments
320 that Diomedes of the great war cry had laid upon him,
  but he held where they were their own single-foot horses
  with their reins tied to the chariot rail, apart from the confusion,

and making a dash for the fluttering-maned horses of Aineias
drove them away from the Trojans among the strong-greaved Achaians,
and gave them to Deïpylos, his close friend, whom beyond all   325
others of his own age he prized, for their hearts were intimate,
to drive away to the hollow ships; meanwhile the warrior
mounted behind his own horses and caught up the shining
reins, and held the strong-footed team toward the son of Tydeus
headlong; and he swung the pitiless bronze at the lady of Kypros,   330
knowing her for a god without warcraft, not of those who,
goddesses, range in order the ranks of men in the fighting,
not Athene and not Enyo, sacker of cities.
Now as, following her through the thick crowd, he caught her,
lunging in his charge far forward the son of high-hearted   335
Tydeus made a thrust against the soft hand with the bronze spear,
and the spear tore the skin driven clean on through the immortal
robe that the very Graces had woven for her carefully,
over the palm's base; and blood immortal flowed from the goddess,
ichor, that which runs in the veins of the blessed divinities;   340
since these eat no food, nor do they drink of the shining
wine, and therefore they have no blood and are called immortal.
She gave a great shriek and let fall her son she was carrying,
but Phoibos Apollo caught him up and away in his own hands,
in a dark mist, for fear that some fast-mounted Danaan   345
might strike the bronze spear through his chest and strip the life from him.
But Diomedes of the great war cry shouted after her:
'Give way, daughter of Zeus, from the fighting and the terror. It is
not then enough that you lead astray women without warcraft?
Yet, if still you must haunt the fighting, I think that now you   350
will shiver even when you hear some other talking of battles.'
   So he spoke, and the goddess departed in pain, hurt badly,
and Iris wind-footed took her by the hand and led her away
from the battle, her lovely skin blood-darkened, wounded and suffering.
There to the left of the fighting she found Ares the violent   355
sitting, his spear leaned into the mist, and his swift horses.
Dropping on one knee before her beloved brother
in deep supplication she asked for his gold-bridled horses:
'Beloved brother, rescue me and give me your horses
so I may come to Olympos where is the place of the immortals.   360

I am in too much pain from the wound of a mortal's spear-stroke,
Tydeus' son's, who would fight now even against Zeus father.'
    So she spoke, and Ares gave her the gold-bridled horses,
    and, still grieved in the inward heart, she mounted the chariot
365 and beside her entering Iris gathered the reins up
    and whipped them into a run, and they winged their way unreluctant.
    Now as they came to sheer Olympos, the place of the immortals,
    there swift Iris the wind-footed reined in her horses
    and slipped them from the yoke and threw fodder immortal before them,
370 and now bright Aphrodite fell at the knees of her mother,
    Dione, who gathered her daughter into the arms' fold
    and stroked her with her hand and called her by name and spoke to her:
    'Who now of the Uranian gods, dear child, has done such
    things to you, rashly, as if you were caught doing something wicked?'
375   Aphrodite the sweetly laughing spoke then and answered her:
    'Tydeus' son Diomedes, the too high-hearted, stabbed me
    as I was carrying my own beloved son out of the fighting,
    Aineias, who beyond all else in the world is dear to me;
    so now this is no horrible war of Achaians and Trojans,
380 but the Danaans are beginning to fight even with the immortals.'
    Then Dione the shining among divinities answered her:
    'Have patience, my child, and endure it, though you be saddened.
    For many of us who have our homes on Olympos endure things
    from men, when ourselves we inflict hard pain on each other.
385 Ares had to endure it when strong Ephialtes and Otos,
    sons of Aloeus, chained him in bonds that were too strong for him,
    and three months and ten he lay chained in the brazen cauldron;
    and now might Ares, insatiable of fighting, have perished,
    had not Eëriboia, their stepmother, the surpassingly lovely,
390 brought word to Hermes, who stole Ares away out of it
    as he was growing faint and the hard bondage was breaking him.
    Hera had to endure it when the strong son of Amphitryon
    struck her beside the right breast with a tri-barbed arrow,
    so that the pain he gave her could not be quieted. Hades
395 the gigantic had to endure with the rest the flying arrow
    when this self-same man, the son of Zeus of the aegis,
    struck him among the dead men at Pylos, and gave him to agony;
    but he went up to the house of Zeus and to tall Olympos

heavy at heart, stabbed through and through with pain, for the arrow
was driven into his heavy shoulder, and his spirit was suffering.   400
But Paiëon, scattering medicines that still pain,
healed him, since he was not made to be one of the mortals.
Brute, heavy-handed, who thought nothing of the bad he was doing,
who with his archery hurt the gods that dwell on Olympos!
It was the goddess grey-eyed Athene who drove on this man   405
against you; poor fool, the heart of Tydeus' son knows nothing
of how that man who fights the immortals lives for no long time,
his children do not gather to his knees to welcome their father
when he returns home after the fighting and the bitter warfare.
Then, though he be very strong indeed, let the son of Tydeus   410
take care lest someone even better than he might fight with him,
lest for a long time Aigialeia, wise child of Adrastos,
mourning wake out of sleep her household's beloved companions,
longing for the best of the Achaians, her lord by marriage,
she, the strong wife of Diomedes, breaker of horses.'   415
    She spoke, and with both hands stroked away from her arm the ichor,
so that the arm was made whole again and the strong pains rested.
But Hera and Athene glancing aside at her began
to tease the son of Kronos, Zeus, in words of mockery:
and the goddess grey-eyed Athene began the talk among them: 420
'Father Zeus, would you be angry with me if I said
something? It must be the lady of Kypros, moving some woman
of Achaia to follow after those Trojans she loves so hopelessly,
laying hold on the fair dresses of the Achaian women,
tore the tenderness of her hand on a golden pin's point.'   425
    So she spoke, and the father of gods and men smiled on her
and spoke to Aphrodite the golden, calling her to him:
'No, my child, not for you are the works of warfare. Rather
concern yourself only with the lovely secrets of marriage,
while all this shall be left to Athene and sudden Ares.'   430
    Now as these were talking in this way with each other
Diomedes of the great war cry made for Aineias.
Though he saw how Apollo himself held his hands over him
he did not shrink even from the great god, but forever forward
drove, to kill Aineias and strip his glorious armour.   435
Three times, furious to cut him down, he drove forward,

[139]

and three times Apollo battered aside the bright shield,
but as a fourth time, like more than man, he charged, Apollo
who strikes from afar cried out to him in the voice of terror:
440 'Take care, give back, son of Tydeus, and strive no longer
to make yourself like the gods in mind, since never the same is
the breed of gods, who are immortal, and men who walk groundling.'
He spoke, and Tydeus' son gave backward, only a little,
avoiding the anger of him who strikes from afar, Apollo,
445 who caught Aineias now away from the onslaught, and set him
in the sacred keep of Pergamos where was built his own temple.
There Artemis of the showering arrows and Leto within
the great and secret chamber healed his wound and cared for him.
But he of the silver bow, Apollo, fashioned an image
450 in the likeness of Aineias himself and in armour like him,
and all about this image brilliant Achaians and Trojans
hewed at each other, and at the ox-hide shields strong circled
guarding men's chests, and at the fluttering straps of the guard-skins.
But Phoibos Apollo spoke now to violent Ares:
455 'Ares, Ares, manslaughtering, blood-stained, stormer of strong walls,
is there no way you can go and hold back this man from the fighting,
Tydeus' son, who would now do battle against Zeus father?
Even now he stabbed in her hand by the wrist the lady
of Kypros, and again, like more than a man, charged even against me.'
460 So he spoke, and himself alighted on the peak of Pergamos
while stark Ares went down to stir the ranks of the Trojans,
in the likeness of the lord of the Thracians, swift-footed Akamas,
and urged onward the god-supported children of Priam:
'O you children of Priam, the king whom the gods love, how long
465 will you allow the Achaians to go on killing your people?
Until they fight beside the strong-builded gates? A man lies
fallen whom we honoured as we honour Hektor the brilliant,
Aineias, who is son of great-hearted Anchises.
Come then, let us rescue our good companion from the carnage.'
470 So he spoke, and stirred the spirit and the strength in each man.
Then Sarpedon spoke in abuse to brilliant Hektor:
'Where now, Hektor, has gone that strength that was yours? You said once
that without companions and without people you could hold this city
alone, with only your brothers and the lords of your sisters.

I can see not one of these men now, I know not where they are;   475
no, but they slink away like hounds who circle the lion,
while we, who are here as your companions, carry the fighting.
I have come, a companion to help you, from a very far place;
Lykia lies far away, by the whirling waters of Xanthos;
there I left behind my own wife and my baby son, there   480
I left my many possessions which the needy man eyes longingly.
Yet even so I drive on my Lykians, and myself have courage
to fight my man in battle, though there is nothing of mine here
that the Achaians can carry away as spoil or drive off.
But you: you stand here, not even giving the word to the rest   485
of your people to stand fast and fight in defence of their own wives.
Let not yourselves, caught as in the sweeping toils of the spun net,
be taken as war-spoil and plunder by the men who hate you,
men who presently will storm your strong-founded citadel.
All these things should lie night and day on your mind, forever,   490
supplication to the lords of your far-renowned companions,
to fight unwearying and hold off the strength of an insult.'
    Sarpedon spoke, and his word bit into the heart of Hektor.
Straightway in all his armour he sprang to the ground from his chariot
and shaking two sharp spears ranged everywhere through the army   495
stirring men up to fight and waking the hateful warfare;
and these pulled themselves about and stood to face the Achaians,
while the Argives held in their close order and would not be broken.
As when along the hallowed threshing floors the wind scatters
chaff, among men winnowing, and fair-haired Demeter   500
in the leaning wind discriminates the chaff and the true grain
and the piling chaff whitens beneath it, so now the Achaians
turned white underneath the dust the feet of the horses
drove far into the brazen sky across their faces
as they rapidly closed and the charioteers wheeled back again.   505
They drove the strength of their hands straight on, as violent Ares
defending the Trojans mantled in dark night the battle
and passed everywhere, since he was carrying out the commandments
of Phoibos Apollo, him of the golden sword, who had bidden him
wake the heart in the Trojans as he saw that Pallas Athene   510
was gone away now, she who stood to defend the Danaans.
And out of the rich secret chamber Apollo sent forth

Aineias, and dropped strength in the heart of the people's shepherd.
So Aineias stood among his friends, who were happy
515 as they saw him coming back, still alive, and unwounded
and full of brave spirit; yet they asked him no question,
for the rest of their fighting work would not let them, that the silver-bow
    god
woke, and manslaughtering Ares, and Hate, whose wrath is relentless.
    Now the two Aiantes and Odysseus and Diomedes
520 stirred the Danaans to fight these; since themselves they did not
fear the force of the men of Troy nor their charges onward,
but stayed where they were, like clouds, which the son of Kronos
stops in the windless weather on the heights of the towering mountains,
motionless, when the strength of the north wind sleeps, and the other
525 tearing winds, those winds that when they blow into tempests
high screaming descend upon the darkening clouds and scatter them.
So the Danaans stood steady against the Trojans, nor gave way.
And Atreus' son ranged through the masses with his many orders:
'Be men now, dear friends, and take up the heart of courage,
530 and have consideration for each other in the strong encounters,
since more come through alive when men consider each other,
and there is no glory when they give way, nor warcraft either.'
    He spoke, and made a swift cast with his spear, and struck down a
    great man
Deïkoön, companion of high-hearted Aineias,
535 Pergasos' son, whom the Trojans honoured as they honoured Priam's
children, since he was a swift man to fight in the foremost.
Powerful Agamemnon struck his shield with spear, nor
could the shield hold off the spear, but the bronze smashed clean through
and was driven on through the belt to the deep of the belly.
540 He fell, thunderously, and his armour clattered upon him.
    Now Aineias killed two great men of the Danaans,
the sons of Diokles, Orsilochos and Krethon,
men whose father dwelt in Phere the strong-founded,
rich in substance, and his generation was of the river
545 Alpheios, who flows wide through the country of the Pylians,
and who got a son, Ortilochos, to be lord over many
men, but the son of Ortilochos was high-hearted Diokles;
and to Diokles in his turn were two twin sons born,

Orsilochos and Krethon, both well skilled in all fighting.
These two as they were grown to young manhood followed along with   550
the Argives in their black ships to Ilion, land of good horses,
winning honour for the sons of Atreus, Agamemnon
and Menelaos; now fulfilment of death was a darkness upon them.
These, as two young lions in the high places of the mountains,
had been raised by their mother in the dark of the deep forest,   555
lions which as they prey upon the cattle and the fat sheep
lay waste the steadings where there are men, until they also
fall and are killed under the cutting bronze in the men's hands;
such were these two who beaten under the hands of Aineias
crashed now to the ground as if they were two tall pine trees.   560
    As these fell warlike Menelaos took pity on them
and he strode out among the champions, helmed in bright bronze,
shaking his spear, and the fury of Ares drove him onward,
minded that he might go down under the hands of Aineias.
But Antilochos, son of high-hearted Nestor, watched him,   565
and he strode among the champions in fear for the shepherd of the
    people,
lest he be hurt, and all their labour slip away into nothing.
So as Aineias and Menelaos raised hand and sharp spear
standing to face each other and furious to do battle,
Antilochos took his stand close beside the shepherd of the people.   570
Nor did Aineias hold his ground, though yet a swift fighter,
as he saw two men staying with each other against him.
These, when they had dragged back the bodies among the Achaian
people, dropped the poor youths into the hands of their company,
and themselves wheeled about once more to fight among the foremost.   575
    There these killed Pylaimenes the equal of Ares,
lord of the Paphlagonian men in armour, high-hearted.
Menelaos the spear-famed, son of Atreus, stabbed him
with the spear as he stood his ground, and struck the collar-bone,
while Antilochos struck down Mydon, his charioteer and   580
henchman, Atymnios' brave son, as he wheeled the single-foot
horses about, with a stone striking mid-elbow, and from his
hands the reins pale with ivory dropped in the dust groundling.
Antilochos charging drove the sword into his temple,
so that gasping he dropped from the carefully wrought chariot   585

[143]

headlong, driven deep in the dust his neck and shoulders;
and there, since he chanced to light in a depth of sand, he stuck fast
while his horses trampled him into the dust with their feet. These
Antilochos lashed and drove back into the host of the Achaians.
590   Hektor saw them across the ranks, and drove on against them
crying aloud, and with him followed the Trojan battalions
in their strength; and Ares led them with the goddess Enyo,
she carrying with her the turmoil of shameless hatred
while Ares made play in his hands with the spear gigantic
595 and ranged now in front of Hektor and now behind him.
    Diomedes of the great war cry shivered as he saw him,
and like a man in his helplessness who, crossing a great plain,
stands at the edge of a fast-running river that dashes seaward,
and watches it thundering into white water, and leaps a pace backward,
600 so now Tydeus' son gave back, and spoke to his people:
'Friends, although we know the wonder of glorious Hektor
to be a fighter with the spear and a bold man of battle,
yet there goe, ever some god beside him, who beats off destruction,
and now, in the likeness of a man mortal, Ares goes with him.
605 Come then, keeping your faces turned to the Trojans, give ground
backward, nor be we eager to fight in strength with divinities.'
    He spoke, and now the Trojans had come very close upon them.
There Hektor cut down two men, well skilled in warcraft,
Anchialos and Menesthes both in a single chariot.
610 As these fell great Telamonian Aias pitied them
and stood close in and made a cast with the shining javelin,
and struck Amphios, Selagos' son, who rich in possessions
and rich in cornland had lived in Paisos, but his own destiny
brought him companion in arms to Priam and the children of Priam.
615 Now Telamonian Aias struck him beneath the war belt
and the far-shadowing spear was fixed in the lower belly,
and he fell, thunderously, and shining Aias ran forward
to strip his armour, but the Trojans showered spears upon him,
sharp spears and glittering, and the great shield caught many.
620 Setting his heel on the chest of the corpse he pulled out the brazen
spear, yet could no longer strip the rest of the glorious
armour from his shoulders, since he was battered with spears thrown,
and he dreaded the strong circle made by the haughty Trojans,

who many and valiant stood over him, gripping their great spears,
and though he was a mighty man and a strong and a proud one   625
thrust him away from them so that he gave ground backward staggering.

So they went at their work all about the strong encounter.
But Herakles' son Tlepolemos the huge and mighty
was driven by his strong destiny against godlike Sarpedon.
Now as these in their advance had come close together,   630
the own son, and the son's son of Zeus cloud-gathering,
it was Tlepolemos of the two who spoke the first word:
'Man of counsel of the Lykians, Sarpedon, why must you
be skulking here, you who are a man unskilled in the fighting?
They are liars who call you issue of Zeus, the holder   635
of the aegis, since you fall far short in truth of the others
who were begotten of Zeus in the generations before us:
such men as, they say, was the great strength of Herakles,
my own father, of the daring spirit, the heart of a lion:
he came here on a time for the sake of Laomedon's horses,   640
with six vessels only and the few men needed to man them,
and widowed the streets of Ilion and sacked the city;
but yours is the heart of a coward and your people are dying.
And I think that now, though you are come from Lykia, you will
bring no help to the Trojans even though you be a strong man,   645
but beaten down by my hands will pass through the gates of Hades.'

In turn the lord of the Lykians, Sarpedon, answered him:
'In truth, Tlepolemos, he did destroy Ilion the sacred
through the senselessness of one man, the haughty Laomedon,
who gave Herakles an evil word in return for good treatment   650
and would not give up the horses for whose sake he had come from far off.
But I tell you, what you will win from me here will be death
and black destruction; and broken under my spear you will give me
glory, and give your soul to Hades of the famed horses.'

So spoke Sarpedon, while the other lifted his ash spear,   655
Tlepolemos; and in a single moment the long shafts
shot from their hands, Sarpedon striking him in the middle
of the throat, and the agonizing spear drove clean through
and over his eyes was mantled the covering mist of darkness.
But Tlepolemos in turn had struck Sarpedon with the long spear   660
in the left thigh, and the spear smashed on through in fury

scraping the bone, but his father fended destruction away from him.
But his brilliant companions carried godlike Sarpedon
out of the fighting, weighted down as he was by the long spear
665 which dragged, yet not one of them noticed nor took thought,
in their urgency, to pull out of his thigh the ash spear
so he might stand, such hard work did they have attending him.
On the other side the strong-greaved Achaians carried Tlepolemos
out of the fighting; but brilliant Odysseus, who held a hardy
670 spirit, saw what had happened, and his heart within was stirred up,
but now he pondered two ways within, in mind and in spirit,
whether first to go after the son of Zeus the loud-thundering
or whether he should strip the life from more of the Lykians.
Yet, as it was not the destiny of great-hearted Odysseus
675 to kill with sharp bronze the strong son of Zeus, therefore
Athene steered his anger against the host of the Lykians.
And there he killed Koiranos, and Chromios, and Alastor,
Halios and Alkandros, and Prytanis and Noemon.
And now might brilliant Odysseus have killed yet more of the Lykians
680 had not tall Hektor of the shining helmet sharply perceived him,
who strode out among the champions helmed in the bright bronze
bringing terror to the Danaans; but Zeus' son, Sarpedon,
was glad as he saw him come up, and piteously bespoke him:
'Son of Priam, do not leave me lying for the Danaans
685 to prey upon, but protect me, since otherwise in your city
my life must come to an end, since I could return no longer
back to my own house and the land of my fathers, bringing
joy to my own beloved wife and my son, still a baby.'
He spoke, but Hektor of the shining helm did not answer
690 but swept on past him in his eagerness with all speed
to push back the Argives and strip the life out of many.
Meanwhile his brilliant companions laid godlike Sarpedon
under a lovely spreading oak of Zeus of the aegis,
and strong Pelagon, one of his beloved companions,
695 pushed perforce through and out of his thigh the shaft of the ash
spear.
And the mist mantled over his eyes, and the life left him,
but he got his breath back again, and the blast of the north wind
blowing brought back to life the spirit gasped out in agony.

But the Argives under the strength of Ares and bronze-armoured
   Hektor
did not ever turn their backs and make for their black ships   700
nor yet stand up to them in fighting, but always backward
gave way, as they saw how Ares went with the Trojans.
   Who then was the first and who the last that they slaughtered,
Hektor, Priam's son, and Ares the brazen? Godlike
Teuthras first, and next Orestes, driver of horses,   705
Trechos the spearman of Aitolia and Oinomaos,
Helenos son of Oinops and Oresbios of the shining
guard, who had lived in Hyle much concerned with his property
in a place hard on the Kephisian mere, and beside him other
men of Boiotia lived and held the fine fertile country.   710
   Now as the goddess Hera of the white arms perceived how
the Argives were perishing in the strong encounter,
immediately she spoke to Pallas Athene her winged words:
'For shame, now, Atrytone, daughter of Zeus of the aegis:
nothing then meant the word we promised to Menelaos,   715
to go home after sacking the strong-walled city of Ilion,
if we are to let cursed Ares be so furious.
Come then, let us rather think of our own stark courage.'
   So she spoke, nor did the goddess grey-eyed Athene
disobey her. But Hera, high goddess, daughter of Kronos   720
the mighty, went away to harness the gold-bridled horses.
Then Hebe in speed set about the chariot the curved wheels
eight-spoked and brazen, with an axle of iron both ways.
Golden is the wheel's felly imperishable, and outside it
is joined, a wonder to look upon, the brazen running-rim,   725
and the silver naves revolve on either side of the chariot,
whereas the car itself is lashed fast with plaiting of gold
and silver, with double chariot rails that circle about it,
and the pole of the chariot is of silver, to whose extremity
Hebe made fast the golden and splendid yoke, and fastened   730
the harness, golden and splendid, and underneath the yoke Hera,
furious for hate and battle, led the swift-running horses.
   Now in turn Athene, daughter of Zeus of the aegis,
beside the threshold of her father slipped off her elaborate
dress which she herself had wrought with her hands' patience,   735

and now assuming the war tunic of Zeus who gathers
the clouds, she armed in her gear for the dismal fighting.
And across her shoulders she threw the betasselled, terrible
aegis, all about which Terror hangs like a garland,
740 and Hatred is there, and Battle Strength, and heart-freezing Onslaught
and thereon is set the head of the grim gigantic Gorgon,
a thing of fear and horror, portent of Zeus of the aegis.
Upon her head she set the golden helm with its four sheets
and two horns, wrought with the fighting men of a hundred cities.
745 She set her feet in the blazing chariot and took up a spear
heavy, huge, thick, wherewith she beats down the battalions of fighting
men, against whom she of mighty father is angered.
Hera laid the lash swiftly on the horses; and moving
of themselves groaned the gates of the sky that the Hours guarded,
750 those Hours to whose charge is given the huge sky and Olympos,
to open up the dense darkness or again to close it.
Through the way between they held the speed of their goaded horses.
They found the son of Kronos sitting apart from the other
gods, upon the highest peak of rugged Olympos.
755 There the goddess of the white arms, Hera, stopping her horses,
spoke to Zeus, high son of Kronos, and asked him a question:
'Father Zeus, are you not angry with Ares for his violent
acts, for killing so many and such good Achaian warriors
for no reason, and out of due order, to grieve me? And meanwhile
760 Kypris and Apollo of the silver bow take their ease and their pleasure
having let loose this maniac who knows nothing of justice.
Father Zeus, would you be angry with me if I were
to smite Ares with painful strokes and drive him out of the fighting?'
     Then in turn the father of gods and men made answer:
765 'Go to it then, and set against him the spoiler Athene,
who beyond all others is the one to visit harsh pains upon him.'
     So he spoke, nor did the goddess of the white arms, Hera,
disobey, but lashed on the horses, and they winged their way unreluctant
through the space between the earth and the starry heaven.
770 As far as into the hazing distance a man can see with
his eyes, who sits in his eyrie gazing on the wine-blue water,
as far as this is the stride of the gods' proud neighing horses.
Now as they came to Troy land and the two running rivers

[148]

where Simoeis and Skamandros dash their waters together,
there the goddess of the white arms, Hera, stayed her horses, 775
slipping them from the chariot, and drifting close mist about them,
and Simoeis grew as grass ambrosia for them to graze on.
  Now these two walked forward in little steps like shivering
doves, in their eagerness to stand by the men of Argos,
after they had come to the place where the most and the bravest 780
stood close huddled about the great strength of the breaker of horses,
Diomedes; in the likeness of lions who rend their meat raw,
or wild pigs, boars, in whom the strength diminishes never,
there standing the goddess of the white arms, Hera, shouted,
likening herself to high-hearted, bronze-voiced Stentor, 785
who could cry out in as great a voice as fifty other men:
'Shame, you Argives, poor nonentities splendid to look on.
In those days when brilliant Achilleus came into the fighting,
never would the Trojans venture beyond the Dardanian
gates, so much did they dread the heavy spear of that man. 790
Now they fight by the hollow ships and far from the city.'
  So she spoke, and stirred the spirit and strength in each man.
But the goddess grey-eyed Athene made straight for Tydeus'
son, and found the king standing by his horses and chariot,
cooling the wound that Pandaros made with the cast of his arrow. 795
For the sweat made him sore underneath the broad strap of the circled
shield; this made him sore, and his arm was tired. He held up
the shield-strap, and wiped the dark blot of blood away from it.
The goddess laid hold of the harnessed horses and spoke to him:
'Tydeus got him a son who is little enough like him, 800
since Tydeus was a small man for stature, but he was a fighter.
Even on that time when I would not consent to his fighting
nor drawing men's eyes, when he went by himself without the Achaians
as a messenger to Thebe among all the Kadmeians,
then I invited him to feast at his ease in their great halls; 805
even so, keeping that heart of strength that was always within him
he challenged the young men of the Kadmeians, and defeated all of them
easily; such a helper was I who stood then beside him.
Now beside you also I stand and ever watch over you,
and urge you to fight confidently with the Trojans. And yet 810
the weariness has entered your limbs from many encounters,

or else it is some poor-spirited fear that holds you. If so,
you are no issue then of the son of wise Oineus, Tydeus.'
    Then in answer powerful Diomedes spoke to her:
815 'Daughter of Zeus who holds the aegis, goddess, I know you,
and therefore will speak confidently to you, and hide nothing.
It is no poor-spirited fear nor shrinking that holds me.
Rather I remember the orders you yourself gave me
when you would not let me fight in the face of the blessed immortals—
820 the rest of them, except only if Aphrodite, Zeus' daughter,
went into the fighting, I might stab at her with the sharp bronze.
Therefore now have I myself given way, and I ordered
the rest of the Argives all to be gathered in this place beside me,
since I see that this who is lord of the fighting is Ares.'
825   Then in turn the goddess grey-eyed Athene answered him:
'Son of Tydeus, you who delight my heart, Diomedes,
no longer be thus afraid of Ares, nor of any other
immortal; such a helper shall I be standing beside you.
Come then, first against Ares steer your single-foot horses,
830 and strike him from close. Be not afraid of violent Ares,
that thing of fury, evil-wrought, that double-faced liar
who even now protested to Hera and me, promising
that he would fight against the Trojans and stand by the Argives.
Now, all promises forgotten, he stands by the Trojans.'
835   So speaking she pushed Sthenelos to the ground from the chariot,
driving him back with her hand, and he leapt away from it lightly,
and she herself, a goddess in her anger, stepped into the chariot
beside brilliant Diomedes, and the oaken axle groaned aloud
under the weight, carrying a dread goddess and a great man.
840 Pallas Athene then took up the whip and the reins, steering
first of all straight on against Ares the single-foot horses.
Ares was in the act of stripping gigantic Periphas,
shining son of Ochesios, far the best of the men of Aitolia.
Blood-stained Ares was in the act of stripping him. But Athene
845 put on the helm of Death, that stark Ares might not discern her.
    Now as manslaughtering Ares caught sight of Diomedes
the brilliant, he let gigantic Periphas lie in the place where
he had first cut him down and taken the life away from him,
and made straight against Diomedes, breaker of horses.

Now as they in their advance had come close together,   850
Ares lunged first over the yoke and the reins of his horses
with the bronze spear, furious to take the life from him.
But the goddess grey-eyed Athene in her hand catching
the spear pushed it away from the car, so he missed and stabbed vainly.
After him Diomedes of the great war cry drove forward   855
with the bronze spear; and Pallas Athene, leaning in on it,
drove it into the depth of the belly where the war belt girt him.
Picking this place she stabbed and driving it deep in the fair flesh
wrenched the spear out again. Then Ares the brazen bellowed
with a sound as great as nine thousand men make, or ten thousand,   860
when they cry as they carry into the fighting the fury of the war god.
And a shivering seized hold alike on Achaians and Trojans
in their fear at the bellowing of battle-insatiate Ares.

   As when out of the thunderhead the air shows darkening
after a day's heat when the stormy wind uprises,   865
thus to Tydeus' son Diomedes Ares the brazen
showed as he went up with the clouds into the wide heaven.
Lightly he came to the gods' citadel, headlong Olympos,
and sat down beside Kronian Zeus, grieving in his spirit,
and showed him the immortal blood dripping from the spear cut.   870
So in sorrow for himself he addressed him in winged words:
'Father Zeus, are you not angry looking on these acts of violence?
We who are gods forever have to endure the most horrible
hurts, by each other's hatred, as we try to give favour to mortals.
It is your fault we fight, since you brought forth this maniac daughter 875
accursed, whose mind is fixed forever on unjust action.
For all the rest, as many as are gods on Olympos,
are obedient to you, and we all have rendered ourselves submissive.
Yet you say nothing and you do nothing to check this girl, letting
her go free, since yourself you begot this child of perdition.   880
See now, the son of Tydeus, Diomedes the haughty,
she has egged on to lash out in fury against the immortal
gods. First he stabbed the Kyprian in the arm by the wrist. Then
like something more than human he swept on even against me.
But my swift feet took me out of the way. Otherwise I should   885
long be lying there in pain among the stark dead men,
or go living without strength because of the strokes of the bronze spear.'

Then looking at him darkly Zeus who gathers the clouds spoke to him:
'Do not sit beside me and whine, you double-faced liar.
890 To me you are most hateful of all gods who hold Olympos.
Forever quarrelling is dear to your heart, wars and battles.
Truly the anger of Hera your mother is grown out of all hand
nor gives ground; and try as I may I am broken by her arguments,
and it is by her impulse, I think, you are suffering all this.
895 And yet I will not long endure to see you in pain, since
you are my child, and it was to me that your mother bore you.
But were you born of some other god and proved so ruinous
long since you would have been dropped beneath the gods of the bright
      sky.'
    So he spoke, and told Paiëon to heal him; and scattering
900 medicines to still pain upon him Paiëon rendered him
well again, since he was not made to be one of the mortals.
As when the juice of the fig in white milk rapidly fixes
that which was fluid before and curdles quickly for one who
stirs it; in such speed as this he healed violent Ares;
905 and Hebe washed him clean and put delicate clothing upon him.
And rejoicing in the glory of his strength he sat down beside Kronion.
    Meanwhile, the two went back again to the house of great Zeus,
Hera of Argos, with Athene who stands by her people,
after they stopped the murderous work of manslaughtering Ares.

S o the grim encounter of Achaians and Trojans was left
to itself, and the battle veered greatly now one way, now in another,
over the plain as they guided their bronze spears at each other
in the space between the waters of Xanthos and Simoeis.
  First Telamonian Aias, that bastion of the Achaians,   5
broke the Trojan battalions and brought light to his own company,
striking down the man who was far the best of the Thracians,
Akamas, the huge and mighty, the son of Eussoros.
Throwing first, he struck the horn of the horse-haired helmet
and the bronze spear-point fixed in his forehead and drove inward   10
through the bone; and a mist of darkness clouded both eyes.
  Diomedes of the great war cry cut down Axylos,
Teuthras' son, who had been a dweller in strong-founded Arisbe,
a man rich in substance and a friend to all humanity
since in his house by the wayside he entertained all comers.   15
Yet there was none of these now to stand before him and keep off
the sad destruction, and Diomedes stripped life from both of them,
Axylos and his henchman Kalesios, who was the driver
guiding his horses; so down to the underworld went both men.
  Now Euryalos slaughtered Opheltios and Dresos,   20
and went in pursuit of Aisepos and Pedasos, those whom the naiad
nymph Abarbare had born to blameless Boukolion.
Boukolion himself was the son of haughty Laomedon,
eldest born, but his mother conceived him in darkness and secrecy.
While shepherding his flocks he lay with the nymph and loved her,   25

and she conceiving bore him twin boys. But now Mekistios'
son unstrung the strength of these and the limbs in their glory,
Euryalos, and stripped the armour away from their shoulders.
    Polypoites the stubborn in battle cut down Astyalos,
30 while Odysseus slaughtered one from Perkote, Pidytes,
with the bronze spear, and great Aretaon was killed by Teukros.
Nestor's son Antilochos with the shining shaft killed
Ableros; the lord of men, Agamemnon, brought death to Elatos,
whose home had been on the shores of Satnioeis' lovely waters,
35 sheer Pedasos. And Leitos the fighter caught Phylakos
as he ran away; and Eurypylos made an end of Melanthios.
    Now Menelaos of the great war cry captured Adrestos
alive; for his two horses bolting over the level land
got entangled in a tamarisk growth, and shattered the curving
40 chariot at the tip of the pole; so they broken free went
on toward the city, where many beside stampeded in terror.
So Adrestos was whirled beside the wheel from the chariot
headlong into the dust on his face; and the son of Atreus,
Menelaos, with the far-shadowed spear in his hand, stood over him.
45 But Adrestos, catching him by the knees, supplicated:
'Take me alive, son of Atreus, and take appropriate ransom.
In my rich father's house the treasures lie piled in abundance;
bronze is there, and gold, and difficultly wrought iron,
and my father would make you glad with abundant repayment
50 were he to hear that I am alive by the ships of the Achaians.'
    So he spoke, and moved the spirit inside Menelaos.
And now he was on the point of handing him to a henchman
to lead back to the fast Achaian ships; but Agamemnon
came on the run to join him and spoke his word of argument:
55 'Dear brother, o Menelaos, are you concerned so tenderly
with these people? Did you in your house get the best of treatment
from the Trojans? No, let not one of them go free of sudden
death and our hands; not the young man child that the mother carries
still in her body, not even he, but let all of Ilion's
60 people perish, utterly blotted out and unmourned for.'
    The hero spoke like this, and bent the heart of his brother
since he urged justice. Menelaos shoved with his hand Adrestos
the warrior back from him, and powerful Agamemnon

stabbed him in the side and, as he writhed over, Atreides,
setting his heel upon the midriff, wrenched out the ash spear. 65
  Nestor in a great voice cried out to the men of Argos:
'O belovèd Danaan fighters, henchmen of Ares,
let no man any more hang back with his eye on the plunder
designing to take all the spoil he can gather back to the vessels;
let us kill the men now, and afterwards at your leisure 70
all along the plain you can plunder the perished corpses.'
  So he spoke, and stirred the spirit and strength in each man.
Then once more would the Trojans have climbed back into Ilion's
wall, subdued by terror before the warlike Achaians,
had not Priam's son, Helenos, best by far of the augurs, 75
stood beside Aineias and Hektor and spoken a word to them:
'Hektor and Aineias, on you beyond others is leaning
the battle-work of Trojans and Lykians, since you are our greatest
in every course we take, whether it be in thought or in fighting:
stand your ground here; visit your people everywhere; hold them 80
fast by the gates, before they tumble into their women's
arms, and become to our enemies a thing to take joy in.
Afterwards, when you have set all the battalions in motion,
the rest of us will stand fast here and fight with the Danaans
though we are very hard hit indeed; necessity forces us; 85
but you, Hektor, go back again to the city, and there tell
your mother and mine to assemble all the ladies of honour
at the temple of grey-eyed Athene high on the citadel;
there opening with a key the door to the sacred chamber
let her take a robe, which seems to her the largest and loveliest 90
in the great house, and that which is far her dearest possession,
and lay it along the knees of Athene the lovely haired. Let her
promise to dedicate within the shrine twelve heifers,
yearlings, never broken, if only she will have pity
on the town of Troy, and the Trojan wives, and their innocent children. 95
So she might hold back from sacred Ilion the son of Tydeus,
that wild spear-fighter, the strong one who drives men to thoughts of
    terror,
who I say now is become the strongest of all the Achaians.
For never did we so fear Achilleus even, that leader
of men, who they say was born of a goddess. This man has gone clean 100

berserk, so that no one can match his warcraft against him.'
    So he spoke, and Hektor did not disobey his brother,
but at once in all his armour leapt to the ground from his chariot
and shaking two sharp spears in his hands ranged over the whole host
105 stirring them up to fight and waking the ghastly warfare.
So they whirled about and stood their ground against the Achaians,
and the Argives gave way backward and stopped their slaughtering,
and thought some one of the immortals must have descended
from the starry sky to stand by the Trojans, the way they rallied.
110 But Hektor lifted his voice and cried aloud to the Trojans:
'You high-hearted Trojans and far-renowned companions,
be men now, dear friends, and remember your furious valour
until I can go back again to Ilion, and there tell
the elder men who sit as counsellors, and our own wives,
115 to make their prayer to the immortals and promise them hecatombs.'
    So spoke Hektor of the shining helm, and departed;
and against his ankles as against his neck clashed the dark ox-hide,
the rim running round the edge of the great shield massive in the middle.
    Now Glaukos, sprung of Hippolochos, and the son of Tydeus
120 came together in the space between the two armies, battle-bent.
Now as these advancing came to one place and encountered,
first to speak was Diomedes of the great war cry:
'Who among mortal men are you, good friend? Since never
before have I seen you in the fighting where men win glory,
125 yet now you have come striding far out in front of all others
in your great heart, who have dared stand up to my spear far-shadowing.
Yet unhappy are those whose sons match warcraft against me.
But if you are some one of the immortals come down from the bright sky,
know that I will not fight against any god of the heaven,
130 since even the son of Dryas, Lykourgos the powerful, did not
live long; he who tried to fight with the gods of the bright sky,
who once drove the fosterers of rapturous Dionysos
headlong down the sacred Nyseian hill, and all of them
shed and scattered their wands on the ground, stricken with an ox-goad
135 by murderous Lykourgos, while Dionysos in terror
dived into the salt surf, and Thetis took him to her bosom,
frightened, with the strong shivers upon him at the man's blustering.
But the gods who live at their ease were angered with Lykourgos,

and the son of Kronos struck him to blindness, nor did he live long
afterwards, since he was hated by all the immortals.   140
Therefore neither would I be willing to fight with the blessed
gods; but if you are one of those mortals who eat what the soil yields,
come nearer, so that sooner you may reach your appointed destruction.'
    Then in turn the shining son of Hippolochos answered:
'High-hearted son of Tydeus, why ask of my generation?   145
As is the generation of leaves, so is that of humanity.
The wind scatters the leaves on the ground, but the live timber
burgeons with leaves again in the season of spring returning.
So one generation of men will grow while another
dies. Yet if you wish to learn all this and be certain   150
of my genealogy: there are plenty of men who know it.
There is a city, Ephyre, in the corner of horse-pasturing
Argos; there lived Sisyphos, that sharpest of all men,
Sisyphos, Aiolos' son, and he had a son named Glaukos,
and Glaukos in turn sired Bellerophontes the blameless.   155
To Bellerophontes the gods granted beauty and desirable
manhood; but Proitos in anger devised evil things against him,
and drove him out of his own domain, since he was far greater,
from the Argive country Zeus had broken to the sway of his sceptre.
Beautiful Anteia the wife of Proitos was stricken   160
with passion to lie in love with him, and yet she could not
beguile valiant Bellerophontes, whose will was virtuous.
So she went to Proitos the king and uttered her falsehood:
"Would you be killed, o Proitos? Then murder Bellerophontes
who tried to lie with me in love, though I was unwilling."   165
So she spoke, and anger took hold of the king at her story.
He shrank from killing him, since his heart was awed by such action,
but sent him away to Lykia, and handed him murderous symbols,
which he inscribed in a folding tablet, enough to destroy life,
and told him to show it to his wife's father, that he might perish.   170
Bellerophontes went to Lykia in the blameless convoy
of the gods; when he came to the running stream of Xanthos, and Lykia,
the lord of wide Lykia tendered him full-hearted honour.
Nine days he entertained him with sacrifice of nine oxen,
but afterwards when the rose fingers of the tenth dawn showed, then   175
he began to question him, and asked to be shown the symbols,

whatever he might be carrying from his son-in-law, Proitos.
Then after he had been given his son-in-law's wicked symbols
first he sent him away with orders to kill the Chimaira
180 none might approach; a thing of immortal make, not human,
lion-fronted and snake behind, a goat in the middle,
and snorting out the breath of the terrible flame of bright fire.
He killed the Chimaira, obeying the portents of the immortals.
Next after this he fought against the glorious Solymoi,
185 and this he thought was the strongest battle with men that he entered;
but third he slaughtered the Amazons, who fight men in battle.
Now as he came back the king spun another entangling
treachery; for choosing the bravest men in wide Lykia
he laid a trap, but these men never came home thereafter
190 since all of them were killed by blameless Bellerophontes.
Then when the king knew him for the powerful stock of the god,
he detained him there, and offered him the hand of his daughter,
and gave him half of all the kingly privilege. Thereto
the men of Lykia cut out a piece of land, surpassing
195 all others, fine ploughland and orchard for him to administer.
His bride bore three children to valiant Bellerophontes,
Isandros and Hippolochos and Laodameia.
Laodameia lay in love beside Zeus of the counsels
and bore him godlike Sarpedon of the brazen helmet.
200 But after Bellerophontes was hated by all the immortals,
he wandered alone about the plain of Aleios, eating
his heart out, skulking aside from the trodden track of humanity.
As for Isandros his son, Ares the insatiate of fighting
killed him in close battle against the glorious Solymoi,
205 while Artemis of the golden reins killed the daughter in anger.
But Hippolochos begot me, and I claim that he is my father;
he sent me to Troy, and urged upon me repeated injunctions,
to be always among the bravest, and hold my head above others,
not shaming the generation of my fathers, who were
210 the greatest men in Ephyre and again in wide Lykia.
Such is my generation and the blood I claim to be born from.'
     He spoke, and Diomedes of the great war cry was gladdened.
He drove his spear deep into the prospering earth, and in winning
words of friendliness he spoke to the shepherd of the people:

'See now, you are my guest friend from far in the time of our fathers.   215
Brilliant Oineus once was host to Bellerophontes
the blameless, in his halls, and twenty days he detained him,
and these two gave to each other fine gifts in token of friendship.
Oineus gave his guest a war belt bright with the red dye,
Bellerophontes a golden and double-handled drinking-cup,   220
a thing I left behind in my house when I came on my journey.
Tydeus, though, I cannot remember, since I was little
when he left me, that time the people of the Achaians perished
in Thebe. Therefore I am your friend and host in the heart of Argos;
you are mine in Lykia, when I come to your country.   225
Let us avoid each other's spears, even in the close fighting.
There are plenty of Trojans and famed companions in battle for me
to kill, whom the god sends me, or those I run down with my swift feet,
many Achaians for you to slaughter, if you can do it.
But let us exchange our armour, so that these others may know   230
how we claim to be guests and friends from the days of our fathers.'
   So they spoke, and both springing down from behind their horses
gripped each other's hands and exchanged the promise of friendship;
but Zeus the son of Kronos stole away the wits of Glaukos
who exchanged with Diomedes the son of Tydeus armour   235
of gold for bronze, for nine oxen's worth the worth of a hundred.
   Now as Hektor had come to the Skaian gates and the oak tree,
all the wives of the Trojans and their daughters came running about him
to ask after their sons, after their brothers and neighbours,
their husbands; and he told them to pray to the immortals,   240
all, in turn; but there were sorrows in store for many.
   Now he entered the wonderfully built palace of Priam.
This was fashioned with smooth-stone cloister walks, and within it
were embodied fifty sleeping chambers of smoothed stone
built so as to connect with each other; and within these slept   245
each beside his own wedded wife, the sons of Priam.
In the same inner court on the opposite side, to face these,
lay the twelve close smooth-stone sleeping chambers of his daughters
built so as to connect with each other; and within these slept,
each by his own modest wife, the lords of the daughters of Priam.   250
There there came to meet Hektor his bountiful mother
with Laodike, the loveliest looking of all her daughters.

She clung to his hand and called him by name and spoke to him: 'Why then,
    child, have you come here and left behind the bold battle?
255 Surely it is these accursed sons of the Achaians who wear you
out, as they fight close to the city, and the spirit stirred you
to return, and from the peak of the citadel lift your hands, praying
to Zeus. But stay while I bring you honey-sweet wine, to pour out
a libation to father Zeus and the other immortals
260 first, and afterwards if you will drink yourself, be strengthened.
In a tired man, wine will bring back his strength to its bigness,
in a man tired as you are tired, defending your neighbours.'
    Tall Hektor of the shining helm spoke to her answering:
'My honoured mother, lift not to me the kindly sweet wine,
265 for fear you stagger my strength and make me forget my courage;
and with hands unwashed I would take shame to pour the glittering
wine to Zeus; there is no means for a man to pray to the dark-misted
son of Kronos, with blood and muck all spattered upon him.
But go yourself to the temple of the spoiler Athene,
270 assembling the ladies of honour, and with things to be sacrificed,
and take a robe, which seems to you the largest and loveliest
in the great house, and that which is far your dearest possession.
Lay this along the knees of Athene the lovely haired. Also
promise to dedicate within the shrine twelve heifers,
275 yearlings, never broken, if only she will have pity
on the town of Troy, and the Trojan wives, and their innocent children,
if she will hold back from sacred Ilion the son of Tydeus,
that wild spear-fighter, the strong one who drives men to thoughts of
    terror.
So go yourself to the temple of the spoiler Athene,
280 while I go in search of Paris, to call him, if he will listen
to anything I tell him. How I wish at this moment the earth might
open beneath him. The Olympian let him live, a great sorrow
to the Trojans, and high-hearted Priam, and all of his children.
If only I could see him gone down to the house of the Death God,
285 then I could say my heart had forgotten its joyless affliction.'
    So he spoke, and she going into the great house called out
to her handmaidens, who assembled throughout the city the highborn
women; while she descended into the fragrant store-chamber.

There lay the elaborately wrought robes, the work of Sidonian
women, whom Alexandros himself, the godlike, had brought home   290
from the land of Sidon, crossing the wide sea, on that journey
when he brought back also gloriously descended Helen.
Hekabe lifted out one and took it as gift to Athene,
that which was the loveliest in design and the largest,
and shone like a star. It lay beneath the others. She went on   295
her way, and a throng of noble women hastened about her.
    When these had come to Athene's temple on the peak of the citadel,
Theano of the fair cheeks opened the door for them, daughter
of Kisseus, and wife of Antenor, breaker of horses,
she whom the Trojans had established to be Athene's priestess.   300
With a wailing cry all lifted up their hands to Athene,
and Theano of the fair cheeks taking up the robe laid it
along the knees of Athene the lovely haired, and praying
she supplicated the daughter of powerful Zeus: 'O lady,
Athene, our city's defender, shining among goddesses: 305
break the spear of Diomedes, and grant that the man be
hurled on his face in front of the Skaian gates; so may we
instantly dedicate within your shrine twelve heifers,
yearlings, never broken, if only you will have pity
on the town of Troy, and the Trojan wives, and their innocent children.' 310
    She spoke in prayer, but Pallas Athene turned her head from her.
    So they made their prayer to the daughter of Zeus the powerful.
But Hektor went away to the house of Alexandros,
a splendid place he had built himself, with the men who at that time
were the best men for craftsmanship in the generous Troad,   315
who had made him a sleeping room and a hall and a courtyard
near the houses of Hektor and Priam, on the peak of the citadel.
There entered Hektor beloved of Zeus, in his hand holding
the eleven-cubit-long spear, whose shaft was tipped with a shining
bronze spearhead, and a ring of gold was hooped to hold it.   320
He found the man in his chamber busy with his splendid armour,
the corselet and the shield, and turning in his hands the curved bow,
while Helen of Argos was sitting among her attendant women
directing the magnificent work done by her handmaidens.
    But Hektor saw him, and in words of shame he rebuked him: 325
'Strange man! It is not fair to keep in your heart this coldness.

The people are dying around the city and around the steep wall
as they fight hard; and it is for you that this war with its clamour
has flared up about our city. You yourself would fight with another
330 whom you saw anywhere hanging back from the hateful encounter.
Up then, to keep our town from burning at once in the hot fire.'
    Then in answer the godlike Alexandros spoke to him:
'Hektor, seeing you have scolded me rightly, not beyond measure,
therefore I will tell, and you in turn understand and listen.
335 It was not so much in coldness and bitter will toward the Trojans
that I sat in my room, but I wished to give myself over to sorrow.
But just now with soft words my wife was winning me over
and urging me into the fight, and that way seems to me also
the better one. Victory passes back and forth between men.
340 Come then, wait for me now while I put on my armour of battle,
or go, and I will follow, and I think I can overtake you.'
    He spoke, but Hektor of the shining helm gave him no answer,
but Helen spoke to him in words of endearment: 'Brother
by marriage to me, who am a nasty bitch evil-intriguing,
345 how I wish that on that day when my mother first bore me
the foul whirlwind of the storm had caught me away and swept me
to the mountain, or into the wash of the sea deep-thundering
where the waves would have swept me away before all these things had
    happened.
Yet since the gods had brought it about that these vile things must be,
350 I wish I had been the wife of a better man than this is,
one who knew modesty and all things of shame that men say.
But this man's heart is no steadfast thing, nor yet will it be so
ever hereafter; for that I think he shall take the consequence.
But come now, come in and rest on this chair, my brother,
355 since it is on your heart beyond all that the hard work has fallen
for the sake of dishonoured me and the blind act of Alexandros,
us two, on whom Zeus set a vile destiny, so that hereafter
we shall be made into things of song for the men of the future.'
    Then tall Hektor of the shining helm answered her: 'Do not, Helen,
360 make me sit with you, though you love me. You will not persuade me.
Already my heart within is hastening me to defend
the Trojans, who when I am away long greatly to have me.
Rather rouse this man, and let himself also be swift to action

so he may overtake me while I am still in the city.
For I am going first to my own house, so I can visit   365
my own people, my beloved wife and my son, who is little,
since I do not know if ever again I shall come back this way,
or whether the gods will strike me down at the hands of the Achaians.'
    So speaking Hektor of the shining helm departed
and in speed made his way to his own well-established dwelling,   370
but failed to find in the house Andromache of the white arms;
for she, with the child, and followed by one fair-robed attendant,
had taken her place on the tower in lamentation, and tearful.
When he saw no sign of his perfect wife within the house, Hektor
stopped in his way on the threshold and spoke among the handmaidens: 375
'Come then, tell me truthfully as you may, handmaidens:
where has Andromache of the white arms gone? Is she
with any of the sisters of her lord or the wives of his brothers?
Or has she gone to the house of Athene, where all the other
lovely-haired women of Troy propitiate the grim goddess?'   380
    Then in turn the hard-working housekeeper gave him an answer:
'Hektor, since you have urged me to tell you the truth, she is not
with any of the sisters of her lord or the wives of his brothers,
nor has she gone to the house of Athene, where all the other
lovely-haired women of Troy propitiate the grim goddess,   385
but she has gone to the great bastion of Ilion, because she heard that
the Trojans were losing, and great grew the strength of the Achaians.
Therefore she has gone in speed to the wall, like a woman
gone mad, and a nurse attending her carries the baby.'
    So the housekeeper spoke, and Hektor hastened from his home   390
backward by the way he had come through the well-laid streets. So
as he had come to the gates on his way through the great city,
the Skaian gates, whereby he would issue into the plain, there
at last his own generous wife came running to meet him,
Andromache, the daughter of high-hearted Eëtion;   395
Eëtion, who had dwelt underneath wooded Plakos,
in Thebe below Plakos, lord over the Kilikian people.
It was his daughter who was given to Hektor of the bronze helm.
She came to him there, and beside her went an attendant carrying
the boy in the fold of her bosom, a little child, only a baby,   400
Hektor's son, the admired, beautiful as a star shining,

whom Hektor called Skamandrios, but all of the others
Astyanax—lord of the city; since Hektor alone saved Ilion.
Hektor smiled in silence as he looked on his son, but she,

405 Andromache, stood close beside him, letting her tears fall,
and clung to his hand and called him by name and spoke to him: 'Dearest,
your own great strength will be your death, and you have no pity
on your little son, nor on me, ill-starred, who soon must be your widow;
for presently the Achaians, gathering together,

410 will set upon you and kill you; and for me it would be far better
to sink into the earth when I have lost you, for there is no other
consolation for me after you have gone to your destiny—
only grief; since I have no father, no honoured mother.
It was brilliant Achilleus who slew my father, Eëtion,

415 when he stormed the strong-founded citadel of the Kilikians,
Thebe of the towering gates. He killed Eëtion
but did not strip his armour, for his heart respected the dead man,
but burned the body in all its elaborate war-gear
and piled a grave mound over it, and the nymphs of the mountains,

420 daughters of Zeus of the aegis, planted elm trees about it.
And they who were my seven brothers in the great house all went
upon a single day down into the house of the death god,
for swift-footed brilliant Achilleus slaughtered all of them
as they were tending their white sheep and their lumbering oxen;

425 and when he had led my mother, who was queen under wooded Plakos,
here, along with all his other possessions, Achilleus
released her again, accepting ransom beyond count, but Artemis
of the showering arrows struck her down in the halls of her father.
Hektor, thus you are father to me, and my honoured mother,

430 you are my brother, and you it is who are my young husband.
Please take pity upon me then, stay here on the rampart,
that you may not leave your child an orphan, your wife a widow,
but draw your people up by the fig tree, there where the city
is openest to attack, and where the wall may be mounted.

435 Three times their bravest came that way, and fought there to storm it
about the two Aiantes and renowned Idomeneus,
about the two Atreidai and the fighting son of Tydeus.
Either some man well skilled in prophetic arts had spoken,
or the very spirit within themselves had stirred them to the onslaught.'

Then tall Hektor of the shining helm answered her: 'All these   440
things are in my mind also, lady; yet I would feel deep shame
before the Trojans, and the Trojan women with trailing garments,
if like a coward I were to shrink aside from the fighting;
and the spirit will not let me, since I have learned to be valiant
and to fight always among the foremost ranks of the Trojans,   445
winning for my own self great glory, and for my father.
For I know this thing well in my heart, and my mind knows it:
there will come a day when sacred Ilion shall perish,
and Priam, and the people of Priam of the strong ash spear.
But it is not so much the pain to come of the Trojans   450
that troubles me, not even of Priam the king nor Hekabe,
not the thought of my brothers who in their numbers and valour
shall drop in the dust under the hands of men who hate them,
as troubles me the thought of you, when some bronze-armoured
Achaian leads you off, taking away your day of liberty,   455
in tears; and in Argos you must work at the loom of another,
and carry water from the spring Messeis or Hypereia,
all unwilling, but strong will be the necessity upon you;
and some day seeing you shedding tears a man will say of you:
"This is the wife of Hektor, who was ever the bravest fighter   460
of the Trojans, breakers of horses, in the days when they fought about
    Ilion."
So will one speak of you; and for you it will be yet a fresh grief,
to be widowed of such a man who could fight off the day of your slavery.
But may I be dead and the piled earth hide me under before I
hear you crying and know by this that they drag you captive.'   465
    So speaking glorious Hektor held out his arms to his baby,
who shrank back to his fair-girdled nurse's bosom
screaming, and frightened at the aspect of his own father,
terrified as he saw the bronze and the crest with its horse-hair,
nodding dreadfully, as he thought, from the peak of the helmet.   470
Then his beloved father laughed out, and his honoured mother,
and at once glorious Hektor lifted from his head the helmet
and laid it in all its shining upon the ground. Then taking
up his dear son he tossed him about in his arms, and kissed him,
and lifted his voice in prayer to Zeus and the other immortals: 475
'Zeus, and you other immortals, grant that this boy, who is my son,

may be as I am, pre-eminent among the Trojans,
great in strength, as am I, and rule strongly over Ilion;
and some day let them say of him: "He is better by far than his father",
480 as he comes in from the fighting; and let him kill his enemy
and bring home the blooded spoils, and delight the heart of his mother.'
    So speaking he set his child again in the arms of his beloved
wife, who took him back again to her fragrant bosom
smiling in her tears; and her husband saw, and took pity upon her,
485 and stroked her with his hand, and called her by name and spoke to her:
'Poor Andromache! Why does your heart sorrow so much for me?
No man is going to hurl me to Hades, unless it is fated,
but as for fate, I think that no man yet has escaped it
once it has taken its first form, neither brave man nor coward.
490 Go therefore back to our house, and take up your own work,
the loom and the distaff, and see to it that your handmaidens
ply their work also; but the men must see to the fighting,
all men who are the people of Ilion, but I beyond others.'
    So glorious Hektor spoke and again took up the helmet
495 with its crest of horse-hair, while his beloved wife went homeward,
turning to look back on the way, letting the live tears fall.
And as she came in speed into the well-settled household
of Hektor the slayer of men, she found numbers of handmaidens
within, and her coming stirred all of them into lamentation.
500 So they mourned in his house over Hektor while he was living
still, for they thought he would never again come back from the fighting
alive, escaping the Achaian hands and their violence.
    But Paris in turn did not linger long in his high house,
but when he had put on his glorious armour with bronze elaborate
505 he ran in the confidence of his quick feet through the city.
As when some stalled horse who has been corn-fed at the manger
breaking free of his rope gallops over the plain in thunder
to his accustomed bathing place in a sweet-running river
and in the pride of his strength holds high his head, and the mane floats
510 over his shoulders; sure of his glorious strength, the quick knees
carry him to the loved places and the pasture of horses;
so from uttermost Pergamos came Paris, the son of
Priam, shining in all his armour of war as the sun shines,
laughing aloud, and his quick feet carried him; suddenly thereafter

he came on brilliant Hektor, his brother, where he yet lingered   515
before turning away from the place where he had talked with his lady.
It was Alexandros the godlike who first spoke to him:
'Brother, I fear that I have held back your haste, by being
slow on the way, not coming in time, as you commanded me.'

    Then tall Hektor of the shining helm spoke to him in answer: 520
'Strange man! There is no way that one, giving judgment in fairness,
could dishonour your work in battle, since you are a strong man.
But of your own accord you hang back, unwilling. And my heart
is grieved in its thought, when I hear shameful things spoken about you
by the Trojans, who undergo hard fighting for your sake.   525
Let us go now; some day hereafter we will make all right
with the immortal gods in the sky, if Zeus ever grant it,
setting up to them in our houses the wine-bowl of liberty
after we have driven out of Troy the strong-greaved Achaians.'

BOOK SEVEN

So speaking Hektor the glorious swept on through the gates,
and with him went Alexandros his brother, both of them minded
in their hearts to do battle and take their part in the fighting.
And as to men of the sea in their supplication the god sends
5   a fair wind, when they are breaking their strength at the smoothed
          oar-sweeps,
driving over the sea, and their arms are weak with weariness,
so these two appeared to the Trojans, who had longed for them.
    Each killed his man: Paris, the son of lord Areïthoös,
Menesthios, who lived in Arne, born to him of the war club
10   Areïthoös, and to ox-eyed Phylomedousa;
while Hektor with the sharp spear struck Eïoneus, under
the circle of the bronze helm, in the neck, and broke his limbs' strength.
And Glaukos, lord of the Lykian men, the son of Hippolochos,
struck down with the spear Iphinoös in the strong encounter,
15   Dexias' son, as he leapt up behind his fast horses, striking him
in the shoulder. He dropped from car to ground, and his limbs' strength
          was broken.
    Now as the goddess grey-eyed Athene was aware of these two
destroying the men of Argos in the strong encounter,
she went down in a flash of speed from the peaks of Olympos
20   to sacred Ilion, where Apollo stirred forth to meet her
from his seat on Pergamos, where he planned that the Trojans should
          conquer.
    These two then encountered each other beside the oak tree,

and speaking first the son of Zeus, lord Apollo, addressed her:
'What can be your desire this time, o daughter of great Zeus,
that you came down from Olympos at the urge of your mighty spirit?   25
To give the Danaans victory in the battle, turning it
back? Since you have no pity at all for the Trojans who are dying.
But if you might only do as I say, it would be far better.
For this day let us put an end to the hatred and the fighting
now; they shall fight again hereafter, till we witness the finish   30
they make of Ilion, since it is dear to the heart of you, who
are goddesses immortal, that this city shall be made desolate.'
    Then in answer the goddess grey-eyed Athene spoke to him:
'Worker from afar, thus let it be. These were my thoughts also
as I came down from Olympos among the Achaians and Trojans.   35
Tell me then, how are you minded to stop these men in their fighting?'
    Now in turn the son of Zeus, lord Apollo, addressed her:
'Let us rouse up the strong heart in Hektor, breaker of horses,
if he might call forth some Danaan to do battle against him,
single man against single man, in bitter combat;   40
and let the strong-greaved Achaians, stirred into admiration,
send forth a single man to do battle with brilliant Hektor.'
    He spoke, nor failed to persuade the goddess grey-eyed Athene.
Now Helenos, Priam's beloved son, gathered into his heart their
deliberation, and all that pleased the musing divinities.   45
He went on his way and stood beside Hektor and spoke a word to him:
'Hektor, o son of Priam and equal of Zeus in counsel,
would you now be persuaded by me, for I am your brother?
Make the rest of the Trojans sit down, and all the Achaians,
and yourself call forth one of the Achaians, their bravest,   50
to fight man to man against you in bitter combat.
Since it is not your destiny yet to die and encounter
fate. For thus I heard it in the speech of the gods everlasting.'
    So he spoke, and Hektor hearing his word was happy,
and went into the space between and forced back the Trojan battalions, 55
holding his spear by the middle, until they were all seated,
while Agamemnon in turn seated the strong-greaved Achaians,
and Athene and the lord of the silver bow, Apollo,
assuming the likenesses of birds, of vultures, settled
aloft the great oak tree of their father, Zeus of the aegis,   60

taking their ease and watching these men whose ranks, dense-settled,
shuddered into a bristle of spears, of shields and of helmets.
As when the shudder of the west wind suddenly rising
scatters across the water, and the water darkens beneath it,
65 so darkening were settled the ranks of Achaians and Trojans
in the plain. And now Hektor spoke forth between them:
'Listen to me, you Trojans and strong-greaved Achaians,
while I speak forth what the heart within my breast urges.
Zeus, son of Kronos, who sits on high, would not bring to fulfilment
70 our oaths, but is found to be of evil intention toward both sides
until that day when you storm Troy of the strong towers, or that day
when you yourselves are broken beside your seafaring vessels.
Seeing now that among you are the bravest of all the Achaians,
let one of you, whose heart stirs him to combat against me,
75 stand forth before all to fight by himself against brilliant Hektor.
Behold the terms that I make, let Zeus be witness upon them.
If with the thin edge of the bronze he takes my life, then
let him strip my armour and carry it back to the hollow ships,
but give my body to be taken home again, so that the Trojans
80 and the wives of the Trojans may give me in death my rite of burning.
But if I take his life, and Apollo grants me the glory,
I will strip his armour and carry it to sacred Ilion
and hang it in front of the temple of far-striking Apollo,
but his corpse I will give back among the strong-benched vessels
85 so that the flowing-haired Achaians may give him due burial
and heap up a mound upon him beside the broad passage of Helle.
And some day one of the men to come will say, as he sees it,
one who in his benched ship sails on the wine-blue water:
"This is the mound of a man who died long ago in battle,
90 who was one of the bravest, and glorious Hektor killed him."
So will he speak some day, and my glory will not be forgotten.'
    So he spoke, and all of them stayed stricken to silence
in shame of refusing him, and in fear to take up his challenge.
But now at long last Menelaos stood forth and addressed them
95 in scorn and reproach, and stirred within the heart to great sorrow:
'Ah me! You brave in words, you women, not men, of Achaia!
This will be a defilement upon us, shame upon shame piled,
if no one of the Danaans goes out to face Hektor.

No, may all of you turn to water and earth, all of you
who sit by yourselves with no life in you, utterly dishonoured.   100
I myself will arm against this man. While above us
the threads of victory are held in the hands of the immortals.'
    So he spoke, and began to put on his splendid armour.
And there, o Menelaos, would have shown forth the end of your life
under the hands of Hektor, since he was far stronger than you were,   105
had not the kings of the Achaians leapt up and caught you;
and the son of Atreus himself, powerful Agamemnon,
caught you by the right hand, and called you by name, and spoke to you:
'Menelaos, beloved of God, you are mad; you have no need
to take leave of your senses thus. Hold fast, though it hurts you,   110
nor long in your pride to fight with a man who is better than you are,
with Hektor, Priam's son. There are others who shudder before him.
Even Achilleus, in the fighting where men win glory,
trembles to meet this man, and he is far better than you are.
Go back now and sit down in the throng of your own companions;   115
the Achaians will set up another to fight against this man,
and even though he is without fear, and can never be glutted
with rough work, I think he will be glad to leave off, even
if he comes off whole from the hateful fighting and bitter combat.'
    The hero spoke like this and bent the heart of his brother   120
since he urged wisely. And Menelaos obeyed him; his henchmen
joyfully thereupon took off the armour from his shoulders.
Nestor among the Argives now stood forth and addressed them:
'Oh, for shame. Great sorrow settles on the land of Achaia.
Surely he would groan aloud, Peleus, the aged horseman,   125
the great man of counsel among the Myrmidons, and their speaker.
Once, as he questioned me in his house, he was filled with great joy
as he heard the generation and blood of all of the Argives.
Now if he were to hear how all cringe away before Hektor,
many a time he would lift up his very hands to the immortals,   130
and the life breath from his limbs would go down into the house of Hades.
If only, o father Zeus, Athene, Apollo,
I were in my youth as when the Pylians assembled
and the spear-fighting Arkadians battled by swirling Keladon,
by the streams of Iardanos and before the ramparts of Pheia.   135
Their champion stood forth, Ereuthalion, a man godlike,

[171]

wearing upon his shoulders the armour of lord Areïthoös,
Areïthoös the brilliant, given by the men of that time
and the fair-girdled women the name club-fighter, because he
140 went into battle armed neither with the bow nor the long spear,
but with a great bar clubbed of iron broke the battalions.
Lykourgos killed this man by craft, not strength, for he met him
in the narrow pass of the way, where the iron club served not to parry
destruction, for Lykourgos, too quick with a stab beneath it,
145 pinned him through the middle with the spear, so he went down
backward
to the ground; and he stripped the armour brazen Ares had given him
and wore the armour thereafter himself through the grind of battle.
But when Lykourgos was grown an old man in his halls, he gave it
to his beloved henchman, Ereuthalion, to carry.
150 Wearing this armour he called forth all the bravest to fight him,
but they were all afraid and trembling: none had the courage,
only I, for my hard-enduring heart in its daring
drove me to fight him. I in age was the youngest of all of them.
And I fought with him, and Pallas Athene gave me the glory.
155 Of all the men I have killed this was the tallest and strongest.
For he sprawled in his great bulk this way and that way. If only
I were young now, as then, and the strength still steady within me;
Hektor of the glancing helm would soon find his battle.
But you, now, who are the bravest of all the Achaians,
160 are not minded with a good will to go against Hektor.'
So the old man scolded them, and nine in all stood forth.
Far the first to rise up was the lord of men, Agamemnon,
and rose after him the son of Tydeus, strong Diomedes,
and next the two Aiantes rose, their fierce strength upon them,
165 and after these Idomeneus, and Idomeneus' companion,
Meriones, a match for the murderous Lord of Battles,
and after these Eurypylos, the glorious son of Euaimon,
and Thoas rose up, Andraimon's son, and brilliant Odysseus.
All of these were willing to fight against brilliant Hektor.
170 Now before them again spoke the Gerenian horseman, Nestor:
'Let the lot be shaken for all of you, to see who wins it.
He shall be the one to gladden the strong-greaved Achaians,
and to be glad within his own heart, if he can come off

whole again from the hateful battle and bitter combat.'
So he spoke, and each of them marked a lot as his own one lot.   175
They threw them in the helmet of Atreus' son, Agamemnon.
and the people, holding up their hands to the gods, prayed to them.
Then would murmur any man, gazing into the wide sky:
'Father Zeus, let Aias win the lot, or else Diomedes,
Tydeus' son, or the king himself of golden Mykenai.'   180
So they spoke, and Nestor the Gerenian horseman shook the lots,
and a lot leapt from the helmet, that one that they all had wished for,
the lot of Aias; and a herald carrying it all through the great throng
showed it from left to right to the great men of the Achaians,
all of them. Each man knew not the mark, and denied it,   185
but as carrying it all through the great throng he showed it to that one
who had marked it as his, and thrown it in the helmet, glorious Aias,
he held forth his hand, and the herald stood by him, and put the lot in it,
and he saw his mark on the lot, and knew it, and his heart was gladdened.
He threw it down on the ground beside his foot, and spoke to them: 190
'See, friends, the lot is mine, and I myself am made happy
in my heart, since I think I can win over brilliant Hektor.
Do this, then: while I put on my armour of fighting,
all of you be praying to the lord Zeus, the son of Kronos,
in silence and each to himself, let none of the Trojans hear you;   195
or openly out loud, since we have nothing to be afraid of
at all, since no man by force will beat me backward unwilling
as he wills, nor by craft either, since I think that the man who was born
and raised in Salamis, myself, is not such a novice.'
So he spoke, and they prayed to the lord Zeus, the son of Kronos.   200
And then would murmur any man, gazing into the wide sky:
'Father Zeus, watching over us from Ida, most high, most honoured,
grant that Aias win the vaunt of renown and the victory;
but if truly you love Hektor and are careful for him,
give to both of them equal strength, make equal their honour.'   205
So they spoke, and meanwhile Aias armed him in shining
bronze. Then when he had girt his body in all its armour,
he strode on his way, as Ares the war god walks gigantic
going into the fighting of men whom the son of Kronos
has driven to fight angrily in heart-perishing hatred.   210
Such was Aias as he strode gigantic, the wall of the Achaians,

smiling under his threatening brows, with his feet beneath him
taking huge strides forward, and shaking the spear far-shadowing.
And the Argives looking upon him were made glad, while the Trojans
215 were taken every man in the knees with trembling and terror,
and for Hektor himself the heart beat hard in his breast, but he could not
any more find means to take flight and shrink back into
the throng of his men, since he in his pride had called him to battle.
Now Aias came near him, carrying like a wall his shield
220 of bronze and sevenfold ox-hide which Tychios wrought him with much
    toil;
Tychios, at home in Hyle, far the best of all workers in leather
who had made him the great gleaming shield of sevenfold ox-hide
from strong bulls, and hammered an eighth fold of bronze upon it.
Telamonian Aias, carrying this to cover
225 his chest, came near to Hektor and spoke to him in words of menace:
'Hektor, single man against single man you will learn now
for sure what the bravest men are like among the Danaans
even after Achilleus the lion-hearted who breaks men in battle.
He lies now apart among his own beaked seafaring
230 ships, in anger at Agamemnon, the shepherd of the people.
But here are we; and we are such men as can stand up against you;
there are plenty of us; so now begin your fight and your combat.'
    Tall Hektor of the glancing helm answered him: 'Aias,
son of Telamon, seed of Zeus, o lord of the people,
235 do not be testing me as if I were some ineffectual
boy, or a woman, who knows nothing of the works of warfare.
I know well myself how to fight and kill men in battle;
I know how to turn to the right, how to turn to the left the ox-hide
tanned into a shield which is my protection in battle;
240 I know how to storm my way into the struggle of flying horses;
I know how to tread my measures on the grim floor of the war god.
Yet great as you are I would not strike you by stealth, watching
for my chance, but openly, so, if perhaps I might hit you.'
    So he spoke, and balanced the spear far-shadowed, and threw it,
245 and struck the sevenfold-ox-hide terrible shield of Aias
in the uttermost bronze, which was the eighth layer upon it,
and the unwearying bronze spearhead shore its way through six folds
but was stopped in the seventh ox-hide. Then after him Aias

the illustrious in turn cast with his spear far-shadowing
and struck the shield of Priam's son on its perfect circle.   250
All the way through the glittering shield went the heavy spearhead,
and crashed its way through the intricately worked corselet;
straight ahead by the flank the spearhead shore through his tunic,
yet he bent away to one side and avoided the dark death.
Both now gripping in their hands the long spears pulled them   255
out, and went at each other like lions who live on raw meat,
or wild boars, whose strength is no light thing. The son of
Priam stabbed then with his spear into the shield's centre,
nor did the bronze point break its way through, but the spearhead bent
     back.
Now Aias plunging upon him thrust at the shield, and the spearhead   260
passed clean through, and pounded Hektor back in his fury,
and tore at his neck passing so that the dark blood broke. Yet
even so Hektor of the shining helmet did not stop fighting,
but gave back and in his heavy hand caught up a stone that
lay in the plain, black and rugged and huge. With this   265
he struck the sevenfold-ox-hide terrible shield of Aias
in the knob of the centre so that the bronze clashed loud about it.
After him Aias in turn lifting a stone far greater
whirled it and threw, leaning into the cast his strength beyond measure,
and the shield broke inward under the stroke of the rock like a millstone, 270
and Hektor's very knees gave, so that he sprawled backward,
shield beaten upon him, but at once Apollo lifted him upright.
And now they would have been stabbing with their swords at close
     quarters,
had not the heralds, messengers of Zeus and of mortals,
come up, one for the bronze-armoured Achaians, one for the Trojans,   275
Idaios and Talthybios, both men of good counsel.
They held their staves between the two men, and the herald Idaios
out of his knowledge of prudent advices spoke a word to them:
'Stop the fight, dear children, nor go on with this battle.
To Zeus who gathers the clouds both of you are beloved,   280
and both of you are fighters; this thing all of us know surely.
Night darkens now. It is a good thing to give way to the night-time.'
     Aias the son of Telamon spoke to him in answer:
'Bid Hektor answer this, Idaios, since it was he who

[175]

285 in his pride called forth all our bravest to fight him.
      Let him speak first; and I for my part shall do as he urges.'
        Tall Hektor of the glancing helm answered him: 'Aias,
      seeing that God has given you strength, stature and wisdom
      also, and with the spear you surpass the other Achaians,
290 let us now give over this fighting and hostility
      for today; we shall fight again, until the divinity
      chooses between us, and gives victory to one or the other.
      Night darkens now. It is a good thing to give way to the night-time.
      Thus you may bring joy to all the Achaians beside their
295 ships, and above all to those who are your own kindred and company;
      and I in the great city of lord Priam will gladden
      the Trojans, and the women of Troy with their trailing robes, who
      will go before the divine assembly in thanksgiving for my sake.
      Come then, let us give each other glorious presents,
300 so that any of the Achaians or Trojans may say of us:
      "These two fought each other in heart-consuming hate, then
      joined with each other in close friendship, before they were parted." '
        So he spoke, and bringing a sword with nails of silver
      gave it to him, together with the sheath and the well-cut sword belt,
305 and Aias gave a war belt coloured shining with purple.
      So separating, Aias went among the Achaian people,
      and Hektor went back to the thronging Trojans, who were made happy
      when they saw him coming alive and unwounded out of the combat,
      escaping the strength and the unconquerable hands of Aias,
310 and they, who had not hoped to see him alive, escorted him
      back to the town. On the other side the strong-greaved Achaians
      led Aias, happy in his victory, to great Agamemnon.
        When these had come to the shelters of the son of Atreus,
      Agamemnon the lord of men dedicated an ox among them,
315 a five-year-old male, to Zeus, all-powerful son of Kronos.
      They skinned the victim and put it in order, and butchered the carcass,
      and cut up the meat expertly into small pieces, and spitted them,
      and roasted all carefully, and took off the pieces.
      Then after they had finished the work and got the feast ready,
320 they feasted, nor was any man's hunger denied a fair portion;
      and Atreus' son, the hero wide-ruling Agamemnon,
      gave to Aias in honour the long cuts of the chine's portion.

But when they had put away their desire for eating and drinking,
the aged man began to weave his counsel before them
first, Nestor, whose advice had shown best before this.   325
He in kind intention toward all stood forth and addressed them:
'Son of Atreus, and you other great men of all the Achaians:
seeing that many flowing-haired Achaians have died here,
whose dark blood has been scattered beside the fair waters of Skamandros
by the fierce war god, while their souls went down into the house of   330
    Hades;
therefore with the dawn we should set a pause to the fighting
of Achaians, and assembling them wheel back the bodies
with mules and oxen; then must we burn them a little apart from
the ships, so that each whose duty it is may carry the bones back
to a man's children, when we go home to the land of our fathers.   335
And let us gather and pile one single mound on the corpse-pyre
indiscriminately from the plain, and build fast upon it
towered ramparts, to be a defence of ourselves and our vessels.
And let us build into these walls gates strongly fitted
that there may be a way through them for the driving of horses;   340
and on the outer side, and close, we must dig a deep ditch
circling it, so as to keep off their people and horses,
that we may not be crushed under the attack of these proud Trojans.'
    So he spoke, and all the kings gave him their approval.
Now there was an assembly of Trojans high on the city of Ilion   345
fiercely shaken to tumult before the doors of Priam,
and among these Antenor the thoughtful began to address them:
'Trojans and Dardanians and companions in arms: hear me
while I speak forth what the heart within my breast urges.
Come then: let us give back Helen of Argos and all her possessions   350
to the sons of Atreus to take away, seeing now we fight with
our true pledges made into lies; and I see no good thing's
accomplishment for us in the end, unless we do this.'
    He spoke thus and sat down again, and among them rose up
brilliant Alexandros, the lord of lovely-haired Helen,   355
who spoke to him in answer and addressed them in winged words:
'Antenor, these things that you argue please me no longer.
Your mind knows how to contrive a saying better than this one.
But if in all seriousness this is your true argument; then

360 it is the very gods who ruined the brain within you.
I will speak out before the Trojans, breakers of horses.
I refuse, straight out. I will not give back the woman.
But of the possessions I carried away to our house from Argos
I am willing to give all back, and to add to these from my own goods.'

365　He spoke thus and sat down again, and among them rose up
Priam, son of Dardanos, equal of the gods in counsel,
who in kind intention toward all stood forth and addressed them:
'Trojans and Dardanians and companions in arms: hear me
while I speak forth what the heart within my breast urges.

370 Take now your supper about the city, as you did before this,
and remember your duty of the watch, and be each man wakeful;
and at dawn let Idaios go to the hollow ships, and speak with
the sons of Atreus, Menelaos and Agamemnon, giving
the word of Alexandros, for whose sake this strife has arisen,

375 and to add this solid message, and ask them if they are willing
to stop the sorrowful fighting until we can burn the bodies
of our dead. We shall fight again until the divinity
chooses between us, and gives victory to one or the other.'
　　So he spoke, and they listened to him with care, and obeyed him;

380 and so took their supper, watch succeeding watch, through the army.
Then at dawn Idaios went down to the hollow ships, where
he found the Danaans, henchmen of the war god, in assembly
beside the stern of Agamemnon's ship; the herald
with the great voice took his stand in their midst, and spoke to them:

385 'Son of Atreus, and you other great men of all the Achaians,
Priam and the rest of the haughty Trojans have bidden me
give you, if this message be found to your pleasure and liking,
the word of Alexandros, for whose sake this strife has arisen.
All those possessions that Alexandros carried in his hollow

390 ships to Troy, and I wish that he had perished before then,
he is willing to give all back, and to add to these from his own goods.
But the very wedded wife of glorious Menelaos
he says that he will not give, though the Trojans would have him do it.
They told me to give you this message also, if you are willing;

395 to stop the sorrowful fighting until we can burn the bodies
of our dead. We shall fight again afterwards, until the divinity
chooses between us, and gives victory to one or the other.'

So he spoke, and all of them stayed quiet in silence;
but now at long last Diomedes of the great war cry addressed them:
'Now let none accept the possessions of Alexandros,   400
nor take back Helen; one who is very simple can see it,
that by this time the terms of death hang over the Trojans.'
So he spoke, and all sons of the Achaians shouted
acclaim for the word of Diomedes, breaker of horses;
and now powerful Agamemnon spoke to Idaios: 405
'Idaios, you hear for yourself the word of the Achaians,
how they are answering you; and such is my pleasure also.
But about the burning of the dead bodies I do not begrudge you;
no, for there is no sparing time for the bodies of the perished,
once they have died, to give them swiftly the pity of burning.   410
Let Zeus, high-thundering lord of Hera, witness our pledges.'
He spoke, and held up the sceptre in the sight of all the gods. Then
Idaios made his way back once more to sacred Ilion.
The Trojans and Dardanians were in session of assembly,
all gathered in one place, awaiting Idaios when he might come   415
back; and he returned to them and delivered his message
standing there in their midst, and they made their swift preparations,
for two things, some to gather the bodies, and the others firewood;
while the Argives on the other side from their strong-benched vessels
went forward, some to gather the bodies, and others firewood.   420

Now the sun of a new day struck on the ploughlands, rising
out of the quiet water and the deep stream of the ocean
to climb the sky. The Trojans assembled together. They found
it hard to recognize each individual dead man;
but with water they washed away the blood that was on them   425
and as they wept warm tears they lifted them on to the wagons.
But great Priam would not let them cry out; and in silence
they piled the bodies upon the pyre, with their hearts in sorrow,
and burned them upon the fire, and went back to sacred Ilion.
In the same way on the other side the strong-greaved Achaians   430
piled their own slain upon the pyre, with their hearts in sorrow,
and burned them upon the fire, and went back to their hollow vessels.

But when the dawn was not yet, but still the pallor of night's edge,
a chosen body of the Achaians formed by the pyre;
and they gathered together and piled one single mound all above it   435

indiscriminately from the plain, and built a fort on it
with towered ramparts, to be a defence for themselves and their vessels;
and they built within these walls gates strongly fitted
that there might be a way through them for the driving of horses;
440 and on the outer side and against it they dug a deep ditch,
making it great and wide, and fixed the sharp stakes inside it.
    So the flowing-haired Achaians laboured, and meanwhile
the gods in session at the side of Zeus who handles the lightning
watched the huge endeavour of the bronze-armoured Achaians;
445 and the god Poseidon who shakes the earth began speaking among them:
'Father Zeus, is there any mortal left on the wide earth
who will still declare to the immortals his mind and his purpose?
Do you not see how now these flowing-haired Achaians
have built a wall landward of their ships, and driven about it
450 a ditch, and not given to the gods any grand sacrifice?
Now the fame of this will last as long as dawnlight is scattered,
and men will forget that wall which I and Phoibos Apollo
built with our hard work for the hero Laomedon's city.'
    Deeply troubled, Zeus who gathers the clouds answered him:
455 'What a thing to have said, earth-shaker of the wide strength.
Some other one of the gods might fear such a thought, one who
is a god far weaker of his hands and in anger than you are;
but the fame of you shall last as long as dawnlight is scattered.
Come then! After once more the flowing-haired Achaians
460 are gone back with their ships to the beloved land of their fathers,
break their wall to pieces and scatter it into the salt sea
and pile again the beach deep under the sands and cover it;
so let the great wall of the Achaians go down to destruction.'
    As these two were talking thus together, the sun went
465 down, and the work of the Achaians was finished. They slaughtered
oxen then beside their shelters, and took their supper.
The ships came over to them from Lemnos bringing them wine, ships
sent over to them in numbers by the son of Jason, Euneos,
whom Hypsipyle had borne to the shepherd of the people, Jason.
470 Apart to the sons of Atreus, Agamemnon and Menelaos,
Jason's son had given wine as a gift, a thousand
measures; and thence the rest of the flowing-haired Achaians
bought wine, some for bronze and others for shining iron,

some for skins and some for the whole oxen, while others
paid slaves taken in war; and they made their feasting abundant.   475
All night long thereafter the flowing-haired Achaians
feasted, and the Trojans and their companions in arms in the city;
but all night long Zeus of the counsels was threatening evil
upon them in the terrible thunderstroke. Green fear took hold of them.
They spilled the wine on the ground from their cups, and none was so   480
    hardy
as to drink, till he had poured to the all-powerful son of Kronos.
They lay down thereafter and took the blessing of slumber.

BOOK EIGHT

Now Dawn the yellow-robed scattered over all the earth. Zeus
who joys in the thunder made an assembly of all the immortals
upon the highest peak of rugged Olympos. There he
spoke to them himself, and the other divinities listened:

5 'Hear me, all you gods and all you goddesses: hear me
while I speak forth what the heart within my breast urges.
Now let no female divinity, nor male god either,
presume to cut across the way of my word, but consent to it
all of you, so that I can make an end in speed of these matters.

10 And any one I perceive against the gods' will attempting
to go among the Trojans and help them, or among the Danaans,
he shall go whipped against his dignity back to Olympos;
or I shall take him and dash him down to the murk of Tartaros,
far below, where the uttermost depth of the pit lies under

15 earth, where there are gates of iron and a brazen doorstone,
as far beneath the house of Hades as from earth the sky lies.
Then he will see how far I am strongest of all the immortals.
Come, you gods, make this endeavour, that you all may learn this.
Let down out of the sky a cord of gold; lay hold of it

20 all you who are gods and all who are goddesses, yet not
even so can you drag down Zeus from the sky to the ground, not
Zeus the high lord of counsel, though you try until you grow weary.
Yet whenever I might strongly be minded to pull you,
I could drag you up, earth and all and sea and all with you,

25 then fetch the golden rope about the horn of Olympos

[182]

and make it fast, so that all once more should dangle in mid air.
So much stronger am I than the gods, and stronger than mortals.'

So he spoke, and all of them stayed stricken to silence,
stunned at his word, for indeed he had spoken to them very strongly.
But now at long last the goddess grey-eyed Athene answered him: 30
'Son of Kronos, our father, o lordliest of the mighty,
we know already your strength and how none can stand up against it.
Yet even so we are sorrowful for the Danaan spearmen
who must fill out an unhappy destiny, and perish.
Still we shall keep out of the fighting, as you command us;   35
yet we will put good counsel in the Argives; if it may help them,
so that not all of them will die because of your anger.'

Then Zeus the gatherer of the clouds smiled at her and answered:
'Tritogeneia, dear daughter, do not lose heart; for I say this
not in outright anger, and my meaning toward you is kindly.'   40

He spoke, and under the chariot harnessed his bronze-shod horses,
flying-footed, with long manes streaming of gold; and he put on
clothing of gold about his own body, and took up the golden
lash, carefully compacted, and climbed up into his chariot,
and whipped them into a run, and they winged their way unreluctant   45
through the space between the earth and the starry heaven.
He came to Ida with all her springs, the mother of wild beasts,
to Gargaron, where was his holy ground and his smoking altar.
There the father of gods and of mortals halted his horses,
and slipped them from their harness, and drifted close mist about them,   50
and himself rejoicing in the pride of his strength sat down on the mountain
looking out over the city of Troy and the ships of the Achaians.

Now the flowing-haired Achaians had taken their dinner
lightly among their shelters, and they put on their armour thereafter;
and on the other side, in the city, the Trojans took up   55
their armour, fewer men, yet minded to stand the encounter
even so, caught in necessity, for their wives and their children.
And all the gates were made open, and the fighting men swept through
          them,
the foot ranks and the horsemen, and the sound grew huge of their onset.

Now as these advancing came to one place and encountered,   60
they dashed their shields together and their spears, and the strength of
armoured men in bronze, and the shields massive in the middle

clashed against each other, and the sound grew huge of the fighting.
There the screaming and the shouts of triumph rose up together
65 of men killing and men killed, and the ground ran blood.

So long as it was early morning and the sacred daylight increasing,
so long the thrown weapons of both took hold and men dropped under
    them.
But when the sun god stood bestriding the middle heaven,
then the father balanced his golden scales, and in them
70 he set two fateful portions of death, which lays men prostrate,
for Trojans, breakers of horses, and bronze-armoured Achaians,
and balanced it by the middle. The Achaians' death-day was heaviest.
There the fates of the Achaians settled down toward the bountiful
earth, while those of the Trojans were lifted into the wide sky;
75 and he himself crashed a great stroke from Ida, and a kindling
flash shot over the people of the Achaians; seeing it
they were stunned, and pale terror took hold of all of them.

Then Idomeneus dared not stand his ground, nor Agamemnon,
nor did the two Aiantes stand, the henchmen of Ares,
80 only Gerenian Nestor stayed, the Achaians' watcher;
not that he would, but his horse was failing, struck by an arrow
from brilliant Alexandros, the lord of lovely-haired Helen;
struck at the point of the head, where the utmost hairs of horses
are grown along the skull, and which is a place most mortal.
85 He reared up in agony as the shaft went into the brain, then
threw the team into confusion writhing upon the bronze point.
Now as the old man hewed away the horse's trace-harness
with a quick sword-cut, meanwhile the fast-running horses of Hektor
came through the flux of the fighting and carried their daring driver,
90 Hektor; and now the old man would have lost his life there, had not
Diomedes of the great war cry sharply perceived him.
He cried out in a terrible voice to rally Odysseus:
'Son of Laertes and seed of Zeus, resourceful Odysseus,
where are you running, turning your back in battle like a coward?
95 Do not let them strike the spear in your back as you run for it,
but stay, so that we can beat back this fierce man from the ancient.'

He spoke, but long-suffering great Odysseus gave no attention
as he swept by on his way to the hollow ships of the Achaians.
The son of Tydeus, alone as he was, went among the champions

and stood before the horses of the old man, the son of Neleus,   100
and uttering his winged words he addressed him: 'Old sir,
in very truth these young fighters are too much for you,
and all your strength is gone, and hard old age is upon you,
your henchman is a man of no worth, and your horses are heavy.
Come then, climb into my chariot, so that you may see   105
what the Trojan horses are like, how they understand their
plain, and how to traverse it in rapid pursuit and withdrawal;
horses I took away from Aineias, who strikes men to terror.
Let the henchmen look after your horses now, while we two
steer these against the Trojans, breakers of horses, so Hektor   110
even may know if my spear also rages in my hands' grip.'
    He spoke, and Nestor the Gerenian horseman obeyed him.
Thereon the two strong henchmen, Sthenelos and the courtly
Eurymedon, looked after the horses of Nestor. The others
both together mounted the chariot of Diomedes.   115
Nestor in his hands took up the glittering reins, then
lashed the horses on, and soon they were close to Hektor,
and as he raged straight forward the son of Tydeus threw at him
and missed his man, but struck the charioteer, his henchman,
Eniopeus, the son of high-hearted Thebaios, striking him   120
in the chest next to the nipple as he gripped the reins of his horses.
He fell out of the chariot, and the fast-footed horses
shied away. And there his life and his strength were scattered.
And bitter sorrow closed over Hektor's heart for his driver,
yet grieving as he did for his friend he left him to lie there,   125
and went on after another bold charioteer; and it was not
long that the horses went lacking a driver, since soon he found one,
Archeptolemos, bold son of Iphitos, and gave into his hands
the reins, and mounted him behind the fast-running horses.
    And now there would have been fighting beyond control, and   130
        destruction,
now they would have been driven and penned like sheep against Ilion,
had not the father of gods and of men sharply perceived them.
He thundered horribly and let loose the shimmering lightning
and dashed it to the ground in front of the horses of Diomedes
and a ghastly blaze of flaming sulphur shot up, and the horses   135
terrified both cringed away against the chariot.

[185]

And the glittering reins escaped out of the hands of Nestor,
and he was afraid in his heart and called out to Diomedes:
'Son of Tydeus, steer now to flight your single-foot horses.
140 Can you not see that the power of Zeus no longer is with you?
For the time Zeus, son of Kronos, gives glory to this man;
for today; hereafter, if he will, he will give it
to us also; no man can beat back the purpose of Zeus, not
even one very strong, since Zeus is by far the greater.'
145   Then in turn Diomedes of the great war cry answered:
'Yes, old sir, all this you have said is fair and orderly.
But this thought comes as a bitter sorrow to my heart and my spirit;
for some day Hektor will say openly before the Trojans:
"The son of Tydeus, running before me, fled to his vessels."
150 So he will vaunt; and then let the wide earth open beneath me.'
    Nestor the Gerenian horseman spoke to him in answer:
'Ah me, son of brave Tydeus; what a thing to have spoken.
If Hektor calls you a coward and a man of no strength, then
the Trojans and Dardanians will never believe him,
155 nor will the wives of the high-hearted Trojan warriors,
    they whose husbands you hurled in the dust in the pride of their
        manhood.'
    So he spoke, and turned to flight the single-foot horses
back again into the rout; and now the Trojans and Hektor
with unearthly clamour showered their baneful missiles upon them,
160 and tall Hektor of the shining helm called out in a great voice:
'Son of Tydeus, beyond others the fast-mounted Danaans honoured you
with pride of place, the choice meats and the filled wine-cups.
But now they will disgrace you, who are no better than a woman.
Down with you, you poor doll. You shall not storm our battlements
165 with me giving way before you, you shall not carry our women
home in your ships; before that comes I will give you your destiny.'
    He spoke, and the son of Tydeus pondered doubtfully, whether
to turn his horses about and match his strength against Hektor.
Three times in his heart and spirit he pondered turning,
170 and three times from the hills of Ida Zeus of the counsels
thundered, giving a sign to the Trojans that the battle was turning.
But Hektor called afar in a great voice to the Trojans:
'Trojans, Lykians and Dardanians who fight at close quarters,

be men now, dear friends, remember your furious valour.
I see that the son of Kronos has bowed his head and assented   175
to my high glory and success, but granted the Danaans
disaster: fools, who designed with care these fortifications,
flimsy things, not worth a thought, which will not beat my strength
back, but lightly my horses will leap the ditch they have dug them.
But after I have come beside their hollow ships, let there   180
be some who will remember to bring me ravening fire,
so that I can set their ships on fire, and cut down
the very Argives mazed in the smoke at the side of their vessels.'
    So he spoke, and called aloud to his horses, and spoke to them:
'Xanthos and you, Podargos, Aithon and Lampos the shining,   185
now repay me for all that loving care in abundance
Andromache the daughter of high-hearted Eëtion
gave you: the sweet-hearted wheat before all the others
and mixed wine with it for you to drink, when her heart inclined to it,
as for me, who am proud that I am her young husband.   190
Follow close now and be rapid, so we may capture
the shield of Nestor, whose high fame goes up to the sky now,
how it is all of gold, the shield itself and the cross-rods;
and strip from the shoulders of Diomedes, breaker of horses,
that elaborate corselet that Hephaistos wrought with much toil.   195
Could we capture these two things, I might hope the Achaians
might embark this very night on their fast-running vessels.'
    So he spoke, boasting, and the lady Hera was angry,
and started upon her throne, and tall Olympos was shaken,
and she spoke straight out to the great god Poseidon: 200
'For shame, now, far-powerful shaker of the earth. In your breast
the heart takes no sorrow for the Danaans who are dying,
they who at Helike and at Aigai bring you offerings
numerous and delightful. Do you then plan that they conquer.
For if all of us who stand by the Danaans only were willing   205
to hurl back the Trojans and hold off Zeus of the broad brows,
he would be desperate, there where he sits by himself on Ida.'
    Deeply troubled, the powerful shaker of the earth answered her
'Hera, reckless of word, what sort of thing have you spoken?
I would not be willing that all the rest of us fight with   210
Zeus, the son of Kronos, since he is so much the greater.'

Now as these two were talking thus to each other, meanwhile
for those others, all that space which the ditch of the wall held
off from the ships was filled with armoured men and with horses
215 penned there; and he who penned them was a man like the rapid war god,
Hektor, Priam's son, since Zeus was giving him glory.
And now he might have kindled their balanced ships with the hot flame,
had not the lady Hera set it in Agamemnon's
heart to rush in with speed himself and stir the Achaians.
220 He went on his way beside the Achaians' ships and their shelters
holding up in his heavy hand the great coloured mantle,
and stood beside the black huge-hollowed ship of Odysseus,
which lay in the midmost, so that he could call out to both sides,
either toward the shelters of Telamonian Aias,
225 or toward Achilleus, since these two had drawn their balanced ships up
at the utter ends, sure of the strength of their hands and their courage.
He lifted his voice and called in a piercing cry to the Danaans:
'Shame, you Argives, poor nonentities splendid to look on.
Where are our high words gone, when we said that we were the bravest?
230 those words you spoke before all in hollow vaunting at Lemnos
when you were filled with abundant meat of the high-horned oxen
and drank from the great bowls filled to the brim with wine, how each
        man
could stand up against a hundred or even two hundred Trojans
in the fighting; now we together cannot match one of them,
235 Hektor, who must presently kindle our ships with the hot fire.
Father Zeus, is it one of our too strong kings you have stricken
in this disaster now, and stripped him of his high honour?
For I say that never did I pass by your fair-wrought altar
in my benched ships when I came here on this desperate journey;
240 but on all altars I burned the fat and the thighs of oxen
in my desire to sack the strong-walled city of the Trojans.
Still, Zeus, bring to pass at least this thing that I pray for.
Let our men at least get clear and escape, and let not
the Achaians be thus beaten down at the hands of the Trojans.'
245   He spoke thus, and as he wept the father took pity upon him
and bent his head, that the people should stay alive, and not perish.
Straightway he sent down the most lordly of birds, an eagle,
with a fawn, the young of the running deer, caught in his talons,

who cast down the fawn beside Zeus' splendid altar
where the Achaians wrought their devotions to Zeus of the Voices.   250
They, when they saw the bird and knew it was Zeus who sent it,
remembered once again their warcraft, and turned on the Trojans.

　　Then, many as the Danaans were, there was no man among them
could claim he held his fast horses ahead of the son of Tydeus
to drive them once more across the ditch and fight at close quarters,   255
but he was far the first to kill a chief man of the Trojans,
Phradmon's son, Agelaos, as he turned his team to escape him.
For in his back even as he was turning the spear fixed
between the shoulders and was driven on through the chest beyond it.
He fell from the chariot, and his armour clattered upon him.   260

　　After him came the Atreidai, Menelaos and Agamemnon,
and the two Aiantes gathering their fierce strength about them,
and with them Idomeneus and Idomeneus' companion
Meriones, a match for the murderous lord of battles,
and after these Eurypylos, the glorious son of Euaimon;   265
and ninth came Teukros, bending into position the curved bow,
and took his place in the shelter of Telamonian Aias'
shield, as Aias lifted the shield to take him. The hero
would watch, whenever in the throng he had struck some man with an
　　arrow,
and as the man dropped and died where he was stricken, the archer   270
would run back again, like a child to the arms of his mother,
to Aias, who would hide him in the glittering shield's protection.

　　Then which of the Trojans first did Teukros the blameless strike down?
Orsilochos first of all, and Ormenos, and Ophelestes,
Daitor and Chromios, and Lykophontes the godlike,   275
and Amopaon, Polyaimon's son, and Melanippos.
All these he felled to the bountiful earth in close succession.
Agamemnon the lord of men was glad as he watched him
laying waste from the strong bow the Trojan battalions;
he went over and stood beside him and spoke a word to him: 280
'Telamonian Teukros, dear heart, o lord of your people,
strike so; thus you may be a light given to the Danaans,
and to Telamon your father, who cherished you when you were little,
and, bastard as you were, looked after you in his own house.
Bring him into glory, though he is far away; and for my part,   285

I will tell you this, and it will be a thing accomplished:
if ever Zeus who holds the aegis and Athene grant me
to sack outright the strong-founded citadel of Ilion,
first after myself I will put into your hands some great gift
290 of honour; a tripod, or two horses and the chariot with them,
or else a woman, who will go up into the same bed with you.'
    Then in answer to him again spoke Teukros the blameless:
'Son of Atreus, most lordly: must you then drive me, who am eager
myself, as it is? Never, so far as the strength is in me,
295 have I stopped, since we began driving the Trojans back upon Ilion;
since then I have been lurking here with my bow, to strike down
fighters. And by this I have shot eight long-flanged arrows,
and all of them were driven into the bodies of young men,
fighters; yet still I am not able to hit this mad dog.'
300   He spoke, and let fly another shaft from the bowstring,
straight for Hektor, and all his heart was straining to hit him;
but missed his man, and struck down instead a strong son of Priam,
Gorgythion the blameless, hit in the chest by an arrow;
Gorgythion whose mother was lovely Kastianeira,
305 Priam's bride from Aisyme, with the form of a goddess.
He bent drooping his head to one side, as a garden poppy
bends beneath the weight of its yield and the rains of springtime;
so his head bent slack to one side beneath the helm's weight.
    But Teukros now let fly another shaft from the bowstring,
310 straight for Hektor, and all his heart was straining to hit him,
yet missed his man once again as Apollo faltered his arrow,
and struck Archeptolemos, bold charioteer of Hektor,
in the chest next to the nipple as he charged into the fighting.
He fell out of the chariot, and the fast-footed horses
315 shied away. And there his life and his strength were scattered.
And bitter sorrow closed over Hektor's heart for his driver,
yet grieving as he did for his friend he left him to lie there,
and called to his brother Kebriones who stood near to take up
the reins of the horses, nor did he disobey him. But Hektor
320 himself vaulted down to the ground from the shining chariot
crying a terrible cry and in his hand caught up a great stone,
and went straight for Teukros, heart urgent to hit him. Now Teukros
had drawn a bitter arrow out of his quiver, and laid it

along the bowstring, but as he drew the shaft by his shoulder,
there where between neck and chest the collar-bone interposes,   325
and this is a spot most mortal; in this place shining-helmed Hektor
struck him in all his fury with the jagged boulder, smashing
the sinew, and all his arm at the wrist was deadened.
He dropped to one knee and stayed, and the bow fell from his hand. Aias
was not forgetful of his fallen brother, but running   330
stood bestriding him and covered him under the great shield.
Thereon Mekisteus, son of Echios, and brilliant Alastor,
two staunch companions, stooping beneath it, caught up Teukros
and carried him, groaning heavily, to the hollow vessels.

Now once again the Olympian filled the Trojans with fury   335
and they piled the Achaians straight backward against the deep ditch,
as Hektor ranged in their foremost ranks in the pride of his great strength.
As when some hunting hound in the speed of his feet pursuing
a wild boar or a lion snaps from behind at his quarters
or flanks, but watches for the beast to turn upon him, so Hektor   340
followed close on the heels of the flowing-haired Achaians,
killing ever the last of the men; and they fled in terror.
But after they had crossed back over the ditch and the sharp stakes
in flight, and many had gone down under the hands of the Trojans,
they reined in and stood fast again beside their ships, calling   345
aloud upon each other, and to all of the gods uplifting
their hands each man of them cried out his prayers in a great voice,
while Hektor, wearing the stark eyes of a Gorgon, or murderous
Ares, wheeled about at the edge his bright-maned horses.

Now seeing them the goddess of the white arms, Hera, took pity   350
and immediately she spoke to Pallas Athene her winged words:
'For shame, daughter of Zeus who wears the aegis! no longer
shall we care for the Danaans in their uttermost hour of destruction?
These must then fill out an evil destiny, and perish
in the wind of one man's fury where none can stand now against him,   355
Hektor, Priam's son, who has wrought so much evil already.'
Then in turn the goddess grey-eyed Athene answered her:
'Yet even this man would have his life and strength taken from him,
dying under the hands of the Argives in his own country;
but it is my father who is so furious in his heart of evil.   360
He is hard, and forever wicked; he crosses my high hopes,

nor remembers at all those many times I rescued his own son,
Herakles, when the tasks of Eurystheus were too much for his strength.
And time and again he would cry out aloud to the heavens,
365 and Zeus would send me down in speed from the sky to help him.
If in the wiliness of my heart I had had thoughts like his,
when Herakles was sent down to Hades of the Gates, to hale back
from the Kingdom of the Dark the hound of the grisly death god,
never would he have got clear of the steep-dripping Stygian water.
370 Yet now Zeus hates me, and is bent to the wishes of Thetis
who kissed his knees and stroked his chin in her hand, and entreated
that he give honour to Achilleus, the sacker of cities.
Yet time shall be when he calls me again his dear girl of the grey eyes.
So then: do you put under their harness our single-foot horses
375 while I go back into the house of Zeus, the lord of the aegis,
and arm me in my weapons of war. So shall I discover
whether the son of Priam, Hektor of the shining helmet,
will feel joy to see us apparent on the outworks of battle,
or see if some Trojan give the dogs and the birds their desire
380 with fat and flesh, struck down beside the ships of the Achaians.'
    She spoke, nor failed to persuade the goddess Hera of the white arms.
And she, Hera, exalted goddess, daughter of Kronos
the mighty, went away to harness the gold-bridled horses.
Now in turn Athene, daughter of Zeus of the aegis,
385 beside the threshold of her father slipped off her elaborate
dress which she herself had wrought with her hands' patience,
and now assuming the war tunic of Zeus who gathers
the clouds, she armed herself in her gear for the dismal fighting.
She set her feet in the blazing chariot, and took up a spear,
390 heavy, huge, thick, wherewith she beats down the battalions of fighting
men, against whom she of the mighty father is angered.
Hera laid the lash swiftly on the horses; and moving
of themselves groaned the gates of the sky that the Hours guarded,
those Hours to whose charge is given the huge sky and Olympos
395 to open up the dense darkness or again to close it.
Through the way between they held the speed of their goaded horses.
    But Zeus father, watching from Ida, was angered terribly
and stirred Iris of the golden wings to run with his message:
'Go forth, Iris the swift, turn them back again, let them not reach me,

since we would close in fighting thus that would be unseemly.   400
For I will say this straight out, and it will be a thing accomplished:
I will lame beneath the harness their fast-running horses,
and hurl the gods from the driver's place, and smash their chariot;
and not in the circle of ten returning years shall they be whole
of the wounds where the stroke of the lightning hits them; so that   405
the grey-eyed goddess may know when it is her father she fights with.
Yet with Hera I am not so angry, neither indignant,
since it is ever her way to cross the commands that I give her.'
     He spoke, and Iris, storm-footed, rose with his message
and took her way from the peaks of Ida to tall Olympos,   410
and at the utmost gates of many-folded Olympos
met and stayed them, and spoke the word that Zeus had given her:
'Where so furious? How can your hearts so storm within you?
The son of Kronos will not let you stand by the Argives.
Since Zeus has uttered this threat and will make it a thing accomplished: 415
that he will lame beneath the harness your fast-running horses,
and hurl yourselves from the driver's place, and smash your chariot;
and not in the circle of ten returning years would you be whole
of the wounds where the stroke of the lightning hits you; so that
you may know, grey-eyed goddess, when it is your father you fight with.   420
Yes, you, bold brazen wench, are audacious indeed, if truly
you dare to lift up your gigantic spear in the face of your father.
Yet with Hera he is not so angry, neither indignant,
since it is ever her way to cross the commands he gives her.'
     So Iris the swift-footed spoke and went away from them,   425
and now Hera spoke a word to Pallas Athene:
'Alas, daughter of Zeus of the aegis: I can no longer
let us fight in the face of Zeus for the sake of mortals.
Let one of them perish then, let another live, as their fortune
wills; let him, as is his right and as his heart pleases,   430
work out whatever decrees he will on Danaans and Trojans.'
     So she spoke, and turned back again her single-foot horses,
and the Hours set free their flowing-maned horses from the harness,
and tethered them at their mangers that were piled with ambrosia
and leaned the chariot against the shining inward wall. Meanwhile   435
the goddesses themselves took their place on the golden couches
among the other immortals, their hearts deep grieving within them.

Now father Zeus steered back from Ida his strong-wheeled chariot
and horses to Olympos, and came among the gods' sessions,
440 while for him the famed shaker of the earth set free his horses,
and put the chariot on its stand, with a cloth spread over it.
Then Zeus himself of the wide brows took his place on the golden
throne, as underneath his feet tall Olympos was shaken.
These two alone, Hera and Athene, stayed seated apart aside
445 from Zeus, and would not speak to him, nor ask him a question;
but he knew the whole matter within his heart, and spoke to them.
'Why then are you two sorrowful, Athene and Hera?
Surely in the battle where men win glory you were not wearied
out, destroying those Trojans on whom you have set your grim wrath.
450 In the whole account, such is my strength and my hand so invincible,
not all the gods who are on Olympos could turn me backward,
but before this the trembling took hold of your shining bodies,
before you could look upon the fighting and war's work of sorrow;
for I will say straight out, and it would now be a thing accomplished:
455 once hit in your car by the lightning stroke you could never
have come back to Olympos, where is the place of the immortals.'

So he spoke; and Athene and Hera muttered, since they were
sitting close to each other, devising evil for the Trojans.
Still Athene stayed silent and said nothing, but only
460 sulked at Zeus her father, and savage anger took hold of her.
But the heart of Hera could not contain her anger, and she spoke forth:
'Majesty, son of Kronos, what sort of thing have you spoken?
We know well already your strength, how it is no small thing.
Yet even so we are sorrowful for the Danaan spearmen
465 who must fill out an unhappy destiny, and perish.
Still we shall keep out of the fighting, as you command us;
yet we will put good counsel in the Argives, if it may help them;
so that not all of them will die because of your anger.'

Zeus who gathers the clouds spoke to her again in answer:
470 'Tomorrow at the dawning, lady Hera of the ox eyes,
you will see, if you have the heart, a still mightier son of Kronos
perishing the ranged numbers of Argive spearmen.
For Hektor the huge will not sooner be stayed from his fighting
until there stirs by the ships the swift-footed son of Peleus
475 on that day when they shall fight by the sterns of the beached ships

in the narrow place of necessity over fallen Patroklos.
This is the way it is fated to be; and for you and your anger
I care not; not if you stray apart to the undermost limits
of earth and sea, where Iapetos and Kronos seated
have no shining of the sun god Hyperion to delight them   480
nor winds' delight, but Tartaros stands deeply about them;
not even if you reach that place in your wandering shall I
care for your sulks; since there is nothing more shameless than you are.'
    So he spoke, and Hera of the white arms gave him no answer.
And now the shining light of the sun was dipped in the Ocean   485
trailing black night across the grain-giving land. For the Trojans
the daylight sank against their will, but for the Achaians
sweet and thrice-supplicated was the coming on of the dark night.
    Now glorious Hektor held an assembly of all the Trojans,
taking them aside from the ships, by a swirling river   490
on clean ground, where there showed a space not cumbered with corpses.
They stepped to the ground from behind their horses and listened to
      Hektor
the loved of Zeus, and the words he spoke to them. He in his hand held
the eleven-cubit-long spear, whose shaft was tipped with a shining
bronze spearhead, and a ring of gold was hooped to hold it.   495
Leaning upon this spear he spoke his words to the Trojans:
'Trojans and Dardanians and companions in arms: hear me.
Now I had thought that, destroying the ships and all the Achaians,
we might take our way back once more to windy Ilion,
but the darkness came too soon, and this beyond all else rescued   500
the Argives and their vessels along the beach where the sea breaks.
But now let us give way to black night's persuasion; let us
make ready our evening meal, and as for your flowing-maned horses,
set them free from their harness, and cast down fodder before them.
And lead forth also out of the city oxen and fat sheep   505
in all speed, and convey out also the kindly sweet wine
with food out of our houses. And heap many piles of firewood,
so that all night long and until the young dawn appears
we may burn many fires, and the glare go up into heaven;
so that not in the night-time the flowing-haired Achaians   510
may set out to run for home over the sea's wide ridges.
No: not thus in their own good time must they take to their vessels,

but in such a way that a man of them at home will still nurse
his wound, the place where he has been hit with an arrow or sharp spear
515 springing to his ship; so that another may shrink hereafter
from bringing down fearful war on the Trojans, breakers of horses.
And let the heralds Zeus loves give orders about the city
for the boys who are in their first youth and the grey-browed elders
to take stations on the god-founded bastions that circle the city;
520 and as for the women, have our wives, each one in her own house,
kindle a great fire; let there be a watch kept steadily
lest a sudden attack get into the town when the fighters have left it.
Let it be thus, high-hearted men of Troy, as I tell you.
Let that word that has been spoken now be a strong one,
525 with that which I speak at dawn to the Trojans, breakers of horses.
For in good hope I pray to Zeus and the other immortals
that we may drive from our place these dogs swept into destruction
whom the spirits of death have carried here on their black ships.
Now for the night we shall keep watch on ourselves, and tomorrow
530 early, before dawn shows, shall arm ourselves in our weapons
and beside their hollow vessels waken the bitter war god;
and I shall know if the son of Tydeus, strong Diomedes,
will force me back from the ships against the wall, or whether I
shall cut him down with the bronze and take home the blooded war-spoils.
535 Tomorrow he will learn his own strength, if he can stand up to
my spear's advance; but sooner than this, I think, in the foremost
he will go down under the stroke, and many companions about him
as the sun goes up into tomorrow. Oh, if I only
could be as this in all my days immortal and ageless
540 and be held in honour as Athene and Apollo are honoured
as surely as this oncoming day brings evil to the Argives.'
    So Hektor spoke among them, and the Trojans shouted approval.
And they set free their sweating horses from under the harness
and tethered them by the reins, each one by his own chariot.
545 They led forth also out of the city oxen and fat sheep
in all speed, and conveyed out also the kindly sweet wine,
with food out of their houses, and heaped many piles of firewood.
They accomplished likewise full sacrifices before the immortals,
and the winds wafted the savour aloft from the plain to the heavens
550 in its fragrance; and yet the blessed gods took no part of it.

They would not; so hateful to them was sacred Ilion,
and Priam, and the city of Priam of the strong ash spear.
   So with hearts made high these sat night-long by the outworks
of battle, and their watchfires blazed numerous about them.
As when in the sky the stars about the moon's shining   555
are seen in all their glory, when the air has fallen to stillness,
and all the high places of the hills are clear, and the shoulders out-jutting,
and the deep ravines, as endless bright air spills from the heavens
and all the stars are seen, to make glad the heart of the shepherd;
such in their numbers blazed the watchfires the Trojans were burning   560
between the waters of Xanthos and the ships, before Ilion.
A thousand fires were burning there in the plain, and beside each
one sat fifty men in the flare of the blazing firelight.
And standing each beside his chariot, champing white barley
and oats, the horses waited for the dawn to mount to her high place.   565

So the Trojans held their night watches. Meanwhile immortal
Panic, companion of cold Terror, gripped the Achaians
as all their best were stricken with grief that passes endurance.
As two winds rise to shake the sea where the fish swarm, Boreas
5 and Zephyros, north wind and west, that blow from Thraceward,
suddenly descending, and the darkened water is gathered
to crests, and far across the salt water scatters the seaweed;
so the heart in the breast of each Achaian was troubled.
    And the son of Atreus, stricken at heart with the great sorrow,
10 went among his heralds the clear-spoken and told them
to summon calling by name each man into the assembly
but with no outcry, and he himself was at work with the foremost.
They took their seats in assembly, dispirited, and Agamemnon
stood up before them, shedding tears, like a spring dark-running
15 that down the face of a rock impassable drips its dim water.
So, groaning heavily, Agamemnon spoke to the Argives:
'Friends, who are leaders of the Argives and keep their counsel:
Zeus son of Kronos has caught me badly in bitter futility.
He is hard: who before this time promised me and consented
20 that I might sack strong-walled Ilion and sail homeward.
Now he has devised a vile deception and bids me go back
to Argos in dishonour having lost many of my people.
Such is the way it will be pleasing to Zeus, who is too strong,
who before now has broken the crests of many cities
25 and will break them again, since his power is beyond all others.

Come then, do as I say, let us all be won over; let us
run away with our ships to the beloved land of our fathers
since no longer now shall we capture Troy of the wide ways.'
    So he spoke, and all of them stayed stricken to silence.
For some time the sons of the Achaians said nothing in sorrow;   30
but at long last Diomedes of the great war cry addressed them:
'Son of Atreus: I will be first to fight with your folly,
as is my right, lord, in this assembly; then do not be angered.
I was the first of the Danaans whose valour you slighted
and said I was unwarlike and without courage. The young men   35
of the Argives know all these things, and the elders know it.
The son of devious-devising Kronos has given you
gifts in two ways: with the sceptre he gave you honour beyond all,
but he did not give you a heart, and of all power this is the greatest.
Sir, sir, can you really believe the sons of the Achaians   40
are so unwarlike and so weak of their hearts as you call them?
But if in truth your own heart is so set upon going,
go. The way is there, and next to the water are standing
your ships that came—so many of them!—with you from Mykenai,
and yet the rest of the flowing-haired Achaians will stay here   45
until we have sacked the city of Troy; let even these also
run away with their ships to the beloved land of their fathers,
still we two, Sthenelos and I, will fight till we witness
the end of Ilion; for it was with God that we made our way hither.'
    So he spoke, and all the sons of the Achaians shouted   50
acclaim for the word of Diomedes, breaker of horses.
And now Nestor the horseman stood forth among them and spoke to them:
'Son of Tydeus, beyond others you are strong in battle,
and in counsel also are noblest among all men of your own age.
Not one man of all the Achaians will belittle your words nor   55
speak against them. Yet you have not made complete your argument,
since you are a young man still and could even be my own son
and my youngest born of all; yet still you argue in wisdom
with the Argive kings, since all you have spoken was spoken fairly.
But let me speak, since I can call myself older than you are,   60
and go through the whole matter, since there is none who can dishonour
the thing I say, not even powerful Agamemnon.
Out of all brotherhood, outlawed, homeless shall be that man

who longs for all the horror of fighting among his own people.
65 But now let us give way to the darkness of night, and let us
make ready our evening meal; and let the guards severally
take their stations by the ditch we have dug outside the ramparts.
This I would enjoin upon our young men; but thereafter
do you, son of Atreus, take command, since you are our kingliest.
70 Divide a feast among the princes; it befits you, it is not
unbecoming. Our shelters are filled with wine that the Achaian
ships carry day by day from Thrace across the wide water.
All hospitality is for you; you are lord over many.
When many assemble together follow him who advises
75 the best counsel, for in truth there is need for all the Achaians
of good close counsel, since now close to our ships the enemy
burn their numerous fires. What man could be cheered to see this?
Here is the night that will break our army, or else will preserve it.'
So he spoke, and they listened hard to him, and obeyed him,
80 and the sentries went forth rapidly in their armour, gathering
about Nestor's son Thrasymedes, shepherd of the people,
and about Askalaphos and Ialmenos, sons both of Ares,
about Meriones and Aphareus and Deïpyros
and about the son of Kreion, Lykomedes the brilliant.
85 There were seven leaders of the sentinels, and with each one a hundred
fighting men followed gripping in their hands the long spears.
They took position in the space between the ditch and the rampart,
and there they kindled their fires and each made ready his supper.
But the son of Atreus led the assembled lords of the Achaians
90 to his own shelter, and set before them the feast in abundance.
They put their hands to the good things that lay ready before them.
But when they had put away their desire for eating and drinking,
the aged man began to weave his counsel before them
first, Nestor, whose advice had shown best before this.
95 He in kind intention toward all stood forth and addressed them:
'Son of Atreus, most lordly and king of men, Agamemnon,
with you I will end, with you I will make my beginning, since you
are lord over many people, and Zeus has given into your hand
the sceptre and rights of judgment, to be king over the people.
100 It is yours therefore to speak a word, yours also to listen,
and grant the right to another also, when his spirit stirs him

to speak for our good. All shall be yours when you lead the way. Still
I will speak in the way it seems best to my mind, and no one
shall have in his mind any thought that is better than this one
that I have in my mind either now or long before now   105
ever since that day, illustrious, when you went from the shelter
of angered Achilleus, taking by force the girl Briseis
against the will of the rest of us, since I for my part
urged you strongly not to, but you, giving way to your proud heart's
anger, dishonoured a great man, one whom the immortals   110
honour, since you have taken his prize and keep it. But let us
even now think how we can make this good and persuade him
with words of supplication and with the gifts of friendship.'
    Then in turn the lord of men Agamemnon spoke to him:
'Aged sir, this was no lie when you spoke of my madness.   115
I was mad, I myself will not deny it. Worth many
fighters is that man whom Zeus in his heart loves, as now
he has honoured this man and beaten down the Achaian people.
But since I was mad, in the persuasion of my heart's evil,
I am willing to make all good, and give back gifts in abundance.   120
Before you all I will count off my gifts in their splendour:
seven unfired tripods; ten talents' weight of gold; twenty
shining cauldrons; and twelve horses, strong, race-competitors
who have won prizes in the speed of their feet. That man would not be
poor in possessions, to whom were given all these have won me,   125
nor be unpossessed of dearly honoured gold, were he given
all the prizes these single-foot horses have won for me.
I will give him seven women of Lesbos, the work of whose hands is
blameless, whom when he himself captured strong-founded Lesbos
I chose, and who in their beauty surpassed the races of women.   130
I will give him these, and with them shall go the one I took from him,
the daughter of Briseus. And to all this I will swear a great oath
that I never entered into her bed and never lay with her
as is natural for human people, between men and women.
All these gifts shall be his at once; but again, if hereafter   135
the gods grant that we storm and sack the great city of Priam,
let him go to his ship and load it deep as he pleases
with gold and bronze, when we Achaians divide the war spoils,
and let him choose for himself twenty of the Trojan women

140 who are the loveliest of all after Helen of Argos.
And if we come back to Achaian Argos, pride of the tilled land,
he may be my son-in-law; I will honour him with Orestes
my growing son, who is brought up there in abundant luxury.
Since, as I have three daughters there in my strong-built castle,
145 Chrysothemis and Laodike and Iphianassa,
let him lead away the one of these that he likes, with no bride-price,
to the house of Peleus, and with the girl I will grant him as dowry
many gifts, such as no man ever gave with his daughter.
I will grant to him seven citadels, strongly settled:
150 Kardamyle, and Enope, and Hire of the grasses,
Pherai the sacrosanct, and Antheia deep in the meadows,
with Aipeia the lovely and Pedasos of the vineyards.
All these lie near the sea, at the bottom of sandy Pylos,
and men live among them rich in cattle and rich in sheepflocks,
155 who will honour him as if he were a god with gifts given
and fulfil his prospering decrees underneath his sceptre.
All this I will bring to pass for him, if he changes from his anger.
Let him give way. For Hades gives not way, and is pitiless,
and therefore he among all the gods is most hateful to mortals.
160 And let him yield place to me, inasmuch as I am the kinglier
and inasmuch as I can call myself born the elder.'
　　Thereupon the Gerenian horseman Nestor answered him:
'Son of Atreus, most lordly and king of men, Agamemnon,
none could scorn any longer these gifts you offer to Achilleus
165 the king. Come, let us choose and send some men, who in all speed
will go to the shelter of Achilleus, the son of Peleus;
or come, the men on whom my eye falls, let these take the duty.
First of all let Phoinix, beloved of Zeus, be their leader,
and after him take Aias the great, and brilliant Odysseus,
170 and of the heralds let Odios and Eurybates go with them.
Bring also water for their hands, and bid them keep words of good
　　　omen,
so we may pray to Zeus, son of Kronos, if he will have pity.'
　　So he spoke, and the word he spoke was pleasing to all of them.
And the heralds brought water at once, and poured it over
175 their hands, and the young men filled the mixing-bowl with pure wine
and passed it to all, pouring first a libation in goblets.

[202]

Then when they had poured out wine, and drunk as much as their hearts
    wished,
they set out from the shelter of Atreus' son, Agamemnon.
And the Gerenian horseman Nestor gave them much instruction,
looking eagerly at each, and most of all at Odysseus,   180
to try hard, so that they might win over the blameless Peleion.
    So these two walked along the strand of the sea deep-thundering
with many prayers to the holder and shaker of the earth, that they
might readily persuade the great heart of Aiakides.
Now they came beside the shelters and ships of the Myrmidons   185
and they found Achilleus delighting his heart in a lyre, clear-sounding,
splendid and carefully wrought, with a bridge of silver upon it,
which he won out of the spoils when he ruined Eëtion's city.
With this he was pleasuring his heart, and singing of men's fame,
as Patroklos was sitting over against him, alone, in silence,   190
watching Aiakides and the time he would leave off singing.
Now these two came forward, as brilliant Odysseus led them,
and stood in his presence. Achilleus rose to his feet in amazement
holding the lyre as it was, leaving the place where he was sitting.
In the same way Patroklos, when he saw the men come, stood up.   195
And in greeting Achilleus the swift of foot spoke to them:
'Welcome. You are my friends who have come, and greatly I need you,
who even to this my anger are dearest of all the Achaians.'
    So brilliant Achilleus spoke, and guided them forward,
and caused them to sit down on couches with purple coverlets   200
and at once called over to Patroklos who was not far from him:
'Son of Menoitios, set up a mixing-bowl that is bigger,
and mix us stronger drink, and make ready a cup for each man,
since these who have come beneath my roof are the men that I love best.'
    So he spoke, and Patroklos obeyed his beloved companion,   205
and tossed down a great chopping-block into the firelight,
and laid upon it the back of a sheep, and one of a fat goat,
with the chine of a fatted pig edged thick with lard, and for him
Automedon held the meats, and brilliant Achilleus carved them,
and cut it well into pieces and spitted them, as meanwhile   210
Menoitios' son, a man like a god, made the fire blaze greatly.
But when the fire had burned itself out, and the flames had died down,
he scattered the embers apart, and extended the spits across them

lifting them to the andirons, and sprinkled the meats with divine salt.

215 Then when he had roasted all, and spread the food on the platters,
Patroklos took the bread and set it out on a table
in fair baskets, while Achilleus served the meats. Thereafter
he himself sat over against the godlike Odysseus
against the further wall, and told his companion, Patroklos,

220 to sacrifice to the gods; and he threw the firstlings in the fire.
They put their hands to the good things that lay ready before them.
But when they had put aside their desire for eating and drinking,
Aias nodded to Phoinix, and brilliant Odysseus saw it,
and filled a cup with wine, and lifted it to Achilleus:

225 'Your health, Achilleus. You have no lack of your equal portion
either within the shelter of Atreus' son, Agamemnon,
nor here now in your own. We have good things in abundance
to feast on; here it is not the desirable feast we think of,
but a trouble all too great, beloved of Zeus, that we look on

230 and are afraid. There is doubt if we save our strong-benched vessels
or if they will be destroyed, unless you put on your war strength.
The Trojans in their pride, with their far-renowned companions,
have set up an encampment close by the ships and the rampart,
and lit many fires along their army, and think no longer

235 of being held, but rather to drive in upon the black ships.
And Zeus, son of Kronos, lightens upon their right hand, showing them
portents of good, while Hektor in the huge pride of his strength rages
irresistibly, reliant on Zeus, and gives way to no one
neither god nor man, but the strong fury has descended upon him.

240 He prays now that the divine Dawn will show most quickly,
since he threatens to shear the uttermost horns from the ship-sterns,
to light the ships themselves with ravening fire, and to cut down
the Achaians themselves as they stir from the smoke beside them.
All this I fear terribly in my heart, lest immortals

245 accomplish all these threats, and lest for us it be destiny
to die here in Troy, far away from horse-pasturing Argos.
Up, then! if you are minded, late though it be, to rescue
the afflicted sons of the Achaians from the Trojan onslaught.
It will be an affliction to you hereafter, there will be no remedy

250 found to heal the evil thing when it has been done. No, beforehand
take thought to beat the evil day aside from the Danaans.

Dear friend, surely thus your father Peleus advised you
that day when he sent you away to Agamemnon from Phthia:
"My child, for the matter of strength, Athene and Hera will give it
if it be their will, but be it yours to hold fast in your bosom   255
the anger of the proud heart, for consideration is better.
Keep from the bad complication of quarrel, and all the more for this
the Argives will honour you, both their younger men and their elders."
So the old man advised, but you have forgotten. Yet even now
stop, and give way from the anger that hurts the heart. Agamemnon   260
offers you worthy recompense if you change from your anger.
Come then, if you will, listen to me, while I count off for you
all the gifts in his shelter that Agamemnon has promised:
Seven unfired tripods; ten talents' weight of gold; twenty
shining cauldrons; and twelve horses, strong, race-competitors   265
who have won prizes in the speed of their feet. That man would not be
poor in possessions, to whom were given all these have won him,
nor be unpossessed of dearly honoured gold, were he given
all the prizes Agamemnon's horses won in their speed for him.
He will give you seven women of Lesbos, the work of whose hands   270
is blameless, whom when you yourself captured strong-founded Lesbos
he chose, and who in their beauty surpassed the races of women.
He will give you these, and with them shall go the one he took from you,
the daughter of Briseus. And to all this he will swear a great oath
that he never entered into her bed and never lay with her   275
as is natural for human people, between men and women.
All these gifts shall be yours at once; but again, if hereafter
the gods grant that we storm and sack the great city of Priam,
you may go to your ship and load it deep as you please with
gold and bronze, when we Achaians divide the war spoils,   280
and you may choose for yourself twenty of the Trojan women,
who are the loveliest of all after Helen of Argos.
And if we come back to Achaian Argos, pride of the tilled land,
you could be his son-in-law; he would honour you with Orestes,
his growing son, who is brought up there in abundant luxury.   285
Since, as he has three daughters there in his strong-built castle,
Chrysothemis and Laodike and Iphianassa,
you may lead away the one of these that you like, with no bride-price,
to the house of Peleus; and with the girl he will grant you as dowry

290 many gifts, such as no man ever gave with his daughter.
He will grant you seven citadels, strongly settled:
Kardamyle and Enope and Hire of the grasses,
Pherai the sacrosanct, and Antheia deep in the meadows,
with Aipeia the lovely, and Pedasos of the vineyards.
295 All these lie near the sea, at the bottom of sandy Pylos,
and men live among them rich in cattle and rich in sheepflocks,
who will honour you as if you were a god with gifts given
and fulfil your prospering decrees underneath your sceptre.
All this he will bring to pass for you, if you change from your anger.
300 But if the son of Atreus is too much hated in your heart,
himself and his gifts, at least take pity on all the other
Achaians, who are afflicted along the host, and will honour you
as a god. You may win very great glory among them.
For now you might kill Hektor, since he would come very close to you
305 with the wicked fury upon him, since he thinks there is not his equal
among the rest of the Danaans the ships carried hither.'
    Then in answer to him spoke Achilleus of the swift feet:
'Son of Laertes and seed of Zeus, resourceful Odysseus:
without consideration for you I must make my answer,
310 the way I think, and the way it will be accomplished, that you may not
come one after another, and sit by me, and speak softly.
For as I detest the doorways of Death, I detest that man, who
hides one thing in the depths of his heart, and speaks forth another.
But I will speak to you the way it seems best to me: neither
315 do I think the son of Atreus, Agamemnon, will persuade me,
nor the rest of the Danaans, since there was no gratitude given
for fighting incessantly forever against your enemies.
Fate is the same for the man who holds back, the same if he fights hard.
We are all held in a single honour, the brave with the weaklings.
320 A man dies still if he has done nothing, as one who has done much.
Nothing is won for me, now that my heart has gone through its
        afflictions
in forever setting my life on the hazard of battle.
For as to her unwinged young ones the mother bird brings back
morsels, wherever she can find them, but as for herself it is suffering,
325 such was I, as I lay through all the many nights unsleeping,
such as I wore through the bloody days of the fighting,

striving with warriors for the sake of these men's women.
But I say that I have stormed from my ships twelve cities
of men, and by land eleven more through the generous Troad.
From all these we took forth treasures, goodly and numerous,   330
and we would bring them back, and give them to Agamemnon,
Atreus' son; while he, waiting back beside the swift ships,
would take them, and distribute them little by little, and keep many.
All the other prizes of honour he gave the great men and the princes
are held fast by them, but from me alone of all the Achaians   335
he has taken and keeps the bride of my heart. Let him lie beside her
and be happy. Yet why must the Argives fight with the Trojans?
And why was it the son of Atreus assembled and led here
these people? Was it not for the sake of lovely-haired Helen?
Are the sons of Atreus alone among mortal men the ones   340
who love their wives? Since any who is a good man, and careful,
loves her who is his own and cares for her, even as I now
loved this one from my heart, though it was my spear that won her.
Now that he has deceived me and taken from my hands my prize of
    honour,
let him try me no more. I know him well. He will not persuade me.   345
Let him take counsel with you, Odysseus, and the rest of the princes
how to fight the ravening fire away from his vessels.
Indeed, there has been much hard work done even without me;
he has built himself a wall and driven a ditch about it,
making it great and wide, and fixed the sharp stakes inside it.   350
Yet even so he cannot hold the strength of manslaughtering
Hektor; and yet when I was fighting among the Achaians
Hektor would not drive his attack beyond the wall's shelter
but would come forth only so far as the Skaian gates and the oak tree.
There once he endured me alone, and barely escaped my onslaught.   355
But, now I am unwilling to fight against brilliant Hektor,
tomorrow, when I have sacrificed to Zeus and to all gods,
and loaded well my ships, and rowed out on to the salt water,
you will see, if you have a mind to it and if it concerns you,
my ships in the dawn at sea on the Hellespont where the fish swarm   360
and my men manning them with good will to row. If the glorious
shaker of the earth should grant us a favouring passage
on the third day thereafter we might raise generous Phthia.

I have many possessions there that I left behind when I came here
365 on this desperate venture, and from here there is more gold, and red
        bronze,
    and fair-girdled women, and grey iron I will take back;
    all that was allotted to me. But my prize: he who gave it,
    powerful Agamemnon, son of Atreus, has taken it back again
    outrageously. Go back and proclaim to him all that I tell you,
370 openly, so other Achaians may turn against him in anger
    if he hopes yet one more time to swindle some other Danaan,
    wrapped as he is forever in shamelessness; yet he would not,
    bold as a dog though he be, dare look in my face any longer.
    I will join with him in no counsel, and in no action.
375 He cheated me and he did me hurt. Let him not beguile me
    with words again. This is enough for him. Let him of his own will
    be damned, since Zeus of the counsels has taken his wits away from him.
    I hate his gifts. I hold him light as the strip of a splinter.
    Not if he gave me ten times as much, and twenty times over
380 as he possesses now, not if more should come to him from elsewhere,
    or gave all that is brought in to Orchomenos, all that is brought in
    to Thebes of Egypt, where the greatest possessions lie up in the houses,
    Thebes of the hundred gates, where through each of the gates two
        hundred
    fighting men come forth to war with horses and chariots;
385 not if he gave me gifts as many as the sand or the dust is,
    not even so would Agamemnon have his way with my spirit
    until he had made good to me all this heartrending insolence.
    Nor will I marry a daughter of Atreus' son, Agamemnon,
    not if she challenged Aphrodite the golden for loveliness,
390 not if she matched the work of her hands with grey-eyed Athene;
    not even so will I marry her; let him pick some other Achaian,
    one who is to his liking and is kinglier than I am.
    For if the gods will keep me alive, and I win homeward,
    Peleus himself will presently arrange a wife for me.
395 There are many Achaian girls in the land of Hellas and Phthia,
    daughters of great men who hold strong places in guard. And of these
    any one that I please I might make my beloved lady.
    And the great desire in my heart drives me rather in that place
    to take a wedded wife in marriage, the bride of my fancy,

to enjoy with her the possessions won by aged Peleus. For not 400
worth the value of my life are all the possessions they fable
were won for Ilion, that strong-founded citadel, in the old days
when there was peace, before the coming of the sons of the Achaians;
not all that the stone doorsill of the Archer holds fast within it,
of Phoibos Apollo in Pytho of the rocks. Of possessions 405
cattle and fat sheep are things to be had for the lifting,
and tripods can be won, and the tawny high heads of horses,
but a man's life cannot come back again, it cannot be lifted
nor captured again by force, once it has crossed the teeth's barrier.
For my mother Thetis the goddess of the silver feet tells me 410
I carry two sorts of destiny toward the day of my death. Either,
if I stay here and fight beside the city of the Trojans,
my return home is gone, but my glory shall be everlasting;
but if I return home to the beloved land of my fathers,
the excellence of my glory is gone, but there will be a long life 415
left for me, and my end in death will not come to me quickly.
And this would be my counsel to others also, to sail back
home again, since no longer shall you find any term set
on the sheer city of Ilion, since Zeus of the wide brows has strongly
held his own hand over it, and its people are made bold. 420
    Do you go back therefore to the great men of the Achaians,
and take them this message, since such is the privilege of the princes:
that they think out in their minds some other scheme that is better,
which might rescue their ships, and the people of the Achaians
who man the hollow ships, since this plan will not work for them 425
which they thought of by reason of my anger. Let Phoinix
remain here with us and sleep here, so that tomorrow
he may come with us in our ships to the beloved land of our fathers,
if he will; but I will never use force to hold him.'
    So he spoke, and all of them stayed stricken to silence 430
in amazement at his words. He had spoken to them very strongly.
But at long last Phoinix the aged horseman spoke out
in a stormburst of tears, and fearing for the ships of the Achaians:
'If it is going home, glorious Achilleus, you ponder
in your heart, and are utterly unwilling to drive the obliterating 435
fire from the fast ships, since anger has descended on your spirit,
how then shall I, dear child, be left in this place behind you

all alone? Peleus the aged horseman sent me forth with you
on that day when he sent you from Phthia to Agamemnon
440 a mere child, who knew nothing yet of the joining of battle
nor of debate where men are made pre-eminent. Therefore
he sent me along with you to teach you of all these matters,
to make you a speaker of words and one who accomplished in action.
Therefore apart from you, dear child, I would not be willing
445 to be left behind, not were the god in person to promise
he would scale away my old age and make me a young man blossoming
as I was that time when I first left Hellas, the land of fair women,
running from the hatred of Ormenos' son Amyntor,
my father; who hated me for the sake of a fair-haired mistress.
450 For he made love to her himself, and dishonoured his own wife,
my mother; who was forever taking my knees and entreating me
to lie with this mistress instead so that she would hate the old man.
I was persuaded and did it; and my father when he heard of it straightway
called down his curses, and invoked against me the dreaded furies
455 that I might never have any son born of my seed to dandle
on my knees; and the divinities, Zeus of the underworld
and Persephone the honoured goddess, accomplished his curses.
Then I took it into my mind to cut him down with the sharp bronze,
but some one of the immortals checked my anger, reminding me
460 of rumour among the people and men's maledictions repeated,
that I might not be called a parricide among the Achaians.
But now no more could the heart in my breast be ruled entirely
to range still among these halls when my father was angered.
Rather it was the many kinsmen and cousins about me
465 who held me closed in the house, with supplications repeated,
and slaughtered fat sheep in their numbers, and shambling horn-curved
cattle, and numerous swine with the fat abundant upon them
were singed and stretched out across the flame of Hephaistos,
and much wine was drunk that was stored in the jars of the old man.
470 Nine nights they slept nightlong in their places beside me,
and they kept up an interchange of watches, and the fire was never
put out; one below the gate of the strong-closed courtyard,
and one in the ante-chamber before the doors of the bedroom.
But when the tenth night had come to me in its darkness,
475 then I broke the close-compacted doors of the chamber

and got away, and overleapt the fence of the courtyard
lightly, unnoticed by the guarding men and the women servants.
Then I fled far away through the wide spaces of Hellas
and came as far as generous Phthia, mother of sheepflocks,
and to lord Peleus, who accepted me with a good will   480
and gave me his love, even as a father loves his own son
who is a single child brought up among many possessions.
He made me a rich man, and granted me many people,
and I lived, lord over the Dolopes, in remotest Phthia,
and, godlike Achilleus, I made you all that you are now,   485
and loved you out of my heart, for you would not go with another
out to any feast, nor taste any food in your own halls
until I had set you on my knees, and cut little pieces
from the meat, and given you all you wished, and held the wine for you.
And many times you soaked the shirt that was on my body   490
with wine you would spit up in the troublesomeness of your childhood.
So I have suffered much through you, and have had much trouble,
thinking always how the gods would not bring to birth any children
of my own; so that it was you, godlike Achilleus, I made
my own child, so that some day you might keep hard affliction from me. 495
Then, Achilleus, beat down your great anger. It is not
yours to have a pitiless heart. The very immortals
can be moved; their virtue and honour and strength are greater than ours
        are,
and yet with sacrifices and offerings for endearment,
with libations and with savour men turn back even the immortals   500
in supplication, when any man does wrong and transgresses.
For there are also the spirits of Prayer, the daughters of great Zeus,
and they are lame of their feet, and wrinkled, and cast their eyes sidelong,
who toil on their way left far behind by the spirit of Ruin:
but she, Ruin, is strong and sound on her feet, and therefore   505
far outruns all Prayers, and wins into every country
to force men astray; and the Prayers follow as healers after her.
If a man venerates these daughters of Zeus as they draw near,
such a man they bring great advantage, and hear his entreaty;
but if a man shall deny them, and stubbornly with a harsh word   510
refuse, they go to Zeus, son of Kronos, in supplication
that Ruin may overtake this man, that he be hurt, and punished.

So, Achilleus: grant, you also, that Zeus' daughters be given
their honour, which, lordly though they be, curbs the will of others.
515 Since, were he not bringing gifts and naming still more hereafter,
Atreus' son; were he to remain still swollen with rancour,
even I would not bid you throw your anger aside, nor
defend the Argives, though they needed you sorely. But see now,
he offers you much straightway, and has promised you more hereafter;
520 he has sent the best men to you to supplicate you, choosing them
out of the Achaian host, those who to yourself are the dearest
of all the Argives. Do not you make vain their argument
nor their footsteps, though before this one could not blame your anger.
Thus it was in the old days also, the deeds that we hear of
525 from the great men, when the swelling anger descended upon them.
The heroes would take gifts; they would listen, and be persuaded.
For I remember this action of old, it is not a new thing,
and how it went; you are all my friends, I will tell it among you.
     The Kouretes and the steadfast Aitolians were fighting
530 and slaughtering one another about the city of Kalydon,
the Aitolians in lovely Kalydon's defence, the Kouretes
furious to storm and sack it in war. For Artemis,
she of the golden chair, had driven this evil upon them,
angered that Oineus had not given the pride of the orchards
535 to her, first fruits; the rest of the gods were given due sacrifice,
but alone to this daughter of great Zeus he had given nothing.
He had forgotten, or had not thought, in his hard delusion,
and in wrath at his whole mighty line the Lady of Arrows
sent upon them the fierce wild boar with the shining teeth, who
540 after the way of his kind did much evil to the orchards of Oineus.
For he ripped up whole tall trees from the ground and scattered them
          headlong
roots and all, even to the very flowers of the orchard.
The son of Oineus killed this boar, Meleagros, assembling
together many hunting men out of numerous cities
545 with their hounds; since the boar might not have been killed by a few men,
so huge was he, and had put many men on the sad fire for burning.
But the goddess again made a great stir of anger and crying
battle, over the head of the boar and the bristling boar's hide,
between Kouretes and the high-hearted Aitolians. So long

as Meleagros lover of battle stayed in the fighting   550
it went the worse for the Kouretes, and they could not even
hold their ground outside the wall, though they were so many.
But when the anger came upon Meleagros, such anger
as wells in the hearts of others also, though their minds are careful,
he, in the wrath of his heart against his own mother, Althaia,   555
lay apart with his wedded bride, Kleopatra the lovely,
daughter of sweet-stepping Marpessa, child of Euenos,
and Idas, who was the strongest of all men upon earth
in his time; for he even took up the bow to face the King's onset,
Phoibos Apollo, for the sake of the sweet-stepping maiden;   560
a girl her father and honoured mother had named in their palace
Alkyone, sea-bird, as a by-name, since for her sake
her mother with the sorrow-laden cry of a sea-bird
wept because far-reaching Phoibos Apollo had taken her;
with this Kleopatra he lay mulling his heart-sore anger,   565
raging by reason of his mother's curses, which she called down
from the gods upon him, in deep grief for the death of her brother,
and many times beating with her hands on the earth abundant
she called on Hades and on honoured Persephone, lying
at length along the ground, and the tears were wet on her bosom,   570
to give death to her son; and Erinys, the mist-walking,
she of the heart without pity, heard her out of the dark places.
Presently there was thunder about the gates, and the sound rose
of towers under assault, and the Aitolian elders
supplicated him, sending their noblest priests of the immortals,   575
to come forth and defend them; they offered him a great gift:
wherever might lie the richest ground in lovely Kalydon,
there they told him to choose out a piece of land, an entirely
good one, of fifty acres, the half of it to be vineyard
and the half of it unworked ploughland of the plain to be furrowed. 580
And the aged horseman Oineus again and again entreated him,
and took his place at the threshold of the high-vaulted chamber
and shook against the bolted doors, pleading with his own son.
And again and again his honoured mother and his sisters
entreated him, but he only refused the more; then his own friends   585
who were the most honoured and dearest of all entreated him;
but even so they could not persuade the heart within him

[213]

until, as the chamber was under close assault, the Kouretes
were mounting along the towers and set fire to the great city.
590 And then at last his wife, the fair-girdled bride, supplicated
Meleagros, in tears, and rehearsed in their numbers before him
all the sorrows that come to men when their city is taken:
they kill the men, and the fire leaves the city in ashes,
and strangers lead the children away and the deep-girdled women.
595 And the heart, as he listened to all this evil, was stirred within him,
and he rose, and went, and closed his body in shining armour.
So he gave way in his own heart, and drove back the day of evil
from the Aitolians; yet these no longer would make good
their many and gracious gifts; yet he drove back the evil from them.
600   Listen, then; do not have such a thought in your mind; let not
the spirit within you turn you that way, dear friend. It would be worse
to defend the ships after they are burning. No, with gifts promised
go forth. The Achaians will honour you as they would an immortal.
But if without gifts you go into the fighting where men perish,
605 your honour will no longer be as great, though you drive back the battle.'
      Then in answer to him spoke Achilleus of the swift feet:
'Phoinix my father, aged, illustrious, such honour is a thing
I need not. I think I am honoured already in Zeus' ordinance
which will hold me here beside my curved ships as long as life's wind
610 stays in my breast, as long as my knees have their spring beneath me.
And put away in your thoughts this other thing I tell you.
Stop confusing my heart with lamentation and sorrow
for the favour of great Atreides. It does not become you
to love this man, for fear you turn hateful to me, who love you.
615 It should be your pride with me to hurt whoever shall hurt me.
Be king equally with me; take half of my honour.
These men will carry back the message; you stay here and sleep here
in a soft bed, and we shall decide tomorrow, as dawn shows,
whether to go back home again or else to remain here.'
620   He spoke, and, saying nothing, nodded with his brows to Patroklos
to make up a neat bed for Phoinix, so the others might presently
think of going home from his shelter. The son of Telamon,
Aias the godlike, saw it, and now spoke his word among them:
'Son of Laertes and seed of Zeus, resourceful Odysseus:
625 let us go. I think that nothing will be accomplished

by argument on this errand; it is best to go back quickly
and tell this story, though it is not good, to the Danaans
who sit there waiting for us to come back, seeing that Achilleus
has made savage the proud-hearted spirit within his body.
He is hard, and does not remember that friends' affection   630
wherein we honoured him by the ships, far beyond all others.
Pitiless. And yet a man takes from his brother's slayer
the blood price, or the price for a child who was killed, and the guilty
one, when he has largely repaid, stays still in the country,
and the injured man's heart is curbed, and his pride, and his anger   635
when he has taken the price; but the gods put in your breast a spirit
not to be placated, bad, for the sake of one single
girl. Yet now we offer you seven, surpassingly lovely,
and much beside these. Now make gracious the spirit within you.
Respect your own house; see, we are under the same roof with you,   640
from the multitude of the Danaans, we who desire beyond all
others to have your honour and love, out of all the Achaians.'
    Then in answer to him spoke Achilleus of the swift feet:
'Son of Telamon, seed of Zeus, Aias, lord of the people:
all that you have said seems spoken after my own mind.   645
Yet still the heart in me swells up in anger, when I remember
the disgrace that he wrought upon me before the Argives,
the son of Atreus, as if I were some dishonoured vagabond.
Do you then go back to him, and take him this message:
that I shall not think again of the bloody fighting   650
until such time as the son of wise Priam, Hektor the brilliant,
comes all the way to the ships of the Myrmidons, and their shelters,
slaughtering the Argives, and shall darken with fire our vessels.
But around my own shelter, I think, and beside my black ship
Hektor will be held, though he be very hungry for battle.'   655
    He spoke, and they taking each a two-handled cup poured out
a libation, then went back to their ships, and Odysseus led them.
Now Patroklos gave the maids and his followers orders
to make up without delay a neat bed for Phoinix.
And these obeyed him and made up the bed as he had commanded,   660
laying fleeces on it, and a blanket, and a sheet of fine linen.
There the old man lay down and waited for the divine Dawn.
But Achilleus slept in the inward corner of the strong-built shelter,

[215]

and a woman lay beside him, one he had taken from Lesbos,
665 Phorbas' daughter, Diomede of the fair colouring.
In the other corner Patroklos went to bed; with him also
was a girl, Iphis the fair-girdled, whom brilliant Achilleus
gave him, when he took sheer Skyros, Enyeus' citadel.
   Now when these had come back to the shelters of Agamemnon,
670 the sons of the Achaians greeted them with their gold cups
uplifted, one after another, standing, and asked them questions.
And the first to question them was the lord of men, Agamemnon:
'Tell me, honoured Odysseus, great glory of the Achaians:
is he willing to fight the ravening fire away from our vessels,
675 or did he refuse, and does the anger still hold his proud heart?'
   Then long-suffering great Odysseus spoke to him in answer:
'Son of Atreus, most lordly, king of men, Agamemnon.
That man will not quench his anger, but still more than ever
is filled with rage. He refuses you and refuses your presents.
680 He tells you yourself to take counsel among the Argives
how to save your ships, and the people of the Achaians.
And he himself has threatened that tomorrow as dawn shows
he will drag down his strong-benched, oarswept ships to the water.
He said it would be his counsel to others also, to sail back
685 home again, since no longer will you find any term set
on the sheer city of Ilion, since Zeus of the wide brows has strongly
held his own hand over it, and its people are made bold.
So he spoke. There are these to attest it who went there with me
also, Aias, and the two heralds, both men of good counsel.
690 But aged Phoinix stayed there for the night, as Achilleus urged him,
so he might go home in the ships to the beloved land of his fathers
if Phoinix will; but he will never use force to persuade him.'
   So he spoke, and all of them stayed stricken to silence
in amazement at his words. He had spoken to them very strongly.
695 For a long time the sons of the Achaians said nothing, in sorrow,
but at long last Diomedes of the great war cry spoke to them:
'Son of Atreus, most lordly and king of men, Agamemnon,
I wish you had not supplicated the blameless son of Peleus
with innumerable gifts offered. He is a proud man without this,
700 and now you have driven him far deeper into his pride. Rather
we shall pay him no more attention, whether he comes in with us

or stays away. He will fight again, whenever the time comes
that the heart in his body urges him to, and the god drives him.
Come then, do as I say, and let us all be won over.
Go to sleep, now that the inward heart is made happy   705
with food and drink, for these are the strength and courage within us.
But when the lovely dawn shows forth with rose fingers, Atreides,
rapidly form before our ships both people and horses
stirring them on, and yourself be ready to fight in the foremost.'

So he spoke, and all the kings gave him their approval,   710
acclaiming the word of Diomedes, breaker of horses.
Then they poured a libation, and each man went to his shelter,
where they went to their beds and took the blessing of slumber.

Now beside their ships the other great men of the Achaians
slept night long, with the soft bondage of slumber upon them;
but the son of Atreus, Agamemnon, shepherd of the people,
was held by no sweet sleep as he pondered deeply within him.
5 As when the lord of Hera the lovely-haired flashes his lightning
as he brings on a great rainstorm, or a hail incessant,
or a blizzard, at such time when the snowfall scatters on ploughlands,
or drives on somewhere on earth the huge edge of tearing battle,
such was Agamemnon, with the beating turmoil in his bosom
10 from the deep heart, and all his wits were shaken within him.
Now he would gaze across the plain to the Trojan camp, wondering
at the number of their fires that were burning in front of Ilion,
toward the high calls of their flutes and pipes, the murmur of people.
Now as he would look again to the ships and the Achaian
15 people, he would drag the hair by its roots from his head, looking
toward Zeus on high, and his proud heart was stricken with lamentation.
Now to his mind this thing appeared to be the best counsel,
first among men to seek out Nestor, the son of Neleus,
to see if Nestor with him could work out a plan that would not fail,
20 and one that might drive the evil away from all the Danaans.
He stood upright, and slipped the tunic upon his body,
and underneath his shining feet he bound the fair sandals,
and thereafter slung across him the tawny hide of a lion
glowing and huge, that swung to his feet, and took up a spear.
25   So likewise trembling seized Menelaos, neither on his eyes

had sweet slumber descending settled, for fear that the Argives
might suffer some hurt, they who for his sake over much water
had come to Troy, bearing their bold attack to the Trojans.
First of all he mantled his broad back in a leopard's
spotted hide, then lifting the circle of a brazen helmet   30
placed it upon his head, and took up a spear in his big hand,
and went on his way to waken his brother, who was the great king
of all Argives, one honoured in his own land as a god is.
He found him putting the splendid armour about his shoulders
beside the stern of his ship, and was welcomed as he came up to him. 35
It was Menelaos of the great war cry who spoke first:
'Why this arming, my brother? Is it some one of your companions
you are stirring to go and spy on the Trojans? Yet I fear sadly
there will not be any man to undertake this endeavour,
going against enemy fighters to spy on them, alone, through   40
the immortal night. Such a man will have to be very bold-hearted.'
    Then in turn powerful Agamemnon answered him:
'You and I, illustrious, o Menelaos, have need now
of crafty counsel, if any man is to defend and rescue
the Argives and their ships, since the heart of Zeus is turned from us. 45
For the sacrifices of Hektor have stirred his heart more than ours have.
No, for I never saw nor heard from the lips of another
of a single man in a day imagining so much evil
as Hektor, beloved of Zeus, has wrought on the sons of the Achaians,
alone, being called true son neither of a god nor a goddess.   50
He has done things I think the Argives will remember with sorrow
long into the future, such harm has he devised the Achaians.
But go now, running lightly beside the ships, and call to us
Idomeneus and Aias, while I shall go after Nestor
the brilliant, and waken him to rise, if he might be willing   55
to approach the sacred duty of the guards, or give orders to them.
Above all, these would listen to him, seeing that his own son
commands the pickets, and with him the follower of Idomeneus,
Meriones. To these above all we entrusted the duty.'
    Then in turn Menelaos of the great war cry answered him: 60
'How then do you intend this order that you have given me?
Shall I wait where I am, with them, and watch for your coming,
or run after you, when I have properly given the order?'

Then in turn the lord of men Agamemnon spoke to him:
65 'Better wait here, so there will be no way we can miss one another
as we come and go. There are many paths up and down the encampment.
Call out wherever you go, and waken each man to give him
your orders, naming him by descent with the name of his father.
Give each man due respect. Let not your spirit be haughty,
70 but let it be you and I ourselves who do the work, seeing
that Zeus cast on us as we were born this burden of evil.'
So he spoke and with careful orders sent off his brother,
and he himself went in search of Nestor, shepherd of the people,
and came on him beside his own shelter and his own black ship
75 in a soft bed, and his bright gear was lying beside him,
the shield, and the two spears, and the glittering helmet, and by him
lay in all its shining the war belt, in which the old man
girt himself, when he armed for the fighting where men die, leading
his own people, since he gave no ground to sorrowful old age.
80 He straightened up and raised his head, leaning on one elbow,
and spoke to the son of Atreus, and asked him a question:
'Who are you, who walk alone through the ships and the army
and through the darkness of night when other mortals are sleeping?
Are you looking for one of your mules, or looking for some companion?
85 Speak, do not come upon me in silence. What would you of me?'
Then in turn the lord of men Agamemnon answered him:
'Nestor, son of Neleus, great glory of the Achaians,
you will know Atreus' son Agamemnon, whom beyond others
Zeus has involved in hard work forever, as long as life's wind
90 stays in my breast, as long as my knees have their spring beneath me.
I am driven thus, because the ease of sleep will not settle
on my eyes, but fighting and the cares of the Achaians perplex me.
Terribly I am in dread for the Danaans, nor does my pulse beat
steadily, but I go distracted, and my heart is pounding
95 through my chest, and my shining limbs are shaken beneath me.
But if you are for action, since sleep comes neither upon you,
let us both go out to the pickets, so that we may see
if they might not have found weariness too much for them, and fallen
asleep, and altogether forgotten their duty, to keep watch.
100 There are men who hate us sitting nearby, nor do we know
that they might not be pondering an attack on us in the darkness.'

Thereupon the Gerenian horseman Nestor answered him:
'Son of Atreus, most lordly and king of men, Agamemnon,
Zeus of the counsels, I think, will not accomplish for Hektor
all his designs and all he hopes for now; I think rather   105
he will have still more hardships to wrestle, if ever Achilleus
turns again the heart within him from its wearisome anger.
Surely, I will go with you, and let us also awaken
others, the son of Tydeus the spear-famed, and Odysseus,
and Aias the swift-footed, and the powerful son of Phyleus.   110
But if one were to go also and call these others I speak of,
Aias the great, the godlike one, and the lord Idomeneus,
why, their ships lie farthest from us, and are not at all close.
But, beloved as he is and respected, I will still blame
Menelaos, even though you be angry, and I will not hide it,   115
for the way he sleeps and has given to you alone all the hard work.
For now he ought to be hard at work going to all the great men
in supplication. This need that has come is no more endurable.'
    Then in turn the lord of men Agamemnon spoke to him:
'Aged sir, other times I also would tell you to blame him,   120
since often he hangs back and is not willing to work hard,
not that he shrinks from it and gives way, nor in the mind's dullness,
but because he looks to me, and waits till I make a beginning.
But this time he woke far before me, and came to rouse me,
and I sent him on to call those you ask after. Therefore   125
let us go. We shall find those others there with the sentries
before the gates, where I told them to form and assemble.'
    Thereupon the Gerenian horseman Nestor answered him:
'Thus no man of the Argives can disobey him nor find fault
with him, whenever he stirs up any of them and gives orders.'   130
    With this speech, he slipped the tunic upon his body
and underneath his shining feet he bound the fair sandals,
and pinned about him a great vermilion mantle sweeping
in a double fold, with a thick fleece of wool upon it.
Then he caught up a powerful spear, edged with sharp bronze,   135
and went on his way down the ships of the bronze-armoured Achaians.
First he came on Odysseus, the equal of Zeus in counsel,
and Nestor the Gerenian horseman wakened him from sleep,
speaking aloud, and the wave of the voice swept quick through his hearing

140 and he came forth from his shelter and called out his word to them:
'Why do you wander thus up and down the ships and the army
alone, through the immortal night? What need is upon you?'
    Thereupon the Gerenian horseman Nestor answered him:
'Son of Laertes and seed of Zeus, resourceful Odysseus,
145 do not be angry; such grief has fallen upon the Achaians.
Come then with us to waken another, for whom it is becoming
to deliberate the question of running away or of fighting.'
    He spoke, and resourceful Odysseus moving back into his shelter
put the bright-patterned shield on his shoulders, and went on with them.
150 They went to the son of Tydeus, Diomedes, and found him
with his gear outside the shelter, and his companions about him
slept with their shields underneath their heads, and their spears beside
        them
stood upright, the heels driven deep in the ground, and the bronze afar off
glared, like the lightning of Zeus father. The hero
155 slept, with the hide of a field-ranging ox laid beneath him,
but underneath his head was laid out a lustrous blanket.
Nestor the Gerenian horseman stood by to waken him
and roused him, stirring him with his heel, and scolded him to his face:
'Son of Tydeus, wake up! Why do you doze in slumber
160 nightlong? Do you not hear how the Trojans at the break of the flat land
are sitting close to our ships, and narrow ground holds them from us?'
    So he spoke, and the other rapidly stirred from his sleeping
and spoke winged words to him and addressed him thus: 'Aged sir,
you are a hard man. You are never finished with working.
165 Now are there not other sons of the Achaians younger than you are
who could be going about everywhere to each of the princes
and waking them up? But you, aged sir, are too much for us.'
    In turn Nestor the Gerenian horseman said to him:
'Yes, dear friend, all this that you said has been fairly spoken.
170 I myself have sons without blame, I have followers,
plenty of them, of whom any could go to summon the princes.
But this difficulty is very great that has come to the Achaians,
since for all of us the decision now stands on the edge of a razor
whether the Achaians shall have life or sorry destruction.
175 But go now to Aias the swift and the son of Phyleus
and waken them—you are younger than I—if truly you have pity.'

He spoke, and the other wrapped his shoulders in the hide of a lion
glowing and huge, that swung to his feet, and took up a spear.
The hero went, and waking the others brought them back with him.
    Now as these men mingled with the sentries assembling   180
they found the leaders of the pickets by no means asleep
but all of them were wide awake, and sat by their weapons.
As dogs about the sheep in a yard are restless in watching
as they hear a wild beast boldly moving, who through the timber
goes among the mountains, and a clamour rises about him   185
of men and of dogs, and all their sleep has been broken from them;
so for these the softness of sleep was broken from their eyes
as they held the bitter midwatch, since they were turning always
toward the plain, where they heard the Trojans coming and going.
The aged man was glad when he saw them, and with speech of good cheer 190
spoke winged words to them and addressed them thus: 'Continue
to keep your watch this way, beloved children, and let not
sleep seize any, lest you become a delight to your enemies.'
    So he spoke, and strode on through the ditch, and there followed with
      him
the kings of the Argives, all who had been called into conclave,   195
and with them went Meriones and Nestor's glorious
son, since the kings themselves called these to take counsel with them.
After they had crossed the deep-dug ditch they settled
on clean ground, where there showed a space not cumbered with corpses
of the fallen, a place whence Hektor the huge had turned back   200
from destroying the Argives, after the night had darkened about him.
There they seated themselves, and opened words to each other,
and the Gerenian horseman Nestor began speaking among them:
'O my friends, is there no man who, trusting in the daring
of his own heart, would go among the high-hearted Trojans?   205
So he might catch some enemy, who straggled behind them,
or he might overhear some thing that the Trojans are saying,
what they deliberate among themselves, and whether they purpose
to stay where they are, close to the ships, or else to withdraw back
into their city, now that they have beaten the Achaians.   210
Could a man learn this, and then come back again to us
unhurt, why huge and heaven-high would rise up his glory
among all people, and an excellent gift would befall him;

for all those who hold by the ships high power as princes,
215 of all these each one of them will give him a black sheep,
female, with a lamb beneath; there shall be no gift like this one,
one that will be forever by at the feasts and festivals.'
    So he spoke, and all of them stayed stricken to silence;
but now Diomedes of the great war cry spoke forth among them:
220 'Nestor, my own heart and my own proud spirit arouse me
to go into the host of the hateful men who lie near us,
the Trojans; but if some other man would go along with me
there would be more comfort in it, and greater confidence.
When two go together, one of them at least looks forward
225 to see what is best; a man by himself, though he be careful,
still has less mind in him than two, and his wits have less weight.'
    He spoke, and many were willing to go with Diomedes.
The two Aiantes were willing, henchman of Ares, and likewise
Meriones, and Nestor's son altogether willing,
230 and Atreus' son was willing, Menelaos the spear-famed,
and patient Odysseus too was willing to enter the multitude
of Trojans, since forever the heart in his breast was daring.
Now it was the lord of men, Agamemnon, who spoke to them:
    'Son of Tydeus, you who delight my heart, Diomedes,
235 pick your man to be your companion, whichever you wish,
the best of all who have shown, since many are eager to do it.
You must not, for the awe that you feel in your heart, pass over
the better man and take the worse, giving way to modesty
and looking to his degree—not even if he be kinglier.'
240   So he spoke, and was frightened for Menelaos of the fair hair.
But now again Diomedes of the great war cry spoke forth:
'If indeed you tell me myself to pick my companion,
how then could I forget Odysseus the godlike, he whose
heart and whose proud spirit are beyond all others forward
245 in all hard endeavours, and Pallas Athene loves him.
Were he to go with me, both of us could come back from the blazing
of fire itself, since his mind is best at devices.'
    Then in turn long-suffering brilliant Odysseus answered him:
'Son of Tydeus, do not praise me so, nor yet blame me.
250 These are the Argives, who know well all these matters you speak of.
But let us go: for the night draws far along, and the dawn nears,

the stars have gone far on their course, and the full of the night has passed
    by,
through two portions, and the third portion is that which is left us.'
    So they spoke, and armed themselves in their weapons of terror,
and Thrasymedes the stubborn in battle gave the son of Tydeus   255
a two-edged sword (his own had been left behind by his vessel)
and a shield; and he put over his head a helmet
of bull's hide, with neither horn nor crest, which is known as
the skull cap, and guards the heads of strong men in battle;
while Meriones gave Odysseus a bow and a quiver   260
and a sword; and he too put over his head a helmet
fashioned of leather; on the inside the cap was cross-strung firmly
with thongs of leather, and on the outer side the white teeth
of a tusk-shining boar were close sewn one after another
with craftsmanship and skill; and a felt was set in the centre.   265
Autolykos, breaking into the close-built house, had stolen it
from Amyntor, the son of Ormenos, out of Eleon,
and gave it to Kytherian Amphidamas, at Skandeia;
Amphidamas gave it in turn to Molos, a gift of guest-friendship,
and Molos gave it to his son Meriones to carry.   270
But at this time it was worn to cover the head of Odysseus.
    When these two had armed themselves in their weapons of terror
they went on their way, and left behind there all the princes,
and on the right near the way they were taking Pallas Athene
sent down a heron to them; indeed, their eyes could not see it   275
through the darkness of night, but they could hear it crying.
And Odysseus was glad at the bird-sign, and prayed to Athene:
'Hear me, daughter of Zeus of the aegis, you who forever
stand beside me in all hard tasks, nor am I forgotten
as I go my ways: now give me the best of your love, Athene,   280
and grant that we come back in glory to the strong-benched vessels
when we have done a great thing that will sadden the Trojans.'
    Diomedes of the great war cry spoke in prayer after him:
'Hear me also, Atrytone, daughter of great Zeus.
Come with me now as you went with my father, brilliant Tydeus,   285
into Thebes, when he went with a message before the Achaians,
and left the bronze-armoured Achaians beside Asopos
while he carried a word of friendship to the Kadmeians

in that place; but on his way back he was minded to grim deeds
290 with your aid, divine goddess, since you stood in goodwill beside him.
So now again be willing to stand by me, and watch over me,
and I in turn will dedicate you a heifer, broad-browed,
one year old, unbroken, that no man ever led under
the yoke. I will drench her horns in gold and offer her to you.'
295   So they spoke in prayer, and Pallas Athene heard them.
Then, after they had made their prayers to the daughter of great Zeus
they went on their way like two lions into the black night
through the carnage and through the corpses, war gear and dark blood.
    Nor did Hektor either permit the high-hearted Trojans
300 to sleep, but had called together in a group all of their great men,
those who were the leaders of Troy and their men of deliberation.
Summoning these he compacted before them his close counsel:
'Who would take upon him this work and bring it to fulfilment
for a huge price? The reward will be one that will suffice him;
305 for I will give a chariot and two strong-necked horses
who are the finest of all beside the fast ships of the Achaians
to him who has the daring, winning honour for himself also,
to go close to the swift-running ships and find out for us
whether the swift ships are guarded, as they were before this,
310 or whether now the Achaians who are beaten under our hands
are planning flight among themselves, and no longer are willing
to guard them by night, now that stark weariness has broken them.'
    So he spoke, and all of them were stricken to silence.
But there was one among the Trojans, Dolon, Eumedes'
315 son, the sacred herald's, a man of much gold and much bronze.
He was an evil man to look on, but was swift-footed;
moreover he was a single son among five sisters.
This man now spoke his word before the Trojans and Hektor:
    'Hektor, my own heart and my proud spirit arouse me
320 to go close to the swift-running ships and to learn about them.
Come then, hold up your sceptre before me, and swear upon it
that you will give me the horses, and the chariot made bright
with bronze, that carry the blameless son of Peleus. I shall not
be a vain spy for you, nor less than your expectation,
325 for I shall go straight on through their army, until I come to
the ship of Agamemnon, where their greatest men must be gathered

to deliberate the question of running away or of fighting.'

He spoke, and Hektor took the staff in his hand, and swore to him:
'Let Zeus, loud-thundering lord of Hera, now be my witness
himself, that no other man of the Trojans shall mount these horses,   330
since I say they shall be utterly yours, and your glory.'

He spoke, and swore to an empty oath, and stirred the man onward.
And at once Dolon cast across his shoulders the bent bow.
He put on about him the pelt of a grey wolf, and on his head set
a cap of marten's hide, and took up a sharp throwing spear   335
and went on his way toward the ships from his own camp, nor was he ever
to come back again from the ships, and carry his word to Hektor.
Now when he had left behind the throng of men and of horses
he went on his way, eagerly, but illustrious Odysseus
was aware of him coming and spoke to Diomedes: 340
'This is some man, Diomedes, on his way from the army.
I do not know whether he comes to spy on our vessels
or to strip some one of the perished corpses, but we must let him
first go on past us a little way in the open
and afterwards we will make a rush and fasten upon him   345
suddenly. But if in the speed of his feet he eludes us
then keep him crowded upon the ships, and away from the army
always, feinting with the spear, nor let him escape to the city.'

So they spoke, and bent aside from their way, through the corpses,
while he in the thoughtlessness of his heart ran swiftly by them.   350
But when he was gone from them as far as the range of a plough yoke
of mules, since these are better beasts than oxen for dragging
the wrought ploughshare through the depth of the harvest land, these two
ran after him, and he heard the thudding of their feet and stopped still.
He thought in his heart these would be friends from among the Trojans   355
to turn him back, and that Hektor had sped them to summon him again.
But when they got to a spear's throw from him, or less even,
he saw that these were enemy men, and moved his knees rapidly
to run away, and these set out in rapid chase of him.
And, as when two rip-fanged hounds have sighted a wild beast,   360
a young deer, or a hare, and go after it, eagerly always
through the spaces of the woods, and the chase runs crying before them,
so the son of Tydeus, and Odysseus, sacker of cities,
kept always hard on his heels and cut him off from his people.

365 But when he was on the point of reaching the Achaian pickets,
as he fled toward the vessels, then Athene put great power
in Tydeus' son, so that no other bronze-armoured Achaian
might win the glory of striking him down, and he come in second.
Powerful Diomedes threatening with the spear spoke to him:
370 'Either wait, or my spear will catch you. I think that you will not
thus get clear from my hands for long, and sudden destruction.'
        He spoke, and let fly with his spear, but missed, on purpose,
his man, as the point of the polished spear went over his right shoulder
and stuck fast in the earth. And Dolon stood still in terror
375 gibbering, as through his mouth came the sound of his teeth's chatter
in green fear; and these two, breathing hard, came up to him
and caught him by the hands, and he broke into tears and spoke to them:
'Take me alive, and I will pay my ransom: in my house
there is bronze, and gold, and difficultly wrought iron,
380 and my father would make you glad with abundant ransom
were he to hear that I am alive by the ships of the Achaians.'
        Then resourceful Odysseus spoke in turn, and answered him:
'Do not fear, and let no thought of death be upon you.
But come, tell me this thing and recite it to me accurately:
385 where is it that you walk alone to the ships from the army
through the darkness of night when other mortals are sleeping?
Is it to strip some one of the perished corpses, or is it
that Hektor sent you out to spy with care upon each thing
beside our hollow ships? Or did your own spirit drive you?'
390   Then Dolon answered him, but his legs were shaking beneath him:
'Hektor has led my mind astray with many deceptions.
He promised me the single-foot horses of proud Achilleus,
Peleus' son, and the chariot bright with bronze, for my gift,
and gave me an order, to go through the running black night,
395 and get close to the enemy men, and find out for him
whether the swift ships are guarded, as they were before this,
or whether now the Achaians who are broken under our hands
are planning flight among themselves, and no longer are willing
to guard them by night, now that stark weariness has broken them.'
400   Then Odysseus the resourceful smiled and spoke to him:
'Surely now, these were mighty gifts that your heart longed after,
the horses of valiant Aiakides. They are difficult horses

[228]

for mortal men to manage, or even to ride behind them
for all except Achilleus, who was born of an immortal mother.
But come, tell me this thing and recite it to me accurately.   405
Where did you leave Hektor, the people's shepherd, when you came here?
Where is his gear of war lying? Where are his horses?
How are the rest of the Trojans disposed, the guards and the sleepers?
What do they deliberate among themselves? Do they purpose
to stay where they are, close to the ships? Or else to withdraw back   410
into the city, now that they have beaten the Achaians?'
    Then in turn Dolon the son of Eumedes spoke to him:
'See, I will accurately recite all these things to you.
Hektor is now among those who are the men of counsel
and they hold their deliberations by the barrow of godlike Ilos   415
apart from the confusion. But those guards that you ask of, hero—
there is no detail that protects the army and guards it.
As for the watchfire hearths of the Trojans, those who must do it
keep awake by the fires and pass on the picket duty
to each other, but their far-assembled companions in battle   420
are sleeping, and pass on to the Trojans the duty of watching,
since their own children do not lie nearby, nor their women.'
    Then resourceful Odysseus spoke in turn, and answered him:
'How, then, are these sleeping? And are they mixed with the Trojans,
breakers of horses, or apart? Tell me, so I may be clear.'   425
    Then in turn Dolon the son of Eumedes answered him:
'See, I will accurately recite all these things to you.
Next the sea are the Karians, and Paionians with their curved bows,
the Leleges and Kaukonians and the brilliant Pelasgians.
By Thymbre are stationed the Lykians and the proud Mysians   430
with the Phrygians who fight from horses, and Maionians, lords of
        chariots.
But why do you question me on all this, each thing in detail?
For if you are minded to get among the mass of the Trojans,
here are the Thracians, new come, separate, beyond all others
in place, and among them Rhesos their king, the son of Eïoneus.   435
And his are the finest horses I ever saw, and the biggest;
they are whiter than snow, and their speed of foot is the winds' speed;
his chariot is fairly ornate with gold and with silver,
and the armour is golden and gigantic, a wonder to look on,

440 that he brought here with him. It is not like armour for mortal
men to carry, but for the immortal gods. And therefore
take me with you to some place by the fast-running vessels,
or else tie me fast here in a pitiless bond, and leave me,
until you can make your venture, and try out the truth of my story,
445 whether I have told you this fairly, or whether I have not.'
     But powerful Diomedes looked darkly at him and spoke then:
'Do not, Dolon, have in your mind any thought of escape
now you have got in our hands, though you brought us an excellent
     message.
For if we let you get away now, or set you free, later
450 you will come back again to the fast ships of the Achaians
either to spy on us once more, or to fight strongly with us.
But if, beaten down under my hands, you lose your life now,
then you will nevermore be an affliction upon the Argives.'
     He spoke, and the man was trying to reach his chin with his strong hand
455 and cling, and supplicate him, but he struck the middle of his neck
with a sweep of the sword, and slashed clean through both tendons,
and Dolon's head still speaking dropped in the dust. They took off
his cap of marten's hide from his head, and stripped off also
the wolf's pelt, and the back-strung bow, and the long spear.
460 Brilliant Odysseus held these up to Athene the Spoiler
high in his hand, and spoke a word, and prayed to Athene:
'Hail, goddess. These are yours. To you first of all the immortals
on Olympos we will give your due share. Only guide us
once again to where the Thracians sleep, and their horses.'
465   So he spoke, and lifting the spoils high from him he placed them
upon a tamarisk bush, and piled a clear landmark beside them,
pulling reeds together and the long branches of tamarisk
that they might not miss them on their way back through the running
     black night.
These two went ahead on their way through war gear and dark blood
470 and came suddenly to the Thracians for whom they were looking.
These were asleep, worn out with weariness, and their armour
lay in splendour and good order on the ground beside them
in three rows, and beside each man stood his team of horses.
Rhesos slept in the centre with his fast horses about him
475 tethered by the reins to the outer rail of the chariot. Odysseus

was the first to see him and pointed him out to Diomedes:
'Here is our man, see, Diomedes, and here are his horses,
those that Dolon, the man we killed, pointed out to us.
Come then, put forward your great strength. Here is no matter
for standing by idle in your weapons. Untie the horses;   480
or else let me look after them, while you kill the people.'
    He spoke, and grey-eyed Athene breathed strength into Diomedes
and he began to kill them one after another. Grim sounds rose
from there as they were stricken with the sword, and the ground reddened
    with blood.
As a lion advancing on the helpless herds unshepherded   485
of sheep or goats pounces upon them with wicked intention,
so the son of Tydeus attacked the Thracian people
until he had killed twelve. Meanwhile resourceful Odysseus
as Tydeus' son stood over each man with the sword, and struck him,
would catch each dead man by the foot from behind, and drag him   490
away, with this thought in his mind, that the bright-maned horses
might pass easily through and not be shaken within them
at stepping on dead men. These horses were not yet used to them.
But when the son of Tydeus came to the king, and this was
the thirteenth man, he stripped the sweetness of life from him   495
as he lay heavily breathing—since a bad dream stood by his head
in the night—no dream, but Oineus' son, by device of Athene.
Meanwhile patient Odysseus was untying the single-foot horses,
and pulled them together with the reins, and drove them from the
    confusion
and whipped them with his bow, since he had not noticed nor taken   500
in his hands the glittering whip that was in the elaborate chariot.
He whistled to brilliant Diomedes as a signal to him.
    But he waited, divided in his mind as to what he would best do,
whether to seize the chariot, wherein lay the bright armour,
and draw it away by the pole, or lift it and carry it off with him,   505
or strip the life from still more of the Thracians. Meanwhile
as he was pondering all this in his heart, Athene
came and stood beside him, and spoke to great Diomedes:
'Think now, son of great-hearted Tydeus, of getting back
to the hollow ships; else you might go back with men pursuing   510
if there should be some other god to waken the Trojans.'

So she spoke, and he knew the voice of the goddess speaking
and lightly mounted behind the horses. Odysseus whipped them
with his bow, and they ran for the rapid ships of the Achaians.
515   Neither did Apollo of the silver bow keep blind watch,
since he saw Athene attending the son of Tydeus. Angered
with her he plunged into the great multitude of the Trojans
and roused a man of counsel among the Thracians, Hippokoön
the lordly cousin of Rhesos; and he, starting out of his sleep,
520 when he saw the place left empty where the fast horses had been standing
and his men in the shambles of slaughter gasping their lives out,
he groaned, and called aloud by name his beloved companion.
And a clamour rose up from the Trojans and a vast turmoil
as they swept together in confusion and stared at the ghastly work done
525 by these two men, before they went back to their hollow vessels.
    But when these had come back to the place where they killed Hektor's
       scout,
Odysseus beloved of Zeus reined in his running horses
while Tydeus' son leaping to the ground took the bloody war spoils
and handed them to Odysseus, and got up behind the horses.
530 Odysseus lashed them on, and they winged their way unreluctant
back to the hollow ships, since this was the way he desired it.
Nestor was the first to hear their thunder, and spoke forth:
'Friends, who are leaders of the Argives and keep their counsel,
shall I be wrong, or am I speaking the truth? My heart tells me.
535 The thunder is beating against my ears of fast-running horses.
Might this only be Odysseus and strong Diomedes
driving rapidly away from the Trojans their single-foot horses!
Yet terribly I fear in my heart that these bravest Achaians
might have suffered some disaster from the loud host of the Trojans.'
540   Yet he had not spoken all his words, and they came. The two men
dismounted to the ground, and their companions rejoicing
congratulated them with clasped hands and with words of welcome.
First to question them was the Gerenian horseman, Nestor:
'Come, tell me, honoured Odysseus, great glory of the Achaians,
545 how did you win these horses? Did you go into the great company
of the Trojans, or did some god meet you and give them to you?
They shine, like the rays of the sun, terribly. Yet over and over
I encounter the Trojans, I say that I am not at all one

to hang back beside the ships, though I am an aged fighter.
Yet I have never seen horses like these, nor laid eyes upon them.   550
I think it must be some god who met you, and gave them to you.
Since both of you are beloved to Zeus who gathers the clouds, both
to the grey-eyed maiden of Zeus who wears the aegis, Athene.'
    Then resourceful Odysseus spoke in turn and answered him:
'Son of Neleus, Nestor, great glory of the Achaians: 555
lightly a god, if he wished, could give us horses even better
than these, seeing that the gods are far stronger than we are.
These horses, aged sir, that you ask about are newcomers
from Thrace, and as for their master brave Diomedes killed him
and at his side killed twelve companions, all of them great men;   560
our thirteenth man killed was their scout, here by the vessels,
one whom Hektor and the rest of the haughty Trojans
had sent out between the lines to spy on our army.'
    He spoke, and guided across the ditch the single-foot horses
laughing aloud, and the rest of the Achaians went with him   565
rejoicing. When they came to Diomedes' strong-fashioned shelter
there they tied up the horses by the carefully cut reins
by the horse trough where already the horses of Diomedes
were standing, rapid of foot, and eating their welcome provender.
And by the stern of the ship Odysseus laid down the bloody   570
battle spoils of Dolon, to dedicate to Athene.
And the men themselves waded into the sea and washed off
the dense sweat from shin and shoulder and thigh. Afterwards
when the surf of the sea had rinsed the dense-running sweat away
from all their skin, and the inward heart had been cooled to refreshment,   575
they stepped into the bathtubs smooth-polished, and bathed there,
and after they had bathed and anointed themselves with olive oil
they sat down to dine, and from the full mixing-bowl drawing
the sweet-hearted wine poured out an offering to Athene.

Now Dawn rose from her bed, where she lay by haughty
   Tithonos,
to carry her light to men and to immortals. Zeus sent down
in speed to the fast ships of the Achaians the wearisome goddess
of Hate, holding in her hands the portent of battle.
5 She took her place on the huge-hollowed black ship of Odysseus
which lay in the middle, so that she could cry out to both flanks,
either as far as the shelters of Telamonian Aias
or to those of Achilleus; since these had hauled their balanced ships up
at the ends, certain of their manhood and their hands' strength.
10 There the goddess took her place, and cried out a great cry
and terrible and loud, and put strength in all the Achaians'
hearts, to go on tirelessly with their fighting of battles.
And now battle became sweeter to them than to go back
in their hollow ships to the beloved land of their fathers.
15   And Atreus' son cried out aloud and drove the Achaians
to gird them, while he himself put the shining bronze upon him.
First he placed along his legs the beautiful greaves linked
with silver fastenings to hold the greaves at the ankles.
Afterwards he girt on about his chest the corselet
20 that Kinyras had given him once, to be a guest present.
For the great fame and rumour of war had carried to Kypros
how the Achaians were to sail against Troy in their vessels.
Therefore he gave the king as a gift of grace this corselet.
Now there were ten circles of deep cobalt upon it,

and twelve of gold and twenty of tin. And toward the opening   25
at the throat there were rearing up three serpents of cobalt
on either side, like rainbows, which the son of Kronos
has marked upon the clouds, to be a portent to mortals.
Across his shoulders he slung the sword, and the nails upon it
were golden and glittered, and closing about it the scabbard   30
was silver, and gold was upon the swordstraps that held it.
And he took up the man-enclosing elaborate stark shield,
a thing of splendour. There were ten circles of bronze upon it,
and set about it were twenty knobs of tin, pale-shining,
and in the very centre another knob of dark cobalt.   35
And circled in the midst of all was the blank-eyed face of the Gorgon
with her stare of horror, and Fear was inscribed upon it, and Terror.
The strap of the shield had silver upon it, and there also on it
was coiled a cobalt snake, and there were three heads upon him
twisted to look backward and grown from a single neck, all three.   40
Upon his head he set the helmet, two-horned, four-sheeted,
with the horse-hair crest, and the plumes nodded terribly above it.
Then he caught up two strong spears edged with sharp bronze
and the brazen heads flashed far from him deep into heaven.
And Hera and Athene caused a crash of thunder about him,   45
doing honour to the lord of deep-golden Mykenai.

    Thereupon each man gave orders to his charioteer
to rein in the horses once again by the ditch, in good order,
while they themselves, dismounted and armed in their war gear, swept
        onward
to the ditch, and their incessant clamour rose up in the morning.   50
In battle array they came to the ditch well ahead of the horseman
and the horseman followed a little behind. And the son of Kronos
drove down the evil turmoil upon them, and from aloft cast
down dews dripping blood from the sky, since he was minded
to hurl down a multitude of strong heads to the house of Hades.   55

    On the other side of the ditch at the break of the plain the Trojans
gathered about tall Hektor and stately Poulydamas
and Aineias, honoured by Trojans in their countryside as a god is,
and the three sons of Antenor, Polybos, and brilliant Agenor,
and Akamas, a young man still, in the likeness of the immortals.   60
And Hektor carried the perfect circle of his shield in the foremost,

[235]

as among the darkened clouds the bale star shows forth
in all shining, then merges again in the clouds and the darkness.
So Hektor would at one time be shining among the foremost,
65 and then once more urging on the last, and complete in bronze armour
glittered like the thunder-flash of Zeus of the aegis, our father.

And the men, like two lines of reapers who, facing each other,
drive their course all down the field of wheat or of barley
for a man blessed in substance, and the cut swathes drop showering,
70 so Trojans and Achaians driving in against one another
cut men down, nor did either side think of disastrous panic.
The pressure held their heads on a line, and they whirled and fought
    like
wolves, and Hate, the Lady of Sorrow, was gladdened to watch them.
She alone of all the immortals attended this action
75 but the other immortals were not there, but sat quietly
remote and apart in their palaces, where for each one of them
a house had been built in splendour along the folds of Olympos.
All were blaming the son of Kronos, Zeus of the dark mists,
because his will was to give glory to the Trojans. To these gods
80 the father gave no attention at all, but withdrawn from them
and rejoicing in the pride of his strength sat apart from the others
looking out over the city of Troy and the ships of the Achaians,
watching the flash of the bronze, and men killing and men killed.

So long as it was early morning and the sacred daylight increasing,
85 so long the thrown weapons of both took hold and men dropped under
    them.
But at that time when the woodcutter makes ready his supper
in the wooded glens of the mountains, when his arms and hands have
    grown weary
from cutting down the tall trees, and his heart has had enough of it,
and longing for food and for sweet wine takes hold of his senses;
90 at that time the Danaans by their manhood broke the battalions
calling across the ranks to each other. First Agamemnon
drove on, and killed a man, Bienor, shepherd of the people,
himself, then his companion Oïleus, lasher of horses;
who, springing down from behind his horses, stood forth to face
    him,
95 but Agamemnon stabbed straight at his face as he came on in fury

with the sharp spear, nor did helm's bronze-heavy edge hold it,
but the spearhead passed through this and the bone, and the inward
brain was all spattered forth. So he beat him down in his fury,
and Agamemnon the lord of men left them lying there
and their white bodies showing, since he had stripped off their tunics.   100
Then he went on to kill and strip Isos and Antiphos,
two sons of Priam, bastard one and one lawful, both riding
in a single chariot. The bastard, Isos, was charioteer
and renowned Antiphos rode beside him. Before this Achilleus
had caught these two at the knees of Ida, and bound them in pliant   105
willows as they watched by their sheep, and released them for ransom.
This time the son of Atreus, wide-powerful Agamemnon,
struck Isos with the thrown spear in the chest above the nipple
and hit Antiphos by the ear with the sword and hurled him from his
          horses,
and in eager haste he stripped off from these their glorious armour   110
which he knew; he had seen these two before by the fast ships
when Achilleus of the swift feet had brought them in from Ida.
And as a lion seizes the innocent young of the running
deer, and easily crunches and breaks them caught in the strong teeth
when he has invaded their lair, and rips out the soft heart from them,   115
and even if the doe be very near, still she has no strength
to help, for the ghastly shivers of fear are upon her also
and suddenly she dashes away through the glades and the timber
sweating in her speed away from the pounce of the strong beast;
so there was no one of the Trojans who could save these two   120
from death, but they themselves were running in fear from the Argives.
     Next he caught Peisandros and Hippolochos stubborn in battle,
sons of Antimachos the wise, who beyond all others
had taken the gold of Alexandros, glorious gifts, so that
he had opposed the return of Helen to fair-haired Menelaos.   125
Powerful Agamemnon caught his two sons riding
in one chariot, who together guided the running horses.
Now the glittering reins escaped from the hands of both of them
and they were stunned with fear, for against them rose like a lion
Atreus' son, and they supplicated him out of the chariot: 130
'Take us alive, son of Atreus, and take appropriate ransom.
In the house of Antimachos the treasures lie piled in abundance,

bronze is there, and gold, and difficultly wrought iron,
and our father would make you glad with abundant repayment
135 were he to hear we were alive by the ships of the Achaians.'
    Thus these two cried out upon the king, lamenting
and in pitiful phrase, but they heard the voice that was without pity:
'If in truth you are the sons of wise Antimachos,
that man who once among the Trojans assembled advised them
140 that Menelaos, who came as envoy with godlike Odysseus,
should be murdered on the spot nor let go back to the Achaians,
so now your mutilation shall punish the shame of your father.'
    He spoke, and spurned Peisandros to the ground from the chariot
with a spear-stroke in the chest, and he crashed on his back to the ground.
    Then
145 Hippolochos sprang away, but Atreides killed him dismounted,
cutting away his arms with a sword-stroke, free of the shoulder,
and sent him spinning like a log down the battle. Thereafter
he left them, and toward that place where the most battalions were shaken
drove, and beside him drove the rest of the strong-greaved Achaians,
150 and footmen killed footmen who fled under strong compulsion
and riders killed riders, and a storm of dust rose up under them
out of the plain uplifted by the thundering feet of their horses.
They killed with the bronze, and among them powerful Agamemnon
went onward always slaying and urged on the rest of the Argives.
155 As when obliterating fire comes down on the timbered forest
and the roll of the wind carries it everywhere, and bushes
leaning under the force of the fire's rush tumble uprooted,
so before Atreus' son Agamemnon went down the high heads
of the running Trojans, and in many places the strong-necked horses
160 rattled their empty chariots along the causeways of battle,
and longed for their haughty charioteers, who were lying
along the ground, to delight no longer their wives, but the vultures.
    But Zeus drew Hektor out from under the dust and the missiles,
out of the place where men were killed, the blood and confusion,
165 while Atreides followed urging the Danaans forever onward.
The Trojans swept in their flight past the barrow of ancient Ilos
Dardanos' son, to the centre of the level ground and the fig tree,
as they made for the city, and he followed them always, screaming,
Atreus' son, his invincible hands spattered with bloody filth.

But when they had made their way to the Skaian gates and the oak tree   170
the Trojans stood their ground, and each side endured the other,
while others still in the middle plain stampeded like cattle
when a lion, coming upon them in the dim night, has terrified
the whole herd, while for a single one sheer death is emerging.
First the lion breaks her neck caught fast in the strong teeth,   175
then gulps down the blood and all the guts that are inward;
so Atreus' son, powerful Agamemnon, went after them
killing ever the last of the men; and they fled in terror.
Many were hurled from behind their horses, face downward or sprawling
under the hands of Atreides who raged with his spear in the forefront.   180
But when he was on the point of making his way to the city
and the steep wall, the father of gods and of men descending
out of the sky took his place along the ridges of Ida
of the fountains, and held fast in his hands the thunderbolt.
He sent on her way Iris of the golden wings with a message: 185
'Go on your way, swift Iris, and carry my word to Hektor:
as long as he beholds Agamemnon, shepherd of the people,
raging among the champions and cutting down the ranged fighters,
so long let him hold back and urge on the rest of his people
to fight against the enemy through this strong encounter.   190
But when, either struck with a spear or hit by a flying arrow,
he springs up behind his horses, then I guarantee power to Hektor
to kill men, till he makes his way to the strong-benched vessels,
until the sun goes down and the blessed darkness comes over.'

He spoke, and swift wind-footed Iris did not disobey him,   195
but went down along the hills of Ida to sacred Ilion,
and found the son of wise Priam, Hektor the brilliant,
standing among the compacted chariots and by the horses.
Iris the swift of foot came close beside and spoke to him:
'Hektor, o son of Priam and equal of Zeus in counsel,   200
Zeus my father has sent me down to tell you this message.
As long as you behold Agamemnon, shepherd of the people,
raging among the champions and cutting down the ranged fighters,
so long hold back from the fighting, but urge on the rest of your people
to fight against the enemy through this strong encounter.   205
But when, either struck with a spear or hit by a flying arrow,
he springs up behind his horses, then Zeus guarantees power to you

to kill men, till you make your way to the strong-benched vessels,
until the sun goes down and the blessed darkness comes over.'
210   Swift-foot Iris spoke to him thus and went away from him,
and Hektor in all his armour leapt to the ground from his chariot
and shaking two sharp spears in his hand ranged over the whole host
stirring them up to fight and waking the ghastly warfare.
So they whirled about and stood their ground against the Achaians,
215 and the Argives against them pulled together their battle lines.
So the fighting grew close and they faced each other, and foremost
Agamemnon drove on, trying to fight far ahead of all others.

     Tell me now, you Muses who have your homes on Olympos,
who was the first to come forth and stand against Agamemnon
220 of the very Trojans, or their renowned companions in battle.
     Iphidamas, Antenor's son, the huge and stalwart
who had been reared in generous Thrace, the mother of sheepflocks.
Kisseus had raised him in his own house when he was little,
his mother's father, whose child was Theano, the girl of the fair cheeks.
225 But when he had arrived at the stature of powerful manhood
Kisseus detained him there and gave him his daughter. Married
he went away from the bride chamber, looking for glory
from the Achaians, with twelve curved ships that followed with him.
These balanced vessels he had left behind in Perkote
230 and gone himself to fight on foot at Ilion; and there
he came face to face with Atreus' son, Agamemnon.
Now when these in their advance were close to each other
the son of Atreus missed with his throw, and the spear was turned past him,
but Iphidamas stabbed to the belt underneath the corselet
235 and leaned in on the stroke in the confidence of his strong hand
but could not get clean through the bright war belt, far sooner
the spearpoint pushed against the silver bent back, like soft lead.
And in his hand wide-powerful Agamemnon catching it
dragged it against him, raging like a lion, and tore it
240 out of his hand, then struck the neck with his sword, and unstrung him.
So Iphidamas fell there and went into the brazen slumber,
unhappy, who came to help his own people, and left his young wife
a bride, and had known no delight from her yet, and given much for
     her.
First he had given a hundred oxen, then promised a thousand

head of goats and sheep, which were herded for him in abundance.   245
Now Agamemnon, son of Atreus, stripped him and went back
to the throng of the Achaians bearing the splendid armour.
　　When Koön, conspicuous among the fighters, perceived him,
he who was Antenor's eldest born, the strong sorrow
misted about his eyes for the sake of his fallen brother.   250
He came from the side and unobserved at great Agamemnon
and stabbed with his spear at the middle arm, underneath the elbow,
and the head of the glittering spear cut its way clean through.
Agamemnon the lord of men shuddered with fear then
but even so did not give up the attack or his fighting   255
but sprang at Koön, gripping a spear that struck with the wind's speed.
Now Koön was dragging his father's son, his brother Iphidamas,
by the foot back eagerly, and cried out on all the bravest,
but as he dragged him into the crowd, Agamemnon thrust at him
with the smoothed bronze spear underneath the knobbed shield, and   260
　　unstrung him,
then came up and hewed off his head over Iphidamas.
There under the king, Atreus' son, the sons of Antenor
filled out their destiny and went down to the house of the death god.
　　But Agamemnon ranged the ranks of the other fighters
with spear and sword and with huge stones that he flung, for such time   265
as the blood was still running warm from the spear-wound.
But after the sore place was dry, and the flow of blood stopped,
the sharp pains began to break in on the strength of Atreides.
As the sharp sorrow of pain descends on a woman in labour,
the bitterness that the hard spirits of childbirth bring on,   270
Hera's daughters, who hold the power of the bitter birthpangs,
so the sharp pains began to break in on the strength of Atreides.
He sprang back into the car, and called to his charioteer
to drive him back to the hollow ships, since his heart was heavy.
He lifted his voice and called in a piercing cry to the Danaans: 275
'Friends, o leaders and men of counsel among the Argives,
you must still continue to defend our seafaring vessels
from the wearying attack, since Zeus of the counsels would not
allow me to do battle daylong against the Trojans.'
　　He spoke, and the charioteer lashed on the bright-maned horses   280
back toward the hollow ships, and they winged their way unreluctant.

The foam ran down their chests, they were powdered with dust from
    beneath them
as they carried the stricken king away from the fighting.
    When Hektor was aware of Agamemnon withdrawing
285 he called out in a great voice to Trojans and Lykians:
'Trojans, Lykians and Dardanians who fight at close quarters,
be men now, dear friends, remember your furious valour.
Their best man is gone, and Zeus, Kronos' son, has consented
to my great glory; but steer your single-foot horses straight on
290 at the powerful Danaans, so win you the higher glory.'
    So he spoke, and stirred the spirit and strength in each man.
As when some huntsman drives to action his hounds with shining
teeth against some savage beast, wild boar or lion,
so against the Achaians Hektor the son of Priam,
295 a man like the murderous war god, lashed on the high-hearted Trojans.
And he himself with high thoughts strode out in the foremost
and hurled himself on the struggle of men like a high-blown storm-cloud
which swoops down from above to trouble the blue sea-water.
    Who then was the first, and who the last that he slaughtered,
300 Hektor, Priam's son, now that Zeus granted him glory?
Asaios first, and then Autonoös and Opites,
and Dolops, Klytios' son, Opheltios and Agelaos,
and Aisymnos, and Oros, and Hipponoös stubborn in battle.
He killed these, who were lords of the Danaans, and thereafter
305 the multitude, as when the west wind strikes in the deepening
whirlstorm to batter the clouds of the shining south wind,
so that the bulging big waves roll hard and the blown spume
scatters high before the force of the veering wind's blast.
So the massed high heads of the people were struck down by Hektor.
310 And now there might have been havoc and hopeless things done, now
the running Achaians might have tumbled back into their own ships
had not Odysseus cried out to Tydeus' son, Diomedes:
'Son of Tydeus, what has happened to us that we have forgotten
our fighting strength? Come here and stand with me, brother. There
    must be
315 shame on us, if Hektor of the glancing helm captures our vessels.'
    Then in answer powerful Diomedes spoke to him:
'Yes, I will stand with you and take what I must, yet

we shall not have our way for long, since Zeus the cloud-gatherer
would wish to give the power to the Trojans rather than to us.'

He spoke, and hurled down Thymbraios to the ground from his horses   320
with a stroke of the spear by the left nipple. Meanwhile Odysseus
killed this lord of battle's henchman, godlike Molion.
They left these to lie there, since they had ended their fighting,
then went into the ranks and wrought havoc, as when two wild boars
hurl themselves in their pride upon the hounds who pursue them.   325
So they whirled on the Trojans again and destroyed them. Meanwhile
the Achaians gladly drew breath again after their flight from great Hektor.

There they took a chariot and two men, lords in their countryside,
sons both of Merops of Perkote, who beyond all men
knew the art of prophecy, and tried to prevent his two sons   330
from going into the battle where men die. Yet these would not
listen, for the spirits of dark death were driving them onward.
Tydeus' son, Diomedes of the renowned spear, stripped them
of life and spirit, and took away their glorious armour
while Odysseus killed Hypeirochos and Hippodamos.   335
There the son of Kronos strained the battle even between them
as he looked down from Ida. They went on killing each other.
Now Tydeus' son stabbed with the spear Agastrophos, a chief
and son of Paion, striking at the hip joint. His horses
were not by for his escape, but he, strongly infatuate,   340
had a henchman holding them aside, while he, dismounted,
raged on among the champions until so he lost his dear life.
Hektor saw it sharply across the ranks and rose up against them
with a great cry, and behind him came on the Trojan battalions.
Diomedes of the great war cry shivered as he saw him   345
and suddenly he spoke to Odysseus as he came near:
'Here is this curse, Hektor the huge, wheeling down upon us.
Let us stand, and hold our ground against him, and beat him off from us.'

So he spoke, and balanced the spear far-shadowed, and threw it
aiming at the head, and struck against his mark, nor missed it,   350
at the high peak of the helm, but the bronze from the bronze was driven
back, nor reached his shining skin, the helmet guarded it,
three-ply and hollow-eyed, which Phoibos Apollo gave him.
But Hektor sprang far away back and merged among his own people,
and dropping to one knee stayed leaning on the ground with his heavy   355

[243]

hand, and a covering of black night came over both eyes.
But while the son of Tydeus was following his spear's cast
far through the front fighters where it fixed in the earth, meanwhile
Hektor got his wind again, and springing back into his chariot
360 drove back into the multitude and avoided the dark death.
Then shaking his spear powerful Diomedes called to him:
'Once again now you escaped death, dog. And yet the evil
came near you, but now once more Phoibos Apollo has saved you,
he to whom you must pray when you go into the thunder of spears
     thrown.
365 Yet I may win you, if I encounter you ever hereafter,
if beside me also there is some god who will help me.
Now I must chase whoever I can overtake of the others.'
     He spoke, and set about stripping the spear-famed son of Paion.
But now Alexandros, the lord of lovely-haired Helen,
370 pulled his bow against Tydeus' son, the shepherd of the people,
leaning against the column, work of men's hand, on the gravemound
of Ilos, Dardanos' son, an elder of the folk in the old days.
Now Diomedes was stripping the corselet of strong Agastrophos
from about his chest, and the shining shield from his shoulders
375 and the heavy helm, as the other pulled his bow at the handgrip
and shot, and the arrow escaping his hand flew not vain
but struck the flat of the right foot, and the shaft driven clean through
stuck in the ground. Then Alexandros, laughing merrily,
sprang from his hiding-place and cried out his speech of triumph:
380 'You are hit, and my arrow flew not in vain. How I wish
I had struck you in the depth of the belly and torn the life from you.
So the Trojans, who shudder before you as bleating goats do
before a lion, would have got their wind again after disaster.'
     Then not at all frightened strong Diomedes answered him:
385 'You archer, foul fighter, lovely in your locks, eyer of young girls.
If you were to make trial of me in strong combat with weapons
your bow would do you no good at all, nor your close-showered arrows.
Now you have scratched the flat of my foot, and even boast of this.
I care no more than if a witless child or a woman
390 had struck me; this is the blank weapon of a useless man, no fighter.
But if one is struck by me only a little, that is far different,
the stroke is a sharp thing and suddenly lays him lifeless,

and that man's wife goes with cheeks torn in lamentation,
and his children are fatherless, while he staining the soil with his red blood
rots away, and there are more birds than women swarming about him.'   395
    He spoke, and Odysseus the spear-famed coming up from nearby
stood in front; so he sat down behind him and pulled out
the sharp arrow from his foot, and the hard pain came over his flesh.
He sprang back into the car and called to his charioteer
to drive him back to the hollow ships, since his heart was heavy.   400
    Now Odysseus the spear-famed was left alone, nor did any
of the Argives stay beside him, since fear had taken all of them.
And troubled, he spoke then to his own great-hearted spirit:
'Ah me, what will become of me? It will be a great evil
if I run, fearing their multitude, yet deadlier if I am caught   405
alone; and Kronos' son drove to flight the rest of the Danaans.
Yet still, why does the heart within me debate on these things?
Since I know that it is the cowards who walk out of the fighting,
but if one is to win honour in battle, he must by all means
stand his ground strongly, whether he be struck or strike down another.'   410
    While he was pondering these things in his heart and his spirit
the ranks of the armoured Trojans came on against him, and penned him
in their midst, but made thereby a wound in their ranks, as when
closing about a wild boar the hounds and the lusty young men
rush him, and he comes out of his lair in the deep of a thicket   415
grinding to an edge the white fangs in the crook of the jawbones,
and these sweep in all about him, and the vaunt of his teeth uprises
as they await him, terrible though he is, without wavering;
so closing on Odysseus beloved of Zeus the Trojans
rushed him. First he stabbed lordly Deïopites   420
in the shoulder, lunging from above with a stroke of the sharp spear,
and after him he killed Thoön and Ennomos, and next
stabbed Chersidamas as he sprang down from behind his horses
in the navel with a spear's stroke underneath the massive
shield, and he dropping in the dust clawed the ground with his hand.   425
        These
he left lying, and stabbed with the spear the son of Hippasos,
Charops, full brother of Sokos, a man rich in substance. And Sokos
moved in, a man like a god, to stand over his fallen brother
and came and stood close by Odysseus and spoke a word to him:

430 'Honoured Odysseus, insatiable of guile and endeavour,
today you will have two sons of Hippasos to vaunt over
for having killed two such men as we and stripping our armour,
or else, stricken underneath my spear, you might lose your own life.'
He spoke, and stabbed Odysseus' shield in its perfect circle.
435 All the way through the glittering shield went the heavy spearhead
and crashed its way through the intricately wrought corselet,
and all the skin was torn away from his ribs, yet Pallas
Athene would not let the point penetrate the man's vitals.
Odysseus saw that the fatal end had not yet come to him,
440 and drew back and spoke a word to Sokos: 'Ah, wretch,
surely now steep destruction is advancing upon you.
It is true, you have stopped my fighting against the Trojans,
but I declare that here and now dark death and slaughter
will come upon you this day, and that beaten down under my spear
445 you will give glory to me and your life to Hades of the horses.'
He spoke, and Sokos turning from him was striding in flight
but in his back even as he was turning the spear fixed
between the shoulders and was driven on through the chest beyond it.
He fell, thunderously, and great Odysseus boasted over him:
450 'Sokos, son of wise Hippasos the breaker of horses,
death was too quick for you and ran you down, you could not
avoid it. Wretch, since now your father and your honoured mother
will not be able to close your eyes in death, but the tearing
birds will get you, with their wings close-beating about you.
455 If I die, the brilliant Achaians will bury me in honour.'
So he spoke, and dragged the heavy spear of wise Sokos
out of his flesh and out of the shield massive in the middle,
and as it was torn out the blood sprang and his heart was sickened.
But the great-hearted Trojans, when they saw the blood of Odysseus,
460 cried aloud through the close battle and all made a charge against him.
He gave back a little way and called out for his companions.
Three times he called, as much voice as a man's head could hold,
and three times Menelaos the warlike heard him shouting
and immediately spoke to Aias, who was near by him:
465 'Son of Telamon, seed of Zeus, Aias, lord of the people,
the war cry of patient Odysseus is ringing about me
with a sound as if he had been cut off by himself, and the Trojans

were handling him violently in the strong encounter. Therefore
let us go to him through the battle. It is better to defend him against them.
I fear that, caught alone, he may be hurt by the Trojans   470
brave as he is, and so a great loss may befall the Danaans.'
    He spoke, and led the way, and the other followed, a mortal
like a god. They found Odysseus beloved of Zeus, and around him
the Trojans crowded, as bloody scavengers in the mountains
crowd on a horned stag who is stricken, one whom a·hunter   475
shot with an arrow from the string, and the stag has escaped him, running
with his feet, while the blood stayed warm, and his knees were springing
        beneath him.
But when the pain of the flying arrow has beaten him, then
the rending scavengers begin to feast on him in the mountains
and the shaded glen. But some spirit leads that way a dangerous   480
lion, and the scavengers run in terror, and the lion eats it;
so about wise much-devising Odysseus the Trojans
crowded now, valiant and numerous, but the hero
with rapid play of his spear beat off the pitiless death-day.
Now Aias came near him, carrying like a wall his shield,   485
and stood forth beside him, and the Trojans fled one way and another.
Then taking Odysseus by the hand warlike Menelaos
led him from the battle, while his henchman drove the horses close up.
    But Aias leaping upon the Trojans struck down Doryklos,
Priam's son, but a bastard, and thereafter stabbed Pandokos,   490
and so also Lysandros and Pyrasos and Pylartes.
As when a swollen river hurls its water, big with rain,
down the mountains to the flat land following rain from the sky god,
and sweeps down with it numbers of dry oaks and of pine trees
numbers, until it hurls its huge driftwood into the salt sea;   495
so now glittering Aias cumbered the plain as he chased them,
slaughtering men and horses alike, nor yet had Hektor
heard, since he was fighting at the left of the entire battle
by the banks of Skamandros river, where more than elsewhere
the high heads of men were dropping, and the tireless clamour   500
rising about tall Nestor and Idomeneus the warlike.
Now Hektor was encountering these and doing grim work
with spear and horsemanship, ruining the battalions of young men.
Yet even so the Achaians would not have given from his path

505 had not Alexandros, the lord of lovely-haired Helen,
stayed from his bravery the shepherd of the people, Machaon,
hitting him with a three-barbed arrow in the right shoulder.
And the Achaians whose wind was fury were frightened for him,
that the enemy might catch him in the backturn of the fighting.
510 At once Idomeneus called out to brilliant Nestor:
'Nestor, son of Neleus, great glory of the Achaians,
quick, get up on your chariot, let Machaon beside you
mount, and steer your single-foot horses to the ships in all speed.
A healer is a man worth many men in his knowledge
515 of cutting out arrows and putting kindly medicines on wounds.'
  He spoke, and the Gerenian horseman Nestor obeyed him.
Immediately he mounted the chariot, and Machaon,
son of the great healer Asklepios, mounted beside him.
He lashed on the horses, and they winged their way unreluctant
520 back toward the hollow ships, since this was the way they desired.
  Now Kebriones, who saw how the Trojans were being driven,
and who stood beside Hektor in the chariot, spoke a word to him:
'Hektor, you and I encounter the Danaans at the utmost
edge of the sorrowful battle, but meanwhile the rest of the Trojans
525 are driven pell-mell upon each other, the men and their horses.
The Telamonian Aias drives them; I know him surely
for he carries the broad shield on his shoulders. So, let us also
steer our horses and chariot that way, since there the horsemen
and the foot-ranks more than elsewhere hurling the wicked war-hate
530 against each other, are destroying, and the ceaseless clamour has risen.'
  So he spoke, and lashed forward the bright-maned horses
with the singing whip, and they at the feel of the stroke lightly
carried the running chariot among Achaians and Trojans,
trampling down dead men and shields, and the axle under
535 the chariot was all splashed with blood and the rails which encircled
the chariot, struck by flying drops from the feet of the horses,
from the running rims of the wheels. So Hektor was straining to plunge
    in
the turmoil of men, and charge them and break them. He hurled the
    confusion
of disaster upon the Danaans, and stayed from the spear's stroke
540 little, but with his spear and his sword and with huge stones flung

ranged about among the ranks of the rest of the fighters
yet kept clear still of the attack of Telamonian Aias.
   But Zeus father who sits on high drove fear upon Aias.
He stood stunned, and swung the sevenfold ox-hide shield behind him
and drew back, throwing his eyes round the crowd of men, like a wild   545
      beast,
turning on his way, shifting knee past knee only a little;
as when the men who live in the wild and their dogs have driven
a tawny lion away from the mid-fenced ground of their oxen,
and will not let him tear out the fat of the oxen, watching
nightlong against him, and he in his hunger for meat closes in   550
but can get nothing of what he wants, for the raining javelins
thrown from the daring hands of the men beat ever against him,
and the flaming torches, and these he balks at for all of his fury
and with the daylight goes away, disappointed of desire;
so Aias, disappointed at heart, drew back from the Trojans   555
much unwilling, but feared for the ships of the Achaians. As when
a donkey, stubborn and hard to move, goes into a cornfield
in despite of boys, and many sticks have been broken upon him,
but he gets in and goes on eating the deep grain, and the children
beat him with sticks, but their strength is infantile; yet at last   560
by hard work they drive him out when he is glutted with eating;
so the high-hearted Trojans and companions in arms gathered
from far places kept after great Aias, the son of Telamon,
stabbing always with their spears at the centre of the great shield.
And now Aias would remember again his furious valour   565
and turn upon them, and beat back the battalions of Trojans,
breakers of horses, and then again would turn and run from them.
He blocked them all from making their way on to the fast ships
and himself stood and fought on in the space between the Achaians
and Trojans, and of the spears thrown by the daring hands of the fighters 570
some that were driven forward stuck fast in the great shield, others
and many in the mid space before they had got to his white skin
stood fast in the ground, though they had been straining to reach his
      body.
   Now as Eurypylos the glorious son of Euaimon
saw how Aias was being overpowered by the dense spears,   575
he came and stood beside him and made a cast with his bright spear

and struck Apisaon, son of Phausias, shepherd of the people,
in the liver under the midriff, and at once took the strength from his knees.
Eurypylos springing forward stripped the armour from his shoulders
580 but godlike Alexandros watched him as he was stripping
the armour of Apisaon, and at once drew his bow, and shot
at Eurypylos, and hit him in the right thigh with the arrow,
and the reed shaft was broken off, and his thigh was heavy with pain.
To avoid death he shrank into the host of his own companions.
585 He lifted his voice and called in a piercing cry to the Danaans:
'Friends, o leaders and men of counsel among the Argives,
turn again and stand and beat off the pitiless death-day
from Aias, who is being overpowered with spears thrown; and I think
he cannot escape out of this sorrowful battle. Therefore
590 stand fast and face them around great Aias, the son of Telamon.'
So spoke wounded Eurypylos, and the others about him
stood in their numbers and sloped their shields over his shoulders, holding
the spears away, and Aias came back to join them. He turned
and stood, when he had got back to the swarm of his own companions.
595   So they fought on in the likeness of blazing fire. And meanwhile
the horses of Neleus sweating carried Nestor away from
the fighting, and carried also the shepherd of the people, Machaon.
Now swift-footed brilliant Achilleus saw him and watched him,
for he was standing on the stern of his huge-hollowed vessel
600 looking out over the sheer war work and the sorrowful onrush.
At once he spoke to his own companion in arms, Patroklos,
calling from the ship, and he heard it from inside the shelter, and came out
like the war god, and this was the beginning of his evil.
The strong son of Menoitios spoke first, and addressed him:
605 'What do you wish with me, Achilleus? Why do you call me?'
Then in answer again spoke Achilleus of the swift feet:
'Son of Menoitios, you who delight my heart, o great one,
now I think the Achaians will come to my knees and stay there
in supplication, for a need past endurance has come to them.
610 But go now, Patroklos beloved of Zeus, to Nestor
and ask him who is this wounded man he brings in from the fighting.
Indeed, seeing him from behind I thought he was like Machaon,
Asklepios' son, in all ways, but I got no sight of the man's face
since the horses were tearing forward and swept on by me.'

So he spoke, and Patroklos obeyed his beloved companion   615
and went on the run along the shelters and ships of the Achaians.
  Now when the others came to the shelter of the son of Neleus,
they themselves dismounted to the prospering earth, and the henchman
Eurymedon unharnessed the horses of the old man
from the chariot. The men wiped off the sweat on their tunics   620
and stood to the wind beside the beach of the sea, and thereafter
went inside the shelter and took their places on settles.
And lovely-haired Hekamede made them a potion, she whom
the old man won from Tenedos, when Achilleus stormed it.
She was the daughter of great-hearted Arsinoös. The Achaians   625
chose her out for Nestor, because he was best of them all in counsel.
First she pushed up the table in front of them, a lovely
table, polished and with feet of cobalt, and on it
she laid a bronze basket, with onion to go with the drinking,
and pale honey, and beside it bread, blessed pride of the barley,   630
and beside it a beautifully wrought cup which the old man brought with
     him
from home. It was set with golden nails, the eared handles upon it
were four, and on either side there were fashioned two doves
of gold, feeding, and there were double bases beneath it.
Another man with great effort could lift it full from the table,   635
but Nestor, aged as he was, lifted it without strain.
In this the woman like the immortals mixed them a potion
with Pramneian wine, and grated goat's-milk cheese into it
with a bronze grater, and scattered with her hand white barley into it.
When she had got the potion ready, she told them to drink it,   640
and both when they had drunk it were rid of their thirst's parching
and began to take pleasure in conversation, talking with each other,
and Patroklos came and stood, a godlike man, in the doorway.
Seeing him the old man started up from his shining
chair, and took him by the hand, led him in and told him to sit down,   645
but Patroklos from the other side declined, and spoke to him:
'No chair, aged sir beloved of Zeus. You will not persuade me.
Honoured, and quick to blame, is the man who sent me to find out
who was this wounded man you were bringing. Now I myself
know, and I see it is Machaon, the shepherd of the people.   650
Now I go back as messenger to Achilleus, to tell him.

You know yourself, aged sir beloved of Zeus, how *he* is;
a dangerous man; he might even be angry with one who is guiltless.'
    Then in turn the Gerenian horseman Nestor answered him:
655 'Now why is Achilleus being so sorry for the sons of the Achaians
who have been wounded with spears thrown, he who knows nothing
of the sorrow that has risen along the host, since the bravest
are lying up among the ships with arrow or spear wounds?
The son of Tydeus, strong Diomedes, was hit by an arrow,
660 and Odysseus has a pike wound, and Agamemnon the spear-famed,
and Eurypylos has been wounded in the thigh with an arrow. And even
    now
I have brought this other one, Machaon, out of the fighting
hit by an arrow from the bowstring. Meanwhile Achilleus
brave as he is cares nothing for the Danaans nor pities them.
665 Is he going to wait then till the running ships by the water
are burned with consuming fire for all the Argives can do, till
we ourselves are killed one after another? Since there is not
any longer in my gnarled limbs the strength that there once was.
If only I were young now, and the strength still steady within me,
670 as that time when a quarrel was made between us and the Eleians
over a driving of cattle, when I myself killed Itymoneus,
the brave son of Hypeirochos who made his home in Elis.
I was driving cattle in reprisal, and he, as he was defending
his oxen, was struck among the foremost by a spear thrown from my hand
675 and fell, and his people who live in the wild fled in terror about him.
And we got and drove off together much spoil from this pastureland:
fifty herds of oxen, as many sheepflocks, as many
droves of pigs, and again as many wide-ranging goatflocks,
and a hundred and fifty brown horses, mares all of them
680 and many with foals following underneath. And all there
we drove inside the keep of Neleian Pylos, making
our way nightwise to the town. And Neleus was glad in his heart
that so much had come my way, who was young to go to the fighting.
And next day as dawn showed the heralds lifted their clear cry
685 for all to come who had anything owed them in shining Elis.
And the men who were chiefs among the Pylians assembling
divided the spoil. There were many to whom the Epeians owed something
since we in Pylos were few and we had been having the worst of it.

For Herakles had come in his strength against us and beaten us
in the years before, and all the bravest among us had been killed.   690
For we who were sons of lordly Neleus had been twelve, and now
I alone was left of these, and all the others had perished,
and grown haughty over this the bronze-armoured Epeians
despised and outraged us, and devised wicked actions against us.
Now the old man took for himself a herd of cattle and a big flock   695
of sheep, choosing out three hundred of them along with the shepherds;
for indeed a great debt was owing to him in shining Elis.
It was four horses, race-competitors with their own chariot,
who were on their way to a race and were to run for a tripod,
but Augeias the lord of men took these, and kept them   700
and sent away their driver who was vexed for the sake of the horses.
Now aged Neleus, angry over things said and things done,
took a vast amount for himself, and gave the rest to the people
to divide among them, so none might go away without a just share.
So we administered all this spoil, and all through the city   705
wrought sacrifices to the gods; and on the third day the Epeians
came all against us, numbers of men and single-foot horses
in full haste, and among them were armoured the two Moliones,
boys still, not yet altogether skilled in furious fighting.
There is a city, Thryoessa, a headlong hill town   710
far away by the Alpheios at the bottom of sandy Pylos.
They had thrown their encampment about that place, furious to smash it.
But when they had swept the entire plain, Athene came running
to us, a messenger from Olympos by night, and warned us
to arm. It was no hesitant host she assembled in Pylos   715
but people straining hard toward the battle. Now Neleus would not
let me be armed among them, and had hidden away my horses
because he thought I was not yet skilled in the work of warfare.
Even so I was pre-eminent among our own horsemen
though I went on foot; since thus Athene guided the battle.   720
There is a river, Minyeïos, which empties its water
in the sea beside Arene. There we waited for the divine Dawn,
we horsemen among the Pylians, and the hordes of the streaming foot-
    soldiers,
and from there having armed in all speed and formed in our armour
we came by broad daylight to the sacred stream of Alpheios.   725

There we wrought fine sacrifices to Zeus in his great strength
and sacrificed a bull to Alpheios, a bull to Poseidon,
but to Athene of the grey eyes a cow from the herds. Then
we took our dinner along the host in divided watches
730 and went to sleep, each man in his own armour, by the current
of the river, and meanwhile the high-hearted Epeians
had taken their places around the city, furious to smash it.
But sooner than this there was shown forth a great work of the war god,
for when the sun in his shining lifted above the earth, then
735 we joined our battle together, with prayers to Zeus and Athene.
Now when the battle came on between Pylians and Epeians,
I was first to kill a man, and I won his single-foot horses.
It was Moulios the spearman who was son-in-law to Augeias
and had as wife his eldest daughter, fair-haired Agamede
740 who knew of all the medicines that are grown in the broad earth.
As he came on I threw and hit him with the bronze-headed spear
and he dropped in the dust, whereupon I springing into his chariot
took my place among the champions, as the high-hearted Epeians
fled one way and another in terror when they saw the man fall
745 who was leader of their horsemen and the best of them all in fighting.
Then I charged upon them like a black whirlwind, and overtook
fifty chariots, and for each of the chariots two men
caught the dirt in their teeth beaten down under my spear.
And now I would have killed the young Moliones, scions
750 of Aktor, had not their father who shakes the earth in his wide strength
caught them out of the battle, shrouding them in a thick mist.
Then Zeus gave huge power into the hands of the Pylians,
for we chased them on over the hollow plain, killing
the men themselves, and picking up their magnificent armour
755 until we brought our horses to Bouprasion of the wheatfields
and the Olenian rock, where there is a hill called the hill
of Alesios. There at last Athene turned back our people.
There I killed my last man and left him. There the Achaians
steered back from Bouprasion to Pylos their fast-running horses,
760 and all glorified Zeus among the gods, but among men Nestor.
That was I, among men, if it ever happened. But Achilleus
will enjoy his own valour in loneliness, though I think
he will weep much, too late, when his people are perished from him.

Dear child, surely this was what Menoitios told you
that day when he sent you out from Phthia to Agamemnon.   765
We two, brilliant Odysseus and I, were inside with you
and listened carefully to everything, all that he told you.
For we had come to the strong-established house of Peleus
assembling fighting men all through generous Achaia. We came
there, and found the hero Menoitios inside, and you,   770
Achilleus beside you, and Peleus the aged horseman was burning
the fat thigh pieces of an ox to Zeus who delights in the thunder
in the garth of the courtyard. He was holding a golden beaker
and pouring the bright wine over the burning dedications. You two
were over the meat of the ox attending to it, and we came   775
and stood in the forecourt, and Achilleus sprang up wondering
and took us by the hand and led us in, and told us to sit down,
and set hospitality properly before us, as is the stranger's
right. Now when we had taken our pleasure of eating and drinking
I began to talk, and invited you both to come with us,   780
and you were altogether willing, and your fathers spoke to you.
And Peleus the aged was telling his own son, Achilleus,
to be always best in battle and pre-eminent beyond all others,
but for you, Menoitios, Aktor's son, had this to say to you:
"My child, by right of blood Achilleus is higher than you are,   785
but you are the elder. Yet in strength he is far the greater.
You must speak solid words to him, and give him good counsel,
and point his way. If he listens to you it will be for his own good."
This is what the old man told you, you have forgotten. Yet even
now you might speak to wise Achilleus, he might be persuaded.   790
Who knows if, with God helping, you might trouble his spirit
by entreaty, since the persuasion of a friend is a strong thing.
But if he is drawing back from some prophecy known in his own heart
and by Zeus' will his honoured mother has told him of something,
let him send you out, at least, and the rest of the Myrmidon people   795
follow you, and you may be a light given to the Danaans.
And let him give you his splendid armour to wear to the fighting,
if perhaps the Trojans might think you are he, and give way
from their attack, and the fighting sons of the Achaians get wind
again after hard work. There is little breathing space in the fighting.   800
You, unwearied, might with a mere cry pile men wearied

back upon their city, and away from the ships and the shelters.'
       So he spoke, and stirred the feeling in the breast of Patroklos,
       and he went on the run along the ships to the son of Aiakos,
805   Achilleus. But as Patroklos came in his running to the ships
       of great Odysseus, where the Achaians had their assembly and dealt out
       rights, and where were established their altars to the immortals,
       there Eurypylos, who had been wounded in the thigh with an arrow,
       met him, the illustrious son of Euaimon, limping
810   away from the battle, and the watery sweat was running
       down his shoulders and face, and from the sore wound dark blood
       continued to drip, and yet the will stayed steady within him.
       And the strong son of Menoitios looked on him in pity
       and was sorrowful over him, and addressed him in winged words:
815   'Poor wretches, you leaders and men of counsel among the Danaans,
       was it your fate then, far from your friends and the land of your fathers,
       to glut with your shining fat the running dogs here in Troy land?
       But tell me this, my lord Eurypylos grown under God's hand:
       will the Achaians somehow be able to hold huge Hektor
820   or must they now perish beaten down under his spear?'
       Then Eurypylos who was wounded answered him in turn:
       'No longer, illustrious Patroklos, can the Achaians
       defend themselves, but they will be piled back into their black ships.
       For all of these who were before the bravest in battle
825   are lying up among the ships with arrow or spear wounds
       under the hands of the Trojans whose strength is forever on the uprise.
       But help save me now at least, leading me away to my black ship,
       and cut the arrow out of my thigh, wash the dark blood running
       out of it with warm water, and put kind medicines on it,
830   good ones, which they say you have been told of by Achilleus,
       since Cheiron, most righteous of the Centaurs, told him about them.
       As for Machaon and Podaleirios, who are healers,
       I think Machaon has got a wound, and is in the shelters
       lying there, and himself is in need of a blameless healer,
835   while the other in the plain is standing the bitter attack of the Trojans.'
       Then in turn the strong son of Menoitios spoke to him:
       'But how shall this be, my lord Eurypylos, how shall we do it?
       I am on my way carrying a message to wise Achilleus
       given me by Gerenian Nestor, the Achaians' watcher.

But even so I will not leave you in your affliction.'   840
    He spoke, and holding the shepherd of the host under the arms led him
to his shelter, and a henchman seeing them spread out some ox-hides,
and Patroklos laid him there and with a knife cut the sharp tearing
arrow out of his thigh, and washed the black blood running from it
with warm water, and, pounding it up in his hands, laid on   845
a bitter root to make pain disappear, one which stayed
all kinds of pain. And the wound dried, and the flow of blood stopped.

So within the shelter the warlike son of Menoitios
tended stricken Eurypylos, and meanwhile the Argives
and Trojans fought on in massed battle, nor was the Danaans'
ditch going to hold them back nor the wide wall above it
5 they had built for the sake of their ships, and driven a deep ditch
about it, and had not given to the gods grand sacrifices
so that it might guard their running ships and their masses
of spoil within it. It had been built in despite of the immortal
gods, and therefore it was not to stand firm for a long time.
10 So long as Hektor was still alive, and Achilleus was angry,
so long as the citadel of lord Priam was a city untaken,
for this time the great wall of the Achaians stood firm. But afterwards
when all the bravest among the Trojans had died in the fighting,
and many of the Argives had been beaten down, and some left,
15 when in the tenth year the city of Priam was taken
and the Argives gone in their ships to the beloved land of their fathers,
then at last Poseidon and Apollo took counsel
to wreck the wall, letting loose the strength of rivers upon it,
all the rivers that run to the sea from the mountains of Ida,
20 Rhesos and Heptaporos, Karesos and Rhodios,
Grenikos and Aisepos, and immortal Skamandros,
and Simoeis, where much ox-hide armour and helmets were tumbled
in the river mud, and many of the race of the half-god mortals.
Phoibos Apollo turned the mouths of these waters together
25 and nine days long threw the flood against the wall, and Zeus rained

incessantly, to break the wall faster and wash it seaward.
And the shaker of the earth himself holding in his hands the trident
guided them, and hurled into the waves all the bastions' strengthening
of logs and stones the toiling Achaians had set in position
and made all smooth again by the hard-running passage of Helle   30
and once again piled the great beach under sand, having wrecked
the wall, and turned the rivers again to make their way down
the same channel where before they had run the bright stream of their
    water.
   Thus, afterwards, Poseidon and Apollo were minded
to put things in place, but at this time battle and clamour were blazing   35
about the strong-founded wall and the bastion timbers were thundering
as they were struck, as the Argives broken under Zeus' lashing
were crowded back on their hollow ships, and struggled to get clear
in dread of Hektor, the strong one who drove men to thoughts of panic.
But Hektor, as he had before, fought on like a whirlwind.   40
As when among a pack of hounds and huntsmen assembled
a wild boar or lion turns at bay in the strength of his fury,
and the men, closing themselves into a wall about him,
stand up to face him, and cast at him with the volleying spears thrown
from their hands, and in spite of this the proud heart feels not   45
terror, nor turns to run, and it is his own courage that kills him;
and again and again he turns on them trying to break the massed men
and wherever he charges the masses of men break away in front of him;
such was Hektor as he went through the battle and rallied his companions
and drove them on to cross over the ditch, but now the fast-footed   50
horses balked at the edge of the lip, and dared not cross, whinnying
loud, since the ditch in its great width frightened them from it,
being not easy for them to overleap, nor to walk through,
since along the whole length the jut of the overhangs stood
on both sides, and the surface of the floor was thickset with pointed   55
palisades, which the sons of the Achaians had paled there
dense and huge, so as to hold off the rage of attackers.
And a horse straining at the strong-wheeled chariot might not easily
enter there, but the dismounted were strong in their effort.
And now Poulydamas stood beside bold Hektor, and spoke to him: 60
   'Hektor, and other lords of the Trojans and companions in battle,
we are senseless trying to drive our fast-footed horses over

this ditch. It is hard indeed to cross, and sharp stakes are planted
inside it, and across from these the wall of the Achaians.
65 There there is no way to get down, no way again to do battle
from horses, for the passage is narrow and I think they must be hurt there.
For now if Zeus who thunders on high in evil intention
toward these is destroying them utterly, sending aid to the Trojans,
this is the way I would wish it, may it happen immediately
70 that the Achaians be destroyed here forgotten and far from
Argos; but if they turn again and a backrush comes on us
out of the ships, and we are driven against the deep ditch,
then I think no longer could one man to carry a message
get clear to the city, once the Achaians have turned back upon us.
75 Come then, do as I say, let us all be persuaded; let us
tell our henchmen to check our horses here by the ditch, then
let ourselves, all of us dismounted and armed in our war gear,
follow Hektor in mass formation. As for the Achaians,
they will not hold, if the bonds of death are fastened upon them.'
80   So spoke Poulydamas, and this counsel of safety pleased Hektor.
And at once in all his armour he leapt to the ground from his chariot,
and the rest of the Trojans assembled, not mounted behind their horses,
but all sprang to the ground, when they saw brilliant Hektor had done it.
Then each man gave orders to his own charioteer
85 to check the horses in good order at the edge of the ditch,
and the fighters formed apart into groups, then closing together
into five well-ordered battalions followed their leaders.

    They who went with Hektor and Poulydamas the blameless,
these were most numerous, and bravest, and beyond others furious
90 to smash the wall and fight their way among the hollow ships,
and Kebriones went with them as third man, while by the chariots
Hektor had left another man, not so good as Kebriones.
Paris led the next group with Alkathoös and Agenor,
and Helenos, with godlike Deïphobos, led the third group,
95 sons both of Priam, and Asios was with them as third man,
Asios, son of Hyrtakos, whom his tall shining horses
had carried over from Arisbe and beside the river Selleëis.
The leader of the fourth group was the strong son of Anchises,
Aineias, and with him were the two sons of Antenor,
100 Archelochos and Akamas, both skilled in all fighting.

Sarpedon led the far-renowned companions in battle,
and had chosen to go with him Glaukos and warlike Asteropaios
since these seemed to him to be marked out as the bravest
of the rest, after himself, but among all he was pre-eminent.
Now when these had closed their wrought ox-hide shields together   105
they charged straight for the Danaans, eagerly, with no thought longer
of being held, but rather to hurl themselves on the black ships.

   Then the rest of the Trojans and renowned companions in battle
were willing to follow the order of blameless Poulydamas. Only
Asios, Hyrtakos' son, lord of men, was unwilling   110
to leave his horses there and a charioteer to attend them
but kept them with him, and so drove on at the fast-running vessels,
poor fool, who by the ships in the pride of his horses and chariot
was not destined to evade the evil spirits of destruction
nor ever to make his way back again to windy Ilion.   115
Before this the dark-named destiny had shrouded about him
through the spear of Idomeneus, proud son of Deukalion.
For he sent his horses to the left of the ships, where the Achaians
were streaming back from the level ground with horses and chariots,
and this way he drove his chariot and horses, and found there   120
the leaves not yet pushed home in the gates, nor the long door-bar,
but men were holding them wide apart, on the chance of rescuing
some one of their companions running for the ships from the battle.
Of a purpose he steered his horses straight there, and his men followed
screaming aloud, since they thought the Achaians no longer   125
would hold, but that they would be driven back on their dark ships.
Fools! since in the gates they found two men of the bravest,
high-hearted sons of the spear-fighting Lapithai, one
the son of Peirithoös, powerful Polypoites,
and one Leonteus, a man like the murderous god of battles.   130
Now these two, who had taken their place in front of the high gates,
stood there like two oaks who rear their crests in the mountains
and through day upon day stand up to the wind and the rainbeat
since their great roots reach far and are gripped in the ground. So
these two, in the confidence of their strength and their hands' work,   135
stood up to tall Asios advancing upon them, nor gave way.
But these, holding up high the tanned leather of their shields, moved
straight in on the strong-built wall with enormous clamour

around Asios their lord and Iamenos and Orestes,
140 and Asios' son Adamas, and Oinomaos and Thoön.
In this time the Lapithai still inside the wall were striving
to stir up the strong-greaved Achaians to defend the vessels,
but among the Danaans, when they saw the Trojans sweeping
on against the wall, a clamour arose, and they gave way;
145 and the two bursting through the gates fought on in front of them.
They were in the likeness of two wild boars who in the mountains
await a rabble of men and dogs advancing upon them
and as they go tearing slantwise and rip the timber about them
to pieces at the stock, the grinding scream of their teeth sounds
150 high, until some man hits them with his throw and takes the life from
        them;
such was the grinding scream from the bright bronze covering their chests
struck hard on by spears, for they fought a very strong battle
in the confidence of their own strength and the people above them.
These flung about them with great stones torn from the strong-founded
155 bastions, as they fought in defence of themselves, and the shelters,
and the fast-running vessels, so that the flung stones dropped to the
        ground
like snowflakes which the winds' blast whirling the shadowy clouds
drifts in their abundance along the prospering earth. So
the missiles flung from the hands of Achaians, and Trojans also,
160 went showering, and the helms and shields massive in the middle
crashed hollow underneath the impact of rocks like millstones.
And now Asios, Hyrtakos' son, groaned aloud and beat on
both thighs with his hands, and spoke aloud in his agony:
'Zeus father, now even you are made utterly a lover
165 of deception. For I never thought the fighting Achaians
would be able to hold our strength and our hands invincible.
But they, as wasps quick-bending in the middle, or as bees
will make their homes at the side of the rocky way, and will not
abandon the hollow house they have made, but stand up to
170 men who come to destroy them, and fight for the sake of their children,
so these, though they are only two, are unwilling to give back
from the gates, until they have killed their men, or are taken.'
    He spoke, but by such talk did not persuade the heart of Zeus
whose desire it was to extend the glory to Hektor.

And now at the various gates various men fought each other.   175
It were too much toil for me, as if I were a god, to tell all this,
for all about the stone wall the inhuman strength of the fire
was rising, and the Argives fought unhappily, yet they must fight
on, to defend their ships. And all the gods who were helpers
of the Danaans in the fighting were dejected in spirit.   180
    But the Lapithai fought on and closed in the hateful fighting,
and there the son of Peirithoös, powerful Polypoites,
struck Damasos with the spear through the bronze-sided helmet,
and the brazen helmet could not hold, but the bronze spearhead
driven on through smashed the bone apart, and the inward   185
brain was all spattered forth. So he beat him down in his fury.
Then he went on to kill Pylon and Ormenos. Meanwhile
Leonteus, the scion of Ares, struck down Antimachos'
son, Hippomachos, with a spear cast into the war belt
and afterwards drawing his sharp sword out of the scabbard   190
made a rush through the crowding men, and struck from close up
Antiphates first, so that he crashed on his back to the ground, then
beat down along the prospering earth Menon and Orestes
and Iamenos, all beaten down in rapid succession.
    Now as these were stripping their men of the shining armour,   195
the fighting men following with Poulydamas and Hektor,
who were most numerous, and bravest, and beyond others furious
to smash the wall, and set fire to the vessels, these still
were divided in doubt as they stood there at the ditch's edge.
As they were urgent to cross a bird sign had appeared to them,   200
an eagle, flying high and holding to the left of the people
and carrying in its talons a gigantic snake, blood-coloured,
alive still and breathing, it had not forgotten its warcraft
yet, for writhing back it struck the eagle that held it
by chest and neck, so that the eagle let it drop groundward   205
in pain of the bite, and dashed it down in the midst of the battle
and itself, screaming high, winged away down the wind's blast.
And the Trojans shivered with fear as they looked on the lithe snake
lying in their midst, a portent of Zeus of the aegis.
And now Poulydamas stood beside bold Hektor and spoke to him: 210
'Hektor, somehow in assembly you move ever against me
though I speak excellently, since indeed there is no good reason

for you, in your skill, to argue wrong, neither in the councils
nor in the fighting, and ever to be upholding your own cause.
215 Now once more I will speak out the way it seems best to me.
Let us not go on and fight the Danaans by their ships. I think
it will end as the portent was accomplished, if the bird sign
that came to the Trojans as we were trying to cross was a true one,
an eagle, flying high and holding to the left of the people
220 and carrying in its talons a gigantic snake, blood-coloured,
alive, but let it drop suddenly before winning his own home,
and could not finish carrying it back to give to his children.
So we, even though in our great strength we break in the gates
and the wall of the Achaians, and the Achaians give way before us,
225 we shall not take the same ways back from the ships in good order;
since we shall leave many Trojans behind us, whom the Achaians
will cut down with the bronze as they fight for themselves by their vessels.
So an interpreter of the gods would answer, one who knew
in his mind the truth of portents, and whom the people believed in.'
230   Looking darkly at him tall Hektor of the shining helm answered:
'Poulydamas, these things that you argue please me no longer.
Your mind knows how to contrive a saying better than this one.
But if in all seriousness this is your true argument, then
it is the very gods who ruined the brain within you,
235 you who are telling me to forget the counsels of thunderous
Zeus, in which he himself nodded his head to me and assented.
But you: you tell me to put my trust in birds, who spread
wide their wings. I care nothing for these, I think nothing of them,
nor whether they go by on our right against dawn and sunrise
240 or go by to the left against the glooming mist and the darkness.
No, let us put our trust in the counsel of great Zeus, he who
is lord over all mortal men and all the immortals.
One bird sign is best: to fight in defence of our country.
Why are you so afraid of war and hostility? Even
245 though all the rest of us were to be cut down around you
among the Argive ships, you would run no danger of dying
since your heart is not enduring in battle nor a fighter's.
But if you shrink away from the murderous work, or turn back
some other man from the fighting, beguiling him with your arguments,
250 at once beaten down under my spear you will lose your own life.'

He spoke, and led the way, and the rest of them came on after him
with unearthly clamour, and over them Zeus who delights in the thunder
drove down from among the hills of Ida the blast of a windstorm
which swept the dust straight against the ships. He was mazing the minds
of the Achaians, and giving glory to the Trojans and Hektor,   255
and they in the confidence of the portents shown, and their own strength,
worked to break down the great wall of the Achaians. They tore
at the projections on the outworks, and broke down the battlements
and shook with levers the jut of the buttresses the Achaians
had stuck in the earth on the outer face to shore their defences.   260
They tore at these, in hope of breaking down the Achaians'
wall, but now the Danaans did not give way in front of them,
but they, fencing the battlements with the hides of oxen,
hurled from the wall at the enemy who came on beneath it.

The two Aiantes, walking up and down the length of the ramparts,   265
urged the men on, stirring up the warcraft of the Achaians,
and stung them along, using kind words to one, to another
hard ones, whenever they saw a man hang back from the fighting:
'Dear friends, you who are pre-eminent among the Argives, you who
are of middle estate, you who are of low account, since   270
all of us are not alike in battle, this is work for all now,
and you yourselves can see it. Now let no man let himself
be turned back upon the ships for the sound of their blustering
but keep forever forward calling out courage to each other.
So may Olympian Zeus who grips the thunderbolt grant us   275
a way to the city, when we beat off the attack of our enemies.'
Such was their far cry, and they stirred the Achaians' war strength.
And they, as storms of snow descend to the ground incessant
on a winter day, when Zeus of the counsels, showing
before men what shafts he possesses, brings on a snowstorm   280
and stills the winds asleep in the solid drift, enshrouding
the peaks that tower among the mountains and the shoulders out-jutting,
and the low lands with their grasses, and the prospering work of men's
    hands,
and the drift falls along the grey sea, the harbours and beaches,
and the surf that breaks against it is stilled, and all things elsewhere   285
it shrouds from above, with the burden of Zeus' rain heavy upon it;
so numerous and incessant were the stones volleyed from both sides,

some thrown on Trojans, others flung against the Achaians
by Trojans, so the whole length of the wall thundered beneath them.
290   And not even then might the Trojans and glorious Hektor
have broken in the gates of the rampart, and the long door-bar,
had not Zeus of the counsels driven his own son, Sarpedon,
upon the Argives, like a lion among horn-curved cattle.
Presently he held before him the perfect circle of his shield,
295 a lovely thing of beaten bronze, which the bronze-smith hammered
out for him, and on the inward side had stitched ox-hides
in close folds with golden staples clean round the circle.
Holding this shield in front of him, and shaking two spears,
he went onward like some hill-kept lion, who for a long time
300 has gone lacking meat, and the proud heart is urgent upon him
to get inside of a close steading and go for the sheepflocks.
And even though he finds herdsmen in that place, who are watching
about their sheepflocks, armed with spears, and with dogs, even so
he has no thought of being driven from the steading without some attack
        made,
305 and either makes his spring and seizes a sheep, or else
himself is hit in the first attack by a spear from a swift hand
thrown. So now his spirit drove on godlike Sarpedon
to make a rush at the wall and break apart the battlements.
And now he spoke in address to Glaukos, son of Hippolochos:
310 'Glaukos, why is it you and I are honoured before others
with pride of place, the choice meats and the filled wine cups
in Lykia, and all men look on us as if we were immortals,
and we are appointed a great piece of land by the banks of Xanthos,
good land, orchard and vineyard, and ploughland for the planting of
        wheat?
315 Therefore it is our duty in the forefront of the Lykians
to take our stand, and bear our part of the blazing of battle,
so that a man of the close-armoured Lykians may say of us:
"Indeed, these are no ignoble men who are lords of Lykia,
these kings of ours, who feed upon the fat sheep appointed
320 and drink the exquisite sweet wine, since indeed there is strength
of valour in them, since they fight in the forefront of the Lykians."
Man, supposing you and I, escaping this battle,
would be able to live on forever, ageless, immortal,

so neither would I myself go on fighting in the foremost
nor would I urge you into the fighting where men win glory.   325
But now, seeing that the spirits of death stand close about us
in their thousands, no man can turn aside nor escape them,
let us go on and win glory for ourselves, or yield it to others.'
    He spoke, nor did Glaukos disobey him nor turn aside from him.
They, leading the great horde of the Lykians, advanced straight onward,   330
and the son of Peteos, Menestheus, shivered as he saw them
since they came against his bastion and carried disaster upon it.
He scanned the rampart of the Achaians in the hope of seeing
some great chief who could beat back the bane from his company,
and saw the two Aiantes, insatiate of battle, standing   335
on the wall, and Teukros even now coming up from the shelter,
and close by, but he was not able to cry out and make them
hear, so great was the clamour about him as the shouts hit skyward,
as shields were battered with missiles, and the helmets crested with
        horse-hair,
and the gates, which all had been slammed shut, and the Trojans standing   340
against them were trying to break them down and force their way in.
At once he sent Thoötes off as a runner to Aias:
'Go on the run, brilliant Thoötes, and call Aias here,
or better, both Aiantes, since that would be far the best thing
that could happen, since here headlong destruction is building against us.   345
Such is the weight of the Lykian lords upon us, who even
before now have shown as deadly men in the strong encounters.
But if in their place also hard work and fury have arisen,
at least let powerful Telamonian Aias come by himself,
and let Teukros follow with him, with his craft in the bow's use.'   350
    He spoke, nor did the herald disobey when he heard him,
but went on the run along the wall of the bronze-armoured Achaians
and came and stood by the two Aiantes, and spoke to them straight out:
'Aiantes, leaders of the bronze-armoured Argives: Menestheus,
beloved son of Peteos engendered of Zeus, desires you   355
to go where he is and meet the danger, if only for a little;
both of you for choice, since that would be far the best thing
that could happen, since there headlong destruction is building against
        him.
Such is the weight of the Lykian lords upon him, who even

360 before now have shown as deadly men in the strong encounters.
But if in this place also hard fighting and fury have arisen,
at least let powerful Telamonian Aias come by himself
and let Teukros follow with him, with his craft in the bow's use.'
He spoke, and huge Telamonian Aias did not disobey him,
365 but at once called out in winged words to Aias, the son of Oïleus:
'Aias, now you two, yourself and strong Lykomedes,
must stand your ground and urge on the Danaans to fight strongly.
I am going over there to meet the attack, and afterwards
I will come back soon, when I have beaten them back from the others.'
370 So speaking Telamonian Aias went away, and with him
went Teukros, his brother by the same father, and following them
was Pandion, who carried the curved bow for Teukros.
They kept inside the wall as they went, till they came to the bastion
of high-hearted Menestheus, and found men who were hard pressed there,
375 for the strong lords and men of counsel among the Lykians
came on against the battlements like a darkening stormwind,
and they charged forward to fight with these, and the clamour rose high.
First to kill his man was Telamonian Aias.
It was Sarpedon's companion in arms, high-hearted Epikles,
380 whom he struck with a great jagged stone, that lay at the inside
of the wall, huge, on top of the battlements. A man could not easily
hold it, not even if he were very strong, in both hands,
of men such as men are now, but he heaving it high threw it,
and smashed in the four-sheeted helm, and pounded to pieces
385 the bones of the head inside it, so that Epikles dropped
like a diver from the high bastion, and the life left his bones.
And Teukros with an arrow struck the strong son of Hippolochos,
Glaukos, as he was swarming aloft the wall's high bastion,
where he saw the arm was bare of defence, and stayed his warcraft;
390 he sprang down from the wall, secretly, for fear some Achaian
might see that he had been hit and vaunt with high words over him.
Sarpedon, as soon as he was aware that Glaukos had gone back,
was downcast, nevertheless he did not forget his warcraft
but striking with his spear at Alkmaon, the son of Thestor,
395 stabbed him, then wrenched the spear out, and he following the spear fell
on his face, and the armour elaborate with bronze clashed about him.
And Sarpedon, grabbing in both ponderous hands the battlements,

pulled, and the whole thing came away in his hands, and the rampart
was stripped defenceless above. He had opened a pathway for many.

Aias and Teukros aimed at him together, and Teukros   400
hit him with an arrow in the shining belt that encircled
his chest to hold the man-covering shield, but Zeus brushed the death
    spirits
from his son, and would not let him be killed there beside the ships' sterns;
and Aias plunging upon him stabbed at the shield, but the spearhead
did not pass clean through. Still, he pounded him back in his fury   405
so that he gave back a little space from the battlement, and yet not
utterly gave way, since his heart was still hopeful of winning glory.
He whirled about and called aloud to the godlike Lykians:
'Lykians, why do you thus let go of your furious valour?
It is a hard thing for me, strong as I am, to break down   410
the wall, single-handed, and open a path to the vessels.
Come on with me then. This work is better if many do it.'

So he spoke, and they, awed at the reproach of their leader,
put on the pressure of more weight around their lord of the counsels.
And on the other side the Argives stiffened their battalions   415
inside the wall, and a huge fight developed between the two sides.
For neither could the powerful Lykians break in the rampart
of the Danaans, and so open a path through to the vessels,
nor had the Danaan spearmen strength to push back the Lykians
from the rampart, once they had won to a place close under it;   420
but as two men with measuring ropes in their hands fight bitterly
about a boundary line at the meeting place of two cornfields,
and the two of them fight in the strait place over the rights of division,
so the battlements held these armies apart, and across them
they hewed at each other, and at the ox-hide shields strong-circled   425
guarding men's chests, and at the fluttering straps of the guard-skins.
Many were torn in their white flesh by the bronze without pity
wherever one of the fighters turning aside laid bare
his back, and many were struck with the spear carried clean through the
    shield.
Everywhere the battlements and the bastions were awash   430
with men's blood shed from both sides, Achaian and Trojan.
But even so they could not drive panic among the Achaians,
but held evenly as the scales which a careful widow

holds, taking it by the balance beam, and weighs her wool evenly
435 at either end, working to win a pitiful wage for her children:
so the battles fought by both sides were pulled fast and even
until that time when Zeus gave the greater glory to Hektor,
Priam's son, who was first to break into the wall of the Achaians.
For he lifted his voice and called in a piercing cry to the Trojans:
440 'Rise up, Trojans, breakers of horses, and wreck the ramparts
of the Argives, and let loose the inhuman fire on their vessels.'
    So he spoke, driving them on, and they all gave ear to him
and steered against the wall in a pack, and at once gripping
still their edged spears caught and swarmed up the wall's projections.
445 Meanwhile Hektor snatched up a stone that stood before the gates
and carried it along; it was blunt-massed at the base, but the upper
end was sharp; two men, the best in all a community,
could not easily hoist it up from the ground to a wagon,
of men such as men are now, but he alone lifted and shook it
450 as the son of devious-devising Kronos made it light for him.
As when a shepherd easily carries the fleece of a wether,
picking it up with one hand, and little is the burden weighting him,
so Hektor lifting the stone carried it straight for the door leaves
which filled the gateway ponderously close-fitted together.
455 These were high and twofold, and double door-bars on the inside
overlapping each other closed it, and a single pin-bolt secured them.
He came and stood very close and taking a strong wide stance threw
at the middle, leaning into the throw, that the cast might not lack
force, and smashed the hinges at either side, and the stone crashed
460 ponderously in, and the gates groaned deep, and the door-bars
could not hold, but the leaves were smashed to a wreckage of splinters
under the stone's impact. Then glorious Hektor burst in
with dark face like sudden night, but he shone with the ghastly
glitter of bronze that girded his skin, and carried two spears
465 in his hands. No one could have stood up against him, and stopped him,
except the gods, when he burst in the gates; and his eyes flashed fire.
Whirling, he called out across the battle to the Trojans
to climb over the wall, and they obeyed his urgency.
Immediately some swarmed over the wall, while others swept in
470 through the wrought gateways, and the Danaans scattered in terror
among their hollow ships, and clamour incessant rose up.

WHEN Zeus had driven against the ships the Trojans and Hektor,
he left them beside these to endure the hard work and sorrow
of fighting without respite, and himself turned his eyes shining
far away, looking out over the land of the Thracian riders
and the Mysians who fight at close quarters, and the proud Hippomolgoi,   5
drinkers of milk, and the Abioi, most righteous of all men.
He did not at all now turn his shining eyes upon Troy land
for he had no idea in mind that any one of the immortals
would come down to stand by either Danaans or Trojans.
    Neither did the powerful shaker of the earth keep blind watch;   10
for he sat and admired the fighting and the run of the battle,
aloft on top of the highest summit of timbered Samos,
the Thracian place; and from there all Ida appeared before him,
and the city of Priam was plain to see, and the ships of the Achaians.
There he came up out of the water, and sat, and pitied the Achaians   15
who were beaten by the Trojans, and blamed Zeus for it in bitterness.
    So presently he came down from the craggy mountain, striding
on rapid feet, and the tall mountains trembled and the timber
under the immortal feet of Poseidon's progress.
He took three long strides forward, and in the fourth came to his goal,   20
Aigai, where his glorious house was built in the waters'
depth, glittering with gold, imperishable forever.
Going there he harnessed under his chariot his bronze-shod horses,
flying-footed, with long manes streaming of gold; and he put on
clothing of gold about his own body, and took up the golden   25

lash, carefully compacted, and climbed up into his chariot
and drove it across the waves. And about him the sea beasts came up
from their deep places and played in his path, and acknowledged their
    master,
and the sea stood apart before him, rejoicing. The horses winged on
30 delicately, and the bronze axle beneath was not wetted.
The fast-running horses carried him to the ships of the Achaians.
    There is a cave, broad and deep down in the gloom of the water,
lying midway between Tenedos and Imbros of the high cliffs.
There Poseidon the shaker of the earth reined in his horses,
35 and slipped them from the yoke, and threw fodder immortal before them
so they could eat, and threw around their feet golden hobbles
not to be broken or slipped from, so they would wait there steadfast
for their lord gone. And Poseidon went to the ships of the Achaians.
    But the Trojans, gathered into a pack, like flame, like a stormcloud,
40 came on after Hektor the son of Priam, raging relentless,
roaring and crying as one, and their hopes ran high of capturing
the ships of the Achaians, and killing the best men beside them,
all of them. But Poseidon who circles the earth and shakes it
rose up out of the deep water to stir on the Argives,
45 likening himself in form and weariless voice to Kalchas.
First he spoke to the Aiantes, who were burning for battle already:
'Aiantes, you two, remembering the spirit of warcraft
and not that of shivering panic, must save the Achaian people.
Elsewhere in truth I do not fear the Trojans' invincible
50 hands, though in full force they have swarmed over our great wall;
since the strong-greaved Achaians will be able to hold the rest of them.
But I fear most terribly disaster to us in the one place
where that berserk flamelike leads them against us, Hektor,
who claims he must be son of Zeus of the high strength. May this
55 be the message some one of the gods gives your minds to carry,
that you stand fast strongly yourselves, urge the rest to stand also.
Thus, hard though he sweeps on, you might stay him beside the fast-
    running
ships, even though the very Olympian wakes him to battle.'
    Poseidon who circles the earth and shakes it spoke, and striking
60 both of them with his staff filled them with powerful valour,
and he made their limbs light, and their feet, and their hands above them,

and burst into winged flight himself, like a hawk with quick wings
who from the huge height of an impassable rock lifting
leans to flight to pursue some other bird over the wide land;
so Poseidon shaker of the earth broke away from the Aiantes.   65
And of the two swift Aias son of Oïleus was first
to know him, and spoke therewith to Aias the son of Telamon;
'Aias, since some one of the gods, whose hold is Olympos,
has likened himself to the seer, and told us to fight by our vessels,
this is not Kalchas, the bird interpreter of the gods, for I knew   70
easily as he went away the form of his feet, the legs' form
from behind him. Gods, though gods, are conspicuous. Therefore
as for me, the spirit inside my inward breast drives me
all the harder to carry on the war and the fighting,
and my feet underneath me are eager and my hands above them.'   75
     Aias the son of Telamon spoke to him in answer:
'So for me also now the invincible hands on my spearshaft
are furious, my strength is rising, and both feet beneath me
are sweeping me onward, so that I long even for single combat
with Hektor, Priam's son, the forever avid of battle.'   80
     Now as these two were saying such things to each other, joyful
in the delight of battle the god had put into their spirits,
meanwhile the earth-encircler stirred up the Achaians behind them
who were cooling the heat of the inward heart back beside their vessels,
for their very limbs were broken with weariness of hard work, and also   85
discouragement of the heart came over them, as they watched
the Trojans, and how in a mass they had overswarmed the great wall.
As they saw them the tears dripped from their eyes; they did not
think they could win clear of the evil, but the earth-shaker
lightly turning their battalions to strength drove them onward.   90
He came first in encouragement to Teukros and Leïtos,
with the fighting Peneleos, and Deïpyros and Thoas,
to Meriones and Antilochos, both urgent for battle.
Calling out to these in winged words he rallied them onward:
'Shame, you Argives, young fighting men, since I for my part   95
have confidence that by fighting you can save our ships from destruction;
but if you yourselves are to go slack from the sorrowful fighting
now is seen your day to be beaten down by the Trojans.
Oh for shame! Here is a great strange thing I see with my own eyes,

100 a terrible thing, and one that I thought never could happen,
that the Trojans could come against our ships, they who in time past
were like fugitive deer before us, who in the forests
are spoil for scavengers and wolves and leopards, who scatter
in absolute cowardice, there is no war spirit within them.
105 So before now the Trojans were unwilling to stand up
against the strength and hands of the Achaians, even for a little,
but now far from their city they fight by the hollow vessels
through the weakness of our leader, and the hanging back of our people
who have made their quarrel with him, and will not stand in defence
110 of the fast-running ships. Instead of this they are killed against them.
Yet even though it be utterly true that the son of Atreus
the hero wide-powerful Agamemnon is guilty
because he did dishonour to Peleus' son, the swift-footed,
still there is no way for us now to hang back from the fighting.
115 No, sooner let us heal it, for the hearts of great men can be healed.
But you can no longer in honour give way from your fighting valour
being all the best men along the host. Even I, for my part,
would not quarrel with any man who hung back from the fighting
because he was a weak thing, but with you my heart must be angry.
120 O friends, soon you will bring to pass some still greater evil
with this hanging back. Let every one of you plant in his heart's depth
discipline and shamefastness. A big battle rises against you.
For Hektor of the great war cry is fighting beside our vessels
in his power, and has broken our gates and the long door-bar.'
125   So urging them on the earth-encircler stirred up the Achaians,
and their battalions formed in strength about the two Aiantes,
battalions the war god could not find fault with, coming among them,
nor Athene lady of storming armies, since there the bravest
formed apart and stood against the Trojans and brilliant Hektor
130 locking spear by spear, shield against shield at the base, so buckler
leaned on buckler, helmet on helmet, man against man,
and the horse-hair crests along the horns of their shining helmets
touched as they bent their heads, so dense were they formed on each other,
and the spears shaken from their daring hands made a jagged battle line.
135 Their thoughts were driving straight ahead in the fury of fighting.
    The Trojans came down on them in a pack, and Hektor led them
raging straight forward, like a great rolling stone from a rock face

that a river swollen with winter rain has wrenched from its socket
and with immense washing broken the hold of the unwilling rock face;
the springing boulder flies on, and the forest thunders beneath it;   140
and the stone runs unwavering on a strong course, till it reaches
the flat land, then rolls no longer for all its onrush;
so Hektor for a while threatened lightly to break through
the shelters and ships of the Achaians and reach the water
cutting his way. But when he collided with the dense battalions   145
he was stopped, hard, beaten in on himself. The sons of the Achaians
against him stabbing at him with swords and leaf-headed spears
thrust him away from them so that he gave ground backward, staggering.
He lifted his voice and called in a piercing cry to the Trojans:
'Trojans, Lykians, Dardanians who fight at close quarters,   150
stand with me. The Achaians will not hold me back for a long time
for all they are building themselves into a bastion against me.
No, I think they will give back under my spear, if truly
I am driven by the greatest of gods, the thunderous lord of Hera.'
    So he spoke, and stirred the spirit and strength in each man.   155
Among them Deïphobos in high purpose had come striding,
Priam's son, who held the perfect circle of his shield before him,
moving lightly on his feet as he walked in the shield's protection.
Meriones aimed at him with the shining spear, and threw it
nor missed his mark, but struck the shield on its perfect circle   160
of bull's hide, but the spear did not get through, but sooner
the long shaft was broken behind the head. Deïphobos
held the bull's-hide shield away from him, his heart frightened
by the spear of wise Meriones, but that hero drew back
into the host of his own companions, deeply angered   165
for two things, the broken spear and the loss of his battle,
and went away back to the shelters and ships of the Achaians
to bring back a long spear that was left behind in his shelter.
    But the rest fought on with clamour incessant rising about them.
Teukros, son of Telamon, was the first to kill his man, Imbrios   170
the spearfighter, son of Mentor of the many horses, one who
before the coming of the sons of the Achaians lived in Pedaios
and had married a bastard daughter of Priam, Medesikaste.
But when the oarswept ships of the Danaans came, he went back
to Ilion, and was a great man among the Trojans, and lived   175

[275]

at Priam's side, who honoured him as he did his own children.
Now the son of Telamon with the long spear stabbed him under
the ear, and wrenched the spear out again, and he dropped like an ash tree
which, on the crest of a mountain glittering far about, cut down
180 with the bronze axe scatters on the ground its delicate leafage;
so he dropped, and the armour elaborate with bronze clashed
about him, and Teukros ran up, eager to strip the armour.
As he came on Hektor threw at him with the shining javelin,
but Teukros with his eyes straight on him avoided the bronze spear
185 by a little, and Hektor struck Amphimachos, son of Aktorian
Kteatos, with a spear in his chest as he swept into battle.
He fell, thunderously, and his armour clattered upon him.
Then Hektor charged in to tear the helm of great-hearted Amphimachos
from his head where it fitted close on the brows, but Aias
190 thrust with the shining spear at Hektor as he came onward;
he could not manage to reach the skin, since this was all shrouded
in the ghastly bronze, but drove at the shield's mass in the middle
and beat him back in great strength so that Hektor gave ground backward
from both corpses. These the Achaians dragged out of the fighting.
195 Then Stichios and brilliant Menestheus, lords of the Athenians,
carried Amphimachos back among the Achaian people.
But the two Aiantes in the fury of their fierce war strength,
as two lions catch up a goat from the guard of rip-fanged
hounds, and carry it into the density of the underbrush,
200 holding it high from the ground in the crook of their jaws, so the lordly
two Aiantes lifted Imbrios high and stripped him
of his armour, and the son of Oïleus, in anger
for Amphimachos, hewed away his head from the soft neck
and threw it spinning like a ball through the throng of fighters
205 until it came to rest in the dust at the feet of Hektor.
     Then Poseidon was angered about the heart at his grandson's
slaying in the bitter hostility, so the god went forth
on his way among the shelters and ships of the Achaians
and stirred the Danaans, and worked disaster against the Trojans.
210 Idomeneus the spear-famed encountered him, on his way
from a companion, who had just before come back from the fighting
wounded in the hollow behind the knee by the sharp bronze.
This man his companions carried away. Idomeneus had given

the healers instructions and gone on to his shelter, still burning
to face the battle, and now the strong earth-shaker spoke to him.   215
Poseidon likened his voice to Thoas, son of Andraimon,
lord of the Aitolians over all Pleuron, and headlong
Kalydon, who was honoured in his countryside as a god is:
'Idomeneus, lord of the Kretans' councils, where are those threats you gave
now, that the sons of the Achaians uttered against the Trojans?'   220
    Then Idomeneus lord of the Kretans answered him in turn:
'Thoas, no man is responsible for this, so far as
my thought goes, since all of us understand how to wage war.
It is not that heartless fear holds anyone, that a man yielding
to dread emerges out of the evil fighting, but rather   225
this way must be pleasurable to Kronos' son in his great strength,
that the Achaians must die here forgotten, and far from Argos.
Since you, Thoas, have been before this a man stubborn in battle
and stirred up another whenever you saw one hang back, so now
also do not give up, and urge on each man as you find him.'   230
    Then in answer spoke the shaker of the earth, Poseidon:
'Idomeneus, may that man who this day wilfully hangs back
from the fighting never win home again out of Troy land,
but stay here and be made dogs' delight for their feasting. Come then,
take up your armour and go with me. We must speed this action   235
together, since we, being two, might bring some advantage.
The warcraft even of sad fighters combined turns courage,
and you and I would have skill to fight even against good men.'
    So he spoke and strode on, a god, through the mortals' struggle.
Idomeneus, when he came back to his strong-built shelter,   240
drew his splendid armour over his body, and caught up two spears,
and went on his way, as a thunderbolt, which the son of Kronos
catching up in his hand shakes from the shining edge of Olympos,
flashes as a portent to men and the bright glints shine from it.
Such was the glitter of bronze that girt his chest in his running.   245
Close to his shelter there encountered him his strong henchman,
Meriones, who was on his way to pick up a bronze spear
and bring it back. Idomeneus in his strength spoke to him:
'Meriones, son of Molos, swift-footed, dearest beloved
companion, why have you come back and left the battle and fighting?   250
Have you been hit somewhere? Does pain of a spear's head afflict you?

Have you come back with someone's message for me? For my part
my desire is to fight, not sit away in the shelters.'
    Meriones, a thoughtful man, spoke to him in answer:
255 'Idomeneus, lord of the counsels of the bronze-armoured Kretans,
I am on my way to bring back a spear, if you have any
left in your shelter. I broke just now the one I was carrying
with a throw made against the shield of haughty Deïphobos.'
    Then Idomeneus lord of the Kretans answered him in turn:
260 'You will find one spear, and twenty spears, if you want them,
standing against the shining inward wall in my shelter,
Trojan spears I win from men that I kill, for my way
is not to fight my battles standing far away from my enemies.
Thereby I have spears there, and shields massive in the middle,
265 and helms and corselets are there in all the pride of their shining.'
    Meriones, a thoughtful man, spoke to him in answer:
'For me also, beside my shelter and beside my black ship,
there are many spoils of the Trojans, but not near for me to get them.
For I tell you, neither am I one who has forgotten his war strength
270 but among the foremost, along the fighting where men win glory,
I take my stand, whenever the quarrel of battle arises.
Let my fighting be forgotten by some other bronze-armoured
Achaian. You are the very one I think must know of it.'
    Then Idomeneus lord of the Kretans answered him in turn:
275 'I know your valour and what you are. Why need you speak of it?
If now beside the ships all the best of us were to assemble
for a hidden position, and there man's courage is best decided,
where the man who is a coward and the brave man show themselves
    clearly:
the skin of the coward changes colour one way and another,
280 and the heart inside him has no control to make him sit steady,
but he shifts his weight from one foot to another, then settles firmly
on both feet, and the heart inside his chest pounds violent
as he thinks of the death spirits, and his teeth chatter together:
but the brave man's skin will not change colour, nor is he too much
285 frightened, once he has taken his place in the hidden position,
but his prayer is to close as soon as may be in bitter division:
and there no man could make light of your battle strength or your hand's
    work.

Even were you to be wounded in your work with spearcast or spear-
   stroke,
the weapon would not strike behind your neck, nor in your back,
but would be driven straight against the chest or the belly   290
as you made your way onward through the meeting of champions.
But come, let us no longer stand here talking of these things
like children, for fear some man may arrogantly scold us.
Go to my shelter and choose for yourself a heavy spear.'
   So he spoke; Meriones, a match for the rapid war god,   295
went into the shelter rapidly, and took up a bronze spear,
and with his mind deeply set on battle followed Idomeneus.
As manslaughtering Ares is when he strides into battle
and Terror goes on beside him, his beloved son, the powerful
and dauntless, who frightens even the patient-hearted warrior: 300
these two come out of Thrace to encounter in arms the Ephyroi
or the great-hearted Phlegyes, but the two will not listen to prayers
from both sides, but give the glory to one side or the other:
such were Meriones and Idomeneus, leaders of armies,
as they went on into the fighting helmed in the bright bronze.   305
First of the two, Meriones, spoke his word to Idomeneus:
'Deukalides, where are you minded to enter the battle?
Would it be on the right of the whole array, or in the centre,
or to the left? Since I think that nowhere else in the fighting
are the flowing-haired Achaians overmatched so badly.'   310
   Idomeneus lord of the Kretans answered him in turn:
'There are others beside us to defend the ships in the centre,
the two Aiantes, and Teukros, best of all the Achaians
in archery, and a good man in the close of standing combat.
They can give Hektor, Priam's son, enough hard hitting,   315
even though he is very strong, and sweeps hard into battle.
Furious though he is for fighting, it will be very steep work
for him to win through their irresistible hands and their war strength
and fire the ships, unless the son of Kronos in person
should hurl the blazing firebrand into our fast-running vessels.   320
Nor would huge Telamonian Aias give way to any man,
one who was mortal and ate bread, the yield of Demeter,
one who could be broken by the bronze and great stones flung at him.
He would not make way for Achilleus who breaks men in battle,

325 in close combat. For speed of feet none can strive with Achilleus.
Hold, as you say, for the left of the army, and thus soonest
shall we see whether we win glory or give it to others.'

He spoke, and Meriones, a match for the running war god,
led the way, till they came to the place in the army he spoke for.
330 These, as they saw Idomeneus like a flame in his valour
himself and his henchman with him in their elaborate war gear,
they called out across the battle and gathered about him,
and an indiscriminate fight rose up by the sterns of the vessels.
And as when under the screaming winds the whirlstorms bluster
335 on that day when the dust lies deepest along the pathways
and the winds in the confusion of dust uplift a great cloud,
such was their indiscriminate battle, and their hearts were furious
to slaughter each other with the sharp bronze through the press of the
fighting.
The battle where men perish shuddered now with the long
340 man-tearing spears they held in their hands, their eyes were blinded
in the dazzle of the bronze light from the glittering helmets,
from the burnished corselets and the shining shields as men came on
in confusion. That man would have to be very bold-hearted
who could be cheerful and not stricken looking on that struggle.
345 Two powerful sons of Kronos, hearts divided against each other,
were wreaking bitter agonies on the fighting warriors,
since Zeus willed the victory for the Trojans and Hektor,
glorifying swift-footed Achilleus, yet not utterly
did he wish the Achaian people to be destroyed before Ilion,
350 but only was giving glory to Thetis and her strong-spirited
son, while Poseidon emerging unseen from the grey salt water
went among the Argives and stirred them, since he was angered
that they were beaten by the Trojans and blamed Zeus for it bitterly.
Indeed, the two were of one generation and a single father,
355 but Zeus was the elder born and knew more. Therefore Poseidon
shrank from openly defending them, but secretly
in a man's likeness was forever stirring them up through the army.
So these two had looped over both sides a crossing
cable of strong discord and the closing of battle, not to be
360 slipped, not to be broken, which unstrung the knees of many.
There Idomeneus, greying though he was, called on the Danaans

and charged in upon the Trojans and drove panic among them,
for he killed Othryoneus, a man who had lived in Kabesos,
who was newly come in the wake of the rumour of war, and had asked
Priam for the hand of the loveliest of his daughters, 365
Kassandra, without bride price, but had promised a great work for her,
to drive back the unwilling sons of the Achaians from Troy land,
and aged Priam had bent his head in assent, and promised
to give her, so Othryoneus fought in the faith of his promises.
Idomeneus aimed at him with the shining spear, and threw it, 370
and hit him as he came onward with high stride, and the corselet
of bronze he wore could not hold, the spear fixed in the middle belly.
He fell, thunderously, and Idomeneus vaunting cried out:
'Othryoneus, I congratulate you beyond all others
if it is here that you will bring to pass what you promised 375
to Dardanian Priam, who in turn promised you his daughter.
See now, we also would make you a promise, and we would fulfil it;
we would give you the loveliest of Atreides' daughters,
and bring her here from Argos to be your wife, if you joined us
and helped us storm the strong-founded city of Ilion. 380
Come then with me, so we can meet by our seafaring vessels
about a marriage; we here are not bad matchmakers for you.'
   The hero Idomeneus spoke and dragged him through the strong
      encounter
caught by the foot, but now Asios came to stand by him
dismounted, ahead of his horses whom his henchman held ever behind him 385
so that they breathed on his shoulders. He was striving in all his fury
to strike Idomeneus, but he, too quick with a spearcast,
struck him in the gorge underneath the chin, and drove the bronze clean
      through.
He fell, as when an oak goes down or a white poplar
or like a towering pine tree which in the mountains the carpenters 390
have hewn down with their whetted axes to make a ship timber.
So he lay there felled in front of his horses and chariot,
roaring, and clawed with his hands at the bloody dust. Meanwhile
the charioteer who was close behind him was stricken in the wits
and shrinking from the hands of the enemy did not have daring 395
to turn the horses about, but Antilochos stubborn in battle
pinned him through the middle with a spearstroke, and the corselet

of bronze he wore could not hold, the spear fixed in the middle belly,
so that he tumbled, gasping, out of the strong-wrought chariot.
400 But for the horses, Antilochos, son of great-hearted Nestor,
drove them away from the Trojans among the strong-greaved Achaians.
    Deïphobos in sorrow for Asios now came close
in on Idomeneus, and with the bright spear made a cast at him,
but Idomeneus with his eyes straight on him avoided the bronze spear
405 since also he was hidden beneath his shield's perfect circle, that shield
he carried, hooped in circles of glaring bronze, and the skins
of oxen, fitted with double cross-stays. He was all gathered
together under this, and the brazen spear shot over him
and the shield gave out a hollow clash as the spear glanced from it.
410 Yet Deïphobos made no utterly vain cast from his strong hand,
but struck Hypsenor, son of Hippasos, shepherd of the people,
in the liver under the midriff, and at once took the strength from his knees.
And Deïphobos vaunted terribly over him, calling in a great voice:
'Asios lies not now all unavenged. I think rather
415 as he goes down to Hades of the Gates, the strong one,
he will be cheerful at heart, since I have sent him an escort.'
    He spoke, and sorrow came over the Argives at his vaunting,
and beyond others stirred the spirit in wise Antilochos,
yet sorrowful though he was he did not forget his companion
420 but running stood and bestrode him and covered him under the great
        shield.
Thereon Mekisteus, son of Echios, and brilliant Alastor,
two staunch companions, stooping beneath it, caught up Hypsenor,
and carried him, groaning heavily, to the hollow vessels.
    Idomeneus did not slacken his great fury, but always
425 was straining to shroud some one of the Trojans in dark night
or go down crashing himself as he fought the bane from the Achaians.
There was a man, loved son of illustrious Aisyetes,
the hero Alkathoös, who was son-in-law of Anchises,
and had married the eldest of his daughters, Hippodameia,
430 dear to the hearts of her father and the lady her mother
in the great house, since she surpassed all the girls of her own age
for beauty and accomplishments and wit; for which reason
the man married her who was the best in the wide Troad.
But now Poseidon beat him down at the hands of Idomeneus,

for he bewitched his shining eyes, made moveless his bright limbs,　435
so that he could not run backward, neither evade him,
but stood like a statue or a tree with leaves towering
motionless, while fighting Idomeneus stabbed at the middle
of his chest with the spear, and broke the bronze armour about him
which in time before had guarded his body from destruction.　440
He cried out then, a great cry, broken, the spear in him,
and fell, thunderously, and the spear in his heart was stuck fast
but the heart was panting still and beating to shake the butt end
of the spear. Then and there Ares the huge took his life away from him.
Idomeneus vaunted terribly over him, calling in a great voice:　445
'Deïphobos, are we then to call this a worthy bargain,
three men killed for one? It was you yourself were so boastful.
Strange man. Do you rather come yourself and stand up against me
so you can see what I am like, Zeus' seed, come here to face you.
Since Zeus first got by Krete Minos, who cared for his people,　450
and to Minos in turn was born a blameless son, Deukalion,
and Deukalion sired me to be lord over many people
in wide Krete, and now my ships have brought me to this place
to be an evil for you and your father and the rest of the Trojans.'
　So he spoke, and the heart in Deïphobos was divided,　455
pondering whether to draw back and find some other high-hearted
Trojan to be his companion, or whether to attempt him singly.
And in the division of his heart this way seemed best to him,
to go for Aineias. He found him at the uttermost edge of the battle
standing, since he was forever angry with brilliant Priam　460
because great as he was he did him no honour among his people.
Deïphobos came and stood close to him and addressed him in winged
　words:
'Aineias, lord of the Trojans' counsels, now there is need of you
to stand by your brother-in-law, if this bond of kinship touches you.
Come then, stand by Alkathoös, who was your sister's husband　465
and in time past nursed you in his house when you were still little.
But now Idomeneus the spear-famed has killed him in battle.'
　So he spoke, and stirred the anger in the breast of Aineias.
He went against Idomeneus, strongly eager for battle,
yet no fear gripped Idomeneus as if he were a stripling,　470
but he stood his ground like a mountain wild boar who in the confidence

of his strength stands up to a great rabble of men advancing
upon him in some deserted place, and bristles his back up,
and both his eyes are shining with fire; he grinds his teeth
475 in his fury to fight off the dogs and the men. So
spear-famed Idomeneus held his ground, and would not give way
to Aineias coming against him, but bellowed to his companions,
looking to Askalaphos, and Aphareus, and Deïpyros,
at Meriones and Antilochos, both urgent for battle,
480 and stirring all these forward called out to them in winged words:
'This way, friends, stand by me, I am alone, and terribly
I fear the attack of swift-footed Aineias advancing upon me,
powerful as he is for the slaying of men in battle.
Likewise the flower of youth is his, where man's strength is highest,
485 since were we two of the same age, and in this same spirit,
soon he would win me in a great battle, or I would win him.'
        So he spoke, and all these, a single spirit within them,
came and stood in their numbers and sloped their shields over his shoulders,
and Aineias on the other side called to his own companions,
490 looking to Deïphobos, and Paris, and brilliant Agenor
who were lords of the Trojans along with him, and the people after them
followed on, as when the sheep follow the lead-ram
as they leave the pasture to drink, and make proud the heart of the
        shepherd,
and thus also the heart of Aineias was gladdened within him
495 as he saw the swarm of the host following his own leadership.
        These then drove on in close combat about Alkathoös
with long spears, and the bronze girding the chests of the fighters
clashed horribly to the spears they threw in the press at each other,
and two men, for warcraft pre-eminent beyond the others,
500 Aineias and Idomeneus, both men like the war god,
were straining with the pitiless bronze to tear at each other.
Aineias was first with a spear cast at Idomeneus,
but he, keeping his eyes straight on him, avoided the bronze spear,
so that the vibrant shaft of Aineias was driven groundward
505 since it had been thrown in a vain cast from his big hand.
But Idomeneus hit Oinomaos in the middle belly
and broke the hollow of the corselet, so that the entrails spurted
from the bronze, and he fell clawing the dust in his fingers.

Idomeneus wrenched out the far-shadowing spear from his body
but had no power to strip the rest of his splendid armour   510
away from his shoulders, since he was beaten back by their missiles,
and no longer in an outrush could his limbs stay steady beneath him
either to dash in after his spear, or to get clear again.
So in close-standing fight he beat off the pitiless death-day
as his feet no longer quick to run took him out of the fighting.   515
As he backed slowly Deïphobos made a cast with the shining
spear, since he held a fixed hatred forever against him,
but missed him yet once again and struck down with the spear the war
    god's
son Askalaphos, so that the powerful spear was driven
through his shoulder, and he dropping in the dust clawed the ground in   520
    his fingers.
But Ares the huge and bellowing had yet heard nothing
of how his son had fallen there in the strong encounter
but he, sheltered under the golden clouds on utmost Olympos,
was sitting, held fast by command of Zeus, where the rest also
of the immortal gods were sitting still, in restraint from the battle.   525
    But the men drove on in close combat about Askalaphos.
Deïphobos tore from Askalaphos the shining helmet;
but now Meriones, a match for the running war god,
plunging upon him stabbed his arm with the spear, and the hollow-eyed
helmet dropped from his hand and fell to the ground clashing.   530
Meriones in yet another swoop like a vulture
plucked out the heavy spear from the arm's base at the shoulder,
then shrank into the host of his own companions. Polites,
Deïphobos' brother, caught him about the waist with both arms
and got him out of the sorrowful fighting, and reached his fast-footed   535
horses, where they stood to the rear of the fighting and the battle
holding their charioteer and the elaborate chariot,
and these carried him, groaning heavily, back to the city
in pain, since the blood was running from his arm's fresh wound.
    But the rest fought on with clamour incessant rising about them.   540
There Aineias lunging at Aphareus, the son of Kaletor,
struck him with the sharp spear in the throat where it was turned toward
    him.
His head bent over to one side, and his shield tumbled,

and the helm, and death breaking the spirit drifted about him.

545 Antilochos, watching Thoön as he turned about, dashed in on him
and slashed at him, and shore away the entire vein
which runs all the way up the back till it reaches the neck. This
he shore away entire, so he sprawled in the dust backward,
reaching out both hands to his beloved companions.

550 Antilochos rushed on him, trying to strip the armour
from his shoulders, but watchful, as the Trojans gathered about him
from all sides, and beat at the shining broad shield, but could not
get within it and tear with the pitiless bronze Antilochos'
tender flesh, for about him the earth-shaker Poseidon

555 guarded the son of Nestor even in the swarm of missiles.
Since he was not making his way back clear of the enemy,
but would turn to face them nor held motionless his spear, always
it was shaken or driven forward, the desire in his heart forever
to strike someone with a spearcast or drive at him in close combat.

560   Adamas, Asios' son, was not blind to how he kept aiming
with his spear in the battle, and charging close stabbed with the sharp
        bronze
at the shield's middle, but Poseidon the dark-haired made void
his spear's stroke, nor would let him win the life of Antilochos,
and half of the spear was stuck fast like a stake fire-hardened

565 in Antilochos' shield, and the other half lay on the ground.
To avoid death he shrank into the host of his own companions;
but as he went back Meriones dogging him threw with the spear
and struck between navel and genitals where beyond all places
death in battle comes painfully to pitiful mortals.

570 There the spear stuck fast driven and he, writhing about it,
gasped as an ox does when among the mountains the herdsmen
have bound him strongly in twisted ropes and drag him unwilling.
So he, stricken, gasped for a little while, but not long,
until fighting Meriones came close and wrenched the spear out

575 from his body, and a mist of darkness closed over both eyes.

    But Helenos closing struck Deïpyros on the temple
with a huge Thracian sword, and broke the helmet to pieces
so that it was knocked off and fell to the ground. An Achaian
picked it up where it rolled among the feet of the fighters;

580 but the darkness of night misted over the eyes of Deïpyros.

Then sorrow caught Atreus' son Menelaos of the great war cry,
and he came on menacing and shaking his sharp spear at Helenos
the lord and fighter, who pulled against him the bow at the handgrip,
and both let fly at each other together, one with a sharp spear
in a javelin cast, and one with the arrow from the bowstring.   585
The son of Priam hit him then on the chest with an arrow
in the hollow of the corselet, but the bitter arrow sprang far back.
As along a great threshing floor from the broad blade
of a shovel the black-skinned beans and the chickpeas bounce high
under the whistling blast and the sweep of the winnowing fan, so   590
back from the corselet of glorious Menelaos the bitter
arrow rebounded far away, being driven hard back.
But Atreus' son Menelaos of the great war cry struck him
in the hand where he held the polished bow, and the bronze spear
was driven clean on through the bow and the hand beyond it.   595
To avoid death he shrank into the host of his own companions,
dangling his wounded hand and dragging the ash spear with it.
But great-hearted Agenor drew from his hand the spear
and bound up his hand with a careful twist of wool fleece
in a sling the henchman held for the shepherd of the people.   600
    Peisandros now came on straight against Menelaos
the glorious, but an evil destiny led him toward death's end,
to be beaten down by you, Menelaos, in the stark encounter.
Now when these in their advance were close to each other
the son of Atreus missed with his throw, and the spear was turned past   605
    him,
but Peisandros stabbed with the spear at the shield of glorious
Menelaos, but could not drive the bronze all the way through it
for the wide shield held against it and the spearshaft was broken
behind the head, yet he was light-hearted and hopeful of victory.
Drawing his sword with the silver nails, the son of Atreus   610
sprang at Peisandros, who underneath his shield's cover gripped
his beautiful axe with strong bronze blade upon a long polished
axe-handle of olive wood. They made their strokes at the same time
and Peisandros chopped at the horn of the helmet crested with horse-hair
at the very peak. Menelaos struck him as he came onward   615
in the forehead over the base of the nose, and smashed the bones, so that
both eyes dropped, bloody, and lay in the dust at his feet before him.

He fell, curling, and Menelaos, setting his heel on
his chest, stripped off his armour and spoke exulting over him:
620 'So, I think, shall you leave the ships of the fast-mounted Danaans,
you haughty Trojans, never to be glutted with the grim war noises,
nor go short of all that other shame and defilement
wherewith you defiled me, wretched dogs, and your hearts knew no fear
at all of the hard anger of Zeus loud-thundering,
625 the guest's god, who some day will utterly sack your steep city.
You who in vanity went away taking with you my wedded
wife, and many possessions, when she had received you in kindness.
And now once more you rage among our seafaring vessels
to throw deadly fire on them and kill the fighting Achaians.
630 But you will be held somewhere, though you be so headlong for battle.
Father Zeus, they say your wisdom passes all others',
of men and gods, and yet from you all this is accomplished
the way you give these outrageous people your grace, these Trojans
whose fighting strength is a thing of blind fury, nor can they ever
635 be glutted full of the close encounters of deadly warfare.
Since there is satiety in all things, in sleep, and love-making,
in the loveliness of singing and the innocent dance. In all these
things a man will strive sooner to win satisfaction
than in war; but in this the Trojans cannot be glutted.'
640   So Menelaos the blameless spoke, and stripping the bloody
armour away from his body gave it to his companions,
and turned back himself to merge in the ranks of the champions.
     Now there sprang forth against him the son of King Pylaimenes,
Harpalion, who had followed his father into the fighting
645 at Troy, and did not come home again to the land of his fathers.
He from close up stabbed with his spear at the shield of Atreides
in the middle, but could not drive the bronze all the way through it.
To avoid death he shrank into the host of his own companions,
looking all about him, for fear somebody might wound him with the
     bronze;
650 but as he went back Meriones let fly at him with a bronze-shod
arrow, and hit him beside the right buttock, so that the arrow
was driven on through under the bone to fix in the bladder.
There, sitting among the arms of his beloved companions,
he gasped out his life, then lay like a worm extended

along the ground, and his dark blood drenched the ground in its running. 655
And the great-hearted Paphlagonians busied about him,
lifted him into a chariot and brought him to sacred Ilion
in sorrow, and his father, weeping tears, walked beside them,
and no man-price came his way for his son's slaying.

But Paris was deeply angered at heart for this man's slaying, 660
since he was his guest friend among many Paphlagonians,
and in anger for him he also let fly a bronze-shod arrow.
There was a man, Euchenor, son of the seer Polyidos,
a rich man and good, who lived in his house at Korinth,
who knew well that it was his death when he went on shipboard, 665
since many times the good old man Polyidos had told him
that he must die in his own house of a painful sickness
or go with the ships of the Achaians and be killed by the Trojans.
He therefore chose to avoid the troublesome price the Achaians
would ask, and the hateful sickness so his heart might not be afflicted. 670
Paris struck him by jaw and ear, and at once the life spirit
fled from his limbs, and the hateful darkness closed in about him.

So they fought on in the likeness of blazing fire. But meanwhile
Hektor beloved of Zeus had not heard of this, and knew nothing
of how to the left of the ships his people were being slaughtered 675
by the Argives, and glory for the Achaians might even have been
accomplished, such was Poseidon who circles the earth and shakes it
as he stirred on the Argives and fought for them and his own strength.
But Hektor held where first he had broken a way through the rampart
and the gates, and shattered the close ranks of the armoured Danaans, 680
where lay the ships of Aias and the ships of Protesilaos
hauled up along the beach of the grey sea; and above these
the wall they had built lay lowest, and there beyond other places
dangerous was the onslaught of the Trojans and of their horses.

There the Boiotians, and Ionians with their trailing tunics, 685
the Lokrians and the Phthians, with the shining Epeians
tried to hold him as he swept hard for the ships, but they could not
avail to beat brilliant flame-like Hektor back from them.
There also were the chosen Athenian men, and among them
Peteos' son Menestheus was lord, and there followed with him 690
Pheidas and Stichios and strong Bias; but the Epeians
were led by Meges, Phyleus' son, Amphion and Drakios,

and before the Phthians were Medon and battle-stubborn Podarkes.
Now of these one, Medon, was bastard son of Oïleus
695 the godlike, and brother of Aias, yet he was living away from
the land of his fathers, in Phylake, since he had killed a man,
the brother of Eriopis, his stepmother and wife of Oïleus;
but the other was son of Iphiklos, the son of Phylakos.
And these in arms at the forefront of the great-hearted Phthians
700 fought beside the Boiotians in defence of their vessels.
    But swift Aias the son of Oïleus would not at all now
take his stand apart from Telamonian Aias,
not even a little; but as two wine-coloured oxen straining
with even force drag the compacted plough through the fallow land,
705 and for both of them at the base of the horns the dense sweat gushes;
only the width of the polished yoke keeps a space between them
as they toil down the furrow till the share cuts the edge of the ploughland;
so these took their stand in battle, close to each other.
Now with the son of Telamon many people and brave ones
710 followed as companions, and took over the great shield from him
whenever the sweat and the weariness came over his body.
But no Lokrians went with the great-hearted son of Oïleus.
The heart was not in them to endure close-standing combat,
for they did not have the brazen helmets crested with horse-hair,
715 they did not have the strong-circled shields and the ash spears,
but rather these had followed to Ilion with all their confidence
in their bows and slings strong-twisted of wool; and with these
they shot their close volleys and broke the Trojan battalions.
So now these others fought in front in elaborate war gear
720 against the Trojans and Hektor the brazen-helmed, and the Lokrians
unseen volleyed from behind, so the Trojans remembered
nothing of the joy of battle, since the shafts struck them to confusion.
    Now pitifully the Trojans might have gone back from the shelters
and the ships, to windy Ilion, had not Poulydamas
725 come and stood beside bold Hektor and spoken a word to him:
'Hektor, you are too intractable to listen to reason.
Because the god has granted you the actions of warfare
therefore you wish in counsel also to be wise beyond others.
But you cannot choose to have all gifts given to you together.
730 To one man the god has granted the actions of warfare,

to one to be a dancer, to another the lyre and the singing,
and in the breast of another Zeus of the wide brows establishes
wisdom, a lordly thing, and many take profit beside him
and he saves many, but the man's own thought surpasses all others.
Now I will tell you the way that it seems best to my mind.   735
For you, everywhere the fighting burns in a circle around you,
but of the great-hearted Trojans since they crossed over the rampart
some are standing back in their war gear, others are fighting
fewer men against many, being scattered among the vessels.
Draw back now, and call to this place all of our bravest,   740
and then we might work out together our general counsel,
whether we can fall upon their benched ships, if the god might
be willing to give such power to us, or whether thereafter
we can win away from the ships unhurt; since I fear
the Achaians might wreak on us requital for yesterday;   745
since beside their ships lurks a man insatiate of fighting
and I think we can no longer utterly hold him from the fighting.'
   So spoke Poulydamas, and this counsel of safety pleased Hektor,
and at once in all his armour he leapt to the ground from his chariot
and spoke to him and addressed him in winged words: 'Poulydamas,   750
do you rather call back to their place all of our bravest.
I am going over there to meet the attack, and afterwards
I will come back soon, when I have properly given my orders.'
   So he spoke, and went on his way like a snowy mountain,
calling aloud, and swept through the Trojans and their companions.   755
But the rest of them rallied quickly around the son of Panthoös,
courtly Poulydamas, each as they heard the command of Hektor.
But Hektor ranged the ranks of the foremost fighters, searching
for Deïphobos, and the strength of Helenos the prince, and for Asios'
son Adamas, and Asios, Hyrtakos' son, if he might   760
find them; but found them no longer utterly unwounded or living,
but some were lying along the sterns of Achaian vessels,
they who had lost their lives at the hands of the Argives, and others
were lying away inside the city with arrow or spear wounds.
But he found one man away to the left of the sorrowful battle,   765
brilliant Alexandros, the lord of lovely-haired Helen,
encouraging his companions and urging them on into battle.
Hektor came and stood near, and in words of shame he rebuked him:

'Evil Paris, beautiful, woman-crazy, cajoling:
770 where is Deïphobos gone, and the strength of the prince Helenos,
Adamas, Asios' son, and Asios, son of Hyrtakos?
Where is Othryoneus? Now all steep Ilion is lost
utterly; now your own headlong destruction is certain.'
Then in turn Alexandros the godlike answered him:
775 'Hektor, since it is your pleasure to blame me when I am blameless,
it would be better some other time to withdraw from the fighting
than now. My mother bore me not utterly lacking in warcraft.
For since that time when by the ships you wakened the battle
of our companions, we have stayed here and fought the Danaans
780 without end. And our companions are killed you ask for.
Only Deïphobos and the strength of the prince Helenos
have gone away, wounded each in the hand by strokes
of the long spears, but the son of Kronos fended death from them.
Now lead on, wherever your heart and spirit command you,
785 and we shall follow you eagerly; I think that we shall not
come short in warcraft, in so far as the strength stays with us.
But beyond his strength no man can fight, although he be eager.'
So the hero spoke, and persuaded the heart of his brother.
They went on, to where the clamour and fighting were greatest,
790 about Kebriones, and Poulydamas the blameless,
about Phalkes, and Orthaios, and godlike Polyphetes,
Palmys, with Askanios and Morys, sons of Hippotion,
who had come over in their turn from fertile Askania
on the dawn before, and now Zeus stirred them into the fighting.
795 They went on, as out of the racking winds the stormblast
that underneath the thunderstroke of Zeus father drives downward
and with gigantic clamour hits the sea, and the numerous
boiling waves along the length of the roaring water
bend and whiten to foam in ranks, one upon another;
800 so the Trojans closing in ranks, some leading and others
after them, in the glare of bronze armour followed their leaders.
And Hektor led them, Priam's son, a man like the murderous
war god, and held the perfect circle of his shield before him
fenced deep in skins, with a great fold of bronze beaten upon it,
805 and about his temples was shaken as he went the glittering helmet.
He would step forward, to probe the Achaian battalions at all points,

if they might give way where he stalked on under his shield's cover,
but could not so confuse the heart in the breasts of the Achaians.
Aias was first to take long strides forward and challenge him:
'Man, you are mad. Come closer. Why try this way to terrify   810
the Argives? It is not that we are so unskilled in fighting,
but by the wicked whiplash of Zeus we Achaians are beaten.
I suppose, then, your heart is hopeful utterly to break up
our ships? We too have prompt hands among us strong to defend them.
Rather, far before this your own strong-founded citadel   815
must go down under our hands, stormed and utterly taken.
And for yourself I say that the time is close, when in flight
you will pray to Zeus father and the other immortals
that your bright-maned horses might be swifter than hawks are
as they carry you through the stirred dust of the plain to your city.' 820
    As he spoke so, an ominous bird winged by at his right hand,
a towering eagle, and the host of the Achaians, made brave
by the bird sign, shouted, but glorious Hektor answered him:
'Aias, you inarticulate ox, what is this you have spoken?
If I could only be called son to Zeus of the aegis   825
all the days of my life, and the lady Hera my mother,
and I be honoured, as Apollo and Athene are honoured,
so surely as this is a day that brings evil to the Argives,
all, and you will be killed with the rest of them, if you have daring
to stand up against my long spear, which will bite your delicate   830
body; yet then you will glut the dogs and birds of the Trojans
with fat and flesh, struck down beside the ships of the Achaians.'
    So he spoke and led the way, and the rest of them followed him
with unearthly clamour, and all the people shouted behind him.
But the Argives on the other side cried out, and would not   835
forget their warcraft, but stood the attack of the bravest Trojans,
and the clamour from both was driven high to Zeus' shining aether.

Now Nestor failed not to hear their outcry, though he was
　drinking
his wine, but spoke in winged words to the son of Asklepios:
'Take thought how these things shall be done, brilliant Machaon.
Beside the ships the cry of the strong young men grows greater.
5　Now, do you sit here and go on drinking the bright wine,
until Hekamede the lovely-haired makes ready a hot bath
for you, warming it, and washes away the filth of the bloodstains,
while I go out and make my way till I find some watchpoint.'
　So he spoke, and took up the wrought shield of his son
10　Thrasymedes, breaker of horses. It lay in the shelter
all shining in bronze. Thrasymedes carried the shield of his father.
Then he caught up a powerful spear edged in sharp bronze
and stood outside the shelter, and at once saw a shameful action,
men driven to flight, and others harrying them in confusion,
15　the great-hearted Trojans, and the wall of the Achaians overthrown.
As when the open sea is deeply stirred to the ground-swell
but stays in one place and waits the rapid onset of tearing
gusts, nor rolls its surf onward in either direction
until from Zeus the wind is driven down to decide it;
20　so the aged man pondered, his mind caught between two courses,
whether to go among the throng of fast-mounted Danaans
or in search of Atreus' son Agamemnon, shepherd of the people.
And in the division of his heart this way seemed best to him,
to go after the son of Atreus, while the rest went on with the murderous
25　battle, and the weariless bronze about their bodies was clashing

as the men were stabbing with swords and leaf-headed spears.
   Now there came toward Nestor the kings under God's hand, they who
had been wounded by the bronze and came back along the ships, Tydeus'
son, and Odysseus, and Atreus' son Agamemnon. For there
were ships that had been hauled up far away from the fighting   30
along the beach of the grey sea. They had hauled up the first ones
on the plain, and by the sterns of these had built their defences;
for, wide as it was, the sea-shore was not big enough to make room
for all the ships, and the people also were straitened; and therefore
they had hauled them up in depth, and filled up the long edge   35
of the whole sea-coast, all that the two capes compassed between them.
These lords walked in a group, each leaning on his spear, to look at
the clamorous battle, and for each the heart inside his body
was sorrowful; and Nestor the aged man who now met them
made still more cast down the spirit inside the Achaians.   40
Now powerful Agamemnon spoke aloud and addressed him:
'Nestor, son of Neleus, great glory of the Achaians,
why have you left the fighting where men die, and come back here?
I am afraid huge Hektor may accomplish that word against me
that he spoke, threatening, among the Trojans assembled,   45
that he would not make his way back from the ships toward Ilion
until he had set the ships on fire, and killed the men in them.
So he spoke then; now all these things are being accomplished.
Oh, shame, for I think that all the other strong-greaved Achaians
are storing anger against me in their hearts, as Achilleus   50
did, and no longer will fight for me by the grounded vessels.'
   Then answered him in turn the Gerenian horseman Nestor:
'All these things have been brought to fulfilment, nor in any other
way could even Zeus who thunders on high accomplish it.
For the wall has gone down in which we put our trust, that it   55
would be a protection for our ships and us, and could not be broken,
and our men beside the fast ships are fighting incessantly
without end, nor could you tell any more, though you looked hard,
from which side the Achaians are broken into confusion,
so indiscriminately are they killed, and their crying goes skyward.   60
We then must take thought together how these things shall be done
if wit can do anything for us now. I think that we must not
enter the fight; a man cannot fight on when he is wounded.'

Then in turn the lord of men Agamemnon spoke to him:
65 'Nestor, since now they are fighting beside the grounded vessels
and the wall we built has done us no good, nor the ditch either
where the Danaans endured so much, and their hearts were hopeful
it would be a protection to their ships and them, and could not be broken,
then such is the way it must be pleasing to Zeus, who is too strong,
70 that the Achaians must die here forgotten and far from Argos.
For I knew it, when with full heart he defended the Danaans,
and I know it now, when he glorifies these people as if they
were blessed gods, and has hobbled our warcraft and our hands' strength.
Come then, do as I say, let us all be won over; let us
75 take all those ships that are beached near the sea in the first line
and haul them down, and row them out on the shining water,
and moor them at anchor stones out on the deep water, until
the immortal Night comes down, if the Trojans will give over fighting
for Night's sake; then we might haul down all the rest of our vessels.
80 There is no shame in running, even by night, from disaster.
The man does better who runs from disaster than he who is caught by it.'
    Then looking darkly at him spoke resourceful Odysseus:
'Son of Atreus, what sort of word escaped your teeth's barrier?
Ruinous! I wish you directed some other unworthy
85 army, and were not lord over us, over us to whom Zeus
has appointed the accomplishing of wars, from our youth
even into our old age until we are dead, each of us.
Are you really thus eager to abandon the wide-wayed city
of the Trojans, over which we have taken so many sorrows?
90 Do not say it; for fear some other Achaian might hear this
word, which could never at all get past the lips of any man
who understood inside his heart how to speak soundly,
who was a sceptred king, and all the people obeyed him
in numbers like those of the Argives, whose lord you are.
95 Now I utterly despise your heart for the thing you have spoken;
you who in the very closing of clamorous battle
tell us to haul our strong-benched ships to the sea, so that even
more glory may befall the Trojans, who beat us already,
and headlong destruction swing our way, since the Achaians
100 will not hold their battle as the ships are being hauled seaward,
but will look about, and let go the exultation of fighting.

There, o leader of the people, your plan will be ruin.'

Then in turn the lord of men Agamemnon answered him:
'Odysseus, you have hit me somewhere deep in my feelings
with this hard word. But I am not telling the sons of the Achaians   105
against their will to drag their benched ships down to the water.
Now let someone speak who has better counsel than this was;
young man or old; and what he says will be to my liking.'

Now among them spoke Diomedes of the great war cry:
'That man is here, we shall not look far for him, if you are willing   110
to listen, and not be each astonished in anger against me
because by birth I am the youngest among you. I also
can boast that my generation is of an excellent father,
Tydeus, whom now the heaped earth covers over in Thebe.
For there were three blameless sons who were born to Portheus,   115
and their home was in Pleuron and headlong Kalydon. Agrios
was first, then Melas, and the third was Oineus the horseman,
the father of my father, and in valour beyond the others.
But Oineus stayed in the land, while my father was driven and settled
in Argos. Such was the will of Zeus and the other immortals.   120
He married one of the daughters of Adrestos, and established
a house rich in substance, and plenty of wheat-grown acres
were his, with many orchards of fruit trees circled about him,
and many herds were his. He surpassed all other Achaians
with the spear. If all this is true, you must have heard of it.   125
Therefore you could not, saying that I was base and unwarlike
by birth, dishonour any word that I speak, if I speak well.
Let us go back to the fighting wounded as we are. We have to.
Once there, we must hold ourselves out of the onfall, clear of
missiles, so that none will add to the wound he has got already,   130
but we shall be there to drive them on, since even before this
they have favoured their anger, and stood far off, and will not fight for us.'

So he spoke, and they listened well to him, and obeyed him,
and went on their way. And the lord of men, Agamemnon, led them.

Neither did the glorious shaker of the earth keep blind watch,   135
but came among them now in the likeness of an old man,
and took hold of Agamemnon, Atreus' son, by the right hand,
and spoke to him and addressed him in winged words: 'Son of Atreus,
I think that now that baleful heart in the breast of Achilleus

140 must be happy as he stares at the slaughter of the Achaians
and their defeat. There is no heart in him, not even a little.
Even so may the god strike him down, let him go to destruction.
But with you the blessed gods are not utterly angry.
There will still be a time when the lords of Troy and their counsellors
145 shall send dust wide on the plain, and you yourself shall look on them
as they take flight for their city away from the ships and the shelters.'
  So he spoke, and swept on over the plain, with a huge cry
like the yell nine thousand men send up, or ten thousand
in battle, as they close in the hateful strife of the war god.
150 So huge was the cry the powerful earth-shaker let go
from his lungs, and in the heart of every Achaian implanted
great strength, to carry the battle on, and fight without flinching.
  Now Hera, she of the golden throne, standing on Olympos'
horn, looked out with her eyes, and saw at once how Poseidon,
155 who was her very brother and her lord's brother, was bustling
about the battle where men win glory, and her heart was happy.
Then she saw Zeus, sitting along the loftiest summit
on Ida of the springs, and in her eyes he was hateful.
And now the lady ox-eyed Hera was divided in purpose
160 as to how she could beguile the brain in Zeus of the aegis.
And to her mind this thing appeared to be the best counsel,
to array herself in loveliness, and go down to Ida,
and perhaps he might be taken with desire to lie in love with her
next her skin, and she might be able to drift an innocent
165 warm sleep across his eyelids, and seal his crafty perceptions.
She went into her chamber, which her beloved son Hephaistos
had built for her, and closed the leaves in the door-posts snugly
with a secret door-bar, and no other of the gods could open it.
There entering she drew shut the leaves of the shining door, then
170 first from her adorable body washed away all stains
with ambrosia, and next anointed herself with ambrosial
sweet olive oil, which stood there in its fragrance beside her,
and from which, stirred in the house of Zeus by the golden pavement,
a fragrance was shaken forever forth, on earth and in heaven.
175 When with this she had anointed her delicate body
and combed her hair, next with her hands she arranged the shining
and lovely and ambrosial curls along her immortal

head, and dressed in an ambrosial robe that Athene
had made her carefully, smooth, and with many figures upon it,
and pinned it across her breast with a golden brooch, and circled   180
her waist about with a zone that floated a hundred tassels,
and in the lobes of her carefully pierced ears she put rings
with triple drops in mulberry clusters, radiant with beauty,
and, lovely among goddesses, she veiled her head downward
with a sweet fresh veil that glimmered pale like the sunlight.   185
Underneath her shining feet she bound on the fair sandals.
Now, when she had clothed her body in all this loveliness,
she went out from the chamber, and called aside Aphrodite
to come away from the rest of the gods, and spoke a word to her:
'Would you do something for me, dear child, if I were to ask you?   190
Or would you refuse it? Are you forever angered against me
because I defend the Danaans, while you help the Trojans?'
    Then the daughter of Zeus, Aphrodite, answered her: 'Hera,
honoured goddess, daughter to mighty Kronos, speak forth
whatever is in your mind. My heart is urgent to do it   195
if I can, and if it is a thing that can be accomplished.'
    Then, with false lying purpose the lady Hera answered her:
'Give me loveliness and desirability, graces
with which you overwhelm mortal men, and all the immortals.
Since I go now to the ends of the generous earth, on a visit   200
to Okeanos, whence the gods have risen, and Tethys our mother
who brought me up kindly in their own house, and cared for me
and took me from Rheia, at that time when Zeus of the wide brows
drove Kronos underneath the earth and the barren water.
I shall go to visit these, and resolve their division of discord,   205
since now for a long time they have stayed apart from each other
and from the bed of love, since rancour has entered their feelings.
Could I win over with persuasion the dear heart within them
and bring them back to their bed to be merged in love with each other
I shall be forever called honoured by them, and beloved.'   210
    Then in turn Aphrodite the laughing answered her:
'I cannot, and I must not deny this thing that you ask for,
you, who lie in the arms of Zeus, since he is our greatest.'
    She spoke, and from her breasts unbound the elaborate, pattern-pierced
zone, and on it are figured all beguilements, and loveliness   215

[299]

is figured upon it, and passion of sex is there, and the whispered
endearment that steals the heart away even from the thoughtful.
She put this in Hera's hands, and called her by name and spoke to her:
'Take this zone, and hide it away in the fold of your bosom.
220 It is elaborate, all things are figured therein. And I think
whatever is your heart's desire shall not go unaccomplished.'
　　So she spoke, and the ox-eyed lady Hera smiled on her
and smiling hid the zone away in the fold of her bosom.
　　So Aphrodite went back into the house, Zeus' daughter,
225 while Hera in a flash of speed left the horn of Olympos
and crossed over Pieria and Emathia the lovely
and overswept the snowy hills of the Thracian riders
and their uttermost pinnacles, nor touched the ground with her feet. Then
from Athos she crossed over the heaving main sea
230 and came to Lemnos, and to the city of godlike Thoas.
There she encountered Sleep, the brother of Death. She clung
fast to his hand and spoke a word and called him by name: 'Sleep,
lord over all mortal men and all gods, if ever
before now you listened to word of mine, so now also
235 do as I ask; and all my days I shall know gratitude.
Put to sleep the shining eyes of Zeus under his brows
as soon as I have lain beside him in love. I will give you
gifts; a lovely throne, imperishable forever,
of gold. My own son, he of the strong arms, Hephaistos,
240 shall make it with careful skill and make for your feet a footstool
on which you can rest your shining feet when you take your pleasure.'
　　Then Sleep the still and soft spoke to her in answer:
'Hera, honoured goddess and daughter of mighty Kronos,
any other one of the gods, whose race is immortal,
245 I would lightly put to sleep, even the stream of that River
Okeanos, whence is risen the seed of all the immortals.
But I would not come too close to Zeus, the son of Kronos,
nor put him to sleep, unless when he himself were to tell me.
Before now, it was a favour to you that taught me wisdom,
250 on the day Herakles, the high-hearted son of Zeus, was sailing
from Ilion, when he had utterly sacked the city of the Trojans.
That time I laid to sleep the brain in Zeus of the aegis
and drifted upon him still and soft, but your mind was devising

evil, and you raised along the sea the blasts of the racking
winds, and on these swept him away to Kos, the strong-founded,   255
with all his friends lost, but Zeus awakened in anger
and beat the gods up and down his house, looking beyond all others
for me, and would have sunk me out of sight in the sea from the bright sky
had not Night who has power over gods and men rescued me.
I reached her in my flight, and Zeus let be, though he was angry   260
in awe of doing anything to swift Night's displeasure.
Now you ask me to do this other impossible thing for you.'
    Then in turn the lady ox-eyed Hera answered him:
'Sleep, why do you ponder this in your heart, and hesitate?
Or do you think that Zeus of the wide brows, aiding the Trojans,   265
will be angry as he was angry for his son, Herakles?
Come now, do it, and I will give you one of the younger
Graces for you to marry, and she shall be called your lady;
Pasithea, since all your days you have loved her forever.'
    So she spoke, and Sleep was pleased and spoke to her in answer: 270
'Come then! Swear it to me on Styx' ineluctable water.
With one hand take hold of the prospering earth, with the other
take hold of the shining salt sea, so that all the undergods
who gather about Kronos may be witnesses to us.
Swear that you will give me one of the younger Graces,   275
Pasithea, the one whom all my days I have longed for.'
    He spoke, nor failed to persuade the goddess Hera of the white arms,
and she swore as he commanded, and called by their names on all those
gods who live beneath the Pit, and who are called Titans.
Then when she had sworn this, and made her oath a complete thing,   280
the two went away from Lemnos, and the city of Imbros,
and mantled themselves in mist, and made their way very lightly
till they came to Ida with all her springs, the mother of wild beasts,
to Lekton, where first they left the water, and went on
over dry land, and with their feet the top of the forest was shaken.   285
There Sleep stayed, before the eyes of Zeus could light on him,
and went up aloft a towering pine tree, the one that grew tallest
at that time on Ida, and broke through the close air to the aether.
In this he sat, covered over and hidden by the pine branches,
in the likeness of a singing bird whom in the mountains   290
the immortal gods call chalkis, but men call him kymindis.

But Hera light-footed made her way to the peak of Gargaros
on towering Ida. And Zeus who gathers the clouds saw her,
and when he saw her desire was a mist about his close heart
295 as much as on that time they first went to bed together
and lay in love, and their dear parents knew nothing of it.
He stood before her and called her by name and spoke to her: 'Hera,
what is your desire that you come down here from Olympos?
And your horses are not here, nor your chariot, which you would ride in.'
300 Then with false lying purpose the lady Hera answered him:
'I am going to the ends of the generous earth, on a visit
to Okeanos, whence the gods have risen, and Tethys our mother,
who brought me up kindly in their own house, and cared for me.
I shall go to visit these, and resolve their division of discord,
305 since now for a long time they have stayed apart from each other
and from the bed of love, since rancour has entered their feelings.
In the foothills by Ida of the waters are standing
my horses, who will carry me over hard land and water.
Only now I have come down here from Olympos for your sake
310 so you will not be angry with me afterwards, if I
have gone silently to the house of deep-running Okeanos.'
   Then in turn Zeus who gathers the clouds answered her:
'Hera, there will be a time afterwards when you can go there
as well. But now let us go to bed and turn to love-making.
315 For never before has love for any goddess or woman
so melted about the heart inside me, broken it to submission,
as now: not that time when I loved the wife of Ixion
who bore me Peirithoös, equal of the gods in counsel,
nor when I loved Akrisios' daughter, sweet-stepping Danaë,
320 who bore Perseus to me, pre-eminent among all men,
nor when I loved the daughter of far-renowned Phoinix, Europa
who bore Minos to me, and Rhadamanthys the godlike;
not when I loved Semele, or Alkmene in Thebe,
when Alkmene bore me a son, Herakles the strong-hearted,
325 while Semele's son was Dionysos, the pleasure of mortals;
not when I loved the queen Demeter of the lovely tresses,
not when it was glorious Leto, nor yourself, so much
as now I love you, and the sweet passion has taken hold of me.'
   Then with false lying purpose the lady Hera answered him:

'Most honoured son of Kronos, what sort of thing have you spoken?   330
If now your great desire is to lie in love together
here on the peaks of Ida, everything can be seen. Then
what would happen if some one of the gods everlasting
saw us sleeping, and went and told all the other immortals
of it? I would not simply rise out of bed and go back   335
again, into your house, and such a thing would be shameful.
No, if this is your heart's desire, if this is your wish, then
there is my chamber, which my beloved son Hephaistos
has built for me, and closed the leaves in the door-posts snugly.
We can go back there and lie down, since bed is your pleasure.'   340
    Then in turn Zeus who gathers the clouds answered her:
'Hera, do not fear that any mortal or any god
will see, so close shall be the golden cloud that I gather
about us. Not even Helios can look at us through it,
although beyond all others his light has the sharpest vision.'   345
    So speaking, the son of Kronos caught his wife in his arms. There
underneath them the divine earth broke into young, fresh
grass, and into dewy clover, crocus and hyacinth
so thick and soft it held the hard ground deep away from them.
There they lay down together and drew about them a golden   350
wonderful cloud, and from it the glimmering dew descended.
    So the father slept unshaken on the peak of Gargaron
with his wife in his arms, when sleep and passion had stilled him;
but gently Sleep went on the run to the ships of the Achaians
with a message to tell him who circles the earth and shakes it,   355
Poseidon, and stood close to him and addressed him in winged words:
'Poseidon, now with all your heart defend the Danaans
and give them glory, though only for a little, while Zeus still
sleeps; since I have mantled a soft slumber about him
and Hera beguiled him into sleeping in love beside her.'   360
    He spoke so, and went away among the famed races
of men, and stirred Poseidon even more to defend the Danaans.
He sprang among their foremost and urged them on in a great voice:
'Argives, now once more must we give the best of it to Hektor,
Priam's son, so he may take our ships and win glory from them?   365
Such is his thought and such is his prayer, because now Achilleus
in the anger of his heart stays still among the hollow ships.

But there will not be too much longing for him, if the others
of us can stir ourselves up to stand by each other.
370 Come; then, do as I say, let us all be won over; let us
take those shields which are best in all the army and biggest
and put them on, and cover our heads in the complete shining
of helmets, and take in our hands our spears that are longest
and go. I myself will lead the way, and I think that no longer
375 Hektor, Priam's son, can stand up to us, for all his fury.
Let the man stubborn in battle who wears a small shield on his shoulder
give it to a worse man, and put on the shield that is bigger.'
    So he spoke, and they listened hard to him, and obeyed him.
The kings in person marshalled these men, although they were wounded,
380 Tydeus' son, and Odysseus, and Atreus' son Agamemnon.
They went among all, and made them exchange their armour of battle,
and the good fighter put on the good armour, and each gave the worse
    gear
to the worse. Then when in the shining bronze they had shrouded their
    bodies
they went forward, and Poseidon the shaker of the earth led them
385 holding in his heavy hand the stark sword with the thin edge
glittering, as glitters the thunderflash none may close with
by right in sorrowful division, but fear holds all men back.
    On the other side glorious Hektor ordered the Trojans,
and now Poseidon of the dark hair and glorious Hektor
390 strained to its deadliest the division of battle, the one
bringing power to the Trojans, and the god to the Argives.
The breaking of the sea washed up to the ships and the shelters
of the Argives. The two sides closed together with a great war cry.
Not such is the roaring against dry land of the sea's surf
395 as it rolls in from the open under the hard blast of the north wind;
not such is the bellowing of fire in its blazing
in the deep places of the hills when it rises inflaming the forest,
nor such again the crying voice of the wind in the deep-haired
oaks, when it roars highest in its fury against them,
400 not so loud as now the noise of Achaians and Trojans
in voice of terror rose as they drove against one another.
    First glorious Hektor made a cast with his spear at Aias
since he had turned straight against him, nor missed with his throw

but struck, there where over his chest were crossed the two straps,
one for the sword with the silver nails, and one for the great shield.   405
These guarded the tenderness of his skin. And Hektor, in anger
because his weapon had been loosed from his hand in a vain cast,
to avoid death shrank into the host of his own companions.
But as he drew away huge Telamonian Aias
caught up a rock; there were many, holding-stones for the fast ships,   410
rolled among the feet of the fighters; he caught up one of these
and hit him in the chest next the throat over his shield rim,
and spun him around like a top with the stroke, so that he staggered
in a circle; as a great oak goes down root-torn under
Zeus father's stroke, and a horrible smell of sulphur uprises   415
from it, and there is no courage left in a man who stands by
and looks on, for the thunderstroke of great Zeus is a hard thing;
so Hektor in all his strength dropped suddenly in the dust, let
fall the spear from his hand, and his shield was beaten upon him,
and the helm, and his armour elaborate with bronze clashed over him.   420
Screaming aloud the sons of the Achaians ran forward
in hope to drag him away, and threw their volleying javelins
against him, yet no man could stab or cast at the shepherd
of the people; sooner the Trojans' bravest gathered about him,
Aineias, and Poulydamas, and brilliant Agenor,   425
Sarpedon, lord of the Lykians, and Glaukos the blameless;
and of the rest no man was heedless of him, but rather
sloped the strong circles of their shields over him, while his companions
caught him in their arms out of the fighting and reached his fast-footed
horses, where they stood to the rear of the fighting and the battle   430
holding their charioteer and the elaborate chariot,
and these carried him, groaning heavily, back toward the city.
    But when they came to the crossing place of the fair-running river,
of whirling Xanthos, whose father was Zeus the immortal,
they moved him from behind his horses to the ground, and splashed   435
water over him. He got his wind again, and his eyes cleared,
and he got up to lean on one knee and vomit a dark clot
of blood, then lay back on the ground again, while over both eyes
dark night misted. His strength was still broken by the stone's stroke.
    But the Argives, when they saw Hektor withdrawing from them,   440
remembered once again their warcraft and turned on the Trojans.

There far before them all swift Aias son of Oïleus
made an outrush, and stabbed with the sharp spear Satnios,
Enops' son, whom the perfect naiad nymph had borne once
445 to Enops, as he tended his herds by Satnioeis river.
The spear-famed son of Oïleus, coming close to this man,
stabbed him in the flank so that he knocked him backward, and over him
Trojans and Danaans closed together in strong encounter.
Poulydamas of the shaken spear came up to stand by him,
450 Panthoös' son, and struck in the right shoulder Prothoënor
son of Areïlykos, and the powerful spear was driven
through the shoulder, and he dropping in the dust clawed the ground in
      his fingers.
Poulydamas vaunted terribly over him, calling in a great voice:
'I think this javelin leaping from the heavy hand of Panthoös'
455 high-hearted son was not thrown away in a vain cast. Rather
some Argive caught it in his skin. I think he has got it
for a stick to lean on as he trudges down into Death's house.'
      He spoke, and sorrow came over the Argives at his vaunting,
and beyond others he stirred the anger in wise Telamonian
460 Aias, for the man had fallen closest to him, and at once
he made a cast with the shining spear at returning Poulydamas.
But Poulydamas himself avoided the dark death
with a quick spring to one side, and Archelochos son of Antenor
caught the spear, since the immortal gods had doomed his destruction.
465 He hit him at the joining place of head and neck, at the last
vertebra, and cut through both of the tendons, so that
the man's head and mouth and nose hit the ground far sooner
than did the front of his legs and knees as he fell. And Aias
spoke aloud in answer to unfaulted Poulydamas:
470 'Think over this, Poulydamas, and answer me truly.
Is not this man's death against Prothoënor's a worthwhile
exchange? I think he is no mean man, nor born of mean fathers,
but is some brother of Antenor, breaker of horses,
or his son; since he is close in blood by the look of him.'
475   He spoke, knowing well what he said, and sorrow fastened on the
      Trojans.
There Akamas, bestriding his brother, stabbed the Boiotian
Promachos with the spear as he tried to drag off the body.

Akamas vaunted terribly over him, calling in a great voice:
'You Argives, arrow-fighters, insatiate of menace. I think
we shall not be the only ones to be given hard work   480
and sorrow, but you too must sometimes die, as this man did.
Think how Promachos sleeps among you, beaten down under
my spear, so that punishment for my brother may not go
long unpaid. Therefore a man prays he will leave behind him
one close to him in his halls to avenge his downfall in battle.'   485
     He spoke, and sorrow came over the Argives at his vaunting,
and beyond others he stirred the anger in wise Peneleos.
He charged Akamas, who would not stand up against the onset
of lord Peneleos. He then stabbed with the spear Ilioneus
the son of Phorbas the rich in sheepflocks, whom beyond all men   490
of the Trojans Hermes loved, and gave him possessions.
Ilioneus was the only child his mother had borne him.
This man Peneleos caught underneath the brow, at the bases
of the eye, and pushed the eyeball out, and the spear went clean through
the eye-socket and tendon of the neck, so that he went down   495
backward, reaching out both hands, but Peneleos drawing
his sharp sword hewed at the neck in the middle, and so dashed downward
the head, with helm upon it, while still on the point of the big spear
the eyeball stuck. He, lifting it high like the head of a poppy,
displayed it to the Trojans and spoke vaunting over it: 500
'Trojans, tell haughty Ilioneus' beloved father
and mother, from me, that they can weep for him in their halls, since
neither shall the wife of Promachos, Alegenor's
son, take pride of delight in her dear lord's coming, on that day
when we sons of the Achaians come home from Troy in our vessels.'   505
     So he spoke, and the shivers came over the limbs of all of them,
and each man looked about him for a way to escape the sheer death.
     Tell me now, you Muses who have your homes on Olympos,
who was first of the Achaians to win the bloody despoilment
of men, when the glorious shaker of the earth bent the way of the battle?   510
First Telamonian Aias cut down Hyrtios, he who
was son to Gyrtios, and lord over the strong-hearted Mysians.
Antilochos slaughtered Phalkes and Mermeros. Morys
and Hippotion were killed by Meriones. Teukros cut down
Periphetes and Prothoön. Next the son of Atreus,   515

[307]

Menelaos, stabbed Hyperenor, shepherd of the people,
in the flank, so the bronze head let gush out the entrails
through the torn side. His life came out through the wound of the spear-
        stab
in beating haste, and a mist of darkness closed over both eyes.
520 But Aias the fast-footed son of Oïleus caught and killed most,
since there was none like him in the speed of his feet to go after
men who ran, once Zeus had driven the terror upon them.

BUT after they had crossed back over the ditch and the sharp stakes
in flight, and many had gone down under the hands of the Danaans,
they checked about once more and stood their ground by the chariots,
green for fear and terrified. But now Zeus wakened
by Hera of the gold throne on the high places of Ida,   5
and stood suddenly upright, and saw the Achaians and Trojans,
these driven to flight, the others harrying them in confusion,
these last Argives, and saw among them the lord Poseidon.
He saw Hektor lying in the plain, his companions sitting
around him, he dazed at the heart and breathing painfully,   10
vomiting blood, since not the weakest Achaian had hit him.
Then the father of gods and men seeing Hektor pitied him
and looked scowling terribly at Hera, and spoke a word to her:
'Hopeless one, it was your evil design, your treachery, Hera,
that stayed brilliant Hektor from battle, terrified his people.   15
I do not know, perhaps for this contrivance of evil
and pain you will win first reward when I lash you with whip strokes.
Do you not remember that time you hung from high and on your feet
I slung two anvils, and about your hands drove a golden
chain, unbreakable. You among the clouds and the bright sky   20
hung, nor could the gods about tall Olympos endure it
and stood about, but could not set you free. If I caught one
I would seize and throw him from the threshold, until he landed
stunned on the earth, yet even so the weariless agony

25 for Herakles the godlike would not let go my spirit.
You with the north wind's aid winning over the stormwinds drove him
on across the desolate sea in evil intention
and then on these swept him away to Kos, the strong-founded.
I myself rescued him there and brought him back once more
30 to horse-pasturing Argos, when he had been through much hardship.
I will remind you of all this, so you will give up
your deceptions, see if your love-making in bed will help you,
that way you lay with me apart from the gods, and deceived me.'
He spoke, and the lady the ox-eyed goddess Hera was frightened
35 and she spoke to him and addressed him in winged words: 'Now let
Earth be my witness in this, and the wide heaven above us,
and the dripping water of the Styx, which oath is the biggest
and most formidable oath among the blessed immortals.
The sanctity of your head be witness, and the bed of marriage
40 between us: a thing by which I at least could never swear vainly.
It is not through my will that the shaker of the earth Poseidon
afflicts the Trojans and Hektor and gives aid to the others,
but it is his own passion that urges him to it and drives him.
He saw the Achaians hard pressed beside their ships, and pitied them.
45 No, but I myself also would give him counsel
to go with you, o dark clouded, that way that you lead us.'
She spoke, and now the father of gods and men smiled on her
and spoke again in answer to her, and addressed her in winged words:
'If even you, lady Hera of the ox eyes, hereafter
50 were to take your place among the immortals thinking as I do,
then Poseidon, hard though he may wish it otherwise,
must at once turn his mind so it follows your heart, and my heart.
If now all this that you say is real, and you speak truthfully,
go now among the generations of the gods, and summon
55 Iris to come here to me, and Apollo the glorious archer,
so that Iris may go among the bronze-armoured people
of the Achaians, and give a message to lord Poseidon
to leave the fighting and come back to the home that is his. Also
let Phoibos Apollo stir Hektor back into battle,
60 breathe strength into him once more, and make him forget the agonies
that now are wearing out his senses. Let him drive strengthless
panic into the Achaians, and turn them back once more;

let them be driven in flight and tumble back on the benched ships
of Achilleus, Peleus' son. And he shall rouse up Patroklos
his companion. And glorious Hektor shall cut down Patroklos   65
with the spear before Ilion, after he has killed many others
of the young men, and among them my own son, shining Sarpedon.
In anger for him brilliant Achilleus shall then kill Hektor.
And from then on I would make the fighting surge back from the vessels
always and continuously, until the Achaians   70
capture headlong Ilion through the designs of Athene.
Before this I am not stopping my anger, and I will not let
any other of the immortals stand there by the Danaans
until the thing asked by the son of Peleus has been accomplished
as I undertook at the first and bent my head in assent to it   75
on that day when embracing my knees immortal Thetis
supplicated honour for Achilleus, sacker of cities.'

    He spoke, and the goddess of the white arms Hera did not disobey him
but went back to tall Olympos from the mountains of Ida.
As the thought flashes in the mind of a man who, traversing   80
much territory, thinks of things in the mind's awareness,
'I wish I were this place, or this', and imagines many things;
so rapidly in her eagerness winged Hera, a goddess.
She came to sheer Olympos and entered among the assembled
immortal gods in the house of Zeus, and they seeing her   85
rose all to swarm about her and lifted their cups in greeting.
But Hera passed by the others and accepted a cup from Themis
of the fair cheeks, since she had first come running to greet her
and had spoken to her and addressed her in winged words: 'Hera,
why have you come? You seem like one who has been terrified.   90
I know, it was the son of Kronos, your husband, frightened you.'

    In turn the goddess Hera of the white arms answered her:
'Ask me nothing of this, divine Themis. You yourself
know what his spirit is, how it is stubborn and arrogant.
Preside still over the gods in their house, the feast's fair division.   95
Yet so much may you hear, and with you all the immortals,
how Zeus discloses evil actions, and I do not think
the heart of all will be pleasured alike, neither among mortals
nor gods either, although one now still feasts at his pleasure.'

    The lady Hera spoke so and sat down, and the gods   100

about the house of Zeus were troubled. Hera was smiling
with her lips, but above the dark brows her forehead
was not at peace. She spoke before them all in vexation:
'Fools, we who try to work against Zeus, thoughtlessly.
105 Still we are thinking in our anger to go near, and stop him
by argument or force. He sits apart and cares nothing
nor thinks of us, and says that among the other immortals
he is pre-eminently the greatest in power and strength. Therefore
each of you must take whatever evil he sends you.
110 Since I think already a sorrow has been wrought against Ares.
His son has been killed in the fighting, dearest of all men
to him, Askalaphos, whom stark Ares calls his own son.'
     So she spoke. Then Ares struck against both his big thighs
with the flats of his hands, and spoke a word of anger and sorrow:
115 'Now, you who have your homes on Olympos, you must not blame me
for going among the ships of the Achaians, and avenging my son's
slaughter, even though it be my fate to be struck by Zeus'
thunderbolt, and sprawl in the blood and dust by the dead men.'
     So he spoke, and ordered Fear and Terror to harness
120 his horses, and himself got into his shining armour.
And there might have been wrought another anger, and bitterness
from Zeus, still greater, more wearisome among the immortals,
had not Athene, in her fear for the sake of all gods,
sprung up and out through the forecourt, left her chair where she was
          sitting,
125 and taken the helmet off from his head, the shield from his shoulders,
and snatched out of his heavy hand the bronze spear, and fixed it
apart, and then in speech reasoned with violent Ares:
'Madman, mazed of your wits, this is ruin! Your ears can listen
still to reality, but your mind is gone and your discipline.
130 Do you not hear what the goddess Hera of the white arms tells us,
and she coming back even now from Zeus of Olympos?
Do you wish, after running the course of many misfortunes
yourself, still to come back to Olympos under compulsion
though reluctant, and plant seed of great sorrow among the rest of us?
135 Since he will at once leave the Achaians and the high-hearted
Trojans, and come back to batter us on Olympos
and will catch up as they come the guilty one and the guiltless.

Therefore I ask of you to give up your anger for your son.
By now some other, better of his strength and hands than your son was,
has been killed, or will soon be killed; and it is a hard thing   140
to rescue all the generation and seed of all mortals.'
     So she spoke, and seated on a chair violent Ares.
But Hera called to come with her outside the house Apollo
and Iris, who is messenger among the immortal
gods, and spoke to them and addressed them in winged words: 'Zeus   145
     wishes
both of you to go to him with all speed, at Ida;
but when you have come there and looked upon Zeus' countenance,
then you must do whatever he urges you, and his orders.'
     So the lady Hera spoke, and once more returning
sat on her throne. They in a flash of speed winged their way onward.   150
They came to Ida with all her springs, the mother of wild beasts,
and found the wide-browed son of Kronos on the height of Gargaron,
sitting still, and fragrant cloud gathered in a circle about him.
These two came into the presence of Zeus the cloud-gatherer
and stood, nor was his heart angry when he looked upon them,   155
seeing they had promptly obeyed the message of his dear lady.
He spoke to Iris first of the two, and addressed her in winged words:
'Go on your way now, swift Iris, to the lord Poseidon,
and give him all this message nor be a false messenger. Tell him
that he must now quit the war and the fighting, and go back   160
among the generations of gods, or into the bright sea.
And if he will not obey my words, or thinks nothing of them,
then let him consider in his heart and his spirit
that he might not, strong though he is, be able to stand up
to my attack; since I say I am far greater than he is   165
in strength, and elder born; yet his inward heart shrinks not from calling
himself the equal of me, though others shudder before me.'
     He spoke, and swift wind-footed Iris did not disobey him
but went down along the hills of Ida to sacred Ilion.
As those times when out of the clouds the snow or the hail whirls   170
cold beneath the blast of the north wind born in the bright air,
so rapidly in her eagerness winged Iris, the swift one,
and stood beside the famed shaker of the earth, and spoke to him:
'I have a certain message for you, dark-haired, earth-encircler,

175 and came here to bring it to you from Zeus of the aegis.
His order is that you quit the war and the fighting, and go back
among the generations of gods, or into the bright sea.
And if you will not obey his words, or think nothing of them,
his threat is that he himself will come to fight with you
180 here, strength against strength, but warns you to keep from under
his hands, since he says he is far greater than you are
in strength, and elder born. Yet your inward heart shrinks not from
   calling
yourself the equal of him, though others shudder before him.'
   Then deeply vexed the famed shaker of the earth spoke to her:
185 'No, no. Great though he is, this that he has said is too much,
if he will force me against my will, me, who am his equal
in rank. Since we are three brothers born by Rheia to Kronos,
Zeus, and I, and the third is Hades, lord of the dead men.
All was divided among us three ways, each given his domain.
190 I when the lots were shaken drew the grey sea to live in
forever; Hades drew the lot of the mists and the darkness,
and Zeus was allotted the wide sky, in the cloud and the bright air.
But earth and high Olympos are common to all three. Therefore
I am no part of the mind of Zeus. Let him in tranquillity
195 and powerful as he is stay satisfied with his third share.
And let him absolutely stop frightening me, as if I were
mean, with his hands. It were better to keep for the sons and the
   daughters
he got himself these blusterings and these threats of terror.
They will listen, because they must, to whatever he tells them.'
200   Then in turn swift wind-footed Iris answered him:
'Am I then to carry, o dark-haired, earth-encircler,
this word, which is strong and steep, back to Zeus from you?
Or will you change a little? The hearts of the great can be changed.
You know the Furies, how they forever side with the elder.'
205   Then in turn the shaker of the earth Poseidon spoke to her:
'Now this, divine Iris, was a word quite properly spoken.
It is a fine thing when a messenger is conscious of justice.
But this thing comes as a bitter sorrow to my heart and my spirit,
when Zeus tries in words of anger to reprimand one who
210 is his equal in station, and endowed with destiny like his.

Still, this time I will give way, for all my vexation.
But I will say this also, and make it a threat in my anger.
If ever, acting apart from me and Athene the spoiler,
apart from Hera and Hermes and the lord Hephaistos,
he shall spare headlong Ilion, and shall not be willing   215
to take it by storm, and bestow great victory on the Argives,
let him be sure, there will be no more healing of our anger.'
    The shaker of the earth spoke, and left the Achaian people,
and went, merging in the sea, and the fighting Achaians longed for him.
After this Zeus who gathers the clouds spoke to Apollo: 220
'Go now, beloved Phoibos, to the side of brazen-helmed Hektor,
since by this he who encircles the earth and shakes it
is gone into the bright sea and has avoided the anger
that would be ours. In truth, this would have been a fight those other
gods would have heard about, who gather to Kronos beneath us.   225
Now this way it was far better for me, and for himself
also, that, for all his vexation before, he gave way
to my hands. We would have sweated before this business was finished.
Now yourself take up in your hands the aegis with fluttering
tassels, and shake it hard to scare the Achaian fighters.   230
Then, striker from afar, let your own concern be glorious Hektor.
So long waken the huge strength in him, until the Achaians
run in flight, and come to the ships and the crossing of Helle.
From there on I myself shall think of the word and the action
to make the Achaians get wind once more, after their hard fighting.'   235
    He spoke so, and Apollo, not disregarding his father,
came down along the mountains of Ida in the likeness of a rapid
hawk, the dove's murderer and swiftest of all things flying.
He found brilliant Hektor, the son of wise Priam, sitting
now, no longer sprawled, as he gathered new strength back into him   240
and recognized his companions about him. The sweat and hard breathing
had begun to stop, once the will in Zeus of the aegis wakened him.
Apollo who works from afar stood beside him, and spoke to him:
'Hektor, son of Priam, why do you sit in such weakness
here apart from the others? Did some disaster befall you?'   245
    In his weakness Hektor of the shining helm spoke to him:
'Who are you, who speak to me face to face, o noblest
of gods? Did you not know how by the Achaians' grounded

ships, Aias of the great war cry struck me in the chest with a boulder
250 as I slaughtered his companions, and stayed my furious valour?
Truly, I thought that on this day I would come to the corpses
and the house of the death god, once I had breathed the inward life from
  me.'
    In turn the lord, the worker from afar, Apollo, spoke to him:
'Take heart; such an avenger am I whom the son of Kronos
255 sent down from Ida, to stand by your side and defend you,
Phoibos Apollo of the golden sword, who in time before this
also have stood to defend yourself and your sheer citadel.
So come now, and urge on your cavalry in their numbers
to drive on their horses against the hollow ships. Meanwhile
260 I shall move on before you and make all the way for the horses
smooth before them, and bend back the Achaian fighters.'
    He spoke, and breathed huge strength into the shepherd of the people.
As when some stalled horse who has been corn-fed at the manger
breaking free of his rope gallops over the plain in thunder
265 to his accustomed bathing place in a sweet-running river
and in the pride of his strength holds high his head and the mane floats
over his shoulders; sure of his glorious strength, the quick knees
carry him to the loved places and the pasture of horses;
so Hektor moving rapidly his feet and his knees went
270 onward, stirring the horsemen when he heard the god's voice speak.
And as when men who live in the wilds and their dogs have driven
into flight a horned stag or a wild goat. Inaccessible
the rocky cliff or the shadowed forest has covered the quarry
so that the men know it was not their fortune to take him;
275 and now by their clamouring shows in the way a great bearded
lion, and bends them to sudden flight for all their eagerness;
so the Danaans until that time kept always in close chase
assembled, stabbing at them with swords and leaf-headed spears,
but when they saw Hektor once more ranging the men's ranks
280 they were frightened, and by their feet collapsed all their bravery.
    Now Thoas spoke forth among them, the son of Andraimon,
far the best of the Aitolians, one skilled in the spear's throw
and brave in close fight. In assembly few of the Achaians
when the young men contended in debate could outdo him.
285 He in kind intention now spoke forth and addressed them:

'Can this be? Here is a strange thing I see with my own eyes,
how this Hektor has got to his feet once more, and eluded
the death spirits. I think in each of us the heart had high hope
he was killed under the hands of Telamonian Aias.
Now some one of the gods has come to his help and rescued   290
Hektor, who has unstrung the knees of so many Danaans.
I think he will do it once more now. It is not without Zeus
the deep-thundering that he stands their champion in all this fury.
Come then, let us do as I say, let us all be persuaded.
Let us tell the multitude to make its way back toward the vessels   295
while we ourselves, who claim we are greatest in all the army,
stand, and see if we can face him first, and hold him off from them
with spears lifted against him, and I think for all of his fury
his heart will be afraid to plunge into our Danaan company.'
      So he spoke, and they listened to him with care, and obeyed him.   300
They who rallied about Aias, the lord Idomeneus,
Teukros, Meriones, and Meges, a man like the war god,
closed their order for hard impact, calling on the bravest
to face Hektor and the Trojans. Meanwhile behind them
the multitude made their way back toward the ships of the Achaians.   305
      The Trojans came down on them in a pack, and Hektor led them
in long strides, and in front of him went Phoibos Apollo
wearing a mist about his shoulders, and held the tempestuous
terrible aegis, shaggy, conspicuous, that the bronze-smith
Hephaistos had given Zeus to wear to the terror of mortals.   310
Gripping this in both hands he led on the Trojan people.
      But the Argives stood in close order against them, and the battle cry
            rose up
in a thin scream from either side, the arrows from the bowstrings
jumping, while from violent hands the numerous thrown spears
were driven, some deep in the bodies of quick-stirring young men,   315
while many in the space between before they had got to the white skin
stood fast in the ground, though they had been straining to reach the
            bodies.
So long as Phoibos Apollo held stilled in his hands the aegis,
so long the thrown weapons of both took hold, and men dropped under
            them.
But when he stared straight into the eyes of the fast-mounted Danaans   320

and shook the aegis, and himself gave a great baying cry, the spirit
inside them was mazed to hear it, they forgot their furious valour.
And they, as when in the dim of the black night two wild beasts
stampede a herd of cattle or big flock of sheep, falling
325 suddenly upon them, when no herdsman is by, the Achaians
fled so in their weakness and terror, since Apollo drove
terror upon them, and gave the glory to the Trojans and Hektor.
     There man killed man all along the scattered encounter.
Hektor first killed Stichios and Arkesilaos,
330 one the leader of the bronze-armoured Boiotians, the other
trusted companion in arms of great-hearted Menestheus.
But Aineias slaughtered Medon and Iasos. Of these
Medon was a bastard son of godlike Oïleus
and therefore brother of Aias, but had made his home in Phylake
335 away from the land of his fathers, having killed a man, a relation
of Eriopis, his stepmother, the wife of Oïleus.
Iasos was a leader appointed of the Athenians,
and was called the son of Sphelos, the son of Boukolos.
Poulydamas killed Mekisteus, and Polites Echios
340 in the first onfall, and brilliant Agenor cut down Klonios.
Paris struck Deïochos from behind at the shoulder's
base, as he ran away through the front ranks, and drove the bronze clean
     through.
     While these stripped the armour from their men, meanwhile the
          Achaians
blundering about the deep-dug ditch and the sharp stakes
345 ran this way and that in terror, forced into their rampart.
But Hektor called aloud in a piercing cry to the Trojans:
'Make hard for the ships, let the bloody spoils be. That man
I see in the other direction apart from the vessels,
I will take care that he gets his death, and that man's relations
350 neither men nor women shall give his dead body the rite of burning.
In the space before our city the dogs shall tear him to pieces.'
     So speaking with a whipstroke from the shoulder he lashed on his
          horses
calling across the ranks to the Trojans, who along with him
all cried aloud as they steered the horses who pulled their chariots,
355 with inhuman clamour, and in front of them Phoibos Apollo

easily, kicking them with his feet, tumbled the banked edges
of the deep ditch into the pit between, and bridged over a pathway
both wide and long, about as long as the force of a spearcast
goes when a man has thrown it to try his strength. They streamed over
in massed formation, with Apollo in front of them holding   360
the tremendous aegis, and wrecked the bastions of the Achaians
easily, as when a little boy piles sand by the sea-shore
when in his innocent play he makes sand towers to amuse him
and then, still playing, with hands and feet ruins them and wrecks them.
So you, lord Apollo, piled in confusion much hard work   365
and painful done by the Argives and drove terror among them.
So they reined in and stood fast again beside their ships, calling
aloud upon each other, and to all of the gods, uplifting
their hands each man of them cried out his prayers in a great voice,
and beyond others Gerenian Nestor, the Achaians' watcher,   370
prayed, reaching out both arms to the starry heavens:
'Father Zeus, if ever in wheat-deep Argos one of us
burning before you the rich thigh pieces of sheep or ox prayed
he would come home again, and you nodded your head and assented,
remember this, Olympian, save us from the day without pity;   375
let not the Achaians be beaten down like this by the Trojans.'
    So he spoke in prayer, and Zeus of the counsels thundered
a great stroke, hearing the prayer of the old man, the son of Neleus.
    But the Trojans, hearing the thunderstroke of Zeus of the aegis,
remembered even more their warcraft, and sprang on the Argives.   380
They, as when the big waves on the sea wide-wandering
wash across the walls of a ship underneath the leaning
force of the wind, which particularly piles up the big waves,
so the Trojans with huge clamour went over the rampart
and drove their horses to fight alongside the grounded vessels,   385
with leaf-headed spears, some at close quarters, others from their horses.
But the Achaians climbing high on their black ships fought from them
with long pikes that lay among the hulls for sea fighting,
shrouded about the heads in bronze that was soldered upon them.
    Meanwhile Patroklos, all the time the Achaians and Trojans   390
were fighting on both sides of the wall, far away from the fast ships,
had sat all this time in the shelter of courtly Eurypylos
and had been entertaining him with words and applying

medicines that would mitigate the black pains to the sore wound.
395 But when he saw the Trojans were sweeping over the rampart
and the outcry and the noise of terror rose from the Danaans
Patroklos groaned aloud then and struck himself on both thighs
with the flats of his hands and spoke a word of lamentation:
'Eurypylos, much though you need me I cannot stay here
400 longer with you. This is a big fight that has arisen.
Now it is for your henchman to look after you, while I
go in haste to Achilleus, to stir him into the fighting.
Who knows if, with God helping, I might trouble his spirit
by entreaty, since the persuasion of a friend is a strong thing.'
405   As he was speaking his feet carried him away. Meanwhile
the Achaians stood steady against the Trojan attack, but they could not
beat the enemy, fewer as they were, away from their vessels,
nor again had the Trojans strength to break the battalions
of the Danaans, and force their way into the ships and the shelters.
410 But as a chalkline straightens the cutting of a ship's timber
in the hands of an expert carpenter, who by Athene's
inspiration is well versed in all his craft's subtlety,
so the battles fought by both sides were pulled fast and even.
Now by the ships others fought in their various places
415 but Hektor made straight for glorious Aias. These two
were fighting hard for a single ship, and neither was able,
Hektor to drive Aias off the ship, and set fire to it,
nor Aias to beat Hektor back, since the divinity
drove him. Shining Aias struck with the spear Kaletor,
420 Klytios' son, in the chest as he brought fire to the vessel.
He fell, thunderously, and the torch dropped from his hand. Then
Hektor, when his eyes were aware of his cousin fallen
in the dust in front of the black ship, uplifting
his voice in a great cry called to the Trojans and Lykians:
425 'Trojans, Lykians, Dardanians who fight at close quarters,
do not anywhere in this narrow place give way from the fighting
but stand by the son of Klytios, do not let the Achaians
strip the armour from him, fallen where the ships are assembled.'
  So he spoke, and made a cast at Aias with the shining
430 spear, but missed him and struck the son of Mastor, Lykophron,
henchman of Aias from Kythera who had been living

with him; for he had killed a man in sacred Kythera.
Hektor struck him in the head above the ear with the sharp bronze
as he stood next to Aias, so that Lykophron sprawling
dropped from the ship's stern to the ground, and his strength was broken.   435
And Aias shuddered at the sight, and spoke to his brother:
'See, dear Teukros, our true companion, the son of Mastor,
is killed, who came to us from Kythera and in our household
was one we honoured as we honoured our beloved parents.
Now great-hearted Hektor has killed him. Where are your arrows   440
of sudden death, and the bow that Phoibos Apollo gave you?'

   He spoke, and Teukros heard and came running to stand beside him
holding in his hand the backstrung bow and the quiver
to hold arrows, and let go his hard shots against the Trojans.
First he struck down Kleitos, the glorious son of Peisenor   445
and companion of Poulydamas, proud son of Panthoös.
Now Kleitos held the reins, and gave all his care to the horses,
driving them into that place where the most battalions were shaken,
for the favour of Hektor and the Trojans, but the sudden evil
came to him, and none for all their desire could defend him,   450
for the painful arrow was driven into his neck from behind him.
He fell out of the chariot, and the fast-footed horses
shied away, rattling the empty car; but Poulydamas
their master saw it at once, and ran first to the heads of the horses.
He gave them into the hands of Astynoös, Protiaon's   455
son, with many orders to be watchful and hold the horses
close; then himself went back into the ranks of the champions.

   But Teukros picked up another arrow for bronze-helmed
Hektor, and would have stopped his fighting by the ships of the Achaians
had he hit him during his bravery and torn the life from him;   460
but he was not hidden from the close purpose of Zeus, who was
     guarding
Hektor, and denied that glory to Telamonian Teukros;
who broke in the unfaulted bow the close-twisted sinew
as Teukros drew it against him, so the bronze-weighted arrow
went, as the bow dropped out of his hands, driven crazily sidewise.   465
And Teukros shuddered at the sight, and spoke to his brother:
'See now, how hard the divinity cuts across the intention
in all our battle, who struck the bow out of my hand, who has broken

the fresh-twisted sinew of the bowstring I bound on
470 this morning, so it would stand the succession of springing arrows.'
    Then in turn huge Telamonian Aias answered him:
'Dear brother, then let your bow and your showering arrows
lie, now that the god begrudging the Danaans wrecked them.
But take a long spear in your hands, a shield on your shoulder,
475 and close with the Trojans, and drive on the rest of your people.
Let them not, though they have beaten us, easily capture
our strong-benched ships. We must remember the frenzy of fighting.'
    He spoke, and Teukros put away the bow in his shelter
and threw across his shoulders the shield of the fourfold ox-hide.
480 Over his mighty head he set the well-fashioned helmet
with the horse-hair crest, and the plumes nodded terribly above it.
Then he caught up a powerful spear, edged with sharp bronze,
and went on his way, running fast, and stood beside Aias.
    But Hektor, when he saw how the arrows of Teukros were baffled,
485 lifted his voice in a great cry to the Trojans and Lykians:
'Trojans, Lykians, Dardanians who fight at close quarters,
be men now, dear friends, remember your furious valour
along the hollow ships, since I have seen with my own eyes
how by the hand of Zeus their bravest man's arrows were baffled.
490 Easily seen is the strength that is given from Zeus to mortals
either in those into whose hands he gives the surpassing
glory, or those he diminishes and will not defend them
as now he diminishes the strength of the Argives, and helps us.
Fight on then by the ships together. He who among you
495 finds by spear thrown or spear thrust his death and destiny,
let him die. He has no dishonour when he dies defending
his country, for then his wife shall be saved and his children afterwards,
and his house and property shall not be damaged, if the Achaians
must go away with their ships to the beloved land of their fathers.'
500   So he spoke, and stirred the spirit and strength in each man.
But Aias on the other side called to his companions:
'Shame, you Argives; here is the time of decision, whether
we die, or live on still and beat back ruin from our vessels.
Do you expect, if our ships fall to helm-shining Hektor,
505 you will walk each of you back dryshod to the land of your fathers?
Do you not hear how Hektor is stirring up all his people,

how he is raging to set fire to our ships? He is not
inviting you to come to a dance. He invites you to battle.
For us there can be no design, no purpose, better than this one,
to close in and fight with the strength of our hands at close quarters.   510
Better to take in a single time our chances of dying
or living, than go on being squeezed in the stark encounter
right up against our ships, as now, by men worse than we are.'
    So he spoke, and stirred the spirit and strength in each man.
There Hektor killed the son of Perimedes, Schedios,   515
lord of the men of Phokis; but Aias killed Laodamas,
leader of the foot-soldiers, and shining son of Antenor.
Then Poulydamas stripped Otos of Kyllene, companion
to Meges, Phyleus' son, and a lord among the great-hearted
Epeians. Meges seeing it lunged at him, but Poulydamas   520
bent down and away, so that Meges missed him. Apollo
would not let Panthoös' son go down among the front fighters,
but Meges stabbed with the spear the middle of the chest of Kroismos.
He fell, thunderously, and Meges was stripping the armour
from his shoulders, but meanwhile Dolops lunged at him, Lampos'   525
son, a man crafty with the spear and strongest of the sons born
to Lampos, Laomedon's son, one skilled in furious fighting.
He from close up stabbed with his spear at the shield of Phyleides
in the middle, but the corselet he wore defended him, solid
and built with curving plates of metal, which in days past Phyleus   530
had taken home from Ephyra and the river Selleëis.
A guest and friend had given him it, lord of men, Euphetes,
to carry into the fighting and beat off the attack of the enemy,
and now it guarded the body of his son from destruction.
But Meges stabbed with the sharp spear at the uttermost summit   535
of the brazen helmet thick with horse-hair, and tore off
the mane of horse-hair from the helmet, so that it toppled
groundward and lay in the dust in all its new shining of purple.
Yet Dolops stood his ground and fought on, in hope still of winning,
but meanwhile warlike Menelaos came to stand beside Meges,   540
and came from the side and unobserved with his spear, and from behind
threw at his shoulder, so the spear tore through his chest in its fury
to drive on, so that Dolops reeled and went down, face forward.
The two of them swept in to strip away from his shoulders

545 the bronze armour, but Hektor called aloud to his brothers,
the whole lot, but first scolded the son of Hiketaon,
strong Melanippos. He in Perkote had tended his lumbering
cattle, in the days before when the enemy were still far off;
but when the oarswept ships of the Danaans came, then
550 he returned to Ilion, and was a great man among the Trojans,
and lived with Priam, who honoured him as he honoured his children.
Now Hektor spoke a word and called him by name and scolded him:
'Shall we give way so, Melanippos? Does it mean nothing
even to you in the inward heart that your cousin is fallen?
555 Do you not see how they are busied over the armour of Dolops?
Come on, then; no longer can we stand far off and fight with
the Argives. Sooner we must kill them, or else sheer Ilion
be stormed utterly by them, and her citizens be killed.'
    He spoke, and led the way, and the other followed, a mortal
560 godlike. But huge Telamonian Aias stirred on the Argives:
'Dear friends, be men; let shame be in your hearts, and discipline,
and have consideration for each other in the strong encounters,
since more come through alive when men consider each other,
and there is no glory when they give way, nor warcraft either.'
565   He spoke, and they likewise grew furious in their defence,
and put his word away in their hearts, and fenced in their vessels
in a circle of bronze, but Zeus against them wakened the Trojans.
Then Menelaos of the great war cry stirred on Antilochos:
'Antilochos, no other Achaian is younger than you are,
570 nor faster on his feet, nor strong as you are in fighting.
You could make an outrush and strike down some man of the Trojans.'
    So speaking, he hastened back but stirred Antilochos onward,
and he sprang forth from the champions and hefted the shining javelin,
glaring round about him, and the Trojans gave way in the face
575 of the man throwing with the spear. And he made no vain cast
but struck Hiketaon's son, Melanippos the high-hearted,
in the chest next to the nipple as he swept into the fighting.
He fell, thunderously, and darkness closed over both eyes.
Antilochos sprang forth against him, as a hound rushes
580 against a stricken fawn that as he broke from his covert
a hunter has shot at, and hit, and broken his limbs' strength.
So Antilochos stubborn in battle sprang, Melanippos,

at you, to strip your armour, but did not escape brilliant Hektor's
notice, who came on the run through the fighting against him.
Antilochos did not hold his ground, although a swift fighter,   585
but fled away like a wild beast who has done some bad thing,
one who has killed a hound or an ox-herd tending his cattle
and escapes, before a gang of men has assembled against him;
so Nestor's son ran away, and after him the Trojans and Hektor
with unearthly clamour showered their groaning weapons against him.   590
He turned and stood when he got into the swarm of his own companions.

But the Trojans in the likeness of ravening lions swept on
against the ships, and were bringing to accomplishment Zeus' orders,
who wakened always the huge strength in them, dazed the courage
of the Argives, and denied their glory, and stirred on the others.   595
Zeus' desire was to give glory to the son of Priam,
Hektor, that he might throw on the curved ships the inhuman
weariless strength of fire, and so make completely accomplished
the prayer of Thetis. Therefore Zeus of the counsels waited
the sight before his eyes of the flare, when a single ship burned.   600
From thereon he would make the attack of the Trojans
surge back again from the ships, and give the Danaans glory.
With this in mind he drove on against the hollow ships Hektor,
Priam's son, though Hektor without the god was in fury
and raged, as when destructive fire or spear-shaking Ares   605
rages among the mountains and dense places of the deep forest.
A slaver came out around his mouth, and under the lowering
brows his eyes were glittering, the helm on his temples
was shaken and thundered horribly to the fighting of Hektor.
Out of the bright sky Zeus himself was working to help him   610
and among men so numerous he honoured this one man
and glorified him, since Hektor was to have only a short life
and already the day of his death was being driven upon him
by Pallas Athene through the strength of Achilleus. And now
he was probing the ranks of men, and trying to smash them,   615
and made for where there were most men together, and the best armour.
But even so he could not break them, for all his fury,
for they closed into a wall and held him, like some towering
huge sea-cliff that lies close along the grey salt water
and stands up against the screaming winds and their sudden directions   620

and against the waves that grow to bigness and burst up against it.
So the Danaans stood steady against the Trojans, nor gave way.
But he, lit about with flame on all sides, charged on their numbers
and descended upon them as descends on a fast ship the battering
625 wave storm-bred from beneath the clouds, and the ship goes utterly
hidden under the foam, and the dangerous blast of the hurricane
thunders against the sail, and the hearts of the seamen are shaken
with fear, as they are carried only a little way out of death's reach.
So the heart in the breast of each Achaian was troubled.

630 Hektor came on against them, as a murderous lion on cattle
who in the low-lying meadow of a great marsh pasture
by hundreds, and among them a herdsman who does not quite know
how to fight a wild beast off from killing a horn-curved
ox, and keeps pace with the first and the last of the cattle
635 always, but the lion making his spring at the middle
eats an ox as the rest stampede; so now the Achaians
fled in unearthly terror before father Zeus and Hektor,
all, but he got one only, Periphetes of Mykenai,
beloved son of Kopreus, who for the lord Eurystheus
640 had gone often with messages to powerful Herakles.
To him, a meaner father, was born a son who was better
for all talents, in the speed of his feet and in battle
and for intelligence counted among the first in Mykenai.
Thereby now higher was the glory he granted to Hektor.
645 For as he whirled about to get back, he fell over the out-rim
of the shield he carried, which reached to his feet to keep the spears from
     him.
Stumbling on this he went over on his back, and the helmet
that circled his temples clashed horribly as he went down.
Hektor saw it sharply, and ran up and stood beside him,
650 and stuck the spear into his chest and killed him before the eyes
of his dear friends, who for all their sorrowing could do nothing
to help their companion, being themselves afraid of great Hektor.

    Now they had got among the ships, and the ends were about them
of the ships hauled up in the first line, but the Trojans swarmed
655 on them. The Argives under force gave back from the first line
of their ships, but along the actual shelters they rallied
in a group, and did not scatter along the encampment. Shame held them

and fear. They kept up a continuous call to each other,
and beyond others Gerenian Nestor, the Achaians' watcher,
supplicated each man by the knees for the sake of his parents. 660
'Dear friends, be men; let shame be in your hearts and discipline
in the sight of other men, and each one of you remember
his children and his wife, his property and his parents,
whether a man's father and mother live or have died. Here now
I supplicate your knees for the sake of those who are absent 665
to stand strongly and not be turned to the terror of panic.'

So he spoke, and stirred the spirit and heart in each man,
and from their eyes Athene pushed the darkness immortal
of mist, and the light came out hard against them on both sides
whether they looked from the ships or from the closing of battle. 670
They knew Hektor of the great war cry, they knew his companions
whether they stood away behind and out of the fighting
or whether alongside the fast ships they fought in the battle.

Nor did it still please great-hearted Aias to stand back
where the other sons of the Achaians had taken position; 675
but he went in huge strides up and down the decks of the vessels.
He wielded in his hands a great pike for sea fighting,
twenty-two cubits long and joined together by clinchers.
And as a man who is an expert rider of horses
who when he has chosen and coupled four horses out of many 680
makes his way over the plain galloping toward a great city
along the travelled road, and many turn to admire him,
men or women, while he steadily and never slipping
jumps and shifts his stance from one to another as they gallop;
so Aias ranged crossing from deck to deck of the fast ships 685
taking huge strides, and his voice went always up to the bright sky
as he kept up a terrible bellow and urged on the Danaans
to defend their ships and their shelters, while on the other side Hektor
would not stay back among the mass of close-armoured Trojans,
but as a flashing eagle makes his plunge upon other 690
flying birds as these feed in a swarm by a river,
whether these be geese or cranes or swans long-throated,
so Hektor steered the course of his outrush straight for a vessel
with dark prows, and from behind Zeus was pushing him onward
hard with his big hand, and stirred on his people beside him. 695

Now once again a grim battle was fought by the vessels;
you would say that they faced each other unbruised, unwearied
in the fighting, from the speed in which they went for each other.
This was the thought in each as they struggled on: the Achaians
700 thought they could not get clear of the evil, but must perish,
while the heart inside each one of the Trojans was hopeful
to set fire to the ships and kill the fighting men of Achaia.
With such thoughts in mind they stood up to fight with each other.
Hektor caught hold of the stern of a grand, fast-running,
705 seafaring ship, that once had carried Protesilaos
to Troy, and did not take him back to the land of his fathers.
It was around his ship that now Achaians and Trojans
cut each other down at close quarters, nor any longer
had patience for the volleys exchanged from bows and javelins
710 but stood up close against each other, matching their fury,
and fought their battle with sharp hatchets and axes, with great
swords and with leaf-headed pikes, and many magnificent
swords were scattered along the ground, black-thonged, heavy-hilted,
sometimes dropping from the hands, some glancing from shoulders
715 of men as they fought, so the ground ran black with blood. Hektor
would not let go of the stern of a ship where he had caught hold of it
but gripped the sternpost in his hands and called to the Trojans:
'Bring fire, and give single voice to the clamour of battle.
Now Zeus has given us a day worth all the rest of them:
720 the ships' capture, the ships that came here in spite of the gods' will
and have visited much pain on us, by our counsellors' cowardice
who would not let me fight by the grounded ships, though I wanted to,
but held me back in restraint, and curbed in our fighters.
But Zeus of the wide brows, though then he fouled our intentions,
725 comes now himself to urge us on and give us encouragement.'
     He spoke, and they thereby came on harder against the Argives.
Their volleys were too much for Aias, who could hold no longer
his place, but had to give back a little, expecting to die there,
back to the seven-foot midship, and gave up the high deck of the
     balanced
730 ship. There he stood and waited for them, and with his pike always
beat off any Trojan who carried persistent fire from the vessels.
He kept up a terrible bellowing, and urged on the Danaans:

'Friends and fighting men of the Danaans, henchmen of Ares,
be men now, dear friends, remember your furious valour.
Do we think there are others who stand behind us to help us?   735
Have we some stronger wall that can rescue men from perdition?
We have no city built strong with towers lying near us, within which
we could defend ourselves and hold off this host that matches us.
We hold position in this plain of the close-armoured Trojans,
bent back against the sea, and far from the land of our fathers.   740
Salvation's light is in our hands' work, not the mercy of battle.'

   He spoke, and came forward with his sharp spear, raging for battle.
And whenever some Trojan crashed against the hollow ships
with burning fire, who sought to wake the favour of Hektor,
Aias would wait for him and then stab with the long pike   745
and so from close up wounded twelve in front of the vessels.

So they fought on both sides for the sake of the strong-benched
  vessel.
Meanwhile Patroklos came to the shepherd of the people, Achilleus,
and stood by him and wept warm tears, like a spring dark-running
that down the face of a rock impassable drips its dim water;
5 and swift-footed brilliant Achilleus looked on him in pity,
and spoke to him aloud and addressed him in winged words: 'Why then
are you crying like some poor little girl, Patroklos,
who runs after her mother and begs to be picked up and carried,
and clings to her dress, and holds her back when she tries to hurry,
10 and gazes tearfully into her face, until she is picked up?
You are like such a one, Patroklos, dropping these soft tears.
Could you have some news to tell, for me or the Myrmidons?
Have you, and nobody else, received some message from Phthia?
Yet they tell me Aktor's son Menoitios lives still
15 and Aiakos' son Peleus lives still among the Myrmidons.
If either of these died we should take it hard. Or is it
the Argives you are mourning over, and how they are dying
against the hollow ships by reason of their own arrogance?
Tell me, do not hide it in your mind, and so we shall both know.'
20   Then groaning heavily, Patroklos the rider, you answered:
'Son of Peleus, far greatest of the Achaians, Achilleus,
do not be angry; such grief has fallen upon the Achaians.
For all those who were before the bravest in battle
are lying up among the ships with arrow or spear wounds.

The son of Tydeus, strong Diomedes, was hit by an arrow,   25
and Odysseus has a pike wound, and Agamemnon the spear-famed,
and Eurypylos has been wounded in the thigh with an arrow.
And over these the healers skilled in medicine are working
to cure their wounds. But you, Achilleus; who can do anything
with you? May no such anger take me as this that you cherish!   30
Cursed courage. What other man born hereafter shall be advantaged
unless you beat aside from the Argives this shameful destruction?
Pitiless: the rider Peleus was never your father
nor Thetis was your mother, but it was the grey sea that bore you
and the towering rocks, so sheer the heart in you is turned from us.   35
But if you are drawing back from some prophecy known in your own
        heart
and by Zeus' will your honoured mother has told you of something,
then send me out at least, let the rest of the Myrmidon people
follow me, and I may be a light given to the Danaans.
Give me your armour to wear on my shoulders into the fighting;   40
so perhaps the Trojans might think I am you, and give way
from their attack, and the fighting sons of the Achaians get wind
again after hard work. There is little breathing space in the fighting.
We unwearied might with a mere cry pile men wearied
back upon their city, and away from the ships and the shelters.'   45
    So he spoke supplicating in his great innocence; this was
his own death and evil destruction he was entreating.
But now, deeply troubled, swift-footed Achilleus answered him:
'Ah, Patroklos, illustrious, what is this you are saying?
I have not any prophecy in mind that I know of;   50
there is no word from Zeus my honoured mother has told me,
but this thought comes as a bitter sorrow to my heart and my spirit
when a man tries to foul one who is his equal, to take back
a prize of honour, because he goes in greater authority.
This is a bitter thought to me; my desire has been dealt with   55
roughly. The girl the sons of the Achaians chose out for my honour,
and I won her with my own spear, and stormed a strong-fenced city,
is taken back out of my hands by powerful Agamemnon,
the son of Atreus, as if I were some dishonoured vagabond.
Still, we will let all this be a thing of the past; and it was not   60
in my heart to be angry forever; and yet I have said

I would not give over my anger until that time came
when the fighting with all its clamour came up to my own ships.
So do you draw my glorious armour about your shoulders;
65 lead the Myrmidons whose delight is battle into the fighting,
if truly the black cloud of the Trojans has taken position
strongly about our ships, and the others, the Argives, are bent back
against the beach of the sea, holding only a narrow division
of land, and the whole city of the Trojans has descended upon them
70 boldly; because they do not see the face of my helmet
glaring close; or else they would run and cram full of dead men
the water-courses; if powerful Agamemnon treated me
kindly. Now the Argives fight for their very encampment.
For the spear rages not now in the hands of the son of Tydeus,
75 Diomedes, to beat destruction aside from the Danaans,
nor have I heard the voice of the son of Atreus crying
from his hated head; no, but the voice of murderous Hektor
calling to the Trojans crashes about my ears; with their war cry
they hold the entire plain as they beat the Achaians in battle.
80 But even so, Patroklos, beat the bane aside from our ships; fall
upon them with all your strength; let them not with fire's blazing
inflame our ships, and take away our desired homecoming.
But obey to the end this word I put upon your attention
so that you can win, for me, great honour and glory
85 in the sight of all the Danaans, so they will bring back to me
the lovely girl, and give me shining gifts in addition.
When you have driven them from the ships, come back; although
        later
the thunderous lord of Hera might grant you the winning of glory,
you must not set your mind on fighting the Trojans, whose delight
90 is in battle, without me. So you will diminish my honour.
You must not, in the pride and fury of fighting, go on
slaughtering the Trojans, and lead the way against Ilion,
for fear some one of the everlasting gods on Olympos
might crush you. Apollo who works from afar loves these people
95 dearly. You must turn back once you bring the light of salvation
to the ships, and let the others go on fighting in the flat land.
Father Zeus, Athene and Apollo, if only
not one of all the Trojans could escape destruction, not one

of the Argives, but you and I could emerge from the slaughter
so that we two alone could break Troy's hallowed coronal.'   100
   Now as these two were talking thus to each other, meanwhile
the volleys were too much for Aias, who could hold no longer
his place. The will of Zeus beat him back, and the proud Trojans
with their spears, and around his temples the shining helmet
clashed horribly under the shower of strokes; he was hit constantly   105
on the strong-wrought cheek-pieces, and his left shoulder was tiring
from always holding up the big glittering shield; yet they could not
beat him out of his place, though they piled their missiles upon him.
His breath came ever hard and painful, the sweat ran pouring
down his body from every limb, he could find no means   110
to catch his breath, but evil was piled on evil about him.
   Tell me now, you Muses who have your homes on Olympos,
how fire was first thrown upon the ships of the Achaians.
   Hektor stood up close to Aias and hacked at the ash spear
with his great sword, striking behind the socket of the spearhead,   115
and slashed it clean away, so that Telamonian Aias
shook there in his hand a lopped spear, while far away from him
the bronze spearhead fell echoing to the ground; and Aias
knew in his blameless heart, and shivered for knowing it, how this
was gods' work, how Zeus high-thundering cut across the intention   120
in all his battle, how he planned that the Trojans should conquer.
He drew away out of the missiles, and the Trojans threw weariless fire
on the fast ship, and suddenly the quenchless flame streamed over it.
So the fire was at work on the ship's stern; but Achilleus
struck his hands against both his thighs, and called to Patroklos: 125
'Rise up, illustrious Patroklos, rider of horses.
I see how the ravening fire goes roaring over our vessels.
They must not get our ships so we cannot run away in them.
Get on your armour; faster; I will muster our people.'
   He spoke, and Patroklos was helming himself in bronze that glittered.   130
First he placed along his legs the beautiful greaves, linked
with silver fastenings to hold the greaves at the ankles.
Afterwards he girt on about his chest the corselet
starry and elaborate of swift-footed Aiakides.
Across his shoulders he slung the sword with the nails of silver,   135
a bronze sword, and above it the great shield, huge and heavy.

Over his mighty head he set the well-fashioned helmet
with the horse-hair crest, and the plumes nodded terribly above it.
He took up two powerful spears that fitted his hand's grip,
140 only he did not take the spear of blameless Aiakides,
huge, heavy, thick, which no one else of all the Achaians
could handle, but Achilleus alone knew how to wield it;
the Pelian ash spear which Cheiron had brought to his father
from high on Pelion to be death for fighters. Patroklos
145 ordered Automedon rapidly to harness the horses,
a man he honoured most, after Achilleus breaker of battles,
who stood most staunchly by him against the fury of fighting.
For him Automedon led the fast-running horses under
the yoke, Xanthos and Balios, who tore with the winds' speed,
150 horses stormy Podarge once conceived of the west wind
and bore, as she grazed in the meadow beside the swirl of the Ocean.
In the traces beside these he put unfaulted Pedasos
whom Achilleus brought back once when he stormed Eëtion's city.
He, mortal as he was, ran beside the immortal horses.
155   But Achilleus went meanwhile to the Myrmidons, and arrayed them
all in their war gear along the shelters. And they, as wolves
who tear flesh raw, in whose hearts the battle fury is tireless,
who have brought down a great horned stag in the mountains, and then
        feed
on him, till the jowls of every wolf run blood, and then go
160 all in a pack to drink from a spring of dark-running water,
lapping with their lean tongues along the black edge of the surface
and belching up the clotted blood; in the heart of each one
is a spirit untremulous, but their bellies are full and groaning;
as such the lords of the Myrmidons and their men of counsel
165 around the brave henchman of swift-footed Aiakides
swarmed, and among them was standing warlike Achilleus
and urged on the fighting men with their shields, and the horses.
    Fifty were the fast-running ships wherein Achilleus
beloved of Zeus had led his men to Troy, and in each one
170 were fifty men, his companions in arms, at the rowing benches.
He had made five leaders among them, and to these entrusted
the command, while he in his great power was lord over all of them.
One battalion was led by Menesthios of the shining

corselet, son of Spercheïos, the river swelled from the bright sky,
born of the daughter of Peleus, Polydore the lovely,   175
to unremitting Spercheïos, when a woman lay with an immortal;
but born in name to Perieres' son, Boros, who married
Polydore formally, and gave gifts beyond count to win her.
The next battalion was led by warlike Eudoros, a maiden's
child, born to one lovely in the dance, Polymele,   180
daughter of Phylas; whom strong Hermes Argeïphontes
loved, when he watched her with his eyes among the girls dancing
in the choir for clamorous Artemis of the golden distaff.
Presently Hermes the healer went up with her into her chamber
and lay secretly with her, and she bore him a son, the shining   185
Eudoros, a surpassing runner and a quick man in battle.
But after Eileithyia of the hard pains had brought out
the child into the light, and he looked on the sun's shining,
Aktor's son Echekles in the majesty of his great power
led her to his house, when he had given numberless gifts to win her,   190
and the old man Phylas took the child and brought him up kindly
and cared for him, in affection as if he had been his own son.
The leader of the third battalion was warlike Peisandros,
Maimalos' son, who outshone all the rest of the Myrmidons
in spear-fighting, next to Peleian Achilleus' henchman.   195
The fourth battalion was led by Phoinix, the aged horseman,
the fifth by Alkimedon, the blameless son of Laerkes.
But after Achilleus gave them their stations all in good order
beside their leaders, he laid his stern injunction upon them:
'Myrmidons: not one of you can forget those mutterings,   200
those threats that beside the running ships you made at the Trojans
in all the time of my anger, and it was I you were blaming,
as: "Hard son of Peleus! Your mother nursed you on gall. You have no
pity, to keep your companions here by the ships unwilling.
We should go back home again, then, in our seafaring vessels   205
now that this wretched anger has befallen your spirit."
Often you would gather in groups and so mutter against me,
and now is shown a great work of that fighting you longed for.
Then let each man take heart of strength to fight with the Trojans.'
   So he spoke, and stirred the spirit and strength in each man,   210
and their ranks, as they listened to the king, pulled closer together.

And as a man builds solid a wall with stones set close together
for the rampart of a high house keeping out the force of the winds, so
close together were the helms and shields massive in the middle.
215 For shield leaned on shield, helmet on helmet, man against man,
and the horse-hair crests along the horns of the shining helmets
touched as they bent their heads, so dense were they formed on each other.
And before them all were two men in their armour, Patroklos
and Automedon, both of them in one single fury
220 to fight in front of the Myrmidons. But meanwhile Achilleus
went off into his shelter, and lifted the lid from a lovely
elaborately wrought chest, which Thetis the silver-footed
had put in his ship to carry, and filled it fairly with tunics
and mantles to hold the wind from a man, and with fleecy blankets.
225 Inside this lay a wrought goblet, nor did any other
man drink the shining wine from it nor did Achilleus
pour from it to any other god, but only Zeus father.
He took this now out of the chest, and cleaned it with sulphur
first, and afterwards washed it out in bright-running water,
230 and washed his own hands, and poured shining wine into the goblet
and stood in his middle forecourt and prayed, and poured the wine,
    looking
into the sky, not unseen by Zeus who delights in the thunder:
'High Zeus, lord of Dodona, Pelasgian, living afar off,
brooding over wintry Dodona, your prophets about you
235 living, the Selloi who sleep on the ground with feet unwashed. Hear me.
As one time before when I prayed to you, you listened
and did me honour, and smote strongly the host of the Achaians,
so one more time bring to pass the wish that I pray for.
For see, I myself am staying where the ships are assembled,
240 but I send out my companion and many Myrmidons with him
to fight. Let glory, Zeus of the wide brows, go forth with him.
Make brave the heart inside his breast, so that even Hektor
will find out whether our henchman knows how to fight his battles
by himself, or whether his hands rage invincible only
245 those times when I myself go into the grind of the war god.
But when he has beaten back from the ships their clamorous onset,
then let him come back to me and the running ships, unwounded,
with all his armour and with the companions who fight close beside him.'

So he spoke in prayer, and Zeus of the counsels heard him.
The father granted him one prayer, and denied him the other.   250
That Patroklos should beat back the fighting assault on the vessels
he allowed, but refused to let him come back safe out of the fighting.
When Achilleus had poured the wine and prayed to Zeus father
he went back into the shelter, stowed the cup in the chest, and came out
to stand in front of the door, with the desire in his heart still   255
to watch the grim encounter of Achaians and Trojans.

Now they who were armed in the company of great-hearted Patroklos
went onward, until in high confidence they charged on the Trojans.
The Myrmidons came streaming out like wasps at the wayside
when little boys have got into the habit of making them angry   260
by always teasing them as they live in their house by the roadside;
silly boys, they do something that hurts many people;
and if some man who travels on the road happens to pass them
and stirs them unintentionally, they in heart of fury
come swarming out each one from his place to fight for their children.   265
In heart and in fury like these the Myrmidons streaming
came out from their ships, with a tireless clamour arising,
and Patroklos called afar in a great voice to his companions:
'Myrmidons, companions of Peleus' son, Achilleus,
be men now, dear friends, remember your furious valour;   270
we must bring honour to Peleus' son, far the greatest of the Argives
by the ships, we, even the henchmen who fight beside him,
so Atreus' son wide-ruling Agamemnon may recognize
his madness, that he did no honour to the best of the Achaians.'

So he spoke, and stirred the spirit and strength in each man.   275
They fell upon the Trojans in a pack, and about them
the ships echoed terribly to the roaring Achaians.
But the Trojans, when they saw the powerful son of Menoitios
himself and his henchman with him in the glare of their war gear,
the heart was stirred in all of them, the battalions were shaken   280
in the expectation that by the ships swift-footed Peleion
had thrown away his anger and chosen the way of friendship.
Then each man looked about him for a way to escape the sheer death.

Patroklos was the first man to make a cast with the shining
spear, straight through the middle fighting, where most men were   285
  stricken,

beside the stern on the ship of great-hearted Protesilaos,
and struck Pyraichmes, who had led the lords of Paionian
horses from Amydon and the wide waters of Axios.
He struck him in the right shoulder, so he dropped in the dust groaning,
290 on his back, and his Paionian companions about him
scattered; for Patroklos drove the fear into all of them
when he cut down their leader, the best of them all in battle.
He drove them from the ships and put out the fire that was blazing,
and that ship was left half-burnt as it was, as the Trojans scattered
295 in terror and unearthly noise, and the Danaans streamed back
along the hollow ships, and clamour incessant rose up.
And as when from the towering height of a great mountain Zeus
who gathers the thunderflash stirs the cloud dense upon it,
and all the high places of the hills are clear and the shoulders out-jutting
300 and the deep ravines, as endless bright air spills from the heavens,
so when the Danaans had beaten from their ships the ravening
fire, they got breath for a little, but there was no check in the fighting;
for the Trojans under the attack of the warlike Achaians
had not yet turned their faces to run away from the black ships.
305 They stood yet against them, but gave way from the ships under pressure.
There man killed man all along the scattered encounter
of the leaders, and first among them, the strong son of Menoitios,
threw and struck Areïlykos in the thigh, as he turned
back, with the sharp point of the spear, and drove the bronze clean
through.
310 The spear smashed in the bone and he fell to the ground headlong
on his face. Meanwhile warlike Menelaos stabbed Thoas
in the chest where it was left bare by the shield, and unstrung his limbs'
strength.
Meges, Phyleus' son, watched Amphiklos as he came on
and was too quick with a stab at the base of the leg, where the muscle
315 of a man grows thickest, so that on the spearhead the sinew
was torn apart, and a mist of darkness closed over both eyes.
Of the sons of Nestor one, Antilochos, stabbed Atymnios
with the sharp spear, and drove the bronze head clean through his
flank, so
that he fell forward; but Maris with the spear from close up
320 made a lunge at Antilochos in rage for his brother

standing in front of the corpse, but before him godlike Thrasymedes
was in with a thrust before he could stab, nor missed his quick stroke
into the shoulder, and the spearhead shore off the arm's base
clear away from the muscles and torn from the bone utterly.
He fell, thunderously, and darkness closed over both eyes.   325
So these two, beaten down under the hands of two brothers,
descended to the dark place, Sarpedon's noble companions
and spear-throwing sons of Amisodaros, the one who had nourished
the furious Chimaira to be an evil to many.
Aias, Oïleus' son, in an outrush caught Kleoboulos   330
alive, where he was fouled in the running confusion, and there
unstrung his strength, hewing with the hilted sword at the neck,
so all the sword was smoking with blood and over both eyes
closed the red death and the strong destiny. Then Peneleos
and Lykon ran up close together, since these with their spear-throws   335
had gone wide of each other, and each had made a cast vainly.
So now the two of them ran together with swords. There Lykon
hacked at the horn of the horse-hair crested helm, but the sword blade
broke at the socket; Peneleos cut at the neck underneath
the ear, and the sword sank clean inside, with only skin left   340
to hold it, and the head slumped aside, and the limbs were loosened.
Meriones on his light feet overtaking Akamas
stabbed him in the right shoulder as he climbed up behind his horses
and the darkness drifted over his eyes as he crashed from the chariot.
Idomeneus stabbed Erymas in the mouth with the pitiless   345
bronze, so that the brazen spearhead smashed its way clean through
below the brain in an upward stroke, and the white bones splintered,
and the teeth were shaken out with the stroke and both eyes filled up
with blood, and gaping he blew a spray of blood through the nostrils
and through his mouth, and death in a dark mist closed in about him.   350
   So these lords of the Danaans killed each his own man.
They as wolves make havoc among lambs or young goats in their fury,
catching them out of the flocks, when the sheep separate in the mountains
through the thoughtlessness of the shepherd, and the wolves seeing them
suddenly snatch them away, and they have no heart for fighting;   355
so the Danaans ravaged the Trojans, and these remembered
the bitter sound of terror, and forgot their furious valour.
   But the great Aias was trying forever to make a spearcast

at bronze-helmed Hektor, but he in his experience of fighting
360 with his broad shoulders huddled under the bull's-hide shield kept
watching always the whistle of arrows, the crash of spears thrown.
He knew well how the strength of the fighting shifted against him,
but even so stood his ground to save his steadfast companions.
     As when a cloud goes deep into the sky from Olympos
365 through the bright upper air when Zeus brings on the hurricane,
so rose from beside the ships their outcry, the noise of their terror.
In no good order they went back, while his fast-running horses
carried Hektor away in his armour; he abandoned the people
of the Trojans, who were trapped by the deep-dug ditch unwilling,
370 and in the ditch many fast horses who pulled the chariots
left, broken short at the joining of the pole, their masters' chariots
while Patroklos was on them, calling hard and loud to the Danaans
with evil intention for the Trojans, who, in clamorous terror,
choked all the ways where they were cut off; from under their feet stirred
375 the dust-storm scattered in clouds, their single-foot horses were straining
to get back to the city away from the ships and the shelters.
But Patroklos, where he saw the stirring of most people,
steered there, shouting, and men went down under the axles
headlong from chariots as the empty cars rattled onward.
380 Straight across the ditch overleapt those swift and immortal
horses the gods had given as shining gifts to Peleus,
hurtling onward, as Patroklos' rage stirred him against Hektor,
whom he tried to strike, but his fast horses carried him out of it.
As underneath the hurricane all the black earth is burdened
385 on an autumn day, when Zeus sends down the most violent waters
in deep rage against mortals after they stir him to anger
because in violent assembly they pass decrees that are crooked,
and drive righteousness from among them and care nothing for what the
     gods think,
and all the rivers of these men swell current to full spate
390 and in the ravines of their water-courses rip all the hillsides
and dash whirling in huge noise down to the blue sea, out of
the mountains headlong, so that the works of men are diminished;
so huge rose the noise from the horses of Troy in their running.
     But Patroklos, when he had cut away their first battalions,
395 turned back to pin them against the ships, and would not allow them

to climb back into their city though they strained for it, but sweeping
through the space between the ships, the high wall, and the river,
made havoc and exacted from them the blood price for many.
There first of all he struck with the shining spear Pronoös
in the chest where it was left bare by the shield, and unstrung his limbs'   400
    strength.
He fell, thunderously, and Patroklos in his next outrush
at Thestor, Enops' son, who huddled inside his chariot,
shrunk back, he had lost all his nerve, and from his hands the reins
slipped—Patroklos coming close up to him stabbed with a spear-thrust
at the right side of the jaw and drove it on through the teeth, then   405
hooked and dragged him with the spear over the rail, as a fisherman
who sits out on the jut of a rock with line and glittering
bronze hook drags a fish, who is thus doomed, out of the water.
So he hauled him, mouth open to the bright spear, out of the chariot,
and shoved him over on his face, and as he fell the life left him.   410
Next he struck Erylaos, as he swept in, with a great stone
in the middle of the head, and all the head broke into two pieces
inside the heavy helmet, and he in the dust face downward
dropped while death breaking the spirit drifted about him.
Afterwards with Erymas, Amphoteros, and Epaltes,   415
Tlepolemos Damastor's son, Echios and Pyris,
Ipheus and Euippos, and Argeas' son Polymelos,
all these he felled to the bountiful earth in rapid succession.
    But Sarpedon, when he saw his free-girt companions going
down underneath the hands of Menoitios' son Patroklos,   420
called aloud in entreaty upon the godlike Lykians:
'Shame, you Lykians, where are you running to? You must be fierce
    now,
for I myself will encounter this man, so I may find out
who this is who has so much strength and has done so much evil
to the Trojans, since many and brave are those whose knees he has   425
    unstrung.'
    He spoke, and sprang to the ground in all his arms from the chariot,
and on the other side Patroklos when he saw him leapt down
from his chariot. They as two hook-clawed beak-bent vultures
above a tall rock face, high-screaming, go for each other,
so now these two, crying aloud, encountered together.   430

And watching them the son of devious-devising Kronos
was pitiful, and spoke to Hera, his wife and his sister:
'Ah me, that it is destined that the dearest of men, Sarpedon,
must go down under the hands of Menoitios' son Patroklos.
435 The heart in my breast is balanced between two ways as I ponder,
whether I should snatch him out of the sorrowful battle
and set him down still alive in the rich country of Lykia,
or beat him under at the hands of the son of Menoitios.'
    In turn the lady Hera of the ox eyes answered him:
440 'Majesty, son of Kronos, what sort of thing have you spoken?
Do you wish to bring back a man who is mortal, one long since
doomed by his destiny, from ill-sounding death and release him?
Do it, then; but not all the rest of us gods shall approve you.
And put away in your thoughts this other thing I tell you;
445 if you bring Sarpedon back to his home, still living,
think how then some other one of the gods might also
wish to carry his own son out of the strong encounter;
since around the great city of Priam are fighting many
sons of the immortals. You will waken grim resentment among them.
450 No, but if he is dear to you, and your heart mourns for him,
then let him be, and let him go down in the strong encounter
underneath the hands of Patroklos, the son of Menoitios;
but after the soul and the years of his life have left him, then send
Death to carry him away, and Sleep, who is painless,
455 until they come with him to the countryside of broad Lykia
where his brothers and countrymen shall give him due burial
with tomb and gravestone. Such is the privilege of those who have
        perished.'
    She spoke, nor did the father of gods and men disobey her;
yet he wept tears of blood that fell to the ground, for the sake
460 of his beloved son, whom now Patroklos was presently
to kill, by generous Troy and far from the land of his fathers.
    Now as these two advancing had come close to each other
there Patroklos threw first at glorious Thrasymelos
who was the strong henchman of lord Sarpedon, and struck him
465 in the depth of the lower belly, and unstrung his limbs' strength.
Sarpedon with the second throw then missed with the shining
spear, but the spear fixed in the right shoulder of Pedasos

the horse, who screamed as he blew his life away, and went down
in shrill noise into the dust, and the life spirit flittered from him.
The other horses shied apart, the yoke creaked, the guide reins   470
were fouled together as the trace horse lay in the dust beside them;
but at this spear-famed Automedon saw what he must do
and wrenching out the long-edged sword from beside his big thigh
in a flashing stroke and without faltering cut loose the trace horse
and the other horses were straightened out, and pulled in the guide reins,   475
and the two heroes came together in the heart-perishing battle.
　　Once again Sarpedon threw wide with a cast of his shining
spear, so that the pointed head overshot the left shoulder
of Patroklos; and now Patroklos made the second cast with the brazen
spear, and the shaft escaping his hand was not flung vainly   480
but struck where the beating heart is closed in the arch of the muscles.
He fell, as when an oak goes down or a white poplar,
or like a towering pine tree which in the mountains the carpenters
have hewn down with their whetted axes to make a ship-timber.
So he lay there felled in front of his horses and chariots   485
roaring, and clawed with his hands at the bloody dust; or as
a blazing and haughty bull in a huddle of shambling cattle
when a lion has come among the herd and destroys him
dies bellowing under the hooked claws of the lion, so now
before Patroklos the lord of the shield-armoured Lykians   490
died raging, and called aloud to his beloved companion:
'Dear Glaukos, you are a fighter among men. Now the need comes
hardest upon you to be a spearman and a bold warrior.
Now, if you are brave, let bitter warfare be dear to you.
First you must go among all men who are lords of the Lykians   495
everywhere, and stir them up to fight for Sarpedon,
and then you yourself also must fight for me with the bronze spear.
For I shall be a thing of shame and a reproach said of you
afterwards, all your days forever, if the Achaians
strip my armour here where I fell by the ships assembled.   500
But hold strongly on and stir up all the rest of our people.'
　　He spoke, and as he spoke death's end closed over his nostrils
and eyes, and Patroklos stepping heel braced to chest dragged
the spear out of his body, and the midriff came away with it
so that he drew out with the spearhead the life of Sarpedon,   505

[343]

and the Myrmidons close by held in the hard-breathing horses
as they tried to bolt away, once free of their master's chariot.
   But when he heard the voice a hard sorrow came upon Glaukos,
and the heart was stirred within him, and he could not defend Sarpedon.
510 He took his arm in his hand and squeezed it, since the wound hurt him
where Teukros had hit him with an arrow shot as he swept in
on the high wall, and fended destruction from his companions.
He spoke in prayer to him who strikes from afar, Apollo:
'Hear me, my lord. You are somewhere in the rich Lykian countryside
515 or here in Troy, and wherever you are you can listen
to a man in pain, as now this pain has descended upon me.
For see, I have this strong wound on me, and my arm on both sides
is driven with sharp pains about, my blood is not able
to dry and stop running, my shoulder is aching beneath it.
520 I cannot hold my spear up steady, I cannot go forward
to fight against the enemy. And the best of men has perished,
Sarpedon, son of Zeus; who will not stand by his children.
No, but you at least, my lord, make well this strong wound;
and put the pains to sleep, give me strength, so that I may call out
525 to my companions, the Lykians, and stir them to fight on,
and I myself do battle over the fallen body.'
   So he spoke in prayer, and Phoibos Apollo heard him.
At once he made the pains stop, and dried away from the hard wound
the dark running of blood, and put strength into his spirit.
530 And Glaukos knew in his heart what was done, and was happy
that the great god had listened to his prayer. And first of all
he roused toward battle all the men who were lords of the Lykians,
going everywhere among them, to fight for Sarpedon;
afterwards he ranged in long strides among the Trojans,
535 by Poulydamas the son of Panthoös and brilliant Agenor,
and went to Aineias and to Hektor of the brazen helmet
and stood near them and addressed them in winged words: 'Hektor,
now you have utterly forgotten your armed companions
who for your sake, far from their friends and the land of their fathers,
540 are wearing their lives away, and you will do nothing to help them.
Sarpedon has fallen, the lord of the shield-armoured Lykians,
who defended Lykia in his strength and the right of his justice.
Now brazen Ares has struck him down by the spear of Patroklos.

Then, friends, stand beside me, let the thought be shame in your spirit
that they might strip away his arms, and dishonour his body,   545
these Myrmidons, in anger for all the Danaans perished,
those whom we Lykians have killed with the spear by the swift ships.'

    He spoke, and the Trojans were taken head to heel with a sorrow
untakeable, not to be endured, since he was their city's
stay, always, though he was an outlander, and many people   550
came with him, but he was the best of them all in battle
always. They went straight for the Danaans, raging, and Hektor
led them, in anger for Sarpedon. Meanwhile the Achaians
roused to the savage heart of Patroklos, the son of Menoitios.
First he spoke to the Aiantes, who were burning for battle already: 555
'Aiantes, now your desire must be to defend yourselves, and be
such as you were among men before, or even more valiant.
The man is fallen who first scaled the wall of the Achaians,
Sarpedon. If only we could win and dishonour his body
and strip the armour from his shoulders, and kill with the pitiless   560
bronze some one of his companions who fight to defend him.'

    He spoke, and they likewise grew furious in their defence,
and when they on either side had made massive their battalions,
Trojans and Lykians, and Myrmidons and Achaians,
they clashed together in battle over the perished body   565
howling terribly, with a high crash of the men in their armour,
while Zeus swept ghastly night far over the strong encounter
that over his dear son might be deadly work in the fighting.

    First the Trojans shouldered back the glancing-eyed Achaians
when a man, and not the worst of the Myrmidons, was struck down,   570
son of high-hearted Agakles, Epeigeus the brilliant.
He was one who was lord before in strong-founded Boudeion,
but now, since he had happened to kill his high-born cousin,
had come suppliant to Peleus and to Thetis the silver-footed,
and these sent him to follow Achilleus, who broke men in battle,   575
to Ilion of the horses and the battle against the Trojans.
As he caught at a dead man glorious Hektor hit him
with a stone in the head, and all the head broke into two pieces
inside the heavy helmet, and he in the dust face downward
dropped, while death breaking the spirit drifted about him.   580
And the sorrow took hold of Patroklos for his fallen companion.

He steered his way through the ranks of the front fighters, like a flying
hawk who scatters into flight the daws and the starlings.
So straight for the Lykians, o lord of horses, Patroklos,
585 you swept, and for the Trojans, heart angered for your companion.
Now he struck Sthenelaos, beloved son of Ithaimenes,
in the neck with a stone, and broke the tendons loose from about it.
The champions of Troy gave back then, and glorious Hektor.
As far as goes the driving cast of a slender javelin
590 which a man throws making trial of his strength, either in a contest
or else in battle, under the heart-breaking hostilities,
so far the Trojans gave way with the Achaians pushing them.
But Glaukos was first, lord of the shield-armoured Lykians,
to turn again, and killed Bathykles the great-hearted, beloved
595 son of Chalkon, who had dwelled in his home in Hellas
conspicuous for wealth and success among all the Myrmidons.
It was he whom Glaukos stabbed in the middle of the chest, turning
suddenly back with his spear as he overtook him. He fell,
thunderously, and the closing sorrow came over the Achaians
600 as the great man went down, but the Trojans were gladdened greatly
and came and stood in a pack about him, nor did the Achaians
let go of their fighting strength, but steered their fury straight at them.
And there Meriones cut down a chief man of the Trojans,
Laogonos, bold son of Onetor, who was Idaian,
605 Zeus' priest, and who was honoured in his countryside as a god is.
Meriones struck him by jaw and ear, and at once the life spirit
fled from his limbs, and the hateful darkness closed in about him.
But Aineias threw his bronze spear at Meriones, hoping
to hit him as he came forward under his shield's covering,
610 but Meriones with his eyes straight on him avoided the bronze spear.
For he bent forward, and behind his back the long spearshaft
was driven into the ground so that the butt end was shaken
on the spear. Then and there Ares the huge took the force from it
[so that the vibrant shaft of Aineias was driven groundward
615 since it had been thrown in a vain cast from his big hand].
But Aineias was angered in his spirit, and called out to him:
'Meriones, though you are a dancer my spear might have stopped you
now and for all time, if only I could have hit you.'
    Then in turn Meriones the spear-famed answered him:

'Aineias, strong fighter though you are, it would be hard for you 620
to quench the strength of every man who might come against you
and defend himself, since you also are made as a mortal.
But if I could throw and hit you with the sharp bronze in the middle,
then strong as you are and confident in your hands' work, you might
give the glory to me, and your soul to Hades of the horses.' 625
   He spoke, but the fighting son of Menoitios reprimanded him:
'Meriones, when you are a brave fighter, why say such things?—
See, dear friend, the Trojans will not give back from the body
for hard words spoken. Sooner the ground will cover them. Warfare's
finality lies in the work of hands, that of words in counsel. 630
It is not for us now to pile up talk, but to fight in battle.'
   He spoke, and led the way, and the other followed, a mortal
like a god. As the tumult goes up from men who are cutting
timber in the mountain valleys, and the sound is heard from far off,
such was the dull crashing that rose from earth of the wide ways, 635
from the bronze shields, the skins and the strong-covering ox-hides
as the swords and leaf-headed spears stabbed against them. No longer
could a man, even a knowing one, have made out the godlike
Sarpedon, since he was piled from head to ends of feet under
a mass of weapons, the blood and the dust, while others about him 640
kept forever swarming over his dead body, as flies
through a sheepfold thunder about the pails overspilling
milk, in the season of spring when the milk splashes in the buckets.
So they swarmed over the dead man, nor did Zeus ever
turn the glaring of his eyes from the strong encounter, 645
but kept gazing forever upon them, in spirit reflective,
and pondered hard over many ways for the death of Patroklos;
whether this was now the time, in this strong encounter,
when there over godlike Sarpedon glorious Hektor
should kill him with the bronze, and strip the armour away from his 650
      shoulders,
or whether to increase the steep work of fighting for more men.
In the division of his heart this way seemed best to him,
for the strong henchman of Achilleus, the son of Peleus,
once again to push the Trojans and bronze-helmed Hektor
back on their city, and tear the life from many. In Hektor 655
first of all he put a temper that was without strength.

He climbed to his chariot and turned to flight, and called to the other
Trojans to run, for he saw the way of Zeus' sacred balance.
Nor did the powerful Lykians stand now, but were all scattered
660 to flight, when they had seen their king with a spear in his heart, lying
under the pile of dead men, since many others had fallen
above him, once Zeus had strained fast the powerful conflict.
But the Achaians took from Sarpedon's shoulders the armour
glaring and brazen, and this the warlike son of Menoitios
665 gave to his companions to carry back to the hollow ships.
And now Zeus who gathers the clouds spoke a word to Apollo:
'Go if you will, beloved Phoibos, and rescue Sarpedon
from under the weapons, wash the dark suffusion of blood from him,
then carry him far away and wash him in a running river,
670 anoint him in ambrosia, put ambrosial clothing upon him;
then give him into the charge of swift messengers to carry him,
of Sleep and Death, who are twin brothers, and these two shall lay him
down presently within the rich countryside of broad Lykia
where his brothers and countrymen shall give him due burial
675 with tomb and gravestone. Such is the privilege of those who have
        perished.'
    He spoke so, and Apollo, not disregarding his father,
went down along the mountains of Ida, into the grim fight,
and lifting brilliant Sarpedon out from under the weapons
carried him far away, and washed him in a running river,
680 and anointed him in ambrosia, put ambrosial clothing upon him,
then gave him into the charge of swift messengers to carry him,
of Sleep and Death, who are twin brothers, and these two presently
laid him down within the rich countryside of broad Lykia.
    But Patroklos, with a shout to Automedon and his horses,
685 went after Trojans and Lykians in a huge blind fury.
Besotted: had he only kept the command of Peleiades
he might have got clear away from the evil spirit of black death.
But always the mind of Zeus is a stronger thing than a man's mind.
He terrifies even the warlike man, he takes away victory
690 lightly, when he himself has driven a man into battle
as now he drove on the fury in the heart of Patroklos.
    Then who was it you slaughtered first, who was the last one,
Patroklos, as the gods called you to your death? Adrestos

first, and after him Autonoös and Echeklos,
Perimos, son of Megas, and Epistor, and Melanippos, 695
and after these Elasos, and Moulios, and Pylartes.
These he killed, while each man of the rest was bent on escaping.

There the sons of the Achaians might have taken gate-towering Ilion
under the hands of Patroklos, who raged with the spear far before them,
had not Phoibos Apollo taken his stand on the strong-built 700
tower, with thoughts of death for him, but help for the Trojans.
Three times Patroklos tried to mount the angle of the towering
wall, and three times Phoibos Apollo battered him backward
with the immortal hands beating back the bright shield. As Patroklos
for the fourth time, like something more than a man, came at him 705
he called aloud, and spoke winged words in the voice of danger:
'Give way, illustrious Patroklos: it is not destined
that the city of the proud Trojans shall fall before your spear
nor even at the hand of Achilleus, who is far better than you are.'

He spoke, and Patroklos gave ground before him a great way, 710
avoiding the anger of him who strikes from afar, Apollo.

But Hektor inside the Skaian Gates held his single-foot horses,
and wondered whether to drive back into the carnage, and fight there,
or call aloud to his people to rally inside the wall. Thus
as he was pondering Phoibos Apollo came and stood by him, 715
assuming the likeness of a man, a young and a strong one,
Asios, who was uncle to Hektor, breaker of horses,
since he was brother of Hekabe, and the son of Dymas,
and had made his home in Phrygia by the stream of Sangarios.
In the likeness of this man Zeus' son Apollo spoke to him: 720
'Hektor, why have you stopped fighting? You should not do it.
If I were as much stronger than you as now I am weaker!
So might you, in this evil way, hold back from the fighting.
But come! Hold straight against Patroklos your strong-footed horses.
You might be able to kill him. Apollo might give you such glory.' 725

He spoke, and went once more, a divinity, into the mortals'
struggle, while glorious Hektor called to wise Kebriones
to lash their horses into the fighting. Meanwhile Apollo
went down into the battle, and launched a deadly confusion
upon the Argives, and gave glory to the Trojans and Hektor. 730
Now Hektor let the rest of the Danaans be, and he would not

[349]

kill them, but drove his strong-footed horses straight for Patroklos.
On the other side Patroklos sprang to the ground from his chariot
holding his spear in his left hand. In the other he caught up
735 a stone, jagged and shining, in the hold of his hand, and threw it,
leaning into the throw, nor fell short of the man he aimed at
nor threw vainly, but hit the charioteer of Hektor,
Kebriones, a bastard son of glorious Priam,
as he held the reins on his horses. The sharp stone hit him in the forehead
740 and smashed both brows in on each other, nor could the bone hold
the rock, but his eyes fell out into the dust before him
there at his feet, so that he vaulted to earth like a diver
from the carefully wrought chariot, and the life left his bones. Now
you spoke in bitter mockery over him, rider Patroklos:
745 'See now, what a light man this is, how agile an acrobat.
If only he were somewhere on the sea, where the fish swarm,
he could fill the hunger of many men, by diving for oysters;
he could go overboard from a boat even in rough weather
the way he somersaults so light to the ground from his chariot
750 now. So, to be sure, in Troy also they have their acrobats.'
    He spoke so, and strode against the hero Kebriones
with the spring of a lion, who as he ravages the pastures
has been hit in the chest, and his own courage destroys him.
So in your fury you pounced, Patroklos, above Kebriones.
755 On the other side Hektor sprang to the ground from his chariot,
and the two fought it out over Kebriones, like lions
who in the high places of a mountain, both in huge courage
and both hungry, fight together over a killed deer.
So above Kebriones these two, urgent for battle,
760 Patroklos, son of Menoitios, and glorious Hektor,
were straining with the pitiless bronze to tear at each other;
since Hektor had caught him by the head, and would not let go of him,
and Patroklos had his foot on the other side, while the other
Trojans and Danaans drove together the strength of their onset.
765   As east wind and south wind fight it out with each other
in the valleys of the mountains to shake the deep forest timber,
oak tree and ash and the cornel with the delicate bark; these
whip their wide-reaching branches against one another
in inhuman noise, and the crash goes up from the splintering timber;

so Trojans and Achaians springing against one another   770
cut men down, nor did either side think of disastrous panic,
and many sharp spears were driven home about Kebriones
and many feathered arrows sprung from the bowstrings, many
great throwing stones pounded against the shields, as they fought on
hard over his body, as he in the turning dust lay   775
mightily in his might, his horsemanship all forgotten.
    So long as the sun was climbing still to the middle heaven,
so long the thrown weapons of both took hold, and men dropped under
        them;
but when the sun had gone to the time for unyoking of cattle,
then beyond their very destiny the Achaians were stronger   780
and dragged the hero Kebriones from under the weapons
and the clamour of the Trojans, and stripped the armour from his
        shoulders.
And Patroklos charged with evil intention in on the Trojans.
Three times he charged in with the force of the running war god,
screaming a terrible cry, and three times he cut down nine men;   785
but as for the fourth time he swept in, like something greater
than human, there, Patroklos, the end of your life was shown forth,
since Phoibos came against you there in the strong encounter
dangerously, nor did Patroklos see him as he moved through
the battle, and shrouded in a deep mist came in against him   790
and stood behind him, and struck his back and his broad shoulders
with a flat stroke of the hand so that his eyes spun. Phoibos
Apollo now struck away from his head the helmet
four-horned and hollow-eyed, and under the feet of the horses
it rolled clattering, and the plumes above it were defiled   795
by blood and dust. Before this time it had not been permitted
to defile in the dust this great helmet crested in horse-hair;
rather it guarded the head and the gracious brow of a godlike
man, Achilleus; but now Zeus gave it over to Hektor
to wear on his head, Hektor whose own death was close to him.   800
And in his hands was splintered all the huge, great, heavy,
iron-shod, far-shadowing spear, and away from his shoulders
dropped to the ground the shield with its shield sling and its tassels.
The lord Apollo, son of Zeus, broke the corselet upon him.
Disaster caught his wits, and his shining body went nerveless.   805

He stood stupidly, and from close behind his back a Dardanian
man hit him between the shoulders with a sharp javelin:
Euphorbos, son of Panthoös, who surpassed all men of his own age
with the throwing spear, and in horsemanship and the speed of his feet. He
810 had already brought down twenty men from their horses
since first coming, with his chariot and his learning in warfare.
He first hit you with a thrown spear, o rider Patroklos,
nor broke you, but ran away again, snatching out the ash spear
from your body, and lost himself in the crowd, not enduring
815 to face Patroklos, naked as he was, in close combat.
    Now Patroklos, broken by the spear and the god's blow, tried
to shun death and shrink back into the swarm of his own companions.
But Hektor, when he saw high-hearted Patroklos trying
to get away, saw how he was wounded with the sharp javelin,
820 came close against him across the ranks, and with the spear stabbed him
in the depth of the belly and drove the bronze clean through. He fell,
thunderously, to the horror of all the Achaian people.
As a lion overpowers a weariless boar in wild combat
as the two fight in their pride on the high places of a mountain
825 over a little spring of water, both wanting to drink there,
and the lion beats him down by force as he fights for his breath, so
Hektor, Priam's son, with a close spear-stroke stripped the life
from the fighting son of Menoitios, who had killed so many,
and stood above him, and spoke aloud the winged words of triumph:
830 'Patroklos, you thought perhaps of devastating our city,
of stripping from the Trojan women the day of their liberty
and dragging them off in ships to the beloved land of your fathers.
Fool! When in front of them the running horses of Hektor
strained with their swift feet into the fighting, and I with my own spear
835 am conspicuous among the fighting Trojans, I who beat from them
the day of necessity. For you, here the vultures shall eat you.
Wretch! Achilleus, great as he was, could do nothing to help you.
When he stayed behind, and you went, he must have said much to you:
"Patroklos, lord of horses, see that you do not come back to me
840 and the hollow ships, until you have torn in blood the tunic
of manslaughtering Hektor about his chest." In some such
manner he spoke to you, and persuaded the fool's heart in you.'
    And now, dying, you answered him, o rider Patroklos:

'Now is your time for big words, Hektor. Yours is the victory
given by Kronos' son, Zeus, and Apollo, who have subdued me   845
easily, since they themselves stripped the arms from my shoulders.
Even though twenty such as you had come in against me,
they would all have been broken beneath my spear, and have perished.
No, deadly destiny, with the son of Leto, has killed me,
and of men it was Euphorbos; you are only my third slayer.   850
And put away in your heart this other thing that I tell you.
You yourself are not one who shall live long, but now already
death and powerful destiny are standing beside you,
to go down under the hands of Aiakos' great son, Achilleus.'

He spoke, and as he spoke the end of death closed in upon him,   855
and the soul fluttering free of his limbs went down into Death's house
mourning her destiny, leaving youth and manhood behind her.
Now though he was a dead man glorious Hektor spoke to him:
'Patroklos, what is this prophecy of my headlong destruction?
Who knows if even Achilleus, son of lovely-haired Thetis,   860
might before this be struck by my spear, and his own life perish?'

He spoke, and setting his heel upon him wrenched out the bronze spear
from the wound, then spurned him away on his back from the spear.
    Thereafter
armed with the spear he went on, aiming a cast at Automedon,
the godlike henchman for the swift-footed son of Aiakos,   865
with the spear as he was carried away by those swift and immortal
horses the gods had given as shining gifts to Peleus.

As Patroklos went down before the Trojans in the hard fighting
he was not unseen by Atreus' son, warlike Menelaos,
who stalked through the ranks of the champions, helmed in the bright
      bronze,
and bestrode the body, as over a first-born calf the mother
5 cow stands lowing, she who has known no children before this.
So Menelaos of the fair hair stood over Patroklos
and held the spear and the perfect circle of his shield before him,
raging to cut down any man who might come forth against him.
Nor did the fall of blameless Patroklos pass unattended
10 by Panthoös' son of the strong ash spear, Euphorbos, who standing
close to face him spoke a word to warlike Menelaos:
'Son of Atreus, Menelaos, illustrious, leader of armies:
give way, let the bloody spoils be, get back from this body,
since before me no one of the Trojans, or renowned companions,
15 struck Patroklos down with the spear in the strong encounter.
Thereby let me win this great glory among the Trojans
before I hit you and strip the sweetness of life away from you.'
   Deeply stirred, Menelaos of the fair hair answered him:
'Father Zeus, it is not well for the proud man to glory.
20 Neither the fury of the leopard is such, not such is the lion's,
nor the fury of the devastating wild boar, within whose breast
the spirit is biggest and vaunts in the pride of his strength, is so great
as goes the pride in these sons of Panthoös of the strong ash spear.
Yet even the strength of Hyperenor, breaker of horses,

[354]

had no joy of his youth when he stood against me and taunted me 25
and said that among all the Danaans I was the weakest
in battle. Yet I think that his feet shall no more carry him
back, to pleasure his beloved wife and his honoured parents.
So I think I can break your strength as well, if you only
stand against me. No, but I myself tell you to get back 30
into the multitude, not stand to face me, before you
take some harm. Once a thing has been done, the fool sees it.'
   He spoke so, but did not persuade Euphorbos, who answered:
'Then, lordly Menelaos, you must now pay the penalty
for my brother, whom you killed, and boast that you did it, 35
and made his wife a widow in the depth of a young bride chamber
and left to his parents the curse of lamentation and sorrow.
Yet I might stop the mourning of these unhappy people
if I could carry back to them your head, and your armour,
and toss them into Panthoös' hands, and to Phrontis the lovely. 40
No, this struggle shall not go long untested between us
nor yet unfought, whether it prove our strength or our terror.'
   He spoke, and stabbed Menelaos' shield in its perfect circle,
nor did the bronze break its way through, but the spearhead bent back
in the strong shield. And after him Atreus' son, Menelaos, 45
made his prayer to father Zeus and lunged with the bronze spear
and as he was drawing back caught him in the pit of the gullet
and leaned in on the stroke in the confidence of his strong hand,
and clean through the soft part of the neck the spearpoint was driven.
He fell, thunderously, and his armour clattered upon him, 50
and his hair, lovely as the Graces, was splattered with blood, those
braided locks caught waspwise in gold and silver. As some
slip of an olive tree strong-growing that a man raises
in a lonely place, and drenched it with generous water, so that
it blossoms into beauty, and the blasts of winds from all quarters 55
tremble it, and it bursts into pale blossoming. But then
a wind suddenly in a great tempest descending upon it
wrenches it out of its stand and lays it at length on the ground; such
was Euphorbos of the strong ash spear, the son of Panthoös,
whom Menelaos Atreides killed, and was stripping his armour. 60
   As when in the confidence of his strength some lion
hill-reared snatches the finest cow in a herd as it pastures;

first the lion breaks her neck caught fast in the strong teeth,
then gulps down the blood and all the guts that are inward
65 savagely, as the dogs and the herdsmen raise a commotion
loudly about him, but from a distance, and are not willing
to go in and face him, since the hard green fear has hold of them;
so no heart in the breast of any Trojan had courage
to go in and face glorious Menelaos. Then easily
70 the son of Atreus might have taken the glorious armour
from Panthoös' son, only Phoibos Apollo begrudged him
and stirred up Hektor, a match for the running war god, against him
in semblance of a man, the leader of the Kikones,
Mentes, and spoke aloud to him, and addressed him in winged words:
75 'While you, Hektor, run after what can never be captured,
the horses of valiant Aiakides; they are difficult horses
for mortal man to manage, or even to ride behind them
for all except Achilleus, who was born of an immortal mother;
meanwhile Menelaos, the warlike son of Atreus,
80 stands over Patroklos and has killed the best man of the Trojans,
Euphorbos, Panthoös' son, and stopped his furious valour.'
     So he spoke, and went back, a god, to the mortals' struggle.
But bitter sorrow closed over Hektor's heart in its darkness.
He looked about then across the ranks, and at once was aware
85 of the two men, one stripping the glorious armour, the other
sprawled on the ground, and blood running from the gash of the
     spear-thrust.
He stalked through the ranks of the champions helmed in the bright
     bronze
with a shrill scream, and looking like the flame of Hephaistos,
weariless. Nor did Atreus' son fail to hear the sharp cry.
90 Deeply troubled, he spoke to his own great-hearted spirit:
'Ah me; if I abandon here the magnificent armour,
and Patroklos, who has fallen here for the sake of my honour,
shall not some one of the Danaans, seeing it, hold it against me?
Yet if I fight, alone as I am, the Trojans and Hektor
95 for shame, shall they not close in, many against one, about me?
Hektor of the shining helm leads all of the Trojans
here. Then why does my own heart within me debate this?
When a man, in the face of divinity, would fight with another

[356]

whom some god honours, the big disaster rolls sudden upon him.
Therefore, let no Danaan seeing it hold it against me   100
if I give way before Hektor, who fights from God. Yet if somewhere
I could only get some word of Aias of the great war cry,
we two might somehow go, and keep our spirit of battle
even in the face of divinity, if we might win the body
for Peleïd Achilleus. It would be our best among evils.'   105
     Now as he was pondering this in his heart and his spirit
meanwhile the ranks of the Trojans came on, and Hektor led them;
and Menelaos backed away from them and left the dead man,
but kept turning on his way like some great bearded lion
when dogs and men drive him off from a steading with weapons   110
and shouts, and in the breast of the lion the strong heart of valour
freezes, and he goes reluctant away from the fenced ground.
So fair-haired Menelaos moved from Patroklos, but turning
stood fast when he had got back to the swarm of his own companions,
and looked all about for huge Aias, the son of Telamon,   115
and saw soon where he was, at the left of the entire battle
encouraging his companions and urging them into the fighting,
since Phoibos Apollo had smitten them all with unearthly terror.
He went on the run, and presently stood beside him and spoke to him:
'This way, Aias, we must make for fallen Patroklos   120
to try if we can carry back to Achilleus the body
which is naked; Hektor of the shining helm has taken his armour.'
     So he spoke, and stirred the spirit in valiant Aias
who strode among the champions, fair-haired Menelaos with him.
But Hektor, when he had stripped from Patroklos the glorious armour,   125
dragged at him, meaning to cut his head from his shoulders with the
     sharp bronze,
to haul off the body and give it to the dogs of Troy; but meanwhile
Aias came near him, carrying like a wall his shield,
and Hektor drew back to the company of his own companions
and sprang to his chariot, but handed over the beautiful armour   130
to the Trojans, to take back to the city and to be his great glory.
Now Aias covering the son of Menoitios under his broad shield
stood fast, like a lion over his young, when the lion
is leading his little ones along, and men who are hunting
come upon them in the forest. He stands in the pride of his great strength 135

hooding his eyes under the cover of down-drawn eyelids.
Such was Aias as he bestrode the hero Patroklos,
while on the other side Atreus' son, warlike Menelaos,
stood fast, feeding still bigger the great sorrow within him.

140   But Glaukos, lord of the Lykian men, the son of Hippolochos,
looked at Hektor, scowling, and laid a harsh word upon him:
'Hektor, splendid to look at, you come far short in your fighting.
That fame of yours, high as it is, belongs to a runner.
Take thought now how to hold fast your town, your citadel

145 by yourself, with those your people who were born in Ilion;
since no Lykian will go forth now to fight with the Danaans
for the sake of your city, since after all we got no gratitude
for our everlasting hard struggle against your enemies.
How then, o hard-hearted, shall you save a worse man in all your

150 company, when you have abandoned Sarpedon, your guest-friend
and own companion, to be the spoil and prey of the Argives,
who was of so much use to you, yourself and your city
while he lived? Now you have not the spirit to keep the dogs from him.
Therefore now, if any of the Lykian men will obey me,

155 we are going home, and the headlong destruction of Troy shall be
        manifest.
For if the Trojans had any fighting strength that were daring
and unshaken, such as comes on men who, for the sake of their country,
have made the hard hateful work come between them and their enemies,
we could quickly get the body of Patroklos inside Ilion.

160 If, dead man though he be, he could be brought into the great city
of lord Priam, if we could tear him out of the fighting,
the Argives must at once give up the beautiful armour
of Sarpedon, and we could carry his body inside Ilion.
Such is the man whose henchman is killed. He is far the greatest

165 of the Argives by the ships, and his men fight hard at close quarters.
No, but you could not bring yourself to stand up against Aias
of the great heart, nor to look at his eyes in the clamour of fighting
men, nor attack him direct, since he is far better than you are.'

     Looking darkly at him tall Hektor of the shining helm answered:
170 'Glaukos, why did a man like you speak this word of annoyance?
I am surprised. I thought that for wits you surpassed all others
of those who dwell in Lykia where the soil is generous; and yet

now I utterly despise your heart for the thing you have spoken
when you said I cannot stand in the face of gigantic Aias.
I am not one who shudders at attack and the thunder of horses.   175
But always the mind of Zeus is a stronger thing than a man's mind.
He terrifies even the warlike man, he takes away victory
lightly, when he himself has driven a man into battle.
Come here, friend, and watch me at work; learn, standing beside me,
whether I shall be a coward all day, as you proclaim me,   180
or whether I stop some Danaan, for all of his fury,
from his fighting strength and from the defence of fallen Patroklos.'
    So speaking he called afar in a great voice to the Trojans:
'Trojans, Lykians, Dardanians who fight at close quarters,
be men now, dear friends, remember your furious valour   185
while I am putting on the beautiful armour of blameless
Achilleus, which I stripped from Patroklos the strong when I killed him.'
    So spoke Hektor of the shining helm, and departed
from the hateful battle, and running caught up with his companions
very soon, since he went on quick feet, and they had not gone far   190
carrying the glorious armour of Peleus' son toward the city.
He stood apart from the sorrowful fighting, and changed his armour,
and gave what he had worn to the fighting Trojans to carry
to sacred Ilion, and himself put on that armour immortal
of Peleïd Achilleus, which the Uranian gods had given   195
to his loved father; and he in turn grown old had given it
to his son; but a son who never grew old in his father's armour.
    When Zeus who gathers the clouds saw him, apart from the others
arming himself in the battle gear of godlike Peleïdes,
he stirred his head and spoke to his own spirit: 'Ah, poor wretch!   200
There is no thought of death in your mind now, and yet death stands
close beside you as you put on the immortal armour
of a surpassing man. There are others who tremble before him.
Now you have killed this man's dear friend, who was strong and gentle,
and taken the armour, as you should not have done, from his shoulders   205
and head. Still for the present I will invest you with great strength
to make up for it that you will not come home out of the fighting,
nor Andromache take from your hands the glorious arms of Achilleus.'
    He spoke, the son of Kronos, and nodded his head with the dark brows.
The armour was fitted to Hektor's skin, and Ares the dangerous   210

war god entered him, so that the inward body was packed full
of force and fighting strength. He went onward calling in a great voice
to his renowned companions in arms, and figured before them
flaming in the battle gear of great-hearted Peleion.

215 He ranged their ranks, and spoke a word to encourage each captain,
to Mesthles and Glaukos, to Thersilochos and Medon,
Deisenor and Hippothoös and Asteropaios,
to Phorkys and Chromios and the bird interpreter Ennomos,
and stirring all of these forward called to them in winged words:

220 'Hear me, you numberless hordes of companions who live at our borders.
It was not for any desire nor need of a multitude
that man by man I gathered you to come here from your cities,
but so that you might have good will to defend the innocent
children of the Trojans, and their wives, from the fighting Achaians.

225 With such a purpose I wear out my own people for presents
and food, wherewith I make strong the spirit within each one of you.
Therefore a man must now turn his face straight forward, and perish
or survive. This is the sweet invitation of battle.
That man of you who drags Patroklos, dead as he is, back

230 among Trojans, breakers of horses, and Aias gives way before him,
I will give him half the spoils for his portion, and keep half
for myself, and his glory shall be as great as mine is.'
    So he spoke, and they lifted their spears and went straight for the
        Danaans
who felt their weight, and inside each man the spirit was hopeful

235 to get the body away from Telamonian Aias.
Fools! Since over the dead man he tore the life out of many.
Then Aias himself spoke to Menelaos of the great war cry:
'Illustrious Menelaos, dear friend, I no longer have hope
that even you and I can win back out of the fighting.

240 My fear is not so much for the dead body of Patroklos
who presently must glut the dogs and the birds of Troy, so much
as I fear for my own head, my life, and what may befall it,
and for yours, since this cloud of war is darkened on all things,
this Hektor, while for you and me sheer death is emerging.

245 Come then, call the great men of the Danaans, if one might hear you.'
    He spoke, and Menelaos of the great war cry obeyed him.
He lifted his voice and called in a piercing cry to the Danaans:

'Friends, o leaders and men of counsel among the Argives,
you that beside Agamemnon and Menelaos, the two sons
of Atreus, drink the community's wine and give, each man, his orders   250
to the people; and from Zeus the respect and honour attend you.
It is hard for me to discriminate among you each man
who is a leader, so big is the bitter fight that has blazed up.
Then let a man come of his own accord, think it shameful
that Patroklos be given to the dogs of Troy to delight them.'   255
    He spoke, and swift Aias son of Oïleus was sharp to hear him
and was first to come running along the battle, and join him,
and after him Idomeneus, and Idomeneus' companion
Meriones, a match for the murderous lord of battles.
But what man could tell forth from his heart the names of the others,   260
all who after these waked the war strength of the Achaians?
    The Trojans came down on them in a pack, and Hektor led them.
As when at the outpouring place of a rain-glutted river
the huge surf of the sea roars against the current, out-jutting
beaches thunder aloud to the backwash of the salt water,   265
with such a bellow the Trojans came on, but now the Achaians
stood fast about the son of Menoitios, in a single courage
and fenced beneath their bronze-armoured shields, while the son of
    Kronos
drifted across the glitter of their helmets a deepening
mist; since before this time he had not hated Menoitios'   270
son, while he lived yet and was Achilleus' companion,
and loathed now that he should become the spoil of the hated
Trojans' dogs, and stirred his companions on to defend him.
    First the Trojans shouldered back the glancing-eyed Achaians,
who abandoned the body and ran for terror, nor did the high-hearted   275
Trojans take any with their spears, for all of their striving,
but dragged at the dead man, only the Achaians were not long destined
to fail him, since they were pulled around in sudden speed
by Aias, who for his beauty and the work of his hands surpassed
all other Danaans, after the blameless son of Peleus.   280
He steered through the front fighters in pride of strength like a savage
wild boar, who among the mountains easily scatters
the dogs and strong young men when he turns at bay in the valley.
So now the son of haughty Telamon, glorious Aias,

285 turned to charge and easily scatter the Trojan battalions,
who had taken their stand bestriding Patroklos, in high hope
of dragging him off to their own city, and so winning honour.
    Indeed, Hippothoös, glorious son of Pelasgian Lethos,
was trying to drag him by the foot through the strong encounter
290 by fastening the sling of his shield round the ankle tendons
for the favour of Hektor and the Trojans, but the sudden evil
came to him, and none for all their desire could defend him.
The son of Telamon, sweeping in through the mass of the fighters,
struck him at close quarters through the brazen cheeks of his helmet
295 and the helm crested with horse-hair was riven about the spearhead
to the impact of the huge spear and the weight of the hand behind it
and the brain ran from the wound along the spear by the eye-hole,
bleeding. There his strength was washed away, and from his hands
he let fall to the ground the foot of great-hearted Patroklos
300 to lie there, and himself collapsed prone over the dead man
far away from generous Larisa, and he could not
render again the care of his dear parents; he was short-lived,
beaten down beneath the spear of high-hearted Aias.
    Again Hektor threw at Aias with the shining javelin,
305 but Aias with his eyes straight on him avoided the bronze spear
by a little, and Hektor struck Schedios, the son of high-hearted
Iphitos and far the best of the Phokians, one who lived
in his home in famous Panopeus and was lord over many people.
He struck him fair beneath the collar-bone, and the pointed
310 bronze head tore clean through and came out by the base of the shoulder.
He fell, thunderously, and his armour clattered upon him.
    But Aias in turn cut at Phorkys, the wise son of Phainops,
in the middle of the belly as he stood over fallen Hippothoös,
and broke the hollow of the corselet, so that the entrails spurted
315 from the bronze, and he went down clawing the dust in his fingers.
The champions of Troy gave back then, and glorious Hektor,
and the Argives gave a great cry and dragged back the bodies
of Hippothoös and Phorkys, and eased the armour from their shoulders.
    Then, once more, might the Trojans have climbed back into Ilion's
320 wall, subdued by terror before the warlike Achaians,
and the Argives, even beyond Zeus' destiny, might have won glory
by their own force and strength, had not Apollo in person

stirred on Aineias; he had assumed the form of the herald
Periphas, Epytos' son, growing old in his herald's office
by Aineias' aged father, and a man whose thoughts were of kindness.   325
In the likeness of this man Zeus' son Apollo spoke to him:
'Aineias, how could you be the men to defend sheer Ilion
even against a god's will, as I have seen other men do it
in the confidence of their own force and strength, their own manhood
and their own numbers, though they had too few people for it?   330
But now Zeus wishes the victory far rather for our side
than the Danaans', only yourselves keep blenching and will not fight
    them.'
    So he spoke, but Aineias knew far-striking Apollo
as he looked him straight in the face, and called in a great voice to Hektor:
'Hektor, and you other lords of the Trojans and their companions,   335
here is a shameful thing! We are climbing back into Ilion's
wall, subdued by terror before the warlike Achaians.
Yet see, some one of the gods is standing beside me, and tells me
that Zeus the supreme counsellor lends his weight to our fighting.
Therefore we must go straight for the Danaans, so that they may not   340
carry thus easily back to their ships the fallen Patroklos.'
    He spoke, and with a long leap stood far before the front fighters,
and the Trojans turned and held their ground against the Achaians.
And now Aineias killed Leiokritos, with a spear-thrust,
the son of Arisbas and noble companion of Lykomedes;   345
but as he fell the warrior Lykomedes pitied him,
and stood close in, and made a cast with the shining javelin
and struck Apisaon, son of Hippasos, shepherd of the people,
in the liver under the midriff, and the strength of his knees was broken.
He was one who had come from Paionia of the rich soil   350
and was best of her men in fighting next to Asteropaios.
    As this man fell, warlike Asteropaios pitied him
and he in turn drove forward eager to fight with the Danaans,
but was not able to do it, for they, standing about Patroklos,
fenced him behind their shields on all sides, and held their spears out-thrust.   355
For Aias ranged their whole extent with his numerous orders,
and would not let any man give back from the body, nor let one
go out and fight by himself far in front of the other Achaians,
but made them stand hard and fast about him and fight at close quarters.

[363]

360 Such were the orders of gigantic Aias. The ground ran
with red blood, the dead men dropped one after another
from the ranks alike of Trojans and their mighty companions
and Danaans also, since these fought not without bloodletting,
but far fewer of them went down, since they ever remembered
365 always to stand massed and beat sudden death from each other.
　　So they fought on in the likeness of fire, nor would you have thought
the sun was still secure in his place in the sky, nor the moon, since
the mist was closed over all that part of the fight where the bravest
stood about Patroklos, the fallen son of Menoitios.
370 Now elsewhere the rest of the Trojans and strong-greaved Achaians
fought naturally in the bright air, with the sun's sharp glitter
everywhere about them, no cloud was showing anywhere
on earth nor on the mountains. They fought their battle by intervals
standing each well off at a distance, avoiding the painful
375 shots from the other side; but they in the middle were suffering
distress in the mist and the fighting, with the cruel bronze wearing them.
These men were the bravest, but there were two men of glory,
Thrasymedes and Antilochos, who had not yet heard
how Patroklos the blameless had been killed, but still thought
380 he was alive and fighting in the first shock with the Trojans.
But these two, watching against death or flight in their company,
fought their separate battle, since such was their order from Nestor
as he was urging them forth from the black ships into the fighting.
　　So for these daylong the hard bitterness of the wearing
385 battle rose. With the ever-relentless sweat and the weariness
knees, legs, and feet that supported from underneath each fighter,
their hands and eyes also were running wet as they fought on
over the brave henchman of swift-footed Aiakides.
As when a man gives the hide of a great ox, a bullock,
390 drenched first deep in fat, to all his people to stretch out;
the people take it from him and stand in a circle about it
and pull, and presently the moisture goes and the fat sinks
in, with so many pulling, and the bull's hide is stretched out level;
so the men of both sides in a cramped space tugged at the body
395 in both directions; and the hearts of the Trojans were hopeful
to drag him away to Ilion, those of the Achaians
to get him back to the hollow ships. And about him a savage

struggle arose. Not Ares who rallies men, not Athene,
watching this fight could have scorned it, not even in some strong anger,
such was the wicked work of battle for men and for horses   400
Zeus strained tight above Patroklos that day. But the brilliant
Achilleus did not yet know at all that Patroklos had fallen.
Since now the men were fighting far away from the fast ships
under the Trojan wall, and Achilleus had no expectation
that Patroklos was dead, but thought he was alive and close under   405
the gates, and would come back. He had not thought that Patroklos
would storm the city without himself, nor with himself either;
for often he had word from his mother, not known to mortals;
she was ever telling him what was the will of great Zeus; but this time
his mother did not tell Achilleus of all the evil   410
that had been done, nor how his dearest companion had perished.
    So they about the body gripping their headed spears kept
inexorably close together, and slaughtered on both sides.
And such would be the saying of some bronze-armoured Achaian:
'Friends, there is no glory for us if we go back again   415
to our hollow ships, but here and now let the black earth open
gaping for all; this would soon be far better for us
if we give up this man to the Trojans, breakers of horses,
to take away to their own city and win glory from him.'
    And such in turn would be the cry of some high-hearted Trojan: 420
'O friends, though it be destined for all of us to be killed here
over this man, still none of us must give ground from the fighting.'
    Thus a man would speak, and stir the spirit in each one
of his fellowship. So they fought on, and the iron tumult
went up into the brazen sky through the barren bright air.   425
But the horses of Aiakides standing apart from the battle
wept, as they had done since they heard how their charioteer
had fallen in the dust at the hands of murderous Hektor.
In truth Automedon, the powerful son of Diores,
hit them over and over again with the stroke of the flying   430
lash, or talked to them, sometimes entreating them, sometimes
        threatening.
They were unwilling to go back to the wide passage of Helle
and the ships, or back into the fighting after the Achaians,
but still as stands a grave monument which is set over

435 the mounded tomb of a dead man or lady, they stood there
holding motionless in its place the fair-wrought chariot,
leaning their heads along the ground, and warm tears were running
earthward from underneath the lids of the mourning horses
who longed for their charioteer, while their bright manes were made dirty
440 as they streamed down either side of the yoke from under the yoke pad.
    As he watched the mourning horses the son of Kronos pitied them,
and stirred his head and spoke to his own spirit: 'Poor wretches,
why then did we ever give you to the lord Peleus,
a mortal man, and you yourselves are immortal and ageless?
445 Only so that among unhappy men you also might be grieved?
Since among all creatures that breathe on earth and crawl on it
there is not anywhere a thing more dismal than man is.
At least the son of Priam, Hektor, shall not mount behind you
in the carefully wrought chariot. I will not let him. Is it not
450 enough for him that he has the armour and glories in wearing it?
But now I will put vigour into your knees and your spirits
so that you bring back Automedon out of the fighting
safe to the hollow ships; since I shall still give the Trojans
the glory of killing, until they win to the strong-benched vessels,
455 until the sun goes down and the blessed darkness comes over.'
    So spoke Zeus, and breathed great vigour into the horses,
and they shaking the dust from their manes to the ground lightly
carried the running chariot among the Achaians and Trojans.
Automedon fought from them, though grieving for his companion.
460 He would dash in, like a vulture among geese, with his horses,
and lightly get away out of the Trojans' confusion
and lightly charge in again in pursuit of a great multitude,
and yet could kill no men when he swept in in chase of them.
He had no way while he was alone in a separate chariot
465 to lunge with the spear and still keep in hand his fast-running horses.
But at last there was one of his companions who laid eyes upon him:
Alkimedon, the son of Laerkes, descended from Haimon.
He stood behind the chariot and called to Automedon:
'Automedon, what god put this unprofitable purpose
470 into your heart, and has taken away the better wits, so that
you are trying to fight the Trojans in the first shock of encounter
by yourself, since your companion has been killed, and Hektor

glories in wearing Aiakides' armour on his own shoulders?'
   In turn Automedon answered him, the son of Diores:
'Alkimedon, which other of the Achaians could handle   475
the management and the strength of immortal horses as you can,
were it not Patroklos, the equal of the immortals in counsel,
while he lived? Now death and fate have closed in upon him.
Therefore take over from me the whip and the glittering guide reins
while I dismount from behind the horses, so I may do battle.'   480
   He spoke, and Alkimedon vaulted up to the charging chariot
and quickly gathered up the reins and the lash in his hands, while
Automedon sprang down. But glorious Hektor saw them
and immediately spoke to Aineias, who stood close beside him:
'Aineias, lord of the counsels of the bronze-armoured Trojans,   485
I see before us the horses of swift-footed Aiakides
who appear now in the fighting with weak charioteers. Therefore
I could be hopeful of their capture, if you were willing
in heart to go with me. If we two went forth against them
they would not dare to stand their ground and do battle against us.'   490
   He spoke, and the strong son of Anchises did not disobey him.
The two went strongly forward, hooding their shoulders in well-tanned
and stubborn hides of oxen with deep bronze beaten upon them.
Along with these went Chromios and godlike Aretos
both together, and the spirit within each had high hopes   495
of killing the men and driving away the strong-necked horses;
poor fools, who were not going to come back from Automedon
without the shedding of blood; and he with a prayer to Zeus father
was filled about the darkening heart with war-strength and courage,
and spoke now to Alkimedon his trusted companion: 500
'Alkimedon, no longer check the horses back from me
but keep them breathing right against my back. I have no thought
that I can stand up to the strength of Hektor the son of Priam.
Sooner, I think, he will kill us and mount behind the mane-floating
horses of Achilleus, and scatter the ranks of the Argive   505
fighting men; or else himself go down in the first rush.'
   He spoke, and called to the two Aiantes and Menelaos:
'Aiantes, lords of the Argives, and Menelaos, we call you
to leave the dead man in the care of those who are fittest
to stand bestriding him and fend off the ranks of the Trojans   510

while you beat back the day without pity from us who are living.
For Hektor and Aineias, the greatest men of the Trojans,
are leaning the weight of their charge this way through the sorrowful
    battle.
Yet all these are things that are lying upon the gods' knees.
515 I myself will cast; and Zeus will look after the issue.'
    So he spoke, and balanced the spear far-shadowed, and threw it,
and struck the shield of Aretos on its perfect circle,
nor could the shield hold off the spear, but the bronze smashed clean
    through
and was driven on through the belt to the deep of the belly.
520 As when a strong-grown man with sharp axe in his hands chops
at an ox, ranger of the fields, behind the horns, cutting
all the way through the sinew, and the ox springing forward topples,
so Aretos sprang forward, then toppled back, and sharp-driven
into the depth of his belly the quivering spear unstrung him.
525 Then Hektor made a cast with the shining spear at Automedon,
but he, keeping his eyes straight on him, avoided the bronze spear.
For he bent forward, and behind his back the long spearshaft
was driven into the ground so that the butt end was shaken
on the spear. Then and there Ares the huge took the force from it.
530 And now they would have gone for each other with swords at close
    quarters,
had not the two Aiantes driven strongly between them,
who came on through the battle at the call of their companion,
and in fear before them Hektor and Aineias and godlike
Chromios gave ground back and away once more, leaving
535 Aretos lying there where he was with a wound in his vitals.
Then Automedon, a match for the running god of battles,
stripped the armour, and spoke a word of boasting above him:
'Now I have put a little sorrow from my heart for Patroklos'
death, although the man I killed was not great as he was.'
540   So he spoke, and took up the bloody war spoils and laid them
inside the chariot, and himself mounted it, the blood running
from hands and feet, as on some lion who has eaten a bullock.
    Once again over Patroklos was close drawn a strong battle
weary and sorrowful, and Athene from the sky descending
545 waked the bitter fighting, since Zeus of the wide brows sent her

down to stir the Danaans, for now his purpose had shifted.
As when in the sky Zeus strings for mortals the shimmering
rainbow, to be a portent and sign of war, or of wintry
storm, when heat perishes, such storm as stops mortals'
work upon the face of the earth, and afflicts their cattle, 550
so Athene shrouded in the shimmering cloud about her
merged among the swarming Achaians, and wakened each man.
And first she spoke, stirring him on, to the son of Atreus,
strong Menelaos, since he was the one who was standing close to her.
She likened herself in form and weariless voice to Phoinix: 555
'Menelaos, this will be a thing of shame, a reproach said
of you, if under the wall of the Trojans the dogs in their fury
can mutilate the staunch companion of haughty Achilleus.
But hold strongly on, and stir up all the rest of your people.'

    Then in turn Menelaos of the great war cry answered her: 560
'Phoinix, my father, aged and honoured, if only Athene
would give me such strength, and hold the volleying missiles off from me!
So for my part I would be willing to stand by Patroklos
and defend him, since in his death he hurt my heart greatly.
Yet Hektor holds still the awful strength of a fire, nor falters 565
in raging with the bronze spear, since Zeus is giving him glory.'

    So he spoke, and the goddess grey-eyed Athene was happy
that first among all the divinities his prayer had bespoken her.
She put strength into the man's shoulders and knees, inspiring
in his breast the persistent daring of that mosquito 570
who though it is driven hard away from a man's skin, even
so, for the taste of human blood, persists in biting him.
With such daring she darkened to fullness the heart inside him.
He stood over Patroklos, and made a cast with the shining
spear. There was one among the Trojans, Podes, Eëtion's 575
son, a rich man and good, whom Hektor prized above others
in the countryside, since he was his friend and ate at his table.
Now fair-haired Menelaos struck this man, at the war belt
as he swept away in flight, and drove the bronze spear clean through it.
He fell, thunderously, and Atreus' son Menelaos 580
dragged the body away from the Trojans among his companions.

    But now Apollo came and stood beside Hektor, and stirred him,
assuming the shape of Phainops, Asios' son, who among all

guest friends was dearest to Hektor, and lived at home in Abydos.
585 In the likeness of this man far-striking Apollo spoke to him:
'Hektor, what other Achaian now shall be frightened before you?
See, you have shrunk before Menelaos, who in times before this
was a soft spearfighter; and now he has gone taking off single-handed
a body from among the Trojans. He has killed your trusted companion,
590 valiant among the champions, Podes, the son of Eëtion.'
     He spoke, and the dark cloud of sorrow closed over Hektor.
He took his way among the champions helmed in the shining
bronze. And now the son of Kronos caught up the betasselled
glaring aegis, and shrouded Ida in mists. He let go
595 a lightning flash and a loud thunderstroke, shaking the mountain,
gave victory to the Trojans, and terrified the Achaians.
     First to begin the flight was Peneleos the Boiotian.
For he, turning always toward the attack, was hit in the shoulder's
end, a slight wound, but the spear of Poulydamas, who had thrown it
600 from a stance very close to him, had grated the bone's edge.
Then Hektor wounded in the hand by the wrist Leïtos,
the son of great-hearted Alektryon, and halted his warcraft,
and he drew back staring about him since his spirit had hope no longer
of holding a spear steady in his hand to fight with the Trojans.
605 Now as Hektor made a rush for Leïtos, Idomeneus
struck him on the corselet over the chest by the nipple,
but the long shaft was broken behind the head, and the Trojans
shouted. Now Hektor made a cast at Deukalian Idomeneus
as he stood in his chariot, and missed him by only a little,
610 but struck the follower and charioteer of Meriones,
Koiranos, who had come with him from strong-founded Lyktos.
Now Idomeneus at the first had come on foot, leaving the oarswept
ships, and now would have given the Trojans a mighty triumph,
had not Koiranos swiftly come up with the fast-running horses;
615 came as light to the other and beat from him the day without pity,
but himself lost his life at the hands of manslaughtering Hektor,
who hit him under the jaw by the ear, and the spearshaft pushed out
his teeth by the roots from the base, and split the tongue through the
     middle.
He toppled from the chariot, with the reins on the ground scattered,
620 but Meriones leaning down caught these up in his own hands

from the surface of the plain, and called aloud to Idomeneus:
'Lash them now, until you can get back to our fast ships.
You see yourself there is no more strength left in the Achaians.'

So he spoke, and Idomeneus whipped the mane-floating horses
back to the hollow ships, with fear fallen upon his spirit.   625

Nor was it unseen by great-hearted Aias how Zeus shifted
the strength of the fighting toward the Trojans, nor by Menelaos.
First of the two to speak was huge Telamonian Aias:
'Shame on it! By now even one with a child's innocence
could see how father Zeus himself is helping the Trojans.   630
The weapons of each of these take hold, no matter who throws them,
good fighter or bad, since Zeus is straightening all of them equally,
while ours fall to the ground and are utterly useless. Therefore
let us deliberate with ourselves upon the best counsel,
how at the same time to rescue the dead body, and also   635
win back ourselves, and bring joy to our beloved companions
who look our way and sorrow for us, and believe no longer
that the fury of manslaughtering Hektor, his hands irresistible,
can be held, but must be driven on to the black ships.
But there should be some companion who could carry the message   640
quickly to Peleus' son, since I think he has not yet heard
the ghastly news, how his beloved companion has fallen.
Yet I cannot make out such a man among the Achaians,
since they are held in the mist alike, the men and their horses.
Father Zeus, draw free from the mist the sons of the Achaians,   645
make bright the air, and give sight back to our eyes; in shining
daylight destroy us, if to destroy us be now your pleasure.'

He spoke thus, and as he wept the father took pity upon him,
and forthwith scattered the mist and pushed the darkness back from them,
and the sun blazed out, and all the battle was plain before them.   650
Now Aias spoke to him of the great war cry, Menelaos:
'Look hard, illustrious Menelaos, if you can discover
Antilochos still living, the son of great-hearted Nestor,
and send him out to run with a message to wise Achilleus
how one who was far the dearest of his companions has fallen.'   655

He spoke, and Menelaos of the great war cry obeyed him,
and went on his way, as from a mid-fenced ground some lion
who has been harrying dogs and men, but his strength is worn out;

they will not let him tear out the fat of the oxen, watching
660 nightlong against him, and he in his hunger for meat closes in
but can get nothing of what he wants, for the raining javelins
thrown from the daring hands of the men beat ever against him,
and the flaming torches, and these he balks at for all of his fury,
and with the daylight goes away, disappointed of desire;
665 so Menelaos of the great war cry went from Patroklos
much unwilling, and was afraid for him, lest the Achaians
under pressure of fear might leave him as spoil for the enemy,
and had much to urge on Meriones and the Aiantes:
'Aiantes, o lords of the Argives, and you, Meriones,
670 now let each one of you remember unhappy Patroklos
who was gentle, and understood how to be kindly toward all men
while he lived. Now death and fate have closed in upon him.'
    So spoke fair-haired Menelaos, and went away from them
peering about on all sides, like an eagle, who, as men say,
675 sees most sharply of all winged creatures under the heaven,
and lofty though he hover the cowering hare, the swift-footed,
escapes not his sight as he crouches in the shaggy bush, but the eagle
plunges suddenly to grab him and tear the life from him.
So now in you, Menelaos, illustrious, the eyes shining
680 circled everywhere your swarming hordes of companions,
if the man might see anywhere Nestor's son, still living,
and saw soon where he was, at the left of the entire battle,
encouraging his companions and urging them into the fighting.
Menelaos the fair-haired stood beside him and spoke to him:
685 'Antilochos, turn this way, illustrious, and hear from me
the ghastly message of a thing I wish never had happened.
You can see for yourself, I think, already, from watching,
how the god is wheeling disaster against the Danaans
and how the Trojans are winning. The best of the Achaians has
        fallen,
690 Patroklos, and a huge loss is inflicted upon the Danaans.
Run then quickly to Achilleus, by the ships of the Achaians,
and tell him. He might in speed win back to his ship the dead body
which is naked. Hektor of the shining helm has taken his armour.'
    So he spoke, and Antilochos hated his word as he listened.
695 He stayed for a long time without a word, speechless, and his eyes

filled with tears, the springing voice was held still within him,
yet even so he neglected not Menelaos' order
but went on the run, handing his war gear to a blameless companion,
Laodokos, who had turned nearby his single-foot horses.

Now as his feet carried him, weeping, out of the battle,   700
with his message of evil for the son of Peleus, Achilleus,
so now, Menelaos, the spirit in you, illustrious,
wished not to defend his stricken companions, after Antilochos
was gone from them, and his loss wrought greatly upon the Pylians;
rather he sent Thrasymedes the brilliant over to help them,   705
while he himself went back again to the hero Patroklos
running, and took his place beside the Aiantes, and spoke to them:
'Now I have sent the man you spoke of back to the fast ships
on his way to swift-footed Achilleus, yet think not even
he can come now, for all his great anger with Hektor the brilliant.   710
There is no way he could fight bare of armour against the Trojans.
We by ourselves must deliberate upon the best counsel
how at the same time to rescue the dead body, and also
ourselves escape death and destiny from the clamouring Trojans.'

Then in turn huge Telamonian Aias answered him: 715
'All you have said, renowned Menelaos, is fair and orderly.
But come: you and Meriones stoop and shoulder the body
at once, and carry it out of the hard fighting. Behind you
we two shall fight off the Trojans and glorious Hektor,
we, who have the same name, the same spirit, and who in times past   720
have stood fast beside each other in the face of the bitter war god.'

He spoke, and they caught the body from the ground in their arms,
        lifting
him high with a great heave, and the Trojan people behind them
shouted aloud as they saw the Achaians lifting the dead man,
and made a rush against them like dogs, who sweep in rapidly   725
on a wounded wild boar, ahead of the young men who hunt him,
and for the moment race in raging to tear him to pieces
until in the confidence of his strength he turns on them, at bay,
and they give ground and scatter for fear one way and another;
so the Trojans until that time kept always in close chase   730
assembled, stabbing at them with swords and leaf-headed spears,
but every time the two Aiantes would swing round to face them

and stand fast, the colour of their skin changed, and no longer
could any endure to sweep in further and fight for the body.

735   So these, straining, carried the dead man out of the battle
and back to the hollow ships, and the fight that was drawn fast between
        them
was wild as fire which, risen suddenly, storming a city
of men sets it ablaze, and houses diminish before it
in the high glare, and the force of the wind on it roars it to thunder;

740 so, as the Danaans made their way back, the weariless roaring
of horses, chariots, and spearmen was ever upon them.
But they, as mules who have put the on-drive of strength upon them
drag down from the high ground along a steep stony trail either
a beam or some big timber for a ship, and the heart in them

745 wearies under the hard work and sweat of their urgent endeavour;
so these, straining, carried the dead man away, and behind them
the two Aiantes held them off, as a timbered rock ridge
holds off water, one that is placed to divide an entire plain,
which, though flood-currents of strong rivers drive sorely against it,

750 holds them off and beats back the waters of them all to be scattered
over the plain, and all the strength of their streams cannot break it;
so behind the Achaians the Aiantes held off forever
the Trojan attack. But these stayed close, and two beyond others,
Aineias, who was son of Anchises, and glorious Hektor.

755 But before these, as goes a cloud of daws or of starlings
screaming terror when they have seen coming forth against them
the hawk, whose coming is murder for the little birds, so now
before Aineias and Hektor the young Achaian warriors
went, screaming terror, all the delight of battle forgotten.

760 Many fine pieces of armour littered the ground on both sides
of the ditch, as the Danaans fled. There was no check in the fighting.

So these fought on in the likeness of blazing fire. Meanwhile,
Antilochos came, a swift-footed messenger, to Achilleus,
and found him sitting in front of the steep-horned ships, thinking
over in his heart of things which had now been accomplished.
Disturbed, Achilleus spoke to the spirit in his own great heart: 5
'Ah me, how is it that once again the flowing-haired Achaians
are driven out of the plain on their ships in fear and confusion?
May the gods not accomplish vile sorrows upon the heart in me
in the way my mother once made it clear to me, when she told me
how while I yet lived the bravest of all the Myrmidons   10
must leave the light of the sun beneath the hands of the Trojans.
Surely, then, the strong son of Menoitios has perished.
Unhappy! and yet I told him, once he had beaten the fierce fire
off, to come back to the ships, not fight in strength against Hektor.'
    Now as he was pondering this in his heart and his spirit,   15
meanwhile the son of stately Nestor was drawing near him
and wept warm tears, and gave Achilleus his sorrowful message:
'Ah me, son of valiant Peleus; you must hear from me
the ghastly message of a thing I wish never had happened.
Patroklos has fallen, and now they are fighting over his body   20
which is naked. Hektor of the shining helm has taken his armour.'
    He spoke, and the black cloud of sorrow closed on Achilleus.
In both hands he caught up the grimy dust, and poured it
over his head and face, and fouled his handsome countenance,
and the black ashes were scattered over his immortal tunic.   25

And he himself, mightily in his might, in the dust lay
at length, and took and tore at his hair with his hands, and defiled it.
And the handmaidens Achilleus and Patroklos had taken
captive, stricken at heart cried out aloud, and came running
30   out of doors about valiant Achilleus, and all of them
     beat their breasts with their hands, and the limbs went slack in each of
         them.
On the other side Antilochos mourned with him, letting the tears fall,
and held the hands of Achilleus as he grieved in his proud heart,
fearing Achilleus might cut his throat with the iron. He cried out
35   terribly, aloud, and the lady his mother heard him
     as she sat in the depths of the sea at the side of her aged father,
     and she cried shrill in turn, and the goddesses gathered about her,
     all who along the depth of the sea were daughters of Nereus.
     For Glauke was there, Kymodoke and Thaleia,
40   Nesaie and Speio and Thoë, and ox-eyed Halia;
     Kymothoë was there, Aktaia and Limnoreia,
     Melite and Iaira, Amphithoë and Agauë,
     Doto and Proto, Dynamene and Pherousa,
     Dexamene and Amphinome and Kallianeira;
45   Doris and Panope and glorious Galateia,
     Nemertes and Apseudes and Kallianassa;
     Klymene was there, Ianeira and Ianassa,
     Maira and Oreithyia and lovely-haired Amatheia,
     and the rest who along the depth of the sea were daughters of Nereus.
50   The silvery cave was filled with these, and together all of them
     beat their breasts, and among them Thetis led out the threnody:
     'Hear me, Nereids, my sisters; so you may all know
     well all the sorrows that are in my heart, when you hear of them from me.
     Ah me, my sorrow, the bitterness in this best of child-bearing,
55   since I gave birth to a son who was without fault and powerful,
     conspicuous among heroes; and he shot up like a young tree,
     and I nurtured him, like a tree grown in the pride of the orchard.
     I sent him away with the curved ships into the land of Ilion
     to fight with the Trojans; but I shall never again receive him
60   won home again to his country and into the house of Peleus.
     Yet while I see him live and he looks on the sunlight, he has
     sorrows, and though I go to him I can do nothing to help him.

Yet I shall go, to look on my dear son, and to listen
to the sorrow that has come to him as he stays back from the fighting.'

So she spoke, and left the cave, and the others together   65
went with her in tears, and about them the wave of the water
was broken. Now these, when they came to the generous Troad,
followed each other out on the sea-shore, where close together
the ships of the Myrmidons were hauled up about swift Achilleus.
There as he sighed heavily the lady his mother stood by him   70
and cried out shrill and aloud, and took her son's head in her arms, then
sorrowing for him she spoke to him in winged words: 'Why then,
child, do you lament? What sorrow has come to your heart now?
Speak out, do not hide it. These things are brought to accomplishment
through Zeus: in the way that you lifted your hands and prayed for,   75
that all the sons of the Achaians be pinned on their grounded vessels
by reason of your loss, and suffer things that are shameful.'

Then sighing heavily Achilleus of the swift feet answered her:
'My mother, all these things the Olympian brought to accomplishment.
But what pleasure is this to me, since my dear companion has perished,   80
Patroklos, whom I loved beyond all other companions,
as well as my own life. I have lost him, and Hektor, who killed him,
has stripped away that gigantic armour, a wonder to look on
and splendid, which the gods gave Peleus, a glorious present,
on that day they drove you to the marriage bed of a mortal.   85
I wish you had gone on living then with the other goddesses
of the sea, and that Peleus had married some mortal woman.
As it is, there must be on your heart a numberless sorrow
for your son's death, since you can never again receive him
won home again to his country; since the spirit within does not drive me   90
to go on living and be among men, except on condition
that Hektor first be beaten down under my spear, lose his life
and pay the price for stripping Patroklos, the son of Menoitios.'

Then in turn Thetis spoke to him, letting the tears fall:
'Then I must lose you soon, my child, by what you are saying,   95
since it is decreed your death must come soon after Hektor's.'

Then deeply disturbed Achilleus of the swift feet answered her:
'I must die soon, then; since I was not to stand by my companion
when he was killed. And now, far away from the land of his fathers,
he has perished, and lacked my fighting strength to defend him.   100

Now, since I am not going back to the beloved land of my fathers,
since I was no light of safety to Patroklos, nor to my other
companions, who in their numbers went down before glorious Hektor,
but sit here beside my ships, a useless weight on the good land,
105 I, who am such as no other of the bronze-armoured Achaians
in battle, though there are others also better in council—
why, I wish that strife would vanish away from among gods and mortals,
and gall, which makes a man grow angry for all his great mind,
that gall of anger that swarms like smoke inside of a man's heart
110 and becomes a thing sweeter to him by far than the dripping of honey.
So it was here that the lord of men Agamemnon angered me.
Still, we will let all this be a thing of the past, and for all our
sorrow beat down by force the anger deeply within us.
Now I shall go, to overtake that killer of a dear life,
115 Hektor; then I will accept my own death, at whatever
time Zeus wishes to bring it about, and the other immortals.
For not even the strength of Herakles fled away from destruction,
although he was dearest of all to lord Zeus, son of Kronos,
but his fate beat him under, and the wearisome anger of Hera.
120 So I likewise, if such is the fate which has been wrought for me,
shall lie still, when I am dead. Now I must win excellent glory,
and drive some one of the women of Troy, or some deep-girdled
Dardanian woman, lifting up to her soft cheeks both hands
to wipe away the close bursts of tears in her lamentation,
125 and learn that I stayed too long out of the fighting. Do not
hold me back from the fight, though you love me. You will not
    persuade me.'
  In turn the goddess Thetis of the silver feet answered him:
'Yes, it is true, my child, this is no cowardly action,
to beat aside sudden death from your afflicted companions.
130 Yet, see now, your splendid armour, glaring and brazen,
is held among the Trojans, and Hektor of the shining helmet
wears it on his own shoulders, and glories in it. Yet I think
he will not glory for long, since his death stands very close to him.
Therefore do not yet go into the grind of the war god,
135 not before with your own eyes you see me come back to you.
For I am coming to you at dawn and as the sun rises
bringing splendid armour to you from the lord Hephaistos.'

So she spoke, and turned, and went away from her son,
and turning now to her sisters of the sea she spoke to them:
'Do you now go back into the wide fold of the water   140
to visit the ancient of the sea and the house of our father,
and tell him everything. I am going to tall Olympos
and to Hephaistos, the glorious smith, if he might be willing
to give me for my son renowned and radiant armour.'

      She spoke, and they plunged back beneath the wave of the water,   145
while she the goddess Thetis of the silver feet went onward
to Olympos, to bring back to her son the glorious armour.

      So her feet carried her to Olympos; meanwhile the Achaians
with inhuman clamour before the attack of manslaughtering Hektor
fled until they were making for their own ships and the Hellespont;   150
nor could the strong-greaved Achaians have dragged the body
of Patroklos, henchman of Achilleus, from under the missiles,
for once again the men and the horses came over upon him,
and Hektor, Priam's son, who fought like a flame in his fury.
Three times from behind glorious Hektor caught him   155
by the feet, trying to drag him, and called aloud on the Trojans.
Three times the two Aiantes with their battle-fury upon them
beat him from the corpse, but he, steady in the confidence of his great
      strength,
kept making, now a rush into the crowd, or again at another time
stood fast, with his great cry, but gave not a bit of ground backward.   160
And as herdsmen who dwell in the fields are not able to frighten
a tawny lion in his great hunger away from a carcass,
so the two Aiantes, marshals of men, were not able
to scare Hektor, Priam's son, away from the body.
And now he would have dragged it away and won glory forever   165
had not swift wind-footed Iris come running from Olympos
with a message for Peleus' son to arm. She came secretly
from Zeus and the other gods, since it was Hera who sent her.
She came and stood close to him and addressed him in winged words:
'Rise up, son of Peleus, most terrifying of all men.   170
Defend Patroklos, for whose sake the terrible fighting
stands now in front of the ships. They are destroying each other;
the Achaians fight in defence over the fallen body
while the others, the Trojans, are rushing to drag the corpse off

175 to windy Ilion, and beyond all glorious Hektor
     rages to haul it away, since the anger within him is urgent
     to cut the head from the soft neck and set it on sharp stakes.
     Up, then, lie here no longer; let shame come into your heart, lest
     Patroklos become sport for the dogs of Troy to worry,
180 your shame, if the body goes from here with defilement upon it.'
     Then in turn Achilleus of the swift feet answered her:
     'Divine Iris, what god sent you to me with a message?'
     Then in turn swift wind-footed Iris spoke to him:
     'Hera sent me, the honoured wife of Zeus; but the son of
185 Kronos, who sits on high, does not know this, nor any other
     immortal, of all those who dwell by the snows of Olympos.'
     Then in answer to her spoke Achilleus of the swift feet:
     'How shall I go into the fighting? They have my armour.
     And my beloved mother told me I must not be armoured,
190 not before with my own eyes I see her come back to me.
     She promised she would bring magnificent arms from Hephaistos.
     Nor do I know of another whose glorious armour I could wear
     unless it were the great shield of Telamonian Aias.
     But he himself wears it, I think, and goes in the foremost
195 of the spear-fight over the body of fallen Patroklos.'
     Then in turn swift wind-footed Iris spoke to him:
     'Yes, we also know well how they hold your glorious armour.
     But go to the ditch, and show yourself as you are to the Trojans,
     if perhaps the Trojans might be frightened, and give way
200 from their attack, and the fighting sons of the Achaians get wind
     again after hard work. There is little breathing space in the fighting.'
     So speaking Iris of the swift feet went away from him;
     but Achilleus, the beloved of Zeus, rose up, and Athene
     swept about his powerful shoulders the fluttering aegis;
205 and she, the divine among goddesses, about his head circled
     a golden cloud, and kindled from it a flame far-shining.
     As when a flare goes up into the high air from a city
     from an island far away, with enemies fighting about it
     who all day long are in the hateful division of Ares
210 fighting from their own city, but as the sun goes down signal
     fires blaze out one after another, so that the glare goes
     pulsing high for men of the neighbouring islands to see it,

in case they might come over in ships to beat off the enemy;
so from the head of Achilleus the blaze shot into the bright air.
He went from the wall and stood by the ditch, nor mixed with the other   215
Achaians, since he followed the close command of his mother.
There he stood, and shouted, and from her place Pallas Athene
gave cry, and drove an endless terror upon the Trojans.
As loud as comes the voice that is screamed out by a trumpet
by murderous attackers who beleaguer a city,   220
so then high and clear went up the voice of Aiakides.
But the Trojans, when they heard the brazen voice of Aiakides,
the heart was shaken in all, and the very floating-maned horses
turned their chariots about, since their hearts saw the coming afflictions.
The charioteers were dumbfounded as they saw the unwearied dangerous   225
fire that played above the head of great-hearted Peleion
blazing, and kindled by the goddess grey-eyed Athene.
Three times across the ditch brilliant Achilleus gave his great cry,
and three times the Trojans and their renowned companions were routed.
There at that time twelve of the best men among them perished   230
upon their own chariots and spears. Meanwhile the Achaians
gladly pulled Patroklos out from under the missiles
and set him upon a litter, and his own companions about him
stood mourning, and along with them swift-footed Achilleus
went, letting fall warm tears as he saw his steadfast companion   235
lying there on a carried litter and torn with the sharp bronze,
the man he had sent off before with horses and chariot
into the fighting; who never again came home to be welcomed.
    Now the lady Hera of the ox eyes drove the unwilling
weariless sun god to sink in the depth of the Ocean,   240
and the sun went down, and the brilliant Achaians gave over
their strong fighting, and the doubtful collision of battle.
    The Trojans on the other side moved from the strong encounter
in their turn, and unyoked their running horses from under the chariots,
and gathered into assembly before taking thought for their supper.   245
They stood on their feet in assembly, nor did any man have the patience
to sit down, but the terror was on them all, seeing that Achilleus
had appeared, after he had stayed so long from the difficult fighting.
First to speak among them was the careful Poulydamas,
Panthoös' son, who alone of them looked before and behind him.   250

He was companion to Hektor, and born on the same night with him,
but he was better in words, the other with the spear far better.
He in kind intention toward all stood forth and addressed them:
'Now take careful thought, dear friends; for I myself urge you
255 to go back into the city and not wait for the divine dawn
in the plain beside the ships. We are too far from the wall now.
While this man was still angry with great Agamemnon,
for all that time the Achaians were easier men to fight with.
For I also used then to be one who was glad to sleep out
260 near their ships, and I hoped to capture the oarswept vessels.
But now I terribly dread the swift-footed son of Peleus.
So violent is the valour in him, he will not be willing
to stay here in the plain, where now Achaians and Trojans
from either side sunder between them the wrath of the war god.
265 With him, the fight will be for the sake of our city and women.
Let us go into the town; believe me; thus it will happen.
For this present, immortal night has stopped the swift-footed
son of Peleus, but if he catches us still in this place
tomorrow, and drives upon us in arms, a man will be well
270 aware of him, be glad to get back into sacred Ilion,
the man who escapes; there will be many Trojans the vultures
and dogs will feed on. But let such a word be out of my hearing!
If all of us will do as I say, though it hurts us to do it,
this night we will hold our strength in the market place, and the great
walls
275 and the gateways, and the long, smooth-planed, close-joined gate timbers
that close to fit them shall defend our city. Then, early
in the morning, under dawn, we shall arm ourselves in our war gear
and take stations along the walls. The worse for him, if he endeavours
to come away from the ships and fight us here for our city.
280 Back he must go to his ships again, when he wears out the strong necks
of his horses, driving them at a gallop everywhere by the city.
His valour will not give him leave to burst in upon us
nor sack our town. Sooner the circling dogs will feed on him.'
    Then looking darkly at him Hektor of the shining helm spoke:
285 'Poulydamas, these things that you argue please me no longer
when you tell us to go back again and be cooped in our city.
Have you not all had your glut of being fenced in our outworks?

There was a time when mortal men would speak of the city
of Priam as a place with much gold and much bronze. But now
the lovely treasures that lay away in our houses have vanished,   290
and many possessions have been sold and gone into Phrygia
and into Maionia the lovely, when great Zeus was angry.
But now, when the son of devious-devising Kronos has given
me the winning of glory by the ships, to pin the Achaians
on the sea, why, fool, no longer show these thoughts to our people.   295
Not one of the Trojans will obey you. I shall not allow it.
Come, then, do as I say and let us all be persuaded.
Now, take your supper by positions along the encampment,
and do not forget your watch, and let every man be wakeful.
And if any Trojan is strongly concerned about his possessions,   300
let him gather them and give them to the people, to use them in common.
It is better for one of us to enjoy them than for the Achaians.
In the morning, under dawn, we shall arm ourselves in our war gear
and waken the bitter god of war by the hollow vessels.
If it is true that brilliant Achilleus is risen beside their   305
ships, then the worse for him if he tries it, since I for my part
will not run from him out of the sorrowful battle, but rather
stand fast, to see if he wins the great glory, or if I can win it.
The war god is impartial. Before now he has killed the killer.'

     So spoke Hektor, and the Trojans thundered to hear him;   310
fools, since Pallas Athene had taken away the wits from them.
They gave their applause to Hektor in his counsel of evil,
but none to Poulydamas, who had spoken good sense before them.
They took their supper along the encampment. Meanwhile the Achaians
mourned all night in lamentation over Patroklos.   315
Peleus' son led the thronging chant of their lamentation,
and laid his manslaughtering hands over the chest of his dear friend
with outbursts of incessant grief. As some great bearded lion
when some man, a deer hunter, has stolen his cubs away from him
out of the close wood; the lion comes back too late, and is anguished,   320
and turns into many valleys quartering after the man's trail
on the chance of finding him, and taken with bitter anger;
so he, groaning heavily, spoke out to the Myrmidons:
'Ah me. It was an empty word I cast forth on that day
when in his halls I tried to comfort the hero Menoitios.   325

I told him I would bring back his son in glory to Opous
with Ilion sacked, and bringing his share of war spoils allotted.
But Zeus does not bring to accomplishment all thoughts in men's minds.
Thus it is destiny for us both to stain the same soil
330   here in Troy; since I shall never come home, and my father,
Peleus the aged rider, will not welcome me in his great house,
nor Thetis my mother, but in this place the earth will receive me.
But seeing that it is I, Patroklos, who follow you underground,
I will not bury you till I bring to this place the armour
335   and the head of Hektor, since he was your great-hearted murderer.
Before your burning pyre I shall behead twelve glorious
children of the Trojans, for my anger over your slaying.
Until then, you shall lie where you are in front of my curved ships
and beside you women of Troy and deep-girdled Dardanian women
340   shall sorrow for you night and day and shed tears for you, those whom
you and I worked hard to capture by force and the long spear
in days when we were storming the rich cities of mortals.'
    So speaking brilliant Achilleus gave orders to his companions
to set a great cauldron across the fire, so that with all speed
345   they could wash away the clotted blood from Patroklos.
They set up over the blaze of the fire a bath-water cauldron
and poured water into it and put logs underneath and kindled them.
The fire worked on the swell of the cauldron, and the water heated.
But when the water had come to a boil in the shining bronze, then
350   they washed the body and anointed it softly with olive oil
and stopped the gashes in his body with stored-up unguents
and laid him on a bed, and shrouded him in a thin sheet
from head to foot, and covered that over with a white mantle.
    Then all night long, gathered about Achilleus of the swift feet,
355   the Myrmidons mourned for Patroklos and lamented over him.
But Zeus spoke to Hera, who was his wife and his sister:
'So you have acted, then, lady Hera of the ox eyes.
You have roused up Achilleus of the swift feet. It must be then
that the flowing-haired Achaians are born of your own generation.'
360   Then the goddess the ox-eyed lady Hera answered him:
'Majesty, son of Kronos, what sort of thing have you spoken?
Even one who is mortal will try to accomplish his purpose
for another, though he be a man and knows not such wisdom as we do.

As for me then, who claim I am highest of all the goddesses,
both ways, since I am eldest born and am called your consort,   365
yours, and you in turn are lord over all the immortals,
how could I not weave sorrows for the men of Troy, when I hate them?'
    Now as these two were saying things like this to each other,
Thetis of the silver feet came to the house of Hephaistos,
imperishable, starry, and shining among the immortals,   370
built in bronze for himself by the god of the dragging footsteps.
She found him sweating as he turned here and there to his bellows
busily, since he was working on twenty tripods
which were to stand against the wall of his strong-founded dwelling.
And he had set golden wheels underneath the base of each one   375
so that of their own motion they could wheel into the immortal
gathering, and return to his house: a wonder to look at.
These were so far finished, but the elaborate ear handles
were not yet on. He was forging these, and beating the chains out.
As he was at work on this in his craftsmanship and his cunning   380
meanwhile the goddess Thetis the silver-footed drew near him.
Charis of the shining veil saw her as she came forward,
she, the lovely goddess the renowned strong-armed one had married.
She came, and caught her hand and called her by name and spoke to her:
'Why is it, Thetis of the light robes, you have come to our house now? 385
We honour you and love you; but you have not come much before this.
But come in with me, so I may put entertainment before you.'
    She spoke, and, shining among divinities, led the way forward
and made Thetis sit down in a chair that was wrought elaborately
and splendid with silver nails, and under it was a footstool.   390
She called to Hephaistos the renowned smith and spoke a word to him:
'Hephaistos, come this way; here is Thetis, who has need of you.'
    Hearing her the renowned smith of the strong arms answered her:
'Then there is a goddess we honour and respect in our house.
She saved me when I suffered much at the time of my great fall   395
through the will of my own brazen-faced mother, who wanted
to hide me, for being lame. Then my soul would have taken much
    suffering
had not Eurynome and Thetis caught me and held me,
Eurynome, daughter of Ocean, whose stream bends back in a circle.
With them I worked nine years as a smith, and wrought many intricate   400

things; pins that bend back, curved clasps, cups, necklaces, working
there in the hollow of the cave, and the stream of Ocean around us
went on forever with its foam and its murmur. No other
among the gods or among mortal men knew about us
405 except Eurynome and Thetis. They knew, since they saved me.
Now she has come into our house; so I must by all means
do everything to give recompense to lovely-haired Thetis
for my life. Therefore set out before her fair entertainment
while I am putting away my bellows and all my instruments.'
410   He spoke, and took the huge blower off from the block of the anvil
limping; and yet his shrunken legs moved lightly beneath him.
He set the bellows away from the fire, and gathered and put away
all the tools with which he worked in a silver strongbox.
Then with a sponge he wiped clean his forehead, and both hands,
415 and his massive neck and hairy chest, and put on a tunic,
and took up a heavy stick in his hand, and went to the doorway
limping. And in support of their master moved his attendants.
These are golden, and in appearance like living young women.
There is intelligence in their hearts, and there is speech in them
420 and strength, and from the immortal gods they have learned how to do
         things.
These stirred nimbly in support of their master, and moving
near to where Thetis sat in her shining chair, Hephaistos
caught her by the hand and called her by name and spoke a word to
         her:
'Why is it, Thetis of the light robes, you have come to our house now?
425 We honour you and love you; but you have not come much before this.
Speak forth what is in your mind. My heart is urgent to do it
if I can, and if it is a thing that can be accomplished.'
    Then in turn Thetis answered him, letting the tears fall:
'Hephaistos, is there among all the goddesses on Olympos
430 one who in her heart has endured so many grim sorrows
as the griefs Zeus, son of Kronos, has given me beyond others?
Of all the other sisters of the sea he gave me to a mortal,
to Peleus, Aiakos' son, and I had to endure mortal marriage
though much against my will. And now he, broken by mournful
435 old age, lies away in his halls. Yet I have other troubles.
For since he has given me a son to bear and to raise up

conspicuous among heroes, and he shot up like a young tree,
I nurtured him, like a tree grown in the pride of the orchard.
I sent him away in the curved ships to the land of Ilion
to fight with the Trojans; but I shall never again receive him   440
won home again to his country and into the house of Peleus.
Yet while I see him live and he looks on the sunlight, he has
sorrows, and though I go to him I can do nothing to help him.
And the girl the sons of the Achaians chose out for his honour
powerful Agamemnon took her away again out of his hands.   445
For her his heart has been wasting in sorrow; but meanwhile the
     Trojans
pinned the Achaians against their grounded ships, and would not
let them win outside, and the elders of the Argives entreated
my son, and named the many glorious gifts they would give him.
But at that time he refused himself to fight the death from them;   450
nevertheless he put his own armour upon Patroklos
and sent him into the fighting, and gave many men to go with him.
All day they fought about the Skaian Gates, and on that day
they would have stormed the city, if only Phoibos Apollo
had not killed the fighting son of Menoitios there in the first ranks   455
after he had wrought much damage, and given the glory to Hektor.
Therefore now I come to your knees; so might you be willing
to give me for my short-lived son a shield and a helmet
and two beautiful greaves fitted with clasps for the ankles
and a corselet. What he had was lost with his steadfast companion   460
when the Trojans killed him. Now my son lies on the ground, heart
     sorrowing.'
     Hearing her the renowned smith of the strong arms answered her:
'Do not fear. Let not these things be a thought in your mind.
And I wish that I could hide him away from death and its sorrow
at that time when his hard fate comes upon him, as surely   465
as there shall be fine armour for him, such as another
man out of many men shall wonder at, when he looks on it.'
     So he spoke, and left her there, and went to his bellows.
He turned these toward the fire and gave them their orders for working.
And the bellows, all twenty of them, blew on the crucibles,   470
from all directions blasting forth wind to blow the flames high
now as he hurried to be at this place and now at another,

[387]

wherever Hephaistos might wish them to blow, and the work went
   forward.
He cast on the fire bronze which is weariless, and tin with it
475 and valuable gold, and silver, and thereafter set forth
upon its standard the great anvil, and gripped in one hand
the ponderous hammer, while in the other he grasped the pincers.
   First of all he forged a shield that was huge and heavy,
elaborating it about, and threw around it a shining
480 triple rim that glittered, and the shield strap was cast of silver.
There were five folds composing the shield itself, and upon it
he elaborated many things in his skill and craftsmanship.
   He made the earth upon it, and the sky, and the sea's water,
and the tireless sun, and the moon waxing into her fullness,
485 and on it all the constellations that festoon the heavens,
the Pleiades and the Hyades and the strength of Orion
and the Bear, whom men give also the name of the Wagon,
who turns about in a fixed place and looks at Orion
and she alone is never plunged in the wash of the Ocean.
490   On it he wrought in all their beauty two cities of mortal
men. And there were marriages in one, and festivals.
They were leading the brides along the city from their maiden chambers
under the flaring of torches, and the loud bride song was arising.
The young men followed the circles of the dance, and among them
495 the flutes and lyres kept up their clamour as in the meantime
the women standing each at the door of her court admired them.
The people were assembled in the market place, where a quarrel
had arisen, and two men were disputing over the blood price
for a man who had been killed. One man promised full restitution
500 in a public statement, but the other refused and would accept nothing.
Both then made for an arbitrator, to have a decision;
and people were speaking up on either side, to help both men.
But the heralds kept the people in hand, as meanwhile the elders
were in session on benches of polished stone in the sacred circle
505 and held in their hands the staves of the heralds who lift their voices.
The two men rushed before these, and took turns speaking their cases,
and between them lay on the ground two talents of gold, to be given
to that judge who in this case spoke the straightest opinion.
   But around the other city were lying two forces of armed men

shining in their war gear. For one side counsel was divided   510
whether to storm and sack, or share between both sides the property
and all the possessions the lovely citadel held hard within it.
But the city's people were not giving way, and armed for an ambush.
Their beloved wives and their little children stood on the rampart
to hold it, and with them the men with age upon them, but meanwhile   515
the others went out. And Ares led them, and Pallas Athene.
These were gold, both, and golden raiment upon them, and they were
beautiful and huge in their armour, being divinities,
and conspicuous from afar, but the people around them were smaller.
These, when they were come to the place that was set for their ambush,   520
in a river, where there was a watering place for all animals,
there they sat down in place shrouding themselves in the bright bronze.
But apart from these were sitting two men to watch for the rest of them
and waiting until they could see the sheep and the shambling cattle,
who appeared presently, and two herdsmen went along with them   525
playing happily on pipes, and took no thought of the treachery.
Those others saw them, and made a rush, and quickly thereafter
cut off on both sides the herds of cattle and the beautiful
flocks of shining sheep, and killed the shepherds upon them.
But the other army, as soon as they heard the uproar arising   530
from the cattle, as they sat in their councils, suddenly mounted
behind their light-foot horses, and went after, and soon overtook them.
These stood their ground and fought a battle by the banks of the river,
and they were making casts at each other with their spears bronze-headed;
and Hate was there with Confusion among them, and Death the   535
    destructive;
she was holding a live man with a new wound, and another
one unhurt, and dragged a dead man by the feet through the carnage.
The clothing upon her shoulders showed strong red with the men's blood.
All closed together like living men and fought with each other
and dragged away from each other the corpses of those who had fallen.   540
    He made upon it a soft field, the pride of the tilled land,
wide and triple-ploughed, with many ploughmen upon it
who wheeled their teams at the turn and drove them in either direction.
And as these making their turn would reach the end-strip of the field,
a man would come up to them at this point and hand them a flagon   545
of honey-sweet wine, and they would turn again to the furrows

in their haste to come again to the end-strip of the deep field.
The earth darkened behind them and looked like earth that has been
　　ploughed
though it was gold. Such was the wonder of the shield's forging.
550　He made on it the precinct of a king, where the labourers
were reaping, with the sharp reaping hooks in their hands. Of the cut
　　swathes
some fell along the lines of reaping, one after another,
while the sheaf-binders caught up others and tied them with bind-ropes.
There were three sheaf-binders who stood by, and behind them
555　were children picking up the cut swathes, and filled their arms with them
and carried and gave them always; and by them the king in silence
and holding his staff stood near the line of the reapers, happily.
And apart and under a tree the heralds made a feast ready
and trimmed a great ox they had slaughtered. Meanwhile the women
560　scattered, for the workmen to eat, abundant white barley.
　　　He made on it a great vineyard heavy with clusters,
lovely and in gold, but the grapes upon it were darkened
and the vines themselves stood out through poles of silver. About them
he made a field-ditch of dark metal, and drove all around this
565　a fence of tin; and there was only one path to the vineyard,
and along it ran the grape-bearers for the vineyard's stripping.
Young girls and young men, in all their light-hearted innocence,
carried the kind, sweet fruit away in their woven baskets,
and in their midst a youth with a singing lyre played charmingly
570　upon it for them, and sang the beautiful song for Linos
in a light voice, and they followed him, and with singing and whistling
and light dance-steps of their feet kept time to the music.
　　　He made upon it a herd of horn-straight oxen. The cattle
were wrought of gold and of tin, and thronged in speed and with lowing
575　out of the dung of the farmyard to a pasturing place by a sounding
river, and beside the moving field of a reed bed.
The herdsmen were of gold who went along with the cattle,
four of them, and nine dogs shifting their feet followed them.
But among the foremost of the cattle two formidable lions
580　had caught hold of a bellowing bull, and he with loud lowings
was dragged away, as the dogs and the young men went in pursuit of him.
But the two lions, breaking open the hide of the great ox,

gulped the black blood and the inward guts, as meanwhile the herdsmen
were in the act of setting and urging the quick dogs on them.
But they, before they could get their teeth in, turned back from the lions,   585
but would come and take their stand very close, and bayed, and kept clear.

And the renowned smith of the strong arms made on it a meadow
large and in a lovely valley for the glimmering sheepflocks,
with dwelling places upon it, and covered shelters, and sheepfolds.

And the renowned smith of the strong arms made elaborate on it   590
a dancing floor, like that which once in the wide spaces of Knosos
Daidalos built for Ariadne of the lovely tresses.
And there were young men on it and young girls, sought for their beauty
with gifts of oxen, dancing, and holding hands at the wrist. These
wore, the maidens long light robes, but the men wore tunics   595
of finespun work and shining softly, touched with olive oil.
And the girls wore fair garlands on their heads, while the young men
carried golden knives that hung from sword-belts of silver.
At whiles on their understanding feet they would run very lightly,
as when a potter crouching makes trial of his wheel, holding   600
it close in his hands, to see if it will run smooth. At another
time they would form rows, and run, rows crossing each other.
And around the lovely chorus of dancers stood a great multitude
happily watching, while among the dancers two acrobats
led the measures of song and dance revolving among them.   605

He made on it the great strength of the Ocean River
which ran around the uttermost rim of the shield's strong structure.

Then after he had wrought this shield, which was huge and heavy,
he wrought for him a corselet brighter than fire in its shining,
and wrought him a helmet, massive and fitting close to his temples,   610
lovely and intricate work, and laid a gold top-ridge along it,
and out of pliable tin wrought him leg-armour. Thereafter
when the renowned smith of the strong arms had finished the armour
he lifted it and laid it before the mother of Achilleus.
And she like a hawk came sweeping down from the snows of Olympos   615
and carried with her the shining armour, the gift of Hephaistos.

Now Dawn the yellow-robed arose from the river of Ocean
to carry her light to men and to immortals. And Thetis
came to the ships and carried with her the gifts of Hephaistos.
She found her beloved son lying in the arms of Patroklos
5   crying shrill, and his companions in their numbers about him
mourned. She, shining among divinities, stood there beside them.
She clung to her son's hand and called him by name and spoke to him:
'My child, now, though we grieve for him, we must let this man lie
dead, in the way he first was killed through the gods' designing.
10 Accept rather from me the glorious arms of Hephaistos,
so splendid, and such as no man has ever worn on his shoulders.'
    The goddess spoke so, and set down the armour on the ground
before Achilleus, and all its elaboration clashed loudly.
Trembling took hold of all the Myrmidons. None had the courage
15 to look straight at it. They were afraid of it. Only Achilleus
looked, and as he looked the anger came harder upon him
and his eyes glittered terribly under his lids, like sunflare.
He was glad, holding in his hands the shining gifts of Hephaistos.
But when he had satisfied his heart with looking at the intricate
20 armour, he spoke to his mother and addressed her in winged words:
'My mother, the god has given me these weapons; they are such
as are the work of immortals. No mortal man could have made them.
Therefore now I shall arm myself in them. Yet I am sadly
afraid, during this time, for the warlike son of Menoitios
25 that flies might get into the wounds beaten by bronze in his body

and breed worms in them, and these make foul the body, seeing
that the life is killed in him, and that all his flesh may be rotted.'
    In turn the goddess Thetis the silver-footed answered him:
'My child, no longer let these things be a care in your mind.
I shall endeavour to drive from him the swarming and fierce things,   30
those flies, which feed upon the bodies of men who have perished;
and although he lie here till a year has gone to fulfilment,
still his body shall be as it was, or firmer than ever.
Go then and summon into assembly the fighting Achaians,
and unsay your anger against Agamemnon, shepherd of the people,   35
and arm at once for the fighting, and put your war strength upon you.'
    She spoke so, and drove the strength of great courage into him;
and meanwhile through the nostrils of Patroklos she distilled
ambrosia and red nectar, so that his flesh might not spoil.
    But he, brilliant Achilleus, walked along by the sea-shore   40
crying his terrible cry, and stirred up the fighting Achaians.
And even those who before had stayed where the ships were assembled,
they who were helmsmen of the ships and handled the steering oar,
they who were stewards among the ships and dispensers of rations,
even these came then to assembly, since now Achilleus   45
had appeared, after staying so long from the sorrowful battle.
And there were two who came limping among them, henchmen of Ares
both, Tydeus' son the staunch in battle, and brilliant Odysseus,
leaning on spears, since they had the pain of their wounds yet upon them,
and came and took their seats in the front rank of those assembled.   50
And last of them came in the lord of men Agamemnon
with a wound on him, seeing that Koön, the son of Antenor,
had stabbed him with the bronze edge of the spear in the strong encounter.
But now, when all the Achaians were in one body together,
Achilleus of the swift feet stood up before them and spoke to them: 55
'Son of Atreus, was this after all the better way for
both, for you and me, that we, for all our hearts' sorrow,
quarrelled together for the sake of a girl in soul-perishing hatred?
I wish Artemis had killed her beside the ships with an arrow
on that day when I destroyed Lyrnessos and took her.   60
For thus not all these too many Achaians would have bitten
the dust, by enemy hands, when I was away in my anger.
This way was better for the Trojans and Hektor; yet I think

the Achaians will too long remember this quarrel between us.
65 Still, we will let all this be a thing of the past, though it hurts us,
and beat down by constraint the anger that rises inside us.
Now I am making an end of my anger. It does not become me
unrelentingly to rage on. Come, then! The more quickly
drive on the flowing-haired Achaians into the fighting,
70 so that I may go up against the Trojans, and find out
if they still wish to sleep out beside the ships. I think rather
they will be glad to rest where they are, whoever among them
gets away with his life from the fury of our spears' onset.'
    He spoke, and the strong-greaved Achaians were pleasured to hear him
75 and how the great-hearted son of Peleus unsaid his anger.
Now among them spoke forth the lord of men Agamemnon
from the place where he was sitting, and did not stand up among them:
'Fighting men and friends, o Danaans, henchmen of Ares:
it is well to listen to the speaker, it is not becoming
80 to break in on him. This will be hard for him, though he be able.
How among the great murmur of people shall anyone listen
or speak either? A man, though he speak very clearly, is baffled.
I shall address the son of Peleus; yet all you other
Argives listen also, and give my word careful attention.
85 This is the word the Achaians have spoken often against me
and found fault with me in it, yet I am not responsible
but Zeus is, and Destiny, and Erinys the mist-walking
who in assembly caught my heart in the savage delusion
on that day I myself stripped from him the prize of Achilleus.
90 Yet what could I do? It is the god who accomplishes all things.
Delusion is the elder daughter of Zeus, the accursed
who deludes all; her feet are delicate and they step not
on the firm earth, but she walks the air above men's heads
and leads them astray. She has entangled others before me.
95 Yes, for once Zeus even was deluded, though men say
he is the highest one of gods and mortals. Yet Hera
who is female deluded even Zeus in her craftiness
on that day when in strong wall-circled Thebe Alkmene
was at her time to bring forth the strength of Herakles. Therefore
100 Zeus spoke forth and made a vow before all the immortals:
    "Hear me, all you gods and all you goddesses: hear me

while I speak forth what the heart within my breast urges.
This day Eileithyia of women's child-pains shall bring forth
a man to the light who, among the men sprung of the generation
of my blood, shall be lord over all those dwelling about him."   105
Then in guileful intention the lady Hera said to him:
"You will be a liar, not put fulfilment on what you have spoken.
Come, then, lord of Olympos, and swear before me a strong oath
that he shall be lord over all those dwelling about him
who this day shall fall between the feet of a woman,   110
that man who is born of the blood of your generation." So Hera
spoke. And Zeus was entirely unaware of her falsehood,
but swore a great oath, and therein lay all his deception.
But Hera in a flash of speed left the horn of Olympos
and rapidly came to Argos of Achaia, where she knew   115
was the mighty wife of Sthenelos, descended of Perseus.
And she was carrying a son, and this was the seventh month for her,
but she brought him sooner into the light, and made him premature,
and stayed the childbirth of Alkmene, and held back the birth pangs.
She went herself and spoke the message to Zeus, son of Kronos: 120
"Father Zeus of the shining bolt, I will tell you a message
for your heart. A great man is born, who will be lord over the Argives,
Eurystheus, son of Sthenelos, of the seed of Perseus,
your generation. It is not unfit that he should rule over
the Argives." She spoke, and the sharp sorrow struck at his deep heart.   125
He caught by the shining hair of her head the goddess Delusion
in the anger of his heart, and swore a strong oath, that never
after this might Delusion, who deludes all, come back
to Olympos and the starry sky. So speaking, he whirled her
about in his hand and slung her out of the starry heaven,   130
and presently she came to men's establishments. But Zeus
would forever grieve over her each time that he saw his dear son
doing some shameful work of the tasks that Eurystheus set him.
So I in my time, when tall Hektor of the shining helm
was forever destroying the Argives against the sterns of their vessels,   135
could not forget Delusion, the way I was first deluded.
But since I was deluded and Zeus took my wits away from me,
I am willing to make all good and give back gifts in abundance.
Rise up, then, to the fighting and rouse the rest of the people.

140 Here am I, to give you all those gifts, as many
as brilliant Odysseus yesterday went to your shelter and promised.
Or if you will, hold back, though you lean hard into the battle,
while my followers take the gifts from my ship and bring them
to you, so you may see what I give to comfort your spirit.'

145   Then in answer to him spoke Achilleus of the swift feet:
'Son of Atreus, most lordly and king of men, Agamemnon,
the gifts are yours to give if you wish, and as it is proper,
or to keep with yourself. But now let us remember our joy in warcraft,
immediately, for it is not fitting to stay here and waste time

150 nor delay, since there is still a big work to be done.
So can a man see once more Achilleus among the front fighters
with the bronze spear wrecking the Trojan battalions. Therefore
let each of you remember this and fight his antagonist.'
    Then in answer to him spoke resourceful Odysseus:

155 'Not that way, good fighter that you are, godlike Achilleus.
Do not drive the sons of the Achaians on Ilion when they are hungry,
to fight against the Trojans, since not short will be the time
of battle, once the massed formations of men have encountered
together, with the god inspiring fury in both sides.

160 Rather tell the men of Achaia here by their swift ships,
to take food and wine, since these make fighting fury and warcraft.
For a man will not have strength to fight his way forward all day
long until the sun goes down if he is starved for food. Even
though in his heart he be very passionate for the battle,

165 yet without his knowing it his limbs will go heavy, and hunger
and thirst will catch up with him and cumber his knees as he moves on.
But when a man has been well filled with wine and with eating
and then does battle all day long against the enemy,
why, then the heart inside him is full of cheer, nor do his limbs

170 get weary, until all are ready to give over the fighting.
Come then, tell your men to scatter and bid them get ready
a meal; and as for the gifts, let the lord of men Agamemnon
bring them to the middle of our assembly so all the Achaians
can see them before their eyes, so your own heart may be pleasured.

175 And let him stand up before the Argives and swear an oath to you
that he never entered into her bed and never lay with her
as is natural for people, my lord, between men and women.

And by this let the spirit in your own heart be made gracious.
After that in his own shelter let him appease you
with a generous meal, so you will lack nothing of what is due you.   180
And you, son of Atreus, after this be more righteous to another
man. For there is no fault when even one who is a king
appeases a man, when the king was the first one to be angry.'
    Then in turn the lord of men Agamemnon answered him:
'Hearing what you have said, son of Laertes, I am pleased with you.   185
Fairly have you gone through everything and explained it.
And all this I am willing to swear to, and my heart urges me,
and I will not be foresworn before the gods. Let Achilleus
stay here the while, though he lean very hard toward the work of the war
        god,
and remain the rest of you all here assembled, until the gifts come   190
back from my shelter and while we cut our oaths of fidelity.
And for you yourself, Odysseus, I give you this errand, this order,
that you choose out excellent young men of all the Achaians
and bring the gifts back here from my ship, all that you promised
yesterday to Achilleus, and bring the women back also.   195
And in the wide host of the Achaians let Talthybios make ready
a boar for me, and dedicate it to Zeus and Helios.'
    Then in answer to him spoke Achilleus of the swift feet:
'Son of Atreus, most lordly and king of men, Agamemnon,
at some other time rather you should busy yourself about these things,   200
when there is some stopping point in the fighting, at some time
when there is not so much fury inside of my heart. But now
as things are they lie there torn whom the son of Priam
Hektor has beaten down, since Zeus was giving him glory,
and then you urge a man to eating. No, but I would now   205
drive forward the sons of the Achaians into the fighting
starving and unfed, and afterwards when the sun sets
make ready a great dinner, when we have paid off our defilement.
But before this, for me at least, neither drink nor food shall
go down my very throat, since my companion has perished   210
and lies inside my shelter torn about with the cutting
bronze, and turned against the forecourt while my companions
mourn about him. Food and drink mean nothing to my heart
but blood does, and slaughter, and the groaning of men in the hard work.'

215   Then in answer to him spoke resourceful Odysseus:
    'Son of Peleus, Achilleus, far greatest of the Achaians,
    you are stronger than I am and greater by not a little
    with the spear, yet I in turn might overpass you in wisdom
    by far, since I was born before you and have learned more things.
220 Therefore let your heart endure to listen to my words.
    When there is battle men have suddenly their fill of it
    when the bronze scatters on the ground the straw in most numbers
    and the harvest is most thin, when Zeus has poised his balance,
    Zeus, who is administrator to men in their fighting.
225 There is no way the Achaians can mourn a dead man by denying
    the belly. Too many fall day by day, one upon another,
    and how could anyone find breathing space from his labour?
    No, but we must harden our hearts and bury the man who
    dies, when we have wept over him on the day, and all those
230 who are left about from the hateful work of war must remember
    food and drink, so that afterwards all the more strongly
    we may fight on forever relentless against our enemies
    with the weariless bronze put on about our bodies. Let one not
    wait longing for any other summons to stir on the people.
235 This summons now shall be an evil on anyone left behind
    by the ships of the Argives. Therefore let us drive on together
    and wake the bitter war god on the Trojans, breakers of horses.'
       He spoke, and went away with the sons of glorious Nestor,
    with Meges, the son of Phyleus, and Meriones, and Thoas,
240 and Lykomedes, the son of Kreion, and Melanippos. These went
    on their way to the shelter of Atreus' son Agamemnon.
    No sooner was the order given than the thing had been done.
    They brought back seven tripods from the shelter, those Agamemnon
    had promised, and twenty shining cauldrons, twelve horses. They brought
       back
245 immediately the seven women the work of whose hands was
    blameless, and the eighth of them was Briseis of the fair cheeks.
    Odysseus weighed out ten full talents of gold and led them
    back, and the young men of the Achaians carried the other gifts.
    They brought these into the midst of assembly, and Agamemnon
250 stood up, and Talthybios in voice like an immortal
    stood beside the shepherd of the people with the boar in his hands.

Atreus' son laid hands upon his work-knife, and drew it
from where it hung ever beside the great sheath of his war sword,
and cut first hairs away from the boar, and lifting his hands up
to Zeus, prayed, while all the Argives stayed fast at their places   255
in silence and in order of station, and listened to their king.
He spoke before them in prayer gazing into the wide sky:
'Let Zeus first be my witness, highest of the gods and greatest,
and Earth, and Helios the Sun, and Furies, who underground
avenge dead men, when any man has sworn to a falsehood,   260
that I have never laid a hand on the girl Briseis
on pretext to go to bed with her, or for any other
reason, but she remained, not singled out, in my shelter.
If any of this is falsely sworn, may the gods give me many
griefs, all that they inflict on those who swear falsely before them.'   265
    So he spoke, and with pitiless bronze he cut the boar's throat.
Talthybios whirled the body about, and threw it in the great reach
of the grey sea, to feed the fishes. Meanwhile Achilleus
stood up among the battle-fond Achaians, and spoke to them:
'Father Zeus, great are the delusions with which you visit men.   270
Without you, the son of Atreus could never have stirred so
the heart inside my breast, nor taken the girl away from me
against my will, and be in helplessness. No, but Zeus somehow
wished that death should befall great numbers of the Achaians.
Go now and take your dinner, so we may draw on the battle.'   275
    So he spoke, and suddenly broke up the assembly.
Now these scattered away each man to his own ship. Meanwhile
the great-hearted Myrmidons disposed of the presents.
They went on their way carrying them to the ship of godlike Achilleus,
and stowed the gifts in the shelters, and let the women be settled,   280
while proud henchmen drove the horses into Achilleus' horse-herd.
    And now, in the likeness of golden Aphrodite, Briseis
when she saw Patroklos lying torn with sharp bronze, folding
him in her arms cried shrilly above him and with her hands tore
at her breasts and her soft throat and her beautiful forehead.   285
The woman like the immortals mourning for him spoke to him:
'Patroklos, far most pleasing to my heart in its sorrows,
I left you here alive when I went away from the shelter,
but now I come back, lord of the people, to find you have fallen.

290 So evil in my life takes over from evil forever.
 The husband on whom my father and honoured mother bestowed me
 I saw before my city lying torn with the sharp bronze,
 and my three brothers, whom a single mother bore with me
 and who were close to me, all went on one day to destruction.
295 And yet you would not let me, when swift Achilleus had cut down
 my husband, and sacked the city of godlike Mynes, you would not
 let me sorrow, but said you would make me godlike Achilleus'
 wedded lawful wife, that you would take me back in the ships
 to Phthia, and formalize my marriage among the Myrmidons.
300 Therefore I weep your death without ceasing. You were kind always.'
   So she spoke, lamenting, and the women sorrowed around her
 grieving openly for Patroklos, but for her own sorrows
 each. But the lords of Achaia were gathered about Achilleus
 beseeching him to eat, but he with a groan denied them:
305 'I beg of you, if any dear companion will listen
 to me, stop urging me to satisfy the heart in me
 with food and drink, since this strong sorrow has come upon me.
 I will hold out till the sun goes down and endure, though it be hard.'
   So he spoke, and caused the rest of the kings to scatter;
310 but the two sons of Atreus stayed with him, and brilliant Odysseus,
 and Nestor, and Idomeneus, and the aged charioteer, Phoinix,
 comforting him close in his sorrow, yet his heart would not
 be comforted, till he went into the jaws of the bleeding battle.
 Remembering Patroklos he sighed much for him, and spoke aloud:
315 'There was a time, ill fated, o dearest of all my companions,
 when you yourself would set the desirable dinner before me
 quickly and expertly, at the time the Achaians were urgent
 to carry sorrowful war on the Trojans, breakers of horses.
 But now you lie here torn before me, and my heart goes starved
320 for meat and drink, though they are here beside me, by reason
 of longing for you. There is nothing worse than this I could suffer,
 not even if I were to hear of the death of my father
 who now, I think, in Phthia somewhere lets fall a soft tear
 for bereavement of such a son, for me, who now in a strange land
325 make war upon the Trojans for the sake of accursed Helen;
 or the death of my dear son, who is raised for my sake in Skyros
 now, if godlike Neoptolemos is still one of the living.

Before now the spirit inside my breast was hopeful
that I alone should die far away from horse-pasturing Argos
here in Troy; I hoped you would win back again to Phthia 330
so that in a fast black ship you could take my son back
from Skyros to Phthia, and show him all my possessions,
my property, my serving men, my great high-roofed house.
For by this time I think that Peleus must altogether
have perished, or still keeps a little scant life in sorrow 335
for the hatefulness of old age and because he waits ever from me
the evil message, for the day he hears I have been killed.'

So he spoke, mourning, and the elders lamented around him
remembering each those he had left behind in his own halls.
The son of Kronos took pity on them as he watched them mourning 340
and immediately spoke in winged words to Athene:
'My child, have you utterly abandoned the man of your choice?
Is there no longer deep concern in your heart for Achilleus?
Now he has sat down before the steep horned ships and is mourning
for his own beloved companion, while all the others 345
have gone to take their dinner, but he is fasting and unfed.
Go then to him and distil nectar inside his chest, and delicate
ambrosia, so the weakness of hunger will not come upon him.'

Speaking so, he stirred Athene, who was eager before this,
and she in the likeness of a wide-winged, thin-crying 350
hawk plummeted from the sky through the bright air. Now the Achaians
were arming at once along the encampment. She dropped the delicate
ambrosia and the nectar inside the breast of Achilleus
softly, so no sad weakness of hunger would come on his knees,
and she herself went back to the close house of her powerful 355
father, while they were scattering out away from the fast ships.
As when in their thickness the snowflakes of Zeus come fluttering
cold beneath the blast of the north wind born in the bright sky,
so now in their thickness the pride of the helms bright shining
were carried out from the ships, and shields massive in the middle 360
and the corselets strongly hollowed and the ash spears were worn forth.
The shining swept to the sky and all earth was laughing about them
under the glitter of bronze and beneath their feet stirred the thunder
of men, within whose midst brilliant Achilleus helmed him.
A clash went from the grinding of his teeth, and his eyes glowed 365

[401]

as if they were the stare of a fire, and the heart inside him
was entered with sorrow beyond endurance. Raging at the Trojans
he put on the gifts of the god, that Hephaistos wrought him with much
    toil.

First he placed along his legs the fair greaves linked with
370 silver fastenings to hold the greaves at the ankles.
Afterward he girt on about his chest the corselet,
and across his shoulders slung the sword with the nails of silver,
a bronze sword, and caught up the great shield, huge and heavy
next, and from it the light glimmered far, as from the moon.
375 And as when from across water a light shines to mariners
from a blazing fire, when the fire is burning high in the mountains
in a desolate steading, as the mariners are carried unwilling
by storm winds over the fish-swarming sea, far away from their loved
    ones;
so the light from the fair elaborate shield of Achilleus
380 shot into the high air. And lifting the helm he set it
massive upon his head, and the helmet crested with horse-hair
shone like a star, the golden fringes were shaken about it
which Hephaistos had driven close along the horn of the helmet.
And brilliant Achilleus tried himself in his armour, to see
385 if it fitted close, and how his glorious limbs ran within it,
and the armour became as wings and upheld the shepherd of the people.
Next he pulled out from its standing place the spear of his father,
huge, heavy, thick, which no one else of all the Achaians
could handle, but Achilleus alone knew how to wield it,
390 the Pelian ash spear which Cheiron had brought to his father
from high on Pelion, to be death for fighters in battle.
Automedon and Alkimos, in charge of the horses,
yoked them, and put the fair breast straps about them, and forced the bits
    home
between their jaws, and pulled the reins back against the compacted
395 chariot seat, and one, Automedon, took up the shining
whip caught close in his hand and vaulted up to the chariot,
while behind him Achilleus helmed for battle took his stance
shining in all his armour like the sun when he crosses above us,
and cried in a terrible voice on the horses of his father:
400 'Xanthos, Balios, Bay and Dapple, famed sons of Podarge,

[402]

take care to bring in another way your charioteer back
to the company of the Danaans, when we give over fighting,
not leave him to lie fallen there, as you did to Patroklos.'

    Then from beneath the yoke the gleam-footed horse answered him,
Xanthos, and as he spoke bowed his head, so that all the mane   405
fell away from the pad and swept the ground by the cross-yoke;
the goddess of the white arms, Hera, had put a voice in him:
'We shall still keep you safe for this time, o hard Achilleus.
And yet the day of your death is near, but it is not we
who are to blame, but a great god and powerful Destiny.   410
For it was not because we were slow, because we were careless,
that the Trojans have taken the armour from the shoulders of Patroklos,
but it was that high god, the child of lovely-haired Leto,
who killed him among the champions and gave the glory to Hektor.
But for us, we two could run with the blast of the west wind   415
who they say is the lightest of all things; yet still for you
there is destiny to be killed in force by a god and a mortal.'

    When he had spoken so the Furies stopped the voice in him,
but deeply disturbed, Achilleus of the swift feet answered him:
'Xanthos, why do you prophesy my death? This is not for you.   420
I myself know well it is destined for me to die here
far from my beloved father and mother. But for all that
I will not stop till the Trojans have had enough of my fighting.'

    He spoke, and shouting held on in the foremost his single-foot horses.

So these now, the Achaians, beside the curved ships were arming
around you, son of Peleus, insatiate of battle,
while on the other side at the break of the plain the Trojans
armed. But Zeus, from the many-folded peak of Olympos,
5 told Themis to summon all the gods into assembly. She went
everywhere, and told them to make their way to Zeus' house.
There was no river who was not there, except only Ocean,
there was not any one of the nymphs who live in the lovely
groves, and the springs of rivers and grass of the meadows, who came not.
10 These all assembling into the house of Zeus cloud gathering
took places among the smooth-stone cloister walks which Hephaistos
had built for Zeus the father by his craftsmanship and contrivance.
   So they were assembled within Zeus' house; and the shaker
of the earth did not fail to hear the goddess, but came up among them
15 from the sea, and sat in the midst of them, and asked Zeus of his counsel:
'Why, lord of the shining bolt, have you called the gods to assembly
once more? Are you deliberating Achaians and Trojans?
For the onset of battle is almost broken to flame between them.'
   In turn Zeus who gathers the clouds spoke to him in answer:
20 'You have seen, shaker of the earth, the counsel within me,
and why I gathered you. I think of these men though they are dying.
Even so, I shall stay here upon the fold of Olympos
sitting still, watching, to pleasure my heart. Meanwhile all you others
go down, wherever you may go among the Achaians and Trojans

and give help to either side, as your own pleasure directs you.   25
For if we leave Achilleus alone to fight with the Trojans
they will not even for a little hold off swift-footed Peleion.
For even before now they would tremble whenever they saw him,
and now, when his heart is grieved and angered for his companion's
death, I fear against destiny he may storm their fortress.'   30
    So spoke the son of Kronos and woke the incessant battle,
and the gods went down to enter the fighting, with purposes opposed.
Hera went to the assembled ships with Pallas Athene
and with Poseidon who embraces the earth, and with generous
Hermes, who within the heart is armed with astute thoughts.   35
Hephaistos went the way of these in the pride of his great strength
limping, and yet his shrunken legs moved lightly beneath him.
But Ares of the shining helm went over to the Trojans,
and with him Phoibos of the unshorn hair, and the lady of arrows
Artemis, and smiling Aphrodite, Leto, and Xanthos.   40
    Now in the time when the gods were still distant from the mortals,
so long the Achaians were winning great glory, since now Achilleus
showed among them, who had stayed too long from the sorrowful
        fighting.
But the Trojans were taken every man in the knees with trembling
and terror, as they looked on the swift-footed son of Peleus   45
shining in all his armour, a man like the murderous war god.
But after the Olympians merged in the men's company
strong Hatred, defender of peoples, burst out, and Athene bellowed
standing now beside the ditch dug at the wall's outside
and now again at the thundering sea's edge gave out her great cry,   50
while on the other side Ares in the likeness of a dark stormcloud
bellowed, now from the peak of the citadel urging the Trojans
sharply on, now running beside the sweet banks of Simoeis.
    So the blessed gods stirring on the opponents drove them
together, and broke out among themselves the weight of their quarrel.   55
From high above the father of gods and men made thunder
terribly, while Poseidon from deep under them shuddered
all the illimitable earth, the sheer heads of the mountains.
And all the feet of Ida with her many waters were shaken
and all her crests, and the city of Troy, the ships of the Achaians.   60
Aïdoneus, lord of the dead below, was in terror

and sprang from his throne and screamed aloud, for fear that above him
he who circles the land, Poseidon, might break the earth open
and the houses of the dead lie open to men and immortals,
65 ghastly and mouldering, so the very gods shudder before them;
such was the crash that sounded as the gods came driving together
in wrath. For now over against the lord Poseidon
Phoibos Apollo took his stand with his feathered arrows,
and against Enyalios the goddess grey-eyed Athene.
70 Against Hera stood the lady of clamour, of the golden distaff,
of the showering arrows, Artemis, sister of the far striker.
Opposite Leto stood the strong one, generous Hermes,
and against Hephaistos stood the great deep-eddying river
who is called Xanthos by the gods, but by mortals Skamandros.
75   Thus gods went on to encounter gods; and meanwhile Achilleus
was straining to plunge into the combat opposite Hektor
Priam's son, since beyond all others his anger was driving him
to glut with his blood Ares the god who fights under the shield's guard.
But it was Aineias whom Apollo defender of people
80 drove straight against Peleion, and inspired vast power within him.
Zeus' son Apollo made his voice like that of Lykaon
Priam's son, and assumed his appearance, and spoke to Aineias:
'Aineias, lord of the Trojans' counsels. Where are those threats gone
which as you drank your wine you made before Troy's kings, solemnly,
85 that you would match your battle strength with Peleian Achilleus?'
    In turn Aineias spoke to him in answer: 'Lykaon
son of Priam, why do you urge me on against my will
to fight in the face of Peleus' son and his too great fury?
Since this will not be the first time I stand up against swift-footed
90 Achilleus, but another time before now he drove me
with the spear from Ida, when he came there after our cattle
the time he sacked Lyrnessos and Pedasos. But Zeus rescued me
when he put strength inside me and made my knees quick. Otherwise
I should have gone down at Achilleus' hands, and those of Athene
95 who goes before him and makes light before him, who then was urging
him on with the brazen spear to destroy Leleges and Trojans.
Thereby it is not for any man to fight with Achilleus.
There is always some one of the gods with him to beat death from him.
Without this, even, his spear wings straight to its mark, nor gives out

until it has gone through a man's body. But if the god only   100
would pull out even the issue of war, he would not so easily
win, not even though he claims to be made all of bronze.'
    In turn the lord the son of Zeus Apollo spoke to him:
'Hero, then make your prayer, you also, to the everlasting
gods, since they say that you yourself are born of Zeus' daughter   105
Aphrodite, but Achilleus was born of a lesser goddess,
Aphrodite being daughter of Zeus, Thetis of the sea's ancient.
Carry your weariless bronze straight against him, let him by no means
turn you back by blustering words and his threats of terror.'
    So speaking, he inspired enormous strength in the shepherd of the   110
        people,
who strode on his way among the champions helmed in the bright bronze,
nor did Hera of the white arms fail to see the son of Anchises
as he went through the thronging men to face the son of Peleus,
and drew the other immortals about her and spoke to them, saying:
'Poseidon and Athene, now take counsel between you   115
and within your hearts as to how these matters shall be accomplished.
Here is Aineias gone helmed in the shining bronze against
Peleus' son, and it was Phoibos Apollo who sent him.
Come then, we must even go down ourselves and turn him
back from here, or else one of us must stand by Achilleus   120
and put enormous strength upon him, and let him not come short
in courage, but let him know that they love him who are the highest
of the immortals, but those who before now fended the fury
of war, as now, from the Trojans are as wind and nothing.
For all of us have come down from Olympos to take our part   125
in this battle, so nothing may be done to him by the Trojans
on this day. Afterwards he shall suffer such things as Destiny
wove with the strand of his birth that day he was born to his mother.
But if Achilleus does not hear all this from gods' voices
he will be afraid, when a god puts out his strength against him   130
in the fighting. It is hard for gods to be shown in their true shape.'
    In turn Poseidon the shaker of the earth answered her:
'Hera, do not be angry without purpose. It does not
become you, since I at least would not have the rest of us gods
encounter in battle, since indeed we are far too strong for them.   135
Let us then go away and sit down together off the path

at a viewing place, and let the men take care of their fighting.
Only if Ares begins to fight, or Phoibos Apollo,
or if they hold Achilleus back and will not let him fight,
140 then at once they will have a quarrel with us on their hands
in open battle. But soon, I think, when they have fought with us
they will get back to Olympos and the throng of the other gods
beaten back by the overmastering strength of our hands.'
     So he spoke, Poseidon of the dark hair, and led the way
145 to the stronghold of godlike Herakles, earth-piled on both sides,
a high place, which the Trojans and Pallas Athene had built him
as a place of escape where he could get away from the Sea Beast
when the charging monster drove him away to the plain from the sea-
     shore.
There Poseidon and the gods who were with him sat down
150 and gathered a breakless wall of cloud to darken their shoulders;
while they of the other side sat down on the brows of the sweet bluffs
around you, lord Apollo, and Ares sacker of cities.
     So they on either side took their places, deliberating
counsels, reluctant on both sides to open the sorrowful
155 attack. But Zeus sitting on high above urged them on.
     But all the plain was filled and shining with bronze of the mortals,
their men and horses, and underneath their feet the earth staggered
as they swept together. Two men far greater than all the others
were coming to encounter, furious to fight with each other,
160 Aineias, the son of Anchises, and brilliant Achilleus.
First of the two Aineias had strode forth in menace, tossing
his head beneath the heavy helm, and he held the stark shield
in front of his chest, and shook the brazen spear. From the other
side the son of Peleus rose like a lion against him,
165 the baleful beast, when men have been straining to kill him, the county
all in the hunt, and he at the first pays them no attention
but goes his way, only when some one of the impetuous young men
has hit him with the spear he whirls, jaws open, over his teeth foam
breaks out, and in the depth of his chest the powerful heart groans;
170 he lashes his own ribs with his tail and the flanks on both sides
as he rouses himself to fury for the fight, eyes glaring,
and hurls himself straight onward on the chance of killing some one
of the men, or else being killed himself in the first onrush.

So the proud heart and fighting fury stirred on Achilleus
to go forward in the face of great-hearted Aineias.   175
Now as these in their advance had come close to each other
first of the two to speak was swift-footed brilliant Achilleus:
'Aineias, why have you stood so far forth from the multitude
against me? Does the desire in your heart drive you to combat
in hope you will be lord of the Trojans, breakers of horses,   180
and of Priam's honour. And yet even if you were to kill me
Priam would not because of that rest such honour on your hand.
He has sons, and he himself is sound, not weakened.
Or have the men of Troy promised you a piece of land, surpassing
all others, fine ploughland and orchard for you to administer   185
if you kill me? But I think that killing will not be easy.
Another time before this, I tell you, you ran from my spear.
Or do you not remember when, apart from your cattle, I caught you
alone, and chased you in the speed of your feet down the hills of Ida
headlong, and that time as you ran you did not turn to look back. 190
Then you got away into Lyrnessos, but I went after you
and stormed that place, with the help of Athene and of Zeus father,
and took the day of liberty away from their women
and led them as spoil, but Zeus and the other gods saved you.
I think they will not save you now, as your expectation   195
tells you they will. No, but I myself urge you to get back
into the multitude, not stand to face me, before you
take some harm. Once a thing has been done, the fool sees it.'
    Then in turn Aineias spoke to him and made his answer:
'Son of Peleus, never hope by words to frighten me   200
as if I were a baby. I myself understand well enough
how to speak in vituperation and how to make insults.
You and I know each other's birth, we both know our parents
since we have heard the lines of their fame from mortal men; only
I have never with my eyes seen your parents, nor have you seen mine. 205
For you, they say you are the issue of blameless Peleus
and that your mother was Thetis of the lovely hair, the sea's lady;
I in turn claim I am the son of great-hearted Anchises
but that my mother was Aphrodite; and that of these parents
one group or the other will have a dear son to mourn for   210
this day. Since I believe we will not in mere words, like children,

meet, and separate and go home again out of the fighting.
Even so, if you wish to learn all this and be certain
of my genealogy: there are plenty of men who know it.
215 First of all Zeus who gathers the clouds had a son, Dardanos
who founded Dardania, since there was yet no sacred Ilion
made a city in the plain to be a centre of peoples,
but they lived yet in the underhills of Ida with all her waters.
Dardanos in turn had a son, the king, Erichthonios,
220 who became the richest of mortal men, and in his possession
were three thousand horses who pastured along the low grasslands,
mares in their pride with their young colts; and with these the North
    Wind
fell in love as they pastured there, and took on upon him
the likeness of a dark-maned stallion, and coupled with them,
225 and the mares conceiving of him bore to him twelve young horses.
Those, when they would play along the grain-giving tilled land
would pass along the tassels of corn and not break the divine yield,
but again, when they played across the sea's wide ridges
they would run the edge of the wave where it breaks on the grey salt
    water.
230 Erichthonios had a son, Tros, who was lord of the Trojans,
and to Tros in turn there were born three sons unfaulted,
Ilos and Assarakos and godlike Ganymedes
who was the loveliest born of the race of mortals, and therefore
the gods caught him away to themselves, to be Zeus' wine-pourer,
235 for the sake of his beauty, so he might be among the immortals.
Ilos in turn was given a son, the blameless Laomedon,
and Laomedon had sons in turn, Tithonos and Priam,
Lampos, Klytios and Hiketaon, scion of Ares;
but Assarakos had Kapys, and Kapys' son was Anchises,
240 and I am Anchises' son, and Priam's is Hektor the brilliant.
Such is the generation and blood I claim to be born from.
Zeus builds up and Zeus diminishes the strength in men,
the way he pleases, since his power is beyond all others'.
But come, let us no longer stand here talking of these things
245 like children, here in the space between the advancing armies.
For there are harsh things enough that could be spoken against us
both, a ship of a hundred locks could not carry the burden.

The tongue of man is a twisty thing, there are plenty of words there
of every kind, the range of words is wide, and their variance.
The sort of thing you say is the thing that will be said to you.   250
But what have you and I to do with the need for squabbling
and hurling insults at each other, as if we were two wives
who when they have fallen upon a heart-perishing quarrel
go out in the street and say abusive things to each other,
much true, and much that is not, and it is their rage that drives them.   255
You will not by talking turn me back from the strain of my warcraft,
not till you have fought to my face with the bronze. Come on then
and let us try each other's strength with the bronze of our spearheads.'
   He spoke, and on the terrible grim shield drove the ponderous
pike, so that the great shield moaned as it took the spearhead.   260
The son of Peleus with his heavy hand held the shield away
from him, in fright, since he thought the far-shadowing spear
of great-hearted Aineias would lightly be driven through it.
Fool, and the heart and spirit in him could not understand
how the glorious gifts of the gods are not easily broken   265
by mortal men, how such gifts will not give way before them.
Nor this time could the ponderous spear of war-wise Aineias
smash the shield, since the gold stayed it, the god's gift. Indeed
he did drive the spear through two folds, but there were three left
still, since the god of the dragging feet had made five folds on it,   270
two of bronze on the outside and on the inside two of tin
and between them the single gold, and in this the ash spear was held fast.
   After him Achilleus let go his spear far shadowing
and struck the shield of Aineias along its perfect circle
at the utter rim where the circle of bronze ran thinnest about it   275
and the oxhide was laid thinnest there. The Pelian ash spear
crashed clean through it there, and the shield cried out as it went through.
Aineias shrank down and held the shield away and above him
in fright, and the spear went over his back and crashed its way
to the ground, and fixed there, after tearing apart two circles   280
of the man-covering shield. But Aineias, free of the long spear,
stood still, and around his eyes gathered the enormous emotion
and fear, that the weapon had fixed so close to him. Now Achilleus
drew his tearing sword and swept in fury upon him
crying a terrible cry, but Aineias now in his hand caught   285

[411]

up a stone, a huge thing which no two men could carry
such as men are now, but by himself he lightly hefted it.
And there Aineias would have hit him with the stone as he swept in,
on helm or shield, which would have fended the bitter death from him,
290 and Peleus' son would have closed with the sword and stripped the life
    from him,
had not the shaker of the earth Poseidon sharply perceived all
and immediately spoken his word out among the immortals:
'Ah me; I am full of sorrow for great-hearted Aineias
who must presently go down to death, overpowered by Achilleus,
295 because he believed the words of Apollo, the far ranging;
poor fool, since Apollo will do nothing to keep grim death from him.
But why does this man, who is guiltless, suffer his sorrows
for no reason, for the sake of others' unhappiness, and always
he gives gifts that please them to the gods who hold the wide heaven.
300 But come, let us ourselves get him away from death, for fear
the son of Kronos may be angered if now Achilleus
kills this man. It is destined that he shall be the survivor,
that the generation of Dardanos shall not die, without seed
obliterated, since Dardanos was dearest to Kronides
305 of all his sons that have been born to him from mortal women.
For Kronos' son has cursed the generation of Priam,
and now the might of Aineias shall be lord over the Trojans,
and his sons' sons, and those who are born of their seed hereafter.'
    In turn the lady of the ox eyes, Hera, answered him:
310 'Shaker of the earth, you yourself must decide in your own heart
about Aineias, whether to rescue him or to let him
go down, for all his strength, before Peleus' son, Achilleus.
For we two, Pallas Athene and I, have taken
numerous oaths and sworn them in the sight of all the immortals
315 never to drive the day of evil away from the Trojans,
not even when all the city of Troy is burned in the ravening
fire, on that day when the warlike sons of the Achaians burn it.'
    When he had heard this, the shaker of the earth Poseidon
went on his way through the confusion of spears and the fighting,
320 and came to where Aineias was, and renowned Achilleus.
There quickly he drifted a mist across the eyes of one fighter,
Achilleus, Peleus' son, and from the shield of Aineias

of the great heart pulled loose the strong bronze-headed ash spear
and laid it down again before the feet of Achilleus;
but Aineias he lifted high from the ground, and slung him through the air   325
so that many ranks of fighting men, many ranks of horses,
were overvaulted by Aineias, hurled by the god's hand.
He landed at the uttermost edge of the tossing battle
where the Kaukonians were arming them for the order of fighting.
And Poseidon, shaker of the earth, came and stood very near him   330
and spoke to him and addressed him in winged words: 'Aineias,
which one of the gods is it who urges you to such madness
that you fight in the face of Peleus' son, against his high courage
though he is both stronger than you and dearer to the immortals?
Give back rather, whenever you find yourself thrown against him,   335
lest beyond your fate you go down into the house of the death god.
But once Achilleus has fulfilled his death and his destiny,
then take courage, and go on, and fight with their foremost,
since there shall be no other Achaian able to kill you.'

He spoke, and left him there, when he had told him all this,   340
and at once scattered the mist away from the eyes of Achilleus
that the gods had sent, and now he looked with his eyes, and saw largely,
and in disgust spoke then to his own great-hearted spirit:
'Can this be? Here is a strange thing I see with my own eyes.
Here is my spear lying on the ground, but I can no longer   345
see the man, whom I was charging in fury to kill him.
Aineias was then one beloved of the immortal
gods. I thought what he said was ineffectual boasting.
Let him go. He will not again have daring to try me
in battle, since even now he was glad to escape my onset.   350
Come! I must urge on the Danaans whose delight is in battle
and go on to face the rest of the Trojans, and see what they can do.'

He spoke, and leapt back into the ranks, and urged each man on:
'No longer stand away from the Trojans, o great Achaians,
but let each one go to face his man, furious to fight him.   355
It is a hard thing for me, for all my great strength, to harry
the flight of men in such numbers or to fight with all of them.
Not Ares, who is a god immortal, not even Athene
could take the edge of such masses of men and fight a way through them.
But what I can do with hands and feet and strength I tell you   360

I will do, and I shall not hang back even a little
but go straight on through their formation, and I think that no man
of the Trojans will be glad when he comes within my spear's range.'
    He spoke, urging them on, but glorious Hektor called out
365 in a great voice to the Trojans, and was minded to face Achilleus:
'Do not be afraid of Peleion, o high-hearted Trojans.
I myself could fight in words against the immortals,
but with the spear it were hard, since they are far stronger than we are.
Even Achilleus will not win achievement of everything
370 he says. Part he will accomplish, but part shall be baulked halfway done.
I am going to stand against him now, though his hands are like flame,
though his hands are like flame, and his heart like the shining of iron.'
    He spoke, urging the Trojans, and they lifted their spears to face them.
Their fury gathered into bulk and their battle cry rose up.
375 But now Phoibos Apollo stood by Hektor and spoke to him:
'Hektor, do not go out all alone to fight with Achilleus,
but wait for him in the multitude and out of the carnage
lest he hit you with the spear or the stroke of the sword from close in.'
    He spoke, and Hektor plunged back into the swarm of the fighting
380 men, in fear, when he heard the voice of the god speaking.
But Achilleus, gathering the fury upon him, sprang on the Trojans
with a ghastly cry, and the first of them he killed was Iphition
the great son of Otrynteus and a lord over numbers of people,
born of a naiad nymph to Otrynteus, sacker of cities,
385 under the snows of Tmolos in the rich countryside of Hydē.
Great Achilleus struck him with the spear as he came in fury,
in the middle of the head, and all the head broke into two pieces.
He fell, thunderously. Great Achilleus vaunted above him:
'Lie there, Otrynteus' son, most terrifying of all men.
390 Here is your death, but your generation was by the lake waters
of Gyge, where is the allotted land of your fathers
by fish-swarming Hyllos and the whirling waters of Hermos.'
    He spoke, vaunting, but darkness shrouded the eyes of the other,
and the running-rims of Achaian chariots cut him to pieces
395 in the van of the onrush. Next, after him, facing Demoleon
lord defender of battle and son of Antenor, Achilleus
stabbed him in the temple through the brazen sides of the helmet,
and the brazen helmet could not hold, but the bronze spearhead

driven on through smashed the bone apart, and the inward
brain was all spattered forth. So he beat him down in his fury.   400
Next he stabbed with a spear-stroke in the back Hippodamas
as he fled away before him and sprang from behind his horses.
He blew his life away, bellowing, as when a bull
bellows as he is dragged for Poseidon, lord of Helike,
and the young men drag him. In such bulls the earth shaker glories.   405
Such was his bellowing as the proud spirit flitted from his bones.
Next he went with the spear after godlike Polydoros,
Priam's son, whom his father would not let go into battle
because he was youngest born of all his sons to him, and also
the most beloved, and in speed of his feet outpassed all the others.   410
But now, in his young thoughtlessness and display of his running
he swept among the champions until thus he destroyed his dear life.
For as he shot by swift-footed brilliant Achilleus hit him
with a spear thrown in the middle of the back where the clasps of the war
    belt
were golden and came together at the joining halves of the corselet.   415
The spearhead held its way straight on and came out by the navel,
and he dropped, moaning, on one knee as the dark mist gathered
about him, and sagged, and caught with his hands at his bowels in front of
    him.
    But now when Hektor saw Polydoros, his own brother,
going limp to the ground and catching his bowels in his hands,   420
the mist closed about his eyes also, he could stand no longer
to turn there at a distance, but went out to face Achilleus
hefting his sharp spear, like a flame. Seeing him Achilleus
balanced his spear in turn, and called out to him, and challenged him:
'Here is the man who beyond all others has troubled my anger,   425
who slaughtered my beloved companion. Let us no longer
shrink away from each other along the edgeworks of battle.'
    He spoke, and looking darkly at brilliant Hektor spoke to him:
'Come nearer, so that sooner you may reach your appointed destruction.'
    But with no fear Hektor of the shining helm answered him: 430
'Son of Peleus, never hope by words to frighten me
as if I were a baby. I myself understand well enough
how to speak in vituperation and how to make insults.
I know that you are great and that I am far weaker than you are.

[415]

435 Still, all this lies upon the knees of the gods; and it may be
    that weaker as I am I might still strip the life from you
    with a cast of the spear, since my weapon too has been sharp before this.'
        He spoke, and balanced the spear and let it fly. But Athene
    blew against it and turned it back from renowned Achilleus
440 with an easy blast. It came back again to glorious Hektor
    and dropped to the ground in front of his feet. Meanwhile Achilleus
    made a furious charge against him, raging to kill him
    with a terrible cry, but Phoibos Apollo caught up Hektor
    easily, since he was a god, and wrapped him in thick mist.
445 Three times swift-footed brilliant Achilleus swept in against him
    with the brazen spear. Three times his stroke went into the deep mist.
    But as a fourth time, like something more than a man, he charged in,
    Achilleus with a terrible cry called in winged words after him:
    'Once again now you escaped death, dog. And yet the evil
450 came near you, but now once more Phoibos Apollo has saved you,
    he to whom you must pray when you go into the thunder of spears
        thrown.
    Yet I may win you, if I encounter you ever hereafter,
    if beside me also there is some god who will help me.
    Now I must chase whoever I can overtake of the others.'
455   He spoke, and with the spear full in the neck stabbed Dryops
    so that he dropped in front of his feet. He left him to lie there
    and with a spear thrown against the knee stopped the charge of Demouchos,
    Philetor's son, a huge man and powerful. After the spearcast
    with an inward plunge of the great sword he took the life from him.
460 Then Achilleus swooping on Dardanos and Laogonos, sons both
    of Bias, dashed them to the ground from behind their horses,
    one with a spearcast, one with a stroke of the sword from close up.
    Now Tros, Alastor's son: he had come up against Achilleus'
    knees, to catch them and be spared and his life given to him
465 if Achilleus might take pity upon his youth and not kill him;
    fool, and did not see there would be no way to persuade him,
    since this was a man with no sweetness in his heart, and not kindly
    but in a strong fury; now Tros with his hands was reaching
    for the knees, bent on supplication, but he stabbed with his sword at the
        liver
470 so that the liver was torn from its place, and from it the black blood

[416]

drenched the fold of his tunic and his eyes were shrouded in darkness
as the life went. Next from close in he thrust at Moulios
with the pike at the ear, so the bronze spearhead pushed through and
    came out
at the other ear. Now he hit Echeklos the son of Agenor
with the hilted sword, hewing against his head in the middle   475
so all the sword was smoking with blood, and over both eyes
closed the red death and the strong destiny. Now Deukalion
was struck in the arm, at a place in the elbow where the tendons
come together. There through the arm Achilleus transfixed him
with the bronze spearhead, and he, arm hanging heavy, waited   480
and looked his death in the face. Achilleus struck with the sword's edge
at his neck, and swept the helmed head far away, and the marrow
gushed from the neckbone, and he went down to the ground at full
    length.
Now he went on after the blameless son of Peires,
Rhigmos, who had come over from Thrace where the soil is rich. This   485
    man
he stabbed in the middle with the spear, and the spear stuck fast in his
    belly.
He dropped from the chariot, but as Areïthoös his henchman
turned the horses away Achilleus stabbed him with the sharp spear
in the back, and thrust him from the chariot. And the horses bolted.
    As inhuman fire sweeps on in fury through the deep angles   490
of a drywood mountain and sets ablaze the depth of the timber
and the blustering wind lashes the flame along, so Achilleus
swept everywhere with his spear like something more than a mortal
harrying them as they died, and the black earth ran blood.
Or as when a man yokes male broad-foreheaded oxen   495
to crush white barley on a strong-laid threshing floor, and rapidly
the barley is stripped beneath the feet of the bellowing oxen,
so before great-hearted Achilleus the single-foot horses
trampled alike dead men and shields, and the axle under
the chariot was all splashed with blood and the rails which encircled   500
the chariot, struck by flying drops from the feet of the horses,
from the running rims of the wheels. The son of Peleus was straining
to win glory, his invincible hands spattered with bloody filth.

BUT when they came to the crossing place of the fair-running
river
of whirling Xanthos, a stream whose father was Zeus the immortal,
there Achilleus split them and chased some back over the flat land
toward the city, where the Achaians themselves had stampeded in terror
5 on the day before, when glorious Hektor was still in his fury.
Along this ground they were streaming in flight; but Hera let fall
a deep mist before them to stay them. Meanwhile the other half
were crowded into the silvery whirls of the deep-running river
and tumbled into it in huge clamour, and the steep-running water
10 sounded, and the banks echoed hugely about them, as they out-crying
tried to swim this way and that, spun about in the eddies.
As before the blast of a fire the locusts escaping
into a river swarm in air, and the fire unwearied
blazes from a sudden start, and the locusts huddle in water;
15 so before Achilleus the murmuring waters of Xanthos
the deep-whirling were filled with confusion of men and of horses.
    But heaven-descended Achilleus left his spear there on the bank
leaning against the tamarisks, and leapt in like some immortal,
with only his sword, but his heart was bent upon evil actions,
20 and he struck in a circle around him. The shameful sound of their groaning
rose as they were struck with the sword, and the water was reddened
with blood. As before a huge-gaping dolphin the other fishes
escaping cram the corners of a deepwater harbour
in fear, for he avidly eats up any he can catch;

so the Trojans along the course of the terrible river   25
shrank under the bluffs. He, when his hands grew weary with killing,
chose out and took twelve young men alive from the river
to be vengeance for the death of Patroklos, the son of Menoitios.
These, bewildered with fear like fawns, he led out of the water
and bound their hands behind them with thongs well cut out of leather,   30
with the very belts they themselves wore on their ingirt tunics,
and gave them to his companions to lead away to the hollow ships,
then himself whirled back, still in a fury to kill men.
    And there he came upon a son of Dardanian Priam
as he escaped from the river, Lykaon, one whom he himself   35
had taken before and led him unwilling from his father's gardens
on a night foray. He with the sharp bronze was cutting young branches
from a fig tree, so that they could make him rails for a chariot,
when an unlooked-for evil thing came upon him, the brilliant
Achilleus, who that time sold him as slave in strong-founded Lemnos   40
carrying him there by ship, and the son of Jason paid for him;
from there a guest and friend who paid a great price redeemed him,
Eëtion of Imbros, and sent him to shining Arisbe;
and from there he fled away and came to the house of his father.
For eleven days he pleasured his heart with friends and family   45
after he got back from Lemnos, but on the twelfth day once again
the god cast him into the hands of Achilleus, who this time
was to send him down unwilling on his way to the death god.
Now as brilliant swift-footed Achilleus saw him and knew him
naked and without helm or shield, and he had no spear left   50
but had thrown all these things on the ground, being weary and
      sweating
with the escape from the river, and his knees were beaten with weariness,
disturbed, Achilleus spoke to his own great-hearted spirit:
'Can this be? Here is a strange thing that my eyes look on.
Now the great-hearted Trojans, even those I have killed already,   55
will stand and rise up again out of the gloom and the darkness
as this man has come back and escaped the day without pity
though he was sold into sacred Lemnos; but the main of the grey sea
could not hold him, though it holds back many who are unwilling.
But come now, he must be given a taste of our spearhead   60
so that I may know inside my heart and make certain

whether he will come back even from there, or the prospering
earth will hold him, she who holds back even the strong man.'
    So he pondered, waiting, and the other in terror came near him
65 in an agony to catch at his knees, and the wish in his heart was
to get away from the evil death and the dark fate. By this
brilliant Achilleus held the long spear uplifted above him
straining to stab, but he under-ran the stroke and caught him
by the knees, bending, and the spear went over his back and stood fast
70 in the ground, for all its desire to tear a man's flesh. Lykaon
with one hand had taken him by the knees in supplication
and with the other held and would not let go of the edged spear
and spoke aloud to him and addressed him in winged words: 'Achilleus,
I am at your knees. Respect my position, have mercy upon me.
75 I am in the place, illustrious, of a suppliant who must be honoured,
for you were the first beside whom I tasted the yield of Demeter
on that day you captured me in the strong-laid garden
and took me away from my father and those near me, and sold me
away into sacred Lemnos, and a hundred oxen I fetched you.
80 My release was ransom three times as great; and this is
the twelfth dawn since I came back to Ilion, after
much suffering. Now again cursed destiny has put me
in your hands; and I think I must be hated by Zeus the father
who has given me once more to you, and my mother bore me
85 to a short life, Laothoë, daughter of aged Altes,
Altes, lord of the Leleges, whose delight is in battle,
and holds headlong Pedasos on the river Satnioeis.
His daughter was given to Priam, who had many wives beside her.
We are two who were born to her. You will have cut the throats
90 of both, since one you beat down in the forefront of the foot-fighters,
Polydoros the godlike, with a cast of the sharp spear. This time
the evil shall be mine in this place, since I do not think
I shall escape your hands, since divinity drove me against them.
Still, put away in your heart this other thing I say to you.
95 Do not kill me. I am not from the same womb as Hektor,
he who killed your powerful and kindly companion.'
    So the glorious son of Priam addressed him, speaking
in supplication, but heard in turn the voice without pity:
'Poor fool, no longer speak to me of ransom, nor argue it.

In the time before Patroklos came to the day of his destiny   100
then it was the way of my heart's choice to be sparing
of the Trojans, and many I took alive and disposed of them.
Now there is not one who can escape death, if the gods send
him against my hands in front of Ilion, not one
of all the Trojans and beyond others the children of Priam.   105
So, friend, you die also. Why all this clamour about it?
Patroklos also is dead, who was better by far than you are.
Do you not see what a man I am, how huge, how splendid
and born of a great father, and the mother who bore me immortal?
Yet even I have also my death and my strong destiny,   110
and there shall be a dawn or an afternoon or a noontime
when some man in the fighting will take the life from me also
either with a spearcast or an arrow flown from the bowstring.'
     So he spoke, and in the other the knees and the inward
heart went slack. He let go of the spear and sat back, spreading   115
wide both hands; but Achilleus drawing his sharp sword struck him
beside the neck at the collar-bone, and the double-edged sword
plunged full length inside. He dropped to the ground, face downward,
and lay at length, and the black blood flowed, and the ground was soaked
     with it.
Achilleus caught him by the foot and slung him into the river   120
to drift, and spoke winged words of vaunting derision over him:
'Lie there now among the fish, who will lick the blood away
from your wound, and care nothing for you, nor will your mother
lay you on the death-bed and mourn over you, but Skamandros
will carry you spinning down to the wide bend of the salt water.   125
And a fish will break a ripple shuddering dark on the water
as he rises to feed upon the shining fat of Lykaon.
Die on, all; till we come to the city of sacred Ilion,
you in flight and I killing you from behind; and there will not
be any rescue for you from your silvery-whirled strong-running   130
river, for all the numbers of bulls you dedicate to it
and drown single-foot horses alive in its eddies. And yet
even so, die all an evil death, till all of you
pay for the death of Patroklos and the slaughter of the Achaians
whom you killed beside the running ships, when I was not with them.'   135
     He spoke, but the anger was rising now in the heart of the river

and he pondered in his heart as to how he could stop the labour
of brilliant Achilleus, and fend destruction away from the Trojans.
And now with the spear far shadowing in his hands Peleus' son
140 was springing, furious to kill him, on Asteropaios
the son of Pelegon; who in turn was born of the wide-running river
Axios, and of Periboia, eldest of the daughters
of Akessamenos, for she lay in love with the deep-whirling river.
Against this man Achilleus rose up, and he came out to face him
145 from the river, holding two spears, for Xanthos had inspired valour
into his heart, in anger for the slaughter of the young men
whom Achilleus had slain beside his waters and taken no pity.
Now as these two in their advance encountered together
first of the two to speak was swift-footed brilliant Achilleus:
150 'What man are you, and whence, who dare stand up to my onset?
Since unhappy are those whose sons match warcraft against me.'
   Then in turn the glorious son of Pelegon answered him:
'High-hearted son of Peleus, why ask of my generation?
I am from Paionia far away, where the soil is generous,
155 and lead the men of Paionia with long spears; and this for me
is the eleventh day since I arrived in Ilion.
For my generation, it is from the broad waters of Axios,
Axios, who floods the land with the loveliest waters.
His son was Pelegon the spear-famed; but men say I am Pelegon's
160 son; now, glorious Achilleus, we shall fight together.'
   So he spoke, challenging, and brilliant Achilleus uplifted
the Pelian ash spear, but the warrior Asteropaios
threw with both spears at the same time, being ambidextrous.
With the one spear he hit the shield but could not altogether
165 break through the shield, since the gold stayed it that the god had given.
With the other spear he struck Achilleus on the right forearm
and grazed it so that the blood gushed out in a dark cloud, and the spear
overpassed him and fixed in the ground, straining to reach his body.
Throwing second Achilleus let fly at Asteropaios
170 with the straight-flying ash spear in a fury to kill him,
but missed his man and hit the high bank, so that the ash spear
was driven half its length and stuck in the bank of the river.
But the son of Peleus, drawing from beside his thigh the sharp sword,
sprang upon him in fury; and Asteropaios could not

with his heavy hand wrench Achilleus' ash spear free of the river-bank.   175
Three times he struggled straining to wrench it clear, and three times
gave over the effort, and now for the fourth time he was bending
over the ash spear of Aiakides, trying to break it,
but before this Achilleus took his life with the sword from close up
for he struck him in the belly next the navel, and all his guts poured   180
out on the ground, and a mist of darkness closed over both eyes
as he gasped life out, and springing upon his chest Achilleus
stripped his armour away and spoke in triumph above him:
'Lie so: it is hard even for those sprung of a river
to fight against the children of Kronos, whose strength is almighty.   185
You said you were of the generation of the wide-running river,
but I claim that I am of the generation of great Zeus.
The man is my father who is lord over many Myrmidons,
Peleus, Aiakos' son, but Zeus was the father of Aiakos.
And as Zeus is stronger than rivers that run to the sea, so   190
the generation of Zeus is made stronger than that of a river.
For here is a great river beside you, if he were able
to help; but it is not possible to fight Zeus, son of Kronos.
Not powerful Acheloios matches his strength against Zeus,
not the enormous strength of Ocean with his deep-running waters,   195
Ocean, from whom all rivers are and the entire sea
and all springs and all deep wells have their waters of him, yet
even Ocean is afraid of the lightning of great Zeus
and the dangerous thunderbolt when it breaks from the sky crashing.'
    So he spoke, and pulled the bronze spear free of the river bluff   200
and left him there, when he had torn the heart of life from him,
sprawled in the sands and drenched in the dark water. And about
Asteropaios the eels and the other fish were busy
tearing him and nibbling the fat that lay by his kidneys.
But Achilleus went on after the Paionians crested with horse-hair   205
who had scattered in fear along the banks of the eddying river
when they had seen their greatest man in the strong encounter
gone down by force under the sword and the hands of Peleïdes.
There he killed Thersilochos and Astypylos and Mydon,
Mnesos and Thrasios, and Ainios and Ophelestes.   210
Now swift Achilleus would have killed even more Paionians
except that the deep-whirling river spoke to him in anger

and in mortal likeness, and the voice rose from the depth of the eddies:
'O Achilleus, your strength is greater, your acts more violent
215 than all men's; since always the very gods are guarding you.
If the son of Kronos has given all Trojans to your destruction,
drive them at least out of me to the plain, and there work your havoc.
For the loveliness of my waters is crammed with corpses, I cannot
find a channel to cast my waters into the bright sea
220 since I am congested with the dead men you kill so brutally.
Let me alone, then; lord of the people, I am confounded.'
    Then in answer to him spoke Achilleus of the swift feet:
'All this, illustrious Skamandros, shall be as you order.
But I will not leave off my killing of the proud Trojans
225 until I have penned them inside their city, and attempted Hektor
strength against strength, until he has killed me or I have killed him.'
    He spoke, and like something more than mortal swept down on the
        Trojans.
And now the deep-whirling river called aloud to Apollo:
'Shame, lord of the silver bow, Zeus' son; you have not kept
230 the counsels of Kronion, who very strongly ordered you
to stand by the Trojans and defend them, until the sun setting
at last goes down and darkens all the generous ploughland.'
    He spoke: and spear-famed Achilleus leapt into the middle water
with a spring from the bluff, but the river in a boiling surge was upon
        him
235 and rose making turbulent all his waters, and pushed off
the many dead men whom Achilleus had killed piled in abundance
in the stream; these, bellowing like a bull, he shoved out
on the dry land, but saved the living in the sweet waters
hiding them under the huge depths of the whirling current.
240 And about Achilleus in his confusion a dangerous wave rose
up, and beat against his shield and pushed it. He could not
brace himself with his feet, but caught with his hands at an elm tree
tall and strong grown, but this uptorn by the roots and tumbling
ripped away the whole cliff and with its dense tangle of roots stopped
245 the run of the lovely current and fallen full length in the water
dammed the very stream. Achilleus uprising out of the whirlpool
made a dash to get to the plain in the speed of his quick feet
in fear, but the great god would not let him be, but rose on him

in a darkening edge of water, minded to stop the labour
of brilliant Achilleus and fend destruction away from the Trojans.   250
The son of Peleus sprang away the length of a spearcast
running with the speed of the black eagle, the marauder
who is at once the strongest of flying things and the swiftest.
In the likeness of this he sped away, on his chest the bronze armour
clashed terribly, and bending away to escape from the river   255
he fled, but the river came streaming after him in huge noise.
And as a man running a channel from a spring of dark water
guides the run of the water among his plants and his gardens
with a mattock in his hand and knocks down the blocks in the channel;
in the rush of the water all the pebbles beneath are torn loose   260
from place, and the water that has been dripping suddenly jets on
in a steep place and goes too fast even for the man who guides it;
so always the crest of the river was overtaking Achilleus
for all his speed of foot, since gods are stronger than mortals.
And every time swift-footed brilliant Achilleus would begin   265
to turn and stand and fight the river, and try to discover
if all the gods who hold the wide heaven were after him, every
time again the enormous wave of the sky-fed river
would strike his shoulders from above. He tried, in his desperation,
to keep a high spring with his feet, but the river was wearing his knees out   270
as it ran fiercely beneath him and cut the ground from under
his feet. Peleïdes groaned aloud, gazing into the wide sky:
'Father Zeus, no god could endure to save me from the river
who am so pitiful. And what then shall become of me?
It is not so much any other Uranian god who has done this   275
but my own mother who beguiled me with falsehoods, who told me
that underneath the battlements of the armoured Trojans
I should be destroyed by the flying shafts of Apollo.
I wish now Hektor had killed me, the greatest man grown in this place.
A brave man would have been the slayer, as the slain was a brave man.   280
But now this is a dismal death I am doomed to be caught in,
trapped in a big river as if I were a boy and a swineherd
swept away by a torrent when he tries to cross in a rainstorm.'
   So he spoke, and Poseidon and Athene swiftly came near him
and stood beside him with their shapes in the likeness of mortals   285
and caught him hand by hand and spoke to him in assurance.

First of them to speak was the shaker of the earth, Poseidon.
'Do not be afraid, son of Peleus, nor be so anxious,
such are we two of the gods who stand beside you to help you,
290 by the consent of Zeus, myself and Pallas Athene.
Thereby it is not your destiny to be killed by the river,
but he shall be presently stopped, and you yourself shall behold it.
  'But we also have close counsel to give you, if you will believe us.
Do not let stay your hands from the collision of battle
295 until you have penned the people of Troy, those who escape you,
inside the famed wall of Ilion. Then when you have taken Hektor's life
go back again to the ships. We grant you the winning of glory.'
    So speaking the two went back again among the immortals,
but Achilleus went on, and the urgency of the gods strongly stirred him,
300 into the plain. But the river filled with an outrush of water
and masses of splendid armour from the young men who had perished
floated there, and their bodies, but against the hard drive of the river
straight on he kept a high spring with his feet, and the river wide running
could not stop him now, since he was given great strength by Athene.
305 But Skamandros did not either abate his fury, but all the more
raged at Peleion, and high uplifting the wave of his waters
gathered it to a crest, and called aloud upon Simoeis:
'Beloved brother, let even the two of us join to hold back
the strength of a man, since presently he will storm the great city
310 of lord Priam. The Trojans cannot stand up to him in battle.
But help me beat him off with all speed, and make full your currents
with water from your springs, and rouse up all of your torrents
and make a big wave rear up and wake the heavy confusion
and sound of timbers and stones, so we can stop this savage man
315 who is now in his strength and rages in fury like the immortals.
For I say that his strength will not be enough for him nor his beauty
nor his arms in their splendour, which somewhere deep down under the
        waters
shall lie folded under the mud; and I will whelm his own body
deep, and pile it over with abundance of sands and rubble
320 numberless, nor shall the Achaians know where to look for
his bones to gather them, such ruin will I pile over him.
And there shall his monument be made, and he will have no need
of any funeral mound to be buried in by the Achaians.'

He spoke, and rose against Achilleus, turbulent, boiling
to a crest, muttering in foam and blood and dead bodies   325
until the purple wave of the river fed from the bright sky
lifted high and caught in its waters the son of Peleus.
But Hera, greatly fearing for Achilleus, cried in a loud voice
lest he be swept away in the huge deep-eddying river,
and at once thereafter appealed to her own dear son, Hephaistos: 330
'Rise up, god of the dragging feet, my child; for we believe
that whirling Xanthos would be fit antagonist for you in battle.
Go now quickly to the help of Achilleus, make shine a great flame
while I raise up and bring in out of the sea a troublesome
storm of the west wind and the whitening south wind, a storm   335
that will burn the heads of the Trojans and burn their armour
carrying the evil flame, while you by the banks of Xanthos
set fire to the trees and throw fire on the river himself, and do not
by any means let him turn you with winning words or revilements.
Do not let your fury be stopped until such time as   340
I lift my voice and cry to you. Then stay your weariless burning.'
   Hera spoke, and Hephaistos set on them an inhuman fire.
First he kindled a fire in the plain and burned the numerous
corpses that lay there in abundance, slain by Achilleus,
and all the plain was parched and the shining water was straitened.   345
As when the north wind of autumn suddenly makes dry
a garden freshly watered and makes glad the man who is tending it,
so the entire flat land was dried up with Hephaistos burning
the dead bodies. Then he turned his flame in its shining
into the river. The elms burned, the willows and tamarisks,   350
the clover burned and the rushes and the galingale, all those
plants that grew in abundance by the lovely stream of the river.
The eels were suffering and the fish in the whirl of the water
who leaped out along the lovely waters in every direction
in affliction under the hot blast of resourceful Hephaistos.   355
The strength of the river was burning away; he gave voice and called out
by name: 'Hephaistos, not one of the gods could stand up against you.
I for one could not fight the flame of a fire like this one.
Leave your attack. Brilliant Achilleus can capture the city
of the Trojans, now, for me. What have I to do with this quarrel?'   360
   He spoke, blazing with fire, and his lovely waters were seething.

And as a cauldron that is propped over a great fire boils up
dancing on its whole circle with dry sticks burning beneath it
as it melts down the fat of swine made tender, so Xanthos'
365 lovely streams were burned with the fire, and the water was boiling
and would not flow along but was stopped under stress of the hot blast
strongly blown by resourceful Hephaistos. And now the river
cried out to Hera in the winged words of strong supplication:
'Hera, why did your son assault me to trouble my waters
370 beyond others'? It is not so much I who have done anything against you
as all the rest of the gods who stand by to help the Trojans.
Now indeed I will leave off, if such is your order,
but let him leave off too, I will swear you a promise
not ever to drive the day of evil away from the Trojans,
375 not even when all the city of Troy is burned in the ravening
fire, on that day when the warlike sons of the Achaians burn it.'
　　Now when the goddess of the white arms, Hera, had heard this
immediately she spoke to her own dear son, Hephaistos:
'Hephaistos, hold, my glorious child, since it is not fitting
380 to batter thus an immortal god for the sake of mortals.'
　　So she spoke, and Hephaistos quenched his inhuman fire. Now
the lovely waters ran their ripples back in the channel.
　　But when the strength of Xanthos had been beaten, these two gods
rested, since Hera, for all she was still angry, restrained them.
385 But upon the other gods descended the wearisome burden
of hatred, and the wind of their fury blew from division,
and they collided with a grand crash, the broad earth echoing
and the huge sky sounded as with trumpets. Zeus heard it
from where he sat on Olympos, and was amused in his deep heart
390 for pleasure, as he watched the gods' collision in conflict.
Thereafter they stood not long apart from each other, for Ares
began it, the shield-stabber, and rose up against Athene
with the brazen spear in his hand, and spoke a word of revilement:
'Why once more, you dogfly, have you stirred up trouble among the gods
395 with the blast of your blown fury, and the pride of your heart driving you?
Do you not remember how you set on Diomedes, Tydeus'
son, to spear me, and yourself laying hold of the far-seen pike
pushed it straight into me and tore my skin in its beauty.
So now I am minded to pay you back for all you have done me.'

He spoke, and stabbed against the ghastly aegis with fluttering   400
straps, which gives way not even before the bolt of Zeus' lightning.
There blood-dripping Ares made his stab with the long spear,
but Athene giving back caught up in her heavy hand a stone
that lay in the plain, black and rugged and huge, one which men
of a former time had set there as boundary mark of the cornfield.   405
With this she hit furious Ares in the neck, and unstrung him.
He spread over seven acres in his fall, and his hair dragged
in the dust, and his armour clashed. But Pallas Athene laughing
stood above him and spoke to him in the winged words of triumph:
'You child; you did not think even this time how much stronger   410
I can claim I am than you, when you match your fury against me.
Therefore you are paying atonement to your mother's furies
since she is angry and wishes you ill, because you abandoned
the Achaians, and have given your aid to the insolent Trojans.'

    She spoke, and turned the shining of her eyes away. But taking   415
Ares by the hand the daughter of Zeus, Aphrodite,
led him away, groaning always, his strength scarce gathered back into him.
But now, as the goddess of the white arms, Hera, noticed her
immediately she spoke to Pallas Athene her winged words:
'For shame now, Atrytone, daughter of Zeus of the aegis.   420
Here again is this dogfly leading murderous Ares
out of the fighting and through the confusion. Quick, go after her!'

    She spoke, and Athene swept in pursuit, heart full of gladness,
and caught up with her and drove a blow at her breasts with her
        ponderous
hand, so that her knees went slack and the heart inside her.   425
Those two both lay sprawled on the generous earth. But Athene
stood above them and spoke to them in the winged words of triumph:
'Now may all who bring their aid to the Trojans be in
such case as these, when they do battle with the armoured Argives,
as daring and as unfortunate, as now Aphrodite   430
came companion in arms to Ares, and faced my fury.
So we should long ago have rested after our fighting
once having utterly stormed the strong-founded city of Ilion.'

    She spoke, and the goddess of the white arms, Hera, smiled on her.
But now the powerful shaker of the earth spoke to Apollo: 435
'Phoibos, why do you and I stand yet apart. It does not suit

when the others have begun, and it were too shameful if without fighting
we go back to the brazen house of Zeus on Olympos.
Begin, you; you are younger born than I; it is not well
440 for me to, since I am elder born than you, and know more.
Young fool, what a mindless heart you have. Can you not even
now remember all the evils we endured here by Ilion,
you and I alone of the gods, when to proud Laomedon
we came down from Zeus and for a year were his servants
445 for a stated hire, and he told us what to do, and to do it?
Then I built a wall for the Trojans about their city,
wide, and very splendid, so none could break into their city,
but you, Phoibos, herded his shambling horn-curved cattle
along the spurs of Ida with all her folds and her forests.
450 But when the changing seasons brought on the time for our labour
to be paid, then headstrong Laomedon violated and made void
all our hire, and sent us away, and sent threats after us.
For he threatened to hobble our feet and to bind our arms,
to carry us away for slaves in the far-lying islands.
455 He was even going to strip with bronze the ears from both of us.
Then you and I took our way back with hearts full of anger
and wrath for our hire which he promised us and would not accomplish it.
Yet to his people you give now your grace, and you will not
try with us to bring destruction on the insolent Trojans
460 evil and complete, with their honoured wives and their children.'
    In turn the lord who strikes from afar, Apollo, answered him:
'Shaker of the earth, you would have me be as one without prudence
if I am to fight even you for the sake of insignificant
mortals, who are as leaves are, and now flourish and grow warm
465 with life, and feed on what the ground gives, but then again
fade away and are dead. Therefore let us with all speed
give up this quarrel and let the mortals fight their own battles.'
    He spoke so and turned away, for he was too modest
to close and fight in strength of hand with his father's brother.
470 But his sister, Artemis of the wild, the lady of wild beasts,
scolded him bitterly and spoke a word of revilement:
'You run from him, striker from afar. You have yielded Poseidon
the victory entire. He can brag, where nothing has happened.
Fool, then why do you wear that bow, which is wind and nothing.

Let me not hear you in the halls of my father boasting   475
ever again, as you did before among the immortals,
that you could match your strength in combat against Poseidon.'
    So she spoke, but Apollo who strikes from afar said nothing
to her; but the august consort of Zeus, full of anger,
scolded the lady of showering arrows in words of revilement: 480
'How have you had the daring, you shameless hussy, to stand up
and face me? It will be hard for you to match your strength with mine
even if you wear a bow, since Zeus has made you a lion
among women, and given you leave to kill any at your pleasure.
Better for you to hunt down the ravening beasts in the mountains   485
and deer of the wilds, than try to fight in strength with your betters.
But if you would learn what fighting is, come on. You will find out
how much stronger I am when you try to match strength against me.'
    She spoke, and caught both of her arms at the wrists in her left hand
and with her right hand stripped away the bow from her shoulders,   490
then with her own bow, smiling, boxed her ears as Artemis
tried to twist away, and the flying arrows were scattered.
She got under and free and fled in tears, as a pigeon
in flight from a hawk wings her way into some rock-hollow
and a cave, since it was not destiny for the hawk to catch her.   495
So she left her archery on the ground, and fled weeping.
Meanwhile the Guide, Argeïphontes, addressed him to Leto:
'Leto, I will not fight with you; since it is a hard thing
to come to blows with the brides of Zeus who gathers the clouds. No,
sooner you may freely speak among the immortal   500
gods, and claim that you were stronger than I, and beat me.'
    So he spoke, but Leto picked up the curved bow and the arrows
which had fallen in the turn of the dust one way and another.
When she had taken up the bow she went back to her daughter.
But the maiden came to the bronze-founded house on Olympos   505
of Zeus, and took her place kneeling at the knees of her father
and the ambrosial veil trembled about her. Her father
Kronides caught her against him, and laughed softly, and questioned
    her:
'Who now of the Uranian gods, dear child, has done such
things to you, rashly, as if you were caught doing something wicked?'   510
    Artemis sweet-garlanded lady of clamours answered him:

[431]

'It was your wife, Hera of the white arms, who hit me,
father, since hatred and fighting have fastened upon the immortals.'
    Now as these two were talking thus to each other, meanwhile
515 Phoibos Apollo went into the sacred city of Ilion,
since he was concerned for the wall of the strong-founded city
lest the Danaans storm it on that day, before they were fated.
The rest of the gods who live forever went back to Olympos,
some in anger and others glorying greatly, and sat down
520 at the side of their father the dark-misted. Meanwhile Achilleus
was destroying alike the Trojans themselves and their single-foot horses;
and as when smoke ascending goes up into the wide sky
from a burning city, with the anger of the gods let loose upon it
which inflicted labour upon them all, and sorrow on many,
525 so Achilleus inflicted labour and sorrow upon the Trojans.
    The aged Priam had taken his place on the god-built bastion,
and looked out and saw gigantic Achilleus, where before him
the Trojans fled in the speed of their confusion, no war strength
left them. He groaned and descended to the ground from the bastion
530 and beside the wall set in motion the glorious guards of the gateway;
'Hold the gates wide open in your hands, so that our people
in their flight can get inside the city, for here is Achilleus
close by, stampeding them, and I think there will be disaster.
But once they are crowded inside the city and get wind again,
535 shut once more the door-leaves closely fitted together.
I am afraid this ruinous man may spring into our stronghold.'
    He spoke, and they spread open the gates and shoved back the door bars
and the gates opening let in daylight. Meanwhile Apollo
sprang out to meet them, so that he could fend off destruction
540 from the Trojans, who, straight for the city and the lift of the rampart
dusty from the plain and throats rugged with thirst, fled
away, and Achilleus followed fiercely with the spear, strong madness
forever holding his heart and violent after his glory.
    There the sons of the Achaians might have taken gate-towering Ilion
545 had not Phoibos Apollo sent on them brilliant Agenor,
a man who was the son of Antenor, blameless and powerful.
He drove courage into his heart, and stood there beside him
in person, so as to beat the dragging death spirits from him,
and leaned there on an oak tree with close mist huddled about him.

When Agenor was aware of Achilleus, sacker of cities,   550
he stood fast, but the heart was a storm in him as he waited,
and deeply disturbed he spoke to his own great-hearted spirit:
'Ah me! if I run away before the strength of Achilleus
in the way that others are stampeded in terror before him,
he will catch me even so and cut my throat like a coward's.   555
But if I leave these men to be driven in flight by Achilleus,
Peleus' son, and run on my feet in another direction
away from the wall to the plain of Ilion, until I come to
the spurs of Ida, and take cover there within the undergrowth,
then in the evening, when I have bathed in the river, and washed off   560
the sweat, I could make my way back again to Ilion.
Yet still, why does the heart within me debate on these things?
This way, he might see me as I started to the plain from the city,
and go in pursuit, and in the speed of his feet overtake me.
Then there will be no way to escape death and the death spirits.   565
He is too strong, his strength is beyond all others'. But then if
I go out in front of the city and stand fast against him,
I think even his body might be torn by the sharp bronze.
There is only one life in him, and people say he is mortal.
It is only that Zeus, the son of Kronos, is granting him glory.'   570
    He spoke, and gathered himself to await Achilleus, and in him
the fighting heart was urgent for the encounter of battle.
But as a leopard emerges out of her timbered cover
to face the man who is hunting her, and takes no terror
in her heart nor thought of flight when she hears them baying against her; 575
and even though one be too quick for her with spear thrust or spear
        thrown
stuck with the shaft though she be she will not give up her fighting
fury, till she has closed with one of them or is overthrown;
so the son of proud Antenor, brilliant Agenor,
was unwilling to run away until he had tested Achilleus,   580
but held the perfect circle of his shield in front of him,
and with the spear aimed at him and cried out in a great voice:
'You must have hoped within your heart, o shining Achilleus,
on this day to storm the city of the proud Trojans.
You fool! There is much hard suffering to be done for its winning,   585
since there are many of us inside, and men who are fighters,

[433]

who will stand before our beloved parents, our wives and our children,
to defend Ilion; but in this place you will find your destiny,
for all you are so headlong and so bold a warrior.'

590   He spoke, and from his heavy hand let fly with the sharp spear
and struck him in the leg below the knee, nor entirely
missed him, and taking the spear the greave of new-wrought tin clattered
horribly, and back from the struck greave the bronze rebounded
without getting through, but the gift of the god defended Achilleus.

595 After him Peleus' son made his spring at godlike Agenor,
but Apollo would no further grant him the winning of glory
but caught Agenor away closing him in a dense mist
and sent him to make his way quietly out of the battle.
Then by deception he kept Peleion away from the people.

600 The striker from afar likened himself in all ways to Agenor
and stood there before his feet, and Achilleus sprang in chase of him
in the speed of his feet; for the time he chased him across the wheat-bearing
plain, turning him toward the deep whirls of the river Skamandros
as he ran a little in front; with the trick Apollo beguiled him

605 so that he hoped ever by running to catch up with him;
all this time the rest of the Trojans fled in a body
gladly into the town, and the city was filled with their swarming.
They dared no longer outside the wall and outside the city
to wait for each other and find out which one had got away

610 and who had died in the battle, so hastily were they streaming
into the city, each man as his knees and feet could rescue him.

BOOK TWENTY-TWO

So along the city the Trojans, who had run like fawns, dried
the sweat off from their bodies and drank and slaked their thirst, leaning
along the magnificent battlements. Meanwhile the Achaians
sloping their shields across their shoulders came close to the rampart.
But his deadly fate held Hektor shackled, so that he stood fast   5
in front of Ilion and the Skaian gates. Now Phoibos
Apollo spoke aloud to Peleion: 'Why, son of Peleus,
do you keep after me in the speed of your feet, being mortal
while I am an immortal god? Even yet you have not
seen that I am a god, but strain after me in your fury.   10
Now hard fighting with the Trojans whom you stampeded means nothing
to you. They are crowded in the city, but you bent away here.
You will never kill me. I am not one who is fated.'
    Deeply vexed Achilleus of the swift feet spoke to him:
'You have balked me, striker from afar, most malignant of all gods,   15
when you turned me here away from the rampart, else many Trojans
would have caught the soil in their teeth before they got back into Ilion.
Now you have robbed me of great glory, and rescued these people
lightly, since you have no retribution to fear hereafter.
Else I would punish you, if only the strength were in me.'   20
    He spoke, and stalked away against the city, with high thoughts
in mind, and in tearing speed, like a racehorse with his chariot
who runs lightly as he pulls the chariot over the flat land.
Such was the action of Achilleus in feet and quick knees.
    The aged Priam was the first of all whose eyes saw him   25

[435]

as he swept across the flat land in full shining, like that star
which comes on in the autumn and whose conspicuous brightness
far outshines the stars that are numbered in the night's darkening,
the star they give the name of Orion's Dog, which is brightest
30 among the stars, and yet is wrought as a sign of evil
and brings on the great fever for unfortunate mortals.
Such was the flare of the bronze that girt his chest in his running.
The old man groaned aloud and with both hands high uplifted
beat his head, and groaned amain, and spoke supplicating
35 his beloved son, who there still in front of the gateway
stood fast in determined fury to fight with Achilleus.
The old man stretching his hands out called pitifully to him:
'Hektor, beloved child, do not wait the attack of this man
alone, away from the others. You might encounter your destiny
40 beaten down by Peleion, since he is far stronger than you are.
A hard man: I wish he were as beloved of the immortal
as loved by me. Soon he would lie dead, and the dogs and the vultures
would eat him, and bitter sorrow so be taken from my heart.
He has made me desolate of my sons, who were brave and many.
45 He killed them, or sold them away among the far-lying islands.
Even now there are two sons, Lykaon and Polydoros,
whom I cannot see among the Trojans pent up in the city,
sons Laothoë a princess among women bore to me.
But if these are alive somewhere in the army, then I can
50 set them free for bronze and gold; it is there inside, since
Altes the aged and renowned gave much with his daughter.
But if they are dead already and gone down to the house of Hades,
it is sorrow to our hearts, who bore them, myself and their mother,
but to the rest of the people a sorrow that will be fleeting
55 beside their sorrow for you, if you go down before Achilleus.
Come then inside the wall, my child, so that you can rescue
the Trojans and the women of Troy, neither win the high glory
for Peleus' son, and yourself be robbed of your very life. Oh, take
pity on me, the unfortunate still alive, still sentient
60 but ill-starred, whom the father, Kronos' son, on the threshold of old age
will blast with hard fate, after I have looked upon evils
and seen my sons destroyed and my daughters dragged away captive
and the chambers of marriage wrecked and the innocent children taken

and dashed to the ground in the hatefulness of war, and the wives
of my sons dragged off by the accursed hands of the Achaians.   65
And myself last of all, my dogs in front of my doorway
will rip me raw, after some man with stroke of the sharp bronze
spear, or with spearcast, has torn the life out of my body;
those dogs I raised in my halls to be at my table, to guard my
gates, who will lap my blood in the savagery of their anger   70
and then lie down in my courts. For a young man all is decorous
when he is cut down in battle and torn with the sharp bronze, and lies
      there
dead, and though dead still all that shows about him is beautiful;
but when an old man is dead and down, and the dogs mutilate
the grey head and the grey beard and the parts that are secret,   75
this, for all sad mortality, is the sight most pitiful.'

So the old man spoke, and in his hands seizing the grey hairs
tore them from his head, but could not move the spirit in Hektor.
And side by side with him his mother in tears was mourning
and laid the fold of her bosom bare and with one hand held out   80
a breast, and wept her tears for him and called to him in winged words:
'Hektor, my child, look upon these and obey, and take pity
on me, if ever I gave you the breast to quiet your sorrow.
Remember all these things, dear child, and from inside the wall
beat off this grim man. Do not go out as champion against him,   85
o hard one; for if he kills you I can no longer
mourn you on the death-bed, sweet branch, o child of my bearing,
nor can your generous wife mourn you, but a big way from us
beside the ships of the Argives the running dogs will feed on you.'

So these two in tears and with much supplication called out   90
to their dear son, but could not move the spirit in Hektor,
but he awaited Achilleus as he came on, gigantic.
But as a snake waits for a man by his hole, in the mountains,
glutted with evil poisons, and the fell venom has got inside him,
and coiled about the hole he stares malignant, so Hektor   95
would not give ground but kept unquenched the fury within him
and sloped his shining shield against the jut of the bastion.
Deeply troubled he spoke to his own great-hearted spirit:
'Ah me! If I go now inside the wall and the gateway,
Poulydamas will be first to put a reproach upon me,   100

since he tried to make me lead the Trojans inside the city
on that accursed night when brilliant Achilleus rose up,
and I would not obey him, but that would have been far better.
Now, since by my own recklessness I have ruined my people,
105 I feel shame before the Trojans and the Trojan women with trailing
robes, that someone who is less of a man than I will say of me:
"Hektor believed in his own strength and ruined his people."
Thus they will speak; and as for me, it would be much better
at that time, to go against Achilleus, and slay him, and come back,
110 or else be killed by him in glory in front of the city.
Or if again I set down my shield massive in the middle
and my ponderous helm, and lean my spear up against the rampart
and go out as I am to meet Achilleus the blameless
and promise to give back Helen, and with her all her possessions,
115 all those things that once in the hollow ships Alexandros
brought back to Troy, and these were the beginning of the quarrel;
to give these to Atreus' sons to take away, and for the Achaians
also to divide up all that is hidden within the city,
and take an oath thereafter for the Trojans in conclave
120 not to hide anything away, but distribute all of it,
as much as the lovely citadel keeps guarded within it;
yet still, why does the heart within me debate on these things?
I might go up to him, and he take no pity upon me
nor respect my position, but kill me naked so, as if I were
125 a woman, once I stripped my armour from me. There is no
way any more from a tree or a rock to talk to him gently
whispering like a young man and a young girl, in the way
a young man and a young maiden whisper together.
Better to bring on the fight with him as soon as it may be.
130 We shall see to which one the Olympian grants the glory.'
    So he pondered, waiting, but Achilleus was closing upon him
in the likeness of the lord of battles, the helm-shining warrior,
and shaking from above his shoulder the dangerous Pelian
ash spear, while the bronze that closed about him was shining
135 like the flare of blazing fire or the sun in its rising.
And the shivers took hold of Hektor when he saw him, and he could no
    longer
stand his ground there, but left the gates behind, and fled, frightened,

and Peleus' son went after him in the confidence of his quick feet.
As when a hawk in the mountains who moves lightest of things flying
makes his effortless swoop for a trembling dove, but she slips away   140
from beneath and flies and he shrill screaming close after her
plunges for her again and again, heart furious to take her;
so Achilleus went straight for him in fury, but Hektor
fled away under the Trojan wall and moved his knees rapidly.
They raced along by the watching point and the windy fig tree   145
always away from under the wall and along the wagon-way
and came to the two sweet-running well springs. There there are double
springs of water that jet up, the springs of whirling Skamandros.
One of these runs hot water and the steam on all sides
of it rises as if from a fire that was burning inside it.   150
But the other in the summer-time runs water that is like hail
or chill snow or ice that forms from water. Beside these
in this place, and close to them, are the washing-hollows
of stone, and magnificent, where the wives of the Trojans and their
   lovely
daughters washed the clothes to shining, in the old days   155
when there was peace, before the coming of the sons of the Achaians.
They ran beside these, one escaping, the other after him.
It was a great man who fled, but far better he who pursued him
rapidly, since here was no festal beast, no ox-hide
they strove for, for these are prizes that are given men for their running.   160
No, they ran for the life of Hektor, breaker of horses.
As when about the turnposts racing single-foot horses
run at full speed, when a great prize is laid up for their winning,
a tripod or a woman, in games for a man's funeral,
so these two swept whirling about the city of Priam   165
in the speed of their feet, while all the gods were looking upon them.
First to speak among them was the father of gods and mortals:
'Ah me, this is a man beloved whom now my eyes watch
being chased around the wall; my heart is mourning for Hektor
who has burned in my honour many thigh pieces of oxen   170
on the peaks of Ida with all her folds, or again on the uttermost
part of the citadel, but now the brilliant Achilleus
drives him in speed of his feet around the city of Priam.
Come then, you immortals, take thought and take counsel, whether

175 to rescue this man or whether to make him, for all his valour,
go down under the hands of Achilleus, the son of Peleus.'
Then in answer the goddess grey-eyed Athene spoke to him:
'Father of the shining bolt, dark misted, what is this you said?
Do you wish to bring back a man who is mortal, one long since
180 doomed by his destiny, from ill-sounding death and release him?
Do it, then; but not all the rest of us gods shall approve you.'
Then Zeus the gatherer of the clouds spoke to her in answer:
'Tritogeneia, dear daughter, do not lose heart; for I say this
not in outright anger, and my meaning toward you is kindly.
185 Act as your purpose would have you do, and hold back no longer.'
So he spoke, and stirred on Athene, who was eager before this,
and she went in a flash of speed down the pinnacles of Olympos.
But swift Achilleus kept unremittingly after Hektor,
chasing him, as a dog in the mountains who has flushed from his covert
190 a deer's fawn follows him through the folding ways and the valleys,
and though the fawn crouched down under a bush and be hidden
he keeps running and noses him out until he comes on him;
so Hektor could not lose himself from swift-footed Peleion.
If ever he made a dash right on for the gates of Dardanos
195 to get quickly under the strong-built bastions, endeavouring
that they from above with missiles thrown might somehow defend him,
each time Achilleus would get in front and force him to turn back
into the plain, and himself kept his flying course next the city.
As in a dream a man is not able to follow one who runs
200 from him, nor can the runner escape, nor the other pursue him,
so he could not run him down in his speed, nor the other get clear.
How then could Hektor have escaped the death spirits, had not
Apollo, for this last and uttermost time, stood by him
close, and driven strength into him, and made his knees light?
205 But brilliant Achilleus kept shaking his head at his own people
and would not let them throw their bitter projectiles at Hektor
for fear the thrower might win the glory, and himself come second.
But when for the fourth time they had come around to the well springs
then the Father balanced his golden scales, and in them
210 he set two fateful portions of death, which lays men prostrate,
one for Achilleus, and one for Hektor, breaker of horses,
and balanced it by the middle; and Hektor's death-day was heavier

and dragged downward toward death, and Phoibos Apollo forsook him.
But the goddess grey-eyed Athene came now to Peleion
and stood close beside him and addressed him in winged words: 'Beloved   215
of Zeus, shining Achilleus, I am hopeful now that you and I
will take back great glory to the ships of the Achaians, after
we have killed Hektor, for all his slakeless fury for battle.
Now there is no way for him to get clear away from us,
not though Apollo who strikes from afar should be willing to undergo   220
much, and wallow before our father Zeus of the aegis.
Stand you here then and get your wind again, while I go
to this man and persuade him to stand up to you in combat.'

So spoke Athene, and he was glad at heart, and obeyed her,
and stopped, and stood leaning on his bronze-barbed ash spear. Meanwhile   225
Athene left him there, and caught up with brilliant Hektor,
and likened herself in form and weariless voice to Deïphobos.
She came now and stood close to him and addressed him in winged words:
'Dear brother, indeed swift-footed Achilleus is using you roughly
and chasing you on swift feet around the city of Priam.   230
Come on, then; let us stand fast against him and beat him back from us.'

Then tall Hektor of the shining helm answered her: 'Deïphobos,
before now you were dearest to me by far of my brothers,
of all those who were sons of Priam and Hekabe, and now
I am minded all the more within my heart to honour you,   235
you who dared for my sake, when your eyes saw me, to come forth
from the fortifications, while the others stand fast inside them.'

Then in turn the goddess grey-eyed Athene answered him:
'My brother, it is true our father and the lady our mother, taking
my knees in turn, and my companions about me, entreated   240
that I stay within, such was the terror upon all of them.
But the heart within me was worn away by hard sorrow for you.
But now let us go straight on and fight hard, let there be no sparing
of our spears, so that we can find out whether Achilleus
will kill us both and carry our bloody war spoils back   245
to the hollow ships, or will himself go down under your spear.'

So Athene spoke and led him on by beguilement.
Now as the two in their advance were come close together,
first of the two to speak was tall helm-glittering Hektor:
'Son of Peleus, I will no longer run from you, as before this   250

I fled three times around the great city of Priam, and dared not
stand to your onfall. But now my spirit in turn has driven me
to stand and face you. I must take you now, or I must be taken.
Come then, shall we swear before the gods? For these are the highest
255 who shall be witnesses and watch over our agreements.
Brutal as you are I will not defile you, if Zeus grants
to me that I can wear you out, and take the life from you.
But after I have stripped your glorious armour, Achilleus,
I will give your corpse back to the Achaians. Do you do likewise.'
260   Then looking darkly at him swift-footed Achilleus answered:
'Hektor, argue me no agreements. I cannot forgive you.
As there are no trustworthy oaths between men and lions,
nor wolves and lambs have spirit that can be brought to agreement
but forever these hold feelings of hate for each other,
265 so there can be no love between you and me, nor shall there be
oaths between us, but one or the other must fall before then
to glut with his blood Ares the god who fights under the shield's
         guard.
Remember every valour of yours, for now the need comes
hardest upon you to be a spearman and a bold warrior.
270 There shall be no more escape for you, but Pallas Athene
will kill you soon by my spear. You will pay in a lump for all those
sorrows of my companions you killed in your spear's fury.'
    So he spoke, and balanced the spear far shadowed, and threw it;
but glorious Hektor kept his eyes on him, and avoided it,
275 for he dropped, watchful, to his knee, and the bronze spear flew over his
         shoulder
and stuck in the ground, but Pallas Athene snatched it, and gave it
back to Achilleus, unseen by Hektor shepherd of the people.
But now Hektor spoke out to the blameless son of Peleus:
'You missed; and it was not, o Achilleus like the immortals,
280 from Zeus that you knew my destiny; but you thought so; or rather
you are someone clever in speech and spoke to swindle me,
to make me afraid of you and forget my valour and war strength.
You will not stick your spear in my back as I run away from you
but drive it into my chest as I storm straight in against you;
285 if the god gives you that; and now look out for my brazen
spear. I wish it might be taken full length in your body.

And indeed the war would be a lighter thing for the Trojans
if you were dead, seeing that you are their greatest affliction.'
    So he spoke, and balanced the spear far shadowed, and threw it,
and struck the middle of Peleïdes' shield, nor missed it,   290
but the spear was driven far back from the shield, and Hektor was angered
because his swift weapon had been loosed from his hand in a vain cast.
He stood discouraged, and had no other ash spear; but lifting
his voice he called aloud on Deïphobos of the pale shield,
and asked him for a long spear, but Deïphobos was not near him.   295
And Hektor knew the truth inside his heart, and spoke aloud:
'No use. Here at last the gods have summoned me deathward.
I thought Deïphobos the hero was here close beside me,
but he is behind the wall and it was Athene cheating me,
and now evil death is close to me, and no longer far away,   300
and there is no way out. So it must long since have been pleasing
to Zeus, and Zeus' son who strikes from afar, this way; though before this
they defended me gladly. But now my death is upon me.
Let me at least not die without a struggle, inglorious,
but do some big thing first, that men to come shall know of it.'   305
    So he spoke, and pulling out the sharp sword that was slung
at the hollow of his side, huge and heavy, and gathering
himself together, he made his swoop, like a high-flown eagle
who launches himself out of the murk of the clouds on the flat land
to catch away a tender lamb or a shivering hare; so   310
Hektor made his swoop, swinging his sharp sword, and Achilleus
charged, the heart within him loaded with savage fury.
In front of his chest the beautiful elaborate great shield
covered him, and with the glittering helm with four horns
he nodded; the lovely golden fringes were shaken about it   315
which Hephaistos had driven close along the horn of the helmet.
And as a star moves among stars in the night's darkening,
Hesper, who is the fairest star who stands in the sky, such
was the shining from the pointed spear Achilleus was shaking
in his right hand with evil intention toward brilliant Hektor.   320
He was eyeing Hektor's splendid body, to see where it might best
give way, but all the rest of the skin was held in the armour,
brazen and splendid, he stripped when he cut down the strength of
    Patroklos;

[443]

yet showed where the collar-bones hold the neck from the shoulders,
325 the throat, where death of the soul comes most swiftly; in this place
brilliant Achilleus drove the spear as he came on in fury,
and clean through the soft part of the neck the spearpoint was driven.
Yet the ash spear heavy with bronze did not sever the windpipe,
so that Hektor could still make exchange of words spoken.
330 But he dropped in the dust, and brilliant Achilleus vaunted above him:
'Hektor, surely you thought as you killed Patroklos you would be
safe, and since I was far away you thought nothing of me,
o fool, for an avenger was left, far greater than he was,
behind him and away by the hollow ships. And it was I;
335 and I have broken your strength; on you the dogs and the vultures
shall feed and foully rip you; the Achaians will bury Patroklos.'
     In his weakness Hektor of the shining helm spoke to him:
'I entreat you, by your life, by your knees, by your parents,
do not let the dogs feed on me by the ships of the Achaians,
340 but take yourself the bronze and gold that are there in abundance,
those gifts that my father and the lady my mother will give you,
and give my body to be taken home again, so that the Trojans
and the wives of the Trojans may give me in death my rite of burning.'
     But looking darkly at him swift-footed Achilleus answered:
345 'No more entreating of me, you dog, by knees or parents.
I wish only that my spirit and fury would drive me
to hack your meat away and eat it raw for the things that
you have done to me. So there is no one who can hold the dogs off
from your head, not if they bring here and set before me ten times
350 and twenty times the ransom, and promise more in addition,
not if Priam son of Dardanos should offer to weigh out
your bulk in gold; not even so shall the lady your mother
who herself bore you lay you on the death-bed and mourn you:
no, but the dogs and the birds will have you all for their feasting.'
355   Then, dying, Hektor of the shining helmet spoke to him:
'I know you well as I look upon you, I know that I could not
persuade you, since indeed in your breast is a heart of iron.
Be careful now; for I might be made into the gods' curse
upon you, on that day when Paris and Phoibos Apollo
360 destroy you in the Skaian gates, for all your valour.'
     He spoke, and as he spoke the end of death closed in upon him,

and the soul fluttering free of the limbs went down into Death's house
mourning her destiny, leaving youth and manhood behind her.
Now though he was a dead man brilliant Achilleus spoke to him:
'Die: and I will take my own death at whatever time   365
Zeus and the rest of the immortals choose to accomplish it.'
   He spoke, and pulled the brazen spear from the body, and laid it
on one side, and stripped away from the shoulders the bloody
armour. And the other sons of the Achaians came running about him,
and gazed upon the stature and on the imposing beauty   370
of Hektor; and none stood beside him who did not stab him;
and thus they would speak one to another, each looking at his neighbour:
'See now, Hektor is much softer to handle than he was
when he set the ships ablaze with the burning firebrand.'
   So as they stood beside him they would speak, and stab him.   375
But now, when he had despoiled the body, swift-footed brilliant
Achilleus stood among the Achaians and addressed them in winged words:
'Friends, who are leaders of the Argives and keep their counsel:
since the gods have granted me the killing of this man
who has done us much damage, such as not all the others together   380
have done, come, let us go in armour about the city
to see if we can find out what purpose is in the Trojans,
whether they will abandon their high city, now that this man
has fallen, or are minded to stay, though Hektor lives no longer.
Yet still, why does the heart within me debate on these things?   385
There is a dead man who lies by the ships, unwept, unburied:
Patroklos: and I will not forget him, never so long as
I remain among the living and my knees have their spring beneath me.
And though the dead forget the dead in the house of Hades,
even there I shall still remember my beloved companion.   390
But now, you young men of the Achaians, let us go back, singing
a victory song, to our hollow ships; and take this with us.
We have won ourselves enormous fame; we have killed the great Hektor
whom the Trojans glorified as if he were a god in their city.'
   He spoke, and now thought of shameful treatment for glorious Hektor. 395
In both of his feet at the back he made holes by the tendons
in the space between ankle and heel, and drew thongs of ox-hide through
    them,
and fastened them to the chariot so as to let the head drag,

and mounted the chariot, and lifted the glorious armour inside it,
400 then whipped the horses to a run, and they winged their way unreluctant.
A cloud of dust rose where Hektor was dragged, his dark hair was falling
about him, and all that head that was once so handsome was tumbled
in the dust; since by this time Zeus had given him over
to his enemies, to be defiled in the land of his fathers.
405 So all his head was dragged in the dust; and now his mother
tore out her hair, and threw the shining veil far from her
and raised a great wail as she looked upon her son; and his father
beloved groaned pitifully, and all his people about him
were taken with wailing and lamentation all through the city.
410 It was most like what would have happened, if all lowering
Ilion had been burning top to bottom in fire.
His people could scarcely keep the old man in his impatience
from storming out of the Dardanian gates; he implored them
all, and wallowed in the muck before them calling on each man
415 and naming him by his name: 'Give way, dear friends,
and let me alone though you care for me, leave me to go out
from the city and make my way to the ships of the Achaians.
I must be suppliant to this man, who is harsh and violent,
and he might have respect for my age and take pity upon it
420 since I am old, and his father also is old, as I am,
Peleus, who begot and reared him to be an affliction
on the Trojans. He has given us most sorrow, beyond all others,
such is the number of my flowering sons he has cut down.
But for all of these I mourn not so much, in spite of my sorrow,
425 as for one, Hektor, and the sharp grief for him will carry me downward
into Death's house. I wish he had died in my arms, for that way
we two, I myself and his mother who bore him unhappy,
might so have glutted ourselves with weeping for him and mourning.'
So he spoke, in tears, and beside him mourned the citizens.
430 But for the women of Troy Hekabe led out the thronging
chant of sorrow: 'Child, I am wretched. What shall my life be
in my sorrows, now you are dead, who by day and in the night
were my glory in the town, and to all of the Trojans
and the women of Troy a blessing throughout their city. They adored you
435 as if you were a god, since in truth you were their high honour
while you lived. Now death and fate have closed in upon you.'

[446]

So she spoke in tears but the wife of Hektor had not yet
heard: for no sure messenger had come to her and told her
how her husband had held his ground there outside the gates;
but she was weaving a web in the inner room of the high house,   440
a red folding robe, and inworking elaborate figures.
She called out through the house to her lovely-haired handmaidens
to set a great cauldron over the fire, so that there would be
hot water for Hektor's bath as he came back out of the fighting;
poor innocent, nor knew how, far from waters for bathing,   445
Pallas Athene had cut him down at the hands of Achilleus.
She heard from the great bastion the noise of mourning and sorrow.
Her limbs spun, and the shuttle dropped from her hand to the ground.
    Then
she called aloud to her lovely-haired handmaidens: 'Come here.
Two of you come with me, so I can see what has happened.   450
I heard the voice of Hektor's honoured mother; within me
my own heart rising beats in my mouth, my limbs under me
are frozen. Surely some evil is near for the children of Priam.
May what I say come never close to my ear; yet dreadfully
I fear that great Achilleus might have cut off bold Hektor   455
alone, away from the city, and be driving him into the flat land,
might put an end to that bitter pride of courage, that always
was on him, since he would never stay back where the men were in
    numbers
but break far out in front, and give way in his fury to no man.'
So she spoke, and ran out of the house like a raving woman   460
with pulsing heart, and her two handmaidens went along with her.
But when she came to the bastion and where the men were gathered
she stopped, staring, on the wall; and she saw him
being dragged in front of the city, and the running horses
dragged him at random toward the hollow ships of the Achaians.   465
The darkness of night misted over the eyes of Andromache.
She fell backward, and gasped the life breath from her, and far off
threw from her head the shining gear that ordered her headdress,
the diadem and the cap, and the holding-band woven together,
and the circlet, which Aphrodite the golden once had given her   470
on that day when Hektor of the shining helmet led her forth
from the house of Eëtion, and gave numberless gifts to win her.

And about her stood thronging her husband's sisters and the wives of his
    brothers
and these, in her despair for death, held her up among them.

475 But she, when she breathed again and the life was gathered back into her,
lifted her voice among the women of Troy in mourning:
'Hektor, I grieve for you. You and I were born to a single
destiny, you in Troy in the house of Priam, and I
in Thebe, underneath the timbered mountain of Plakos

480 in the house of Eëtion, who cared for me when I was little,
ill-fated he, I ill-starred. I wish he had never begotten me.
Now you go down to the house of Death in the secret places
of the earth, and left me here behind in the sorrow of mourning,
a widow in your house, and the boy is only a baby

485 who was born to you and me, the unfortunate. You cannot help him,
Hektor, any more, since you are dead. Nor can he help you.
Though he escape the attack of the Achaians with all its sorrows,
yet all his days for your sake there will be hard work for him
and sorrows, for others will take his lands away from him. The day

490 of bereavement leaves a child with no agemates to befriend him.
He bows his head before every man, his cheeks are bewept, he
goes, needy, a boy among his father's companions,
and tugs at this man by the mantle, that man by the tunic,
and they pity him, and one gives him a tiny drink from a goblet,

495 enough to moisten his lips, not enough to moisten his palate.
But one whose parents are living beats him out of the banquet
hitting him with his fists and in words also abuses him:
"Get out, you! Your father is not dining among us."
And the boy goes away in tears to his widowed mother,

500 Astyanax, who in days before on the knees of his father
would eat only the marrow or the flesh of sheep that was fattest.
And when sleep would come upon him and he was done with his playing,
he would go to sleep in a bed, in the arms of his nurse, in a soft
bed, with his heart given all its fill of luxury.

505 Now, with his dear father gone, he has much to suffer:
he, whom the Trojans have called Astyanax, lord of the city,
since it was you alone who defended the gates and the long walls.
But now, beside the curving ships, far away from your parents,
the writhing worms will feed, when the dogs have had enough of you,

on your naked corpse, though in your house there is clothing laid up   510
that is fine-textured and pleasant, wrought by the hands of women.
But all of these I will burn up in the fire's blazing,
no use to you, since you will never be laid away in them;
but in your honour, from the men of Troy and the Trojan women.'

So she spoke, in tears; and the women joined in her mourning.   515

So they were mourning through the city. Meanwhile, the Achaians,
after they had made their way back to their ships and the Hellespont,
scattered, the rest of them, each man to his own ship. Except
Achilleus would not allow the Myrmidons to be scattered,
5 but called out to his companions whose delight was in battle:
'Myrmidons, you of the fast horses, my steadfast companions,
we must not yet slip free of the chariots our single-foot horses,
but with these very horses and chariots we must drive close up
to Patroklos and mourn him, since such is the privilege of the perished.
10 Then, when we have taken full satisfaction from the sorrowful
dirge, we shall set our horses free, and all of us eat here.'
 He spoke, and all of them assembled moaned, and Achilleus led them.
Three times, mourning, they drove their horses with flowing manes about
the body, and among them Thetis stirred the passion for weeping.
15 The sands were wet, and the armour of men was wet with their tears. Such
was their longing after Patroklos, who drove men to thoughts of terror.
Peleus' son led the thronging chant of their lamentation,
and laid his manslaughtering hands over the chest of his dear friend:
'Good-bye, Patroklos. I hail you even in the house of the death god.
20 All that I promised you in time past I am accomplishing,
that I would drag Hektor here and give him to the dogs to feed on
raw, and before your burning pyre to behead twelve glorious
children of the Trojans for my anger over your slaying.'
 He spoke, and thought of shameful treatment for glorious Hektor.

He laid him on his face in the dust by the bier of Menoitios'   25
son. Meanwhile the others took off each man his glittering
brazen armour, and all unyoked their proud neighing horses
and sat down in their thousands beside the ship of swift-footed
Aiakides, who set the funeral feast in abundance
before them; and many shining oxen were slaughtered with the stroke   30
of the iron, and many sheep and bleating goats and numerous
swine with shining teeth and the fat abundant upon them
were singed and stretched out across the flame of Hephaistos.
The blood ran and was caught in cups all around the dead man.

    But now the kings of the Achaians brought the swift-footed   35
lord, the son of Peleus, to great Agamemnon, hardly
persuading him, since his heart was still angered for his companion.
When these had made their way to the shelter of Agamemnon
straightway they gave orders to the heralds, the clear crying,
to set a great cauldron over the fire, if so they might persuade   40
the son of Peleus to wash away the filth of the bloodstains,
but he denied them stubbornly and swore an oath on it:
'No, before Zeus, who is greatest of gods and the highest,
there is no right in letting water come near my head, until
I have laid Patroklos on the burning pyre, and heaped the mound over   45
    him,
and cut my hair for him, since there will come no second sorrow
like this to my heart again while I am still one of the living.
Then let us now give way to the gloomy feast; and with the dawn
cause your people to rise, o lord of men Agamemnon,
and bring in timber and lay it by, with all that is fitting   50
for the dead man to have when he goes down under the gloom and the
    darkness,
so that with the more speed the unwearying fire may burn him
away from our eyes, and the people turn back to that which they must do.'

    So he spoke, and they listened well to him and obeyed him,
and in speed and haste they got the dinner ready, and each man   55
feasted, nor was any men's hunger denied a fair portion.
But when they had put aside their desire for eating and drinking,
they went away to sleep, each man into his own shelter,
but along the beach of the thunderous sea the son of Peleus
lay down, groaning heavily, among the Myrmidon numbers   60

in a clear place where the waves washed over the beach; and at that time
sleep caught him and was drifted sweetly about him, washing
the sorrows out of his mind, for his shining limbs were grown weary
indeed, from running in chase of Hektor toward windy Ilion;
65 and there appeared to him the ghost of unhappy Patroklos
all in his likeness 'for stature, and the lovely eyes, and voice,
and wore such clothing as Patroklos had worn on his body.
The ghost came and stood over his head and spoke a word to him:
'You sleep, Achilleus; you have forgotten me; but you were not
70 careless of me when I lived, but only in death. Bury me
as quickly as may be, let me pass through the gates of Hades.
The souls, the images of dead men, hold me at a distance,
and will not let me cross the river and mingle among them,
but I wander as I am by Hades' house of the wide gates.
75 And I call upon you in sorrow, give me your hand; no longer
shall I come back from death, once you give me my rite of burning.
No longer shall you and I, alive, sit apart from our other
beloved companions and make our plans, since the bitter destiny
that was given me when I was born has opened its jaws to take me.
80 And you, Achilleus like the gods, have your own destiny;
to be killed under the wall of the prospering Trojans. There is one
more thing I will say, and ask of you, if you will obey me:
do not have my bones laid apart from yours, Achilleus,
but with them, just as we grew up together in your house,
85 when Menoitios brought me there from Opous, when I was little,
and into your house, by reason of a baneful manslaying,
on that day when I killed the son of Amphidamas. I was
a child only, nor intended it, but was angered over a dice game.
There the rider Peleus took me into his own house,
90 and brought me carefully up, and named me to be your henchman.
Therefore, let one single vessel, the golden two-handled
urn the lady your mother gave you, hold both our ashes.'
    Then in answer to him spoke swift-footed Achilleus:
'How is it, o hallowed head of my brother, you have come back to me
95 here, and tell me all these several things? Yet surely
I am accomplishing all, and I shall do as you tell me.
But stand closer to me, and let us, if only for a little,
embrace, and take full satisfaction from the dirge of sorrow.'

So he spoke, and with his own arms reached for him, but could not
take him, but the spirit went underground, like vapour,   100
with a thin cry, and Achilleus started awake, staring,
and drove his hands together, and spoke, and his words were sorrowful:
'Oh, wonder! Even in the house of Hades there is left something,
a soul and an image, but there is no real heart of life in it.
For all night long the phantom of unhappy Patroklos   105
stood over me in lamentation and mourning, and the likeness
to him was wonderful, and it told me each thing I should do.'
  So he spoke, and stirred in all of them the passion of mourning,
and Dawn of the rose fingers showed on them as still they mourned
about the forlorn body. Now powerful Agamemnon   110
gave order for men and mules to assemble from all the shelters
and bring in timber, and a great man led them in motion,
Meriones, the henchman of courtly Idomeneus. These then
went out and in their hands carried axes to cut wood
and ropes firmly woven, and their mules went on ahead of them.   115
They went many ways, uphill, downhill, sidehill and slantwise;
but when they came to the spurs of Ida with all her well springs,
they set to hewing with the thin edge of bronze and leaning
their weight to the strokes on towering-leafed oak trees that toppled
with huge crashing; then the Achaians splitting the timbers   120
fastened them to the mules and these with their feet tore up
the ground as they pulled through the dense undergrowth to the flat
      land.
All the woodcutters carried logs themselves; such was the order
of Meriones, the henchman of courtly Idomeneus. These then
threw down their burdens in order along the beach, where Achilleus   125
had chosen place for a huge grave mound, for himself and Patroklos.
  Then when on all sides they had thrown down abundance of timber,
they sat down where they were, assembled. And now Achilleus
gave order at once to the Myrmidons, whose delight was in battle,
to belt themselves in bronze and each man to yoke his horses   130
to the chariot. And they rose up and got into their armour
and stepped up, charioteer and sideman, into the chariots
with the horsemen in front, and behind them came on a cloud of
      foot-soldiers
by thousands; and in the midst his companions carried Patroklos.

135 They covered all the corpse under the locks of their hair, which they
cut off
and dropped on him, and behind them brilliant Achilleus held the head
sorrowing, for this was his true friend he escorted toward Hades.
    When these had come to the place Achilleus had spoken of to them
they laid him down, and quickly piled up abundant timber.
140 And now brilliant swift-footed Achilleus remembered one more thing.
He stood apart from the pyre and cut off a lock of fair hair
which he had grown long to give to the river Spercheios, and gazing
in deep distress out over the wine-blue water, he spoke forth:
'Spercheios, it was in vain that Peleus my father vowed to you
145 that there, when I had won home to the beloved land of my fathers,
I would cut my hair for you and make you a grand and holy
sacrifice of fifty rams consecrate to the waters
of your springs, where is your holy ground and your smoking altar.
So the old man vowed, but you did not accomplish his purpose.
150 Now, since I do not return to the beloved land of my fathers,
I would give my hair into the keeping of the hero Patroklos.'
    He spoke, and laid his hair in the hands of his beloved
companion, and stirred in all of them the passion of mourning.
And now the light of the sun would have set on their lamentation
155 had not Achilleus soon stood by Agamemnon and spoken:
'Son of Atreus, beyond others the people of the Achaians
will obey your words. There can be enough, even in mourning.
Now cause them to scatter from the fire and bid them make ready
their dinner; and we, who are most nearly concerned with the dead man,
160 shall do this work; except only let the leaders stay near us.'
    Then the lord of men, Agamemnon, when he had heard this,
at once caused the people to disperse among the balanced ships,
but the close mourners stayed by the place and piled up the timber,
and built a pyre a hundred feet long this way and that way,
165 and on the peak of the pyre they laid the body, sorrowful
at heart; and in front of it skinned and set in order numbers
of fat sheep and shambling horn-curved cattle; and from all
great-hearted Achilleus took the fat and wrapped the corpse in it
from head to foot, and piled up the skinned bodies about it.
170 Then he set beside him two-handled jars of oil and honey
leaning them against the bier, and drove four horses with strong necks

swiftly aloft the pyre with loud lamentation. And there were
nine dogs of the table that had belonged to the lord Patroklos.
Of these he cut the throats of two, and set them on the pyre;
and so also killed twelve noble sons of the great-hearted Trojans   175
with the stroke of bronze, and evil were the thoughts in his heart against
    them,
and let loose the iron fury of the fire to feed on them.
Then he groaned, and called by name on his beloved companion:
'Good-bye, Patroklos. I hail you even in the house of the death god
For all that I promised you in time past I am accomplishing.   180
Here are twelve noble sons of the great-hearted Trojans
whom the fire feeds on, all, as it feeds on you. But I will not
give Hektor, Priam's son, to the fire, but the dogs, to feast on.'
    So he spoke his threat. But the dogs did not deal with Hektor,
for Aphrodite, daughter of Zeus, drove the dogs back from him   185
by day and night, and anointed him with rosy immortal
oil, so Achilleus, when he dragged him about, might not tear him.
And Phoibos Apollo brought down a darkening mist about him
from the sky to the plain, and covered with it all the space that was taken
by the dead man, to keep the force of the sun from coming   190
first, and wither his body away by limbs and sinews.
    But the pyre of dead Patroklos would not light. Then swift-footed
brilliant Achilleus thought of one more thing that he must do.
He stood apart from the pyre and made his prayer to the two winds
Boreas and Zephyros, north wind and west, and promised them splendid   195
offerings, and much outpouring from a golden goblet entreated them
to come, so that the bodies might with best speed burn in the fire
and the timber burst into flame. And Iris, hearing his prayer,
went swiftly as messenger to the winds for him. Now the winds
assembled within the house of storm-blowing Zephyros   200
were taking part in a feast, and Iris paused in her running
and stood on the stone doorsill; but they, when their eyes saw her,
sprang to their feet, and each one asked her to sit beside him.
But she refused to be seated and spoke her word to them: 'I must not
sit down. I am going back to the running waters of Ocean   205
and the Aithiopians' land, where they are making grand sacrifice
to the immortals; there I, too, shall partake of the sacraments.
But Achilleus' prayer is that Boreas and blustering Zephyros

may come to him, and he promises them splendid offerings,
210 so that you may set ablaze the funeral pyre, whereon lies
Patroklos, with all Achaians mourning about him.'
　　She spoke so, and went away, and they with immortal
clamour rose up, and swept the clouds in confusion before them.
They came with a sudden blast upon the sea, and the waves rose
215 under the whistling wind. They came to the generous Troad
and hit the pyre, and a huge inhuman blaze rose, roaring.
Nightlong they piled the flames on the funeral pyre together
and blew with a screaming blast, and nightlong swift-footed Achilleus
from a golden mixing-bowl, with a two-handled goblet in his hand,
220 drew the wine and poured it on the ground and drenched the ground
　　　with it,
and called upon the soul of unhappy Patroklos. And as
a father mourns as he burns the bones of a son, who was married
only now, and died to grieve his unhappy parents,
so Achilleus was mourning as he burned his companion's
225 bones, and dragged himself by the fire in close lamentation.
　　At that time when the dawn star passes across earth, harbinger
of light, and after him dawn of the saffron mantle is scattered
across the sea, the fire died down and the flames were over.
The winds took their way back toward home again, crossing
230 the Thracian water, and it boiled with a moaning swell as they crossed it.
The son of Peleus turned aside and away from the burning
and lay down exhausted, and sweet sleep rose upon him. But now
they who were with the son of Atreus assembled together
and the sound and murmur of their oncoming wakened Achilleus,
235 who straightened himself and sat upright and spoke a word to him:
'Son of Atreus, and you other greatest of all the Achaians,
first put out with gleaming wine the pyre that is burning,
all that still has on it the fury of fire; and afterwards
we shall gather up the bones of Patroklos, the son of Menoitios,
240 which we shall easily tell apart, since they are conspicuous
where he lay in the middle of the pyre and the others far from him
at the edge burned, the men indiscriminately with the horses.
And let us lay his bones in a golden jar and a double
fold of fat, until I myself enfold him in Hades.
245 And I would have you build a grave mound which is not very great

but such as will be fitting, for now; afterwards, the Achaians
can make it broad and high—such of you Achaians as may be
left to survive me here by the benched ships, after I am gone.'
   So he spoke, and they did as swift-footed Peleion told them.
First with gleaming wine they put out the pyre that was burning,   250
as much as was still aflame, and the ashes dropped deep from it.
Then they gathered up the white bones of their gentle companion,
weeping, and put them into a golden jar with a double
fold of fat, and laid it away in his shelter, and covered it
with a thin veil; then laid out the tomb and cast down the holding walls   255
around the funeral pyre, then heaped the loose earth over them
and piled the tomb, and turned to go away. But Achilleus
held the people there, and made them sit down in a wide assembly,
and brought prizes for games out of his ships, cauldrons and tripods,
and horses and mules and the powerful high heads of cattle   260
and fair-girdled women and grey iron. First of all
he set forth the glorious prizes for speed of foot for the horsemen:
a woman faultless in the work of her hands to lead away
and a tripod with ears and holding twenty-two measures
for the first prize; and for the second he set forth a six-year-old   265
unbroken mare who carried a mule foal within her.
Then for the third prize he set forth a splendid unfired
cauldron, which held four measures, with its natural gloss still upon it.
For the fourth place he set out two talents' weight of gold, and for
the fifth place set forth an unfired jar with two handles.   270
He stood upright and spoke his word out among the Argives:
'Son of Atreus and all you other strong-greaved Achaians,
these prizes are in the place of games and wait for the horsemen.
Now if we Achaians were contending for the sake of some other
hero, I myself should take the first prize away to my shelter.   275
You know how much my horses surpass in their speed all others;
yes, for they are immortal horses, and Poseidon gave them
to Peleus my father, who in turn gave them into my hands.
But I stay here at the side, and my single-foot horses stay with me;
such is the high glory of the charioteer they have lost,   280
the gentle one, who so many times anointed their manes with
soft olive oil, after he had washed them in shining water.
Therefore these two horses stand here and grieve, and their manes

are swept along the ground as they stand with hearts full of sorrow.
285 But take, the rest of you, places in the field, whichever Achaian
has confidence in his horses and his compacted chariot.'
So spoke the son of Peleus, and the swift riders gathered.
Far the first to rise up was the lord of men Eumelos,
own son of Admetos, who surpassed in horsemanship. After
290 him rose up the son of Tydeus, strong Diomedes,
and led under the yoke the Trojan horses whom he had taken
by force from Aineias, but Aineias himself was saved by Apollo.
After him rose the son of Atreus, fair-haired Menelaos
the sky-descended, and led beneath the yoke the swift horses,
295 Aithe, Agamemnon's mare, and his own Podargos.
Echepolos, son of Anchises, gave her to Agamemnon
as a gift, so as not to have to go with him to windy Ilion
but stay where he was and enjoy himself, since Zeus had given him
great wealth, and he made his home in the wide spaces of Sikyon.
300 This mare, who was straining hard for the race, Menelaos harnessed.
Fourth to order his horses with flowing manes was Antilochos,
the glorious son of Nestor, Neleus' son, the high-hearted
lord, and fast-running horses out of the breed of Pylos
pulled his chariot, and his father standing close beside him
305 gave well-intentioned advice to his own good understanding:
'Antilochos, you are young indeed, but Zeus and Poseidon
have loved you and taught you horsemanship in all of its aspects.
Therefore there is no great need to instruct you; you yourself
know well how to double the turning-post. Yet in this race your horse
310 should run slowest. Therefore I think your work will be heavy.
The horses of these men are faster, but they themselves do not
understand any more than you of the science of racing.
Remember then, dear son, to have your mind full of every
resource of skill, so that the prizes may not elude you.
315 The woodcutter is far better for skill than he is for brute strength.
It is by skill that the sea captain holds his rapid ship
on its course, though torn by winds, over the wine-blue water.
By skill charioteer outpasses charioteer. He
who has put all his confidence in his horses and chariot
320 and recklessly makes a turn that is loose one way or another
finds his horses drifting out of the course and does not control them.

But the man, though he drive the slower horses, who takes his advantage,
keeps his eye always on the post and turns tight, ever watchful,
pulled with the ox-hide reins on the course, as in the beginning,
and holds his horses steady in hand, and watches the leader.   325
I will give you a clear mark and you cannot fail to notice it.
There is a dry stump standing up from the ground about six feet,
oak, it may be, or pine, and not rotted away by rain-water,
and two white stones are leaned against it, one on either side,
at the joining place of the ways, and there is smooth driving around it. 330
Either it is the grave-mark of someone who died long ago,
or was set as a racing goal by men who lived before our time.
Now swift-footed brilliant Achilleus has made it the turning-post.
You must drive your chariot and horses so as to hug this,
and yourself, in the strong-fabricated chariot, lean over   335
a little to the left of the course, and as for your right horse, whip him
and urge him along, slackening your hands to give him his full rein,
but make your left-hand horse keep hard against the turning-post
so that the hub's edge of your fashioned wheel will seem to be
touching it, yet take care not really to brush against it,   340
for, if so, you might damage your horses and break your chariot,
and that will be a thing of joy for the others, and a failure
for you. So, dear son, drive thoughtfully and be watchful.
For if you follow the others but get first by the turning-post,
there is none who could sprint to make it up, nor close you, nor pass you, 345
not if the man behind you were driving the great Arion,
the swift horse of Adrestos, whose birth is from the immortals,
or Laomedon's horses, who were the pride of those raised in this country.'
   So spoke Nestor the son of Neleus, and turned back to his place
and sat down, having talked to his son of each stage in the contest.   350
   Fifth to order his horses with flowing manes was Meriones.
They climbed to the chariots and deposited the lots. Achilleus
shook them, and the first to fall out was that of Antilochos,
Nestor's son, and strong Eumelos drew next after him,
and after him the son of Atreus, Menelaos the spear-famed.   355
Meriones drew the next lane to drive, and the last for the driving
of horses was drawn by far the best of them all, Diomedes.
They stood in line for the start, and Achilleus showed them the turn-post
far away on the level plain, and beside it he stationed

360   a judge, Phoinix the godlike, the follower of his father,
      to mark and remember the running and bring back a true story.
         Then all held their whips high-lifted above their horses,
      then struck with the whip thongs and in words urged their horses onward
      into speed. Rapidly they made their way over the flat land
365   and presently were far away from the ships. The dust lifting
      clung beneath the horses' chests like cloud or a stormwhirl.
      Their manes streamed along the blast of the wind, the chariots
      rocking now would dip to the earth who fosters so many
      and now again would spring up clear of the ground, and the drivers
370   stood in the chariots, with the spirit beating in each man
      with the strain to win, and each was calling aloud upon his own
      horses, and the horses flew through the dust of the flat land.
      But as the rapid horses were running the last of the race-course
      back, and toward the grey sea, then the mettle of each began to
375   show itself, and the field of horses strung out, and before long
      out in front was the swift-stepping team of the son of Pheres,
      Eumelos, and after him the stallions of Diomedes,
      the Trojan horses, not far behind at all, but close on him,
      for they seemed forever on the point of climbing his chariot
380   and the wind of them was hot on the back and on the broad shoulders
      of Eumelos. They lowered their heads and flew close after him.
      And now he might have passed him or run to a doubtful decision,
      had not Phoibos Apollo been angry with Diomedes,
      Tydeus' son, and dashed the shining whip from his hands, so
385   that the tears began to stream from his eyes, for his anger
      as he watched how the mares of Eumelos drew far ahead of him
      while his own horses ran without the whip and were slowed. Yet
      Athene did not fail to see the foul play of Apollo
      on Tydeus' son. She swept in speed to the shepherd of the people
390   and gave him back his whip, and inspired strength into his horses.
      Then in her wrath she went on after the son of Admetos
      and she, a goddess, smashed his chariot yoke, and his horses
      ran on either side of the way, the pole dragged, and Eumelos
      himself was sent spinning out beside the wheel of the chariot
395   so that his elbows were all torn, and his mouth, and his nostrils,
      and his forehead was lacerated about the brows, and his eyes
      filled with tears, and the springing voice was held fast within him.

Then the son of Tydeus, turning his single-foot horses to pass him,
went far out in front of the others, seeing that Athene
had inspired strength in his horses and to himself gave the glory.   400
After him came the son of Atreus, fair-haired Menelaos.
But Antilochos cried out aloud to his father's horses:
'Come on, you two. Pull, as fast as you can! I am not
trying to make you match your speed with the speed of those others,
the horses of Tydeus' valiant son, to whom now Athene   405
has granted speed and to their rider has given the glory.
But make your burst to catch the horses of the son of Atreus
nor let them leave you behind, for fear Aithe who is female
may shower you in mockery. Are you falling back, my brave horses?
For I will tell you this, and it will be a thing accomplished.   410
There will be no more care for you from the shepherd of the people,
Nestor, but he will slaughter you out of hand with the edge
of bronze, if we win the meaner prize because you are unwilling.
Keep on close after him and make all the speed you are able.
I myself shall know what to do and contrive it, so that   415
we get by in the narrow place of the way. He will not escape me.'
    So he spoke, and they fearing the angry voice of their master
ran harder for a little while, and presently after this
battle-stubborn Antilochos saw where the hollow way narrowed.
There was a break in the ground where winter water had gathered   420
and broken out of the road, and made a sunken place all about.
Menelaos shrinking from a collision of chariots steered there,
but Antilochos also turned out his single-foot horses
from the road, and bore a little way aside, and went after him;
and the son of Atreus was frightened and called out aloud to Antilochos: 425
'Antilochos, this is reckless horsemanship. Hold in your horses.
The way is narrow here, it will soon be wider for passing.
Be careful not to crash your chariot and wreck both of us.'
    So he spoke, but Antilochos drove on all the harder
with a whiplash for greater speed, as if he had never heard him.   430
As far as is the range of a discus swung from the shoulder
and thrown by a stripling who tries out the strength of his young
        manhood,
so far they ran even, but then the mares of Atreides gave way
and fell back, for he of his own will slackened his driving

[461]

435 for fear that in the road the single-foot horses might crash
and overturn the strong-fabricated chariots, and the men
themselves go down in the dust through their hard striving for victory.
But Menelaos of the fair hair called to him in anger:
'Antilochos, there is no other man more cursed than you are.
440 Damn you. We Achaians lied when we said you had good sense.
Even so, you will not get this prize without having to take oath.'
He spoke, and lifted his voice and called aloud to his horses:
'Never hold back now, never stop, for all your hearts are
sorrowful. The feet of these and their knees will weary
445 before yours do, seeing that the youth is gone from those horses.'
So he spoke, and they fearing the angry voice of their master
ran the harder, and soon were close up behind the others.
Now the Argives who sat in their assembly were watching
the horses, and the horses flew through the dust of the flat land.
450 Idomeneus, lord of the Kretans, was first to make out the horses,
for he sat apart from the others assembled, and higher up, where
he could see all ways, and from far off he heard Diomedes
calling, and knew him, and made out one horse ahead of the others
who was conspicuous, all red, except on his forehead
455 there was a white mark, round, like the full moon. Idomeneus
rose to his feet upright and spoke his word out to the Argives:
'Friends, who are leaders of the Argives and keep their counsel:
am I the only one who can see the horses, or can you
also? It seems to me there are other horses leading
460 and I make out another charioteer. The mares of Eumelos
must have come to grief somewhere in the plain, who led on the way out,
for those I saw running out in front as they made the turn-post
I can see no longer anywhere, though I watch and though my eyes
look everywhere about the plain of Troy. But it must be
465 that the reins got away from the charioteer, or he could not hold them
well in hand at the goal and failed to double the turn-post.
There I think he must have been thrown out and his chariot broken,
and the mares bolted away with the wildness upon their spirit.
But you also stand up and look for yourselves; I cannot
470 well make out, but it seems to me the man who is leading
is an Aitolian by birth, but lord of the Argives,
the son of Tydeus, breaker of horses, strong Diomedes.'

Swift Aias, son of Oïleus, spoke shamefully to him in anger:
'Idomeneus, what was all this windy talk? The light-footed
horses are still far where they sweep over the great plain.   475
You are not by so much the youngest among the Argives,
nor do the eyes in your head see so much sharper than others.
But forever you are windy with your words, and you should not
be a windy speaker. There are others here better than you are.
The horses who are in front are the same as before, and they are   480
those of Eumelos, and he stands holding the reins behind them.'
      The lord of the Kretans answered him to his face in anger:
'Aias, surpassing in abuse, yet stupid, in all else
you are worst of the Argives with that stubborn mind of yours. Come
      then,
let us put up a wager of a tripod or cauldron   485
and make Agamemnon, son of Atreus, witness between us
as to which horses lead. And when you pay, you will find out.'
      So he spoke, and swift Aias, son of Oïleus, was rising
up, angry in turn, to trade hard words with him. And now
the quarrel between the two of them would have gone still further,   490
had not Achilleus himself risen up and spoken between them:
'No longer now, Aias and Idomeneus, continue
to exchange this bitter and evil talk. It is not becoming.
If another acted so, you yourselves would be angry.
Rather sit down again among those assembled and watch for   495
the horses, and they in their strain for victory will before long
be here. Then you each can see for himself, and learn which
of the Argives horses have run first and which have run second.'
      He spoke, and now Tydeus' son in his rapid course was close on them
and he lashed them always with the whipstroke from the shoulder. His   500
      horses
still lifted their feet light and high as they made their swift passage.
Dust flying splashed always the charioteer, and the chariot
that was overlaid with gold and tin still rolled hard after
the flying feet of the horses, and in their wake there was not much
trace from the running rims of the wheels left in the thin dust.   505
The horses came in running hard. Diomedes stopped them
in the middle of where the men were assembled, with the dense sweat
      starting

and dripping to the ground from neck and chest of his horses.
He himself vaulted down to the ground from his shining chariot
510 and leaned his whip against the yoke. Nor did strong Sthenelos
delay, but made haste to take up the prizes, and gave the woman
to his high-hearted companions to lead away and the tripod
with ears to carry, while Diomedes set free the horses.
    After him Neleian Antilochos drove in his horses,
515 having passed Menelaos, not by speed but by taking advantage.
But even so Menelaos held his fast horses close on him.
As far as from the wheel stands the horse who is straining
to pull his master with the chariot over the flat land;
the extreme hairs in the tail of the horse brush against the running
520 rim of the wheel, and he courses very close, there is not much
space between as he runs a great way over the flat land;
by so much Menelaos was left behind by Antilochos
the blameless. At first he was left behind the length of a discus
thrown, but was overhauling him fast, with Aithe
525 of the fair mane, Agamemnon's mare, putting on a strong burst.
If both of them had had to run the course any further,
Menelaos would have passed him, and there could have been no argument.
But Meriones, strong henchman of Idomeneus, was left
a spearcast's length behind by glorious Menelaos.
530 For his horses with splendid manes were slowest of all, and likewise
he himself was of least account for the racing of chariots.
Last and behind them all came in the son of Admetos
dragging his fine chariot and driving his horses before him,
and seeing this, brilliant swift-footed Achilleus took pity upon him
535 and stood forth among the Argives and spoke to them all in winged
        words:
'The best man is driving his single-foot horses in last.
Come then, we must give some kind of prize, and well he deserves it;
second prize; let first place go to the son of Tydeus.'
    So he spoke, and all gave approval to what he was urging,
540 and he would have given him the horse, since all the Achaians
approved, had not Antilochos, son of great-hearted Nestor,
stood up to answer Peleid Achilleus, and argue:
'Achilleus, I shall be very angry with you if you accomplish
what you have said. You mean to take my prize away from me,

with the thought in mind that his chariot fouled and his running horses   545
but he himself is great. He should have prayed to the immortal
gods. That is why he came in last of all in the running.
But if you are sorry for him and he is dear to your liking,
there is abundant gold in your shelter, and there is bronze there
and animals, and there are handmaidens and single-foot horses.   550
You can take from these, and give him afterwards a prize still greater
than mine, or now at once, and have the Achaians applaud you.
But the mare I will not give up, and the man who wants her
must fight me for her with his hands before he can take her.'
        So he spoke, but brilliant swift-footed Achilleus, favouring   555
Antilochos, smiled, since he was his beloved companion,
and answered him and addressed him in winged words: 'Antilochos,
if you would have me bring some other thing out of my dwelling
as special gift for Eumelos, then for your sake I will do it.
I will give him that corselet I stripped from Asteropaios;   560
it is bronze, but there is an overlay circled about it
in shining tin. It will be a gift that will mean much to him.'
        He spoke, and told Automedon, his beloved companion,
to bring it out of the shelter, and he went away, and brought it back,
and put it in Eumelos' hands. And he accepted it joyfully.   565
        But now Menelaos, heart full of bitterness, stood up among them
in relentless anger against Antilochos, and the herald
put the staff into his hand and gave the call for the Argives
to be silent. And he stood forth, a man like a god, and spoke to them:
'Antilochos, you had good sense once. See what you have done.   570
You have defiled my horsemanship, you have fouled my horses
by throwing your horses in their way, though yours were far slower.
Come then, o leaders of the Argives and their men of counsel:
judge between the two of us now; and without favour;
so that no man of the bronze-armoured Achaians shall say of us: 575
"Menelaos using lies and force against Antilochos
went off with the mare he won, for his horses were far slower
but he himself was greater in power and degree." Or rather
come, I myself will give the judgment, and I think no other
man of the Danaans can call it in question, for it will be right.   580
Antilochos, beloved of Zeus, come here. This is justice.
Stand in front of your horses and chariot, and in your hand take

up the narrow whip with which you drove them before, then
lay your hand on the horses and swear by him who encircles
585 the earth and shakes it you used no guile to baffle my chariot.'
　　Then in turn Antilochos of the good counsel answered him:
'Enough now. For I, my lord Menelaos, am younger
by far than you, and you are the greater and go before me.
You know how greedy transgressions flower in a young man, seeing
590 that his mind is the more active but his judgment is lightweight. Therefore
I would have your heart be patient with me. I myself will give you
the mare I won, and if there were something still greater you asked for
out of my house, I should still be willing at once to give it
to you, beloved of Zeus, rather than all my days
595 fall from your favour and be in the wrong before the divinities.'
　　He spoke, the son of Nestor the great-hearted, and leading
the mare up gave her to Menelaos' hands. But his anger
was softened, as with dew the ears of corn are softened
in the standing corn growth of a shuddering field. For you also
600 the heart, o Menelaos, was thus softened within you.
He spoke to him aloud and addressed him in winged words: 'Antilochos,
I myself, who was angry, now will give way before you,
since you were not formerly loose-minded or vain. It is only
that this time your youth got the better of your intelligence.
605 Beware another time of playing tricks on your betters.
Any other man of the Achaians might not have appeased me.
But you have suffered much for me, and done much hard work,
and your noble father, too, and your brother for my sake. Therefore
I will be ruled by your supplication. I will even give you
610 the mare, though she is mine, so that these men too may be witnesses
that the heart is never arrogant nor stubborn within me.'
　　He spoke, and gave Antilochos' companion, Noëmon,
the mare to lead away, and himself took the glittering cauldron.
Fourth, in the order he had driven, Meriones took up
615 the two talents' weight of gold. But the fifth prize, the two-handled
jar, was left. Achilleus carried it through the assembly
of the Argives, and gave it to Nestor, and stood by and spoke to him:
'This, aged sir, is yours to lay away as a treasure
in memory of the burial of Patroklos; since never
620 again will you see him among the Argives. I give you this prize

for the giving; since never again will you fight with your fists nor wrestle,
nor enter again the field for the spear-throwing, nor race
on your feet; since now the hardship of old age is upon you.'
   He spoke, and put it in the hands of Nestor, who took it
joyfully and spoke in answer and addressed him in winged words: 625
'Yes, child: all this you said to me was true as you said it.
My limbs are no longer steady, dear friend; not my feet, neither
do my arms, as once they did, swing light from my shoulders.
I wish I were young again and the strength still unshaken within me
as once, when great Amaryngkeus was buried by the Epeians   630
at Bouprasion, and his sons gave games for a king's funeral.
There there was no man like me, not among the Epeians
nor yet of the Pylians themselves or great-hearted Aitolians.
At boxing I won against Klytomedes, the son of Enops,
at wrestling against Angkaios of Pleuron, who stood up against me.   635
In the foot-race, for all his speed, I outran Iphiklos,
and with the spear I out-threw Polydoros and Phyleus.
It was only in the chariot-race that the sons of Aktor
defeated me, crossing me in the crowd, so intent on winning
were they, for the biggest prizes had been left for the horse-race.   640
Now these sons of Aktor were twins; one held the reins at his leisure,
held the reins at his leisure while the other lashed on the horses.
This was I, once. Now it is for the young men to encounter
in such actions, and for me to give way to the persuasion
of gloomy old age. But once I shone among the young heroes.   645
Go now, and honour the death of your companion with contests.
I accept this from you gratefully, and my heart is happy
that you have remembered me and my kindness, that I am not forgotten
for the honour that should be my honour among the Achaians.
May the gods, for what you have done for me, give you great happiness.' 650
   He spoke, and Peleides went back among the great numbers
of Achaians assembled, when he had listened to all the praise spoken
by Neleus' son, and set forth the prizes for the painful boxing.
He led out into the field and tethered there a hard-working
six-year-old unbroken jenny, the kind that is hardest   655
to break; and for the loser set out a two-handled goblet.
He stood upright and spoke his word out among the Argives:
'Son of Atreus, and all you other strong-greaved-Achaians,

we invite two men, the best among you, to contend for these prizes
660 with their hands up for the blows of boxing. He whom Apollo
grants to outlast the other, and all the Achaians witness it,
let him lead away the hard-working jenny to his own shelter.
The beaten man shall take away the two-handled goblet.'
    He spoke, and a man huge and powerful, well skilled in boxing,
665 rose up among them; the son of Panopeus, Epeios.
He laid his hand on the hard-working jenny, and spoke out:
'Let the man come up who will carry off the two-handled goblet.
I say no other of the Achaians will beat me at boxing
and lead off the jenny. I claim I am the champion. Is it not
670 enough that I fall short in battle? Since it could not be
ever, that a man could be a master in every endeavour.
For I tell you this straight out, and it will be a thing accomplished.
I will smash his skin apart and break his bones on each other.
Let those who care for him wait nearby in a huddle about him
675 to carry him out, after my fists have beaten him under.'
    So he spoke, and all of them stayed stricken to silence.
Alone Euryalos stood up to face him, a godlike
man, son of lord Mekisteus of the seed of Talaos;
of him who came once to Thebes and the tomb of Oidipous after
680 his downfall, and there in boxing defeated all the Kadmeians.
The spear-famed son of Tydeus was his second, and talked to him
in encouragement, and much desired the victory for him.
First he pulled on the boxing belt about his waist, and then
gave him the thongs carefully cut from the hide of a ranging
685 ox. The two men, girt up, strode into the midst of the circle
and faced each other, and put up their ponderous hands at the same time
and closed, so that their heavy arms were crossing each other,
and there was a fierce grinding of teeth, the sweat began to run
everywhere from their bodies. Great Epeios came in, and hit him
690 as he peered out from his guard, on the cheek, and he could no longer
keep his feet, but where he stood the glorious limbs gave.
As in the water roughened by the north wind a fish jumps
in the weeds of the beach-break, then the dark water closes above him,
so Euryalos left the ground from the blow, but great-hearted Epeios
695 took him in his arms and set him upright, and his true companions
stood about him, and led him out of the circle, feet dragging

as he spat up the thick blood and rolled his head over on one side.
He was dizzy when they brought him back and set him among them.
But they themselves went and carried off the two-handled goblet.

Now Peleides set forth the prizes for the third contest,   700
for the painful wrestling, at once, and displayed them before the Danaans.
There was a great tripod, to set over fire, for the winner.
The Achaians among themselves valued it at the worth of twelve oxen.
But for the beaten man he set in their midst a woman
skilled in much work of her hands, and they rated her at four oxen.   705
He stood upright and spoke his word out among the Argives:
'Rise up, two who would endeavour this prize.' So he spoke
and presently there rose up huge Telamonian Aias,
and resourceful Odysseus rose, who was versed in every advantage.
The two men, girt up, strode out into the midst of the circle,   710
and grappled each other in the hook of their heavy arms, as when
rafters lock, when a renowned architect has fitted them
in the roof of a high house to keep out the force of the winds' spite.
Their backs creaked under stress of violent hands that tugged them
stubbornly, and the running sweat broke out, and raw places   715
frequent all along their ribs and their shoulders broke out
bright red with blood, as both of them kept up their hard efforts
for success and the prize of the wrought tripod. Neither Odysseus
was able to bring Aias down or throw him to the ground, nor
could Aias, but the great strength of Odysseus held out against him.   720
But now as they made the strong-greaved Achaians begin to be restless,
at last great Telamonian Aias said to the other:
'Son of Laertes and seed of Zeus, resourceful Odysseus:
lift me, or I will lift you. All success shall be as Zeus gives it.'

He spoke, and heaved; but not forgetting his craft Odysseus   725
caught him with a stroke behind the hollow of the knee, and unnerved
the tendons, and threw him over backward, so that Odysseus
fell on his chest as the people gazed upon them and wondered.
Next, brilliant much-enduring Odysseus endeavoured to lift him
and budged him a little from the ground, but still could not raise him   730
clear, then hooked a knee behind, so that both of them went down
together to the ground, and lay close, and were soiled in the dust. Then
they would have sprung to their feet once more and wrestled a third fall,
had not Achilleus himself stood up and spoken to stop them:

735 'Wrestle no more now; do not wear yourselves out and get hurt.
You have both won. Therefore take the prizes in equal division
and retire, so the rest of the Achaians can have their contests.'
      So he spoke, and they listened close to him and obeyed him
and wiped the dust away from their bodies, and put on their tunics.

740   At once the son of Peleus set out prizes for the foot-race:
a mixing-bowl of silver, a work of art, which held only
six measures, but for its loveliness it surpassed all others
on earth by far, since skilled Sidonian craftsmen had wrought it
well, and Phoenicians carried it over the misty face of the water

745 and set it in the harbour, and gave it for a present to Thoas.
Euneos, son of Jason, gave it to the hero Patroklos
to buy Lykaon, Priam's son, out of slavery, and now
Achilleus made it a prize in memory of his companion,
for that man who should prove in the speed of his feet to run lightest.

750 For second place he set out a great ox with fat deep upon him,
and for the last runner half a talent's weight of gold. He stood
upright then and spoke his word out among the Argives:
'Rise up, you who would endeavour this prize.' So he spoke
and presently there rose up swift Aias, the son of Oïleus,

755 and Odysseus the resourceful rose up, and after him Nestor's
son, Antilochos, the best runner among all the young men.
They stood in line for the start, and Achilleus showed them the turn-post.
The field was strung out from the scratch, and not long afterwards
Oïleus' son was out in front, but brilliant Odysseus

760 overhauled him close, as near as to the breast of a woman
fair-girdled is the rod she pulls in her hands carefully
as she draws the spool out and along the warp, and holds it
close to her chest. So Odysseus ran close up, but behind him,
and his feet were hitting the other's tracks before the dust settled.

765 Great Odysseus was breathing on the back of the head of Aias
as he ran and held his speed, and all the Achaians were shouting
for his effort to win, and hallooed him hard along in his running.
But as they were running the last part of the race, then Odysseus
said a prayer inside his own mind to grey-eyed Athene:

770 'Hear me, goddess; be kind; and come with strength for my footsteps.'
      So he spoke in prayer, and Pallas Athene heard him.
She made his limbs light, both his feet and the hands above them.

Now as they were for making their final sprint for the trophy,
there Aias slipped in his running, for Athene unbalanced him,
where dung was scattered on the ground from the bellowing oxen   775
    slaughtered
by swift-footed Achilleus, those he slew to honour Patroklos;
and his mouth and nose were filled with the cow dung, so that Odysseus
the great and much enduring took off the mixing-bowl, seeing
he had passed him and come in first, and the ox went to glorious Aias.
He stood there holding in his hands the horn of the field-ox,   780
spitting the dung from his mouth, and spoke his word to the Argives:
'Ah, now! That goddess made me slip on my feet, who has always
stood over Odysseus like a mother, and taken good care of him.'
    He spoke, and all the rest of them laughed happily at him.
In turn Antilochos took up prize for last place, and carried it   785
off, and grinning spoke his word out among the Argives:
'Friends, you all know well what I tell you, that still the immortals
continue to favour the elder men. For see now, Aias
is elder than I, if only by a little, but this man
is out of another age than ours and one of the ancients.   790
But his, they say, is a green old age. It would be a hard thing
for any Achaian to match his speed. Except for Achilleus.'
    So he spoke, and glorified the swift-footed Peleion.
And Achilleus gave him an answer for what he said, and spoke to him:
'Antilochos, your good word for me shall not have been spoken   795
in vain. I shall give you another half-talent of gold in addition.'
    He spoke, and put it in Antilochos' hands, who received it joyfully.
Then the son of Peleus carried into the circle and set down
a far-shadowing spear, and set down beside it a shield and a helmet:
the armour of Sarpedon, that Patroklos stripped from his body.   800
He stood upright and spoke his word out among the Argives:
'We invite two men, the best among you, to contend for these prizes.
Let them draw their armour upon them and take up the rending bronze
    spears
and stand up to each other in the trial of close combat. The fighter
who is first of the two to get in a stroke at the other's fair body, 805
to get through armour and dark blood and reach to the vitals,
to that man I will give this magnificent silver-nailed
sword of Thrace I stripped from the body of Asteropaios.

[471]

But let both men carry off this armour and have it in common;
810 and we shall set out a brave dinner before them both in our shelters.'
    So he spoke, and there rose up huge Telamonian Aias,
and next the son of Tydeus rose up, strong Diomedes.
When these were in their armour on either side of the assembly,
they came together in the middle space, furious for the combat,
815 with dangerous looks, and wonder settled on all the Achaians.
Then as, moving forward, the two were closing in on each other,
there were three charges, three times they swept in close. Then Aias
stabbed at Diomedes' shield on its perfect circle
but did not get through to the skin, for the corselet inside it guarded him.
820 The son of Tydeus, over the top of the huge shield, was always
menacing the neck of Aias with the point of the shining
spear, but when the Achaians saw it in fear for Aias
they called for them to stop and divide the prizes evenly.
But the hero Achilleus carried the great sword, with its scabbard
825 and carefully cut sword belt, and gave it to Diomedes.
    Now the son of Peleus set in place a lump of pig-iron,
which had once been the throwing-weight of Eëtion in his great strength;
but now swift-footed brilliant Achilleus had slain him and taken
the weight away in the ships along with the other possessions.
830 He stood upright and spoke his word out among the Argives:
'Rise up, you who would endeavour to win this prize also.
For although the rich demesnes of him who wins it lie far off
indeed, yet for the succession of five years he will have it
to use; for his shepherd for want of iron will not have to go in
835 to the city for it, nor his ploughman either. This will supply them.'
    So he spoke, and up stood Polypoites the stubborn in battle,
and Leonteus in his great strength, a godlike man, and there rose up
Aias, the son of Telamon, and brilliant Epeios.
They stood in order to throw, and great Epeios took up the weight
840 and whirled and threw it, and all the Achaians laughed when they saw
        him.
Second to throw in turn was Leonteus, scion of Ares,
and third in turn huge Telamonian Aias threw it
from his ponderous hand, and overpassed the marks of all others.
But when Polypoites stubborn in battle caught up the iron,
845 he overthrew the entire field by as far as an ox-herd

can cast with his throwing stick which spins through the air and comes
    down
where the cattle graze in their herds, and all the Achaians applauded,
and the companions of powerful Polypoites uprising
carried the prize of the king away to the hollow vessels.

    But Achilleus set gloomy iron forth once more, for the archers.   850
He set ten double-bladed axes forth, ten with single
blades, and planted far away on the sands the mast pole
of a dark-prowed ship, and tethered a tremulous wild pigeon to it
by a thin string attached to her foot, then challenged the archers
to shoot at her: 'Now let the man who hits the wild pigeon   855
take up and carry away home with him all the full axes.
But if one should miss the bird and still hit the string, that man,
seeing that he is the loser, still shall have the half-axes.'
    So he spoke, and there rose up in his strength the lord Teukros,
and Meriones rose up, Idomeneus' powerful henchman.   860
They chose their lots, and shook them up in a brazen helmet,
and Teukros was allotted first place to shoot. He let fly
a strong-shot arrow, but did not promise the lord of archery
that he would accomplish for him a grand sacrifice of lambs first born.
He missed the bird, for Apollo begrudged him that, but he did hit   865
the string beside the foot where the bird was tied, and the tearing
arrow went straight through and cut the string, and the pigeon
soared swift up toward the sky, while the string dropped and dangled
toward the ground. But still the Achaians thundered approval.
Meriones in a fury of haste caught the bow from his hand,   870
but had had out an arrow before, while Teukros was aiming,
and forthwith promised to the one who strikes from afar, Apollo,
that he would accomplish for him a grand sacrifice of lambs first born.
Way up under the clouds he saw the tremulous wild dove
and as she circled struck her under the wing in the body   875
and the shaft passed clean through and out of her, so that it dropped
    back
and stuck in the ground beside the foot of Meriones, but the bird
dropped and fell on top of the mast of the dark-prowed vessel
and drooped her neck and the beating wings went slack, and the spirit
of life fled swift away from her limbs. Far down from the mast peak   880
she dropped to earth. And the people gazed upon it and wondered.

Then Meriones gathered up all ten double axes,
but Teukros carried the half-axes back to the hollow ships.
    Then the son of Peleus carried into the circle and set down
885 a far-shadowing spear and an unfired cauldron with patterns
of flowers on it, the worth of an ox. And the spear-throwers rose up.
The son of Atreus rose, wide-powerful Agamemnon,
and Meriones rose up, Idomeneus' powerful henchman.
But now among them spoke swift-footed brilliant Achilleus:
890 'Son of Atreus, for we know how much you surpass all others,
by how much you are greatest for strength among the spear-throwers,
therefore take this prize and keep it and go back to your hollow
ships; but let us give the spear to the hero Meriones;
if your own heart would have it this way, for so I invite you.'
895   He spoke, nor did Agamemnon lord of men disobey him.
The hero gave the bronze spear to Meriones, and thereafter
handed his prize, surpassingly lovely, to the herald Talthybios.

 AND the games broke up, and the people scattered to go away, each man
to his fast-running ship, and the rest of them took thought of their dinner
and of sweet sleep and its enjoyment; only Achilleus
wept still as he remembered his beloved companion, nor did sleep
who subdues all come over him, but he tossed from one side to the other   5
in longing for Patroklos, for his manhood and his great strength
and all the actions he had seen to the end with him, and the hardships
he had suffered; the wars of men; hard crossing of the big waters.
Remembering all these things he let fall the swelling tears, lying
sometimes along his side, sometimes on his back, and now again   10
prone on his face; then he would stand upright, and pace turning
in distraction along the beach of the sea, nor did dawn rising
escape him as she brightened across the sea and the beaches.
Then, when he had yoked running horses under the chariot
he would fasten Hektor behind the chariot, so as to drag him,   15
and draw him three times around the tomb of Menoitios' fallen
son, then rest again in his shelter, and throw down the dead man
and leave him to lie sprawled on his face in the dust. But Apollo
had pity on him, though he was only a dead man, and guarded
the body from all ugliness, and hid all of it under the golden   20
aegis, so that it might not be torn when Achilleus dragged it.
    So Achilleus in his standing fury outraged great Hektor.
The blessed gods as they looked upon him were filled with compassion
and kept urging clear-sighted Argeïphontes to steal the body.
There this was pleasing to all the others, but never to Hera   25

nor Poseidon, nor the girl of the grey eyes, who kept still
their hatred for sacred Ilion as in the beginning,
and for Priam and his people, because of the delusion of Paris
who insulted the goddesses when they came to him in his courtyard
30 and favoured her who supplied the lust that led to disaster.
But now, as it was the twelfth dawn after the death of Hektor,
Phoibos Apollo spoke his word out among the immortals:
'You are hard, you gods, and destructive. Now did not Hektor
burn thigh pieces of oxen and unblemished goats in your honour?
35 Now you cannot bring yourselves to save him, though he is only
a corpse, for his wife to look upon, his child and his mother
and Priam his father, and his people, who presently thereafter
would burn his body in the fire and give him his rites of burial.
No, you gods; your desire is to help this cursed Achilleus
40 within whose breast there are no feelings of justice, nor can
his mind be bent, but his purposes are fierce, like a lion
who when he has given way to his own great strength and his haughty
spirit, goes among the flocks of men, to devour them.
So Achilleus has destroyed pity, and there is not in him
45 any shame; which does much harm to men but profits them also.
For a man must some day lose one who was even closer
than this; a brother from the same womb, or a son. And yet
he weeps for him, and sorrows for him, and then it is over,
for the Destinies put in mortal men the heart of endurance.
50 But this man, now he has torn the heart of life from great Hektor,
ties him to his horses and drags him around his beloved companion's
tomb; and nothing is gained thereby for his good, or his honour.
Great as he is, let him take care not to make us angry;
for see, he does dishonour to the dumb earth in his fury.'
55 Then bitterly Hera of the white arms answered him, saying:
'What you have said could be true, lord of the silver bow, only
if you give Hektor such pride of place as you give to Achilleus.
But Hektor was mortal, and suckled at the breast of a woman,
while Achilleus is the child of a goddess, one whom I myself
60 nourished and brought up and gave her as bride to her husband
Peleus, one dear to the hearts of the immortals, for you all
went, you gods, to the wedding; and you too feasted among them
and held your lyre, o friend of the evil, faithless forever.'

In turn Zeus who gathers the clouds spoke to her in answer:
'Hera, be not utterly angry with the gods, for there shall not   65
be the same pride of place given both. Yet Hektor also
was loved by the gods, best of all the mortals in Ilion.
I loved him too. He never failed of gifts to my liking.
Never yet has my altar gone without fair sacrifice,
the smoke and the savour of it, since that is our portion of honour.   70
The stealing of him we will dismiss, for it is not possible
to take bold Hektor secretly from Achilleus, since always
his mother is near him night and day; but it would be better
if one of the gods would summon Thetis here to my presence
so that I can say a close word to her, and see that Achilleus   75
is given gifts by Priam and gives back the body of Hektor.'
     He spoke, and Iris storm-footed sprang away with the message,
and at a point between Samos and Imbros of the high cliffs
plunged in the dark water, and the sea crashed moaning about her.
She plummeted to the sea floor like a lead weight which, mounted   80
along the horn of an ox who ranges the fields, goes downward
and takes death with it to the raw-ravening fish. She found Thetis
inside the hollow of her cave, and gathered about her
sat the rest of the sea goddesses, and she in their midst
was mourning the death of her blameless son, who so soon was destined   85
to die in Troy of the rich soil, far from the land of his fathers.
Iris the swift-foot came close beside her and spoke to her:
'Rise, Thetis. Zeus whose purposes are infinite calls you.'
     In turn Thetis the goddess, the silver-footed, answered her:
'What does he, the great god, want with me? I feel shamefast   90
to mingle with the immortals, and my heart is confused with sorrows.
But I will go. No word shall be in vain, if he says it.'
     So she spoke, and shining among the divinities took up
her black veil, and there is no darker garment. She went
on her way, and in front of her rapid wind-footed Iris   95
guided her, and the wave of the water opened about them.
They stepped out on the dry land and swept to the sky. There they
     found
the son of Kronos of the wide brows, and gathered about him
sat all the rest of the gods, the blessed, who live forever.
She sat down beside Zeus father, and Athene made a place for her.   100

Hera put into her hand a beautiful golden goblet
and spoke to her to comfort her, and Thetis accepting drank from it.
The father of gods and men began the discourse among them:
'You have come to Olympos, divine Thetis, for all your sorrow,
105 with an unforgotten grief in your heart. I myself know this.
But even so I will tell you why I summoned you hither.
For nine days there has risen a quarrel among the immortals
over the body of Hektor, and Achilleus, stormer of cities.
They keep urging clear-sighted Argeïphontes to steal the body,
110 but I still put upon Achilleus the honour that he has, guarding
your reverence and your love for me into time afterwards. Go then
in all speed to the encampment and give to your son this message:
tell him that the gods frown upon him, that beyond all other
immortals I myself am angered that in his heart's madness
115 he holds Hektor beside the curved ships and did not give him
back. Perhaps in fear of me he will give back Hektor.
Then I will send Iris to Priam of the great heart, with an order
to ransom his dear son, going down to the ships of the Achaians
and bringing gifts to Achilleus which might soften his anger.'
120   He spoke and the goddess silver-foot Thetis did not disobey him
but descended in a flash of speed from the peaks of Olympos
and made her way to the shelter of her son, and there found him
in close lamentation, and his beloved companions about him
were busy at their work and made ready the morning meal, and there
125 stood a great fleecy sheep being sacrificed in the shelter.
His honoured mother came close to him and sat down beside him,
and stroked him with her hand and called him by name and spoke to him:
'My child, how long will you go on eating your heart out in sorrow
and lamentation, and remember neither your food nor going
130 to bed? It is a good thing even to lie with a woman
in love. For you will not be with me long, but already
death and powerful destiny stand closely above you.
But listen hard to me, for I come from Zeus with a message.
He says that the gods frown upon you, that beyond all other
135 immortals he himself is angered that in your heart's madness
you hold Hektor beside the curved ships and did not redeem him.
Come, then, give him up and accept ransom for the body.'
    Then in turn Achilleus of the swift feet answered her:

'So be it. He can bring the ransom and take off the body,
if the Olympian himself so urgently bids it.'   140

So, where the ships were drawn together, the son and his mother
conversed at long length in winged words. But the son of Kronos
stirred Iris to go down to sacred Ilion, saying:
'Go forth, Iris the swift, leaving your place on Olympos,
and go to Priam of the great heart within Ilion, tell him   145
to ransom his dear son, going down to the ships of the Achaians
and bringing gifts to Achilleus which might soften his anger:
alone, let no other man of the Trojans go with him, but only
let one elder herald attend him, one who can manage
the mules and the easily running wagon, so he can carry   150
the dead man, whom great Achilleus slew, back to the city.
Let death not be a thought in his heart, let him have no fear;
such an escort shall I send to guide him, Argeïphontes
who shall lead him until he brings him to Achilleus. And after
he has brought him inside the shelter of Achilleus, neither   155
will the man himself kill him, but will hold back all the others,
for he is no witless man nor unwatchful, nor is he wicked,
but will in all kindness spare one who comes to him as a suppliant.'

He spoke, and storm-footed Iris swept away with the message
and came to the house of Priam. There she found outcry and mourning.   160
The sons sitting around their father inside the courtyard
made their clothes sodden with their tears, and among them the old man
sat veiled, beaten into his mantle. Dung lay thick
on the head and neck of the aged man, for he had been rolling
in it, he had gathered and smeared it on with his hands. And his daughters   165
all up and down the house and the wives of his sons were mourning
as they remembered all those men in their numbers and valour
who lay dead, their lives perished at the hands of the Argives.
The messenger of Zeus stood beside Priam and spoke to him
in a small voice, and yet the shivers took hold of his body: 170
'Take heart, Priam, son of Dardanos, do not be frightened.
I come to you not eyeing you with evil intention
but with the purpose of good toward you. I am a messenger
of Zeus, who far away cares much for you and is pitiful.
The Olympian orders you to ransom Hektor the brilliant,   175
to bring gifts to Achilleus which may soften his anger:

alone, let no other man of the Trojans go with you, but only
let one elder herald attend you, one who can manage
the mules and the easily running wagon, so he can carry
180 the dead man, whom great Achilleus slew, back to the city.
Let death not be a thought in your heart, you need have no fear,
such an escort shall go with you to guide you, Argeïphontes
who will lead you till he brings you to Achilleus. And after
he has brought you inside the shelter of Achilleus, neither
185 will the man himself kill you but will hold back all the others;
for he is no witless man nor unwatchful, nor is he wicked
but will in all kindness spare one who comes to him as a suppliant.'
    So Iris the swift-footed spoke and went away from him.
Thereupon he ordered his sons to make ready the easily rolling
190 mule wagon, and to fasten upon it the carrying basket.
He himself went into the storeroom, which was fragrant
and of cedar, and high-ceilinged, with many bright treasures inside it.
He called out to Hekabe his wife, and said to her:
'Dear wife, a messenger came to me from Zeus on Olympos,
195 that I must go to the ships of the Achaians and ransom my dear son,
bringing gifts to Achilleus which may soften his anger.
Come then, tell me. What does it seem best to your own mind
for me to do? My heart, my strength are terribly urgent
that I go there to the ships within the wide army of the Achaians.'
200   So he spoke, and his wife cried out aloud, and answered him:
'Ah me, where has that wisdom gone for which you were famous
in time before, among outlanders and those you rule over?
How can you wish to go alone to the ships of the Achaians
before the eyes of a man who has slaughtered in such numbers
205 such brave sons of yours? The heart in you is iron. For if
he has you within his grasp and lays eyes upon you, that man
who is savage and not to be trusted will not take pity upon you
nor have respect for your rights. Let us sit apart in our palace
now, and weep for Hektor, and the way at the first strong Destiny
210 spun with his life line when he was born, when I gave birth to him,
that the dogs with their shifting feet should feed on him, far from his
        parents,
gone down before a stronger man; I wish I could set teeth
in the middle of his liver and eat it. That would be vengeance

for what he did to my son; for he slew him when he was no coward
but standing before the men of Troy and the deep-girdled women   215
of Troy, with no thought in his mind of flight or withdrawal.'
    In turn the aged Priam, the godlike, answered her saying:
'Do not hold me back when I would be going, neither yourself be
a bird of bad omen in my palace. You will not persuade me.
If it had been some other who ordered me, one of the mortals,   220
one of those who are soothsayers, or priests, or diviners,
I might have called it a lie and we might rather have rejected it.
But now, for I myself heard the god and looked straight upon her,
I am going, and this word shall not be in vain. If it is my destiny
to die there by the ships of the bronze-armoured Achaians,   225
then I wish that. Achilleus can slay me at once, with my own son
caught in my arms, once I have my fill of mourning above him.'
    He spoke, and lifted back the fair covering of his clothes-chest
and from inside took out twelve robes surpassingly lovely
and twelve mantles to be worn single, as many blankets,   230
as many great white cloaks, also the same number of tunics.
He weighed and carried out ten full talents of gold, and brought forth
two shining tripods, and four cauldrons, and brought out a goblet
of surpassing loveliness that the men of Thrace had given him
when he went to them with a message, but now the old man spared not   235
even this in his halls, so much was it his heart's desire
to ransom back his beloved son. But he drove off the Trojans
all from his cloister walks, scolding them with words of revilement:
'Get out, you failures, you disgraces. Have you not also
mourning of your own at home that you come to me with your sorrows?   240
Is it not enought that Zeus, son of Kronos, has given me sorrow
in losing the best of my sons? You also shall be aware of this
since you will be all the easier for the Achaians to slaughter
now he is dead. But, for myself, before my eyes look
upon this city as it is destroyed and its people are slaughtered,   245
my wish is to go sooner down to the house of the death god.'
    He spoke, and went after the men with a stick, and they fled outside
before the fury of the old man. He was scolding his children
and cursing Helenos, and Paris, Agathon the brilliant,
Pammon and Antiphonos, Polites of the great war cry,   250
Deïphobos and Hippothoös and proud Dios. There were nine

sons to whom now the old man gave orders and spoke to them roughly:
'Make haste, wicked children, my disgraces. I wish all of you
had been killed beside the running ships in the place of Hektor.
255 Ah me, for my evil destiny. I have had the noblest
of sons in Troy, but I say not one of them is left to me,
Mestor like a god and Troilos whose delight was in horses,
and Hektor, who was a god among men, for he did not seem like
one who was child of a mortal man, but of a god. All these
260 Ares has killed, and all that are left me are the disgraces,
the liars and the dancers, champions of the chorus, the plunderers
of their own people in their land of lambs and kids. Well then,
will you not get my wagon ready and be quick about it,
and put all these things on it, so we can get on with our journey?'
265   So he spoke, and they in terror at the old man's scolding
hauled out the easily running wagon for mules, a fine thing
new-fabricated, and fastened the carrying basket upon it.
They took away from its peg the mule yoke made of boxwood
with its massive knob, well fitted with guiding rings, and brought forth
270 the yoke lashing (together with the yoke itself) of nine cubits
and snugged it well into place upon the smooth-polished wagon-pole
at the foot of the beam, then slipped the ring over the peg, and lashed it
with three turns on either side to the knob, and afterwards
fastened it all in order and secured it under a hooked guard.
275 Then they carried out and piled into the smooth-polished mule wagon
all the unnumbered spoils to be given for the head of Hektor,
then yoked the powerful-footed mules who pulled in the harness
and whom the Mysians gave once as glorious presents to Priam;
but for Priam they led under the yoke those horses the old man
280 himself had kept, and cared for them at his polished manger.
    Now in the high house the yoking was done for the herald
and Priam, men both with close counsels in their minds. And now came
Hekabe with sorrowful heart and stood close beside them
carrying in her right hand the kind, sweet wine in a golden
285 goblet, so that before they went they might pour a drink-offering.
She stood in front of the horses, called Priam by name and spoke to him:
'Here, pour a libation to Zeus father, and pray you may come back
home again from those who hate you, since it seems the spirit
within you drives you upon the ships, though I would not have it.

Make your prayer then to the dark-misted, the son of Kronos   290
on Ida, who looks out on all the Troad, and ask him
for a bird of omen, a rapid messenger, which to his own mind
is dearest of all birds and his strength is the biggest, one seen
on the right, so that once your eyes have rested upon him
you can trust in him and go to the ships of the fast-mounted Danaans.   295
But if Zeus of the wide brows will not grant you his own messenger,
then I, for one, would never urge you on nor advise you
to go to the Argive ships, for all your passion to do it.'
     Then in answer to her again spoke Priam the godlike:
'My lady, I will not disregard this wherein you urge me.   300
It is well to lift hands to Zeus and ask if he will have mercy.'
     The old man spoke, and told the housekeeper who attended them
to pour unstained water over his hands. She standing beside them
and serving them held the washing-bowl in her hands, and a pitcher.
He washed his hands and took the cup from his wife. He stood up   305
in the middle of the enclosure, and prayed, and poured the wine out
looking up into the sky, and gave utterance and spoke, saying:
'Father Zeus, watching over us from Ida, most high, most honoured:
grant that I come to Achilleus for love and pity; but send me
a bird of omen, a rapid messenger which to your own mind   310
is dearest of all birds and his strength is biggest, one seen
on the right, so that once my eyes have rested upon him
I may trust in him and go to the ships of the fast-mounted Danaans.'
     So he spoke in prayer, and Zeus of the counsels heard him.
Straightway he sent down the most lordly of birds, an eagle,   315
the dark one, the marauder, called as well the black eagle.
And as big as is the build of the door to a towering chamber
in the house of a rich man, strongly fitted with bars, of such size
was the spread of his wings on either side. He swept through the city
appearing on the right hand, and the people looking upon him   320
were uplifted and the hearts made glad in the breasts of all of them.
     Now in urgent haste the old man mounted into his chariot
and drove out through the forecourt and the thundering close. Before him
the mules hauled the wagon on its four wheels, Idaios
the sober-minded driving them, and behind him the horses   325
came on as the old man laid the lash upon them and urged them
rapidly through the town, and all his kinsmen were following

much lamenting, as if he went to his death. When the two men
had gone down through the city, and out, and come to the flat land,
330 the rest of them turned back to go to Ilion, the sons
and the sons-in-law. And Zeus of the wide brows failed not to notice
the two as they showed in the plain. He saw the old man and took pity
upon him, and spoke directly to his beloved son, Hermes:
'Hermes, for to you beyond all other gods it is dearest
335 to be man's companion, and you listen to whom you will, go now
on your way, and so guide Priam inside the hollow ships
of the Achaians, that no man shall see him, none be aware of him,
of the other Danaans, till he has come to the son of Peleus.'
He spoke, nor disobeyed him the courier, Argeïphontes.
340 Immediately he bound upon his feet the fair sandals
golden and immortal, that carried him over the water
as over the dry land of the main abreast of the wind's blast.
He caught up the staff, with which he mazes the eyes of those mortals
whose eyes he would maze, or wakes again the sleepers. Holding
345 this in his hands, strong Argeïphontes winged his way onward
until he came suddenly to Troy and the Hellespont, and there
walked on, and there took the likeness of a young man, a noble,
with beard new grown, which is the most graceful time of young
    manhood.
Now when the two had driven past the great tomb of Ilos
350 they stayed their mules and horses to water them in the river,
for by this time darkness had descended on the land; and the herald
made out Hermes, who was coming toward them at a short distance.
He lifted his voice and spoke aloud to Priam: 'Take thought,
son of Dardanos. Here is work for a mind that is careful.
355 I see a man; I think he will presently tear us to pieces.
Come then, let us run away with our horses, or if not, then
clasp his knees and entreat him to have mercy upon us.'
So he spoke, and the old man's mind was confused, he was badly
frightened, and the hairs stood up all over his gnarled body
360 and he stood staring, but the kindly god himself coming closer
took the old man's hand, and spoke to him and asked him a question:
'Where, my father, are you thus guiding your mules and horses
through the immortal night while other mortals are sleeping?
Have you no fear of the Achaians whose wind is fury,

who hate you, who are your enemies, and are near? For if one   365
of these were to see you, how you are conveying so many
treasures through the swift black night, what then could you think of?
You are not young yourself, and he who attends you is aged
for beating off any man who might pick a quarrel with you.
But I will do you no harm myself, I will even keep off   370
another who would. You seem to me like a beloved father.'
    In answer to him again spoke aged Priam the godlike:
'Yes, in truth, dear child, all this is much as you tell me;
yet still there is some god who has held his hand above me,
who sent such a wayfarer as you to meet me, an omen   375
of good, for such you are by your form, your admired beauty
and the wisdom in your mind. Your parents are fortunate in you.'
    Then in turn answered him the courier Argeïphontes:
'Yes, old sir, all this that you said is fair and orderly.
But come, tell me this thing and recite it to me accurately.   380
Can it be you convey these treasures in all their numbers and beauty
to outland men, so that they can be still kept safe for you?
Or are all of you by now abandoning sacred Ilion
in fear, such a one was he who died, the best man among you,
your son; who was never wanting when you fought against the Achaians.'   385
    In answer to him again spoke aged Priam the godlike:
'But who are you, o best of men, and who are your parents?
Since you spoke of my ill-starred son's death, and with honour.'
    Then in turn answered him the courier Argeïphontes:
'You try me out, aged sir. You ask me of glorious Hektor   390
whom many a time my eyes have seen in the fighting where men win
glory, as also on that time when he drove back the Argives
on their ships and kept killing them with the stroke of the sharp bronze,
and we stood by and wondered at him; for then Achilleus
would not let us fight by reason of his anger at Agamemnon.   395
For I am Achilleus' henchman, and the same strong-wrought vessel
brought us here; and I am a Myrmidon, and my father
is Polyktor; a man of substance, but aged, as you are.
He has six sons beside, and I am the seventh, and I shook
lots with the others, and it was my lot to come on this venture.   400
But now I have come to the plain away from the ships, for at daybreak
the glancing-eyed Achaians will do battle around the city.

They chafe from sitting here too long, nor have the Achaians'
kings the strength to hold them back as they break for the fighting.'
405 In answer to him again spoke aged Priam the godlike:
'If then you are henchman to Peleïd Achilleus,
come, tell me the entire truth, and whether my son lies
still beside the ships, or whether by now he has been hewn
limb from limb and thrown before the dogs by Achilleus.'
410 Then in turn answered him the courier Argeïphontes:
'Aged sir, neither have any dogs eaten him, nor have
the birds, but he lies yet beside the ship of Achilleus
at the shelters, and as he was; now here is the twelfth dawn
he has lain there, nor does his flesh decay, nor do worms feed
415 on him, they who devour men who have fallen in battle.
It is true, Achilleus drags him at random around his beloved
companion's tomb, as dawn on dawn appears, yet he cannot
mutilate him; you yourself can see when you go there
how fresh with dew he lies, and the blood is all washed from him,
420 nor is there any corruption, and all the wounds have been closed up
where he was struck, since many drove the bronze in his body.
So it is that the blessed immortals care for your son, though
he is nothing but a dead man; because in their hearts they loved him.'
  He spoke, and the old man was made joyful and answered him, saying:
425 'My child, surely it is good to give the immortals
their due gifts; because my own son, if ever I had one,
never forgot in his halls the gods who live on Olympos.
Therefore they remembered him even in death's stage. Come, then,
accept at my hands this beautiful drinking-cup, and give me
430 protection for my body, and with the gods' grace be my escort
until I make my way to the shelter of the son of Peleus.'
  In turn answered him the courier Argeïphontes:
'You try me out, aged sir, for I am young, but you will not
persuade me, telling me to accept your gifts when Achilleus
435 does not know. I fear him at heart and have too much reverence
to rob him. Such a thing might be to my sorrow hereafter.
But I would be your escort and take good care of you, even
till I came to glorious Argos in a fast ship or following
on foot, and none would fight you because he despised your escort.'
440 The kind god spoke, and sprang up behind the horses and into

the chariot, and rapidly caught in his hands the lash and the guide reins,
and breathed great strength into the mules and horses. Now after
they had got to the fortifications about the ships, and the ditch, there
were sentries, who had just begun to make ready their dinner,
but about these the courier Argeïphontes drifted   445
sleep, on all, and quickly opened the gate, and shoved back
the door-bars, and brought in Priam and the glorious gifts on the wagon.
But when they had got to the shelter of Peleus' son: a towering
shelter the Myrmidons had built for their king, hewing
the timbers of pine, and they made a roof of thatch above it   450
shaggy with grass that they had gathered out of the meadows;
and around it made a great courtyard for their king, with hedgepoles
set close together; the gate was secured by a single door-piece
of pine, and three Achaians could ram it home in its socket
and three could pull back and open the huge door-bar; three other   455
Achaians, that is, but Achilleus all by himself could close it.
At this time Hermes, the kind god, opened the gate for the old man
and brought in the glorious gifts for Peleus' son, the swift-footed,
and dismounted to the ground from behind the horses, and spoke forth:
'Aged sir, I who came to you am a god immortal,   460
Hermes. My father sent me down to guide and go with you.
But now I am going back again, and I will not go in
before the eyes of Achilleus, for it would make others angry
for an immortal god so to face mortal men with favour.
But go you in yourself and clasp the knees of Peleion   465
and entreat him in the name of his father, the name of his mother
of the lovely hair, and his child, and so move the spirit within him.'

   So Hermes spoke, and went away to the height of Olympos,
but Priam vaulted down to the ground from behind the horses
and left Idaios where he was, for he stayed behind, holding   470
in hand the horses and mules. The old man made straight for the dwelling
where Achilleus the beloved of Zeus was sitting. He found him
inside, and his companions were sitting apart, as two only,
Automedon the hero and Alkimos, scion of Ares,
were busy beside him. He had just now got through with his dinner,   475
with eating and drinking, and the table still stood by. Tall Priam
came in unseen by the other men and stood close beside him
and caught the knees of Achilleus in his arms, and kissed the hands

that were dangerous and manslaughtering and had killed so many
480 of his sons. As when dense disaster closes on one who has murdered
a man in his own land, and he comes to the country of others,
to a man of substance, and wonder seizes on those who behold him,
so Achilleus wondered as he looked on Priam, a godlike
man, and the rest of them wondered also, and looked at each other.
485 But now Priam spoke to him in the words of a suppliant:
'Achilleus like the gods, remember your father, one who
is of years like mine, and on the door-sill of sorrowful old age.
And they who dwell nearby encompass him and afflict him,
nor is there any to defend him against the wrath, the destruction.
490 Yet surely he, when he hears of you and that you are still living,
is gladdened within his heart and all his days he is hopeful
that he will see his beloved son come home from the Troad.
But for me, my destiny was evil. I have had the noblest
of sons in Troy, but I say not one of them is left to me.
495 Fifty were my sons, when the sons of the Achaians came here.
Nineteen were born to me from the womb of a single mother,
and other women bore the rest in my palace; and of these
violent Ares broke the strength in the knees of most of them,
but one was left me who guarded my city and people, that one
500 you killed a few days since as he fought in defence of his country,
Hektor; for whose sake I come now to the ships of the Achaians
to win him back from you, and I bring you gifts beyond number.
Honour then the gods, Achilleus, and take pity upon me
remembering your father, yet I am still more pitiful;
505 I have gone through what no other mortal on earth has gone through;
I put my lips to the hands of the man who has killed my children.'
   So he spoke, and stirred in the other a passion of grieving
for his own father. He took the old man's hand and pushed him
gently away, and the two remembered, as Priam sat huddled
510 at the feet of Achilleus and wept close for manslaughtering Hektor
and Achilleus wept now for his own father, now again
for Patroklos. The sound of their mourning moved in the house. Then
when great Achilleus had taken full satisfaction in sorrow
and the passion for it had gone from his mind and body, thereafter
515 he rose from his chair, and took the old man by the hand, and set him
on his feet again, in pity for the grey head and the grey beard,

and spoke to him and addressed him in winged words: 'Ah, unlucky,
surely you have had much evil to endure in your spirit.
How could you dare to come alone to the ships of the Achaians
and before my eyes, when I am one who have killed in such numbers   520
such brave sons of yours? The heart in you is iron. Come, then,
and sit down upon this chair, and you and I will even let
our sorrows lie still in the heart for all our grieving. There is not
any advantage to be won from grim lamentation.
Such is the way the gods spun life for unfortunate mortals,   525
that we live in unhappiness, but the gods themselves have no sorrows.
There are two urns that stand on the door-sill of Zeus. They are unlike
for the gifts they bestow: an urn of evils, an urn of blessings.
If Zeus who delights in thunder mingles these and bestows them
on man, he shifts, and moves now in evil, again in good fortune.   530
But when Zeus bestows from the urn of sorrows, he makes a failure
of man, and the evil hunger drives him over the shining
earth, and he wanders respected neither of gods nor mortals.
Such were the shining gifts given by the gods to Peleus
from his birth, who outshone all men beside for his riches   535
and pride of possession, and was lord over the Myrmidons. Thereto
the gods bestowed an immortal wife on him, who was mortal.
But even on him the god piled evil also. There was not
any generation of strong sons born to him in his great house
but a single all-untimely child he had, and I give him   540
no care as he grows old, since far from the land of my fathers
I sit here in Troy, and bring nothing but sorrow to you and your children.
And you, old sir, we are told you prospered once; for as much
as Lesbos, Makar's hold, confines to the north above it
and Phrygia from the north confines, and enormous Hellespont,   545
of these, old sir, you were lord once in your wealth and your children.
But now the Uranian gods brought us, an affliction upon you,
forever there is fighting about your city, and men killed.
But bear up, nor mourn endlessly in your heart, for there is not
anything to be gained from grief for your son; you will never   550
bring him back; sooner you must go through yet another sorrow.'
    In answer to him again spoke aged Priam the godlike:
'Do not, beloved of Zeus, make me sit on a chair while Hektor
lies yet forlorn among the shelters; rather with all speed

555 give him back, so my eyes may behold him, and accept the ransom
we bring you, which is great. You may have joy of it, and go back
to the land of your own fathers, since once you have permitted me
to go on living myself and continue to look on the sunlight.'
     Then looking darkly at him spoke swift-footed Achilleus:
560 'No longer stir me up, old sir. I myself am minded
to give Hektor back to you. A messenger came to me from Zeus,
my mother, she who bore me, the daughter of the sea's ancient.
I know you, Priam, in my heart, and it does not escape me
that some god led you to the running ships of the Achaians.
565 For no mortal would dare come to our encampment, not even
one strong in youth. He could not get by the pickets, he could not
lightly unbar the bolt that secures our gateway. Therefore
you must not further make my spirit move in my sorrows,
for fear, old sir, I might not let you alone in my shelter,
570 suppliant as you are; and be guilty before the god's orders.'
     He spoke, and the old man was frightened and did as he told him.
The son of Peleus bounded to the door of the house like a lion,
nor went alone, but the two henchmen followed attending,
the hero Automedon and Alkimos, those whom Achilleus
575 honoured beyond all companions after Patroklos dead. These two
now set free from under the yoke the mules and the horses,
and led inside the herald, the old king's crier, and gave him
a chair to sit in, then from the smooth-polished mule wagon
lifted out the innumerable spoils for the head of Hektor,
580 but left inside it two great cloaks and a finespun tunic
to shroud the corpse in when they carried him home. Then Achilleus
called out to his serving-maids to wash the body and anoint it
all over; but take it first aside, since otherwise Priam
might see his son and in the heart's sorrow not hold in his anger
585 at the sight, and the deep heart in Achilleus be shaken to anger;
that he might not kill Priam and be guilty before the god's orders.
Then when the serving-maids had washed the corpse and anointed it
with olive oil, they threw a fair great cloak and a tunic
about him, and Achilleus himself lifted him and laid him
590 on a litter, and his friends helped him lift it to the smooth-polished
mule wagon. He groaned then, and called by name on his beloved
     companion:

'Be not angry with me, Patroklos, if you discover,
though you be in the house of Hades, that I gave back great Hektor
to his loved father, for the ransom he gave me was not unworthy.
I will give you your share of the spoils, as much as is fitting.'   595
    So spoke great Achilleus and went back into the shelter
and sat down on the elaborate couch from which he had risen,
against the inward wall, and now spoke his word to Priam:
'Your son is given back to you, aged sir, as you asked it.
He lies on a bier. When dawn shows you yourself shall see him   600
as you take him away. Now you and I must remember our supper.
For even Niobe, she of the lovely tresses, remembered
to eat, whose twelve children were destroyed in her palace,
six daughters, and six sons in the pride of their youth, whom Apollo
killed with arrows from his silver bow, being angered   605
with Niobe, and shaft-showering Artemis killed the daughters;
because Niobe likened herself to Leto of the fair colouring
and said Leto had borne only two, she herself had borne many;
but the two, though they were only two, destroyed all those others.
Nine days long they lay in their blood, nor was there anyone   610
to bury them, for the son of Kronos made stones out of
the people; but on the tenth day the Uranian gods buried them.
But she remembered to eat when she was worn out with weeping.
And now somewhere among the rocks, in the lonely mountains,
in Sipylos, where they say is the resting place of the goddesses   615
who are nymphs, and dance beside the waters of Acheloios,
there, stone still, she broods on the sorrows that the gods gave her.
Come then, we also, aged magnificent sir, must remember
to eat, and afterwards you may take your beloved son back
to Ilion, and mourn for him; and he will be much lamented.'   620
    So spoke fleet Achilleus and sprang to his feet and slaughtered
a gleaming sheep, and his friends skinned it and butchered it fairly,
and cut up the meat expertly into small pieces, and spitted them,
and roasted all carefully and took off the pieces.
Automedon took the bread and set it out on the table   625
in fair baskets, while Achilleus served the meats. And thereon
they put their hands to the good things that lay ready before them.
But when they had put aside their desire for eating and drinking,
Priam, son of Dardanos, gazed upon Achilleus, wondering

[491]

630 at his size and beauty, for he seemed like an outright vision
of gods. Achilleus in turn gazed on Dardanian Priam
and wondered, as he saw his brave looks and listened to him talking.
But when they had taken their fill of gazing one on the other,
first of the two to speak was the aged man, Priam the godlike:
635 'Give me, beloved of Zeus, a place to sleep presently, so that
we may even go to bed and take the pleasure of sweet sleep.
For my eyes have not closed underneath my lids since that time
when my son lost his life beneath your hands, but always
I have been grieving and brooding over my numberless sorrows
640 and wallowed in the muck about my courtyard's enclosure.
Now I have tasted food again and have let the gleaming
wine go down my throat. Before, I had tasted nothing.'
    He spoke, and Achilleus ordered his serving-maids and companions
to make a bed in the porch's shelter and to lay upon it
645 fine underbedding of purple, and spread blankets above it
and fleecy robes to be an over-all covering. The maid-servants
went forth from the main house, and in their hands held torches,
and set to work, and presently had two beds made. Achilleus
of the swift feet now looked at Priam and said, sarcastic:
650 'Sleep outside, aged sir and good friend, for fear some Achaian
might come in here on a matter of counsel, since they keep coming
and sitting by me and making plans; as they are supposed to.
But if one of these come through the fleeting black night should notice you,
he would go straight and tell Agamemnon, shepherd of the people,
655 and there would be delay in the ransoming of the body.
But come, tell me this and count off for me exactly
how many days you intend for the burial of great Hektor.
Tell me, so I myself shall stay still and hold back the people.'
    In answer to him again spoke aged Priam the godlike:
660 'If you are willing that we accomplish a complete funeral
for great Hektor, this, Achilleus, is what you could do and give
me pleasure. For you know surely how we are penned in our city,
and wood is far to bring in from the hills, and the Trojans are frightened
badly. Nine days we would keep him in our palace and mourn him,
665 and bury him on the tenth day, and the people feast by him,
and on the eleventh day we would make the grave-barrow for him,
and on the twelfth day fight again; if so we must do.'

Then in turn swift-footed brilliant Achilleus answered him:
'Then all this, aged Priam, shall be done as you ask it.
I will hold off our attack for as much time as you bid me.' 670
    So he spoke, and took the aged king by the right hand
at the wrist, so that his heart might have no fear. Then these two,
Priam and the herald who were both men of close counsel,
slept in the place outside the house, in the porch's shelter;
but Achilleus slept in the inward corner of the strong-built shelter, 675
and at his side lay Briseis of the fair colouring.
    Now the rest of the gods and men who were lords of chariots
slept nightlong, with the easy bondage of slumber upon them,
only sleep had not caught Hermes the kind god, who pondered
now in his heart the problem of how to escort King Priam 680
from the ships and not be seen by the devoted gate-wardens.
He stood above his head and spoke a word to him, saying:
'Aged sir, you can have no thought of evil from the way
you sleep still among your enemies now Achilleus has left you
unharmed. You have ransomed now your dear son and given much for 685
    him.
But the sons you left behind would give three times as much ransom
for you, who are alive, were Atreus' son Agamemnon
to recognize you, and all the other Achaians learn of you.'
    He spoke, and the old man was afraid, and wakened his herald,
and lightly Hermes harnessed for them the mules and the horses 690
and himself drove them through the encampment. And no man knew of
    them.
    But when they came to the crossing-place of the fair-running river,
of whirling Xanthos, a stream whose father was Zeus the immortal,
there Hermes left them and went away to the height of Olympos,
and dawn, she of the yellow robe, scattered over all earth, 695
and they drove their horses on to the city with lamentation
and clamour, while the mules drew the body. Nor was any other
aware of them at the first, no man, no fair-girdled woman,
only Kassandra, a girl like Aphrodite the golden,
who had gone up to the height of the Pergamos. She saw 700
her dear father standing in the chariot, his herald and crier
with him. She saw Hektor drawn by the mules on a litter.
She cried out then in sorrow and spoke to the entire city:

[493]

'Come, men of Troy and Trojan women; look upon Hektor
705 if ever before you were joyful when you saw him come back living
from battle; for he was a great joy to his city, and all his people.'
    She spoke, and there was no man left there in all the city
nor woman, but all were held in sorrow passing endurance.
They met Priam beside the gates as he brought the dead in.
710 First among them were Hektor's wife and his honoured mother
who tore their hair, and ran up beside the smooth-rolling wagon,
and touched his head. And the multitude, wailing, stood there about them.
And now and there in front of the gates they would have lamented
all day till the sun went down and let fall their tears for Hektor,
715 except that the old man spoke from the chariot to his people:
'Give me way to get through with my mules; then afterwards
you may sate yourselves with mourning, when I have him inside the
      palace.'
    So he spoke, and they stood apart and made way for the wagon.
And when they had brought him inside the renowned house, they laid
      him
720 then on a carved bed, and seated beside him the singers
who were to lead the melody in the dirge, and the singers
chanted the song of sorrow, and the women were mourning beside them.
Andromache of the white arms led the lamentation
of the women, and held in her arms the head of manslaughtering Hektor:
725 'My husband, you were lost young from life, and have left me
a widow in your house, and the boy is only a baby
who was born to you and me, the unhappy. I think he will never
come of age, for before then head to heel this city
will be sacked, for you, its defender, are gone, you who guarded
730 the city, and the grave wives, and the innocent children,
wives who before long must go away in the hollow ships,
and among them I shall also go, and you, my child, follow
where I go, and there do much hard work that is unworthy
of you, drudgery for a hard master; or else some Achaian
735 will take you by hand and hurl you from the tower into horrible
death, in anger because Hektor once killed his brother,
or his father, or his son; there were so many Achaians
whose teeth bit the vast earth, beaten down by the hands of Hektor.
Your father was no merciful man in the horror of battle.

Therefore your people are grieving for you all through their city, 740
Hektor, and you left for your parents mourning and sorrow
beyond words, but for me passing all others is left the bitterness
and the pain, for you did not die in bed, and stretch your arms to me,
nor tell me some last intimate word that I could remember
always, all the nights and days of my weeping for you.' 745
    So she spoke in tears, and the women were mourning about her.
Now Hekabe led out the thronging chant of their sorrow:
'Hektor, of all my sons the dearest by far to my spirit;
while you still lived for me you were dear to the gods, and even
in the stage of death they cared about you still. There were others 750
of my sons whom at times swift-footed Achilleus captured,
and he would sell them as slaves far across the unresting salt water
into Samos, and Imbros, and Lemnos in the gloom of the mists. You,
when he had taken your life with the thin edge of the bronze sword,
he dragged again and again around his beloved companion's 755
tomb, Patroklos', whom you killed, but even so did not
bring him back to life. Now you lie in the palace, handsome
and fresh with dew, in the likeness of one whom he of the silver
bow, Apollo, has attacked and killed with his gentle arrows.'
    So she spoke, in tears, and wakened the endless mourning. 760
Third and last Helen led the song of sorrow among them:
'Hektor, of all my lord's brothers dearest by far to my spirit:
my husband is Alexandros, like an immortal, who brought me
here to Troy; and I should have died before I came with him;
and here now is the twentieth year upon me since I came 765
from the place where I was, forsaking the land of my fathers. In this time
I have never heard a harsh saying from you, nor an insult.
No, but when another, one of my lord's brothers or sisters, a fair-robed
wife of some brother, would say a harsh word to me in the palace,
or my lord's mother—but his father was gentle always, a father 770
indeed—then you would speak and put them off and restrain them
by your own gentleness of heart and your gentle words. Therefore
I mourn for you in sorrow of heart and mourn myself also
and my ill luck. There was no other in all the wide Troad
who was kind to me, and my friend; all others shrank when they saw me.' 775
    So she spoke in tears, and the vast populace grieved with her.
Now Priam the aged king spoke forth his word to his people:

[495]

'Now, men of Troy, bring timber into the city, and let not
your hearts fear a close ambush of the Argives. Achilleus
780 promised me, as he sent me on my way from the black ships,
that none should do us injury until the twelfth dawn comes.'

He spoke, and they harnessed to the wagons their mules and their oxen
and presently were gathered in front of the city. Nine days
they spent bringing in an endless supply of timber. But when
785 the tenth dawn had shone forth with her light upon mortals,
they carried out bold Hektor, weeping, and set the body
aloft a towering pyre for burning. And set fire to it.

But when the young dawn showed again with her rosy fingers,
the people gathered around the pyre of illustrious Hektor.
790 But when all were gathered to one place and assembled together,
first with gleaming wine they put out the pyre that was burning,
all where the fury of the fire still was in force, and thereafter
the brothers and companions of Hektor gathered the white bones
up, mourning, as the tears swelled and ran down their cheeks. Then
795 they laid what they had gathered up in a golden casket
and wrapped this about with soft robes of purple, and presently
put it away in the hollow of the grave, and over it
piled huge stones laid close together. Lightly and quickly
they piled up the grave-barrow, and on all sides were set watchmen
800 for fear the strong-greaved Achaians might too soon set upon them.
They piled up the grave-barrow and went away, and thereafter
assembled in a fair gathering and held a glorious
feast within the house of Priam, king under God's hand.

Such was their burial of Hektor, breaker of horses.

GLOSSARY

NOTE. It is a frequent, though not universal, practice to latinize Greek names, then anglicize the Latin forms, at least in pronunciation. I have generally avoided this practice, but have followed it on some occasions. Names ending in *ees* have been made to end in *es*; some names end (falsely) in *an*, as *Danaan, Boiotian*. Some endings in *e* have been changed to *a*, as *Ida* (not *Ide*), *Hera* (not *Here*). Other Anglo-Latin forms are: Apollo, Argives, Athens, Centaurs, Egypt, Hades, Helen, Hermes, Jason, Myrmidons, Priam, Rhodes, Thrace and Thracian, Titans, Trojans, Troy.

This glossary is not meant to be a complete index, but gives at least one reference for each name in question (frequently there is only one) except in the case of major characters, for whom only a complete index would be useful. References are to book and line.

Aban'tes: The people of Euboia, 2. 536.
Abar'bare: A nymph, 6. 22.
A'bas: Trojan killed by Diomedes, 5. 148.
A'bioi: Barbarians of the north, 13. 6.
Able'ros: Trojan killed by Antilochos, 6. 33.
Aby'dos: A city on the Hellespont, 2. 836.
Achai'a: Greece.
Achai'ans: Greeks.
Acheloi'os: (1) A river in west-central Greece, 21. 194. (2) A river in Phrygia, 24. 616.
Achill'eus: Son of Peleus and Thetis, (Pelei'on, Pele'ides) leader of the Myrmidons, 1. 7, etc.
A'damas: Trojan killed by Meriones, 13. 560 sqq.
Adme'tos: King in Thessaly, husband of Alkestis, father of Eumelos, 2. 713.
Adrestei'a: City near Troy, 2. 828.
Adres'tos: (1) King of Sikyon, 2. 572. (2) Warrior from Adresteia, 2. 830; killed

by Diomedes, 11. 328 sqq. (3) Trojan killed by Agamemnon and Menelaos 6. 37 sqq. (4) Trojan killed by Patroklos, 16. 693.

Ag'akles: Father of Epeigeus, 16. 571.

Agame'de: Wife of Moulios, 11. 740.

Agamem'non: Son of Atreus (therefore sometimes called Atreides), brother of Menelaos, king of Mykenai and chief leader of the Achaians, 1. 24, etc.

Agape'nor: Leader of the Arkadians, 2. 609.

Agas'thenes: Of Elis, father of Polyxeinos, 2. 624.

Agas'trophos: Trojan killed by Diomedes, 11. 338.

Agathon: Son of Priam, 24. 249.

Agau'e: A Nereid, 18. 42.

Agela'os: (1) Trojan killed by Diomedes, 8. 257. (2) Achaian killed by Hektor, 11. 302.

Age'nor: Son of Antenor, one of the great captains and fighters of Troy. Fights Achilleus, 21. 544 sqq.

Aglai'a: Mother of Nireus, 2. 672.

A'grios: A prince of Kalydon, 14. 116.

Aia'kides: Meaning 'descendent of Aiakos', used of Achilleus.

Ai'akos: Son of Zeus, father of Peleus, 21. 189.

Aian'tes: The two called Aias when spoken of together.

Ai'as: (1) Son of Telamon, 'Telamonian' Aias, of Salamis, 2. 557, etc. (2) Son of Oïleus, of Lokris, 2. 527–530, etc.

Aïdo'neus: Another name for Hades.

Ai'gai: City in Achaia, 8. 203.

Aigai'os: God of the sea, father of Briareos, 1.404.

Ai'geus: Father of Theseus, 1. 265.

Aigialei'a: Wife of Diomedes, 5. 412.

Aigi'alos: City in Paphlagonia, 2. 855.

Ai'gilips: City or locality in the domain of Odysseus, 2. 633.

Aigi'na: Island in the domain of Argos, 2. 562.

Ai'gion: City in Achaia, 2. 574.

Ainei'as: Son of Anchises and Aphrodite, leader of the Dardanians, 2. 820, etc.

Ai'nios: Paionian killed by Achilleus, 21. 210.

Ai'nos: City in Thrace, 4. 520.

Ai'olos: Father of Sisyphos, 6. 154.

Aipei'a: Town in Pylos, 9. 152.

Ai'py: City near Pylos, 2. 592.

Ai'pytos: Hero of Arkadia, 2. 604.

Aise'pos: (1) River near Zeleia, 2. 825. (2) Trojan killed by Euryalos, 6. 21.

Aisye'tes: (1) Hero buried in the Trojan plain, 2. 793. (2) Father of Alkathoös, 13. 427.

Aisy'me: City in Thrace, 8. 304.

Aisym'nos: Achaian killed by Hektor, 11. 303.

Ai'the: Mare belonging to Agamemnon, 23. 295.

Aithi'kes: A people of Thessaly, 2. 744.

Ai'thon: One of Hektor's horses, 8. 185.

Ai'thre: One of Helen's handmaidens, 3. 144.

Aito'lians: People of Aitolia in western Greece, led by Thoas, 2. 638–644, etc.

A'kamas: (1) Son of Antenor and companion of Aineias, killed by Meriones, 16. 342. (2) Thracian killed by Aias, 6. 8.

Akessa'menos: A Thracian chief, 21. 143.

Akri'sios: Father of Danaë, 14. 319.

Aktai'e: A Nereid, 18. 41.

Ak'tor: (1) Father of Astyoche, 2. 513. (2) Apparently, an ancestor of Kteatos and Eurytos, 2. 621. (3) Father of Menoitios, so grandfather of Patroklos, 11. 785. (4) Father of Echekles, 16. 189.

Alas'tor: (1) Follower of Nestor, 4. 295. (2) Lykian, killed by Odysseus, 5. 677. (3) Father of Tros (2), 20. 463.

Alege'nor: Father of Promachos, 14. 504.

Alei'os: A plain in Asia, 6. 201.

Alexan'dros: Another, and in the Iliad more usual, name for Paris, q.v.

Alkan'dros: Lykian killed by Odysseus, 5. 678.

Alkath'oös: Brother-in-law of Aineias, killed by Idomeneus, 13. 427–444.

Alkes'tis: Wife of Admetos, mother of Eumelos, 2. 715.

Alkim'edon: A Myrmidon chief, 16. 197.

Al'kimos: Follower of Achilleus, 19. 392.

Alkma'on: Achaian killed by Sarpedon, 12. 394.

Alkme'ne: Mother of Herakles, 14. 323.

Alky'one: 'Sea-bird', a by-name for Marpessa, 9. 562.

Alo'eus: Father of Ephialtes and Otos, 5. 386.

Al'ope: Town in the domain of Achilleus, 2. 682.

Al'os: Town in the domain of Achilleus, 2. 682.

Alphei'os: A river in the western Peloponnese, 2. 592, etc.

Al'tes: King of the Leleges, whose daughter, Laothoë, was one of Priam's wives, 21. 85.

Althai'a: Mother of Meleagros, 9. 555.

Al'ybē: The city of the Halizones, on the south shore of the Black Sea, 2. 857.

Amaryng'keus: An Elean hero, father of Diores, 2. 622.

Amathei'a: A Nereid, 18. 48.

A'mazons: A race of warrior women who invaded Asia Minor, 3. 189; 6. 186.

Amiso'daros: A lord of Lykia, father of Atymnios and Maris, 16. 328.

Amopa'on: Trojan killed by Teukros, 8. 276.

Amphi'damas: (1) A hero of Kythera, 10. 268. (2) A hero of Opous, 23. 87.

Amphigenei'a: City near Pylos, 2. 593.

Amphi'klos: Trojan killed by Meges, 16. 313.

Amphi'machos: (1) A leader of the Epeians, killed by Hektor, 13. 185. (2) A leader of the Karians, 2. 870.

Amphi'nomē: A Nereid, 18. 44.

Amphi'on: A leader of the Epeians, 13. 692.

Amphi'os: (1) Trojan ally from Adresteia, son of Merops, 2. 830; killed by Diomedes, 11. 328. (2) Trojan ally, son of Selagos, killed by Aias, 5. 612.

Amphi'thoë: A Nereid, 18. 42.

Amphi'tryon: Putative father of Herakles, 5. 392.

Ampho'teros: Trojan killed by Patroklos, 16. 415.

A'mydon: City of the Paionians, 2. 849.

Amy'klai: City near Sparta, 2. 584.

Amyn'tor: Father of Phoinix, 9. 448.

Anchi'alos: Achaian killed by Hektor, 5. 609.

Anchi'ses: Second cousin of Priam, lover of Aphrodite, father of Aineias, 5. 268–273; 20. 230–240.

Andrai'mon: Father of Thoas, 2. 638.

Andro'machē: Daughter of Eëtion, wife of Hektor, 6. 371.

Anemorei'a: City in Phokis, 2. 521.

Angkai'os: (1) Father of Agapenor, 2. 609. (2) Of Pleuron, a wrestler beaten by Nestor, 23. 635.

Antei'a: Wife of Proitos, who tempted Bellerophontes, 6. 160.

Ante'nor: An important counsellor of Priam and the Trojans, father of numerous sons who figure in the Iliad, 3. 148; 7. 347, etc.

Anthe'don: Town in Boiotia, 2. 508.

Anthei'a: Town near Pylos, 11. 151.

Anthe'mion: Father of Simoeisios, 4. 473.

Anti'lochos: Son of Nestor, close friend of Achilleus, a prominent warrior, 4. 457, etc.

Anti'machos: Father of Peisandros (1) and Hippolochos (2), and of Hippomachos, 11. 123; 12. 188.

Anti'phates: Trojan killed by Leonteus, 12. 192.

Anti'phonos: Son of Priam, 24. 250.

An'tiphos: (1) A leader of the men from Kos and adjacent islands, 2. 678. (2) A leader of the Maionians, 2. 864. (3) Son of Priam, killed by Agamemnon, 11. 101.

An'tron: City in Thessaly, in the domain of Protesilaos, 2. 697.

Apai'sos: City in the Troad, 2. 828.

A'phareus: Achaian killed by Aineias, 13. 541.

Aphrodi'te: Daughter of Zeus and Dione, mother of Aineias, protectress of Helen, called also the Lady of Kypros, 3. 374, etc.

Apisa'on: (1) Trojan killed by Eurypylos, 11. 578. (2) Trojan killed by Lykomedes, 17. 348.

Apollo: Son of Zeus and Leto, chief protector of the Trojans, 1. 9, etc.

Apseu'des: A Nereid, 18. 46.

Araithyr'ea: City in the domain of Agamemnon, 2. 571.

Arche'lochos: Son of Antenor, killed by Aias, 14. 463.

Archepto'lemos: Charioteer of Hektor, killed by Teukros, 8. 312.

Areï'lykos: (1) Father of Prothoënor, 14. 451. (2) Trojan killed by Patroklos, 16. 308.

Areï'thoös: (1) 'The club-fighter', father of Menesthios, killed by Lykourgos (2), 7. 8; 137. (2) Trojan killed by Achilleus, 20. 487.

Are'ne: City near Pylos, 2. 591.

A'res: Son of Zeus and Hera, fights on the side of the Trojans, 5. 30, etc.

Areta'on: Trojan killed by Teukros, 6. 31.

Are'tos: Trojan killed by Automedon, 17. 517.

Ar'geas: Father of Polyme'los, 16. 417.

Argeïphon'tes: A name given to Hermes.

Argis'sa: City in Thessaly, in the domain of Polypoites, 2. 738.

Ar'gives: The same as Achaians.

Ar'gos: (1) Place-name denoting sometimes a city (under the sway of Diomedes), sometimes a larger district in the north-east Peloponnese, and used also to mean simply 'Greece'. (2) Pelasgian Argos, the domain of Achilleus.

Ariad'ne: Daughter of Minos, 18. 592.

Ar'imoi: A people of Kilikia, 2. 783.

Ari'on: A famous race-horse, 23. 346.

Aris'bas: Father of Leiokritos, 17. 345.

Aris'be: City in the Troad, 2. 836.

Ar'ne: City in Boiotia, 2. 507.

Arsi'noös: Father of Hekamede, 11. 626.

Ar'temis: Sister of Apollo, 5. 51, etc.

Asai'os: Achaian killed by Hektor, 11. 301.

A'sinē: City near Argos, 2. 560.

A'sios: (1) Son of Hyrtakos, a Trojan ally, killed by Idomeneus, 13. 389. (2) Brother of Hekabe and uncle of Hektor, 16. 717.

Aska'laphos: Son of Ares, a chief of Orchomenos, 2. 511; killed by Deïphobos, 13. 519.

Aska'nia: City in Phrygia, 2. 863.

Aska'nios: Leader from Askania, 13. 792.

Askle'pios: The great healer, father of Machaon and Podalei'rios; 2. 731.

Aso'pos: River in Boiotia, 4. 383.

Asple'don: City of the Minyai, near Orchomenos, 2. 511.

Assar'akos: Son of Tros, brother of Ilos, great-grandfather of Aineias, 20. 232.

Aster'ion: City in Thessaly, in the domain of Eurypylos, 2. 735.

Asteropai'os: Leader of the Paionians, one of the greatest of the Trojan allies, 12. 102; killed by Achilleus, 21. 140–183.

Asty'alos: Trojan killed by Polypoites, 6. 29.

Asty'anax: Hektor's infant son, 6. 403.

Asty'noös: (1) Trojan killed by Diomedes, 5. 144. (2) A Trojan charioteer, 15. 455.

Asty'ochē: Mother, by Ares, of Askalaphos and Ialmenos, 2. 513.

Astyochei'a: Mother of Tlepolemos, 2. 658.

Asty'pylos: Paionian killed by Achilleus, 21. 209.

Athe'ne: or Pallas Athene, also called Tritogeneia, daughter of Zeus, protectress of the Achaians, particularly Achilleus, Diomedes and Odysseus, 1. 194, etc.

Ath'ens: The city of Erechtheus, in east-central Greece, 2. 546.

Ath'os: Mountain and promontory in the northern Aegean, 14. 229.

Atrei'des: 'Son of Atreus', used of Agamemnon, less often of Menelaos.

At'reus: Father of Agamemnon and Menelaos, 2. 105.

Atryto'ne: Epithet of Athene, 1. 157.

Atym'nios: (1) Father of Mydon, 5. 581. (2) Trojan, brother of Maris, killed by Antilochos, 16. 317.

Augei'ai: (1) City in Lokris, 2. 532. (2) City in Lakedaimon, 2. 583.

Augei'as: Lord of Elis, 11. 701.

Au'lis. A city at the narrows between Euboia and the mainland, where the ships of the Achaians assembled for the expedition to Troy, 2. 303.

Auto'lykos: Maternal grandfather of Odysseus, 10. 266.

Auto'medon: Follower and charioteer of Achilleus and Patroklos, a considerable warrior in his own right, 16. 145; 17. 429.

Auto'noös: (1) Achaian killed by Hektor, 11. 301. (2) Trojan killed by Patroklos, 16. 694.

Auto'phonos: Father of Polyphontes, 4. 395.

Ax'ios: A river, and river-god, in Paionia, 2. 849.

Ax'ylos: Trojan ally from Arisbe, killed by Diomedes, 6. 12.

A'zeus: Father, or ancestor, of Aktor (1), 2. 513.

Bal'ios: One of the immortal horses of Achilleus, 16. 149.

Bath'ykles: Myrmidon killed by Glaukos, 16. 594.

Bellerophon'tes: Hero from Korinth, killer of the Chimaira, grandfather of Sarpedon and Glaukos (now usually called Bellerophon), 6. 155–202.

Bes'sa: City in Lokris, 2. 532.

Bias: (1) Leader under Nestor, 4. 296. (2) Athenian, leader under Menestheus, 13. 691. (3) Father of Dardanos (2) and Laogonos (2), 20. 461.

Bie'nor: Trojan killed by Agamemnon, 11. 92.

Boag'rios: River in Lokris, 2. 533.

Boi'be: Thessalian city in the domain of Eumelos, 2. 712.

Boibe'is: The lake by which Boibe was situated, 2. 711.

Boio'tians: The people of Boiotia, in central Greece north-west of Attica, 2. 494.

Bor'eas: The north (more accurately north-east) wind, 9. 4.

Bo'ros: (1) Father of Phaistos, 5. 44. (2) Husband of Polydore, 16. 177.

Boudei'on: Town in the territory of the Myrmidons, 16. 572.

Boukol'ion: Son of Laomedon, father of Aisepos (2) and Pedasos (1), 6. 22.

Bou'kolos: Father of Sphelos, grandfather of Iasos, 15. 338.

Boupra'sion: City in Elis, 2. 615.

Briar'eos: A hundred-handed giant, 1. 403.

Brise'is: The captive mistress of Achilleus, 1. 184; her life-story, 19. 282–300.

Bri'seus: Father of Briseis, 1. 392.

Brysei'ai: City in Lakedaimon, 2. 583.

Cen'taurs: Creatures, part human and part beast, at home around Mount Pelion, 11. 832.

Chal'kis: (1) City in Euboia, 2. 537. (2) City in Aitolia, 2. 640. (3) Name of a bird, 14. 291.

Chalko'don: Father, or ancestor, of Elephenor, 2. 541.

Charis: Goddess, wife of Hephaistos, 18. 382–393.

Char'opos: Father of Nireus, 2. 672.

Charops: Trojan killed by Odysseus, 11. 427.

Chei'ron: 'Most righteous of the Centaurs', friend and teacher of Asklepios, 4. 219; of Achilleus, 11. 832; of Peleus, 16. 143.

Chersi'damas: Trojan killed by Odysseus, 11. 423.

Chimai'ra: Lykian monster killed by Bellerophontes, 6. 179.

Chro'mios: (1) Follower (in the Odyssey, 11. 286, brother) of Nestor, 4. 295. (2) Son of Priam killed by Diomedes, 5. 160. (3) Lykian killed by Odysseus, 5. 677. (4) Trojan killed by Teukros, 8. 275. (5) A Trojan captain, 17. 218.

Chromis: Leader of the Mysians, killed by Achilleus, 2. 858.

Chry'se: Town near Troy, the home of Chryses, 1. 37.

Chryse'is: Daughter of Chryses, captive mistress of Agamemnon, released by him to her father (later Criseyde, Cressida), 1. 111, etc.

Chryses: Priest of Apollo, father of Chryseis, 1. 11.

Chryso'themis: Daughter of Agamemnon, 9. 145.

Dai'dalos: Builder in Krete, 18. 592.

Dai'tor: Trojan killed by Teukros, 8. 275.

Dam'asos: Trojan killed by Polypoites, 12. 183.

Damas'tor: Father of Tlepolemos (2), 16. 416.

Dan'aäns: Achaians, Argives.

Dan'aë: Mother, by Zeus, of Perseus, 14. 319.

Dardan'ia: The domain of Dardanos, 20. 216.

Dardanian, Dardanians: Of Dardania, or descended from, or pertaining to, Dardanos. Used of the group of Trojans whose lord was Aineias, 2. 819.

Dar'danos: (1) Son of Zeus, father of Erichthonios, ancestor of the Trojan kings, 20. 215. (2) Son of Bias, killed by Achilleus, 20. 460.

Dar'es: Priest of Hephaistos in Troy, father of Phegeus and Idaios (2), 5. 9.

Dau'lis: City near Pytho, 2. 520.

Deï'koön: Companion of Aineias, killed by Agamemnon, 5. 534.

Deï'ochos: Achaian killed by Paris, 15. 341.

Deïopi'tes: Trojan killed by Odysseus, 11. 420.

Deï'phobos: Son of Priam, one of the more powerful Trojan fighters, 13. 156; 402; impersonated by Athene in order to swindle Hektor, 22. 227–295.

Deï'pylos: Companion of Sthenelos, 5. 325.

Deï'pyros: Achaian killed by Helenos, 13. 576.

Deise'nor: Trojan captain, 17. 217.

Deme'ter: Sister of Zeus, goddess of the earth as giver of food, 5. 500, etc.

Demo'koön: Bastard son of Priam, killed by Odysseus, 4. 499.

Demo'leon: Son of Antenor, killed by Achilleus, 20. 395.

Demou'chos: Trojan killed by Achilleus, 20. 457.

Deuka'lion: (1) Hero of Krete, father of Idomeneus, 12. 117; 13. 451. (2) Trojan killed by Achilleus, 20, 477.

Dexa'menē: A Nereid, 18. 44.

Dex'ios: Father of Iphinoös, 7. 15.

Dio'kles: Father of Orsilochos (1) and Krethon, 5. 542.

Diome'de: Captive mistress of Achilleus, 9. 665.

Diome'des: Son of Tydeus, lord, with Sthenelos and Euryalos, of Argos proper, one of the greatest of the Achaian fighters, prominent in battle until wounded by Paris, 11. 368–400.

Di'on: City in Euboia, 2. 538.

Dio'ne: Mother of Aphrodite, 5. 370–417.

Diony'sos: Son of Zeus and Semele, driven into the sea by Lykourgos, 6. 132–137.

Dio'res: (1) A leader of the Epeians, 2. 622; killed by Peiros, 4. 517. (2) Father of Automedon, 17. 429.

Di'os: Son of Priam, 24. 251.

Dodo'na: Place in Epeiros in extreme north-west Greece, site of an oracle of Zeus, 2. 750; 16. 233.

Do'lon: Trojan scout, killed by Diomedes and Odysseus, 10. 313–464.

Dol'opes: People 'in remotest Phthia' ruled over by Phoinix, 9. 484.

Dolopi'on: Priest of Skamandros in Troy, father of Hypsenor (1), 5. 77.

Dol'ops: (1) Achaian killed by Hektor, 11. 302. (2) Trojan killed by Menelaos, 15. 525–543.

Doris: A Nereid, 18. 45.

Dory'klos: Son of Priam, killed by Aias, 11. 489.

Doto: A Nereid, 18. 43.

Douli'chion: Island in the domain of Meges, 2. 625.

Dra'kios: A leader of the Epeians, 13. 692.

Dry'as: (1) Hero of the generation of Nestor, 1. 263. (2) Father of Lykourgos (1), 6. 130.

Dry'ops: Trojan killed by Achilleus, 20. 455.

Dy'mas: Father of Hekabe and of Asios (2), 16. 718.

Dyna'menē: A Nereid, 18. 43.

Eche'kles: Myrmidon, son of Aktor (4), husband of Polymele, 16. 189.

Eche'klos: (1) Trojan killed by Patroklos, 16. 694. (2) Trojan, son of Agenor, killed by Achilleus, 20. 474.

Echem'mon: Son of Priam, killed by Diomedes, 5. 160.

Echepo'los: (1) Trojan killed by Antilochos, 4. 458. (2) Son of Anchises, 23. 296.

Echi'nai: Islands in the domain of Meges, 2. 625.

E'chios: (1) Father of Mekisteus, 8. 332. (2) Achaian killed by Polites, 15. 339. (3) Lykian killed by Patroklos, 16. 416.

Eëriboi'a: Stepmother of Ephialtes and Otos, 5. 389.

Eë'tion: (1) King of Thebe, father of Andromache, killed by Achilleus, 6. 414–420. (2) Father of Podes, 17. 575 (perhaps identical with the afore-mentioned). (3) A lord of Imbros, 21. 43.

Eileithy'ia: Goddess of childbirth, 16. 187.

Eile'sion: City in Boiotia, 2. 499.

Ei'ones: City near Argos, 2. 561.

Ei'oneus: (1) Achaian killed by Hektor, 7. 11. (2) Father of Rhesos, 10. 435.

El'asos: Trojan killed by Patroklos, 16. 696.

El'atos: Trojan ally killed by Agamemnon, 6. 33.

Elei'ans: The people of Elis, 11. 673.

El'eon: City in Boiotia, 2. 500.

Elephe'nor: Leader of the Abantes, 2. 540; killed by Agenor, 4. 463–469.

Elis: City and district of the western Peloponnese, adjoining the domain of Nestor, 2. 615, etc.

Elo'ne: City in Thessaly, in the domain of Polypoites, 2. 739.

Ema'thia: District to the north-west of the Aegean, later part of Macedonia, 14. 226.

En'etoi: A Paphlagonian tribe, 2. 852.

GLOSSARY

Enie'nes: People from the extreme north-west of Thessaly, 2. 749.

Eni'opeus: Charioteer of Hektor, killed by Diomedes, 8. 120.

Enis'pe: Town in Arkadia, 2. 606.

En'nomos: (1) Leader of the Mysians and augur, killed by Achilleus, 2. 858–861. (2) Trojan killed by Odysseus, 11. 422.

En'opē: Town near Pylos, 9. 150.

En'ops: (1) Father of Satnios, 14. 444. (2) Father of Thestor, 16. 402 (perhaps identical with the afore-mentioned). (3) Father of Klytomedes, 23. 634.

Eny'eus: King of Skyros, 9. 668.

Eny'o: War goddess, 5. 333.

Epal'tes: Lykian killed by Patroklos, 16. 415.

Epei'ans: People of Elis, 2. 619.

Epei'geus: Myrmidon killed by Hektor, 16. 570–580.

Epei'os: Achaian, a great boxer and winner of this event in the games for Patroklos, 23. 664–699 (in the Odyssey, 8. 493, builder of the Trojan Horse).

Ephial'tes: Giant who with his brother Otos imprisoned Ares, 5. 385.

Eph'yra or Eph'yrē: (1) A place on the river Selleëis, exact location unknown, 2. 659. (2) Homeric name for Korinth, 6. 152.

Eph'yroi: A northern people visited by Ares, 13. 301.

Epidau'ros: City in the domain of Diomedes, 2. 561.

Epi'kles: Lykian killed by Aias, 12. 379.

Epis'tor: Trojan killed by Patroklos, 16. 695.

Epis'trophos: (1) Leader of the men of Phokis, 2. 517. (2) Prince of Lyrnessos, killed by Achilleus, 2. 692. (3) Leader of the Halizones, 2. 856.

Ep'ytos: Father of Periphas, 17. 324.

Erech'theus: Hero of Athens, 2. 547.

Ereutha'lion: Arkadian hero killed by Nestor, 7. 136.

Erichthon'ios: Son of Dardanos, ancestor of the kings of Troy, 20. 219.

Erin'ys: Spirit of vengeance, 9. 571.

Erio'pis: Wife of Oïleus (1) and stepmother of Medon (1), 13. 697.

Eryla'os: Trojan killed by Patroklos, 16. 411.

Er'ymas: (1) Trojan killed by Idomeneus, 16. 345. (2) Trojan killed by Patroklos, 16. 415.

Erythi'noi: Place in Paphlagonia, 2. 855.

Ery'thrai: City in Boiotia, 2. 499.

Eteo'kles: Son of Oidipous, defender of Thebes against the Argives, 4. 386.

Eteo'nos: City in Boiotia, 2. 497.

Euai'mon: Father of Eurypylos (1), 2. 736.

Euboi'a: Island lying close off east-central Greece, 2. 536.

Euche'nor: Achaian killed by Paris, 13. 663–672.

Eudor'os: Son of Hermes and Polymele, a Myrmidon captain, 16. 179.

Eue'nos: (1) Father of Epistrophos (2) and Mynes, 2. 693. (2) Father of Marpessa, 9. 557.

Euip'pos: Lykian killed by Patroklos, 16. 417.

Eume'des: Herald in Troy, father of Dolon, 10. 314.

Eume'los: Son of Admetos and Alkestis, lord of the Thessalians from Pherai, 2. 713. Prominent in the chariot-race in the games for Patroklos, 23. 288–565.

Eune'os: Son of Jason and Hypsipyle, lord in Lemnos, 7. 468.

Euphe'mos: Trojan ally, leader of the Kikonians, 2. 846.

Euphe'tes: Lord of Ephyra (1), 15. 532.

Euphor'bos: Dardanian, son of Panthoös, who struck down Patroklos, 16. 806–815; killed by Menelaos, 17. 43–60.

Euro'pa: Daughter of Phoinix, mother of Minos and Rhadamanthys, 14. 321.

Eury'alos: Leader, with Diomedes and Sthenelos, of the men of Argos proper, 2. 565.

Eury'bates: (1) Herald for Agamemnon, 1. 320. (2) Herald for Odysseus, 2. 184. (The two are probably the same person.)

Eury'damas: A dream-interpreter, father of Abas and Polyidos (1), 5. 149.

Eury'medon: (1) Charioteer of Agamemnon, 4. 228. (2) Charioteer of Nestor, 8. 114.

Eury'nomē· Daughter of Ocean, 18. 398.

Eury'pylos: (1) Son of Euaimon, lord of a district in Thessaly which has not been certainly located, 2. 736; wounded and put out of action by Paris, 11.'575–595, etc. (2) Hero of Kos, 2. 677.

Eurys'theus: Taskmaster of Herakles, 8. 363; 19. 107–125.

Eu'rytos: (1) Hero of Oichalia, 2. 596. (2) Father of Thalpios, brother of Kteatos, 2. 621; he and his brother called Moliones, 11. 709; 750.

Eusso'ros: Father of Akamas (2), 6. 8.

Eutre'sis: City in Boiotia, 2. 502.

Exa'dios: Hero of the generation of Nestor, 1. 264.

Galatei'a: A Nereid, 18. 45.

Ganyme'des: Son of Tros (1), caught up among the gods and made immortal, 20. 232–235.

Gar'garon or Gar'garos: The peak of Ida, 8. 48.

Gere'nian: Epithet of Nestor, 2. 336, etc.

Gla'phyrai: Thessalian city in the domain of Eumelos, 2. 712.

Glau'ke: A Nereid, 18. 39.

Glau'kos: (1) Companion of Sarpedon, second in command of the Lykians, 2. 876; wounded by Teukros, 12. 387–389. (2) Father of Bellerophontes, great-grandfather of Glaukos (1), 6. 154–155.

Glisas: City in Boiotia, 2. 504.

Gonoës'sa: Achaian city in the domain of Agamemnon, 2. 573.

Gor'gon: A staring monster, 5. 741.

Gorgy'thion: Son of Priam and Kastianeira, killed by Teukros, 8. 302–308.

Gor'tyna: City in Krete, 2. 646.

Gou'neus: Lord of the peoples around Dodona, 2. 748.

Grai'a: City in Boiotia, 2. 498.

Greni'kos: River of the Troad, 12. 21.

Gygai'an: Of a lake in Mysia, 2. 865.

Gy'ge: The same lake, 20. 391.

Gyr'tios: Father of Hyrtios, 14. 512.

Gyrto'ne: Thessalian city in the domain of Polypoites, 2. 738.

Ha'des: Properly Aï'des. Son of Kronos and Rhea, full brother of Zeus, Poseidon, Hera and Demeter, 15. 187–192. Lord over the dead, loc. cit.; i. 3, etc. (N.B. A person, not a place.)

Hai'mon: (1) Companion of Nestor, 4. 296. (2) Father of Maion, 4. 394. (3) Father of Laerkes, 17. 467.

Ha'lia: A Nereid, 18. 40.

Haliar'tos: City in Boiotia, 2. 503.

Ha'lios: Lykian killed by Odysseus, 5. 678.

Halizo'nes: A tribe from the Black Sea district, led by Odios (1) and Epistrophos (3), 2. 856.

Harma: City in Boiotia, 2. 499.

Harmon'ides: Smith in Troy, father of Phereklos, 5. 60.

Harpal'ion: Paphlagonian ally of Troy killed by Meriones, 13. 643–659.

He'be: Or Youth, daughter of Zeus and Hera, ministrant to other Olympians, 4. 2; 5. 722, etc.

Hek'abē: Daughter of Dymas, Priam's queen, 6. 251; 22. 79, etc.

Hekame'de: Captive mistress of Nestor, 11. 624.

Hektor: Son of Priam, field commander of the Trojans and their greatest fighter, killer of Patroklos, 16. 816–842; killed by Achilleus, 22. 273–363.

Helen: Wife of Menelaos who ran away with Paris, the cause of the war, 3. 121, etc.

Hel'enos: (1) Achaian killed by Hektor, 5. 707. (2) Son of Priam, augur and fighter, 6. 76; 576, etc.

Helika'on: Son of Antenor, husband of Laodike, 3. 123.

Hel'ikē: Place in the domain of Agamemnon, on the Corinthian Gulf, 2. 575.

Hellas: The domain, or part of the domain, of Peleus, 2. 683, etc.

Hellenes: The people of Hellas, 2. 684.

Hel'lespont: Strait between the Troad and Thrace, now Dardanelles, 2. 845, etc.

Helos: (1) City in Lakedaimon, 2. 584. (2) City near Pylos, 2. 594.

Hephais'tos: Son of Hera, 1. 571; artificer, 1. 607, etc.; fire god, 21. 330–381, etc.

Hepta'poros: River in the Troad, 12. 20.

Hera: Daughter of Kronos and Rhea, full sister and wife of Zeus, protector of the Achaians, 1. 55, etc.

Her'akles: Son of Alkmene and Zeus, 14. 324; father of Tlepolemos (1), 2. 658; of Thessalos, 2. 679.

Her'mes: Son of Zeus, called guide and Argeïphontes, 2. 104, etc.

Hermi'onē: City in the domain of Diomedes, 2. 560.

Hermos: River in Phrygia, 20. 392.

Hesper: The evening star, 22. 318.

Hiketa'on: Son of Laomedon, 20. 238; father of Melanippos (2), 15. 546.

Hippo'damas: Trojan killed by Achilleus, 20. 401.

Hippodamei'a: (1) Wife of Peirithoös, mother of Polypoites, 2. 472. (2) Daughter of Anchises, wife of Alkathoös, 13. 429.

Hippo'damos: Trojan killed by Odysseus, 11. 335.

Hippo'koön: Cousin of Rhesos, 10. 518.

Hippo'lochos: (1) Father of Glaukos (1), 6. 119. (2) Trojan killed by Agamemnon, 11. 122–147.

Hippo'machos: Trojan killed by Leonteus, 12. 189.

Hippomol'goi: A northern tribe, 'horse-milkers', presumably nomads, 13. 5.

Hippo'noös: Achaian killed by Hektor, 11. 303.

Hippo'thoös: (1) Trojan ally, leader of the Pelasgians, 2. 840; killed by Aias, 17. 293. (2) Son of Priam, 24. 251.

Hippo'tion: Chief from Askania, 13. 793; killed by Meriones, 14. 514.

Hi're: Town near Pylos, 9. 150.

Histiai'a: City in Euboia, 2. 537.

Hy'adēs: The stars still so called, 18. 486.

Hyam'polis: City in Phokis, 2. 521.

Hy'de: District around Mount Tmolos, 20. 385.

Hy'le: City in Boiotia, 2. 500.

Hyl'los: River in Mysia, 20. 392.

Hypei'rochos: (1) Trojan killed by Odysseus, 11. 335. (2) Father of Itymoneus, 11. 673.

Hypei'ron: Trojan killed by Diomedes, 5. 144.

Hyperei'a: A spring in the domain of Eurypylos, 2. 734.

Hypere'nor: Son of Panthoös, killed by Menelaos, 14. 516; 17. 24.

Hypere'sia: Achaian city in the domain of Agamemnon, 2. 573.

Hyper'ion: Epithet of Helios, the Sun, 8. 480.

Hypse'nor: (1) Trojan killed by Eurypylos, 5. 76–83. (2) Achaian killed by Deïphobos, 13. 411.

Hypsi'pyle: Mother, by Jason, of Euneos, 7. 469.

Hy'ria: City in Boiotia, 2. 496.

Hyrmi'ne: City in Elis, 2. 616.

Hyr'takos: Father of Asios (1), 2. 837.

Hyr'tios: Mysian killed by Aias, 14. 511.

Iai'ra: A Nereid, 18. 42.

Ial'menos: A leader of the Minyai from Orchomenos, 2. 512.

Ialy'sos: City in Rhodes, 2. 656.

Ia'menos: Trojan killed by Leonteus, 12. 194.

Ianas'sa: A Nereid, 18. 47.

Ianei'ra: A Nereid, 18. 47.

Ia'petos: One of the Titans, 8. 479.

Iar'danos: River apparently on the borders of Pylos and Arkadia, 7. 135.

I'asos: Athenian killed by Aineias, 15. 332–338.

Ida: Mountain and range in the Troad, 2. 821, etc.

Idai'os: (1) Herald of Priam, 3. 248; 7. 381–397. (2) Trojan, son of Dares and
   brother of Phegeus, rescued from Diomedes by Hephaistos, 5. 11–24.

Idas: Husband of Marpessa and father of Kleopatra, who contended against Apollo
   for the sake of Marpessa, 9. 556–560.

Ido'meneus: Son of Deukalion, lord of Krete, one of the great princes and fighters
   of the Achaians, 2. 645, etc.

Ika'ria: Island off the coast of Asia Minor, 2. 145.

Ilion: Or Ilios; Troy, the city of Ilos.

Ili'oneus: Trojan killed by Peneleos, 14. 489–499.

Ilos: Eldest son of Tros, father of Laomedon, grandfather of Priam, 20. 232.

Im'brasos: Thracian, father of Peiros, 4. 520.

Im'brios: Trojan ally from Pedaios, killed by Teukros, 13. 170.

Im'bros: Island north-west of Troy, 13. 33.

Iol'kos: Thessalian town in the domain of Eumelos, 2. 712.

Io'nians: A people closely associated with, perhaps identified with, the Athenians,
   13. 685.

Iph'eus: Lykian killed by Patroklos, 16. 417.

Iphianas'sa: Daughter of Agamemnon, 9. 145.

Iphi'damas: Son of Antenor, killed by Agamemnon, 11. 221–247.

Iphi'klos: Runner defeated by Nestor, 23. 636.

Iphi'noös: Achaian killed by Glaukos, 7. 14.

Iphis: Captive mistress of Patroklos, 9. 667.

Iphi'tion: Lydian killed by Achilleus, 20. 382.

Iph'itos: (1) Father of Schedios (1) and Epistrophos (1), 2. 518. (2) Father of
   Archeptolemos, 8. 128.

Iris: The messenger of the gods, 2. 786, etc.

Isan'dros: Son of Bellerophontes, 6. 197.

Isos: Son of Priam, killed by Agamemnon, 11. 111–121

Ithai'menes: Father of Sthenelaos, 16. 586.

Ith'aka: Island off west-central Greece, the home of Odysseus, 2. 632, etc.

Itho'me: Thessalian city in the domain of Podaleirios and Machaon, 2. 729.

Iton: Thessalian city in the domain of Protesilaos, 2. 696.

Ity'moneus: Eleian killed by Nestor in his youth, 11. 672.

Ixi'on: Putative father of Peirithoös, 14. 317.

Jason: The Argonaut, father of Euneos, 7. 468.

Kabe'sos: City, location unknown, on the Trojan side, 13. 363.

Kadmei'ans: Thebans, 4. 388, etc.

Kai'neus: Hero of the generation of Nestor, 1. 264.

Kal'chas: Augur for the Achaians, 1. 68–100; 2. 300–332. Impersonated by Poseidon, 13. 45.

Kale'sios: Charioteer of Axylos, killed by Diomedes, 6. 18.

Kale'tor: (1) Father of Aphareus, 13. 541. (2) Trojan killed by Aias, 15. 419.

Kallianas'sa: A Nereid, 18. 46.

Kallianei'ra: A Nereid, 18. 44.

Kalli'aros: City in Lokris, 2. 531.

Kalyd'nai: Islands in the south-east Aegean, 2. 677.

Kal'ydon: City of Aitolia, its men led by Thoas, 2. 640. For a part of the Kalydonian Saga, see 9. 529–599.

Kamei'ros: City of Rhodes, 2. 656.

Kap'aneus: Father of Sthenelos, 2. 564.

Kap'ys: Son of Assarakos, father of Anchises, so grandfather of Aineias, 20. 239.

Karda'mylē: Town near Pylos, 9. 150.

Kare'sos: River in the Troad, 12. 20.

Kar'ians: People of Asia Minor who held the city of Miletos, 2. 867.

Karys'tos: City of Euboia, 2. 539.

Ka'sos: Island near Kos, 2. 676.

Kassan'dra: Daughter of Priam, 13. 366; 24. 699.

Kastianei'ra: Mother, by Priam, of Gorgythion, 8. 304.

Kastor: Brother of Helen, 3. 237.

Kaukon'ians: People of Asia Minor allied to the Trojans, 10. 429.

Kaÿst'rian: Of the river Kaÿstros in Asia Minor, 2. 461.

Ke'as: Father of Troizenos, 2. 847.

Kebri'ones: Brother of Hektor, 8. 318; killed by Patroklos, 16. 737–776.

Kel'adon: River apparently on the borders of Pylos and Arkadia, 7. 134.

Kephalle'nia: Island off west-central Greece, in the domain of Odysseus, 2. 631.

Kephisian mere: A lake, more commonly called Kopa'is, in Boiotia, 5. 709.

Kephi'sos: River in Phokis (and Boiotia), 2. 522.

Kerin'thos: City in Euboia, 2. 538.

Kikonian: Of a Thracian people, also called Kiko'nes, 2. 846.

Kili'kians: In Homer, only of the people in Asian Thebe, 6. 397; 415.

Kil'la: Town in the Troad, 1. 38.

Kin'yras: King of Cyprus who gave a corselet to Agamemnon, 11. 20.

Kis'seus: Father of Theano, 11. 223.

Klei'tos: Charioteer of Poulydamas, killed by Teukros, 15. 445–453.

Kleobou'los: Trojan killed by Aias (2), 16. 330–334.

Kleo'nai: City in the domain of Agamemnon, 2. 570.

Kleopat'ra: Daughter of Idas and Marpessa, wife of Meleagros, 9. 556.

Klo'nios: A leader of the Boiotians, 2. 495; killed by Agenor, 15. 340.

Kly'menē: (1) One of Helen's handmaidens, 3, 144. (2) A Nereid, 18. 47.

Klytaimes'tra: Wife of Agamemnon, 1. 113.

Kly'tios: (1) Son of Laomedon, brother of Priam, father of Kaletor, 3. 147; 15. 419; 20. 238. (2) Father of Dolops (1), 11. 302.

Klytome'des: Boxer defeated by Nestor in his youth, 23. 634.

Kno'sos: City in Krete, 2. 646.

Koi'ranos: (1) Lykian killed by Odysseus, 5. 677. (2) Charioteer of Meriones, killed by Hektor, 17. 610–619.

Ko'on: Son of Antenor, killed by Agamemnon after wounding him, 11. 248–263.

Ko'pai: City in Boiotia, 2. 502.

Kop'reus: Herald of Eurystheus, father of Periphetes, 15. 639.

Kor'inth: City in the domain of Agamemnon, 2. 570.

Koronei'a: City in Boiotia, 2. 503.

Koro'nos: Father of Leonteus, 2. 746.

Kos: Island in the south-east Aegean, 2. 677.

Koure'tes: A people at war with the Aitolians, 9. 529–599.

Kran'aë: Island on the homeward route of Paris from Lakedaimon, 3. 445.

Kra'pathos: Island in the south-east Aegean, 2. 676.

Krei'on: Father of Lykomedes, 9. 84.

Krete: Large island south of the Aegean, the domain of Idomeneus, 2. 649.

Kre'thon: Achaian killed by Aineias, 5. 541–560.

Krisa: City in Phokis, 2. 519.

Krois'mos: Trojan killed by Meges, 15. 523.

Krokylei'a: Place on or near Ithaka, 2. 633.

Krom'na: City in Paphlagonia, 2. 855.

Kronos: Father of Zeus, Hades, Poseidon, Hera, Demeter, 1. 498, etc.; overthrown and in Tartaros, 8. 479–481.

Kte'atos: Brother of Eurytos (2), q.v.; father of Amphimachos (1), 2. 620–621.

Kylle'ne: Mountain bounding Arkadia to the north, 2. 603.

Kymin'dis: Name for a bird, 14. 291.

Kymo'dokē: A Nereid, 18. 39.

Kymo'thoë: A Nereid, 18. 41.

Kynos: City in Lokris, 2. 531.

Kyparisse'eis: City near Pylos, 2. 593.

Kyparis'sos: City in Phokis, 2. 519.

Ky'phos: City of Gouneus, 2. 748.

Kythe'ra: Island off the southern tip of Lakedaimon, 15. 431.

Kyto'ros: City in Paphlagonia, 2. 853.

La'as: City in Lakedaimon, 2. 585.

Laër'kes: Myrmidon, father of Alkimedon, 16. 197.

Laër'tes: Father of Odysseus, 2. 173.

Lakedai'mon: The city, with its surrounding country, of Menelaos, in south-eastern Greece, 2. 581, etc.

Lampos: (1) Son of Laomedon, father of Dolops (2), 15. 525–527. (2) One of Hektor's horses, 8. 185.

Lao'damas: Trojan, son of Antenor, killed by Aias, 15. 516.

Laodamei'a: Daughter of Bellerophontes, mother, by Zeus, of Sarpedon, 6. 197–199.

Lao'dikē: (1) Daughter of Priam and wife of Helikaon, impersonated by Iris, 3. 121–124. (2) Daughter of Agamemnon, 9. 145.

Lao'dokos: (1) Son of Antenor, impersonated by Athene, 4. 87. (2) Charioteer of Antilochos, 17. 699.

Lao'gonos: (1) Trojan killed by Meriones, 16. 603–607. (2) Trojan killed by Achilleus, 20. 460.

Lao'medon: King of Troy, son of Ilos and father of Priam, Tithonos, Lampos (1), Klytios (1) and Hiketaon, 20. 236–238; who earned the hatred of Poseidon by his treatment of him and Apollo, 21. 443–460.

Lao'thoë: Daughter of Altes, mother, by Priam, of Lykaon (2) and Polydoros (1), 21. 84–91.

La'pithai: Thessalian people led by Polypoites and Leonteus, 12. 128–130.

Laris'sa: City, location unknown, allied to Troy, 2. 841.

Leio'kritos: Achaian killed by Aineias, 17. 344.

Le'itos: Leader, with Peneleos, of the Boiotians, 2. 494; wounded and put out of action by Hektor, 17. 601–604.

Lektos: Or Lekton, promontory of the Troad, 14. 284.

Le'leges: People of Asia Minor allied to the Trojans, 10. 429.

Lemnos: Island in the Aegean, west of Troy, 1. 593; 2. 722, etc.

Leon'teus: Leader, with Polypoites, of the Lapithai from Argissa, etc., 2. 745.

Lesbos: Island and city close to the coast of Asia Minor south of Troy, 9. 129, etc.

Lethos: Lord of Larissa, 2. 843.

Leto: Mother (by Zeus) of Apollo and Artemis, 1. 9; 21. 498–504; 24. 607–609.

Leu'kos: Companion of Odysseus, killed by Antiphos (3), 4. 489–493.

Likym'nios: Uncle of Herakles, killed by Tlepolemos (1) who was his great-nephew, 2. 663.

Lilai'a: City in Phokis, 2. 523.

Limnorei'a: A Nereid, 18. 41.

Lindos: City in Rhodes, 2. 656.

Lok'rians: People of Lokris, 2. 535.

Lokris: District in east-central Greece, the domain of Aias the son of Oïleus, 2. 527.

Lyka'on: (1) Father of Pandaros, 2. 826, etc. (2) Son of Priam and Laothoë, killed by Achilleus, 21. 34–135.

Lykas'tos: City in Krete, 2. 647.

Ly'kia: (1) District on the southern coast of Asia Minor, the domain of Sarpedon and Glaukos (1), 2. 877, etc. (2) Apparently the country around Zeleia, close to Troy, home of Pandaros, 5. 105; 173.

Lykome'des: Achaian, killer of Apisaon (2), 17. 345–349.

Lykon: Trojan killed by Peneleos, 16. 334–341.

Lykophon'tes: Trojan killed by Teukros, 8. 275.

Ly'kophron: Achaian from Kythera, friend of Aias, killed by Hektor, 15. 429–435.

Lykour'gos: (1) Son of Dryas, who assaulted Dionysos and was punished by the gods, 6. 130–140. (2) Hero who killed Areïthoös (1), 7. 142–149.

Lyktos: City in Krete, 2. 647.

Lyrnes'sos: City in the Troad, the home of Briseis, 2. 690, etc.

Lysan'dros: Trojan killed by Aias, 11. 491.

Macha'on: Son of Asklepios, fighter and healer, with his brother Podaleirios leader of the Thessalians from Trikka and Oichalia, 2. 729–733; ministers to the wounded Menelaos, 4. 192–218; wounded and put out of action by Paris, 11. 504–520.

Magne'sians: People of Thessaly led by Prothoös, 2. 756.

Maian'dros: River of Asia Minor emptying near Miletos (2), 2. 869.

Mai'malos: Father of Peisandros (3), 16. 194.

Mai'on: Kadmeian who led an ambuscade against Tydeus, 4. 393–398.

Maio'nians: People from around the lake of Gyge, 2. 864.

Mai'ra: A Nereid, 18. 48.

Makar: Lord of Lesbos, 24. 544.

Mantinei'a: City in Arkadia, 2. 607.

Maris: Lykian killed by Thrasymedes, 16. 319–329.

Marpes'sa: Daughter of Euenos, wife of Idas, 9. 557.

Ma'ses: City in the domain of Diomedes, 2. 562.

Mastor: Father of Lykophron, 15. 430.

Med'eon: City in Boiotia, 2. 501.

Medesikas'te: Daughter of Priam, wife of Imbrios, 13. 173.

Medon: (1) Bastard son of Oïleus (1), 13. 694–697; killed by Aineias, 15. 332. (2) A captain on the Trojan side, 17. 216.

Megas: Father of Perimos, 16. 695.

Me'ges: Leader of the men from Doulichion, son of Phyleus, 2. 627; leader of the Epeians, 13. 692.

Mekis'teus: (1) Father of Euryalos, 2. 566 (and one of the Seven against Thebes); a great boxer in his youth, 23. 678–680. (2) Achaian killed by Poulydamas, 15. 339.

Melanip'pos: (1) Trojan killed by Teukros, 8. 276. (2) Trojan, son of Hiketaon, killed by Antilochos, 15. 576. (3) Trojan killed by Patroklos, 16. 695. (4) A younger Achaian chief, 19. 240.

Melan'thios: Trojan killed by Eurypylos, 6. 36.

Melas: Son of Portheus, brother of Oineus, 14. 117.

Melea'gros: Son of Oineus and prince of Kalydon, 9. 529–599.

Meliboi'a: Thessalian city in the domain of Philoktetes, 2. 717.

Mel'itē: A Nereid, 18. 42.

Menela'os: Son of Atreus, brother of Agamemnon, first husband of Helen, lord of Lakedaimon, 2. 581–590, etc.

Menes'thes: Achaian killed by Hektor, 5. 609.

Menes'theus: Leader of the Athenians, 2. 552–556.

Menes'thios: (1) Achaian from Arne killed by Paris, 7. 9. (2) Myrmidon leader under Achilleus, 16. 173–178.

Menoi'tios: Son of Aktor (3) and father of Patroklos, 1. 307, etc.

Menon: Trojan killed by Leonteus, 12. 193.

Men'tes: Leader of the Kikones impersonated by Apollo, 17. 73.

Mentor: Father of Imbrios, 13. 171.

Meri'ones: Companion in arms of Idomeneus, one of the most prominent of the younger Achaian warriors, charioteer and archer, 2. 651; 13. 244–329, etc.

Mer'meros: Trojan killed by Antilochos, 14. 513.

Merops: Augur in Perkote, father of Adrestos (2) and Amphios (1), 2. 831.

Mes'se: City in Lakedaimon, 2. 582.

Messe'is: Wellspring in Greece, exact location unknown, 6. 457.

Mesth'les: Leader of the Maionians, 2. 864.

Mestor: Son of Priam, 24. 257.

Metho'ne: Thessalian city in the domain of Philoktetes, 2. 716.

Midei'a: City in Boiotia, 2. 507.

Mile'tos: (1) City in Krete, 2. 647. (2) City of the Karians, 2. 868.

Minos: Son of Zeus and Europa, father of Deukalion, king of Krete, 13. 450–454; 14. 321–322.

Min'yai: People of Orchomenos (1) led by Askalaphos and Ialmenos, 2. 511.

Minyei'os: River on the border of Nestor's domain, 11. 722.

Mnesos: Paionian killed by Achilleus, 21. 210.

Moli'on: Follower of Thymbraios, killed by Odysseus, 11. 322.

Moli'ones: Eurytos (2) and Kteatos (qq.v.), 11. 709.

Molos: Father of Meriones, 10. 270.

Morys: Trojan killed by Meriones, 14. 513.

Mou'lios: (1) Epeian hero killed by Nestor in his youth, 11. 739. (2) Trojan killed by Patroklos, 16. 696. (3) Trojan killed by Achilleus, 20. 472.

Mydon: (1) Charioteer of Pylaimenes, killed by Antilochos, 5. 580. (2) Paionian killed by Achilleus, 21. 209.

Mygdon: King of Phrygia, 3. 186.

My'kalē: Promontory across the bay from Miletos (2), 2. 869.

Mykales'sos: City in Boiotia, 2. 498.

Myke'nai: Agamemnon's capital, a few miles north of the city of Argos, 2. 569, etc.

My'nes: King of Lyrnessos, 19. 296.

Myri'ne: Heroine after whom a hill before Troy was named, 2. 814.

Myr'midons: The people of Phthia, subjects of Peleus and led by Achilleus, 2. 684, etc.

Myr'sinos: City in Elis, 2. 616.

My'sians: A people living to the east of Troy and allied to the Trojans, 2. 858.

Nai'ad: A well-nymph, 6. 21.

Nas'tes: Leader of the Karians, killed by Achilleus, 2. 867–875.

Nau'bolos: Phokian hero, father of Iphitos, 2. 518.

Ne'leus: King of Pylos, father of Nestor, 11. 692, etc.

Nemer'tes: A Nereid, 18. 46.

Neopto'lemos: Son of Achilleus, 19. 327.

Ne'reïds: The daughters of Nereus, nymphs of the sea, 18. 36–49.

Ne'reus: Aged god of the sea, father of Thetis, 1. 556; and of the other Nereids, 18. 36.

Ne'ritos or Ne'riton: Mountain on Ithaka, 2. 632.

Nesai'e: A Nereid, 18. 40.

Nestor: Leader of the Pylians, once a great warrior and still active as a commander and counsellor, 1. 247–284, etc.; Father of Antilochos, 5. 565; of Thrasymedes, 9. 81.

Ni'obē: Heroine of Asia, whose six daughters and six sons were killed by Apollo and Artemis, 24. 602–617.

Ni'reus: Leader from Syme, handsomest (next to Achilleus) of the Achaians, 2. 671.

Ni'sa: City in Boiotia, 2. 508.

Nisy'ros: Island near Kos, 2. 676.

Noë'mon: (1) Lykian killed by Odysseus, 5. 678. (2) Henchman of Antilochos, 23. 612.

Nomi'on: Father of Amphimachos (2) and Nastes, 2. 871.

Nysei'an: Of a mountain sacred to Dionysos, 6. 133.

Ocean or Oke'anos: The waters surrounding the world and the god of those waters, 1. 423; 14. 201, etc.

Odys'seus: Son of Laertes, lord of Ithaka and the neighbouring islands, great fighter and counsellor, close friend of Agamemnon, 2. 631, etc.

Oicha'lia: Thessalian city of Eurytos (1) in the domain of Podaleirios and Machaon, 2. 730.

Oche'sios: Father of Periphas, 5. 843.

Oid'ipous: Hero of Thebes (1), 23. 679. (In Homer, strictly, Oidipodes.)

Oï'leus: (1) Lokrian hero, father of Aias (2), 2. 527. (2) Trojan killed by Agamemnon, 11. 93.

Oi'neus: Hero of Kalydon, son of Portheus, 14. 117; father of Tydeus, 5. 813; of Meleagros, 5. 981.

Oino'maos: (1) Achaian killed by Hektor, 5. 706. (2) Trojan killed by Idomeneus, 13. 506.

Oi'nops: Father of Helenos (1), 5. 707.

Oi'tylos: City in Lakedaimon, 2. 585.

Okal'ea: City in Boiotia, 2. 501.

Olen'ian Rock: Landmark on the borders of Elis, 2. 617.

O'lenos: City in Aitolia, 2. 639.

Oli'zon: Thessalian city in the domain of Philoktetes, 2. 717.

Oloös'son: Thessalian city in the domain of Polypoites, 2. 739.

Olym'pos: Mountain north of Thessaly, the home of the gods, 1. 499, etc.

Onches'tos: City of Boiotia, 2. 506.

One'tor: Father of Laogonos (1), 16. 604.

Opheles'tes: (1) Trojan killed by Teukros, 8. 274. (2) Paionian killed by Achilleus, 21. 210.

Ophel'tios: (1) Trojan killed by Euryalos, 6. 20. (2) Achaian killed by Hektor, 11. 302.

Opi'tes: Achaian killed by Hektor, 11. 301.

Op'oeis or O'pous: City in Lokris, 2. 531.

Orcho'menos: (1) City of the Minyai, adjoining the territory of the Boiotians, 2. 511. (2) City in Arkadia, 2. 605.

Oreithy'ia: A Nereid, 18. 48.

GLOSSARY

Ores'bios: Boiotian killed by Hektor, 5. 707–710.

Ores'tes: (1) Achaian killed by Hektor, 5. 705. (2) Son of Agamemnon, 9. 142. (3) Trojan killed by Leonteus, 12. 193.

Ori'on: The constellation, 18. 486.

Orme'nion: Thessalian city in the domain of Eurypylos, 2. 734.

Or'menos: (1) Trojan killed by Teukros, 8. 274. (2) Father of Amyntor, 9. 448. (3) Trojan killed by Polypoites, 12. 187.

Ornei'ai: City in the domain of Agamemnon, 2. 571.

Oros: Achaian killed by Hektor, 11. 303.

Orsi'lochos: (1) Achaian killed by Aineias, 5. 542–560. (2) Trojan killed by Teukros, 8. 274.

Orthai'os: A Trojan captain, 13. 791.

Or'the: Thessalian city in the domain of Polypoites, 2. 739.

Orti'lochos: Father of Diokles, 5. 546.

Othry'oneus: Suitor of Kassandra, killed by Idomeneus, 13. 363–382.

Otos: (1) Giant who with his brother Ephialtes imprisoned Ares, 5. 385. (2) Achaian from Kyllene, killed by Poulydamas, 15. 518.

Ot'reus: Lord of Phrygia, 3. 186.

Otryn'teus: Father of Iphition, 20. 382–384.

Ouka'legon: An elder in Troy, 3. 148.

Paië'on: The healing god, 5. 899.

Paio'nia: A district, its people allied to the Trojans, in what was later Macedonia, 17. 350.

Pai'sos: Apparently the same as Apaisos (q.v.), 5. 612.

Pallas: Epithet of Athene, 1. 200, etc.

Pal'mys: A Trojan captain, 13. 792.

Pammon: Son of Priam, 24. 250.

Pan'daros: Son of Lykaon (1), leader of the Trojans from Zeleia, 2. 824–827; but spoken of as being from Lykia, 5. 173; breaks the truce by treacherously wounding Menelaos, 4. 85–140; wounds Diomedes, 5. 95–105; killed by him, 5. 280–296.

Pandi'on: Henchman of Teukros, 12. 372.

Pan'dokos: Trojan killed by Aias, 11. 490.

Pan'opē: A Nereid, 18. 45.

Pan'opeus: (1) City in Phokis, 2. 520. (2) Father of Epeios, 23. 665.

Pan'thoös: An elder of Troy, 3. 147; father of Poulydamas, 13. 756; of Euphorbos, 16. 808; of Hyperenor, 17. 19–35.

Paphla'gonēs: People of Paphlagonia on the southern shore of the Black Sea, allied to the Trojans, 2. 851.

Paris: Son of Priam and Hekabe, who carried Helen from Lakedaimon, 3. 15, etc. (in the Iliad more frequently called by his other name, Alexandros).

Parrha'sia: City in Arkadia, 2. 608.

Parthe'nios: River in Paphlagonia, 2. 854.

Pasi'thea: One of the Graces, 14. 269.

Patro'klos: Son of Menoitios, henchman and close friend of Achilleus, killed by Hektor, 1. 307, etc.

Pedai'on or Pedai'os: City in the Troad, 13. 172.

Pedai'os: Trojan, son of Antenor, killed by Meges, 5. 69–75.

Pe'dasos: (1) Trojan killed by Euryalos, 6. 21. (2) City on the river Satnioeis, 6. 35. (3) Town near Pylos, 9. 152. (4) One of the horses of Achilleus, 16. 152.

Peirai'os: Father of Ptolemaios, 4. 228.

Pei'res: Father of Rhigmos, 20. 484.

Peiri'thoös: Son of Zeus, father of Polypoites, 2. 741.

Pei'ros: Thracian killed by Thoas, 4. 517–538.

Peisan'dros: (1) Trojan killed by Agamemnon, 11. 122–144. (2) Trojan killed by Menelaos, 13. 601–619. (3) One of the leaders of the Myrmidons, 16. 193.

Peise'nor: Father of Kleitos, 15. 445.

Pel'agon: (1) Follower of Nestor, 4. 295. (2) Follower of Sarpedon, 5. 694.

Pelas'gian: A term of disputed and apparently variable significance. Applied to Argos (2), the home of Achilleus, 2. 681; but the Pelasgians of Larissa are allied with the Trojans, 2. 840–843.

Pel'egon: Father of Asteropaios, 21. 141.

Pel'eus: Son of Aiakos, 21. 189; father of Achilleus, 1. 1, etc.; husband of Thetis, 18. 85, etc.

Pel'ian: Of the spear of Achilleus, cut from Mount Pelion, 16. 143.

Pel'ias: Father of Alkestis, 2. 715.

Pelle'ne: Achaian city in the domain of Agamemnon, 2. 574.

Pelops: Lord of Argos, father of Atreus, 2. 104.

Penei'os: The chief river of Thessaly, 2. 752.

Pene'leos: Leader, with Leïtos, of the Boiotians, 2. 494.

Perei'a: Place where Apollo had bred the mares of Eumelos, 2. 766.

Per'gamos or Per'gamon: The citadel of Troy, 4. 508, etc.

Per'gasos: Father of Deïkoön, 5. 535.

Periboi'a: Mother, by the river Axios, of Pelegon, 21. 142.

Perie'res: Father of Boros, 16. 177.

Perime'des: Father of Schedios (2), 15. 515.

Per'imos: Trojan killed by Patroklos, 16. 695.

Per'iphas: (1) Aitolian killed by Ares, 5. 842. (2) Herald of Anchises, 17. 324.

Periphe'tes: (1) Trojan killed by Teukros, 14. 515. (2) Achaian from Mykenai, killed by Hektor, 15. 638–652.

Perko'te: City in the Troad, 2. 835.

Perrhai'bians: People from the region of Dodona, led by Gouneus, 2. 749.

Perse'phonē: Wife of Hades and queen of the dead, 9. 457.

Per'seus: Son of Zeus and Danaë, 14. 320; grandfather of Eurystheus, 19. 116.

Pe'teon: City in Boiotia, 2. 500.

Pe'teos: Father of Menestheus, 2. 552.

Phai'nops: (1) Father of Xanthos (2) and Thoön (1), 5. 152. (2) Father of Phorkys, 17. 312.

Phais'tos: (1) City in Krete, 2. 648. (2) Maionian killed by Idomeneus, 5. 43.

Phal'kes: Trojan killed by Antilochos, 14. 513.

Pharis: City in Lakedaimon, 2. 582.

Phau'sias: Father of Apisaon (1), 11. 578.

Phe'geus: Trojan killed by Diomedes, 5. 9–19.

Phe'ia: City on the borders of Pylos and Arkadia, 7. 135.

Phei'das: Captain under Menestheus, 13. 691.

Pheidip'pos: A leader of the men from Kos and the adjacent islands, 2. 678.

Phe'neos: City in Arkadia, 2. 605.

Phe'rai: (1) Thessalian city of Eumelos, 2. 711. (2) City near Pylos, 5. 543; 9. 151.

Phere'klos: Builder in Troy, who made ships for Paris, killed by Meriones, 5. 59–68.

Phe'res: Father of Admetos, grandfather of Eumelos, 2. 763.

Pherou'sa: A Nereid, 18. 43.

Phile'tor: Father of Demouchos, 20. 458.

Philokte'tes: Leader of the Thessalians from Methone and thereabouts, archer, during the action of the Iliad ill of an infection in Lemnos, 2. 716–725.

Phleg'yes: A northern people visited by Ares, 13. 302.

Phoenicians: A nation, well known as seafarers, living on the Syrian coast, 23. 744.

Phoi'bos: Epithet of Apollo, 1. 43, etc.

Phoi'nix: (1) Son of Amyntor, a refugee befriended by Peleus, companion and tutor of Achilleus; his story, 9. 430–495. (2) Father of Europa, 14. 321.

Phokis: District in central Greece, adjoining Boiotia, 2. 517.

Phor'bas: (1) Man of Lesbos, father of Diomede, 9. 665. (2) Father of Ilioneus, 14. 490.

Phor'kys: Phrygian killed by Aias, 17. 312.

Phrad'mon: Father of Agelaos (1), 8. 257.

Phron'tis: Wife of Panthoös, 17. 40.

Phry'gia: District east of the Troad, allied with Troy, 2. 862, etc.

Phthi'a: The home of Achilleus, in southern Thessaly, 2. 683, etc.

Phthi'ron: Mountain near Miletos (2), 2. 868.

Phyl'akē: Thessalian city in the domain of Protesilaos, 2. 695.

Phy'las: Father of Polymele, 16. 181.

Phy'leus: Father of Meges, 2. 628, etc.; defeated in spear-throwing by Nestor, 23. 637.

Phylomedou'sa: Wife of Areïthoös (1), 7. 10.

Pidy'tes: Trojan ally from Perkote, killed by Odysseus, 6. 30.

Piē'ria: The region around Olympos, 14. 226.

Pit'theus: Father of Aithre, 3. 144.

Pityei'a: City on the Hellespont, 2. 829.

Plak'os: Mountain dominating Thebe (2), 6. 396.

Platai'a: City in Boiotia, 2. 504.

Plei'ades: The constellation, 18. 486.

Pleu'ron: City in Aitolia, 2. 639.

Podalei'rios: Son of Asklepios, fighter and healer, with his brother Machaon leader of the men from Oichalia and thereabouts, 2. 732.

Podar'ge: Harpy, mother by the West Wind of the horses of Achilleus, 16. 150.

Podar'gos: (1) One of the horses of Hektor, 8. 185. (2) One of the horses of Menelaos, 23. 295.

Podar'kes: Brother of Protesilaos, succeeding him as leader of the men from Phylake, etc., 2. 703–708.

Po'des: Son of Eëtion, friend (possibly brother-in-law) of Hektor, killed by Menelaos, 17. 575–581.

Poli'tes: Son of Priam, 2. 791, etc.

Polyai'mon: Father of Amopaon, 8. 276.

Pol'ybos: Son of Antenor, 11. 59.

Polydeu'kes: Brother of Helen, 3. 237.

Polydo're: Daughter of Peleus, mother, by the river Spercheios, of Menesthios, 16. 173–178.

Polydo'ros: (1) Youngest son of Priam, killed by Achilleus, 20. 407–418. (2) Spear-thrower defeated by Nestor, 23. 637.

Polyi'dos: (1) Trojan killed by Diomedes, 5. 148–151. (2) Augur in Korinth, father of Euchenor, 13. 663.

Polyk'tor: Named as his father by Hermes to Priam, 24. 398.

Polyme'le: Mother, by Hermes, of Eudoros, 16. 179–190.

Polyme'los: Lykian killed by Patroklos, 16. 417.

Polynei'kes: Son of Oidipous, leader of the Seven against Thebes, 4. 377.

Polyphe'mos: Hero of the generation of Nestor, 1. 264.

Polyphe'tes: A Trojan captain, 13. 791.

Polyphon'tes: Kadmeian killed by Tydeus, 4. 395.

Polypoi'tes: Son of Peirithoös, leader of the Lapithai from Argissa, etc., 2. 740, etc.

Polyxei'nos: A leader of the Epeians, 2. 623.

Por'theus: Aitolian hero, father of Agrios, Melas and Oineus, 14. 115.

Posei'don: Son of Kronos and Rheia, so younger brother of Zeus, lord of the sea, 15. 185–192; protector of the Achaians, 13. 10–124, etc.

Pouly'damas: Son of Panthoös, fighter and careful counsellor, frequently opposed to the reckless strategy of Hektor, 12. 210–229; 18. 249–283, etc.

Prak'tios: River in the Troad, 2. 835.

Pramnei'an wine: A wine used medicinally, origin unknown, 11. 639.

Priam: Son of Laomedon, king of Troy, father of Hektor, Paris and many other children (fifty sons, 24. 495), 3. 161, etc.

Proi'tos: King of Ephyra, who designed against the life of Bellerophontes, 6. 156–170.

Pro'machos: Boiotian killed by Akamas (1), 14. 476.

Pro'noös: Trojan killed by Patroklos, 16. 399.

Protesila'os: Leader of the men from Phylake, etc., first of the Achaians to land at Troy and first to be killed, 2. 695–709.

Prothoë'nor: A Boiotian leader, 2. 495; killed by Poulydamas, 14. 450.

Pro'thoön: Trojan killed by Teukros, 14. 515.

Pro'thoös: Leader of the Magnesians from Pelion, 2. 756.

Protia'on: Father of Astynoös (2), 15. 455.

Proto: A Nereid, 18. 43.

Pry'tanis: Lykian killed by Odysseus, 5. 678.

Ptel'eos: (1) City in the domain of Nestor, 2. 594. (2) City in the domain of Protesilaos, 2. 697.

Ptolemai'os: Father of Eurymedon (1), 4. 228.

Pygmai'ans: That small infantry warred on by cranes, 3. 6.

Pylai'menes: Lord of the Paphlagonians, killed by Menelaos, 5. 576–579.

Pylai'os: Leader, with his brother Hippothoös, of the Pelasgians from Larissa, 2. 842.

Pylar'tes: (1) Trojan killed by Aias, 11. 491. (2) Trojan killed by Patroklos, 16. 696.

Pyle'ne: City in Aitolia, 2. 639.

Py'lon: Trojan killed by Polypoites, 12. 187.

Py'los: The city of Nestor, with the district surrounding it, on the western coast of the Peloponnese (south Greece: exact location disputed), 1. 252; 2. 591, etc.

Pyraich'mes: Paionian chief killed by Patroklos, 16. 287.

Pyr'asos: (1) City in the domain of Protesilaos, 2. 695. (2) Trojan killed by Aias, 11. 491.

Py'ris: Trojan killed by Patroklos, 16. 416.

Py'tho: Place in Phokis sacred to Apollo, later called Delphoi, 2. 519; 9. 404–405.

Rhadaman'thys: Son of Zeus and Europa, brother of Minos, 14. 321–322.

Rhe'a, or Rhei'a: Mother, by Kronos, of Zeus, Poseidon, Hades, Hera and Demeter, 15. 187–188.

Rhe'ne: Mother, by Oïleus (1) of Medon (1), 2. 728.

Rhe'sos: (1) King of the Thracians, killed by Diomedes, 10. 432–502. (2) River of the Troad, 12. 20.

Rhig'mos: Thracian killed by Achilleus, 20. 484–489.

Rhi'pe: City in Arkadia, 2. 606.

Rhodes: Island just south-east of the Aegean, its men led by Tlepolemos (1), 2. 654.

Rho'dios: River of the Troad, 12. 20.

Rhy'tion: City in Krete, 2. 648.

Sal'amis: Island off the shore by Athens, home of Aias (1), 2. 557.

Sa'mos: (1) Large island, later called Kephallenia, near Ithaka and part of the domain of Odysseus, 2. 634. (2) Island, later called Samothrace, in the northern Aegean or Thracian Sea, 13. 13; 24. 78.

Sangar'ios: River in Phrygia, 3. 187.

Sarpe'don: Son of Zeus and Laodameia, lord of the Lykians, 2. 876; 6. 198–199; one of the strongest fighters on the Trojan side, kills Tlepolemos, 5. 629–662; killed by Patroklos, 16. 462–507.

Satni'oeis: River of the Troad, 6. 34, etc.

Sat'nios: Trojan killed by Aias (2), 14. 443.

Sche'dios: (1) Son of Iphitos (1) and a leader of the Phokians, 2. 517; killed by Hektor, 17. 304–311. (2) Son of Perimedes, also leader of the Phokians and killed by Hektor, 15. 515. (It is quite possible that there is confusion in the tradition here, and that the same man is meant.)

Schoi'nos: City in Boiotia, 2. 497.

Sel'agos: Father of Amphios (2), 5. 612.

Sele'pios: Father of Euenos, 2. 693.

Selle'eis: (1) River of unknown location associated with Ephyra (1), 2. 659; 15. 531. (2) River of the Troad, 2. 839.

Sel'loi: Prophets of Zeus at Dodona, 16. 235.

Sem'elē: Mother, by Zeus, of Dionysos, 14. 323–325.

Se'samos: City of the Paphlagones, 2. 853.

Ses'tos: City on the European side of the Hellespont, its people allies of Troy, 2. 836.

Sidon: City of the Phoenicians, 6. 291.

Sik'yon: City once ruled by Adrestos (1) in the domain of Agamemnon, 2. 572.

Sim'oeis: River by Troy, tributary of Skamandros, 5. 774, etc.

Simoei'sios: Trojan named after the river, killed by Aias, 4. 473–489.

Sin'tians: People of Lemnos, 1. 594.

Sip'ylos: Mountain in Lydia, 24. 615.

Sis'yphos: Hero of Ephyre (2), grandfather of Bellerophontes, 6. 153.

Skai'an: Of one of the gates of Troy, 3. 145, etc.

Skaman'drios: (1) Trojan huntsman and fighting man killed by Menelaos, 5. 49-58. (2) Another name for Astyanax, 6. 402.

Skaman'dros: Chief river of the Trojan plain, 2. 465, etc.; as a god, fights and discomfits Achilleus, 21. 211-382; called also, by the gods, Xanthos, 20. 74.

Skandei'a: City on Kythera, 10. 268.

Skar'phe: City in Lokris, 2. 532.

Skolos: City in Boiotia, 2. 497.

Sky'ros: Island off Euboia, 9. 668; 19. 332.

Smin'theus: Epithet of Apollo, 1. 39.

Sokos: Trojan killed by Odysseus, but only after wounding and nearly killing him, 11. 427-455.

Sol'ymoi: Tribe in Asia Minor; Bellerophontes fought against them, 6. 184-185.

Spar'ta: The same as Lakedaimon (q.v.) except that the name Sparta applies only to the city, Lakedaimon to the district as well, 2. 582, etc.

Spei'o: A Nereid, 18. 40.

Sperchei'os: River running through the domain of Peleus and Achilleus, 16. 174, etc.

Sphe'los: Father of Iasos, 15. 338.

Sten'tor: Achaian with a big voice, impersonated by Hera, 5. 785.

Sthenela'os: Trojan killed by Patroklos, 16. 586.

Sthen'elos: (1) Son of Kapaneus, leader, with Diomedes and Euryalos, of the men of Argos (1), 2. 563-564; companion in arms and charioteer of Diomedes, 5. 108, etc. (2) Father of Eurystheus, 19. 116; 123.

Sti'chios: A leader of the Athenians, killed by Hektor, 15. 329-331.

Stra'tia: City in Arkadia, 2. 606.

Stro'phios: Father of Skamandrios (1), 5. 50.

Stympha'los: City in Arkadia, 2. 608.

Sty'ra: City of Euboia, 2. 539.

Styx: The river (later, at least, a river of the dead, and see 8. 369) by which the gods swear, 2. 755, etc.

Sy'me: Island just north of Rhodes, its people led by Nireus, 2. 671.

Talai'menes: Father of Mesthles and Antiphos (2), 2. 865.

Tal'aos: Father of Mekisteus (1), 2. 566.

Talthy'bios: Herald of Agamemnon, 1. 320, etc.

Tar'ne: City of the Maionians, 5. 44.

Tar'phe: City in Lokris, 2. 533.

Tar'taros: The pit of perdition, 8. 13-16; 478-481.

Te'gea: City in Arkadia, 2. 607.

Tel'amon: Father of Aias (1) and Teukros, 2. 528; 8. 283, etc.

Tele'machos: Son of Odysseus, 2. 260.

Ten'edos: Island off the coast of the Troad, 1. 38.

Tenthre'don: Father of Prothoös, 2. 756.

Terei'a: Hill near the Hellespont, 2. 829.

Te'thys: Wife of Okeanos, 14. 201.

Teukros: Bastard son of Telamon, so half-brother of Aias (1), archer and spear-fighter, 8. 266–334, etc.

Teu'tamos: Father of Lethos, 2. 843.

Teu'thras: (1) Achaian killed by Hektor, 5. 705. (2) Father of Axylos, 6. 13.

Thalei'a: A Nereid, 18. 39.

Thal'pios: Son of Eurytos (2), leader of the Epeians, 2. 620.

Thaly'sias: Father of Echepolos (1), 4. 458.

Tha'myris: Thracian singer ruined by the Muses, 2. 594–600.

Thauma'kia: City in the domain of Philoktetes, 2. 716.

Thea'no: Wife of Antenor, 5. 70, etc.; priestess of Athene, 6. 298–311.

Thebai'os: Father of Eniopeus, 8. 120.

The'be or Thebes: (1) City of Eëtion near Troy, sacked by Achilleus, 1. 366, etc. (2) City of the Kadmeians in Boiotia, attacked by Polyneikes and his companions, 4. 376–381; and taken by their sons, 4. 404–409; only the lower city remaining at the time of the Trojan War, 2. 505. (3) City of Egypt, 9. 381–382.

The'mis: Olympian goddess of order and custom, 15. 87; 20. 5.

Thersi'lochos: Paionian killed by Achilleus, 21. 209.

Thersi'tes: Achaian of indefinite social and military status, ugly and scurrilous and eloquent, squelched by Odysseus, 2. 211–277.

The'seus: Hero of Athens, 1. 265.

Thespei'a: City in Boiotia, 2. 498.

Thes'salos: Son of Herakles, father of Antiphos (1) and Pheidippos, 2. 679.

Thes'tor: (1) Father of Kalchas, 1. 69. (2) Father of Alkmaon, 12. 394. (3) Trojan killed by Patroklos, 16. 402.

The'tis: Nereid, given by the gods in marriage to the mortal Peleus, and by him mother of Achilleus, 1. 351–457; 18. 35–147, etc.

This'be: City in Boiotia, 2. 502.

Tho'as: (1) Son of Andraimon, leader of the Aitolians, 2. 638; one of the more important younger chiefs, characterized, 15. 281–284. (2) King in Lemnos, 14. 230. (3) Trojan killed by Menelaos, 16. 311.

Tho'e: A Nereid, 18. 40.

Tho'on: (1) Trojan killed by Diomedes, 5. 152. (2) Trojan killed by Odysseus, 11. 422. (3) Trojan killed by Antilochos, 13. 545.

Thoö'tes: Henchman or herald of Menestheus, 12. 342.

Thrace: The seaboard and inlying territory north of the Aegean, the inhabitants called Thracians, 9. 5; 10. 434, etc.

Thra'sios: Paionian killed by Achilleus, 21. 210.

Thrasyme'des: Son of Nestor, 9. 81, etc.

Thrasyme'los: Henchman of Sarpedon, killed by Patroklos, 16. 463.

Thro'nion: Lokrian city, 2. 533.

Thryoes'sa: Town in Pylos by the Alpheios, 11. 711.

Thry'on: City in the domain of Nestor, on the Alpheios, probably identical with the foregoing, 2. 592.

Thyes'tes: Son of Pelops and brother of Atreus, 2. 106.

Thymbrai'os: Trojan killed by Diomedes, 11. 320.

Thym'bre: Town or village near Troy, 10. 430.

Thymoi'tes: Elder of Troy, 3. 146.

Tir'yns: Argive city in the domain of Diomedes, 2. 559.

Ti'tanos: A place in the domain of Eurypylos (1), 2. 735.

Ti'tans: The elder gods in Tartaros, 14. 279.

Titares'sos: Thessalian river, tributary of the Peneios, 2. 751.

Titho'nos: Son of Laomedon and brother of Priam, 20. 237; husband of the Dawn, 11. 1.

Tlepo'lemos: (1) Son of Herakles and leader of the men from Rhodes, 2. 653–670; killed, after severely wounding him, by Sarpedon, 5. 628–669. (2) Lykian killed by Patroklos, 16. 416.

Tmo'los: Mountain in Maionia, 2. 866.

Tra'chis: City near the Spercheios in the domain of Peleus and Achilleus, 2. 682.

Tre'chos: Aitolian killed by Hektor, 5. 706.

Trik'ke: Thessalian city in the domain of Machaon, 2. 729.

Tritogenei'a: Epithet of Athene, 4. 515.

Tro'ad: Term used for the whole country of the Trojans, of which Troy was the capital, 6. 315, etc.

Tro'ilos: Son of Priam, killed at some time before Hektor, 24. 257.

Troi'zen: City on the Argive coast in the domain of Diomedes, 2. 561.

Troize'nos: Father of Euphemos, 2. 847.

Tros: (1) Son of Erichthonios, father of Ilos, Assarakos and Ganymedes, thus ancestor of the kings and princes of Troy, 20. 230–240. (2) Trojan killed by Achilleus, 20. 463–471.

Troy: Ilion, the city of Tros and of the Trojans, 1. 128, etc.

Ty'chios: Leatherworker of Hyle, who made the great shield of Aias, 7. 220–224.

Ty'deus: Son of Oineus and father of Diomedes; his genealogy and history, 14. 113–125.

Typho'eus: Giant (later called Typhon) put underground in the land of the Arimoi, 2. 783.

Xan'thos: (1) River of Lykia, 2. 877, etc. (2) River of the Troad, also called
   Skamandros (q.v.), 6. 4, etc. (3) Trojan killed by Diomedes, 5. 152. (4) One
   of Hektor's horses, 8. 185. (5) One of the horses of Achilleus, 16. 149, etc.

Zakyn'thos: Island off the western coast of Greece, part of the domain of Odysseus,
   2. 634.
Zelei'a: City of the Troad, its men led by Pandaros, 2. 824–827.
Ze'phyros: The west wind, 9. 5.
Zeus: Son of Kronos, brother and husband of Hera, most powerful of the gods,
   1. 5, etc.